The WTO, Trade and the Environment

Critical Perspectives on the Global Trading System and the WTO

Series Editors: Kym Anderson
Professor of Economics and Executive Director,
Centre for International Economic Studies
University of Adelaide, Australia
and Lead Economist, Development Research Group
World Bank, USA
Bernard Hoekman
Research Manager, International Trade
World Bank, USA

1. The WTO, Intellectual Property Rights and the Knowledge Economy
   Keith E. Maskus
2. The WTO and Agriculture (Volumes I and II)
   Kym Anderson and Tim Josling
3. The WTO and International Trade Law/Dispute Settlement
   Petros C. Mavroidis and Alan O. Sykes
4. The WTO and Technical Barriers to Trade
   Spencer Henson and John S. Wilson
5. The WTO, Trade and the Environment
   Gary Sampson and John Whalley

Future titles will include:

The WTO and Anti-Dumping
Douglas R. Nelson and Hylke Vandenbussche

The International Trading System, Globalization and History
Kevin O'Rourke

The WTO's Core Rules and Disciplines
Kym Anderson and Bernard Hoekman

The WTO and Government Procurement
Simon J. Evenett and Bernard Hoekman

Wherever possible, the articles in these volumes have been reproduced as originally published using facsimile reproduction, inclusive of footnotes and pagination to facilitate ease of reference.

The WTO, Trade and the Environment

Edited by

Gary Sampson

Senior Counsellor
World Trade Organization, Geneva, Switzerland
and Professor of International Economic Governance
Institute of Advanced Studies, United Nations University, Japan

and

John Whalley

Co-Director
Center for the Study of International Economic Relations (CSIER),
University of Western Ontario, Canada

CRITICAL PERSPECTIVES ON THE GLOBAL TRADING SYSTEM AND THE WTO

An Elgar Reference Collection
Cheltenham, UK • Northampton, MA, USA

Published by
Edward Elgar Publishing Limited
Glensanda House
Montpellier Parade
Cheltenham
Glos GL50 1UA
UK

Edward Elgar Publishing, Inc.
136 West Street
Suite 202
Northampton
Massachusetts 01060
USA

A catalogue record for this book is available from the British Library

ISBN 1 84376 839 9

Printed and bound in Great Britain by MPG Books Ltd, Bodmin, Cornwall

Contents

Acknowledgements

The editors and publishers wish to thank the authors and the following publishers who have kindly given permission for the use of copyright material.

American Economic Association for articles: Hemamala Hettige, Robert E.B. Lucas and David Wheeler (1992), 'The Toxic Intensity of Industrial Production: Global Patterns, Trends, and Trade Policy', *American Economic Review*, **82** (2), May, 478–81; Werner Antweiler, Brian R. Copeland and M. Scott Taylor (2001), 'Is Free Trade Good for the Environment?', *American Economic Review*, **91** (4), September, 877–908.

Blackwell Publishing Ltd for articles: James A. Tobey (1990), 'The Effects of Domestic Environmental Policies on Patterns of World Trade: An Empirical Test', *Kyklos*, **43** (2), 191–208; John Whalley (1991), 'The Interface between Environmental and Trade Policies', *Economic Journal*, **101** (405), March, 180–89; Arvind Subramanian (1992), 'Trade Measures for Environment: A Nearly Empty Box?', *World Economy*, **15** (1), January, 135–52; Carlo Perroni and Randall M. Wigle (1994), 'International Trade and Environmental Quality: How Important are the Linkages?', *Canadian Journal of Economics*, **XXVII** (3), August, 551–67; John Beghin, David Roland-Holst and Dominique van der Mensbrugghe (1995), 'Trade Liberalization and the Environment in the Pacific Basin: Coordinated Approaches to Mexican Trade and Environment Policy', *American Journal of Agricultural Economics*, **77** (3), August, 778–85; Lisandro Abrego, Carlo Perroni, John Whalley and Randall M. Wigle (2001), 'Trade and Environment: Bargaining Outcomes from Linked Negotiations', *Review of International Economics*, **9** (3), 414–28; Gary P. Sampson (2001), 'Effective Multilateral Environment Agreements and Why the WTO Needs Them', *World Economy*, **24** (9), September, 1109–34.

Cambridge University Press for excerpt: Hiro Lee and David W. Roland-Holst (1997), 'Trade and the Environment', in Joseph F. Francois and Kenneth A. Reinert (eds), *Applied Methods for Trade Policy Analysis: A Handbook*, Chapter 16, 517–50.

Cameron May Ltd for excerpt: James Cameron (1998), 'Dispute Settlement and Conflicting Trade and Environment Regimes', in Agata Fijalkowski and James Cameron (eds), *Trade and the Environment: Bridging the Gap*, Chapter 1, 16–26.

Earthscan for excerpt: Duncan Brack (2000), 'Multilateral Environmental Agreements: An Overview', in Halina Ward and Duncan Brack (eds), *Trade, Investment and the Environment: Proceedings of the Royal Institute of International Affairs Conference, Chatham House, London, October 1998*, 122–37.

Elsevier for article: Brian R. Copeland and M. Scott Taylor (1999), 'Trade, Spatial Separation, and the Environment', *Journal of International Economics*, **47** (1), February, 137–68.

Journal of World Intellectual Property for article: Graham Dutfield (2002), 'Sharing the Benefits of Biodiversity: Is there a Role for the Patent System?', *Journal of World Intellectual Property*, **5** (6), November, 899–931.

Kluwer Academic Publishers BV for article: Lars Bergman (1991), 'General Equilibrium Effects of Environmental Policy: A CGE-Modeling Approach', *Environmental and Resource Economics*, **1** (1), 43–61.

Kluwer Law International for article: C. Ford Runge (2001), 'A Global Environment Organization (GEO) and the World Trading System', *Journal of World Trade*, **35** (4), August, 399–426.

MIT Press for excerpts: Gene M. Grossman and Alan B. Krueger (1993), 'Environmental Impacts of a North American Free Trade Agreement', in Peter M. Garber (ed.), *The Mexico-U.S. Free Trade Agreement*, Chapter 2, 13–56; Jagdish Bhagwati and T.N. Srinivasan (1996), 'Trade and the Environment: Does Environmental Diversity Detract from the Case for Free Trade?', in Jagdish Bhagwati and Robert E. Hudec (eds), *Fair Trade and Harmonization: Prerequisites for Free Trade?*, Volume 1: Economic Analysis, Chapter 4, 159–99, 215–23.

Norwegian Institute of International Affairs for article: Steve Charnovitz (1998), 'The World Trade Organization and the Environment', *Yearbook of International Environmental Law*, **8**, 98–116.

Oxford University Press for article: Daniel C. Esty (1998), 'Non-Governmental Organizations at the World Trade Organization: Cooperation, Competition, or Exclusion', *Journal of International Economic Law*, **1** (1), March, 123–47.

Tulane Environmental Law Journal for article: Howard Mann (2000), 'NAFTA and the Environment: Lessons for the Future', *Tulane Environmental Law Journal*, **13** (2), Summer, 387–410.

United Nations University Press for excerpts: Magda Shahin (2002), 'Trade and Environment: How Real Is the Debate?', in Gary P. Sampson and W. Bradnee Chambers (eds), *Trade, Environment, and the Millennium*, Chapter 2, 45–80; Arthur E. Appleton (2002), 'Environmental Labelling Schemes Revisited: WTO Law and Developing Country Implications', in Gary P. Sampson and W. Bradnee Chambers (eds), *Trade, Environment, and the Millennium*, Chapter 8, 235–66.

University of Michigan Press for excerpt: Richard H. Snape (1992), 'The Environment, International Trade and Competitiveness', in Kym Anderson and Richard Blackhurst (eds), *The Greening of World Trade Issues*, Chapter 4, 73–92.

World Bank and the Copyright Clearance Center for excerpts: Robert E.B. Lucas, David Wheeler and Hemamala Hettige (1992), 'Economic Development, Environmental Regulation and the International Migration of Toxic Industrial Pollution: 1960–88', in Patrick Low (ed.), *International Trade and the Environment*, Chapter 5, World Bank Discussion Paper No. 159, 67–86, references; Patrick Low (1992), 'Trade Measures and Environmental Quality: The Implications for Mexico's Exports', in Patrick Low (ed.), *International Trade and the Environment*, Chapter 7, World Bank Discussion Paper No. 159, 105–20, references.

World Trade Organization for excerpt: General Agreement on Tariffs and Trade (1992), 'Trade and the Environment', *International Trade 1990–91*, Volume I, Chapter III, 19–39.

Every effort has been made to trace all the copyright holders but if any have been inadvertently overlooked the publishers will be pleased to make the necessary arrangement at the first opportunity.

In addition the publishers wish to thank the Marshall Library of Economics, Cambridge University, the Library of the University of Warwick and the Library of Indiana University at Bloomington, USA for their assistance in obtaining these articles.

Introduction: Seeing Red Over Green

Gary Sampson and John Whalley

This volume contains key readings on issues associated with the trade and environment debate; the clash between the market-opening principles of free trade reflected in the institutional focus of the World Trade Organization (WTO), and the environmental quality and market-regulating instincts of environmentalists. The readings cover the basic conceptual issues, as well as the genesis of trade and environment as it has been dealt with in the WTO.

Much, if not most, of the earlier literature on trade and environment (see General Agreement on Tariffs and Trade (GATT) (1992, Chapter 19), Charnovitz (1998, Chapter 18) and Whalley (1991, Chapter 11)) concerns itself with whether policy linkages between trade and the environment can be justified. Is there a rationale for special trade rules to reflect environmental concerns? When does more trade help or hurt the environment? Should countries use trade measures to achieve environmental goals? Should there be trade provisions in multilateral environment agreements if they override – or conflict with – provisions of trade treaties?

There is a natural linkage between trade and environment through the use of policy instruments. This is largely because actual, or threatened, trade measures can support environmental objectives as demonstrated through their use in some Multilateral Environment Agreements (MEAs). Although little discussed, environmental actions can, in principle, also support trade objectives of exporting countries (see Antweiler, Copeland and Taylor (2001, Chapter 1) and Copeland and Taylor (1999, Chapter 10)). Such a linkage was accepted at the 1994 Marrakesh Ministerial Meeting which concluded the Uruguay Round and established the WTO Committee on Trade and Environment (CTE). The CTE presented its initial report at the first WTO ministerial meeting in Singapore in December 1996. How this linkage should be reflected in the wider post-Singapore trading system is now the more pertinent issue, rather than whether a justification for a linkage exists (see Whalley (1996, Chapter 7)).

Both because of the technical problems and wider precedents created through a change in GATT/WTO rules, as well as the North–South divisions generated by the issue, there has been limited support on the part of the trade community to modify the rules to accommodate the concerns of environmentalists. As the work of the CTE has been largely focused on exploring the implications of the linkages, progress has been incremental rather than bold as environmental groups would wish to see. Indeed, even after extensive debate, nothing near a consensus emerged on feasible options as to how to proceed in the WTO. In fact, the unadopted text proposed by trade negotiators for the Fifth meeting of trade ministers in Cancun in September 2003 did nothing more than 'take note' of the progress made by the CTE in developing 'a common understanding of concepts'. The CTE also agreed to invite secretariats of MEAs, United Nations Environment Programme (UNEP) and United Nations Conference on Trade and Development

(UNCTAD) to its meetings 'in accordance with current practice'. Because of the debacle in Cancun, even this text was not adopted. In short, there is no consensus on how to proceed in the WTO on the trade and environment agenda.

It is perhaps necessary to go further than the WTO to see the potential evolution of the trade and environment debate. Future developments will most likely be driven by factors outside the WTO rather than within it. New global environmental arrangements will emerge, some with potentially large trade implications (such as carbon emission limitation agreements). A credible argument is that the focus thus far on trade and environment issues is of symbolic but limited quantitative significance. This seems poised to change as discussion (outside of the WTO) of possible global environmental measures with potentially large trade effects accelerates. (The potential dimensions of this are discussed in Abrego, Perroni, Whalley and Wigle (2001, Chapter 8) and Perroni and Wigle (1994, Chapter 3).)

It is also worth emphasizing the potential that the trade and environment debate has for reigniting the North–South divide that has been relatively dormant in this area in recent years. Developing countries fear that trade barriers may well be erected in the name of meeting environmental objectives, with the result that their exports are restricted and their growth and development retarded. Trade measures are espoused by some public interest groups in the developed world as a means for dealing with environmental problems. Environmental groups in the developed world argue that environmental issues are so serious that these should be dominant considerations in the setting of the global policy framework, rather than trade concerns. On the other hand, language such as 'green' or 'eco' imperialism is employed on occasions, coupled with the argument that developing countries should be compensated for showing restraint in avoiding environmentally damaging practices that may well contribute significantly to their export earnings.

If the run-up to the meeting of ministers in Cancun revealed anything, it was that trade and environment remains an issue in flux, and one which is unlikely to be resolved quickly or through future WTO negotiations. Also, to treat trade and environment as solely a WTO issue risks missing the wider potential significance of environmental policy issues for the trading system; as well as its ability to resurrect North–South divisions in the trading system. This is especially the case given the complicating precedents the issue raises for core labour standards and other potential trade linkages.

The Trade and Environment Issue

In reality, in the trade and environment debate, there is no one single issue. Rather, there is a series of inter-related sub-issues which together fuel an ongoing debate as to what should be done both within the framework of the WTO and more broadly (see Bhagwati and Srinivasan (1996, Chapter 17) and Whalley (1996, Chapter 7)). An early argument was that the increased trade inevitably implies increased consumption and production and, hence, lower environmental quality. This theme was reflected in Congressional debates on the North America Free Trade Area (NAFTA) in the United States in 1991 and 1992. The argument went through various stages, where extreme environmental problems in the Maquiladora zone, including large untreated discharges into rivers, high infection rates in US border communities attributed to shared US–Mexican aquifers and other related problems, were seen as inevitably worsening under a NAFTA with increased US–Mexican trade. (Grossman and Krueger (1993, Chapter 13) discuss NAFTA and the environment. Mexican trade and environmental policy are also discussed in Low (1992, Chapter 15) and Beghin, Roland-Holst and van der Mensbrugghe (1995, Chapter 12).)

The view that environmental worsening necessarily follows from increased trade is, however, now widely seen as overly simplistic (see Subramanian (1992, Chapter 5) and Tobey (1990, Chapter 6)). In the last few decades, developing countries which have been more outward oriented in their trade policies (e.g. Korea compared with India up to the late 1980s) seem to have achieved higher, rather than lower, environmental standards. In part, this is due to their need to sell into higher income markets with higher environmental standards, and therefore produce according to higher environmental standards (Snape (1992, Chapter 4) discusses some of these effects). In achieving high growth rates for significant periods of time, and hence higher living standards, these same countries have witnessed a positive impact on environmental quality, reflecting, in part, the income elasticity of their own demand for environmental quality. OECD countries' standards for air and water quality are also considerably higher today than they were 50 years ago (again due to higher incomes and a positive income elasticity of demand for environmental quality), even though these same economies now trade considerably more as a percentage of GDP than formerly. The 1992 GATT Annual Report built on these observations to argue that because gains are achievable through trade, real incomes will rise with increased trade; and if these income gains are spent on environmental protection, higher, rather than lower, environmental quality will result.[1]

At quite another level, the debate on trade and environment linkages centres on the claim that environmental problems are now so serious that new and much needed environmental policy cannot be allowed to be thwarted by concerns over trade policy (see the assessment of possible quantitative orders of magnitude involved in Lee and Roland-Holst (1997, Chapter 2)). The argument is that the use of trade-restricting measures on environmental grounds should be allowed, even if presently not sanctioned by GATT/WTO. Thus, special trade promotion devices related to environmental objectives (such as export subsidies for pollution control equipment) should be allowed; trade restrictions which offset the effect of low environmental standards are justifiable; and provisions contained in existing trade treaties (such as GATT/WTO or the Treaty of Rome) should not preclude the use of trade instruments in new environmental arrangements, simply on grounds of precedent. The line of argument is that it is necessary to develop appropriate global management strategies for scarce environmental resources, and that trade policy is a key supporting mechanism to implement such resource management, rather than a policy to be decided upon solely on the grounds of trade considerations.

The counter-arguments reflect the contention that the benefits of an open trading system in the form of gains from trade have been systematically built up over 50 years of multilateral negotiation and should not be surrendered to new protectionism sanctioned by environmental concerns. Any special treatment for the environment under existing trade rules is also seen as setting a dangerous precedent. A domino theory of the trading system is sometimes raised; that is, that special treatment for one issue will lead to special treatment for others, with, eventually, a severe weakening of the rules-based multilateral trading system as we know it today. Reinforcing these concerns is the risk of environmental capture; that is, that trade policy could become more protectionist, not due to genuine environmental considerations motivating trade policy, but rather from protectionist interests using environmental arguments for their own ends and legitimizing their narrow sectional interests by appeal to environmental rationales.

Trade and Environment in the WTO

Within the WTO, the trade and environment issue has also steadily grown in profile in recent years. In its first 40 years, relatively few environmental cases came before the GATT dispute settlement system, and the somewhat oblique environmental content of GATT contained in Article XX remained little clarified by dispute case resolution.[2] Hudec (1996) discusses GATT/WTO dispute settlement and environmental cases.

A central event in changing this situation was the report of the 1991 GATT panel requested by Mexico following US trade actions based on the practices of tuna fishermen off the Mexican west coast.[3] The issue was that tuna were being caught in nets which incidentally entangled dolphins, causing some of the dolphins to be killed. The US responded by restricting imports of tuna from Mexico, and Mexico responded by claiming the US measures violated GATT rules. The fact that the panel ruled in Mexico's favour attracted widespread attention from environmental groups protesting the case and emphasizing what they saw as the anti-environment sentiment of the GATT.[4] In their view, concern for preservation of dolphins did not figure in a decision that reflected only trade interests. Subsequently, dissatisfaction with how the GATT dealt with the environment grew on several fronts. The US Congress saw GATT as overriding the content of domestic US legislation to protect marine life; and more broadly the environmental content of GATT was seen as vague, weak and in need of clarification.

Despite the profile of the trade and environment issue in the mid to late stages of the Uruguay Round,[5] the negotiations conducted in the Round did not deal directly with trade and environment issues. This was largely a reflection of the absence of reference to the environment in the agenda of the Uruguay Round. As a consequence, the WTO Agreements that emerged from the Round did not deal with environment as a standalone issue. Environmental groups made much of the fact that their concerns were not reflected in the 500 pages of legal texts that emerged from the Round, including the tariff schedules, running to some 26 000 pages.[6] This perceived neglect of the WTO to deal directly with environmental problems was seen by environmentalists as squandering a crucial chance to centrally address the trade and environment issue and establish broad principles to guide the WTO in its future work.

On other environmental-related matters, the Uruguay Round generated results with varying degrees of ambiguity. In the area of standards, the thrust of the agreements from the Round was to discipline trade barriers while allowing for differences in non-border measures. Exactly how much discipline would be exerted on national regulations, especially in the case of sanitary and phytosanitary standards, and what would constitute sufficient scientific justification for standards that were higher than international standards, remained unclear. Under the subsidies agreement the use of countervailing measures to deal with 'unfair' trade practices in the form of lax environmental standards was not permitted. But the agreement did imply that subsidies that take the form of foregone revenue for environmental taxes can be countervailable if they are specific.

Nonetheless, trade and environment issues were important in developments running parallel to the negotiations themselves, and in particular played a role in defining the work programme for the WTO following the Round. At the ministerial meeting in Marrakesh in April 1994, governments agreed that trade and environment should be on the future agenda for the WTO, and that a new Committee on Trade and the Environment should be formed to assess trade and environment linkages.[7]

It was agreed that the agenda for the CTE work on trade and environment would be far reaching and cover: (i) the relationship between multilateral environmental arrangements and the GATT/WTO; (ii) how environmental policies with significant trade effects impact the trading system; (iii) how environmental taxes and charges interact with trade rules; (iv) eco-labelling issues; (v) WTO dispute settlement and MEAs; (vi) environmental policy measures and market access; and (vii) domestically prohibited goods. Progress on most of these issues has been slow. In essence, a handful of developed countries, especially the European Union, have argued for modifications to GATT/WTO disciplines for environmental reasons; while developing countries, fearful of legitimizing protection against their exports, have taken a more cautious stance. Nothing of substance in terms of creating new WTO rules for the environment areas has been concluded.

However, trade and environment continues to be repeatedly cited as a major component of the likely future focus for global trade policy negotiation and debate. Renato Ruggiero, an earlier Director General of the WTO, identified trade and environment as one of four issues (along with competitive policy, labour standards and investment) which will shape the future work programme of the WTO and eventually form the lead issues of a future multilateral negotiating Round. Immediately after the Uruguay Round, there were several calls for a new negotiating Round to be a 'Green Round', and such calls, while less frequent, are still heard.

This high profile for trade and environment within the WTO seemingly coexists with difficulties in reaching decisions on new rules coupled with clear divisions between developed and developing countries. The trade and environment component of any future negotiation would also be a rule-writing rather than traditional reciprocity-based negotiation, and one with precedents for other potential rule-writing exercises (such as labour standards). While the Uruguay Round established precedents creating agreements on new areas such as intellectual property rights, it is unlikely that a similar 'non-traditional' agreement would emerge for the environment in a future multilateral negotiating Round.

Responding Multilaterally

International concern about the impact of environmental policies on trade as well as the impact of trade on the environment has been evident since at least the UN Stockholm Conference on the Human Environment in 1972.[8] While the ensuing years have witnessed a great deal of international action on the environment front, including the negotiation of many global and regional conventions, it was not until the 1990s that trade and environment figured prominently on the trade agenda. The 1990s, however, saw a marked intensification of the debate and a proliferation of scholarly contributions. The 'Greening of the GATT' and 'GATTing the Greens' became catch cries for those interested in the trade and environment debate.

A GATT Secretariat study (1992, Chapter 19) sets out the trade and environment issues as seen from a trade perspective in the early 1990s. The argument advanced runs along the lines that when adverse production and consumption externalities are adequately integrated into decision-making processes, trade liberalization and the attainment of environment objectives can be mutually supportive. The argument continues that trade liberalization leads to real growth, more resources available for environmental management programmes, and an increase in the availability of environment-related goods and services through market liberalization.

The link with environmental policy is that for these benefits to be realized, and for trade-induced growth to be sustainable, appropriate environmental policies determined at the national level need to be put in place. For environmental policy making, life cycle analysis of a product – that is, the way it is produced and ultimately disposed of as waste – is important to ensure that the environmental impact of both production and consumption is fully taken into account. But regulations of this nature may well differ significantly across countries for a host of reasons. Here lies the question that is central to the trade and environment debate and, in particular, the formulation and interpretation of trade rules: can a legitimate case be made for allowing one country to independently use trade measures to try to reduce a source of environmental degradation by requiring that imported products meet process standards established by the importing country?

In the view of Charnovitz (1998), the multilateral response by the WTO requires a focus on both production and consumption of goods and services and a questioning of the preference on the part of trade policy analysts for trade rules that treat 'like' products equivalently regardless of their method of production. What is needed is an integrative scenario that would seek to harmonize international trade law with international law generally, and take seriously the goal in the WTO Preamble to use the world's resources in accordance with the objective of sustainable development.

Bhagwati and Srinivasan (1996) take up the same issue of the link between trade and environmental standards by asking the question of under what circumstances – if any – should trade be restricted because of the absence of harmonized environmental policies among countries? Answering this key question underpins much of the discussion of the key items on the multilateral trade and environment agenda. Their view is that the potency of the contention that harmonization of domestic policies across trading partners is a precondition for free trade should not be underestimated today. It is nowhere more manifest, or more compelling in its policy appeal, than in the area of environmental standards.

Bhagwati and Srinivasan analyse the issue in terms of the criticisms of social dumping: the condition of free trade in the absence of harmonized environmental standards. In this respect, a key question is the following: Why should anyone object to free trade with any country on the grounds that its preferred solutions to intrinsically domestic environmental questions are unacceptable, and therefore incompatible with the case for gains from free trade? In addressing this question, they explore the following arguments: diverse environmental standards could lead to unfair trade due to a lack of a level playing field; the related argument that lower environmental standards coupled with free trade could lead to a lowering of environmental standards in order to compete; incompatible ethical preferences based on methods of production mean that some trade should be abandoned or banned; and finally institutional considerations whereby low-standard countries accuse high-standard countries of protectionist motivations – particularly in the GATT.

The authors argue that diversity in environmental standards is perfectly legitimate. This can arise not merely because the environment is differently valued between countries but also because of the differences in endowments and technology across countries.

Settling Disputes

As the 1990s progressed, it was clear that many in the environment community would have liked the WTO to have more permissive rules when it came to accommodating their environmental concerns.[9] An important question addressed by Hudec (1996) in this respect is one of law-making strategies. If differences between trade officials and environmentalists are to be resolved, should this be through the negotiation of special rules in the WTO, or can the differences be resolved through common law interpretation of GATT legal texts and the WTO dispute settlement process?

Hudec examines the GATT legal status of international environment agreements and identifies two questions: do WTO members waive their GATT rights when they accept the trade provision of environment agreements, and can WTO members which have not signed the agreements be barred from asserting their GATT rights against WTO members that apply trade measures authorized by the environmental agreements? Hudec also analyses a number of GATT trade and environment disputes to inquire into the use of unilateral measures as a means of coercing the adoption of certain process-related standards in exporting countries. He concludes that while countries have considerable flexibility in adopting standards within their own territories, the same discretion does not apply with respect to the environmental practices of other countries. He cautions (within the context of Article III of GATT 1994) that permitting governments to make imports comply with process regulations imposed on domestic firms would allow them to insist that imports comply with minimum wage regulations, collective bargaining regulations, record-keeping regulations and any and all safety regulations.

But why have environment disputes gravitated towards the WTO? Like a number of others who have compared compliance mechanisms in different treaties, Cameron (1998, Chapter 20) comments that environmental regimes lack the power of the WTO dispute settlement mechanism; it has been 'astoundingly popular' with states because it can 'offer rewards for use' with political and economic benefits that can be cashed in, and 'There is no comparable mechanism in multilateral environment agreements'. In addition, many of the obligations in MEAs are not subject to judicial application; they are simply too general, leaving too much discretion to parties on how they choose to implement them. Cameron concludes that what the environment community must pay attention to is that the WTO will remain open and available to settle trade-related environment disputes if countries choose to make claims in the language of WTO law.

In terms of policy recommendations, Cameron notes that in cases such as the shrimp turtle case it would have been productive to have considered whether mediation would have been a more appropriate way to settle the dispute. Further, an amendment to Article XX to include specific reference to 'measures taken pursuant to' MEAs would have provided a better legal backcloth for the institutions of the dispute settlement understanding to work with. He also concludes that there is a need for a rational system for distributing jurisdiction among competing regimes in international law and to protect the WTO from taking on cases which it should not hear.

WTO and Multilateral Environment Agreements

Since its establishment, one of the most actively discussed topics in the WTO has been the relationship between its provisions and the use of trade measures in MEAs.[10] The debate has centred on the possibility of a conflict arising over trade-related measures contained in MEAs: namely, their potential inconsistency with WTO rules, and how conflict in these rules could be avoided or dealt with.[11]

Duncan Brack (1999, Chapter 21) notes that some of the most important MEAs permit discrimination between parties on the basis of production processes and making use of quantitative restrictions, and in doing so are inconsistent with WTO rules. Given the success of the use of these trade measures in the MEAs he reviews, he concludes that they are likely to continue to be important; therefore the potential for conflict should be dealt with. He notes the experience of exceptions sought for environment purposes under Article XX of the GATT 1994, and that each of the environmental measures was found to be unacceptable because the measures were not the least trade restrictive, were extra-jurisdictional in nature or were applied in an arbitrary or unjustifiable manner.

Brack argues that the present situation creates an unstable and uncertain situation, threatens direct conflict between two important global regimes, weakens the effectiveness of future environment agreements, and does nothing to remove the perception that the WTO threatens the environment. His recommendations (destined for the ill-fated Millennium Round of negotiations to be launched in Seattle – but still appropriate today) are particularly timely as governments in the Doha Development Agenda negotiations grapple with the tasks mandated by ministers to negotiate the relationship between existing WTO rules and specific trade obligations set out in MEAs. His preference is for a specific agreement in the WTO that would not amend existing WTO rules and would apply only to MEAs.

Sampson (2001, Chapter 22) offers a number of suggestions as to how the relationship between the WTO and MEAs could be improved. In general terms, he considers that environmental matters should be dealt with by those institutions that have both the mandate and expertise to do so. For example, if WTO-inconsistent measures are provided for in an environment agreement, they should be clearly defined and enforced by a robust dispute settlement system within the MEA itself. In this context he argues that it is in the interest of the WTO to have effective MEAs to avoid environment-related disputes and other matters gravitating towards the WTO.

Among the many MEAs in existence, the Convention on Biological Diversity (CBD) is regularly singled out because of its relationship to the WTO and its agreements. The interest relates not to the possible inconsistency between the trade measures of a MEA but rather whether the Convention and a WTO agreement – in this case the Trade Intellectual Property Rights (TRIPs) Agreement – are mutually supportive. The Convention on Biological Diversity has as its objective 'the conservation of biological diversity, the sustainable use of its components and the fair and equitable sharing of the benefits arising out of the utilization of genetic resources'. As Graham Dutfield (2002, Chapter 23) points out, the TRIPs Agreement makes no reference to access and benefits sharing, traditional knowledge or, for that matter, the Convention on Biological Diversity.

The linkage comes from the fact that the Convention recognizes the sovereign rights of States over their natural resources and their authority to determine access to genetic resources. It also recognizes that access, where granted, is to be on mutually agreed terms and subject to prior informed consent of the provider party. Intellectual property considerations are clearly important. A critical question in this respect is whether instruments contained in the TRIPs Agreement for the protection of intellectual property rights promote the sharing of benefits between the commercial users of genetic resources and indigenous communities and the coherence and mutual supportiveness of the TRIPs Agreement and the Convention on Biological Diversity. Dutfield argues that they do not and suggests what to do about it.

Developing Country Concerns

What stands out as an issue that flags many of the concerns of developing countries is eco-labelling, the goal of which is to discriminate against products that are perceived to be less environmentally sound. Appleton (2002, Chapter 24) notes that while the overall goal is laudable, eco-labels are of both a systemic and commercial concern to developing countries. From a commercial perspective, producers in developing countries lack the resources and political expertise to influence the development of foreign labelling criteria. Also, developed countries may formulate eco-labelling criteria on the basis of conditions in their own countries that are not appropriate for developing countries. Further, wage considerations, regulatory requirements and the enforcement of regulations are often viewed as sources of comparative advantage. Labelling schemes that alert consumers to serious discrepancies in the above may disadvantage developing countries and be based on what can be very subjective factors.

Developing countries have seen little value in much of the trade and environment debate. Shahin (2002, Chapter 25) provides an overview of the various key trade and environment issues from a developing country perspective. Her examination covers a range of issues, including MEAs, eco-labelling and trade-related intellectual property rights. She clearly articulates the developing countries' mistrust of the use of process-related environmental standards.[12] She argues they are frequently based on values that differ from one society to another; in particular, those in developing countries. This concern permeates much of her article; such as her rejection of an environmental window for Article XX of GATT 1994 and justifications for unilateral actions in particular, and her suspicion of the motivations behind some eco-labelling schemes as well as proposals for clarifying the relationship between WTO rules and MEAs. She notes that setting ecological standards for process-related production standards could be used as an opening for over-stretching the concept in the future and taking it as a precedent to incorporate other non-trade-related goals. In this respect she identifies the specific areas of concern for a number of developing countries: labour standards, human rights, good governance and other standards that have no relationship with the WTO.

Systemic Considerations

One phenomenon of a systemic nature that raises considerable concern among trade officials is the continuing proliferation of regional trade agreements. Not only are their numbers increasing rapidly, the nature of the obligations they contain frequently reaches deep into the regulatory structure of the parties concerned. One such area where regional trade agreements are extending to new disciplines is environmental protection.

Mann (2000, Chapter 27) examines the side agreement to the North America Free Trade Area between Canada, Mexico and the United States which was developed to support the environmental provisions of the NAFTA. He notes that the two types of environmental provision found in the NAFTA text relate to traditional trade disciplines and their impact on environmental law and management practices. This, for example, encompasses identifying environmental protection as a legitimate purpose for which trade measures may be taken or a specific regime for measures pursuant to multilateral trade agreements. The second type of provision is non-binding and states that the parties should not waive or derogate from existing environmental protection standards in order to attract investment. Other commitments relate to each party agreeing to effectively enforce its environmental laws and pursue the necessary legal means to seek appropriate remedies for violations and report on the state of its environment.

Another systemic consideration of particular concern to Non-Governmental Organizations (NGOs) is their lack of representation in the WTO processes and rule making. Esty (1998, Chapter 26) presents the view of many NGOs that it is in the interests of the WTO itself to be more receptive to their views and involvement. He says that NGOs are a mechanism whereby the WTO can 'connect' to citizens around the world. He acknowledges that the WTO has an important role to play in facilitating collective action among nations to support liberalized trade and overcome market failures that would otherwise disrupt the efficient workings and potential welfare-enhancing effect of the international market place. But he notes that if the WTO is to play its role effectively, it must be seen as having legitimacy, it must be authoritative and carry out its business with a commitment to fairness. NGOs, he argues, can help the WTO to achieve these goals.

Perhaps what is needed to deal effectively with trade and environment issues at the global level is a new institution.[13] Runge (2001, Chapter 28) notes that there have been many schemes and proponents of a World or Global Environment Organization. However, he argues that a Global Environmental Organization (GEO) is an idea whose time will surely come. He says that a GEO should be considered as part of a wider effort to better coordinate international environmental policy and protect and insulate the WTO from responsibilities towards which it is disinclined and unprepared. In promoting the idea of a GEO, Runge offers what he considers solutions to many trade-related problems – a number of which have been addressed in the various articles reproduced in this book. He argues that a GEO offers the trading system the opportunity to disentangle trade from environmental matters, allowing the WTO to focus where it should: on expansion of market access and reductions in trade protectionism, saving attention for environmental measures only in cases of obvious trade distortion. A GEO could be of considerable assistance to the WTO in clarifying where environmental exceptions to the GATT articles are justified (under Article XX) and providing guidelines for minimally trade-distorting MEAs. At the same time, a GEO could help fill the institutional gap in dispute resolution and coordination surrounding the many MEAs and institutions now responsible for global environmental issues.

Future Developments

The outcome of the Fourth WTO Ministerial Conference in Doha, Qatar from 9–14 November 2001 was the launch of a new round of multilateral trade negotiations – the Doha Development Agenda. How the WTO should deal with trade and environment in the coming years was certainly one of the most contentious issues under review and the outcome was potentially far reaching.

In particular, after years of discussions in the CTE, governments agreed that *negotiations* on trade and environment will now be undertaken. The fact that governments are to negotiate potentially elevates the past process considerably in WTO terms. Ministers decided that the negotiations would be conducted with a view to enhancing the mutual supportiveness of trade and environment, and addressing the relationship between existing WTO rules and specific trade obligations set out in MEAs. Procedures for regular information exchange between MEA Secretariats and the relevant WTO committees were to be established, and the thorny question of the criteria for deciding which institutions would have observer status in WTO meetings would be dealt with. The reduction or elimination of tariff and non-tariff barriers to environmental goods and services was also to be addressed.

Ministers also instructed the CTE to give particular attention to the effect of environmental measures on market access, especially in relation to least-developed and developing countries, and the situations in which the elimination or reduction of trade restrictions and distortions would benefit trade, the environment and development. Attention was also to be given to the relevant provisions of the TRIPs Agreement and labelling requirements for environmental purposes. Ministers encouraged Members to pursue national environmental reviews of trade policies on a voluntary basis, and to share expertise and experience among themselves regarding the performance of such reviews. The CTE was to report to the Fifth Session of the Ministerial Conference in Cancun in Mexico in September 2003, and make recommendations with respect to future action, including the desirability of negotiations.

Not surprisingly, in the period between the Doha and Cancun Ministerial meetings there was intensive work in the CTE, particularly in the context of negotiations on the relationship between existing WTO rules and specific trade obligations set out in MEAs. Notwithstanding that, very little progress was registered in this area as well as other parts of the trade and environment negotiating agenda. As noted above, the draft Ministerial Declaration prepared for the Cancun Ministerial meeting did little more than take note of the regular work of the CTE and reaffirm the commitment of governments to the negotiations envisaged in the Doha Development Agenda. As the Cancun meeting failed, even this extremely modest text did not survive.

In addressing the link between trade and environment it would appear that at the inter-governmental level the accepted approach is that trade and environmental policies can complement each other. Environmental protection preserves the natural resource base on which economic growth is premised and trade liberalization leads to the economic growth needed for adequate environmental protection. However, to ensure success, it is important that environmental policies do not act as obstacles to trade liberalization, and that trade rules do not stand in the way of adequate domestic environmental protection. In other words, there is a real need for cooperation between those institutions dealing with the environment and those dealing with trade matters. In any negotiations, it is critical to have the information in hand to negotiate from a well-informed standpoint. The work of the research community has been critical in providing the information that has permitted a better understanding of the issues involved and consequences of decisions that could be taken in the negotiating process. The chapters included in this volume have all contributed importantly in their own way to throwing more light and less heat on what is at times a very emotional debate.

Notes

1. A particularly useful study by Brian Copeland critically reviews both theoretical and empirical work to explore the question of what we know about the relationship between international trade, economic growth and the environment. See Brian R. Copeland, *Trade Growth and the Environment*, National Bureau of Economic Research Working Paper Series, Number 9823, July 2003.
2. Appendix C of Esty (1994) outlines both previous GATT cases and relevant US and EU case law. Some of the earlier GATT cases which touched on environmental issues involved excise duties on imported petroleum and products in the US to fund environmental clean-up (the 1971 Superfund case); Canadian restrictions on export of unprocessed fish products from the West Coast fishery (1988) and import bans on cigarettes in Thailand (1990).
3. For a comprehensive description of this and all other environmental cases dealt with by GATT and the WTO see WTO Secretariat (2002), *GATT/WTO Dispute Settlement Practice Relating to GATT Article XX* (WT/CTE/W/203), Geneva: WTO, 1–47.
4. The panel finding on behalf of Mexico ruled that the US ban was a violation of GATT Article III, and that the Article XX exceptions in GATT could not be applied on an extraterritorial basis, ruling them inapplicable in this case. However, the panel report ruled in favour of the US on the labelling issue. The panel report was not pushed forward to adoption by the GATT Council for a variety of reasons, including Mexico's then emerging NAFTA negotiation; so the EC subsequently brought a second complaint on tuna–dolphin dealing with import bans in the US Marine Mammal Protection Act from third countries who trade with countries against whom primary actions are taken. The panel report (Tuna–Dolphin II) in 1994 ruled against the US, but on somewhat different grounds. See Esty (1994) pp. 268–9.
5. A number of events contributed to raising the profile of trade and environment (virtually unheard of at its launch in Punta del Este in 1986) during the later part of the Uruguay Round besides the tuna/dolphin dispute. These included the Earth Summit at Rio in June 1992, the vocal opposition of environmentalists to NAFTA, and the efforts of environmental groups to block adoption of both NAFTA and the Uruguay Round decisions in the US.
6. For a summary of the Uruguay Round agreements, see Whalley and Hamilton (1996).
7. For a comprehensive description of the world of the CTE see Gregory C. Shaffer, 'The World Trade Organization Under Challenge: Democracy and the Law and Politics of the WTO's Treatment of Trade and Environment Matters', *Harvard Environmental Law Review*, Volume 25, Number 1, 2001.
8. As a contribution to the 1972 Stockholm Conference on the Human Environment, the Secretariat of GATT advanced the concern of trade officials that environmental policies could not only become obstacles to trade, but could constitute a new form of protectionism. See GATT, *Industrial Pollution Control and International Trade*, GATT Studies on International Trade, No. 1, Geneva, July 1971.
9. For a comprehensive overview, see Ernst-Ulrich Petersmann, 'Clarification and Development of GATT/WTO Law through the GATT/WTO Dispute Settlement System: The Case Law on Trade-Related Environmental Measures', Chapter 3 in Ernst-Ulrich Petersmann, *The GATT/WTO Dispute Settlement System: International Law, International Organizations and Dispute Settlement*, Kluwer Law International, 1997.
10. A number of these issues are also dealt with in Richard G. Tarasofsky, 'Minimising Conflicts and Enhancing Complementarity between Multilateral Environment Agreements and WTO Agreement', in *Legal Aspects of International Trade, Proceedings of a World Bank Seminar*, The World Bank, Washington, 2001.
11. See also Konrad Von Moltke, *Whither MEAs – The Role of International Environment Management in the Trade and Environment Agenda*, International Institute for Sustainable Development, Winnipeg, Canada, July 2001.
12. Veena Jha and Rene Vossenaar also argue that there are sound reasons for developing countries to oppose broad WTO negotiations based on environmental considerations. The authors caution against the use of unilateral trade measures as well as the acceptance of non-product-related production measures, particularly in the context of eco-labelling. See Veena Jha and Rene Vossenaar, 'Trade, Environment and Development', in *Positive Agenda and Future Trade Negotiations*, United Nations

Conference on Trade and Development, Chapter 3, New York and Geneva: United Nations, 2000, 367–401

13. There is a comprehensive discussion of the issues surrounding the establishment of a World Environment Organization in several articles contained in *The World Economy*, Volume 25, Issue 5, May, 2002.

References

Esty, Dan (1994), *Greening the GATT*, International Institute for Economics, Washington DC.

Hudec, Robert (1996), 'The GATT/WTO Dispute Settlement Process: Can it Reconcile Trade Rules and Environmental Needs', in Rudiger Wolfrum (ed.), *Enforcing Environmental Standards: Economic Mechanisms as Viable Means*, Berlin: Springer-Verlag.

Whalley, J. and Colleen Hamilton (1996), 'The Trading System after the Uruguay Round' (out of print).

Part I
General Linkage Discussion

[1]

Is Free Trade Good for the Environment?

By WERNER ANTWEILER, BRIAN R. COPELAND, AND M. SCOTT TAYLOR*

This paper investigates how openness to international goods markets affects pollution concentrations. We develop a theoretical model to divide trade's impact on pollution into scale, technique, and composition effects and then examine this theory using data on sulfur dioxide concentrations. We find international trade creates relatively small changes in pollution concentrations when it alters the composition of national output. Estimates of the trade-induced technique and scale effects imply a net reduction in pollution from these sources. Combining our estimates of all three effects yields a somewhat surprising conclusion: freer trade appears to be good for the environment. (*JEL* F11, Q25)

The debate over the role international trade plays in determining environmental outcomes has at times generated more heat than light. Theoretical work has been successful in identifying a series of hypotheses linking openness to trade and environmental quality, but the empirical verification of these hypotheses has seriously lagged. Foremost among these is the pollution haven hypothesis that suggests relatively low-income developing countries will be made dirtier with trade. Its natural alternative, the simple factor endowment hypothesis, suggests that dirty capital-intensive processes will relocate to the relatively capital-abundant developed countries with trade. Empirical work by James A. Tobey (1990), Gene M. Grossman and Alan B. Krueger (1993), and Adam B. Jaffe et al. (1995) cast serious doubt on the strength of the simple pollution haven hypothesis because they find that trade flows are primarily determined by factor endowment considerations and apparently not by differences in pollution abatement costs. Does this mean that trade has no effect on the environment?

This paper investigates how "openness" to international markets affects pollution levels to assess the environmental consequences of international trade. We develop a theoretical model to divide trade's impact on pollution into scale, technique, and composition effects and then examine this theory using data on sulfur dioxide concentrations from the Global Environment Monitoring Project. The decomposition of trade's effect into scale, technique, and composition effects has proven useful in other contexts [see Grossman and Krueger (1993); Copeland and Taylor (1994, 1995)] and here we move one step forward to provide estimates of their magnitude.

We find that international trade creates relatively small changes in sulfur dioxide concentrations when it alters the composition, and hence the pollution intensity, of national output. Combining this result with our estimates of scale and technique effects yields a somewhat surprising conclusion: if trade liberalization

* Antweiler: Faculty of Commerce, University of British Columbia, 2053 Main Mall, Vancouver, BC, V6T 1Z2 Canada. (e-mail: werner@economics.ca); Copeland: Department of Economics, University of British Columbia, 997-1873 East Mall, Vancouver, BC, V6T 1Z1 Canada (e-mail: copeland@econ.ubc.ca); Taylor: Department of Economics, Social Science Building 6448, University of Wisconsin, 1180 Observatory Drive, Madison, WI 53706 (e-mail: staylor@ssc.wisc.edu). An earlier version of this paper was circulated under the title, "Trade and the Environment: Theory and Empirical Results" (August 1997). We express our thanks to, without implicating, P. Beaudry, D. Green, H. Emery, G. Heal, K. Head, K. Scholz, J. McGregor, two anonymous referees, seminar participants at numerous universities, the NBER Summer Institute Workshop on Public Policy and the Environment, the NBER Trade, Resources, and the Environment conference, and the Research Institute for Economics and Business in Kobe, Japan. Financial support was provided by the SSRHC, the Hampton Fund, and the NSF.

raises GDP per person by 1 percent, then pollution concentrations fall by about 1 percent. Free trade is good for the environment.[1]

We obtain this conclusion by estimating a very simple model highlighting the interaction of factor endowments and income differences in determining the pattern of trade. Our approach, although relatively straightforward, is novel in four respects. First, by exploiting the panel structure of our data set, we are able to distinguish empirically between the negative environmental consequences of scalar increases in economic activity—the scale effect—and the positive environmental consequences of increases in income that call for cleaner production methods—the technique effect. This distinction is important for many reasons.[2] Grossman and Krueger (1993) interpret their hump-shaped "Kuznets curve" as reflecting the relative strength of scale versus technique effects, but they do not provide separate estimates of their magnitude. Our estimates indicate that a 1-percent increase in the scale of economic activity raises pollution concentrations by 0.25 to 0.5 percent for an average country in our sample, but the accompanying increase in income drives concentrations down by 1.25–1.5 percent via a technique effect.

Second, we devise a method for determining how trade-induced changes in the composition of output affect pollution concentrations. Many empirical studies include some measure of openness to capture the impact trade has in altering the composition (and hence the cleanliness) of national output, but there is very little reason to believe that openness affects the composition of output in all countries similarly. Both the pollution haven hypothesis and the factor endowment hypothesis predict that openness to trade will alter the composition of national output in a manner that depends on a nation's comparative advantage.

For example, under the pollution haven hypothesis, poor countries get dirtier with trade, whereas rich countries get cleaner.[3] As a result, simply adding openness to trade as an additional explanatory variable for pollution (across a panel of both rich and poor countries) is unlikely to be fruitful. Instead we look for trade's effect by conditioning on country characteristics. We find that openness conditioned on country characteristics has a highly significant, but relatively small, impact on pollution.

Third, we show how to combine economic theory with our estimates of scale, composition, and technique effects to arrive at an assessment of the environmental impact of freer trade. Grossman and Krueger's influential study of NAFTA presented an argument based on the relative strength of these same three effects, but their estimate of the composition effect of trade was obtained from methods and data unrelated to their complementary work estimating the relative strength of scale and technique effects. Moreover, their evidence on composition effects was specific to the situation of Mexico. Here we estimate all three effects jointly on a data set that includes over 40 developed and developing countries.

Finally, our approach forces us to distinguish between the pollution consequences of income growth brought about by increased openness from those created by capital accumulation or technological progress. We find that income gains brought about by further trade or neutral technological progress tend to lower pollution, whereas income gains brought about by capital accumulation raise pollution. The key difference is that capital accumulation necessarily favors the production of pollution-intensive goods, whereas neutral technological progress and further trade do not. One immediate implication of this finding is that the pollution consequences of economic growth are dependent on the underlying source of growth.[4]

[1] Free trade appears to lower sulfur dioxide concentrations for an average country in our sample, but may of course worsen the environment through other channels. Our evidence is specific to sulfur dioxide; however, sulfur dioxide emissions are highly correlated with other airborne emissions.

[2] For example, income transfers across countries raise national income but not output, whereas foreign direct investment raises output more than national income. To evaluate the environmental consequences of either we need separate estimates of technique and scale effects.

[3] That is, the composition effect of trade for poor countries makes them dirtier, whereas the composition effect for rich countries makes them cleaner. The full effect of trade may be positive even for poor countries, depending on the strength of the technique and scale effects. See, for example, Proposition 2.

[4] Another more speculative implication of our results is that pollution concentrations should at first rise and then fall

The theoretical literature on trade and the environment contains many papers in which pollution policy differences across countries drive pollution-intensive industries to countries with lax regulations.[5] One criticism of these papers is that, although they are successful in predicting trade patterns in a world where policy is fixed and unresponsive, their results may be a highly misleading guide to policy in a world where environmental protection responds endogenously to changing conditions.

Empirical work by Grossman and Krueger (1993) suggests that it is important to allow policy to change endogenously with income levels, and in our earlier work (Copeland and Taylor, 1994, 1995) we investigated how income-induced differences in pollution policy determine trade patterns. Although this earlier work produced several insights, it ignored the role factor abundance could play in determining trade patterns.

In contrast, the model we develop here allows income differences and factor abundance differences to jointly determine trade patterns. The model contains as one limiting case the canonical Heckscher–Ohlin–Samuelson (HOS) model of international trade and as another limiting case a simple pollution haven model. Considering these two motivations for trade is especially important in an empirical investigation because many of the most polluting industries are also highly capital intensive.[6] Moreover, it allows us to examine whether changes in dirty goods production brought about by trade is better explained by factor abundance motives or by pollution haven motives arising from an unequal distribution of world income.

The empirical literature in this area has progressed in three distinct ways. One influential group of studies asks: "How does economic growth affect the environment?". This literature was initiated by early work by Grossman and Krueger (1993, 1995) and has since produced a sizable and fast growing empirical literature examining what has come to be known as the "Environmental Kuznets curve."[7] Many of these studies also investigate the role of trade by adding a measure of openness as an additional regressor. The defining feature of this literature is its lack of explicit theory. Although the results from these studies are often interpreted within the context of scale, composition, and technique effects, they do not provide separate estimates of their magnitudes.

Our work is most closely related to this branch of the literature, but differs in that we employ an explicit theoretical model to guide our estimation; we present separate estimates of scale, composition, and technique elasticities; and we provide a methodology for adding up these effects to assess the environmental implications of freer trade. Despite the fact that this earlier work lacks a formal theory, some of their conclusions receive support in our work. Most notably, Grossman and Krueger's (1993) study of NAFTA had at its core the argument that technique effects offset scale effects—at least for Mexico—and that the composition effect created by further United States–Mexico trade was likely to be driven more by factor endowment considerations than by differences in environmental regulation. Our work supports these conclusions: income effects appear to be economically and statistically significant, and the trade-induced composition effects are not driven by differences in pollution regulations.

There is a second group of studies examining the link between the costs of pollution abatement cost and trade flows. This approach was pioneered by Tobey (1990) and was employed in the context of the NAFTA agreement by Grossman and Krueger (1993).[8] This branch of the literature asks a slightly different question: "How do environmental regulations affect trade flows?". Nevertheless some of their results are also relevant to our work. For example, a common result from these studies is that measures

with increases in income per capita, if capital accumulation becomes a less important source of growth as development proceeds.

[5] For example, Rüdiger Pethig (1976), Horst Siebert et al. (1980), and Martin C. McGuire (1982) all present models where the costs of pollution-intensive goods are lower in the region with no environmental policy.

[6] See Muthukumara Mani and David Wheeler (1997) and Werner Antweiler et al. (1998), Appendix Section B.1, for evidence linking capital intensity and pollution intensity.

[7] Some authors refer to it as the Grossman–Krueger Kuznets Curve. Other early contributions to this literature are Thomas M. Selden and Daqing Song (1994) and Nemat Shafik (1994).

[8] Arik Levinson (1996) reviews this work.

of environmental stringency have little effect on trade flows. This result immediately casts doubt on the pollution haven hypothesis, which holds that trade in dirty goods primarily responds to cross-country differences in regulations. Although our work is quite different in approach and method, we too find little support for the pollution haven hypothesis. We do not infer from this, however, that the cost of regulations does not matter to trade flows; instead, we suggest it is because other offsetting factors more than compensate for the costs of tight regulation in developed economies.

Finally, there are those studies that employ either the U.S. Toxic Release Inventory, U.S. emission intensity data, or simple rules to categorize goods industries as dirty or clean, to construct measures of the toxic (or pollution) intensity of production and trade flows. Work along these lines includes Patrick Low and Alexander Yeats (1992), Robert E. B. Lucas et al. (1992), and Mani and Wheeler (1997). The strength of this branch of the literature is its broad cross-country coverage; its weakness is that this coverage arises from the construction of data under various assumptions regarding the similarity of emission intensities across countries. This literature typically asks: "How has the pollution intensity of exports or production changed over time?" By comparing the answer to this question across countries differing in development level, income, or trade stance, the authors hope to identify links between various policy options, country characteristics, and environmental outcomes. Although this work is useful in documenting trends in the pollution intensity of output and trade, it cannot answer why these trends exist. Our work differs from this method by using theory to identify those factors we believe to be crucial to environmental outcomes, and by using regression analysis to hold all else equal when evaluating the links between country characteristics and environmental outcomes.

The overall impression one gets from this literature is that, even though there are many interesting findings, a consensus view does not exist—and the path to building such a consensus view is unclear. The unsettled nature of the literature arises, at least in part, because existing studies are hamstrung by the lack of a well-defined theory. This naturally makes inference difficult. Additional difficulties arise because good data on pollution levels are scarce, and even the best data reflect not only anthropogenic influences but also the little-understood natural processes of dispersion and absorption. As a consequence, our simple first-generation pollution and trade model carries a heavy burden in providing us with the structure needed to isolate and identify the implications of international trade. Although this is a concern, we suggest that earlier empirical investigations failed to find a strong and convincing link between environmental outcomes and freer trade precisely because they lacked a strong theoretical underpinning. With a more complete theoretical framework to guide us, we are able to look in the "right directions" for trade's effect. Moreover, our simple pollution demand-and-supply model may play a useful role in focusing future efforts in this area.

The rest of the paper is organized as follows. In Section I we develop a relatively simple general equilibrium model of trade to determine how a fall in trade barriers affects pollution levels. In Section II we then describe our strategy for dealing with econometric difficulties and present our estimating equation. In Section III we present our empirical results. Section IV concludes. Appendices A and B contain proofs of propositions and a description of our data. An additional Technical Appendix, available on request from the authors, contains further supporting materials.

I. Theory

A. *The Model*

A population of N agents lives in a small open economy that produces two final goods, X and Y, with two primary factors, labor L and capital K. Industry Y is labor intensive and does not pollute. Industry X is capital intensive and generates pollution as a by-product. We assume constant returns to scale, and hence the production technology for X and Y can be described by unit cost functions $c^X(w, r)$ and $c^Y(w, r)$. Let Y be the numeraire, and denote the relative price of X by p. Because countries differ in their location, proximity to suppliers, and existing trade barriers, domestic prices will not be identical to world prices. Accordingly we write

$$p = \beta p^w, \tag{1}$$

where β measures the importance of trade frictions and p^w is the common world relative price of X. Note $\beta > 1$ if a country imports X and $\beta < 1$ if a country exports X.[9]

Pollution Abatement.—We denote pollution emissions by Z. Pollution is generated by X production, but firms have access to an abatement technology. Abatement is costly but uses the same factor intensities as all other activities in the X industry; hence, we simply treat units of X as inputs into abatement. If a firm has a gross output of x units, and allocates x_a units to abatement, then its net output is $x_n = x(1 - \theta)$, where $\theta = x_a/x$ is a measure of the intensity of abatement. If pollution is proportional to output and abatement is a constant returns activity, then we can write pollution emissions as

$$z = e(\theta)x, \tag{2}$$

where $e(\theta)$ is emissions per unit of X produced and is decreasing in θ.[10] We assume abatement is worthwhile [$e'(0) = -\infty$], but with physical limits [$e(1) > 0$].

The government uses pollution emission taxes to reduce pollution. Given the pollution tax τ, the profits π^x for a firm producing X are given by revenue less factor payments, pollution taxes, and abatement costs. Using (1) and our definition of θ, we may write profits succinctly as

$$\pi^x = p^N x - wL_x - rK_x, \tag{3}$$

where $p^N = p(1 - \theta) - \tau e(\theta)$ is the net producer price for gross output. Because of constant returns, the output of an individual firm is indeterminate, but for any level of output, the first-order condition for the choice of θ implies

$$p = -\tau e'(\theta). \tag{4}$$

Hence, we have $\theta = \theta(\tau/p)$ with $\theta' > 0$ and we can write emissions per unit output as

$$e = e(\tau/p), \tag{5}$$

where $e' < 0$. The production side equilibrium conditions are simply (2), (4), and the standard zero profit and full employment conditions:

$$p^N = c^X(w, r) \qquad 1 = c^Y(w, r) \tag{6}$$

$$K = c_r^X x + c_r^Y y \qquad L = c_w^X x + c_w^Y y.$$

Consumers.—For most of our analysis, consumers differ only in their preferences over pollution. There are two groups in society: N^g Green consumers who care greatly about the environment (Greens), and $N^b = N - N^g$ Brown consumers (Browns) who care less about the environment. Each consumer maximizes utility, treating pollution as given. For simplicity, we write the indirect utility function of a consumer in the ith group as

$$V^i(p, G/N, z) = u\left(\frac{G/N}{\rho(p)}\right) - \delta^i z \tag{7}$$

for $i = \{g, b\}$ and where $\delta^g > \delta^b \geq 0$, G is national income (so G/N is per capita income), $\rho(p)$ is a price index, and u is increasing and concave. Implicit in (7) is the assumption of homothetic preferences over consumption goods. Pollution is a pure public bad, but Greens suffer a greater disutility than Browns. It is now convenient to define real per capita income as $I = [G/N]/\rho(p)$ and rewrite indirect utility as simply $u(I) - \delta^i z$.

Government.—We model the policy process very simply. We assume the government

[9] For example, let υ be the level of iceberg transport costs (that is, $\upsilon < 1$ is the fraction of the good that arrives at the destination when a unit is exported). Then if the good is exported from home, we have $p^d = \upsilon p^w$, and if the good is imported, we have $p^d = p^w/\upsilon$. Freer trade (an increase in υ) raises p^d if X is exported and lowers p^d if X is imported.

[10] When x units of gross output are produced, and x_a units are devoted to abatement, emissions are given by $E(x_a, x)$. Given our assumptions, E is decreasing in x_a, increasing in x, strictly convex in x_a, and linearly homogeneous in x and x_a together. Convexity in abatement inputs follows from diminishing returns to the variable factor and implies increasing marginal abatement costs. Linear homogeneity follows from constant returns. Using the linear homogeneity of E, we then write $E(x_a, x) = e(\theta)x$.

chooses a pollution tax to maximize a weighted sum of each group's preferences. It solves

$$\max_{\tau} N[\lambda V^g + (1 - \lambda)V^b], \tag{8}$$

where λ is the weight put on Greens. λ may vary across governments.[11] We introduce this formulation to allow for the realistic possibility that government behavior varies across countries (perhaps across Communist and non-Communist countries), while allowing for an endogenous link between pollution policy and economic conditions.

The optimal pollution tax maximizes the weighted sum of utilities in (8) subject to private sector behavior, production possibilities, fixed world prices, and fixed trade frictions (see, however, Section III, subsection E, for a consideration of optimal tariffs). Private sector behavior can be represented by a standard GNP function giving maximized private sector (net of tax) revenue as $R(p^N, K, L)$.[12] Overall income is private sector revenue plus rebated taxes $G = R(p^N, K, L) + \tau z$. The first-order condition yields

$$u'(I)\frac{dI}{d\tau} - [\lambda\delta^g + (1 - \lambda)\delta^b]\frac{dz}{d\tau} = 0.$$

With world prices fixed we have

$$\frac{dI}{d\tau} = \frac{1}{N\rho(p)}\left[R_{p^N}\frac{dp^N}{d\tau} + z + \tau\frac{dz}{d\tau}\right]$$

$$= \frac{\tau}{N\rho(p)}\frac{dz}{d\tau}.$$

Rearranging our first-order condition now yields an amended Samuelson rule:

$$\tau = N[\lambda MD^g(p, I) + (1 - \lambda)MD^b(p, I)], \tag{9}$$

where $MD^i(p, I) = \delta^i\rho(p)/u'$ is marginal damage per person, and $MD_I^i > 0$ given the concavity of the utility function. Simplifying allows us to rewrite (9) slightly as:

$$\tau = T\phi(p, I). \tag{10}$$

We refer to $T = \lambda N\delta^g + (1 - \lambda)N\delta^b$ as "country type" and $T\phi(p, I)$ as effective marginal damage (MD). Pollution policy therefore varies with economic conditions and government type.

B. *Pollution Demand and Supply*

Our model yields a relatively simple reduced form linking pollution emissions to a short list of (predetermined) economic factors. To isolate the role of trade, it is important to understand how these different economic factors affect the demand for, and supply of, pollution. To do so, we use the terminology of scale, composition, and technique effects. We start by noting the private sector's demand for pollution is implicitly defined by (2). To rewrite this demand in a more convenient form for empirical work, we define an economy's scale as the value of national output at base-year world prices. In obvious notation, our measure of scale S is

$$S = p_x^0 x + p_y^0 y. \tag{11}$$

Choosing units so that base-year prices are unity, we now write pollution emissions as

$$z = ex = e\varphi S, \tag{12}$$

where φ is the share of X in total output. Equation (12) provides a simple decomposition: pollution depends on the pollution intensity of the dirty industry $e(\theta)$, the relative importance of the dirty industry in the economy φ, and the overall scale of the economy S. In differential form,

$$\hat{z} = \hat{S} + \hat{\varphi} + \hat{e}, \tag{13}$$

where hats denote percent change. The first term is the scale effect. It measures the increase in pollution generated if the economy were simply scaled up, holding constant the mix of goods produced φ and production techniques $e(\theta)$.

[11] For example, if the government is utilitarian, then $\lambda = N^g/N$; if the government is controlled by the Greens, $\lambda = 1$, and if controlled by Browns, $\lambda = 0$.

[12] See Avinash K. Dixit and Victor Norman (1980) and Alan D. Woodland (1982).

For example, if all endowments of the economy grew by 10 percent, and if there was no change in the composition of output or emission intensities, then we should expect to see a 10-percent increase in pollution. The second term in (13) is the composition effect. If we hold the scale of the economy and emissions intensities constant, then an economy that devotes more of its resources to producing the polluting good will pollute more. Finally, we have the technique effect, captured by the last term. All else constant, an increase in the emission intensity will increase pollution.

We will use a quantity index of output to measure the scale effect. Because a change in prices creates opposing composition and technique effects, however, it is necessary to divide each into its more primitive determinants. Using (6) we can solve for the share of X in total output φ as a function of the capital/labor ratio $\kappa = K/L$, the net producer price p^N and base-year world prices (suppressed here). That is, the composition of output is $\varphi = \varphi(\kappa, p^N)$, and we have the composition effect given by

$$(14) \qquad \hat{\varphi} = \varepsilon_{\varphi\kappa}\hat{\kappa} + \varepsilon_{\varphi p}\hat{p}^N,$$

where the elasticity of φ with respect to κ and p^N are both positive. Next differentiate p^N and employ (1) and (4) to find

$$(15) \qquad \hat{p}^N = (\hat{\beta} + \hat{p}^w)(1 + a) - a\hat{\tau},$$

where $a = e(\theta)\tau/p^N$. Similarly, using (1) and (5) we find

$$(16) \qquad \hat{e} = \varepsilon_{e,p/\tau}(\hat{\beta} + \hat{p}^w - \hat{\tau}),$$

where the elasticity of emission intensity with respect to p/τ is positive.[13] Combining (13)–(16) we obtain a decomposition of the private sector's demand for pollution:

$$(17) \qquad \hat{z} = \hat{S} + \varepsilon_{\varphi,\kappa}\hat{\kappa} + [(1 + a)\varepsilon_{\varphi,p} + \varepsilon_{e,p/\tau}]\hat{\beta} + [(1 + a)\varepsilon_{\varphi,p} + \varepsilon_{e,p/\tau}]\hat{p}^w - [a\varepsilon_{\varphi,p} + \varepsilon_{e,p/\tau}]\hat{\tau}.$$

All elasticities are positive. If we draw this derived demand in $\{z, \tau\}$-space, then (17) shows that an increase in scale, capital abundance, or the world price of dirty goods shifts the pollution demand curve to the right. A movement of β toward 1 captures a reduction in trade frictions. However, because β is greater than 1 for a dirty good importer this implies $\hat{\beta} < 0$; and because β is less than 1 for a dirty good exporter, a reduction in trade frictions implies $\hat{\beta} > 0$. Therefore, a reduction in trade frictions shifts the pollution demand curve to the right for a dirty good exporter, but to the left for a dirty good importer.

Increases in the pollution tax reduce the quantity demanded of pollution through two channels. First they lower the demand for pollution by raising abatement and lowering the emissions per unit of X produced. This is captured by the elasticity $\varepsilon_{e,p/\tau} > 0$. Second, higher pollution taxes lower the producer price of X and induce a shift in the composition of output that lowers X output for any given emissions intensity. The strength of this effect depends on the importance of pollution taxes in the net producer price (a) and the elasticity of φ with respect to a change in producer prices, $\varepsilon_{\varphi,p}$.

Pollution supply is in effect given by government policy that sets the price for polluting. From (1) and (10) we obtain a decomposition of pollution supply:

$$(18) \qquad \hat{\tau} = \hat{T} + \varepsilon_{MD,p}\hat{\beta} + \varepsilon_{MD,p}\hat{p}^w + \varepsilon_{MD,I}\hat{I},$$

where $\varepsilon_{MD,p} > 0$ and $\varepsilon_{MD,I} > 0$. If we draw (18) in $\{z, \tau\}$-space, then increases in real income, relative prices, or country type shift the pollution supply curve upward. For example, if Greens are given a greater weight in social welfare, or become a larger fraction of the population over time, then policy becomes more stringent and pollution supply shifts upward. Similarly, an increase in real income will increase the demand for environmental quality and shift up the pollution supply curve. An increase in the world relative price of X makes consumption of market goods more expensive relative to environmental protection. This creates a pure substitution effect toward more environmental protection,

[13] It is convenient to define elasticities so that they are positive. Note that e is decreasing in τ/p, and therefore increasing in p/τ.

reflected in (18) by $\varepsilon_{MD,p} > 0$. As a result pollution supply shifts up. An identical substitution effect is at work when trade frictions fall.

A Reduced Form.—Combining supply in (17) and demand in (18) yields a simple reduced form linking pollution emissions to a small set of economic factors:

$$(19) \qquad \hat{z} = \pi_1 \hat{S} + \pi_2 \hat{\kappa} - \pi_3 \hat{I} + \pi_4 \hat{\beta} + \pi_5 \hat{p}^w - \pi_6 \hat{T},$$

where all π_i are positive, and none of the right-hand-side variables are determined simultaneously with emissions. Two features of (19) warrant further comment. First, because a change in domestic prices shifts pollution supply and demand in opposing directions, it is not obvious that π_4 and π_5 are positive. We evaluate this claim more formally in Proposition 1 below. Second, we claim "a reduced form" links emissions to our economic factors, despite the fact that emissions and these same factors are clearly endogenous variables. In our framework, emissions are determined endogenously, but recursively. As a result, the factors on the right-hand side of (19) are not simultaneously determined with or by the level of emissions.[14] This feature of our simple general equilibrium model has the benefit of providing us a simple, straightforward, and parsimonious reduced form linking pollution emissions to economic determinants. We evaluate our first claim below.

The Trade-Induced Composition Effect.

PROPOSITION 1: *Consider two economies that differ only in their trade frictions: (i) if both countries export the polluting good, then pollution is higher in the country with lower trade frictions; (ii) if both import the polluting good, then pollution is lower in the country with lower trade frictions.*

PROOF:
See Appendix A.

Proposition 1 isolates the *trade-induced composition effect.* The sign of this composition effect differs across countries. For an exporter of the polluting good, β rises with freer trade and this raises the relative price of the dirty good X. This shifts a dirty good exporter's pollution demand curve to the right and shifts its pollution supply curve up. Pollution demand shifts out for two reasons: the composition of national output shifts toward X; and emission intensities rise because abatement inputs are now more costly. The shift in the pollution supply curve dampens this increase in pollution as the pure substitution effect of the goods price increase leads the government to raise the pollution tax. However, the direct demand-side effects swamp the substitution effect in supply, and pollution rises.[15] Consequently, holding all other determinants of pollution supply and demand constant, emissions must rise. This increase in emissions represents the trade-induced composition effect for a dirty good exporter.

In contrast, β falls with freer trade for an importer of the polluting good. This raises the relative price of the clean good Y, and again shifts both pollution demand and supply. Demand-side determinants dominate and emissions fall. This reduction in emissions represents the trade-induced composition effect for a clean good exporter.

[14] To see this, note that $R(p^N, K, L) + \tau z = p(1 - \theta)x + y$, which is independent of z. Next, note that (4), (6), and (10) solve for I, τ, and θ, given world prices. With τ, θ, and p determined, p^N is given. Outputs are determined by p^N, and z follows from $z = e(\theta)x$. This result follows for two reasons. First, a society may decide to spend some of its potential income on improving environmental quality and the remainder on consumption goods—but higher pollution does not *cause* higher real income. Second, because marginal damage is independent of z, the equilibrium level of emissions does not affect the pollution tax. As a result, a change in emissions does not cause second-order changes in the composition of output or our measures of scale and income. As a result of these two features, real income, scale, and the pollution tax are set simultaneously, whereas emissions are set recursively.

[15] To see this, note that the increase in τ is less than proportional to the increase in β, because the increase in τ induced by β is a pure substitution effect, which is proportional to the share of X in consumption (which is less than one). This ensures both that emission intensity e rises, and that the share of X in production rises. Details are in the Appendices.

Proposition 1 therefore implies that, if we look across all countries and hold other determinants of emissions constant, we should not expect to find openness per se related in any systematic way to emissions. Although Proposition 1 is useful, it is limited in two respects. First, although it isolates the trade-induced composition effect, any fall in trade frictions will alter the scale of output and income per capita of the liberalizing country as well. Therefore, to account for the full environmental impact of a fall in trade frictions we must also account for the accompanying scale and technique effects. Proposition 1 captures the partial effect of trade liberalization; an overall assessment needs the full effect. Second, the results from the proposition are conditional on trade patterns, but the proposition itself is silent on the determinants of trade patterns. We treat each of these issues in turn below.

The Full Impact of Openness.—To find the full impact of a change in trade frictions we must account for the change created in real incomes, the scale of output, and its composition. Differentiate (12) with respect to β, holding world prices, country type, and factor endowments constant, to find

$$\frac{dz}{d\beta}\frac{\beta}{z} = \pi_1 \frac{dS}{d\beta}\frac{\beta}{S} - \pi_3 \frac{dI}{d\beta}\frac{\beta}{I} + \pi_4. \quad (20)$$

A fall in trade frictions produces a scale effect, a technique effect, and the trade-induced composition effect, discussed previously. To understand how these three effects interact to determine the environmental consequences of trade, we employ Figure 1.

In the top panel of Figure 1 we depict the production response of a dirty good exporter to a fall in trade frictions. In the bottom panel we depict the pollution consequences of these changes. Before the reduction in trade frictions, production is at point A, the world price is p^w, and the net price is p^N. We have assumed this country is an exporter of the dirty good and therefore has consumption at a point to the northwest of A along the economy's budget constraint (not drawn). Note that the value (in world prices) of domestic output at A measures this economy's scale. In the bottom panel we

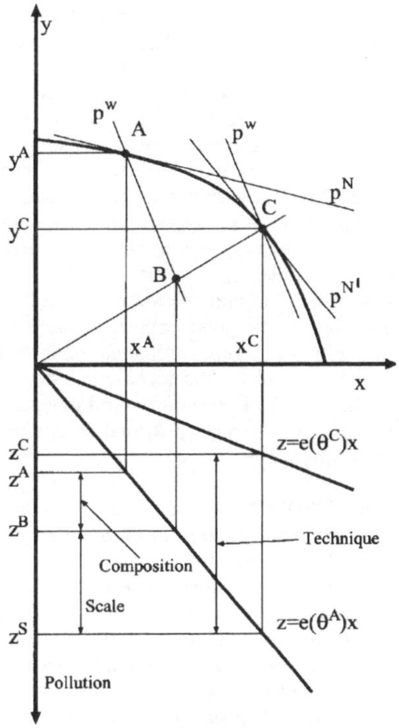

FIGURE 1. A DIRTY GOOD EXPORTER

depict the equilibrium pollution level both before and after the fall in trade frictions. Recall that $z = e(\theta)x$. Hence when production is at A, and emissions intensity is $e(\theta^A)$, pollution is given by z^A.

When trade frictions fall the domestic price approaches the world price and production moves to point C at the new producer price of $p^{N'}$. At C, real income is higher and there is a change in the techniques of production. The emissions intensity falls to $e(\theta^C)$ and overall pollution falls to z^C. Our methodology divides the movement from z^A to z^C into three component parts. First, holding both the scale of the economy and the techniques of production fixed, trade creates a change in the composition of output given by the movement from A to B. Corresponding to this movement is the increase in pollution from z^A to z^B in the bottom panel. This is the trade-induced composition effect isolated in Proposition 1.

The movement in the top panel from point B to point C is the scale effect. The increase in pollution from z^B to z^S in the bottom panel gives the pollution consequences of this scale effect. Finally, note that the value of output measured at world prices rises because of trade and this real income gain (indirectly) creates the technique effect shown in the bottom panel. The technique effect is the fall in pollution from z^S to z^C as producers switch to cleaner techniques with lower emissions intensity.

In total the diagram shows that trade liberalization for a dirty good exporter leads to less pollution if the composition and scale effects are overwhelmed by the technique effect. Because this is only a possibility, and not a necessity within our model, we formalize our results in Proposition 2.

PROPOSITION 2: *Consider a small reduction in trade frictions for our small open economy, then:*

(*i*) *if the small open economy exports the clean good, the full effect of this trade liberalization is to lower pollution emissions;*

(*ii*) *if the small open economy exports the dirty good and the elasticity of marginal damage with respect to income is below one, then the full effect of this trade liberalization is to raise its pollution emissions;*

(*iii*) *if the small open economy exports the dirty good and the elasticity of marginal damage with respect to income is sufficiently above one, then the full effect of this trade liberalization is to lower its pollution emissions.*

PROOF:

See Appendix A.

The first part of the proposition concerns dirty good importers. For dirty good importers the trade-induced composition effect is negative and because X production falls, the sum of composition and scale effects must also be negative.[16] Consequently, pollution emissions will fall for a dirty good importer. For a dirty good exporter, both the trade-induced composition effect and the scale effect are positive. Pollution demand shifts right from these two forces, and Proposition 2 indicates that if the policy response is sufficiently weak (an elasticity of marginal damage with respect to income less than one) emissions will rise. That is, the upward shift in pollution supply is overwhelmed by the demand shifts. Alternatively, if the elasticity of marginal damage is sufficiently strong, then emissions will fall as the technique effect dominates. The full effect of a trade liberalization differs from the partial effect because of two additional effects, and because these new effects can be strong enough to overwhelm the composition effect.

C. *Adding Up Scale, Composition, and Technique Effects*

The amount of information required to implement an adding-up exercise akin to (20) is great. In our empirical work we develop estimates for π_1, π_3, and π_4. But even with these estimates in hand we are faced with disentangling the effects of trade liberalization on income growth from all other potential sources. Because attempts to link trade to growth and income levels are the subject of an already large and somewhat controversial literature, we do not attempt to measure trade's effect on GDP ($dS/d\beta$) or GNP per person ($dI/d\beta$). Instead we employ economic theory to add up our estimated scale, composition, and technique effects. Taking factor endowments as fixed, a lowering of transport costs or trade barriers raises the value of domestic output and real income in a small open economy. The value of output and income rise by the same percentage and this creates both scale and technique effects.[17] Therefore, we can simplify (20) slightly and write

$$\text{(21)} \qquad \frac{dz}{d\beta}\frac{\beta}{z} = [\pi_1 - \pi_3]\frac{dI}{d\beta}\frac{\beta}{I} + \pi_4.$$

In some circumstances we can add up these three effects to come to an overall assessment of

[16] This is a product of our two-good model. With many polluting goods the scale effect may dominate the composition effect, leading to a rise in pollution from these two sources.

[17] If GNP differs from GDP because of receipts or payments from abroad, then we would need to correct for the (generally small) share of these payments in GNP.

trade without knowledge of trade's effect on income or scale. For example, consider a dirty good exporter. Note that $dI/d\beta$ is positive because an increase in β represents lower trade frictions. If we find $\pi_1 > \pi_3$ and $\pi_4 > 0$, then we conclude that trade liberalization raises pollution for a dirty good exporter: scale effects dominate technique and the trade-induced composition effect is positive. Under these same circumstances, trade liberalization would have an ambiguous effect on emissions for a clean good exporter. Consequently, even to implement our more limited adding-up exercise, it is necessary to ask: who exports dirty goods and why?

Pollution Haven versus Factor Abundance Motives.—In our model comparative advantage is primarily a function of relative factor abundance and relative incomes. Although limiting cases of our model reflect only pollution haven motives or pure factor endowment motives, in general we expect both determinants of comparative advantage to matter. To investigate further, we solve for autarky prices. Let $RD(p)$ denote the demand for good X relative to good Y. Then the relative price of good X is determined by the intersection of the (net) relative supply and demand curves

$$RD(p) = (1 - \theta)\chi(\kappa, p^N), \tag{22}$$

where $\chi = x/y$ is determined from (6), and net relative supply is $(1 - \theta)\chi$. Totally differentiating, using (15), (16), and (18), and rearranging gives an expression linking autarky prices to real income and endowments:

$$\hat{p} = \frac{\varepsilon_{MD,I}\left[a\varepsilon_{\chi,p^N} + \dfrac{\theta}{1-\theta}\varepsilon_{\theta,\tau/p}\right]\hat{I} - \varepsilon_{\chi,\kappa}\hat{\kappa}}{\Delta}, \tag{23}$$

where all elasticities and Δ are positive. Equation (23) shows that in general, the pattern of trade is determined by both factor abundance and income-driven differences in pollution policy. For example, unless both the dirty and clean sectors use identical factor proportions then $\varepsilon_{\chi,\kappa}$ is not zero and capital abundance matters to comparative advantage. Similarly, if the environment is a normal good, then $\varepsilon_{MD,I}$ is nonzero and real income matters as well.

The Role of Factor Endowments.—Standard factor endowment theories predict capital abundant countries export capital-intensive goods. In our model this need not be true because pollution policy can reverse this pattern of trade. Nevertheless, capital abundance is still a key determinant of comparative advantage in our model. Because X is relatively capital intensive, an increase in κ, holding all else constant, increases Home's relative supply of X, and lowers Home's autarky relative price of X. Using (23) we obtain $\hat{p} < 0$ because $\varepsilon_{\chi,\kappa} > 0$. All else equal, an increase in the abundance of the factor used intensively in the pollution-intensive sector increases the likelihood that a country will be an exporter of pollution-intensive goods. We can show that if the country is *sufficiently* capital abundant, it must export the capital intensive (polluting) good:

PROPOSITION 3: *Suppose the world price p^w is fixed. Then, for a given level of real income I, there exists a $\underline{\kappa}$ such that if $\kappa > \underline{\kappa}$, then Home exports X. Moreover, for such a country, the trade-induced composition effect will be positive.*

PROOF:
See Appendix A.

The Role of Income Differences.—An alternative theory of trade patterns is the *pollution haven hypothesis.* According to this view, poor countries have a comparative advantage in dirty goods because they have lax pollution policy, and rich countries have a comparative advantage in clean goods because of their stringent pollution policy.[18] This result can be obtained as a special case of our model: if all countries have the same relative factor endowments, but differ in per capita incomes, then richer countries will have stricter pollution policy and this will lead to a comparative advantage in clean goods. Using (23) we obtain $\hat{p} > 0$ whenever

[18] See Copeland and Taylor (1994) for a model that explores this issue.

$\hat{I} > 0$. When countries differ in factor endowments and income levels, we can show that if the country is *sufficiently* rich, it must export the labor-intensive (clean) good.

PROPOSITION 4: *Suppose the world price p^w is fixed and there exists an ε such that $\varepsilon_{MD,I} > \varepsilon > 0$. Then, for a given level of the capital/labor ratio κ, there exists an $\underline{I}$, such that if $I > \underline{I}$, then Home exports Y. Moreover, for such a country, the trade-induced composition effect will be negative.*

PROOF:
See Appendix A.

From Theory to Estimation.—Proposition 1 contains a very simple message: comparative advantage matters. If we compare countries with similar incomes and scale, openness should be associated with higher pollution in dirty good exporters and lower pollution in dirty good importers. Therefore to isolate the trade-induced composition effect, we must condition on country characteristics. This observation begs three questions: how are we to measure openness, what country characteristics should we use, and how should we condition on these characteristics?

Various measures of "openness" exist. We need a measure with both time-series variation and a wide cross-country coverage. In our theory a lowering of trade frictions brings domestic prices closer to world prices and it does not matter whether this occurs because of a fall in transport and communication costs or (apart from revenue effects) because of a GATT-inspired reduction in trade restrictions.[19] However, because we do not observe movements in β directly we must make use of an observable consequence of heightened integration: increases in a country's trade intensity ratio (defined as the ratio of exports plus imports to GDP valued at world prices). We formalize this link below.

PROPOSITION 5: *If preferences over consumption goods are homothetic, trade intensity rises as β approaches* 1.

PROOF:
See Appendix A.

Proposition 5 links unobservable trade frictions with observable trade intensity. Lower trade frictions means greater trade intensity, regardless of a country's comparative advantage. Therefore, in our empirical application we replace unobservable trade frictions with observable trade intensity.[20]

To address our second question, interpret the hat notation in equation (23) as describing small differences across countries. With this interpretation, (23) links differences in autarky relative prices across countries to differences in their relative factor abundance and real income levels. If we take the rest of the world as our small country's partner in this exercise, then the strength and direction of country i's comparative advantage will depend on its capital abundance relative to a world average (denoted by κ_i), and its real income relative to a world average (denoted by ι_i). Although other factors play a role in determining comparative advantage, capital abundance and real income are the key country characteristics within our model.

Finally, to condition on these characteristics we let Ψ be a function measuring the partial effect of an increase in trade intensity on pollution. Our theory tells us that we can write $\Psi = \Psi(\kappa_i, \iota_i)$, but does not give us much more guidance in this regard. The interaction between factor abundance and pollution haven motives depends quite delicately on elasticities of substitution, factor shares, and (unknown) third derivative properties of our more basic functions. This is apparent from (23) because the elasticities in this expression are functions of prices, incomes, and trade frictions. Consequently, we adopt a flexible approach to capturing these influences by adopting a second-order Taylor series approximation to Ψ in our empirical work. That is, we employ

[19] See, however, Section III, subsection E, on the tariff-substitution effect in a large open economy.

[20] If trade frictions are not exogenous, but are endogenously determined along with pollution policy, then our proxy (trade intensity) may be correlated with unmeasured determinants of pollution policy. In Section III, subsection E, we discuss the likely implications of such a link between trade and pollution policy.

$$(24)\quad \Psi_i \cong \psi_0 + \psi_1\kappa_i + \psi_2\kappa_i^2 + \psi_3\iota_i + \psi_4\iota_i^2 + \psi_5\kappa_i\iota_i,$$

and then interact this measure with trade intensity to capture the trade-induced composition effect.

This method has several advantages. It allows the impact of further openness on pollution to depend on country characteristics. It does not dictate whether one or both motives are present in the data or how they interact. And we can evaluate Ψ using our estimates to provide some simple reality checks. For example, does the pollution demand curve shift right for some countries and not for others (i.e., does Ψ_i vary in sign depending on country characteristics)? For which countries does it shift right? Are these countries poor countries as predicted by the pollution haven hypothesis, or are they capital abundant countries as predicted by the factor abundance hypothesis? Finally, the formulation is a relatively parsimonious and reasonably flexible method for estimating an unknown nonlinear function.

II. Empirical Strategy

This section describes how we move from our theory to an estimating equation. To do so we need to discuss our data, its sources and limitations (subsection A), and address the links between theory and our estimating equation (subsection B).

A. *Data Sources and Measurement Issues*

A real-world pollutant useful for our purposes would: (1) be a by-product of goods production; (2) be emitted in greater quantities per unit of output in some industries than others; (3) have strong local effects; (4) be subject to regulations because of its noxious effect on the population; (5) have well known abatement technologies available for implementation; and (6), for econometric purposes, have data available from a mix of developed and developing as well as "open" and "closed" economies. An almost perfect choice for this study is sulfur dioxide.

Sulfur dioxide (SO_2) is a noxious gas produced by the burning of fossil fuels. Natural sources include volcanoes, decaying organic matter, and sea spray. Anthropogenic sources are thought to be responsible for somewhere between one-third to one-half of all emissions (United Nations Environment Programme, 1991; Jack J. Kraushaar and Robert A. Ristinen, 1998). SO_2 is primarily emitted as either a direct or indirect product of goods production and is not strongly linked to automobile use. Because energy-intensive industries are also typically capital intensive, a reasonable proxy for dirty SO_2-creating activities may be physical capital-intensive production processes. Readily available, although costly, methods for the control of emissions exist and their efficacy is well established. In addition, in many countries SO_2 emissions have been actively regulated for some time.

The Global Environment Monitoring System (GEMS) has been recording SO_2 concentrations in major urban areas in developed and developing countries since the early 1970's. Our data set consists of 2,555 observations from 290 observation sites located in 108 cities representing 43 countries spanning the years 1971–1996. The GEMS network was set up to monitor the concentrations of several pollutants in a cross section of countries using comparable measuring devices.[21] The panel of countries includes primarily developed countries in the early years, but from 1976 to the early 1990's the United Nations Environment Programme provided funds to expand and maintain the network. The coverage of developing economies grew over time until the late 1980's. In the 1990's coverage fell with data from the United States only for 1996. The World Health Organization (1984) reports that until the late 1970's data comparability may be limited as monitoring capabilities were being assessed, many new countries were added, and procedures were being developed to ensure validated samples. Accordingly, we investigate the sensitivity of our findings to the time period.

The GEMS data are comprised of summary statistics for the yearly distribution of concentrations at each site. In this study we use the log

[21] The range of sophistication of monitoring techniques used in the network varies quite widely, but the various techniques have been subject to comparability tests over the years. Some stations offer continuous monitoring, whereas others measure only at discrete intervals.

of median SO_2 concentrations at a given site, for each year, as our dependent variable. We use a log transform because the distribution of yearly summary statistics for SO_2 appears to be lognormal (WHO, 1984). Previous work in this area by the WHO and others has argued that a lognormal distribution is appropriate because temperature inversions or other special pollution episodes often lead to large values for some observations. In contrast, even weather very helpful to dissipation cannot drive the level of the pollutant below zero.

In addition to the data on concentrations, the GEMS network also classifies each site within a city as either city center, suburban, or rural in land type, and we employ these land-type categories in our analysis. A list of the cities involved, the years of operation of GEMS stations, and the number of observations from each city along with a frequency distribution of SO_2 emissions is given in our Technical Appendix (available upon request).

In moving from our theoretical model to its empirical counterpart we need to include variables to reflect scale, technique, and composition effects. As well, we have to include site-specific variables to account for meteorological conditions. Our estimations will require the use of data on real GDP per capita, capital-to-labor ratios, population densities, and various measures of "openness." The majority of the economic data were obtained from the Penn World Tables 5.6. The remainder was obtained from several sources. A description of data sources and our methods for collection are provided in Appendix B together with a table of means, standard deviations, and units of measurement for the data.

B. *The Estimating Equation*

In moving from our theoretical model to estimation we face several issues. Here we discuss three: identification, excluded variables, and functional form.

Identification.—The private sector's demand for pollution, written in differential form, is given by (17). The pollution supply curve is given by (18). A problem arises because most measures of the scale of economic activity that shifts pollution demand (for example real GDP or real GDP per person) will be highly or perfectly correlated with real income per capita that shifts pollution supply.

We address this problem by exploiting three different sources of variation in our data. First, we note that changes in the scale of output must have contemporaneous effects on pollution concentrations, whereas pollution policy is likely to respond slowly, if at all, to changes in income levels. Consequently, we use as our proxy for income a one-period lagged, three-year moving average of income per capita, but link pollution concentrations to a contemporaneous measure of economic activity. To the extent that there is significant variation over time in activity measures, this source of variation will help in our identification.[22]

Second, the scale of economic activity should be measured by economic activity within a country's borders (i.e., GDP), whereas the income relevant to the technique effect should reflect the income of residents wherever it is earned (i.e., GNP). Therefore, we can exploit the difference between GDP and GNP measures to separate technique from scale effects. Even though the gap between these two figures is not large for most economies, it is significant for some. This cross-country variation will be useful in separating scale from technique.

Finally, we measure the scale of economic activity S at any site by an intensive measure of economic activity per unit area. This intensive measure is GDP per square kilometer. Lacking detailed data on "Gross City Product," we construct GDP per square kilometer for each city and each year by multiplying city population density with country GDP per person. As a result, scale is now measured in intensive form, as is our dependent variable.[23] To explain *concentrations of pollution* we need a measure of scale

[22] For example, we expect that a significant recession would drive down concentrations (a scale effect) but not lead to a rewriting of pollution control laws (i.e., a technique effect). This source of variation in pollution data has been exploited before. See Kenneth Y. Chay and Michael B. Greenstone (1999).

[23] This is admittedly a rough measure of economic activity, and the quality of this proxy may vary systematically with a country's development level. To investigate this concern we have allowed the scale effect to vary across countries divided by income category, by allowing for nonlinearities in the response to scale, and by excluding the perhaps most troubling rural observations. Our results are similar to those reported for

reflecting the *concentration of economic activity* within the same geographical area. Other possible measures of scale fail this test. Moreover, since we assume pollution policy is determined by national averages for income per capita and the number of exposed individuals, we are in effect fixing the pollution supply curve for all cities within a given country. This "allows" us to employ the within-country variation in scale across cities to separate the influence of scale from that of technique.

Unobservable Variables: Fixed or Random Effects?—Several variables relevant to our theory are unobservable. To account for these exclusions we estimate an individual effects model for ε_{ijkt} given by

$$\varepsilon_{ijkt} = \xi_t + \theta_{ijk} + \nu_{ijkt}, \tag{25}$$

where ξ_t is a time-specific effect, θ_{ijk} is a site-specific effect, and ν_{ijkt} is an idiosyncratic measurement error for observation station i in city j in country k in year t.

Our common-to-world but time-specific effect is included to capture changes in knowledge concerning pollution, changes in the world relative price of dirty goods, and improvements in abatement technologies. Although proxies for some of these variables could be constructed, choosing proxies will of course introduce new issues of data quality, coverage, and so forth. Instead we note that, because each of these variables affects all countries in a similar way, a preferred method may be to treat them as unobservable. For example, a rise in the world price of dirty goods affects all countries in a similar way. Accordingly, we capture these common-to-world excluded variables with a set of unrestricted time dummies.

θ_{ijk} is a site-specific effect representing excluded site (or country-specific) variables such as excluded economic determinants or excluded meteorological variables. For example, country type T appears in (19) but is virtually unobservable in that it relies on both knowledge of the weight governments apply to Greens and Browns in their economy and the share of each in the overall population. Because the panel is relatively short for almost all countries, we take these country-type and distribution parameters as fixed over time. As well, there are unmeasured topographical and meteorological features that undoubtedly affect the dissipation of pollution at each site. Finally, we allow for an idiosyncratic measurement error ν_{ijkt}. Two sources of this error would be machine error in reading concentrations and human error in calculation or tabulation.

Throughout we present both fixed- and random-effects estimates for every model. Whereas random-effects estimation is in theory more efficient, it is unclear whether excluded country-specific effects subsumed in our error term are uncorrelated with our regressors. Although fixed-effects estimation is preferable in just these cases, fixed effects limits the cross-sectional variation we can exploit for separating scale from technique effects.

Functional Form.—Our model predicts emission levels but our data are on concentrations. Meteorological models mapping emissions from a (single) stack into measured concentrations at a receptor are functions of emission rates, stack height, the distance to the receptor, wind speed, temperature gradients, and turbulence. Much of this information is not presently available. In view of these limitations we adopt a linear approximation to measured concentrations by writing concentrations at site ijk, at time t as

$$\begin{aligned} (26)\quad Z^C_{ijkt} &= X'_{jkt}\alpha + Y'_{ijkt}\gamma + \varepsilon_{ijkt} \\ X'_{jkt}\alpha &= \alpha_0 + \alpha_1 \mathrm{SCALE}_{jkt} + \alpha_2 \mathrm{KL}_{kt} \\ &\quad + \alpha_3 \mathrm{INC}_{kt} + \alpha_4 \Psi_{kt} \mathrm{TI}_{kt} \\ \Psi_{kt} &= \psi_0 + \psi_1 \mathrm{REL.KL}_{kt} \\ &\quad + \psi_2 \mathrm{REL.KL}^2_{kt} \\ &\quad + \psi_3 \mathrm{REL.INC}_{kt} \\ &\quad + \psi_4 \mathrm{REL.INC}^2_{kt} \\ &\quad + \psi_5 \mathrm{REL.KL}_{kt} \mathrm{REL.INC}_{kt}, \end{aligned}$$

where SCALE is city-specific GDP/km^2, KL is the national capital-to-labor ratio, INC is a

our simpler specification. For one such sensitivity test see Table 2.

one-period-lagged three-year moving average of GNP/N, TI is the trade intensity (X+M)/GDP, REL.KL is country k's capital-to-labor ratio measured relative to the world average, and REL.INC is country k's real income measured relative to the world average (see Appendix B for further details). Note that world price and country-type variables are captured in (25), and trade intensity has replaced trade frictions in (19), as discussed previously. Y contains site-specific weather variables and site-specific physical characteristics (discussed below), and ε_{ijkt} is a site-specific error reflecting unmeasured economic and physical variables. We refer to equation (26) as Model A in our estimations.

Model A follows from our reduced form if we assume linearity in the response to scale, technique, and composition variables. This linearity assumption is, however, somewhat at odds with our theory. In theory, the impact of capital accumulation on pollution depends on the techniques of production in place. But when countries differ in income per capita, they will also differ in producer prices and hence their techniques of production. Consequently, the Rybczyinski derivatives embedded in (26) will differ across countries. As well, the impact of capital accumulation on the composition of output is not a linear function of KL. Similarly, the impact of income gains on pollution depends on the existing composition of output and hence the existing capital-to-labor ratio and income per capita. To account for these possibilities we amend Model A by adding the squares of income per capita (INC_{kt}^2) and the capital-to-labor ratio (KL_{kt}^2) as well as their cross-product ($\mathrm{INC}_{kt}\mathrm{KL}_{kt}$). We refer to this amended form of (26) as Model B. As a consequence, the impact of factor accumulation can now differ across countries and over time in closer accord with our theory. Finally, we consider a further nonlinearity by adding SCALE_{kt}^2 to Model B. A nonlinearity in the impact of scale could arise from nonhomotheticities in production or consumption. We refer to this slightly amended model as Model C.

Models A, B, and C differ from those previously estimated in several regards. For example, empirical work within the Environmental Kuznets curve tradition employ measures only of site-specific attributes and income per capita as regressors, leaving out a role for factor endowments or scale to play independent effects. Grossman and Krueger (1993, 1995) are the most prominent examples of this approach, but there are many others. Lewis Gale and Jose A. Mendez (1998) add measures of factor endowments to a Kuznet's curve regression, but their (one-year) cross-sectional analysis cannot distinguish between constant-over-time site attributes and scale effects. Empirical work using (constructed) cross-country emission data or emission intensity data has tried to link country characteristics (factor endowments, growth in income, fuel use, etc.) to environmental outcomes, but these studies always fail to condition the impact of openness on country characteristics. For example, see Low and Yeats (1992) and Lucas et al. (1992). As a result, we are not aware of even one study where the impact of trade is conditioned on those country characteristics determining comparative advantage, despite the fact that the trade-induced composition effect should vary across countries according to comparative advantage.

III. Empirical Results

A. *Main Results*

Table 1 presents the main results from our estimations. We present estimates from Models A, B, and C in Table 1 using both random and fixed effects.

Scale, Composition, and Technique Effects.—Consider our core variables representing scale, composition, and technique effects. In all columns of Table 1 we find a positive and significant relationship between the scale of economic activity as measured by GDP/km^2 and concentrations. From the bottom of Table 1 we see that the coefficient estimates imply a sample-mean elasticity of concentrations to an increase in scale somewhere between 0.1 and 0.4. The scale elasticity estimates increases in magnitude as we move from Model A through to Model C, although the estimates differ only slightly across random and fixed effects. Because the models are nested, we can test the restrictions imposed in Models A and B via a likelihood ratio (LR) test. It appears there is

TABLE 1—ALTERNATIVE HYPOTHESES TESTS

Estimation method:	Random effects			Fixed effects		
Model specification:	A	B	C	A	B	C
Variable/column:	(1)	(2)	(3)	(4)	(5)	(6)
Intercept	−2.865***	−3.279***	−3.311***	−2.506***	−4.324***	−4.299***
City economic intensity GDP/km^2	0.042***	0.058***	0.070***	0.024*	0.058***	0.089*
(City economic intensity)^2/1,000			−0.244			−0.340
Capital abundance (K/L)	0.102**	0.293**	0.286*	0.165**	0.461**	0.437*
(K/L)^2		0.014	0.013		0.006	0.008
Lagged per capita income	−0.982***	−1.248***	−1.312***	−1.326***	−0.096	−0.228
(Income)^2		0.708***	0.669***		0.559***	0.578***
$(K/L) \times (I)$		−0.309***	−0.285***		−0.381***	−0.386***
Trade intensity TI = $(X+M)$/GDP	−0.915	−0.488	−0.510	−3.677***	−3.142**	−3.216**
TI × REL.K/L	−0.462	−1.952*	−1.828*	0.159	−2.252*	−2.121
TI × (REL.K/L)^2	0.018	−0.230	−0.248	−0.168	−0.123	−0.176
TI × REL.INC	0.470	1.056*	1.011*	2.128**	2.687***	2.614***
TI × (REL.INC)^2	0.118	−0.308*	−0.285*	−0.108	−0.595**	−0.584**
TI × (REL.K/L) × (REL.INC)	−0.165	0.870***	0.822***	−0.280	0.900**	0.924**
Suburban dummy	−0.299	−0.435*	−0.422*			
Rural dummy	−0.623	−0.674	−0.631			
Communist country (C.C.) dummy	0.312	−0.252	−0.257			
C.C. dummy × income	−0.283	4.569*	4.641*	1.170	9.621**	9.639**
C.C. dummy × (income)^2		−5.755**	−5.788**		−8.931***	−8.806**
Average temperature	−0.055***	−0.052***	−0.052***	−0.060*	−0.057*	−0.056*
Precipitation variation:	3.446	5.860	6.158	8.599	10.810*	10.716*
Helsinki Protocol:	−0.232*	−0.092	−0.114	−0.179	0.016	0.016
Observations	2,555	2,555	2,555	2,555	2,555	2,555
Groups	290	290	290	290	290	290
R^2	0.3395	0.3737	0.374	0.2483	0.131	0.1499
Log-likelihood	−2550	−2523	−2522	−3964	−3906	−3905
LR test/χ^2 (df)	55.596***	1.604		118.42***	2.035	
Hausman test/Wald χ^2 (df)	65.761**	15.158	53.789			
Scale elasticity	0.192***	0.265***	0.315***	0.112*	0.266***	0.398**
Composition elasticity	0.583**	0.948***	0.993***	0.945**	1.006**	0.975*
Technique elasticity	−0.905***	−1.577***	−1.577***	−1.222***	−1.153**	−1.266**
Trade intensity elasticity	−0.436***	−0.388***	−0.394***	−0.641***	−0.864***	−0.882***

Notes: To conserve space, no standard errors or t-statistics are shown. The dependent variable is the log of the median of SO_2 concentrations at each observation site. Model A follows directly from our empirical implementation, whereas model B allows for additional interaction between capital abundance and income. In addition to model B, model C allows for nonlinearity in our scale variable. All model specifications use time-fixed effects. Elasticities are evaluated at sample means using the Delta method.

* Significance at the 95-percent confidence level.
** Significance at the 99-percent confidence level.
*** Significance at the 99.9-percent confidence level.

little gained in moving to the slightly more general Model C from Model B; conversely, the restrictions imposed by Model A are rejected by the data as shown by the significant LR test statistics in columns (1) and (4). These empirical results together with our knowledge of theory suggest that less emphasis be placed on the estimates from Model A.

Next consider the impact of a nation's capital-to-labor ratio. In all columns of Table 1, we find a positive composition effect arising from an increase in capital-to-labor ratios. The estimated effect is typically quite large. With the exception of column (1), we find a 1-percent increase in a nation's capital-to-labor ratio—holding scale, income, and other determinants constant—leads to perhaps a 1-percent-point increase in pollution. Our success in finding a link between factor endowments and pollution may appear surprising given the universal difficulties researchers have had in finding a strong link between factor endowments and trade flows. We would note, however, that the production side of the HOS model has received some support (see especially James Harrigan 1995, 1997), and our model focuses on a highly aggregate relationship between overall pollution intensive output and factor endowments.

The estimates in Table 1 also predict a strong and significantly negative relationship between per capita income levels and concentrations. The elasticity of concentrations to an increase in income is typically quite large and is always significant. Using the estimates from Table 1, the technique elasticity varies between −0.9 and −1.5. This technique effect seems surprisingly strong, but the result appears to be robust. Alternative specifications (discussed below) lead to somewhat different conclusions, although the elasticity is almost universally estimated to be greater than −1 in magnitude, suggesting a strong policy response to income gains.

The Trade-Induced Composition Effect.—Next consider the estimates for the trade-induced composition effect. In all columns we reject the hypothesis that the terms reflecting the trade-induced composition effect are jointly zero.[24] Although the sign and significance of some individual coefficients vary across specifications, the results from Model B and Model C in both random and fixed effects are very similar. At the sample mean, the overall elasticity of concentrations to an increase in trade intensity is relatively constant, ranging from approximately −0.4 to −0.9. Therefore, for an average country in our sample the trade-induced composition effect is negative. Considering the individual coefficients, it is clear that country characteristics describing both relative income and abundance are important, but it is difficult to evaluate the relative strength of pollution haven and factor abundance motives. We present several methods of evaluation below.

Site-Specific and Country-Type Considerations.—Because income gains may not equally translate into policy responses we note it is important to distinguish between Communist and non-Communist countries. The Communist country interactions with income and income squared in Models B and C suggest that the technique effect is very small or nonexistent in Communist countries. For example, using the fixed-effects results from column (6), we cannot reject the hypothesis of a zero technique effect in Communist countries! In the random-effects case in column (3), the technique elasticity is fully one-third of that for our average, non-Communist country.[25] We investigated other country-type effects by including a dummy variable for those years a country was bound by the Helsinki protocol on acid rain. Our results indicate this variable has little explanatory power. The results, however, do indicate that site-specific land use and weather variables have a bearing on concentrations as expected. Higher temperatures both dissipate pollution faster and reduce the need for home heating; precipitation highly concentrated in one season reduces the ability of rain to wash out concentrations.

B. *Discussion and Evaluation*

Although the results in Table 1 appear to be supportive of our theory, it is important to go beyond sign and significance tests to investigate whether the magnitude of these estimates are in some sense plausible. We pursue several of these reality checks below.

To start note that the implied scale, composition, and technique elasticities are not implausibly high, and all are significantly different from zero. Together these elasticities provide some simple reality checks. For example, suppose our average economy experienced neutral technological progress of 1 percent, raising both GDP and GNP per person by 1 percent.

[24] This is in contrast to the case where trade intensity appears alone or is replaced by other measures of "openness." We investigated this issue more fully in Antweiler et al. (1998 Table 2 p. 29).

[25] The technique elasticity in the random-effects case is much smaller −0.50 but is significantly different from zero; the technique elasticity in the fixed-effects case is −0.062 with a 95-percent confidence interval of [−0.90, 0.78].

According to our estimates from Table 1, the positive scale effect from this growth will always be dominated by the negative technique effect.[26] Although the estimates differ across columns, in all cases our results indicate neutral technological progress lowers pollution concentrations. Alternatively, when an increase in income and production is fueled entirely by capital accumulation, the picture is far less favorable to the environment. If we assume a share of capital in output of ⅓, then the full impact of capital accumulation working through scale, composition, and technique effects is to raise pollution concentrations.[27] Even though these two exercises are not tests of our theory, the results are reassuringly close to what we may have expected *ex ante*.

To assess the plausibility of our trade intensity elasticity, we calculated the trade intensity elasticity for all countries in our sample. From Proposition 1 we note that the sign of the trade-induced composition effect should reflect a country's comparative advantage in clean versus dirty goods. Therefore it is not plausible that all countries in the world have negative trade intensity elasticities. Although we have only a sample of countries it seems reasonable to expect both positive and negative elasticities.

As a check on our theory we present in Figures 2 and 3 below a plot of country-specific elasticities against relative income using estimates from Model B in columns (2) and (5) of Table 1. Although there are more positive elasticities in Figure 2 than 3, in both there is a distribution of elasticities around zero. Our inference is simply that some countries' pollution demand shifts right with a fall in trade frictions and some shift left *because countries differ in their comparative advantage*.[28] For example, from either Figure 2 or Figure 3 we would conclude a small trade liberalization in Canada, all else equal, shifts its pollution demand curve to the right. The inference is that, despite Canada's relatively high income, its comparative advantage lies in capital-intensive dirty products. Alternatively, we would conclude a small trade liberalization in India shifts its pollution demand curve to the left, the inference being that, despite its relatively low income, its comparative advantage lies in labor-intensive and relatively clean goods production. Although these two countries estimates may accord well with our intuition, other country-specific elasticities are harder to explain [e.g., why is Malaysia's elasticity (MYS) so negative and Switzerland's (CHE) so positive?]. Because our country-specific estimates do vary across specifications, we caution the reader from drawing too strong an inference from any one of them.

Pollution Haven and Factor Abundance Motives.—The second feature of note in Figures 2 and 3 is that the elasticity estimates increase with relative income. Note that if the simple pollution haven hypothesis were literally true and the sole determinant of trade in dirty products, we would expect just the opposite—a strong negative correlation between relative income and the magnitude of our country-specific elasticities. This is because, under the pollution haven hypothesis, poor countries specialize in dirty goods and rich countries specialize in clean goods. A small movement toward free trade would shift the pollution demand curve inward for a rich country and outward for a poor country. In fact, as shown in the figures, the relationship is definitely nonnegative and, in

[26] Holding input use constant (capital, labor, and pollution), neutral technological progress raises output in our model. Each unit of pollution is more productive than before, and this via a scale effect argues for more pollution. Because real incomes are now higher, however, pollution may in fact fall from a technique effect. Whether we have more or less pollution in equilibrium after the shock therefore depends on the relative strength of these two effects.

[27] Take, for example, the estimates from column (6). Then our estimates indicate that a 1-percent increase in the capital-to-labor ratio raises concentrations by perhaps 1 percent, all else equal. However, an increase in the capital-to-labor ratio will have accompanying impacts on the scale of economic activity and on real incomes. If we make a back-of-the-envelope calculation by taking capital's share in the value of domestic output at 1/3, then capital accumulation leading to a 1-percent increase in the capital-to-labor ratio creates a 1/3-percentage-point increase in GDP per capita and GDP/km^2. Therefore, capital accumulation also creates an induced technique effect of approximately $-1.2/3 = -0.4$ and an induced scale effect of perhaps $0.13 = 0.39/3$. Adding the direct composition effect to these estimates suggests that economic growth fueled entirely by capital accumulation raises pollution concentrations.

[28] The random-effects implementation in Figure 2 has more positive point elasticities than the fixed effects in Figure 3, but relatively minor changes in specifications moves the entire set of fixed-effects estimates upward.

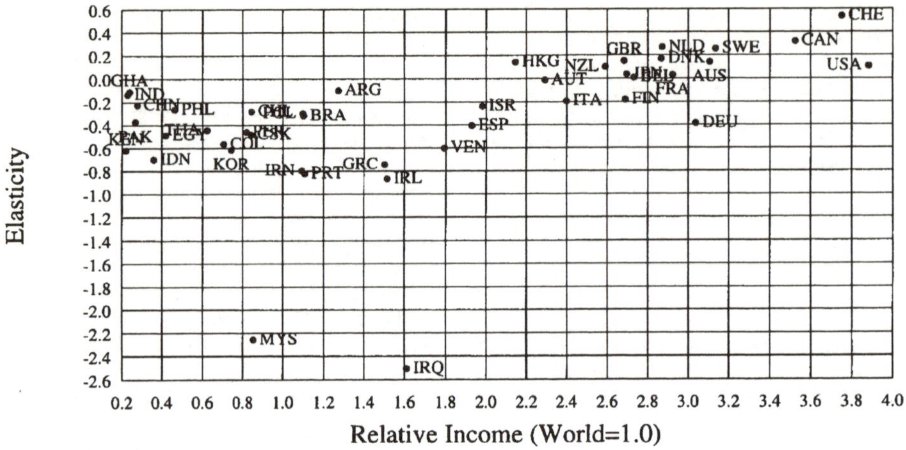

FIGURE 2. COUNTRY-SPECIFIC TRADE ELASTICITIES [MODEL B, RANDOM EFFECTS, CORRESPONDING TO TABLE 1 COLUMN (2)]

fact, slightly positive.[29] It appears that if anything, high-income countries have a comparative advantage in dirty capital-intensive products.

In total, although changes in trade intensity seem to matter, the magnitude of the induced change in pollution concentrations appears relatively small. In Figure 2 the vast majority of countries have trade intensity elasticities less than 1 in absolute value; in Figure 3 the majority of countries also satisfy this requirement.

One explanation for these findings is simple: low-income countries typically have both low incomes per capita and low capital-to-labor ratios. The pollution haven hypothesis suggests that a low-income economy should be made dirtier by trade, but if pollution-intensive industries are also capital-intensive then, whatever benefits accrue from lax pollution regulation could be largely undone by the relatively higher price of capital in this capital-scarce country. As a result, further openness to trade will have a very small effect on the pollution intensity of output for low-income countries. Similarly, high-income countries have both high income and high capital-to-labor ratios. The former argues in favor of trade lowering the pollution intensity of output, whereas the latter argues in favor of trade raising it.

Judging from Figure 2 and 3 it appears that, if anything, factor endowment motives are offsetting tighter pollution policy in relatively rich countries. This may explain why other investigations have failed to find a significant relationship between the strictness of pollution regulations and decreased trade in capital-intensive dirty goods. It may also explain why previous researchers have found it quite difficult to find pollution haven effects in the data. It is not that the (ceterus paribus) pollution haven hypothesis is wrong, or that the (ceterus paribus) factor endowment driven basis for trade is absent. But rather, because these two partial theories work against each other, the net result of the potentially very large composition effects predicted by either theory turn out to be rather small in practice.

C. *An Environmental Assessment of Freer Trade*

Taking factor endowments as fixed, a lowering of transport costs or trade barriers raises the value of domestic output and real income in a small open economy. The value of output and the value of income rise by (approximately) the

[29] Even excluding the strongly negative elasticities of Malaysia (MYS) and Iraq (IRQ), the relationship is significantly positive in both Figures 2 and 3.

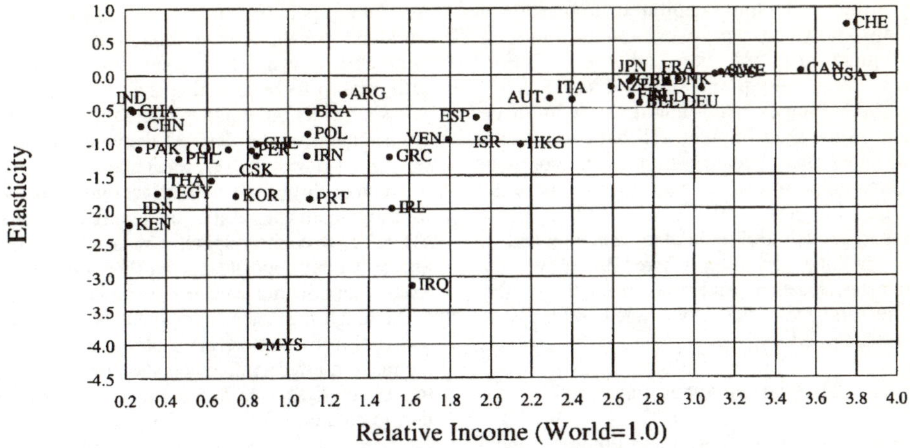

FIGURE 3. COUNTRY-SPECIFIC TRADE ELASTICITIES [MODEL B, FIXED EFFECTS, CORRESPONDING TO TABLE 1 COLUMN (5)]

same percentage, and this creates both scale and technique effects. Using the estimates from either Model B or Model C in Table 1, the net effect of a 1-percent change in income created by trade is a 0.8–0.9-percent fall in emissions: that is, using (21) we have $\pi_1 - \pi_3 < 0$. The composition effect of trade for our average country is also negative; that is, from (21) we have $\pi_4 < 0$. Therefore, for an average country in our sample, the full impact of further openness to international trade—through scale, technique, and composition effects—will be a reduction in SO_2 concentrations!

Similar results follow from all of our specifications: the scale elasticity is dominated by the technique elasticity, whereas the trade-induced composition effect of trade is typically small in magnitude.[30] How large a reduction any one country reaps from a fall in trade frictions will, of course, depend on country characteristics, the impact further trade has on domestic income and output, and how the ongoing process of globalization is affecting country characteristics elsewhere in the world. Given that countries will differ somewhat in their particular elasticities, some may indeed be made dirtier from a reduction in trade frictions, but we expect that trade's effect—whether positive or negative—will be small.[31] After all, the estimated impact of even a large trade liberalization on GDP is small, and when this small increase in GDP is filtered through our estimated scale and technique elasticities, the net effect is likely to be smaller still. Although, in theory, trade's impact on the pollution intensity of output can be large, in practice our estimates suggest a much more muted response.

These conclusions, however, rely on our assumption that factor endowments and technology remain fixed when trade frictions fall.

[30] In the Technical Appendix we investigate a two-equation two-stage least-squares (2SLS) fixed-effects model where our city scale measure and pollution are determined simultaneously. We find a scale elasticity in excess of 1, but also a much larger technique elasticity (approaching −2). As a result, our conclusion on their relative magnitude remains unchanged.

[31] Averaging across countries and years, the average trade intensity is 41 percent with a standard deviation of 32 percentage points. A one-standard-deviation change in trade intensity is then equal to a 79 percent change in trade intensity from its average value, whereas a one-standard-deviation change in pollution concentrations is equivalent to a 203-percent change from its average value. Using our fixed-effects estimate of the trade intensity elasticity from Table 1, column (6), a 79-percent increase in trade intensity amounts to a 69-percent reduction in pollution concentrations, or about one-third of a standard deviation of pollution concentration. Using the random-effects estimate from column (3) in Table 1, the same one-standard-deviation change in trade intensity amounts to a change of less than one-sixth of the standard deviation in pollution concentration.

If further trade spurs capital accumulation or brings knowledge spillovers and hastens technological progress, then other calculations must come into play. Whether these trade-induced changes bring about a net improvement in the environment will depend on their estimated size because they have opposing effects on pollution concentrations. There is a burgeoning empirical literature linking openness to growth and technology adoption and we have nothing new to add here. But clearly our estimates, together with input from these other sources, might provide another method for assessing trade's full impact.

D. *Alternative Specifications*

The results from Table 1 and Figures 2 and 3 suggest that our approach of dividing the determinants of pollution into scale, technique, and composition effects is fruitful. It is, however, important to investigate whether our results are robust to reasonable changes in specification, time period, and so forth. We have conducted numerous sensitivity tests of our specification and report four alternatives in Table 2. Additional results are available in our Technical Appendix, available upon request from the authors. In all columns we amend our full Model C from Table 1 to include other determinants, investigate other time periods, or adopt more flexible specifications.

In columns (1) and (5) we have restricted the time period of our analysis to the years 1976–1991. Before 1976 only a few countries participated and after funding ceased in 1991 country coverage is reduced. To allow for possible data quality and sample selection problems we consider this shorter time period. This shortened period has 489 fewer observations, although as shown in columns (1) and (5) the results are similar both in terms of elasticity estimates and significance levels. Our overall conclusions regarding the relative strength of scale versus technique effects remains, as does the muted response to changes in trade intensity.

In columns (2) and (6) we investigate the importance of other factor endowments. In our parsimonious model of pollution demand and supply "factor endowments" enter directly only through the inclusion of the capital-to-labor ratio. Other potential factor endowments were excluded because, even though they are undoubtedly relevant to income levels, there is little reason to believe that they have an *independent* effect on either the demand for a clean environment or the derived demand for pollution emissions; however, local abundance either in clean or dirty fuels may affect emissions. We investigate this possibility by adding in columns (2) and (6) country-specific measures of hard and soft coal deposits per worker. Overall the results support our earlier conclusions.

Although a greater endowment of high sulfur soft coal leads to more concentrations, at least in the random-effects implementation in column (2), this effect disappears in the fixed-effects estimation in column (6). These results are not surprising: an abundance of soft coal means that countries like China will have higher concentrations, all else equal, but because mineral endowments have very little time series variation they will be well captured by country fixed effects. Consequently, although abundance of high sulfur coal surely adds to emissions, its explicit inclusion has very little effect on our results.

In columns (3) and (6) we investigate the impact foreign direct investment may have on our results. If multinational corporations have common production methods in both developed and developing countries for engineering, quality control, or other reasons, then the pollution intensity of their production will be determined by the income per capita of the source country. As a result, a larger multinational presence in a poor country may mean it is cleaner, all else equal; however, there is an alternative hypothesis working in the other direction. If multinationals locate in poor countries because of their lax environmental protection, then we may instead find a positive relationship between foreign direct investment (FDI) and pollution. To investigate this issue we have calculated for each year and country in our sample the ratio of its inward stock of FDI to its overall capital stock.[32] We refer to this as FDI intensity: it measures the share of the domestic capital stock

[32] In theory we may want to distinguish between acquisitions of brownfields, capacity expansions, and greenfield investments because greenfield investors are perhaps more likely to bring their own plant-specific technology to the foreign country.

TABLE 2—SENSITIVITY TESTS

Estimation method:	Random effects				Fixed effects			
Model specification:	Time	Factors	FDI	Scale	Time	Factors	FDI	Scale
Variable/column:	(1)	(2)	(3)	(4)	(5)	(6)	(7)	(8)
Intercept	−2.545***	−3.141***	−3.650***	−3.635***	−1.697	−4.679***	−4.679***	−4.345***
City economic intensity GDP/km^2	0.068***	0.075***	0.070***	0.154***	0.091*	0.087*	0.092*	0.029
(City economic intensity)^2/1,000	−0.054	−0.275	−0.231		−0.254	−0.329	−0.373	
Capital abundance (K/L)	−0.115	0.289*	0.439***	0.279*	−0.077	0.426*	0.754***	0.489**
(K/L)^2	0.036**	0.012	−0.002	0.010	0.032	0.008	−0.024	0.006
Lagged per capita income	−1.771***	−1.629***	−1.451***	−0.852*	−3.109**	−0.428	−0.981	−0.052
(Income)^2	0.585***	0.717***	0.660***	0.611***	0.512*	0.757***	0.563***	0.564***
$(K/L) \times (I)$	−0.147*	−0.276***	−0.255***	−0.278***	−0.041	−0.401***	−0.297***	−0.400***
Trade intensity TI = $(X+M)$/GDP	−2.466***	−0.671	−0.198	−0.501	−7.161***	−3.333**	−3.747***	−2.964**
TI × REL.K/L	0.934	−1.758*	−2.879**	−1.890*	1.699	−2.281*	−2.737*	−2.541*
TI × (REL.K/L)^2	−0.876**	−0.252	0.304	−0.142	−1.043**	−0.131	0.811	−0.112
TI × REL.INC.	1.344**	1.167*	1.518**	1.212*	4.495***	3.097***	2.720**	2.677***
TI × (REL.INC.)^2	−0.228	−0.309*	−0.308*	−0.354**	−0.742**	−0.723***	−0.360	−0.617**
TI × (REL.K/L) × (REL.INC.)	0.333	0.803***	0.519	0.784**	0.164	0.922**	0.092	0.993**
Suburban dummy	−0.284	−0.424*	−0.445*	−0.490**				
Rural dummy	−0.519	−0.620	−0.655	−0.730*				
Inward FDI stock/capital stock			0.039				1.234*	
FDI/K × poor countries			4.736				6.314	
FDI/K × rich countries			−0.362				−0.828	
Communist country (C.C.) dummy	−0.971*	−0.326	−0.110	−0.475				
C.C. dummy × income	7.785***	4.602*	4.201	5.668**	16.809***	11.751***	10.271**	9.819**
C.C. dummy × (income)^2	−8.683***	−5.683*	−5.677*	−7.127**	−14.13***	−10.84***	−8.840**	−9.039***
Average temperature	−0.061***	−0.056***	−0.051***	−0.052***	−0.072*	−0.055*	−0.049	−0.062*
Precipitation variation	8.867*	5.859	7.633	5.882	14.298**	10.893*	13.972**	11.471*
Hard coal (per worker)		−0.690				4.217		
Soft coal (per worker)		2.998*				4.120		
Helsinki Protocol	−0.242*	−0.157	−0.092	−0.094	−0.173	−0.054	0.036	0.035
Observations	2066	2555	2525	2555	2066	2555	2525	2555
Groups	274	290	284	290	274	290	284	290
R^2	0.3243	0.3779	0.3684	0.389	0.1677	0.0605	0.1577	0.1337
Log-likelihood	−2030	−2519	−2496	−2512	−2982	−3900	−3858	−3899
Hausman test/Wald χ^2 (df)	94.211***	55.536	84.269***	59.331*				
Scale elasticity (all/middle)	0.314***	0.333***	0.318***	0.499***	0.414*	0.388*	0.412**	0.094
Scale elasticity (poor countries)				0.643***				0.355*
Scale elasticity (rich countries)				0.537***				0.598***
Composition elasticity	0.985***	1.008***	1.026***	0.803***	1.442**	0.864*	1.150**	1.056**
Technique elasticity	−1.425***	−1.740***	−1.551***	−1.218***	−2.220***	−1.230**	−1.505***	−1.204**
Trade intensity elasticity	−0.266**	−0.351***	−0.364**	−0.292**	−0.543**	−0.791***	−1.189***	−0.899***
FDI elasticity (poor countries)			0.091				0.143	
FDI elasticity (middle)			0.004				0.121*	
FDI elasticity (rich countries)			−0.039				0.049	

Notes: No standard errors or t-statistics are shown. The dependent variable is the log of the median of SO_2 concentrations at each observation site. All model specifications use time fixed effects. Elasticities are evaluated at sample means using the Delta method. Model "Time" includes only the years 1976–1991 of the primary GEMS phase; model "Factors" introduces factor endowment-related variables; and model "FDI" allows for an an inward foreign direct investment stock relative to the overall capital stock, interacted with income. The terms rich countries and poor countries refer to the top and bottom 30 percent of countries in the Penn World Tables with respect to per capita GDP.

* Significance at the 95-percent confidence level.

** Significance at the 99-percent confidence level.

*** Significance at the 99.9-percent confidence level.

that may have cleaner than expected techniques of production. We then interact this measure with a categorical variable representing a country's income per capita to allow the multinational effect to differ across rich and poor countries. The results from this exercise are mixed. In the fixed-effects estimation, there is a slight positive relationship between FDI and concentrations for poor, middle-income, and rich countries. Only the middle-income relationship is statistically significant. Moreover, the coefficient estimates imply that a 10 percentage point increase in the *ratio* of the FDI stock to K stock would raise concentrations by about 1 percent. This is a small effect on pollution concentrations arising from a very large change in FDI. In the random-effects estimation, none of the coefficients is significantly different from zero. Overall, we find little relationship between the extent of FDI in an economy (even a poor one) and its pollution level. Again our elasticity estimates are changed only slightly from our earlier specification.

Finally, in columns (4) and (8) we investigate whether our scale effect differs significantly across countries categorized by income per capita levels. If there were important nonhomotheticities in production or consumption, or if our method of constructing scale was more appropriate for some income categories than others, this may show up when we allow for disaggregation. The results in column (4) indicate that, whereas separate estimation of scale across income categories tends to raise the overall elasticity estimates to approximately 0.5 or 0.6, the results are very similar to those presented earlier. In column (8) we find similar results for the poor and rich categories, but the middle-income group has a much lower elasticity and it is not precisely estimated. The middle-income group results may be a consequence of the exclusive reliance of fixed effects on the (now smaller) within-group variation for estimation. Despite these caveats, the elasticity estimates, although different across classes, are not significantly different from each other.[33]

E. *Alternative Theories: Tariff Substitution and Distributional Motives*

In our framework, governments use pollution policy only to target pollution, and not for other purposes, such as to influence the terms of trade or to redistribute income. As a result, the pollution tax is always equal to effective marginal damage, and changes in openness affect our pollution supply curve only through its impact on real income and relative prices. More generally, pollution policy and openness may be linked through other channels if governments use pollution policy for other purposes. To examine this possibility further we need to specify the potential theoretical links involved and then ask what variation in the data such a link would create. There are (at least) two reasons why trade and environmental policies may be linked. Each of these links is probably deserving of a paper-length treatment of both theory and further empirical work, but here our goal is merely to sketch two possibilities and identify their probable impact on our empirical results.

Tariff Substitution.—The first link arises from market power. If countries were large and had complete discretion in setting both trade and pollution policy, then both instruments would be targeted: the tariff would be set at its optimal level according to the inverse elasticity rule, and the pollution tax would equal effective marginal damage as in our small open economy case. But if tariff choices are constrained by international agreements, then governments may find it useful to substitute environmental policy for trade policy. We will refer to this as the *tariff substitution motive.* To proceed further consider the optimal pollution tax for a large open economy:

$$\tau = T\phi(p, I) + pE_p^*\left(t - \frac{1}{\varepsilon^*}\right)\left|\frac{dp/d\tau}{dz/d\tau}\right|, \tag{27}$$

where ε^* is the elasticity of foreign export supply, E_p^* is the price derivative of foreign export supply, and t is the ad valorem tariff. To highlight the tariff substitution motive, rewrite (27) to obtain the gap between the pollution tax and effective marginal damage:

$$\tau - T\phi(p, I) = pE_p^*\left(t - \frac{1}{\varepsilon^*}\right)\left|\frac{dp/d\tau}{dz/d\tau}\right|. \tag{28}$$

This gap reflects the tariff substitution motive. Consider first a dirty good importer. When the

[33] In our random-effects implementation we can go further and divide the components of our scale measure into population density and contemporaneous GDP/N. Doing so yields an elasticity of concentrations to population density of 0.57; an elasticity with respect to contemporaneous GDP/N of 0.25; and an overall scale elasticity of 0.65. We cannot reject our restriction that both population density and contemporaneous GDP/N share the same elasticity.

tariff is set at its optimal level, the right-hand side of (28) is zero: each instrument is targeted and there is no tariff substitution motive. If the tariff is constrained to be below its optimal level, then the right-hand side of (28) is negative and a dirty good importer sets the pollution tax below marginal damage to substitute for the tariff. Increased openness therefore induces a loosening of pollution policy that was not accounted for in our empirical work.[34] For a dirty good exporter, a similar argument works in reverse: as trade restrictions are reduced below their optimal level, there is an incentive to tighten pollution policy because pollution taxes can be used as a substitute for an export tax. Increased openness in this case leads to a tightening of pollution policy not accounted for in the empirical work.

The Redistribution Motive.—Even if countries are small in world markets, governments may adjust pollution taxes to try to undo the redistribution of income caused by increased openness. We refer to this as the *redistributive motive.* To illustrate this motive, retain our small open economy framework, but now assume Greens and Browns differ in factor ownership, with Browns having greater capital per person than Greens; for simplicity, let $u(I) = \ln(I)$. Then given the government's weight λ on Greens, the pollution tax will be used both to target pollution and also to influence the income distribution. This again yields a gap between the pollution tax and effective marginal damage:

$$(29) \quad \tau - T\phi(p, I) = \frac{\lambda - s}{s(1 - s)} G \left| \frac{ds/d\tau}{dz/d\tau} \right|,$$

where s is the share of Greens in national income. Note that if the weight given to Greens exceeds their current share of national income, then the pollution tax is higher than marginal damage. This is because higher pollution taxes lower the producer price of X and raise the real return to labor. Alternatively, if the weight given to Browns is greater than their current income share, the right-hand side of (29) is negative: the pollution tax is set below marginal damage to raise the real return to capital.

Consider the effects of increased openness, starting from the position where $\lambda = s$. In this case, the pollution tax in a dirty good exporting country rises above marginal damage to compensate for the Greens' loss in income.[35] Increased openness hurts workers in this case, and the government cushions the blow by tightening the pollution tax to raise wages. For a dirty good importer, the result is reversed: increased openness leads to a loosening of pollution policy to compensate for Browns' loss in income.

Implications of the Theories.—Each theory adds a country-specific unmeasured factor to our simpler determinants of pollution. The factor is a country-type effect, and it is relevant to both a country's degree of openness and its pollution supply curve. In the large-country case, the unmeasured country type is described by its trade pattern and market power; and in the redistributive theory, by its preferred and actual income distribution.

The impact these country-type effects have on our empirical results depends on whether they are time varying. If the country differences are simple level effects and do not vary over time, then our fixed-effects implementation is appropriate, even if country type is correlated with other right-hand-side regressors. If country type is uncorrelated with the right-hand-side variables, then our random-effects estimation is more efficient and still unbiased. On average, countries of different types would have different pollution levels, but they would respond similarly to changes in openness, scale, and so forth. Given that the panel is quite short for many countries, this constant-over-time country-type assumption may be appropriate.

If these country-type effects are time varying, then they will be correlated with our measure of

[34] We know that the gap is zero when tariffs are optimal and is negative when tariffs are zero, so "on average" we expect an increase in openness to widen the gap. However, it should be noted that because the right-hand side of (28) includes the elasticity of foreign export supply, world prices, and so forth, the gap between τ and marginal damage may not increase monotonically as tariffs fall.

[35] Let $\Gamma = \tau - T\phi(p, I)$. Then, evaluating at $\lambda = s$, we have $d\Gamma/d\beta = -s_\beta G|s_\tau|/[|z_\tau|s(1 - s)] > 0$, because $s_\beta < 0$ (an increase in openness reduces workers' share of income).

openness. Consequently, our results concerning the effects of further openness and income on pollution may be undermined. To assess whether these motives could be responsible for our results, consider what is left out by our simpler specification. Start with tariff substitution. When tariffs are reduced and openness rises, tariff substitution creates an unaccounted-for upward shift in pollution supply for a dirty good exporter. This leads to *less* pollution than our model would predict. Alternatively, tariff substitution produces an unaccounted-for downward shift in pollution supply for a dirty good importer. In this case, tariff substitution leads to *more* pollution than our model would predict. In both cases, unaccounted-for shifts in supply work against the shift in pollution demand created by further openness. Similarly, the redistributive motive shifts the pollution supply curve up for a dirty good exporter and down for a dirty good importer in response to increased openness. Again, we find that this additional potential determinant of pollution tends to dampen the composition effect created by further openness.

Could tariff substitution or redistribution motives be responsible for the large technique effects we find? Both of these alternative theories lead to an unmeasured positive relationship between pollution and openness for some countries. Therefore, it is difficult to see how the omission of either of these two additional determinants would manifest itself in a stronger measured negative relationship between income and pollution.

These two alternative theories, however, do suggest a smaller (than we would otherwise predict) change in the composition of output created by a fall in trade frictions. As such, another interpretation of our findings of a small trade-induced composition effect is that governments may be simultaneously dampening the impact of increased openness on pollution with compensating changes in pollution taxes. To disentangle the additional shifts in pollution supply suggested by either theory from the other effects in our data would require us to obtain information on changes in both tariff levels and pollution regulations over time for many countries in our sample; or employ knowledge about the preferred and actual income distribution in many countries over time. But good cross-country and time-series data on pollution regulations and trade protection are unavailable, and the preferred income distribution is unobservable. These two alternative theories are perhaps best examined within a single country context where data on regulations, tariffs, and income distribution are available.[36]

IV. Conclusions

This paper investigates how openness to trading opportunities affects pollution concentrations. We started with a theoretical specification highlighting scale, technique, and composition effects and then showed how this theoretical decomposition is useful in thinking about the relationship between openness to international markets and the environment. In our empirical section we adopted a specification directly linked to our earlier theory. We then estimated this specification, paying special attention to the potentially confounding influences introduced by the panel structure of our data set. Our results consistently indicate that scale, technique, and composition effects are not just theoretical constructs with no empirical counterparts; rather, these theoretical constructs can be identified and their magnitude measured. Moreover, once measured they can play a useful role in determining the likely environmental consequences of technological progress, capital accumulation, or increased trade. These estimates may also be useful in aggregate CGE modeling of the effects of various free trade agreements and other trade reforms [see, e.g., Michael J. Ferrantino and Linda A. Linkins (1996)].

Our work is distinguished by the endogeneity of pollution policy and the close connection we have tried to draw between theory and empirical estimation. Although it represents a useful first step toward answering our title's question, it is clearly not the last. The benefits of our approach are transparency, simplicity, and explicitness.

[36] We discuss here the extreme case where pollution policy is the only available instrument. There are many other instruments (such as production subsidies), which are a better substitute for a tariff; and similarly there are many other instruments (such as income transfers), which can redistribute income. To the extent that these other instruments are available, then the dampening shift in pollution supply that we find above will be less relevant.

We have presented an explicit model of trade and pollution and we have moved from theory to empirical estimation in a transparent manner. Transparency immediately leads to suggestions for extension along both theoretical and empirical lines. Simplicity means additional questions can be addressed within our framework. And the benefit of presenting an explicit pollution demand-and-supply model is that researchers should now be drawn to deeper questions concerning endogeneity, omitted variables, and sample selection. We view this paper's attempt at integrating theory with empirical work as its major contribution to ongoing research in this area.

Several extensions seem natural. One cost of reduced-form estimation is that structural parameters remain hidden. Reduced-form estimation was essentially forced on us by the lack of data on regulations in many developing countries. If we adopt similar methods but restrict the sample to industrialized countries, we could then employ measures of pollution stringency as proxies for pollution regulations. With data on both the quantity and "price" of pollution, the identification of structural parameters seems possible. A shift to a narrower set of countries with more detailed data may also allow us to examine the tariff substitution and redistributive motives we discussed, but did not estimate, here. Finally, our method for adding up scale, composition, and technique effects could be enhanced by direct estimates of the income gains brought about by trade liberalization, and improved by explicit consideration of foreign direct investment and technology transfer.

As with any empirical exercise some questions remain unanswered, but overall our estimates indicate that increases in a country's exposure to international markets create small but measurable changes in pollution concentrations by altering the pollution intensity of national output. Although our estimates indicate that greater trade intensity creates only relatively small changes in pollution via a composition effect, economic theory and numerous empirical studies demonstrate that trade also raises the value of national output and income. These associated increases in output and incomes will then exert an impact on pollution concentrations via our estimated scale and technique effects. Our estimates of the scale and technique elasticities indicate that, if openness to international markets raises both output and income by 1 percent, pollution concentrations fall by approximately 1 percent. Putting this calculation together with our earlier evidence on composition effects yields a somewhat surprising conclusion with regard to sulfur dioxide: freer trade is good for the environment.

Appendix: A: Proof of Propositions

PROOF OF PROPOSITION 1:

Use (17) and (18), and hold T, S, I, K/L, and p^w constant:

$$\hat{z} = [(1 + a)\varepsilon_{\varphi,p} + \varepsilon_{e,p/\tau}]\hat{\beta} - [a\varepsilon_{\varphi,p} + \varepsilon_{e,p/\tau}]\hat{\tau} = [\varepsilon_{\varphi,p} + (a\varepsilon_{\varphi,p} + \varepsilon_{e,p/\tau})(1 - \varepsilon_{MD,p})]\hat{\beta}.$$

Using Roy's identity, we can show that $\varepsilon_{MD,p}$ is equal to the share of x in consumption (note that when calculating this elasticity, real income I is held constant, and so we obtain a pure substitution effect). Hence, $\varepsilon_{MD,p} < 1$, and z rises as β rises. For a dirty good exporter, increased openness corresponds to an increase in β, and hence all else equal, a reduction in trade frictions raises pollution. For a dirty good importer, a reduction in trade frictions lowers β, and pollution falls.

PROOF OF PROPOSITION 2:

Note $z = -R_\tau$ (where $R_\tau = -eR_{p^N}$ and $R_{\tau\tau} > 0$). Then

$$dz = -[R_{\tau\tau}\, d\tau + p^w(1 - \theta)R_{\tau p^N}\, d\beta] = R_{\tau\tau}\left[p^w \frac{d\tau}{dp}\bigg|_z d\beta - d\tau\right],$$

where the last step follows from differentiating $z = -R_\tau$, holding z constant. Next eliminate $d\tau$ by differentiating (10), noting that $I = G/(N\rho)$ and that $dG = p^w(1 - \theta)R_{p^N}\, d\beta + \tau\, dz$. Rearranging and converting to elasticity form yields

$$\frac{dz}{d\beta} = \left[\frac{p}{\tau}\frac{d\tau}{dp}\bigg|_z - \varepsilon_{MD,p} + \varepsilon_{MD,I}\frac{pM}{G}\right] \Big/ H,$$

where M is imports of X and H is a positive expression. From the proof of Proposition 1,

$\varepsilon_{MD,p} < 1$. But $(p/\tau)(d\tau/dp)|_z > 1$ because $z = ex$ and e is decreasing in τ/p. (An increase in p raises x, and so to keep z constant, we need τ/p to rise.) Hence, if $M > 0$, then $dz/d\beta > 0$ and so increased openness reduces pollution for a dirty good importer (β falls). For a dirty good exporter, $M < 0$ and β rises when openness rises. From the proof of Proposition 1, $\varepsilon_{MD,p}$ is the share of X in consumption, and so with $\varepsilon_{MD,I} \leq 1$, we have

$$\frac{dz}{d\beta} > \left[\frac{p}{\tau}\frac{d\tau}{dp}\bigg|_z - \frac{px}{G}\right] \bigg/ H > 0,$$

where $px/G < 1$ is the share of X in output at domestic prices. So pollution rises for a dirty good exporter if $\varepsilon_{MD,I} \leq 1$. Finally, if $\varepsilon_{MD,I}$ is sufficiently large, the sign of $dz/d\beta$ is reversed for a dirty good exporter and pollution falls as openness rises.

PROOF OF PROPOSITION 3:

For a given p and I, Home's relative demand $RD(p)$ is fixed. For given p and I, the unit input coefficients given in (6) are fixed, and hence χ approaches infinity as κ rises. Consequently, there exists a $\underline{\kappa}$ such that for $\kappa > \underline{\kappa}$, χ exceeds relative demand, and Home exports X. The increase in pollution via the trade-induced composition effect follows from Proposition 1.

PROOF OF PROPOSITION 4:

The relative producer price of X is $p^N < p(1 - \theta) - \tau e(1)$, where $e(1) > 0$. Because $\varepsilon_{MD,I} > \varepsilon > 0$, τ increases without bound as income rises given (18). Moreover, θ rises from (4), and hence there exists some I for which p^N falls to 0, in which case X output is 0. The relative demand for X is, however, independent of income. Hence for sufficiently large I, Home must import X and export Y. The fall in pollution from the trade-induced composition effect follows from Proposition 1.

PROOF OF PROPOSITION 5:

Define trade intensity as the value of exports plus imports at world prices (excluding transportation services). Using the trade balance constraint,

$$\mathrm{TI} = 2p^w \frac{|M_x|}{p^w(1 - \theta)x + y},$$

where M_x is imports of X. Consider first an importer of X ($M_x > 0$). Let $G^w = p^w(1 - \theta)x + y$, and $G = \beta p^w(1 - \theta)x + y$. By homotheticity, we can write the demand for X as $D^x = h(p)G$. Letting $\delta^x = p^w D^x/G^w$, and $\varphi = p^w(1 - \theta)x/G^w$, we have $\mathrm{TI} = 2(\delta^x - \varphi)$. With some rearranging, we can write

$$\delta^x = p^w h[1 + (\beta - 1)\varphi].$$

Then

$$\frac{1}{2}\frac{\partial TI}{\partial \beta} = \frac{\partial \delta^x}{\partial \beta} - \frac{\partial \varphi}{\partial \beta}$$

$$= \frac{(p^w)^2}{G^w}\left[\frac{\partial D^x}{\partial p}\bigg|_u - \frac{\partial D^x}{\partial G}M_x\right]$$

$$+ [p^w h(\beta - 1) - 1]\varphi_\beta < 0,$$

where we have used the Slutsky decomposition. Note that the substitution effect in demand is negative ($\partial D^x/\partial p|_u < 0$) and the income effect ($\partial D^x/\partial G$) is positive, so the bracketed term involving demand changes is negative. As well, $p^w \beta h < 1$ from the consumer's budget constraint, and $\varphi_\beta > 0$ (an increase in β shifts production toward X) and so the last term is negative as well. Thus $\partial \mathrm{TI}/\partial \beta < 0$ for an importer of X. Hence a fall in β (a movement toward 1) increases trade intensity. For an exporter of X, one can proceed most simply by replacing $|p^w M_x|$ with imports of Y, M_y in the definition of trade intensity and following a similar analysis as earlier to conclude that an increase in β (a movement toward 1) raises trade intensity.

APPENDIX B: DATA SET DESCRIPTION

The dependent variable in our study is the concentration of sulfur dioxide at observation sites in major cities around the world as obtained through the GEMS/AIR data set supplied by the World Health Organization. Measurements are carried out using comparable methods. Each observation station reports annual summary statistics of SO_2 concentrations such as the median, the arithmetic and geometric mean, as well as 90th and 95th percentiles.

We have chosen to use a logarithmic transformation of the median SO_2 concentration as our dependent variable. The distribution of concentrations is highly skewed toward zero when viewed on a linear scale. As was pointed out in the WHO (1984) report about the GEMS/AIR project, concentrations are more suitably described by a lognormal distribution with a number of observations concentrated at the measurement threshold of the measurement devices. There is also an ambient level of SO_2 in the air that has natural causes.

A large share of observations were from the United States because of this country's extensive network of air quality measurement stations. Other large contributor countries were China, Canada, and Japan. Many of the other observation stations provided short or discontinuous streams of data while participating in the GEMS/AIR project. All in all, our analysis is based on over 2,600 observations from 293 observation stations in 109 cities around the world; these cities are located in 44 countries.

The primary source for our data is the *AIRS Executive International Database* that contains information about ambient air pollution in nations that voluntarily provide data to the GEMS/AIR program sponsored by the United Nations World Health Organization.[37] We had problems with the identification of several observation stations. The longitude and latitude information provided in one of the ancillary files was in some cases incorrect and was corrected case by case based on the description of the location.

Additional data sources for our regressors include the *Penn World Tables*[38] for macroeconomic data, the *World Investment Report*[39] for inward FDI stock data, the CIESIN *Global Population Distribution Database*[40] for population density data, the World Resources Institute *World Resources Database*[41] for natural resources and physical endowments, and data from the *Global Historical Climatology Network*[42] (GHCN) for weather conditions at the observation stations. Yet more time series were obtained for tariff and nontariff trade barriers[43] and educational attainment.[44]

Summary statistics for the major variables appear in Table B1. Some of the variables warrant further explanation. First, our scale measure of economic activity GDP per square kilometer is calculated by multiplying a country's real per capita GDP ($/person) with each city's population density (people/km^2). Extrapolations for per capita GDP were carried out for the years past 1993 based on real growth rates obtained from the IMF/IFS statistics. Population densities were available only for 1990.

The capital abundance (K/L) of countries was obtained from the physical capital stock per worker variable in the Penn World Tables. We have adjusted this series for human capital by applying a 0–1 average education index (in

[37] This package is available from the United States Environmental Protection Agency (US-EPA) at http://www.epa.gov/airs/aexec.html. The US-EPA kindly provided a much more complete version of this data set that included not only averages but also median and other percentiles of SO_2 concentrations. We would like to express our gratitude to Jonathan Miller of the US-EPA for providing additional GEMS/air data not contained in the public release of the data base, and for patiently answering our numerous technical questions.

[38] Robert Summers and Alan Heston, "The Penn World Table (Mark 5): An Expanded Set of International Comparisons, 1950–1988." *Quarterly Journal of Economics,* May 1991, *106*(2), pp. 327–68. Available in revision 5.6 from the Center for International Comparisons at the University of Pennsylvania at http://pwt.econ.upenn.edu/.

[39] United Nations Centre on Transnational Corporations, 1992 and 1999 volumes.

[40] This data set from the Consortium for International Earth Science Information Network (CIESIN) is available only for 1990. It can be obtained freely from the United Nations Environmental Programme server maintained by the U.S. Geological Survey at http://grid2.cr.usgs.gov/globalpop/1-degree/description.html.

[41] *World resources 1998–1999: A guide to the global environment,* Oxford: Oxford University Press, 1998.

[42] Information is available on monthly average temperatures, monthly precipitation, and atmospheric pressure. The raw data and description file are available from the National Climatic Data Center of the U.S. National Oceanic and Atmospheric Administration at ftp://ftp.ncdc.noaa.gov/pub/data/ghcn/.

[43] See Jeffrey D. Sachs and Andrew M. Warner: "Economic Convergence and Economic Policies." National Bureau of Economic Research (Cambridge, MA) Working Paper No. 5039, February 1995.

[44] These figures were obtained from Robert J. Barro and Jong-Wha Lee's (1994) study, available from the NBER website at http://www.nber.org/pub/barro.lee/ZIP/.

TABLE B1—SUMMARY STATISTICS

Variable	Dimension	Number of observations	Mean	SD	Min	Max
Log of SO_2	$\log_{10}$ (ppm)	2,555	−2.112	0.481	−3.000	−0.939
City economic intensity	\$m per km^2	2,555	0.790	0.878	0.010	5.934
GDP per capita (current)	\$10k	2,555	1.478	0.862	0.109	2.718
Population density	1,000 people/km^2	2,555	0.063	0.055	0.001	0.276
Capital abundance (adjusted)	\$10k/worker	2,555	5.612	2.497	0.829	17.189
Capital abundance (unadjusted)	\$10k/worker	2,555	3.207	1.763	0.130	7.750
Education attainment	0–1 range	2,555	0.540	0.226	0.088	0.799
GNP per capita, 3-yr average	\$10k	2,555	1.396	0.815	0.111	2.635
Communist country (C.C.)	[—]	2,555	0.125	0.331	0.000	1.000
C.C. × income	\$10k	319	0.302	0.208	0.127	0.716
Trade intensity $(X+M)$/GDP	[—]	2,555	0.409	0.322	0.088	2.617
Relative (K/L) (adjusted)	World = 1.00	2,555	1.357	0.605	0.203	4.174
Relative income	World = 1.00	2,555	2.500	1.392	0.221	4.138
Inward FDI stock/capital stock	[—]	2,525	0.106	0.250	0.001	2.193
Average temperature	°C	2,555	14.689	5.600	2.617	28.967
Precipitation coefficient of variation	[—]	2,555	0.011	0.006	0.001	0.054
Hard coal reserves	GJoule/worker	2,555	0.040	0.043	0.000	0.146
Soft coal reserves	GJoule/worker	2,555	0.038	0.052	0.000	0.348

Notes: All monetary figures are in 1995 U.S. dollars. The interaction term for income with the Communist countries dummy shows the case only where the dummy is equal to 1; thus the mean for this line is the mean for the Communist countries only.

which 1 represents 16 years of schooling) obtained from the Barro/Lee data set. Relative capital abundance is obtained by dividing each country's capital abundance by the corresponding world average for the given year, where "world average" is defined by all the countries in the Penn World Tables.

Our income (I) variable is the three-year average of lagged GNP per capita. This addresses two problems. First, contemporaneous income and the level of pollution may be determined simultaneously. Lagged income, however, is exogenous. Second, it is reasonable to assume that income changes translate only slowly into policy changes. We therefore smooth out some of the variation introduced through business cycles and include three years of data. (We also experimented with longer lags, without much effect on our results.) More concretely, for a given year t we compute $I_t = (y_{t-1} + y_{t-2} + y_{t-3})/3$. Relative income is constructed in the same fashion as our relative capital-abundance measure. GNP figures were obtained by adjusting GDP figures with a GNP/GDP correction factor obtained from the International Monetary Fund's *International Financial Statistics*. However, such correction factors were unavailable for the former Czechoslovakia, Egypt, Hong Kong, Iraq, Peru, Poland, and the former Yugoslavia. Unadjusted GDP figures were used in these cases.

The data on foreign direct investment (FDI) were obtained as percentages of the stock of inward FDI relative to GDP, and interpolated where necessary. These figures were then divided by GDP to capital stock ratios obtained from the Penn World Tables to obtain the percentage of inward FDI stock relative to a country's entire capital stock.

The suburban and rural location type dummy variables are from the original GEMS/AIR data set. The third (default) location type is central city. Our trade intensity measure is calculated as the sum of exports and imports expressed as a percentage of gross domestic product. The Communist country dummy used in our study identifies the following countries: China, Czechoslovakia, Poland, and Yugoslavia. The country dummy for the Helsinki Protocol identifies Austria, Belgium, Bulgaria, Canada, Czechoslovakia, Denmark, Finland, France, Germany, Hungary, Italy, Luxembourg, The Netherlands, Norway, and Switzerland, in the years after 1985.

For the purpose of calculating sample-mean elasticities we used averages of the relevant variables calculated as follows. An average country value for variable X is calculated by first averaging X's values over time for each country, and then averaging across countries. This procedure gives equal weight to all countries.

REFERENCES

Antweiler, Werner; Copeland, Brian R. and Taylor, M. Scott. "Is Free Trade Good for the Environment?" National Bureau of Economic Research (Cambridge, MA) Working Paper 6707, August 1998.

Chay, Kenneth Y. and Greenstone, Michael B. "The Impact of Air Pollution on Infant Mortality: Evidence from Geographic Variation in Pollution Shocks Induced by a Recession." National Bureau of Economic Research (Cambridge, MA) Working Paper No. 7442, December 1999.

Copeland, Brian R. and Taylor, M. Scott. "North-South Trade and the Environment." *Quarterly Journal of Economics,* August 1994, *109*(3), pp. 755–87.

______. "Trade and Transboundary Pollution." *American Economic Review,* September 1995, *85*(4), pp. 716–37.

Dixit, Avinash K. and Norman, Victor. *Theory of international trade.* Cambridge: Cambridge University Press, 1980.

Ferrantino, Michael J. and Linkins, Linda A. "Global Trade Liberalization and Toxic Releases." U.S. International Trade Commission discussion paper, 1996.

Gale, Lewis and Mendez, Jose A. "The Empirical Relationship between Trade, Growth and the Environment." *International Review of Economics and Finance,* 1998, *7*(1), pp. 53–61.

Grossman, Gene M. and Krueger, Alan B. "Environmental Impacts of a North American Free Trade Agreement," in Peter M. Garber, ed., *The U.S.–Mexico free trade agreement.* Cambridge, MA: MIT Press, 1993, pp. 13–56.

______. "Economic Growth and the Environment." *Quarterly Journal of Economics,* May 1995, *110*(2), pp. 353–77.

Harrigan, James. "Factor Endowments and the International Location of Production: Econometric Evidence for the OECD, 1970–1985." *Journal of International Economics,* August 1995, *39*(1–2), pp. 123–41.

______. "Technology, Factor Supplies, and International Specialization: Estimating the Neoclassical Model." *American Economic Review,* September 1997, *87*(4), pp. 475–94.

Jaffe, Adam B.; Peterson, Steven R.; Portney, Paul R. and Stavins, Robert N. "Environmental Regulation and the Competitiveness of U.S. Manufacturing: What Does the Evidence Tell Us?" *Journal of Economic Literature,* March 1995, *33*(1), pp. 132–63.

Kraushaar, Jack J. and Ristinen, Robert A. *Energy and problems of a technical society.* New York: Wiley, 1998.

Levinson, Arik. "Environmental Regulations and Industry Location: International and Domestic Evidence," in J. N. Bhagwati and R. E. Hudec, eds., *Fair trade and harmonization: Prerequisites for free trade?* Cambridge, MA: MIT Press, 1996, pp. 429–57.

Low, Patrick and Yeats, Alexander. "Do 'Dirty' Industries Migrate," in Patrick Low, ed., *International trade and the environment.* World Bank Discussion Paper No. 159. Washington, DC: World Bank, 1992, pp. 89–104.

Lucas, Robert E. B.; Wheeler, David and Hettige, Hemamala. "Economic Development, Environmental regulation and the International Migration of Toxic Industrial Pollution: 1960–1988," in Patrick Low, ed., *International trade and the environment.* World Bank Discussion Paper No. 159. Washington, DC: World Bank, 1992, pp. 67–86.

Mani, Muthukumara and Wheeler, David. "In Search of Pollution Havens?: Dirty Industry Migration in the World Economy." World Bank Working Paper No. 16, April 1997.

McGuire, Martin C. "Regulation, Factor Rewards, and International Trade." *Journal of Public Economics,* April 1982, *17*(3), pp. 335–54.

Pethig, Rüdiger. "Pollution, Welfare, and Environmental Policy in the Theory of Comparative Advantage." *Journal of Environmental Economics and Management,* February 1976, 2(3), pp. 160–69.

Selden, Thomas M. and Song, Daqing. "Environmental Quality and Development: Is There a Kuznets Curve for Air Pollution Emissions?" *Journal of Environmental Economics and*

Management, September 1994, *27*(2), pp. 147–62.

Shafik, Nemat. "Economic Development and Environmental Quality: An Econometric Analysis." *Oxford Economic Papers,* October 1994, Supp. *46*, pp. 757–73.

Siebert, Horst; Eichberger, Jürgen.; Gronych, R. and Pethig, Rüdiger. *Trade and the environment: A theoretical enquiry.* Amsterdam: Elsevier/North-Holland, 1980.

Tobey, James A. "The Effects of Domestic Environmental Policies on Patterns of World Trade: An Empirical Test." *Kyklos,* 1990, *43*(2), pp. 191–209.

United Nations Environment Programme. *Urban air pollution.* Nairobi: UNEP, 1991.

Woodland, Alan D. *International trade and resource allocation.* Amsterdam: North-Holland, 1982.

World Health Organization. *Urban air pollution: 1973–1980.* Geneva: Published under the joint sponsorship of United Nations Environment Programme and the World Health Organization, 1984.

[2]

Trade and the Environment

Hiro Lee and David W. Roland-Holst

I Introduction

The environmental implications of international trade are becoming an important part of multilateral and domestic policy agendas. This is particularly the case for trade relations between developing and developed countries. To what extent developing countries should devote their resources to lowering domestic environmental costs for their own welfare and that of the world as a whole has frequently been debated. The debate stems from the widely held view that a tradeoff between economic growth and environmental quality exists. Many policymakers in developing countries argue that they have the right to pursue the same material aspirations by the same means as did the industrialized world during its developmental stages and are thus willing to spend smaller percentages of their productive resources for pollution abatement than developed countries.

If it is accepted that differing domestic practices yield different environmental effects, how might trade exert its own environmental influence? It is increasingly recognized that the import of goods and services entails an implicit transfer of environmental effects to the exporting country. Given the hierarchical nature of technology in the development process, one might infer that less developed countries would be net losers in the environmental transfer scheme which underlies trade. The data presented in this chapter indicate that trade between Indonesia and Japan has occasioned a large and sustained net transfer of effluents during the 1965–90 period. For example, the implied unit effluent content of Indonesian exports to Japan has been about six times that of its imports from Japan. This appears to suggest that more outward orientation would be harmful to the Indonesian environment.

We thank Sébastien Dessus, David O'Connor, David Turnham, and Dominique van der Mensbrugghe for helpful comments.

A number of empirical studies (e.g., Grossman and Krueger, 1992; Hettige et al., 1992; Lucas et al., 1992) have shown an inverse U-shaped relationship between gross domestic product (GDP) per capita and industrial pollution intensity. Birdsall and Wheeler (1992) suggest that the normal good characteristic of environmental quality, relatively high costs of monitoring and enforcing pollution standards, and increase in output shares of manufactures during industrialization are some of the major factors leading to relatively high pollution levels per unit of output in developing countries, while Hettige et al. (1992) and Lucas et al. (1992) indicate that the declining portion in the inverse U relationship is due solely to a shift from industry to services and not a shift toward a less toxic mix of manufacturing output.

Despite an intense pressure from environmentalists and some policy-makers to include environmental standards in recent trade agreements such as North American Free Trade Area (NAFTA) and the Uruguay Round of the General Agreement on Tariffs and Trade (GATT), economists have long argued that trade is not the root cause of environmental degradation. Low and Safadi (1992) suggest that freer trade may provide benefits to the environment through its effects on resource allocation and income levels. Lucas et al. (1992) find that among developing countries, the more closed economies experienced very rapid shifts toward toxic-intensive structures in the 1970s and 1980s. This is because import-substituting industrialization protected mainly capital- and pollution-intensive sectors. Thus, previous studies suggest that trade does not necessarily lead to degradation of national environment and that trade policy should not be used to remedy environmental problems.[1]

We use an applied general equilibrium model which incorporates detailed industrial pollution data to examine the environmental implication of trade and tax policies in Indonesia. Indonesia is well suited to our analysis because it has comparative advantage in pollution-intensive industries and its trade has conferred asymmetric environmental effects. An important empirical result of this chapter is that a combination of trade liberalization and a cost-effective tax policy could raise both the country's welfare and its environmental quality.

In Section II, we review the literature on pollution and appropriate policy instruments, environmental accounting, and recent applied models which link economic activities and the environment. Section III presents some statistics on the embodied pollution service trade between Indonesia and

1 See Beghin, Roland-Holst, and van der Mensbrugghe (1995), Cropper and Oates (1992), and Dean (1992) for a survey of literature on trade and the environment. O'Connor (1994) reviews recent Asian Pacific experience.

Japan during 1965–90. Section IV describes the two-country computable general equilibrium (CGE) model used in this study, followed by the appraisal of the environmental implications of Indonesia's trade liberalization in Section V and the evaluation of the welfare effect of pollution abatement by alternative instruments in Section VI. The chapter closes with general conclusions and remarks about how this work might fruitfully be extended.

II Linkages Between Economic Activities and the Environment

When economic activities generate negative externalities such as environmental degradation, two principal market-oriented instruments which correct external effects are regarded as first-best policies in the absence of other distortions in the economy. The first is corrective effluent taxes, equal to the difference between social and private costs of the activity, as established by Pigou (1920), and the second is a system of tradable emission permits (TEP) suggested by Dales (1968).[2] Trade policy instruments, such as tariffs and export taxes, are inferior to Pigouvian taxes or an assignment of property rights unless trade is the source of externalities. An example of inefficient trade instrument is a pollution abatement and control expenditure (PACE) equalization tax, a U.S. import tax on Mexican exports of "dirty" products designed to equalize expenditures by U.S. and Mexican industries on pollution abatement (Low, 1992).

In the real world, other distortions such as various taxes and imperfectly competitive markets exist. Thus, the first-best instruments may not lead to the most efficient outcome under a second-best setting. For example, Markusen (1975) suggests that although trade is not a source of the environmental problem, for a large country second-best trade taxes could produce an allocation superior to free trade. Krutilla (1991) shows that the optimal environmental tax is greater than the standard Pigouvian tax if the regulating country is large and a net exporter of goods with negative production externality. By contrast, Anderson (1992) suggests that even if a country has comparative advantage in the production of pollution-intensive goods, free trade would still raise welfare unambiguously, so long as an optimal pollution tax is introduced. Thus, theoretical ambiguity exists concerning the welfare impact of trade in the presence of environmental externalities.

2 The idea of tradable emission rights is derived from Coase (1960), who viewed externalities as arising from an absence of property rights. These market-based mechanisms have been employed to mitigate pollution in a number of instances. For example, tradable permits have been introduced in the United States for sulfur dioxide, lead additives, and water discharge rights, whereas in Europe emission charges have been used to limit air and water pollution.

Hahn and Stavins (1992) point out that incentive-based instruments such as effluent taxes and TEP are not well suited when there are political and technological constraints. For example, source-specific standards may be more appropriate for highly localized pollution problems with nonlinear damage functions. The polluter-pays principle was recommended by the Organization for Economic Cooperation and Development (OECD) in the early 1970s (OECD, 1975). It represents an allocation of property rights on the environment to consumers, making polluters (producers) pay the social damage. Since it incorporates the internalization of environmental externalities into the production cost, it is consistent with efficient pollution abatement.[3]

When environmental problems transcend national boundaries such as emissions of CO_2 and other greenhouse gases (GHGs), it is usually not possible to implement first-best policy instruments because there is no supra-national agency to enforce them (Anderson and Blackhurst, 1992). In addition, there is a great deal of uncertainty about the impact of global warming on potential damage resulting from a rise in atmospheric concentration of GHGs. Although some attempts have been made to estimate the magnitude of climate change impacts (e.g., Cline, 1992; Mendelsohn, 1995; Nordhaus, 1991), the estimates vary substantially across studies.[4] As a result, many of the previous studies have emphasized cost effectiveness and distributional implications of alternative policies.[5] While different models yield different cost estimates of any given carbon emission reductions relative to the baseline, qualitatively similar results are derived. First, because marginal abatement costs differ substantially across countries, a uniform carbon tax could reduce significantly the global costs of achieving a given emission curtailment target compared with country-specific carbon taxes. Second, because a common emission tax tends to shift the burden of reducing global emissions from developed to developing countries, the likelihood of securing an international cooperation depends upon the level of transfers from the former to the latter. Third, a TEP system will also lead to the equalization of abatement cost across countries. However, compared with TEP for local pollutants, implementation of a global scheme like a uniform carbon tax or TEP for CO_2 may be difficult since it requires substantial preparations

3 See Low and Safadi (1992) for a discussion of the polluter-pays principle.

4 Estimates of the impact of global warming on agricultural production also vary significantly depending upon assumptions and are associated with a great deal of uncertainty. See, e.g., IPCC (1990). Mendelsohn et al. (1994), R. and Tobey et al. (1992).

5 See, for example, Burniaux et al. (1992), Coppel and Lee (1996), Jorgenson et al. (1992), Manne and Richels (1992), OECD (1993, 1994), and Perroni and Rutherford (1993). An important exception is a study by Nordhaus (1992), who examines optimal emissions over time using a dynamic integrated climate–economy (DICE) model.

and negotiations between countries on distributional issues, monitoring, and enforcement. Furthermore, as an efficient outcome requires equalization of marginal benefit and marginal cost, these policy instruments designed to minimize global abatement costs are second best.

Estimation of damage associated with externalities is an important direction for future research as economic accounting of environmental costs and benefits would be essential for comprehensive integration of trade and environmental policies. While the new System of National Accounts (SNA) does not recommend modifying the basic flow aggregates in the national accounts to account for environmental damages and changes in the stock of natural resources, it lays out the structure of satellite accounts on the environment which complements the SNA (United Nations, 1993a,b). Satellite accounts combine physical information from environmental statistics and natural resource accounts with conventional national accounts. The UN System of Environmental and Economic Accounting (SEEA) advocates the inclusion of estimated physical and monetary flows associated with the depletion and degradation of natural resources.[6]

The Bureau of Economic Analysis (BEA) of the U.S. Department of Commerce has introduced the framework for integrated economic and environmental satellite accounts (IEESAs), which are fashioned after SEEA and aim to provide interactions between the economy and the environment (U.S. Department of Commerce, 1994). For example, degradation of air and water quality could lead to such economic feedback as lower timber yields and fish harvests, additional cleaning costs, and increased pollution abatement and health expenditures. In IEESAs natural resources and environmental resources are regarded as productive assets, and the depletion of mineral reserves is treated like the depreciation of fixed capital assets. For a measure of sustainable income, the BEA suggests the use of net domestic product, which is GDP less depreciation and depletion. However, many valuation and measurement issues have to be resolved before an IEESA production account can be completed.

Keuning (1992) suggests that the publication of "green GDP" is not advisable because it may create an erroneous impression that it is an appropriate measure for the level of sustainable income. He indicates that there are no proper valuation methods for resource depletion and environmental degradation. Instead, he proposes an environmental module linked to SNA, the National Accounting Matrix including Environmental Accounts (NAMEA). This module is based on the social accounting matrix (SAM),

6 See U.S. Department of Commerce (1994) for a detailed discussion of the UN System of Environmental and Economic Accounting.

and two new accounts are added to record emissions and extraction of environmental agents/resources and changes in environmental assets. Because those environmental flows and stocks with no market transactions are valued at a zero price in NAMEA, all accounts present complete balance in both value and volume terms. NAMEA can then be used as the database for a CGE model, where, for example, alternative assumptions on prices for depletion and degradation may be simulated.

An attempt to model interactions between the economy and the environment explicitly has been made by Bergman (1993). He includes an environmental quality measure in his CGE model of the Swedish economy. A household maximizes the utility function over final goods and environmental quality, which is negatively affected by the amount of CO_2 and SO_2 emissions. Since taxes on CO_2 and SO_2 emissions are assumed to reflect marginal damage costs, they are used as proxies for the marginal willingness to pay (MWTP) for emission reductions. It is assumed that SO_2 emissions lower the total factor productivity and that a system of tradable emission permits is implemented to attain different SO_2 abatement targets. The preliminary results indicate that the environmental quality adjusted NNP (denoted ENP) is maximized when SO_2 emissions are reduced by 20–30 percent while the aggregated MWTP and marginal cost for SO_2 abatement are equalized when the emissions are curtailed by 30–35 percent. Bergman attributes the different SO_2 abatement results for the two criteria to the terms of trade losses and suggests that the market clearing price of emission permits does not reflect the true social cost of emission curtailment.

A three-region world CGE model that incorporates local and global environmental externalities is constructed by Perroni and Wigle (1994). It is assumed that private marginal benefits are equal to a constant elasticity of transformation (CET) aggregation of unit local and global emission fees. Unit abatement costs are independent of production levels but rise as sectors reduce the ratios of emissions to output. Environmental quality is the difference between endowments of environmental quality and damage, which enters a CES utility function with per capita consumption. Through payments of emission fees, polluting parties internalize part or all of the external cost. It is shown that while international trade tends to cause some negative effect on environmental quality, changes in trade policies have little impact on the magnitude of the welfare effects of environmental policies. Although the main conclusion is robust to alternative values of many of the parameters, the internalization rate and the elasticity of marginal valuation with respect to damages are found to affect the size of benefits of internalization crucially.

The empirical results of Bergman (1993) and Perroni and Wigle (1994) suggest that while incorporating externalities into the models is possible, additional work is needed to improve the quality of pollution data and consensus values for key elasticity parameters. It is highly unlikely that the issue of social valuation of environmental quality will ever be resolved. Since results derived from the models that include environmental externalities critically depend upon the assumptions of the model structure and parameters, they must be interpreted with caution. Nevertheless, these models provide insights on the linkages between trade and the environment.

III Patterns of Effluent Transfer Between Indonesia and Japan

This section presents some historical evidence on how international trade influences the transfer of environmental effects. We introduce the concept of embodied effluent trade (EET) to capture the idea that traded commodities embody an environmental service: the amount of pollution emitted domestically when goods are produced for export. For example, if countries impose different costs on pollution, the ability to pollute might become a source of comparative advantage. In such a case, one would expect to see a pattern of relatively high EET in exports from countries with low environmental standards and relatively low EET in their imports, while the opposite would prevail in countries with higher environmental standards.

The evidence we have obtained for Indonesia and Japan shows a significant degree of EET imbalance between the two countries. The data indicate that Indonesia's net embodied effluents per unit exported to Japan are over six times the reverse flow and 29 percent higher than for its exports to the rest of the world. For Japan's part, imports from Indonesia have about twice the embodied effluent content per unit of its imports from elsewhere. This trend has remained relatively stable over the 1965–90 period, and the result is a sustained and significant transfer of environmental costs between the two countries.

Before reviewing the detailed results, a few definitions are required to clarify interpretation. To measure the effluent levels embodied in tradable commodities, we began with estimates of unit effluents in domestic production. To measure average effluent levels embodied in tradable commodities, the acute human toxic linear (AHTL) index developed by Wheeler (1992) is used. AHTL is a weighted average of various effluents with weights representing their human health risk. The index of sectoral effluent output is defined as

$$e_i = \frac{\varepsilon_i}{\sum_i \varepsilon_i q_i} \quad (16.1)$$

where ε_i denotes the sectoral AHTL emission rate per unit of output in U.S. manufacturing and q_i denotes sector i's share in total domestic output.[7] If these indices are multiplied by 1985 U.S. sectoral output shares, they sum to unity. For any other country, such a sum measures the effluent potential of domestic output in units relative to the United States. Thus in 1985, for example, Japanese output shares give a value of $E=\Sigma e_i=0.86$, indicating that, under the same technologies, the effluent intensity of Japanese domestic production would be 14 percent below that of the United States by this index. The comparable figure for Indonesia is 2.45.[8] Thus E serves as an index of aggregate effluent levels for a given composition of domestic production. If the structure of the economy shifts toward relatively cleaner activities, such as services, E will decrease. E is unaffected by the absolute level of output, but simply allows comparison across countries of one representative unit of domestic product.

This measure can also be used to evaluate the implicit effluent content of trade. The indices

$$E_x^f = \sum_i e_i x_i^f \quad (16.2)$$

and

$$E_m^f = \sum_i e_i m_i^f \quad (16.3)$$

measure the embodied effluent content of exports and imports, respectively. x_i^f and m_i^f are the sectoral shares of exports to destination f (f=bilateral partner, rest of the world [ROW]) and the sectoral shares of imports from origin f. If E_x^f exceeds unity, for example, the composition of the country's existing exports represents (in their production) a higher level of pollution per unit than representative output in the United States. Values less than unity mean that the country's overall exports are "cleaner" than overall U.S. domestic output.

7 Such detailed emission rates are at the moment only available for U.S. manufacturing sectors, obliging us to apply them to both Japan and Indonesia.

8 In the light of differing environmental standards in the two countries, the disparity is likely to be greater than the indexes would indicate. Japan's effluent controls are more stringent than those of the United States, and thus the compositional index for the former is likely to overstate Japanese effluent levels. Likewise, Indonesia's environmental controls are weaker than those of the reference country, so its actual effluent levels are probably underestimated by E.

Table 16.1. *Trends in embodied effluent content of exports and imports*

	1965	*1970*	*1975*	*1980*	*1985*	*1990*	*Avg*
Indonesia							
Exports to							
Japan	11.32	11.45	15.34	13.43	11.77	10.41	12.29
Rest of World	7.28	6.49	14.14	12.20	10.59	7.23	9.66
Imports from							
Japan	2.10	2.17	2.03	1.80	1.99	1.67	1.96
Rest of World	2.29	2.73	2.79	4.44	4.16	3.34	3.29
Effluent Trade Ratio (Ex/Em)							
Japan	5.38	5.29	7.57	7.47	5.93	6.24	6.31
Rest of World	3.18	2.38	5.06	2.75	2.54	2.17	3.01
Japan							
Exports to							
Indonesia	2.10	2.17	2.03	1.80	1.99	1.67	1.96
Rest of World	1.75	1.62	1.69	1.60	1.52	1.54	1.62
Imports from							
Indonesia	11.32	11.45	15.34	13.43	11.77	10.41	12.29
Rest of World	4.09	3.87	7.63	8.86	7.39	4.78	6.10
Effluent Trade Ratio (Ex/Em)							
Indonesia	0.19	0.19	0.13	0.13	0.17	0.16	0.16
Rest of World	0.43	0.42	0.22	0.18	0.21	0.32	0.30

These indices measure embodied effluent content of exports and imports relative to the emission intensity of overall U.S. domestic output. Values greater than unity imply that the country's overall exports by destination or imports by origin are more pollution-intensive than the U.S. output.

Sources: Wheeler (1992), United Nations' COMTRADE database, and authors' calculations.

The indices E_x and E_m thus measure the embodied effluent trade (EET) for a given composition of exports and imports per unit of trade. E_x and E_m for Indonesia–Japan bilateral trade and their trade with the rest of the world are presented in Table 16.1. These estimates were constructed for the 1965–90 period at five-year intervals, with detailed trade data from the United Nations' COMTRADE tables. The ratios of E_x to E_m are also given in the table.[9]

It is quite apparent from these results that the effluent composition of trade varies from that of domestic output for both countries, but that this

9 The pollution content of U.S. exports and imports has been estimated by Walter (1973). He estimated environmental-control loadings entering U.S. trade flows and found that the pollution content of U.S. exports exceeded that of imports in thirty-one of seventy-eight sectors in 1971.

disparity is much greater for Indonesia. Indonesia's export industries appear to be generating three to four times as much effluent as overall domestic output, while Japanese exports are about twice the effluent intensity of domestic product as a whole. One reason for this is the omission of agriculture and services in the effluent database. Although this omission would be unlikely to bias the trade comparisons between the two countries (the two sectors are insignificant in bilateral trade), they do understate the pollution content of production for the domestic market.

The most arresting feature of Table 16.1, however, is the imbalance in direct EET between the two trading partners. This can be seen more clearly in two extreme graphs of Figure 16.1. Over the last two and a half decades, Indonesia's production for export to Japan has been about six times more effluent-intensive than Japanese exports to Indonesia. In a long-term situation of relatively balanced bilateral trade, this implies a sustained and significant transfer of environmental costs from Japan to Indonesia. Although the trend in recent years has reduced this disparity, it is still quite significant.

These results are even more striking when compared to each country's trade with the rest of the world. Indonesia's imports from Japan are about half as effluent-intensive as what Indonesia buys from other countries and its exports to Japan are about 30 percent as effluent-intensive as other countries' exports to Japan. Trade between countries at different stages of modernization has long exhibited hierarchical properties which are correlated with technology levels and environmental effects.

Identification of this problem is only the first step, however, since it has implications for sustainable living standards in both countries. It is often argued that environmental damage at the early stages of industrialization is a transitory phenomenon, and cleaner technologies and resource conservation are inevitably concurrent with rising living standards. The evidence presented here may support a shifting correlation between the level of development and better environmental conditions, but it does nothing to establish a causality in either direction.

Possible explanations of these trends fall into three general categories: institutions, technology, and economic structure. In each of these general respects, the two countries have important differences which might contribute to an explanation of the effluent asymmetry in their trade patterns. The first category, institutions, includes all those influences of private and public rules and behavior, including differences in economic and environmental regulation and enforcement and behavior patterns which exploit them. Examples of this might be protection or taxation patterns which promote domestic or foreign pollution, differing levels of domestic environmental

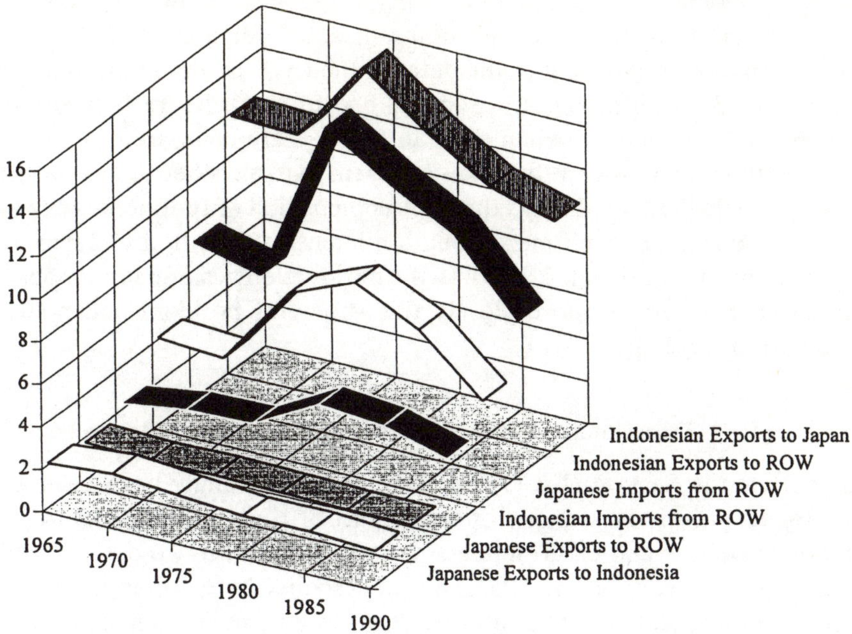

Figure 16.1. *Trends in embodied effluent trade*

stringency, and private or public sector behavior which might facilitate the creation of pollution havens. On the basis of the specific evidence for Indonesia and Japan, as well as the general verdict of economic literature on this subject, we reject institutional factors as decisive in explaining these historical trends. Despite all the public attention and controversy surrounding the pollution haven issue, there is very little evidence to indicate that trade patterns between these two countries can be substantively explained by this phenomenon.[10]

Significant technological disparities between the two countries certainly exist in a variety of industrial activities, and these could reinforce the observed inequality of pollution levels. However, Indonesian–Japanese technology differences have no bearing on the present results, since they were obtained by applying the same (U.S.) effluent coefficients to both countries. Although country-specific data are likely to yield even larger asymmetries, the present results call for and are quite sufficient to justify closer inspection.

10 For a general appraisal of this issue, see Cropper and Oates (1992).

Can economic structure alone explain Indonesia's higher pollution intensities in production, for both domestic and foreign consumption? As will be apparent in a review of the data for the CGE model later, there are indeed significant differences in sectoral and trade structure between the two countries. Moreover, when these differences are compared to sectoral data on effluent intensity, it becomes apparent that, all other things (institutions, technologies, etc.) being equal, the composition of Indonesia's current economic activity is much more pollution-intensive than that of Japan (its export composition even more so). In the next section, a simulation model is developed to examine more closely this structural problem and policies which can mitigate it.

IV A Two-Country CGE Model for Indonesia and Japan

As indicated in Section II, CGE models have increasingly been used as a tool for empirical assessments of the impact of trade and tax policies on economic welfare and environmental quality. While the two-country computable general equilibrium (CGE) model described here is in most respects typical of comparative static, multi-sectoral, economywide models in use today, we incorporate detailed sectoral emission data in the model.[11] Model equations are summarized in Appendix 16.1. An important feature of this model is its endogenous specification of domestic supply, demand, and bilateral trade for the two countries at the sectoral level. This is particularly important for Indonesia as its bilateral trade with Japan as a percentage of the total trade was 47 percent for exports and 21 percent for imports in 1985. While trade between the two countries is modeled endogenously, we assume that their individual trade flows with the rest of the world (ROW) are each governed by the small country assumption.[12] The resulting six sets of sectoral trade flows are then directed by two endogenous price systems (Indonesia–Japan imports and exports) and four exogenous price systems (Indonesia–ROW and Japan–ROW imports and exports).

As has been employed in many other CGE models, a differentiated product specification is used for the demand and supply for tradable commodities. Domestic demand is a CES composite of goods differentiated by origin (domestic goods, imports from the bilateral trading partner, and imports from ROW), while domestic production is a CET composite of goods differ-

11 See Chapter 6 of this volume by Devarajan, Go, Lewis, Robinson, and Sinko on simple general equilibrium models.

12 Lee and Roland-Holst (1993) treat Japan as a large country so as to affect prices in the ROW market. For the moderate trade flow adjustments for Japan described in this study, however, the small country assumption makes almost no change in the results of simulation experiments.

entiated by destination (domestic market, exports to bilateral partner, and exports to ROW).[13]

Every sector is characterized by constant returns to scale and perfect competition, and sectoral prices adjust until they are equal to average costs of composite supply.[14] Sectoral emission levels by pollutant and destination of supply are computed as

$$EMI_{ih}^{k} = \varepsilon_{ih} P_{Si}^{k} S_{i}^{k} \quad (16.4)$$

where ε_{ih} are sectoral effluent intensities of pollutant h, and P_{Si}^{k} and S_i^k are domestic producer price and production for supply to destination k. Ad valorem domestic production taxes, t_{Si}, are the sum of ad valorem indirect taxes, t_{Di}, and ad valorem effluent taxes

$$t_{Si} = t_{Di} + \sum_{h} \tau_{ih} \varepsilon_{ih} \quad (16.4)$$

where τ_{ih} are excise taxes on emissions (\$/ton of pollutant h).

We assume both countries have a fixed aggregate stock of domestic productive capital which is mobile between sectors, while the economywide average rental rate adjusts to equate aggregate capital demand to the fixed total supply. We also assume that labor in both countries is mobile between sectors, but the total labor supply is specified as a function of the wage rate and household income. In the product markets, prices are normalized by a fixed numéraire chosen to be the GDP price deflator. Finally, we assume that the real exchange rate is flexible while the current account balances for the two countries are fixed at the baseline values.[15]

The Indonesia–Japan CGE model is calibrated to a 1985 SAM constructed by the authors.[16] The principal data source used to estimate the SAM was a 128-sector input–output table constructed by the Institute of Developing Economies (1991). Structural parameters of the model are obtained by calibration, direct estimation, or imputation from other sources. Calibrated values are obtainable for most share parameters, input–output coefficients, nominal ad valorem taxes, and tariff rates from the SAM itself. Sectoral employment and capital stock data are obtained from official publications of both countries. Elasticity parameters have been obtained from a variety of published and unpublished sources.

13 See equations (A16.9) and (A16.11) in Appendix 16.1.

14 While varying returns to scale does affect the magnitude of impact of trade and tax policies, the key results of this chapter are robust and not affected by different specifications on market conduct (e.g., oligopolistic behavior) and returns to scale.

15 Since there are no assets in the model, the real exchange rate is the relative price of tradables to nontradables.

16 See Chapter 4 of this volume by Reinert and Roland-Holst on social accounting matrices.

Table 16.2. *Economic structure of Indonesia and Japan, 1985 (all figures in percentages)*

	Indonesia	(1) *S shr*	(2) *D shr*	(3) *X shr*	(4) *M shr*	(5) *X/S*	(6) *M/D*	(7) *Xb/X*	(8) *Xr/X*	(9) *Mb/M*	(10) *Mr/M*	(11) *tm*
1	Agriculture	22.8	22.8	9.5	5.3	5.7	2.4	15.3	84.7	0.3	99.7	9.8
2	Petroleum	15.8	8.3	64.2	8.7	55.1	11.1	62.6	37.4	0.3	99.7	5.2
3	Mining	0.8	0.8	1.0	1.4	17.4	18.2	90.1	9.9	9.1	90.9	4.8
4	FoodProc	5.1	5.3	1.2	1.1	3.2	2.1	7.0	93.0	9.5	90.5	20.2
5	Textile	1.9	1.7	2.5	1.0	17.6	5.8	2.0	98.0	40.3	59.7	35.3
6	LumWood	1.4	0.8	4.4	0.0	43.8	0.2	15.2	84.8	15.9	84.1	8.6
7	PulpPaper	0.3	0.4	0.1	1.7	4.7	41.0	3.8	96.2	9.1	90.9	32.0
8	IndChem	0.1	0.7	0.2	6.4	47.0	94.5	10.0	90.0	25.7	74.3	12.8
9	OtherChem	1.5	2.2	0.8	7.4	7.6	35.5	3.1	96.9	19.7	80.3	12.3
10	Plastic	0.4	0.4	0.1	0.3	2.8	7.5	0.6	99.4	47.8	52.2	27.5
11	NonMtMnr	0.9	1.0	0.1	1.4	1.5	13.8	2.8	97.2	62.9	37.1	28.7
12	Steel	0.5	0.9	0.1	3.8	4.1	46.5	45.2	54.8	63.3	36.7	9.0
13	NonferMtl	0.5	0.3	2.6	1.6	70.4	51.4	60.4	39.6	13.3	86.7	10.1
14	MetalProd	0.6	1.2	0.0	5.0	0.4	44.1	1.0	99.0	39.6	60.4	24.0
15	MachPrcls	0.6	2.7	0.2	19.3	3.2	76.2	1.1	98.9	29.9	70.1	26.6
16	ElecMach	0.4	0.8	0.4	3.6	11.4	48.5	0.1	99.9	31.3	68.7	30.8
17	TranspEq	1.1	2.4	0.2	11.8	2.9	52.8	0.1	99.9	22.8	77.2	25.9
18	OtherMfg	0.9	1.0	0.2	0.7	2.6	7.9	34.4	65.6	39.1	60.9	34.0
19	Services	44.3	46.2	12.1	19.6	3.7	4.5	16.2	83.8	7.4	92.6	5.0
Total/Wgt Avg		100.0	100.0	100.0	100.0	13.6	10.6	47.1	52.9	20.8	79.2	16.2
	Japan											
1	Agriculture	4.4	5.3	0.3	13.9	0.5	15.6	0.3	99.7	5.5	94.5	4.8
2	Petroleum	1.9	4.0	0.7	34.9	2.6	52.5	0.2	99.8	20.6	79.4	4.7
3	Mining	0.6	1.0	0.1	7.1	1.5	41.1	5.9	94.1	2.4	97.6	0.0
4	FoodProc	3.8	4.0	0.5	2.3	0.9	3.5	1.0	99.0	2.5	97.5	16.2
5	Textile	2.0	2.1	2.3	2.9	8.2	8.4	0.9	99.1	1.5	98.5	6.8
6	LumWood	0.6	0.6	0.0	1.1	0.6	10.5	0.3	99.7	9.4	90.6	1.5
7	PulpPaper	1.3	1.3	0.5	0.9	2.7	4.3	1.6	98.4	0.1	99.9	2.7
8	IndChem	1.2	1.3	1.5	2.1	8.6	9.9	6.5	93.5	0.3	99.7	3.3
9	OtherChem	2.2	2.2	3.1	2.5	10.0	6.9	2.7	97.3	0.6	99.4	3.4
10	Plastic	1.2	1.2	0.6	0.4	3.4	1.9	1.5	98.5	0.2	99.8	2.9
11	NonMtMnr	1.3	1.3	1.2	0.5	6.5	2.4	4.7	95.3	0.1	99.9	2.7
12	Steel	4.1	3.8	6.5	1.2	11.2	1.8	2.3	97.7	0.9	99.1	1.9
13	NonferMtl	0.8	1.0	0.7	5.0	7.0	29.2	1.5	98.5	5.0	95.0	2.3
14	MetalProd	2.0	1.9	2.2	0.4	8.0	1.3	5.6	94.4	0.1	99.9	3.5
15	MachPrcls	6.6	5.5	19.4	4.5	21.3	4.9	1.7	98.3	0.1	99.9	2.8
16	ElecMach	4.1	3.1	15.2	1.5	26.9	2.9	0.4	99.6	0.0	100.0	2.9
17	TranspEq	5.1	3.5	24.3	2.1	34.3	3.5	0.7	99.3	0.0	100.0	4.2
18	OtherMfg	2.9	2.9	2.9	2.2	7.1	4.6	0.6	99.4	2.4	97.6	4.6
19	Services	53.8	54.1	18.1	14.4	2.4	1.6	0.5	99.5	4.6	95.4	0.0
Total/Wgt Avg		100.0	100.0	100.0	100.0	7.2	6.0	1.2	98.8	9.3	90.7	3.7

(1) Gross output shares, (2) composite demand shares, (3) export shares, (4) import shares, (5) ratios of exports to gross output, (6) ratios of imports to total demand, (7) ratios of bilateral exports to total exports, (8) ratios of ROW exports to total exports, (9) ratios of bilateral imports to total imports, (10) ratios of ROW imports to total imports, and (12) nominal tariff rates.

The data in Table 16.2 reveal significant structural differences between the two economies. These differences are characteristic of their respective stages of development and arise from three distinct but interdependent sources: endowments, demand, and degree of industrialization. A highly aggregated service sector accounts for a large proportion of total output, but Japan's share is about 10 percentage points higher than Indonesia's. Among the remaining eighteen sectors, the composition of output is considerably more diversified for Japan, which has higher levels of technology and income and is thus less endowment-driven than Indonesia.

The role of demand can be seen in column 2, where lower Indonesian incomes lead to narrower emphasis on subsistence and tertiary goods and services. External demand (column 3) also plays a significant role for Indonesia, and this reinforces the endowment-driven focus on primary products (especially petroleum). Japan's demand for imports is negatively endowment-driven, and thus the two countries settle into a finely delineated relationship of comparative advantage (columns 7 and 9), with Japan supplying a significant portion of Indonesia's advanced manufactures in exchange for Indonesian primary products.

The weighted averages at the bottom of each subtable give general indications about the orientation of each economy. For example, Indonesia's exports (column 3) are 13.6 percent of its gross output, making it almost twice as export-dependent as Japan.[17] Indonesia is also more import-dependent (column 4) than Japan, although the difference here is smaller. The bilateral relationship is also much more important to Indonesia than to Japan, accounting for 47.1 percent of its exports and 20.8 percent of its imports on average, while the corresponding Japanese figures are 1.2 and 9.3 percent, respectively. Finally, Indonesia has higher levels of average nominal tariff protection than Japan (16.2 versus 3.7 percent). This, coupled with the greater trade dependence, indicates that Indonesia has greater potential for efficiency gains and structural change from trade liberalization.

Each sector in the model has effluent coefficients, linear in output, for a variety of pollutants. We have used the database for the Industrial Pollution Projection System of the World Bank to calibrate sectoral effluent coefficients.[18] This database provides emission rates, as a proportion of base-year output value, for seven air pollutants, two water pollutants, and two toxic pollutants at a four-digit SIC level of sectoral detail. The data are then mapped to four-digit output share data for Indonesia and Japan to obtain

17 Total exports as percentages of GDP are 23.0 for Indonesia and 14.9 for Japan.
18 See Martin et al. (1991) and Wheeler (1992).

Table 16.3. *Sectoral effluent intensities (pound/year/$1,000 unless indicated otherwise)*

	Indonesia	*PARTIC*	*SO2*	*NO2*	*LEAD*	*VOC*	*CO*	*BOD*	*SS*	*TOX*	*METAL*
1	Agriculture	n.a.	n.a.	n.a.	n.a.	n.a.	n.a.	n.a.	n.a.	n.a.	n.a.
2	Petroleum	11.90	35.89	7.65	14.41	3.54	1.43	1.06	1.27	2.54	.13
3	Mining	9.29	44.35	3.65	.88	4.53	43.57	18.01	259.35	8.92	6.15
4	FoodProc	1.55	1.40	4.05	.04	.82	1.12	16.64	4.30	.65	.01
5	Textile	1.11	6.23	10.83	.00	2.65	2.05	.04	.07	3.28	.15
6	LumWood	9.26	3.14	6.83	.00	9.25	11.76	.00	.00	4.52	.04
7	PulpPaper	3.06	29.49	11.93	1.51	6.29	17.02	21.82	87.99	6.84	.03
8	IndChem	1.39	9.01	8.71	.07	9.16	12.34	20.75	46.49	29.91	.18
9	OtherChem	1.19	12.12	5.94	.21	5.68	7.28	5.61	1.60	3.74	.04
10	Plastic	.35	3.00	.89	.00	9.97	.26	.00	.01	7.48	.20
11	NonMtMnr	15.72	15.22	16.81	.63	1.18	3.05	.00	.00	3.39	.83
12	Steel	4.12	9.74	4.40	13.47	2.31	33.66	.04	27.35	7.64	4.10
13	NonferMtl	9.12	44.90	3.39	.00	4.59	46.30	19.11	276.09	9.33	6.54
14	MetalProd	.56	.37	1.80	.49	9.33	.21	1.21	25.82	4.59	.66
15	MachPrcls	1.49	.81	.61	.43	1.82	.22	.00	.00	1.56	.25
16	ElecMach	.12	.38	.22	.33	4.50	.26	.00	.04	1.80	.31
17	TranspEq	.84	.20	.13	.00	1.87	.05	.00	.02	1.11	.05
18	OtherMfg	1.02	.48	.15	.00	9.08	.07	.00	.00	2.71	.60
19	Services	n.a.	n.a.	n.a.	n.a.	n.a.	n.a.	n.a.	n.a.	n.a.	n.a.
	Japan										
1	Agriculture	n.a.	n.a.	n.a.	n.a.	n.a.	n.a.	n.a.	n.a.	n.a.	n.a.
2	Petroleum	11.90	35.89	7.65	14.41	3.54	1.43	1.06	1.27	2.54	.13
3	Mining	25.47	121.56	9.99	2.40	12.41	119.43	49.37	710.91	24.45	16.86
4	FoodProc	2.06	1.86	5.39	.05	1.09	1.48	22.12	5.72	.86	.01
5	Textile	1.05	5.89	10.23	.00	2.50	1.94	.04	.07	3.10	.14
6	LumWood	15.48	5.24	11.41	.00	15.46	19.65	.00	.00	7.56	.06
7	PulpPaper	.66	6.37	2.58	.33	1.36	3.68	4.71	19.00	1.48	.01
8	IndChem	.68	4.43	4.29	.04	4.51	6.07	10.21	22.88	14.72	.09
9	OtherChem	1.85	18.82	9.22	.33	8.83	11.30	8.71	2.48	5.81	.05
10	Plastic	.12	1.06	.31	.00	3.52	.09	.00	.00	2.64	.07
11	NonMtMnr	10.90	10.55	11.65	.44	.82	2.11	.00	.00	2.35	.57
12	Steel	4.12	9.74	4.40	13.47	2.31	33.66	.04	27.35	7.64	4.10
13	NonferMtl	9.12	44.90	3.39	.00	4.59	46.30	19.11	276.09	9.33	6.54
14	MetalProd	.56	.37	1.80	.49	9.33	.21	1.21	25.82	4.59	.66
15	MachPrcls	.20	.11	.08	.06	.24	.03	.00	.00	.21	.03
16	ElecMach	.02	.05	.03	.04	.57	.03	.00	.00	.23	.04
17	TranspEq	.20	.05	.03	.00	.45	.01	.00	.00	.27	.01
18	OtherMfg	1.02	.48	.15	.00	9.08	.07	.00	.00	2.71	.60
19	Services	n.a.	n.a.	n.a.	n.a.	n.a.	n.a.	n.a.	n.a.	n.a.	n.a.

Sources: Martin et al. (1991), Wheeler (1992), and authors' calculations.

Definition of pollutants:

Air pollutants: particulates (PARTIC), sulphur dioxide (SO2), nitrogen dioxide (NO2), lead (pound/year/$billion), volatile organic compounds (VOC), carbon monoxide (CO).

Water pollutants: biochemical oxygen demand (BOD), suspended solids (SS).

Toxic pollutants / all media: total toxic release (TOX), bioaccumulative metals (METAL).

weighted emission coefficients for the nineteen sectors of the model. The results of this conversion are presented in Table 16.3.[19]

Eight of the nineteen sectors could be roughly classified as pollution-intensive, namely, petroleum, mining, lumber and wood, pulp and paper, industrial chemicals, nonmetallic minerals (consisting of cement and stone products), steel, and nonferrous metals.[20] For example, petroleum has high effluent intensities for particulates, SO_2, NO_2, and lead, while mining and nonferrous metals have high pollution coefficients on particulates, SO_2, carbon monoxide, the two water pollutants, and the two toxic pollutants. Indonesia's heavy export dependence on petroleum is the most significant factor explaining the high effluent content of its exports, but relatively high export shares of lumber and wood and nonferrous metals also contributed to high EET in exports. By contrast, except for steel, Japan's exports are concentrated in sectors with low pollution intensities, resulting in low effluents embodied in its exports.

The matrix of effluent intensities by sector and type of pollutant, $\{\varepsilon_{ih}\}$, forms the basis for calculating environmental effects resulting from policy changes, such as tariff liberalization and effluent taxes. A limitation of this approach at the moment is that there is no scope for technical substitution within sectors, and thus emissions are proportional to output regardless of relative prices and differential effluent taxes. The main advantage of this approach over previous modeling with these coefficients is the general equilibrium nature of the simulations, which allow for changing composition of domestic output, a large medium-term source of pollution mitigation.[21]

V Trade and Domestic Pollution in Indonesia

The evidence discussed in Section III suggests that Indonesia may be realizing its export potential at a disadvantage in terms of the environmental costs it absorbs vis-à-vis trading partners. The two-country CGE model is used to assess the linkage between trade and the environment by removing Indonesia's nominal tariffs on all imports. Table 16.4 summarizes the aggregate results. The tariff removal leads to an increase in Indonesia's real GDP by 0.87 percent and economywide employment by 1.87 percent. Equivalent variation (EV) income, which measures the change in real consumer purchasing power, rises by less than the increase in real GDP because of a fall

19 We aggregated emission coefficients for suspended particulates and fine particulates.

20 Of the remaining eleven sectors, other chemicals and plastics are relatively more pollution intensive than the other sectors.

21 Compare to, e.g., Anderson (1992) and Ten Kate (1993).

Table 16.4. *Aggregate results of Indonesia's tariff liberalization (percentage changes)*

	Indonesia	*Japan*
Real GDP	0.87	0.00
EV Income	0.53	0.03
Wage Rate	1.10	0.05
Employment	1.87	0.00
Rental Rate on Capital	3.31	0.04
Real Exchange Rate	5.26	-0.07
Total Imports	5.81	0.14
Total Exports	5.72	-0.07

in the bilateral terms of trade with Japan.[22] The wage rate and the rental rate on capital both increase, but the latter increases more because an increase in labor supply in response to higher wages raises the marginal productivity of capital. Indonesia's tariff removal induces real depreciation of rupiah and the subsequent increase in its exports. It has a negligible effect on the Japanese economy, with all aggregate measures changing by a small fraction of 1 percent.

As is usual with trade policy, relatively small aggregate adjustments can mask dramatic shifts in the composition of sectoral trade and output. Table 16.5 gives a more detailed picture of the consequences of Indonesian tariff removal. Although the data on Indonesian tariffs (Table 16.2) do not differentiate between Japan and the rest of the world, the import adjustments vary significantly for two reasons. First, the initial trade flows from the two sources are quite different (Table 16.2, columns 9 and 10), leading to different proportional adjustments to domestic demand changes. Second, because Indonesia is assumed to be a small country with respect to ROW, it imports from this source at fixed prices, while terms of trade with respect to Japan are endogenous. Thus, Japanese exporters benefit less in relative terms from Indonesian liberalization than do Indonesia's other trading partners taken as a group. A similar effect can be detected in the composition of Indonesian exports, but the exchange rate depreciation is large enough to offset most terms of trade effects.

22 The terms of trade with the rest of the world are unaffected because of the small country assumption.

Table 16.5. *Sectoral results for Indonesia's tariff liberalization (percentage changes)*

	Indonesia	Output	Total exports	Exp to Japan	Total Imports	Imp from Japan	Labor demand	Capital demand
1	Agriculture	-0.04	5.99	2.91	10.11	5.43	2.01	-0.60
2	Petroleum	4.11	5.64	4.80	1.65	0.45	6.72	3.98
3	Mining	1.56	3.68	3.53	1.96	0.52	2.93	0.29
4	FoodProc	-0.26	2.42	1.49	15.29	6.27	1.79	-0.82
5	Textile	0.06	3.35	2.47	28.50	9.37	1.70	-0.91
6	LumWood	4.33	9.31	6.15	3.24	1.19	6.31	3.58
7	PulpPaper	-18.25	-11.56	-8.38	13.39	3.89	-16.69	-18.82
8	IndChem	33.53	41.12	28.21	0.10	0.05	34.62	31.17
9	OtherChem	-2.44	1.00	0.73	5.81	1.89	-0.27	-2.83
10	Plastic	-1.20	2.41	1.75	20.94	7.84	0.88	-1.71
11	NonMtMnr	-3.11	-1.11	-0.90	19.49	6.66	-1.32	-3.85
12	Steel	-5.69	-3.38	-3.02	1.56	0.50	-3.35	-5.83
13	NonferMtl	9.01	11.16	10.18	-5.58	-1.36	10.92	8.08
14	MetalProd	-9.89	-6.83	-5.15	11.59	3.80	-8.28	-10.64
15	MachPrcls	4.67	18.64	12.85	6.39	2.23	6.65	3.91
16	ElecMach	-6.54	0.68	0.51	11.33	4.21	-4.78	-7.22
17	TranspEq	-7.27	3.94	2.52	10.53	4.24	-5.71	-8.13
18	OtherMfg	-1.56	1.67	1.36	29.91	9.59	-0.03	-2.60
19	Services	0.28	4.39	2.27	0.58	0.28	1.69	-0.92

	Japan	Output	Total exports	Exp to Indonesia	Total Imports	Imp from Indonesia	Labor demand	Capital demand
1	Agriculture	-0.02	-0.16	5.43	0.14	2.91	-0.03	-0.02
2	Petroleum	-0.22	-0.02	0.45	0.14	4.80	-0.22	-0.21
3	Mining	-0.07	-0.05	0.52	0.03	3.53	-0.08	-0.06
4	FoodProc	0.02	0.03	6.27	0.11	1.49	0.02	0.03
5	Textile	0.02	0.07	9.37	0.12	2.47	0.02	0.03
6	LumWood	-0.07	-0.16	1.19	0.58	6.15	-0.07	-0.05
7	PulpPaper	0.00	0.01	3.89	0.11	-8.38	-0.01	0.01
8	IndChem	0.00	0.02	0.05	0.00	28.21	0.00	0.01
9	OtherChem	0.00	0.02	1.89	0.08	0.73	0.00	0.01
10	Plastic	-0.01	0.07	7.84	0.10	1.75	-0.01	0.00
11	NonMtMnr	0.03	0.33	6.66	0.01	-0.90	0.03	0.04
12	Steel	-0.03	-0.05	0.50	0.14	-3.02	-0.03	-0.02
13	NonferMtl	-0.23	-0.27	-1.36	0.29	10.18	-0.24	-0.22
14	MetalProd	0.03	0.20	3.80	0.10	-5.15	0.02	0.03
15	MachPrcls	0.00	-0.02	2.23	0.15	12.85	-0.01	0.00
16	ElecMach	-0.02	-0.06	4.21	0.16	0.51	-0.03	-0.01
17	TranspEq	-0.12	-0.20	4.24	0.18	2.52	-0.12	-0.11
18	OtherMfg	0.00	0.01	9.59	0.13	1.36	0.00	0.01
19	Services	0.01	-0.08	0.28	0.13	2.27	0.01	0.02

Domestic structural adjustments in Indonesia are driven by a combination of import penetration and export expansion. These two effects generally promote expansion of primary and basic industries such as petroleum and mining, lumber, chemicals and nonferrous metals, with contractions in many of the manufacturing sectors (Table 16.5, column 1). Those sectors with the largest percentage output adjustments (e.g., pulp and paper, industrial chemicals) are quite small in the economy (Table 16.2, column 1), but petroleum accounts for 16 percent of real domestic output and its expansion may have serious implications for the environment in Indonesia. Given the assumption of an upward-sloping labor supply schedule, the adjustment to trade liberalization entails a substitution of labor for capital across most sectors. Results for Japan are again very small, except for the bilateral trade adjustments. There is some shift of resources toward Japanese export sectors and a slight diversion of import demand in response to the rupiah depreciation.

These results indicate that Indonesian tariff removal can induce significant changes in the composition of domestic production, which can in turn be expected to influence the level and composition of domestic effluent emissions. While removing tariff protection leads to expanded trade and greater economywide efficiency, in the absence of new technologies it entails an increase in the total emission levels. Table 16.6 reports the effects on emission levels of each pollutant embodied in domestic output supplied to different destinations (domestic market, bilateral partner, and ROW). Emissions from the production of goods supplied domestically increase for three pollutants (particulates, SO_2, and lead) while those decrease for the other pollutants. Trade expansion would, however, increase emissions quite substantially from the production of goods that are exported to both Japan and the rest of the world for all pollution categories included in the study. The net effect is an increase in the emission level of all the pollutants generated from total output. The right panel of Table 16.6 reports the effects on emissions from output produced in Japan resulting from Indonesia's tariff removal, which are significantly smaller than those in Indonesia in percentage terms.

The result that trade liberalization leads to higher pollution levels is not surprising because it leads to an increase in real output. A more interesting result is that it leads to an increase in the relative output shares of dirty industries, causing higher average pollution intensities for almost all major pollution categories. The only exception is biochemical oxygen demand (water pollution), whose emission level rises by a smaller percentage (0.51 percent) than the increase in real output. For all other pollutants, the per-

Table 16.6. *Emission levels by destination of supply (percentage changes)*

	Indonesia				Japan			
	Domestic	*Japan*	*ROW*	*Total*	*Domestic*	*Indonesia*	*ROW*	*Total*
PARTIC	0.89	4.94	7.40	3.27	-0.08	2.82	-0.07	-0.08
SO2	1.04	5.01	7.23	3.41	-0.10	1.58	-0.07	-0.09
NO2	-0.24	4.89	6.96	2.04	-0.03	2.97	-0.04	-0.03
LEAD	1.57	4.79	7.02	3.73	-0.09	0.70	-0.06	-0.09
VOC	-1.15	5.07	7.80	1.47	-0.03	2.77	-0.06	-0.03
CO	-1.20	6.71	9.49	1.73	-0.06	0.67	-0.08	-0.06
BOD	-0.83	6.43	8.66	0.51	-0.02	1.05	-0.07	-0.02
SS	-0.76	7.66	11.71	2.55	-0.09	0.75	-0.12	-0.09
TOX	-0.89	5.46	9.38	1.95	-0.04	1.45	-0.06	-0.03
METAL	-0.91	6.99	9.80	1.83	-0.06	1.00	-0.08	-0.06
AHTL Index	-0.16	5.16	8.76	2.64	-0.03	1.11	-0.05	-0.03

Percentage changes in emission levels of pollutants embodied in output supplied to different destinations resulting from unilateral tariff liberalization by Indonesia. See Table 16.3 for the definition of pollutants.

centage change in emission levels (1.47–3.73 percent) exceeds the percentage change in real output, resulting in higher emission intensities. Thus, it is reasonable to conclude that the historical asymmetry in the effluent content of trade is not a result of the existing pattern of Indonesian protection because the asymmetry only intensifies with the removal of Indonesian tariffs.

VI Trade and Tax Policy Instruments for Improving Environmental Quality

For Indonesia, the results of the previous section amplify the policy challenge of addressing the environmental consequences of trade-based economic growth. In light of the trade-off between outward-oriented industrialization and the environment, we evaluate relative effectiveness of alternative instruments to curtail pollution. Since the uncertainties on marginal benefits of pollution abatement would make the calculation of an optimal tax rate impossible, our approach is to set a particular level of emission target and assess empirically the relative cost of alternative instruments that achieve the target.[23] In the first three experiments, we

23 An optimal rate of effluent tax would equalize marginal damage and marginal abatement cost of 1 ton of pollutant. On the cost side, Hartman, Wheeler, and Singh (1994) provide comprehensive estimates on abatement of seven air pollutants for thirty-seven US manufacturing industries.

evaluate the cost of mitigating emissions of various pollutants by 5 percent using three policy instruments: an export tax, sector-specific effluent taxes, and a uniform effluent tax.[24] No taxes are levied on the agricultural or service sector because no emission data are incorporated for these sectors. An AHTL tax is equivalent to a set of taxes on the major air pollutants (particulates, SO_2, NO_2, lead, volatile organic compounds, and carbon monoxide) which act to reduce AHTL by 5 percent. In the fourth experiment, the combination of a uniform effluent tax and tariff removal is simulated to evaluate whether it is possible to increase real output and reduce emissions at the same time. While these experiments were conducted for each pollutant, for simplicity we only report the aggregate results for SO_2 and the AHTL index in Tables 16.7 and 16.8.[25]

In the first experiment, an export tax is chosen as a policy instrument because in Indonesia exports are on average considerably more pollution-intensive than goods supplied domestically (Section III). Since the root cause of the pollution problem is production (regardless of destination), however, the imposition of a tax only on exports would be less efficient than a tax on output supplied domestically and exported. Column (1) in both Tables 16.7 and 16.8 indicates that the cost of achieving the emission target with an export tax, in terms of lost real GDP or EV income, is highest among the three policy instruments. The reduction in total exports is partly offset by a large real depreciation of the rupiah but is still over 10 percent of the baseline quantity. The sharp contraction of trade causes additional reduction in real GDP and EV.

A neoclassical economist would naturally argue that an export tax is an inefficient instrument to control pollution decisions at the producer level. In experiment 2, sector-specific effluent taxes are levied to lower SO_2 emissions or the AHTL index by 5 percent in every sector.[26] While effluent taxes are imposed on all output regardless of destination, an enforcement of the same abatement target in all industrial sectors imposes an extremely high cost on some. This is because SO_2 abatement costs in some sectors, such as metal products, transport equipment, and other manufactures, are significantly higher than those in industrial chemicals, nonferrous metals, pulp

24 Different abatement targets have also been tried, but the relative efficiency of these instruments was not affected by the choice of abatement targets.

25 SO_2 is chosen because it is a pollutant that is known to affect local environmental conditions adversely, including acidification of soils and water and corrosion of materials.

26 Sector-specific taxes required to mitigate emissions by 5 percent will lead to the same results regardless of the pollutant chosen except for the effluent tax results, which depend upon the effluent intensities of the pollutant in different sectors.

Table 16.7. *Aggregate results for alternative trade and tax policies to reduce SO_2 emissions (percentage changes)*

Indonesia	(1) *Export tax*	(2) *Sec-specific effluent taxes*	(3) *Uniform effluent tax*	(4) *Uniform tax and liberaliz*
Real GDP	-1.65	-1.22	-0.56	0.30
EV Income	-1.18	-1.14	-0.34	0.25
Employment	-3.07	-2.46	-0.15	1.82
Wage Rate	-2.53	-2.16	-1.15	0.03
Rental Rate on Capital	-5.75	-5.46	-2.49	0.80
Real Exchange Rate	17.67	4.81	3.61	9.02
Total Imports	-11.87	-1.94	-1.45	4.20
Total Exports	-10.87	-2.26	-2.15	3.31
SO2 Emissions	-5.00	-5.00	-5.00	-2.03

Table 16.8. *Aggregate results for alternative trade and tax policies to lower the AHTL index (percentage changes)*

Indonesia	(1) *Export tax*	(2) *Sec-specific effluent taxes*	(3) *Uniform effluent tax*	(4) *Uniform tax and liberaliz*
Real GDP	-2.26	-1.22	-0.54	0.33
EV Income	-1.67	-1.14	-0.45	0.14
Employment	-3.99	-2.46	-0.97	0.92
Wage Rate	-3.57	-2.16	-1.09	0.14
Rental Rate on Capital	-7.68	-5.46	-2.78	0.56
Real Exchange Rate	24.70	4.81	3.54	9.03
Total Imports	-15.58	-1.94	-1.47	4.09
Total Exports	-14.25	-2.26	-1.64	3.81
AHTL Index	-5.00	-5.00	-5.00	-3.07

and paper, petroleum and mining.[27] Thus, regulation which would require every sector to cut emissions by the same proportion would also be highly inefficient.

Given the large disparity in marginal abatement costs, a uniform effluent tax would significantly reduce the costs of achieving a given emission curtailment target (experiment 3). The cost of cutting SO_2 emissions by 5 percent

27 SO_2 tax rates are computed under alternative emission targets. It is found that some high-cost sectors would have to spend more than 100 times as much in curtailing SO_2 by the same percentage compared with such low-cost sectors as industrial chemicals and nonferrous metals.

in terms of a loss in real GDP under a uniform tax is less than half (0.56 vs. 1.22 percent) compared with sector-specific taxes (Table 16.7, columns 2 and 3). Under this scheme each sector will abate SO_2 until the marginal abatement cost is equal to the uniform tax rate. Many high abatement cost sectors will not abate any SO_2 emissions at all.

While a uniform effluent tax will tend to minimize the cost of a given mitigation target, those sectors with low marginal abatement cost would bear much of the cost in terms of loss in real output. A system of tradable emission permits is an alternative cost-effective instrument to a uniform tax, but can be more supportive to equity issues. Under this system a fixed number of permits to emit a specified quantity of the pollutant is issued to emitters. Those firms or sectors with low abatement cost can sell permits to those with high abatement cost at a market-clearing permit price, thereby receiving compensation for further abatement in emissions. The equilibrium permit price is determined by demand and supply of permits, which should equal the uniform tax rate required to achieve the same emission curtailment target. In the absence of transaction costs and regulatory distortions, a uniform tax and tradable emission permits would both achieve a given level of environmental quality at minimum cost.

In the final experiment, the same uniform tax scheme implemented in the third experiment is combined with the removal of all tariffs. This experiment is conducted to illustrate a critical point, that the combination of trade liberalization and a cost-effective emission abatement instrument can lead to both an improvement in welfare (in terms of real GDP or EV) and a reduction in pollution (Tables 16.7 and 16.8, column 4). This is possible because the benefits of tariff removal are greater than the cost of cutting pollution by the magnitude which more than offsets pollution induced by trade liberalization. The twin objectives of a welfare improvement and an emission curtailment can be achieved under a range of ex ante abatement targets for each pollutant. It should be recalled that no pollution externalities have been introduced in our model because of the uncertainties regarding marginal damage. In the presence of externalities, therefore, the net social benefits of the combined policy would be even greater than our estimates would suggest.

Table 16.9 summarizes the output results for the four trade and tax policies to curtail SO_2 emissions. Levying export taxes causes large percentage reductions in the output levels of the sectors with high exports to total supply ratios (petroleum, lumber and wood, industrial chemicals, and nonferrous metals). By design, sector-specific taxes would lower output of all sectors except agriculture and services by 5 percent, while a uniform tax tends to

Table 16.9. *Output results for alternative trade and tax policies to reduce SO_2 emissions (percentage changes)*

	Indonesia	(1) *Export tax*	(2) *Sec-specific effluent taxes*	(3) *Uniform effluent tax*	(4) *Uniform tax and liberaliz*
1	Agriculture	-0.1	1.9	1.8	1.9
2	Petroleum	-5.9	-5.0	-5.1	-1.4
3	Mining	2.8	-5.0	-5.0	-3.9
4	FoodProc	-0.1	-5.0	0.4	0.2
5	Textile	-3.2	-5.0	0.3	0.6
6	LumWood	-7.8	-5.0	4.9	10.4
7	PulpPaper	14.0	-5.0	-4.3	-21.6
8	IndChem	-31.8	-5.0	-4.0	26.9
9	OtherChem	4.9	-5.0	1.3	-1.0
10	Plastic	-0.5	-5.0	-0.1	-1.3
11	NonMtMnr	1.9	-5.0	-0.2	-3.3
12	Steel	14.3	-5.0	2.0	-3.7
13	NonferMtl	-13.9	-5.0	-19.8	-13.7
14	MetalProd	8.2	-5.0	1.4	-8.6
15	MachPrcls	-2.8	-5.0	0.6	5.7
16	ElecMach	2.0	-5.0	2.2	-4.2
17	TranspEq	6.6	-5.0	2.4	-4.9
18	OtherMfg	0.3	-5.0	0.2	-1.2
19	Services	-0.4	-0.5	0.0	0.4

reduce output of the sectors with low abatement cost. When a cost-effective tax policy is combined with tariff liberalization, the agricultural and service sectors, which together account for two-thirds of Indonesia's total output, both expand. The percentage reduction in petroleum output is small compared with other policy scenarios, but the overall SO_2 emission level is lower than in the baseline case.

VII Conclusions and Extensions

The ability of international trade to alter the composition of domestic production activities allows it to exert an important influence on the environment. Export-oriented growth could cause high and unsustainable pollution levels, especially when the country has comparative advantage in dirty industries. This chapter has used data on the economy of Indonesia to appraise the environmental risks of its trade orientation and to evaluate some alternative policy instruments for reducing these risks, including export taxes, sector-specific effluent taxes, and uniform effluent taxes. In addition, a combination of uniform tax and tariff removal is simulated to examine the possibility of lowering domestic emissions and raising material welfare simultaneously.

Four principal conclusions emerge from this preliminary research. First of all, Indonesia's historical trade orientation has been environmentally asymmetric in the sense that it occasioned significant transfers of pollution services from its trading partners, particularly from Japan, to the domestic economy. Second, although trade liberalization would improve Indonesian real income, it would also raise the emission level of major industrial pollutants. Third, our results indicate that a uniform effluent tax is the most cost-effective instrument in abating SO_2 emissions. This result holds for abatement of other industrial pollutants and for different abatement targets. Neither the imposition of an export tax nor uniform emission reduction with sector-specific taxes is recommended as an alternative policy. Pollution abatement using these instruments would result in a loss of real GDP that is significantly greater than achievement of the same target using a uniform effluent tax. Last but not least, it is possible to abate industrial pollution while maintaining or even increasing real output when uniform taxation is combined with trade liberalization. In other words, trade liberalization should not be discouraged because of its environmental effects, and environmental taxation need not be contractionary if distortions can be removed elsewhere.

Much work remains to be done with the data and analytical resources developed in this research. The following areas should be given priority:

1 Broadening the model specifications to include possibilities for technical substitution.
2 Taking account of pollution arising from consumption activities, such as vehicular emissions and fertilizer use.
3 Incorporating direct foreign investment into the model to allow firms to relocate to different regions.
4 Disaggregating domestic institutions to facilitate more clear understanding of the real incidence of economic and environmental effects.
5 Including emissions from agriculture and service activities in the pollution database.
6 Estimating country-specific pollution intensities and abatement costs.

As this family of more extended models is developed, they should be subjected to exhaustive policy experimentation to elucidate the complex environmental role of individual and combined economic instruments. The importance of all this work is to strengthen the empirical foundation for research on the environmental implications of commercial policy and the trade implications of environmental policy, two essential steps to secure the basis for sustainable development.

Appendix 16.1

Structural Equations for the Indonesia–Japan CGE Model

I Country-Specific Equations

Emission Levels by Destination of Supply

$$EMI_h^k = \sum_{i=1}^{n} \varepsilon_{ih} P_{Si}^k S_i^k \tag{A16.1}$$

$k=\{d,b,r\}$, where d=domestic, b=bilateral partner, and r=ROW
h=\{PARTIC, SO_2, NO_2, LEAD, VOD, CO, BOD, SS, TOX, METAL, AHTL\}

Consumer Behavior

$$C_i = LES_C(P_{Di}, Y) = \gamma_i + \frac{\eta_i}{P_{Di}}\left(Y - \sum_{j=1}^{n} P_{Dj}\gamma_j\right) \tag{A16.2}$$

Production Technology

$$S_i = \min\left[CES_S(L_{Di}, K_{Di}; \phi_i), \frac{V_{1i}}{a_{1i}}, \ldots, \frac{V_{ni}}{a_{ni}}\right] \tag{A16.3}$$

$$V_{ij} = a_{ij} S_j \tag{A16.4}$$

Factor Demands

$$\frac{LD_i}{KD_i} = \Psi\left(\frac{w}{r_{Di}; \Phi_i}\right) \tag{A16.5}$$

$$KD_i = KD_i^d + \sum_f KD_i^f \tag{A16.6}$$

Factor Supplies

$$LS = LES_L(w, Y) \tag{A16.7}$$

$$KS_i = KS_i^d + \sum_f KS_i^f \tag{A16.8}$$

Commodity Demands, Supplies, and Allocation of Traded Goods

$$D_i = \overline{A}_{Di}\left[\sum_k \beta_i^k \left(D_i^k\right)^{(\sigma_i-1)/\sigma_i}\right]^{\sigma_i/(\sigma_i-1)} \quad \text{(A16.9)}$$

$$\frac{D_i^f}{D_i^d} = g_D\left(\frac{P_{Di}^f}{P_{Di}^d};\sigma_i\right) \quad \text{(A16.10)}$$

$$S_i = \overline{A}_{Si}\left[\sum_k \delta_i^k \left(S_i^k\right)^{(\lambda_i+1)/\lambda_i}\right]^{\lambda_i/(\lambda_i+1)} \quad \text{(A16.11)}$$

$$\frac{S_i^f}{S_i^d} = g_S\left(\frac{P_{Si}^f}{P_{Si}^d};\lambda_i\right) \quad \text{(A16.12)}$$

Composite Domestic Prices

$$P_{Di}D_i = \sum_k P_{Di}^k D_i^k \quad \text{(A16.13)}$$

$$P_{Si}S_i = \sum_k P_{Si}^k S_i^k \quad \text{(A16.14)}$$

Indirect and Effluent Taxes

$$t_{Si}^d = t_{Di}^d + \sum_h \tau_{ih}\varepsilon_{ih} \quad \text{(A16.15)}$$

Domestic Market Equilibrium

$$D_i = C_i + \sum_{j=1}^n V_{ij} \quad \text{(A16.16)}$$

$$D_i^d = S_i^d \quad \text{(A16.17)}$$

$$LS = \sum_{i=1}^n LD_i \quad \text{(A16.18)}$$

$$\sum_{i=1}^n KD_i^d = \sum_{i=1}^n KS_i^d \quad \text{(A16.19)}$$

Income and Government Revenue

$$Y = (1-t_L)\sum_{i=1}^n wLD_i + (1-t_K)\sum_{i=1}^n r_{Di}KD_i + Y_G \quad \text{(A16.20)}$$

$$Y_G = t_L\sum_i wLD_i + t_k\sum_i r_{Di}KD_i + \sum_k\sum_i\left(t_{Di}^k P_{Di}^k D_i^k + t_{Si}^k P_{Si}^k S_i^k\right) \quad \text{(A16.21)}$$

Balance of Payments

$$B^f = \sum_i \left[PW_{Si}^f S_i^f - PW_{Di}^f D_i^f \right] \quad \text{(A16.22)}$$

Foreign Commodity Prices

$$P_{Di}^f = \left(1 + t_{Di}^f\right) e PW_{Di}^f \quad \text{(A16.23)}$$

$$P_{Si}^f = \left[\frac{1}{\left(1 + t_{Si}^f\right)} \right] e PW_{Si}^f \quad \text{(A16.24)}$$

Foreign Demand and Supply Functions

$$D_i^{h,ROW} = \overline{A}_{Mi} \left(PW_{Si}^{h,ROW} \right)^{\zeta_i} \quad \text{(A16.25)}$$

$$S_i^{h,ROW} = \overline{A}_{Ei} \left(PW_{Di}^{h,ROW} \right)^{\xi_i} \quad \text{(A16.26)}$$

Trade Flow and Price Equivalence

$$D_i^{h,f} = S_i^{f,h} \quad \text{(A16.27)}$$

$$P_{Di}^{h,f} = P_{Si}^{f,h} \quad \text{(A16.28)}$$

Numéraire

$$\sum_i \omega_i P_{Di}^d = 1 \quad \text{(A16.29)}$$

II Variable and Parameter Definitions

Price Variables

e = Exchange rates (domestic/foreign currency)
$P_{Di}^{h,f}$ = Demand price by destination (h) and origin (f)
$P_{Si}^{h,f}$ = Supply price by origin (h) and destination (f)
P_{Di}^{d} = Domestic purchaser prices of domestic goods
P_{Di}^{f} = Domestic purchaser price of imports from region f (equivalent to $P_{Di}^{d,f}$)
P_{Si}^{d} = Domestic producer price in the domestic market
P_{Si}^{f} = Domestic producer price for exports to region f (equivalent to $P_{Si}^{d,f}$)
P_{Di} = Purchaser price of composite domestic demand
P_{Si} = Producer price of domestic output
$PW_{Di}^{h,f}$ = World demand price by destination (h) and origin (f)
$PW_{Si}^{h,f}$ = World supply price by origin (h) and destination (f)
PW_{Di}^{f} = World price of imports from region f

PW^f_{Si} = World price of exports to region f
r_{Di} = Rental rate on capital
w = Average wage rate

Quantity Variables

C_i = Personal consumption
$D_i^{h,f}$ = Demand by destination (h) and origin (f)
D_i^d = Domestic demand for domestic goods
D_i^f = Domestic demand for imports from region f (equivalent to $D_i^{d,f}$)
D_i = Composite goods for domestic consumption
EMI_h^k = Domestic emission levels by destination of supply (domestic market, bilateral country, ROW) for pollutant h
KD_i^d = Domestic demand for domestic capital
KD_i^f = Domestic demand for imported capital (inward direct foreign investment stock) from region f (exogenous)
KS_i^d = Domestic supply of domestic capital
KS_i^f = Outward direct foreign investment stock in region f (exogenous)
LD_i = Demand for labor
LS = Aggregate labor supply
$S_i^{h,f}$ = Supply by origin (h) and destination (f)
S_i^d = Domestic production for domestic use
S_i^f = Domestic production for export to region f (equivalent to $S_i^{d,f}$)
S_i = Gross domestic output
V_{ij} = Demand for intermediate good i in sector j

Nominal Variables

B^f = Net foreign borrowing from region f (exogenous)
Y = Nominal domestic income
Y_G = Government income

Structural and Policy Parameters

a_{ij} = Intermediate use coefficients (Leontief technology)
$\varepsilon_{i,h}$ = Sectoral effluent intensities of pollutant h
γ_i = Subsistence consumption of good i
η_i = Marginal budget share for consumption of good i
ϕ_i = Elasticity of substitution between labor and capital in domestic production
σ_i = Elasticity of substitution between domestic and imported products
λ_i = Elasticity of transformation between domestic and exported products
ζ_i = ROW import supply elasticity
ξ_i = ROW export demand elasticity
$\overline{A}_{Di}$ = Calibrated intercept parameter for composite product demand
$\overline{A}_{Si}$ = Calibrated intercept parameter for composite product supply
$\overline{A}_{Mi}$ = Calibrated intercept parameter for ROW import supply
$\overline{A}_{Ei}$ = Calibrated intercept parameter for ROW export demand
β_i^k = Base share parameter of demand by origin in the composite demand

δ_i^k = Base share parameter of supply by destination in the composite demand
τ_{ih} = Excise taxes on emissions (\$/pound of pollutant h)
t_{Di}^d = Indirect tax rate on domestic sector production
t_{Di}^f = Ad valorem tariff rate on imports from region f
t_K = Tax rate on capital income
t_L = Tax rate on labor income
t_{Si}^d = Producer tax or subsidy on domestic deliveries
t_{Si}^f = Tax or subsidy on exports to region f
ω_i = Domestic expenditure shares

References

Anderson, K. 1992. "The standard welfare economics of policies affecting trade and the environment." In *The Greening of World Trade Issues*, edited by K. Anderson and R. Blackhurst. Ann Arbor: University of Michigan Press.

Anderson, K. and R. Blackhurst. 1992. "Trade, the environment and public policy." In *The Greening of World Trade Issues*, edited by K. Anderson and R. Blackhurst. Ann Arbor: University of Michigan Press.

Barde, J.-P. 1994. "Economic instruments in environmental policy: Lessons from OECD experience and their relevance to developing economies." Technical Paper No. 92, Paris: OECD Development Centre.

Beghin, J., D.W. Roland-Holst, and D. van der Mensbrugghe. 1995. "A survey of the trade and environment nexus: Global dimensions." *OECD Economic Studies* 23:167–192.

Bergman, L. 1993. "General equilibrium costs and benefits of environmental policies: Some preliminary results based on Swedish data." Stockholm School of Economics, Mimeograph.

Birdsall, N. and D. Wheeler. 1992. "Trade policy and industrial pollution in Latin America: Where are the pollution havens?" In *International Trade and the Environment*, edited by P. Low. Discussion Paper No. 159, Washington, D.C.: World Bank.

Burniaux, J.-M., G. Nicoletti, and J. Oliveira Martins. 1992. "GREEN: A global model for quantifying the costs of policies to curb CO_2 emissions." *OECD Economic Studies* 19:49–92.

Chichilnisky, G. and G.M. Heal. 1994. "Markets for tradeable CO_2 emission quotas: Principles and practice." Graduate School of Business, Columbia University, Mimeograph.

Cline, W.R. 1992. *The Economics of Global Warming*. Washington, D.C.: Institute of International Economics.

Coase, R.H. 1960. "The problem of social costs." *Journal of Law and Economics* 3:1–44.

Coppel, J. and H. Lee. 1996. "The framework convention and climate change policy in Asia." In *The Economics of Pollution Control in the Asian Pacific*, edited by R. Mendelsohn and D. Shaw. London: Edward Elgar.

Cropper, M.L. and W.E. Oates. 1992. "Environmental economics: A survey." *Journal of Economic Literature* 30:675–740.

Dales, J.H. 1968. *Pollution, Property and Prices*. Toronto: University of Toronto Press.

Dean, J.M. 1992. "Trade and the environment: A survey of the literature." In *International Trade and the Environment*, edited by P. Low. Discussion Paper No. 159, Washington, D.C.: World Bank.

Devarajan, S. Delfin Go, J.D. Lewis, S. Robinson, and P. Sinko. 1995. "Simple general equilibrium modeling." In *Applied Methods for Trade Policy Analysis*, edited by J.F. Francois and K.A. Reinert. Cambridge: Cambridge University Press.

Grossman, G.M. and A.O. Krueger. 1992. "Environmental aspects of a North American free trade agreement." Working Paper No. 644, London: Centre for Economic Policy Research.

Hahn, R.W. and R.N. Stavins. 1992. "Economic incentives for environmental protection: Integrating theory and practice." *American Economic Review* 82:464–468.

Hamilton, K. 1994. "Environmental accounting for decision-making." Paper presented at the OECD Seminar on Environmental Accounting for Decision-Making, 27–28 September, Paris.

Hartman, R.S., D. Wheeler, and M. Singh. 1994. "The cost of air pollution abatement." Policy Research Department, Washington, D.C., World Bank, Mimeograph.

Hettige, H., R.E.B. Lucas, and D. Wheeler. 1992. "The toxic intensity of industrial production: Global patterns, trends, and trade policy." *American Economic Review* 82:478–481.

Institute of Developing Economies. 1991. *International Input–Output Table: Indonesia-Japan, 1985*. Statistical Data Series No. 57, Tokyo: IDE.

Intergovernmental Panel on Climate Change. 1990. *Climate Change: The IPCC Scientific Assessment*, edited by J.T. Houghton, G.J. Jenkins, and J.J. Ephraums. Cambridge: Cambridge University Press.

Jorgenson, D.W., D.T. Slesnick, and P.J. Wilcoxen. 1992. "Carbon taxes and economic welfare." *Brookings Papers on Economic Activity: Microeconomics*: 393–431.

Keuning, S.J. 1992. "National accounts and the environment: The case for a systems approach." Occasional Paper No. NA-053. Amsterdam: Netherlands Central Bureau of Statistics.

Krutilla, K. 1991. "Environmental regulation in an open economy." *Journal of Environmental Economics and Management* 20:127–142.

Lee, H. and D.W. Roland-Holst. 1993. "Cooperation or confrontation in US-Japan trade? Some general equilibrium estimates." Irvine Economics Paper No. 92-93-08, University of California, Irvine.

Lloyd, P.J. 1992. "The problem of optimal environmental policy choice." In *The Greening of World Trade Issues*, edited by K. Anderson and R. Blackhurst. Ann Arbor: University of Michigan Press.

Low, P. 1992. "Trade measures and environmental quality: The implications for Mexico's exports." In *International Trade and the Environment*, edited by P. Low. Discussion Paper No. 159, Washington, D.C.: World Bank.

Low, P. and R. Safadi. 1992. "Trade policy and pollution." In *International Trade and the Environment*, edited by P. Low. Discussion Paper No. 159, Washington, D.C.: World Bank.

Lucas, R.E.B., D. Wheeler, and H. Hettige. 1992. "Economic development, environmental regulation and the international migration of toxic industrial pollution: 1960–1988." In *International Trade and the Environment*, edited by P. Low. Discussion Paper No. 159, Washington, D.C.: World Bank.

Manne, A.S. and R.G. Richels. 1992. *Buying Greenhouse Insurance: The Economic Costs of CO_2 Emission Limits*. Cambridge; Massachusetts: MIT Press.
Markusen, J.R. 1975. "International Externalities and Optimal Tax Structures." *Journal of International Economics* 5:15–29.
Martin, P., D. Wheeler, H. Hettige, and R. Stengren. 1991. "The industrial pollution projection system: Concept, initial development, and critical assessment." Washington, D.C.: World Bank, Mimeograph.
Mendelsohn, R. 1996. "The impact of global warming on Pacific rim countries." In *The Economics of Pollution Control in the Asian Pacific*, edited by R. Mendelsohn and D. Shaw. London: Edward Elgar.
Mendelsohn, R., W.D. Nordhaus, and D. Shaw. 1994. "The impact of global warming on agriculture: A Ricardian analysis." *American Economic Review* 84:753–771.
Nordhaus, W.D. 1991. "To slow or not to slow: The economics of the greenhouse effect." *Economic Journal* 101:920–937.
Nordhaus, W.D. 1992. "Rolling the 'DICE': An optimal transition path for controlling greenhouse gases." *Science* 258:1315–1319.
O'Connor, D. 1992. "Measuring the costs of environmental damage: A review of methodological approaches with an application to Bangkok, Thailand." Paris: OECD Development Centre, Mimeograph.
O'Connor, D. 1994. "The use of economic instruments in environmental management: The experience of East Asia." In *Economic Instruments for Environmental Management in Developing Countries*. Paris: OECD.
OECD. 1975. *The Polluter Pays Principle*. Paris: OECD.
OECD. 1993. *The Costs of Cutting Carbon Emissions: Results from Global Models*. Paris: OECD.
OECD. 1994. *Policy Response to the Threat of Global Warming*. Working Party No. 1 Report of the Economic Policy Committee, ECO/CPE/WP1(94)5, Paris: OECD.
Perroni, C. and T. Rutherford. 1993. "International trade in carbon emission rights and basic materials: General equilibrium calculations for 2020." *Scandinavian Journal of Economics* 95:257–278.
Perroni, C. and R.M. Wigle. 1994. "International trade and environmental quality: How important are the links?" *Canadian Journal of Economics* 27:551–567.
Pigou, A.C. 1920. *The Economics of Welfare*. London: Macmillan.
Radetzki, M. 1992. "Economic growth and the environment." In *International Trade and the Environment*, edited by P. Low. Discussion Paper No. 159, Washington, D.C.: World Bank.
Reinert, K.A. and D.W. Roland-Holst. 1995. "Social accounting matrices." In *Applied Methods for Trade Policy Analysis*, edited by J.F. Francois and K.A. Reinert. Cambridge: Cambridge University Press.
Roland-Holst, D.W. 1992. "Stabilization and structural adjustment in Indonesia: An intertemporal general equilibrium analysis." Technical Paper No. 83, Paris: OECD Development Centre.
Ten Kate, A. 1993. "Industrial development and the environment in Mexico." Working Paper No. 1125, Policy Research Department. Washington, D.C.: World Bank.
Tobey, J., J. Reilly, and S. Kane. 1992. "Economic implications of global climate change for world agriculture." *Journal of Agricultural and Resource Economics* 17:195–204.

United Nations. 1993a. *System of National Accounts 1993*. New York: United Nations.

United Nations. 1993b. *Integrated Environmental and Economic Accounting*, Series F, No. 61. New York: United Nations.

U.S. Department of Commerce, Bureau of Census. 1988. *Manufacturers' Pollution Abatement Capital Expenditures and Operations Costs*. Washington, D.C.: U.S. Government Printing Office.

U.S. Department of Commerce, Bureau of Economic Analysis. 1994. "Integrated economic environmental satellite accounts." *Survey of Current Business* 74:33–49.

Walter, I. 1973. "The pollution content of American trade." *Western Economic Journal* 11:61–70.

Wheeler, D. 1992. "The economics of industrial pollution control." Industry Series Paper No. 60, Industry and Energy Department. Washington, D.C.: World Bank.

World Bank, 1992. *Development and the Environment: World Bank Development Report, 1992*. Washington, D.C.: World Bank.

[3]

International trade and environmental quality: how important are the linkages?

CARLO PERRONI University of Western Ontario
RANDALL M. WIGLE Wilfrid Laurier University

Abstract. This paper develops a numerical general equilibrium model of the world economy with local and global environmental externalities. The model is then used to investigate the relationship between trade and the environment. Our results suggest that international trade has little impact on environmental quality. Furthermore, the magnitude of the welfare effects of environmental policies is not significantly affected by changes in trade policies. At the same time, the size and distribution of the gains from trade liberalization appear to be little affected by changes in environmental policies.

Commerce international et qualité de l'environnement: quelle est l'importance des liens? Ce mémoire développe un modèle numérique d'équilibre général de l'économie mondiale qui tient compte des effets externes locaux et globaux sur l'environnement. Le modèle est utilisé pour explorer le rapport entre commerce international et environnement. Les résultats obtenus suggèrent que le commerce international a peu d'effet sur la qualité de l'environnement. De plus, la taille des effets de bien-être des politiques environnementales n'est pas affectée de manière significative par les changements dans les politiques commerciales. D'autre part, la taille et la répartition des gains provenant de la libéralisation du commerce semblent peu affectées par les changements dans les politiques environnementales.

I. INTRODUCTION

The last few years have seen a remarkable increase in environmental concerns, both in the public at large and among policy makers. One particular focus of these concerns is the interrelationship between international trade and the environment. A widely held view is that international trade is a primary contributor to environmental

This paper was presented at the CEA annual meetings in June 1992, and at the EEA annual meetings in March 1993. The authors wish to thank participants in workshops at Brock University, the University of Western Ontario, and the University of Guelph. We also wish to thank Nick Hanley, Glenn Harrison, and a number of anonymous referees for their comments on earlier drafts. Financial support from the Social Sciences and Humanities Research Council of Canada is gratefully acknowledged. Perroni acknowledges support from the Ford Foundation.

Canadian Journal of Economics Revue canadienne d'Economique, XXVII, No. 3
August août 1994. Printed in Canada Imprimé au Canada

0008-4085 / 94 / 551–67 $1.50 © Canadian Economics Association

degradation (Shrybman 1990). Trade liberalization has also come under criticism on the grounds that domestic environmental policies can be significantly undercut through trade diversion and relocation of dirty industries to 'pollution havens,' particularly when governments are restricted by trade treaties.[1]

The implications of the environmental externalities for the theory of comparative advantage have been extensively explored in the literature. Environmental emissions affect the pattern of comparative advantage: countries with comparatively higher levels of environmental assimilative capacity, or with comparatively lower valuations of environmental quality have a comparative advantage in the production of pollution-intensive goods (Siebert 1977; Blackhurst 1977). Less than full internalization of environmental externalities may have implications both for equity (if the victims of the externalities are not compensated) and for efficiency (emission levels will be above optimal). With respect to international trade, the lack of internalization distorts the pattern of comparative advantage, resulting in non-optimal levels of trade. In addition to these efficiency effects, the lack of internalization affects the distribution of the gains from trade. In this situation, a country might find autarky to be preferable to free trade (Pethig 1976).

The thrust of the literature on trade and the environment is mainly theoretical and few of the results are even qualitatively robust. Nevertheless, there appears to be some consensus among economists that trade barriers are a very poor substitute for domestic environmental policies (Bhagwati 1981a), and that trade liberalization and environmental protection may be treated as separable objectives, but to our knowledge no previous study has attempted to provide quantitative support for this conjecture.

This paper represents an attempt to assess the relative contribution of international trade to environmental degradation, and the extent to which environmental policies affect the size and distribution of the gains from trade liberalization. To this end we formulate an operational general equilibrium model encompassing international trade and environmental externalities, which is calibrated to a consistent world data set for 1986. We employ the model to explore the quantitative significance of the links between international trade and the environment.

The main obstacle to performing such an exercise is simply our limited information on how economic activities affect the natural environment, and on how individuals value environmental quality. Although there is a large literature on the valuation of environmental damages, there are many parameters we use for our model for which there are no estimates. In this respect our results are of necessity speculative. Nevertheless, we feel that the urgency of the debate on trade and environment warrants a first attempt to assess the importance of these linkages.

Given our parameterization, numerical simulations indicate that although trade liberalization appears to have a discernible impact on the environment, its relative contribution to environmental degradation is very limited, and that this impact is likely to be virtually zero when appropriate environmental policies are in place.

1 Specific GATT rules have come under attack, especially those concerning subsidies and 'National Treatment' (see Whalley 1991).

Furthermore, we find that environmental policies and trade policies are not as interdependent as some appear to believe. Specifically, environmental policy seems to have little effect on the size and distribution of the gains from trade liberalization. Similarly, we find that trade policy has a very limited impact on the welfare effects of environmental policies.

The plan of the paper is as follows. Section II outlines the general methodology employed to model environmental externalities, while section III details the structure of our model. Section IV describes the data set and the calibration procedure. Our experiments and numerical results are presented in section V.

II. ENVIRONMENTAL EXTERNALITIES IN THE GLOBAL ECONOMY

The processes that link environmental externalities to both the damage caused by them and the costs of reducing them can be grouped into four categories.

- *Institutional processes.* While there is normally a market mechanism to mediate transactions in private goods, there may be no private market for environmental quality. In the absence of a market or some other corrective policy, polluters do not pay for their 'use' of environmental resources.
- *Technological processes.* Production activities generate emissions that reduce environmental quality. These emissions can be reduced by switching to cleaner technologies or through the cleaning up of existing technologies ('end-of-pipe treatment'). Just as there are different technical processes for production, there are alternative processes of abatement.
- *Natural and geographical processes.* The impact of emissions on environmental quality varies across regions, depending on the nature of the emissions (local/transnational/global) and on the assimilative capacity of the environment. The latter will depend on the geographical pattern of emissions and on the local characteristics of the natural environment.
- *Subjective processes.* The value placed by consumers on environmental quality depends on consumers' preferences and there is a strong presumption among economists that the willingness to pay for environmental quality is positively correlated with lifetime wealth.[2]

The connections between these processes, the economy's agents and the environment are summarized in figure 1.

These categories may become quite blurred in practice. For instance, we may observe that the valuation of environmental externalities appears to be higher in rich countries than it is in poor ones, but it is hard to tell whether this effect is mainly due to differences in assimilative capacity or differences in income levels. Also, the distinction between technological and physical processes is largely conventional and depends on how we define the pollutant being emitted. Thus, unless

2 There is limited evidence on the matter. Braden and Kolstad (1991) give a good discussion of the associated problems. The general conclusion of Radetzki (1992) is consistent with the view that valuation rises with income.

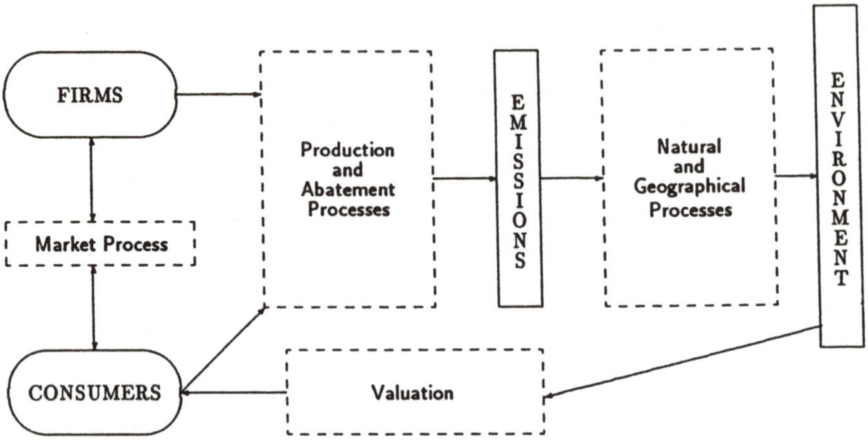

FIGURE 1 Economy–environment linkages

detailed information on the various aspects of environmental externalities is available, one may be tempted to abandon some of the above distinctions. In our view, however, maintaining these distinctions is important *precisely because of* the lack of detailed information: a careful categorization provides structure to the analysis and order to the policy debate. Also, maintaining such distinctions is essential for an interdisciplinary approach to the problem of environmental externalities.

The fact that these distinctions are often subtle means that they are often ignored in quantitative models; the need for preserving these distinctions in a model with fully integrated international trade spurred our modelling efforts. In order to explore the relationship between trade and the environment, in the next section we develop a model of the global economy that attempts explicitly to include all of the above aspects of environmental externalities.

III. MODEL STRUCTURE

This section describes the structure of our model, with a special emphasis on the modelling of environmental externalities. A complete description of the model is available from the authors by request.

1. Emissions and abatement

As mentioned above, we distinguish between externalities arising from production and from consumption activities, as well as between local and global externalities.[3] Gross environmental emissions, in the absence of any regulation, represent a fixed

3 There is nothing in the model structure to prevent us from having 'regional' externalities that affect only geographically close countries. Since our country aggregation is not based on geography, such a categorization becomes meaningless.

proportion of activity levels. To illustrate, let us denote by m^L and m^G, respectively, the local and global emission coefficients of a given production or consumption sector.[4] Then the sector's gross emissions are simply equal to m^LX and m^GX, where X represents the level of output or consumption. Net emissions depend on gross emissions and on the degree of emission abatement. Denoting by A^L and A^G, respectively, the proportional abatement of local and global emissions by this sector, its net emissions can be expressed as $m^LX\ (1 - A^L)$ and $m^GX\ (1 - A^G)$.

Abatement activities are sector specific. We assume that there exists some degree of output complementarity in the 'production' of abatement of local and global emissions. This is achieved by postulating a constant-elasticity transformation (CET) function linking 'aggregate abatement,' A, with the proportional abatement levels for local and global emissions with elasticity of transformation τ between the two types of abatement. Unit abatement costs are assumed to be independent of production levels; as sectors increase the level of abatement as a proportion of their emissions (i.e., as they decrease their per-unit emissions), however, unit emission abatement costs rise (Ballard and Medema 1988). We represent this cost structure by means of a constant-elasticity unit cost function of the form

$$\frac{F(\vec{p}, A)}{A} = \frac{f(\vec{p})}{1+\eta}A^{\eta}, \tag{1}$$

where $F(\vec{p}, A)$ is the cost of abating a given proportion, A, of emissions for each unit of output or consumption, $\vec{p}$ is a vector of input prices, and η (which is positive) is the elasticity of unit abatement costs with respect to A. Marginal abatement costs as a function of A are then

$$f(\vec{p})A^{\eta}. \tag{2}$$

The government levies unit local and global emission fees. The resulting emission charges, z^jL and z^jG, paid on each physical unit of the 'unabated' portion of output or consumption, are equal to the emission fee times the amount of emissions per unit of output or consumption (i.e., the emission coefficient). For given emission fees, producers and consumers select cost-minimizing abatement levels for which marginal abatement costs equal private marginal abatement benefits. The latter are equal to a CET aggregation of unit emission charges. Notice that we assume abatement technologies to be identical in all regions, which implies that differences in abatement choices across regions arise exclusively from differences in emission charges or in factor prices.[5]

2. Damage and valuation

Total local emissions experienced by a certain region, E^L, are the sum of net local emissions by all sectors in that region. Total global emissions experienced

4 By consumption sector, we mean merely the domestic consumption of the good in question.
5 We assume that no region is inherently 'dirtier' than others.

by a region, E^G, are the sum of net global emissions by all sectors in all regions. The relationship between emissions experienced and environmental damage D is modelled by means of convex, constant-elasticity damage functions:

$$D^L(E^L) = k^L(E^L)^{\rho^L} \tag{3}$$

$$D^G(E^G) = k^G(E^G)^{\rho^G}, \tag{4}$$

where k^L and k^G are constants, and ρ^L and ρ^G represent elasticities of damage with respect to emissions (assumed to be greater than unity) (Dewees 1992). These elasticities are likely to be different for different types of emissions and to vary across regions to reflect differences in assimilative capacity. Further discussion of the parameters of the damage functions follows below.

We also distinguish between a local dimension and a global dimension of environmental quality on the consumption side of the economy. Environmental quality is equal to the difference between endowments of environmental quality and damage:

$$Q^L = \bar{Q}^L - D^L(E^L) \tag{5}$$

$$Q^G = \bar{Q}^G - D^G(E^G). \tag{6}$$

It follows that the marginal valuation of emissions experienced by a region is simply equal to

$$p_E^L = Np_Q^L \frac{dD^L}{dE^L} \tag{7}$$

$$p_E^G = Np_Q^G \frac{dD^G}{dE^G}, \tag{8}$$

where N is population, and p_Q^L and p_Q^G are individual marginal valuations for local and global environmental quality, respectively.

The individual valuations of environmental quality in turn depend on the level of environmental quality and on per capita consumption of goods. We model this relationship via a utility function defined over consumption goods and environmental quality. First we aggregate the two types of environmental quality by means of a constant-elasticity of substitution (CES) function with an elasticity of substitution of σ. Combined environmental quality then enters a CES utility function together with per capita consumption, with an elasticity of substitution equal to γ.[6] It can be easily shown that the reciprocal of γ equals the income elasticity of environmental quality valuation, ω.[7] Also notice that the degree of responsiveness of the marginal

6 We assume strong separability between consumption and environmental quality, which enables us to treat environmental quality as a single consumption aggregate (Forster 1981).

7 Notice that since individuals are rationed in their consumption of environmental quality, and since observable income does not include the value of environmental quality consumed, it is possible to obtain a positive income elasticity of the marginal valuation of environmental quality from a homothetic formulation of preferences (Lucas et al., 1992).

valuation of environmental quality to an increase in damage depends on the size of environmental quality endowments. Thus, we can choose these endowments so as to reflect an exogenously selected value for the elasticity of marginal valuation with respect to damage, ζ.

Because of the static nature of the model, we implicitly assume that environmental quality is a renewable resource. If all pollutants were 'fund' pollutants (i.e., if the environment has some assimilative capacity for them) this inaccuracy may not be too serious. For 'stock' pollutants (those for which the assimilative capacity is very small or zero), this assumption leads to an underestimation of the social cost of environmental emissions.[8]

3. Environmental policies

Environmental controls are modelled as emission fees that force the emitting party to internalize part or all of the external cost. For local emissions generated by a sector in region j, emission charges per unit of unabated output or consumption are

$$z^j L = \pi_D^j p_E^{jL} m^L, \tag{9}$$

where π_D^j represents the rate at which the emitter is forced to internalize the externality. For global emissions, charges are

$$z^j G = \pi j_D p_E^{jG} m^G + \pi_X^j \sum_{r \neq j} p_E^{rG} m^G, \tag{10}$$

where π_D^j is an internalization rate for the domestic component of the externality, and π_X^j is the rate of internalization for international spillovers. Even when π_X^j is greater than zero, we assume that the revenue of emission charges is transferred not to the affected parties but to the residents of the country where the emissions originate. In our model structure this approach – unlike real-world environmental regulatory schemes – is inherently efficient, though not necessarily equitable.

4. Key parameters

The respective shapes of the marginal cost and benefit functions for emission abatement are crucial determinants of optimal abatement choices and their responsiveness to policy changes. This subsection summarizes how the key parameters and variables in our environmental submodel affect the shape of these functions.

The level of marginal abatement costs depends on factor prices and is increasing in the proportion of emissions abated. The marginal cost schedule is steeper the larger is the elasticity of unit abatement costs with respect to proportional abatement, η. This relation merely reflects the fact that a given incremental reduction in emissions is easier to achieve when emissions are high than when almost all emissions have been eliminated.

8 The terms 'stock' and 'fund' pollutants are suggested in Tietenberg (1991).

The marginal benefits of abatement depend on internalization rates, population size, and the marginal valuation of environmental quality, which in turn depends directly on per capita income and inversely on the level of environmental quality. The marginal benefit schedule is decreasing in the level of abatement, since an increase in environmental quality results in a reduced marginal valuation of environmental quality and thus in lower emission charges for a given rate of internalization. The marginal benefit schedule is steeper the larger are the elasticity of environmental damage with respect to emissions, ρ, and the elasticity of damage valuation with respect to damage, ζ.

5. *Production and trade*

The environmental submodel described above is embedded in a multisectoral-multiregional trade model with non-homogeneous traded goods. Primary factors, labour and capital, are domestically mobile but internationally immobile, and factor endowments differ across regions. Because of capital immobility, and the static nature of the model, dirty industries are prevented from relocating to regions with low emission charges, a possibility that some authors indicate as a primary source of environmental 'leakage' (Lucas et al., 1992). As we shall mention below, we view this as a main limitation to our analysis. Production technologies are identical across regions and are modelled by means of constant returns to scale CES production functions. Preferences are modelled through homothetic nested CES functions, as discussed above. Substitution elasticities are identical across regions, but demand share parameters are region specific. In order to accommodate cross-hauling in trade flows, we adopt an 'Armington' structure: goods of the same type produced in different regions are less than perfect substitutes.[9]

IV. DATA AND PARAMETER CALIBRATION

In this section we describe the basic data used to calibrate the model. The commodities were chosen with the idea of identifying goods by their factor intensities in labour, skills, capital, and 'environmental inputs.' As a result, there are six goods (and sectors) chosen to separate industries with more emissions from those with less and also to separate higher-technology industries from lower-technology industries.

Countries were grouped according to their per capita incomes (since it is an important determinant of the valuation of environmental quality) and the relative levels of environmental quality they enjoy. The following abbreviations are used:

NA United States and Canada (assumed to have relatively low unit emissions and limited assimilative capacity)

9 From a theoretical point of view an Armington structure is inconsistent with the assumption that technologies are identical across regions. Nevertheless, in a model with aggregated flows, the assumption of imperfect substitutability between imports and domestically produced goods may be justified by the existence of discrepancies in the commodity compositions of trade and production flows.

OD Other Developed Countries (assumed to have relatively low unit emissions and limited assimilative capacity).

LI Low- and Middle-Income Countries (assumed to have relatively high unit emissions and abundant assimilative capacity).

For standard CGE models the calibration procedure is straightforward, but for the environmental portion of our model, calibration is complicated by the inadequacy of data, and specifically by the absence of markets for environmental quality.

Population, trade, demand and value added data were used to calibrate the model to 1986.[10]

Sectoral abatement costs as a percentage of total costs in NA were obtained from Lucas et al. (1992) and Low (1992b). Since data on abatement costs for consumption emissions were not available to us, we simply assumed that these costs are one-half of the abatement costs in the corresponding production sectors. For this specification, total abatement costs represent less than 1 per cent of GNP, which is in line with typical estimates (Low 1992a).

Although the choice of a reference abatement level is somewhat arbitrary, if we assume a 50 per cent abatement level in conjunction with a value of 1/3 for η (the elasticity of unit abatement costs with respect to proportional abatement), the resulting abatement cost schedules behave consistently with empirical findings.[11]

The parameters of damage functions are specified as follows. For global emissions we assume identical parameters for all regions. With respect to local emissions, we specify different scale coefficients in the various regions. These coefficients, k^{jL}, reflect the degree of dispersion of local emissions in the local environment and are likely to be different for different pollutants and to depend on the size and physical characteristics of the local environment. Since we were not able to find aggregate estimates for these coefficients, as a first approximation they were specified according to the formula $k^{jL} = \kappa^L (N^j)^{-\rho^{jL}}$, where N^j is the population of region j, and κ^L is a scaling parameter that is endogenously determined by our calibration procedure. Given this specification, if two regions of different size (and with an identical ρ^L) experienced local emissions that are in proportion to their respective population sizes, then they would experience the same level of local environmental damage. For the elasticities of damage with respect to emissions, we employ educated guesses based on a comparison of emission data with concentration levels for selected air and water pollutants in different regions (World Resources Institute 1990).

To calculate emission coefficients, we first compute marginal abatement costs, given our choice of η (see above) and for given unit abatement costs. Notice that our choice of functional form implies that marginal abatement cost is simply equal to average cost times $(1 + \eta)$. These marginal abatement costs provide an

10 Further details are available from the authors by request.

11 Maloney and Yandle (1984) focus on the price elasticity of demand for emission permits, which, given our specification of abatement costs, can be expressed as $\Omega = A/[\eta(1 - A)]$. For $A = 0.5$ and $\eta = 1/3$ one obtains $\Omega = 3$, which is consistent with their findings (they report values of 3 and above).

estimate of the implied emission charges (which equal the marginal benefit of abatement). We then employ an exogenous imputation scheme to obtain separate local and global emission charges.[12] For given domestic internalization rates, and assuming zero internalization rates for international spillovers, we can compute net emissions values per unit of output. Given reference abatement levels, we obtain gross emission values. We then arbitrarily choose units for physical emission so that, in the benchmark equilibrium, the marginal valuation in NA is equal to unity. We thus obtain physical sectoral unit coefficients of gross emissions, which we adopt for all regions.

Clearly, the absolute size of environmental externalities that we obtain through this process is crucially dependent on the choice of benchmark internalization rates: the higher the benchmark rate of internalization rate, the smaller the implied external effects in the benchmark equilibrium. Since no reliable estimate is available for the value of environmental damages generated by economic activities, any choice of internalization rates must by necessity be purely speculative. In order to reflect this indeterminacy, we choose a base case value of 0.33 for the domestic internalization rate in all regions and subsequently perform sensitivity analysis around this central value. Notice that assuming identical internalization rates for all regions does *not* contradict the idea that environmental controls are tighter in high-income countries, since, for a given internalization rate, emission charges and abatement levels will be higher in high-income regions, where the marginal valuation for environmental quality is higher.[13]

For the income elasticity of the marginal valuation of environmental quality, ω, the elasticity of marginal valuation of environmental quality with respect to environmental damage, ζ, and the elasticity of substitution between local and global environmental quality, σ, we select, respectively, central-case values of 1.0, 0.5, and 1. Although the available evidence on the parameters characterizing preferences for environmental quality is rather scant,[14] there seems to be an agreement that, given a certain level of environmental quality, its marginal valuation would be substantially higher in rich countries than in low- and middle-income countries. Given our choice of parameters, we obtain equilibrium values for the social marginal valuation of environmental quality in different regions that do not conflict with our prior beliefs: 1.0 for NA, 0.63 for OD, and 0.12 for LI.

For all production and abatement functions, as well as for the aggregation of domestic demand, we employ a Cobb-Douglas specification, which implies a unitary

12 For production emissions, we assume that local emissions charges account for 80 per cent of total emission charges. For consumption emissions, 100 per cent of emission charges are assumed to account for local emission charges in all sectors except EH, where this share is reduced to 80 per cent (to reflect the presence of taxes on consumption of fossil fuels).

13 This assumption, however, contradicts the observation that internalization rates appear to differ across countries by type of emission. For example, taxes on fossil fuels in the EEC are substantially higher than they are in North America, suggesting that the internalization rate for global emissions is higher in the EEC than in North America.

14 'Economists are as far now from placing a single dollar value on fishable water, unimpaired scenery, or other environmental phenomena as they were two decades ago, perhaps farther' (Braden and Kolstad 1991, 324).

elasticity of substitution. Finally, for the elasticity of substitution between domestically produced goods and imports we use a value of 2.5, while the elasticity of substitution between imports of different origin is made equal to 5 (see discussion in Jomini et al. 1991).

When the model is calibrated, a direct computation of benchmark emissions and abatement levels in all regions would require a previous knowledge of the values of the marginal valuations of environmental quality in all regions, which in turn depend on net emissions. This requirement forces us to resort to a simultaneous calibration procedure: all parameters are endogenized, and the model is augmented by a set of calibration restrictions. This augmented model, together with our assumed data and parameters, is sufficient to identify all the parameters of the model. The final step of our calibration procedure consists of solving the augmented model numerically to obtain a set of parameters that is consistent with our data set.[15] The calibration procedure is detailed in model documentation available from the authors.

V. SIMULATIONS AND RESULTS

We performed simulations with our model to assess the relative contribution of international trade (including trade policy changes) to environmental degradation and to explore the implications of environmental externalities for the size and distribution of the gains from trade liberalization. Specifically, we explore the effects on environmental quality and welfare of all combinations of the following trade-policy configurations:

1. Business as usual (current levels of environmental protection)
2. A move to full, global internalization (i.e., $\pi_D^j = 1$ and $\pi_X^j = 1$ in all regions)
3. Unilateral domestic environmental action by NA (i.e., $\pi_D^j = 1$ in NA);

   and of the following three trade-policy scenarios:

   a. Benchmark trade barriers (benchmark)
   b. A removal of all trade barriers (free trade)
   c. A three-fold increase in trade barriers (trade wars).

The results of our simulations for all cases are summarized in tables 1 and 2.[16] The rest of this section is devoted to a discussion of our findings. Some limited sensitivity analysis is presented in subsection 1.

At the benchmark levels of internalization, international trade does appear to have some negative impact on environmental quality. A move to free trade slightly

15 The model is conceived and solved using MPS/GE (Rutherford 1988).

16 The numbers in these tables should all be interpreted as percentage changes compared with the initial situation (benchmark trade barriers and benchmark internalization in all countries). Given our parameterization, in the benchmark equilibrium a 1 per cent increase in net emissions produces approximately a 1 per cent decrease in the level of environmental quality in the NA bloc. Admittedly, the figures representing changes in environmental quality cannot be given any cardinal interpretation, since in our model environmental quality is defined only in a conventional fashion; these figures, however, may provide information on the *relative* effects of different policies. Percentage welfare changes are computed as equivalent variations as a proportion of benchmark full income (income plus the value of environmental quality enjoyed by consumers).

TABLE 1
Per cent changes in combined environmental quality – central case

Region	NA	OD	LI
	Benchmark internalization		
Benchmark	0.0	0.0	0.0
Free trade	−1.3	−0.9	−0.7
Trade wars	+0.8	+0.5	+0.4
	Global internalization		
Benchmark	+95.9	+68.1	+39.4
Free trade	+95.5	+67.5	+39.5
Trade wars	+96.1	+68.6	+39.5
	Unilateral action by NA		
Benchmark	+45.7	+2.0	+2.3
Free trade	+44.5	+1.2	+1.7
Trade wars	+46.5	+2.5	+2.7

TABLE 2
Per cent welfare changes – central case

Region	NA	OD	LI
	Benchmark internalization		
Benchmark	0.0	0.0	0.0
Free trade	+0.4	+1.3	0.0
Trade wars	−1.1	−2.6	−1.6
	Global internalization		
Benchmark	+1.3	+0.8	+0.8
Free trade	+1.7	+2.2	+0.8
Trade wars	+0.2	−1.8	−0.8
	Unilateral action by NA		
Benchmark	+0.4	+0.1	+0.2
Free trade	+0.8	+1.4	+0.1
Trade wars	−0.7	−2.5	−1.4

worsens the environment, while an increase in trade barriers has a small but positive impact on the environment. Trade liberalization produces sizable welfare gains only for NA and OD. On the other hand, an increase in trade barriers has a substantial negative welfare impact on all regions.

Full internalization of all externalities causes marked improvements in environmental quality in all regions. All countries that fully internalize externalities experience an improvement in environmental quality of more than 39 per cent, regardless of the trade policy regime. By contrast, the improvement in environmental quality brought about by a move from free trade to a trade war is never more than 2 per cent. Full internalization also yields substantial welfare gains for all regions.

The most striking message of the results is that compared with environmental policies, trade policies have very little impact on environmental quality. This finding suggests that the relative contribution of international trade to environmental degradation is quite modest. Notice also that the size and the distribution of the gains from trade liberalization are not substantially affected by the change in environmental policies.

Unilateral domestic internalization by NA causes a marked improvement in NA environmental quality, but the addition of trade restrictions has virtually no added effect on environmental quality. However, trade restrictions still cause a large welfare loss. The idea that appropriate environmental policies, when implemented unilaterally, must be buttressed by trade restrictions is not supported by our results. Even though NA internalizes only the 'domestic' impact of the emissions, such a policy still produces a reduction in global emissions. As a result, the welfare of non-participants rises and their environmental quality improves.

The *qualitative* effect of trade policy on environmental quality is unrelated to the environmental policy regime. Liberalization causes small quality losses, and trade restriction causes small gains in environmental quality. In most cases, environmental quality is highest for all environmental policies when trade is restricted. In the LI region, virtually the same environmental quality is achieved when global internalization is combined with free trade as it is when it is combined with trade wars. In the other cases, the reduction in environmental quality caused by free trade is smallest (sometimes almost zero), however, when appropriate environmental policies are in place. Stated differently, the indirect negative impact of trade liberalization on environmental quality is likely to be smaller the higher the level of internalization of environmental externalities.

1. Sensitivity analysis

Given the acknowledged uncertainty about many of our parameters, we performed some limited sensitivity runs on two experiments (Global internalization and Trade Wars). The central case elasticities and alternate values used are reported in table 3. The choice of values was based on a number of considerations. First, where we had some evidence (as in the case of the elasticity of marginal abatement cost with respect to the degree of abatement), we used this evidence to choose the midpoint. Where there was no directly applicable evidence, we adopted values that seemed plausible. We also did a run corresponding to the case where the internalization rates in the developed regions are higher (0.5) than the low-middle income region (0.33). This run is reported in the last column of our sensitivity results. (See tables 4 and 5.)

The main message from the sensitivity runs is that the main conclusion of our analysis is robust to the range of parameters we tried. In all configurations, trade restrictions have relatively minor effects on environmental quality and cause significant welfare losses to all regions, whereas following appropriate environ-

TABLE 3
Parameter values used in sensitivity analysis

Parameter	LOW	CC	HIGH
Domestic internalization rate (π_D^j)	0.10	0.33	0.50
MAC w.r.t. degree of abatement (η)	0.25	0.33	0.50
Valuation w.r.t. income (ω)	0.95	1.00	1.05
Valuation w.r.t. damage (ζ)	0.25	0.50	0.75
Local-global substitution (σ)	0.85	1.00	1.15

TABLE 4
Sensitivity: global internalization

Environmental quality (per cent changes)

		π_D^j		η		ω		ζ		σ		$\pi_D^{NA,OD} = 0.5$
Region	CC	L	H	L	H	L	H	L	H	L	H	$\pi_D^{LI} = 0.33$
NA	95.9	100.0	77.2	98.5	91.7	97.4	94.2	49.9	132.3	95.9	95.8	81.7
OD	68.1	106.2	54.0	72.5	60.9	64.9	69.8	37.3	95.1	68.4	67.9	63.1
LL	39.4	42.8	38.1	43.0	34.1	32.3	43.9	21.7	54.5	39.9	39.1	50.5

Welfare (per cent changes)

		π_D^j		η		ω		ζ		σ		$\pi_D^{NA,OD} = 0.5$
Region	CC	L	H	L	H	L	H	L	H	L	H	$\pi_D^{LI} = 0.33$
NA	1.3	5.6	0.6	1.4	1.2	1.0	1.5	1.6	1.1	1.3	1.3	1.0
OD	0.8	5.4	0.3	0.9	0.7	0.6	1.0	1.0	0.7	0.8	0.8	0.7
LL	0.8	2.8	0.5	0.8	0.8	0.8	0.8	0.9	0.7	0.8	0.8	0.6

mental policies significantly improves environmental quality and raises economic welfare.

The analysis also identifies two parameters that are crucial to the analysis. The first is the domestic internalization rate (π_D^j). The lower the benchmark internalization rate, the higher the (welfare and environmental quality) returns to internalization. The other important parameter is the elasticity of marginal valuation with respect to damages. The higher this value is, the higher are the returns to liberalization as well.

2. Summary of results

Our numerical findings must be viewed as exploratory for a number of reasons, not least of which is our limited knowledge of precisely how environmental emissions affect the environment. The main qualifications to our results fall into the following categories.

TABLE 5
Sensitivity: trade wars

Environmental quality (per cent changes)

		π_D^j		η		ω		ζ		σ		$\pi_D^{NA,OD} = 0.5$
Region	CC	L	H	L	H	L	H	L	H	L	H	$\pi_D^{LI} = 0.33$
NA	0.8	0.8	0.8	0.8	0.8	0.8	0.8	0.6	0.9	0.8	0.8	0.6
OD	0.5	0.9	0.4	0.5	0.5	0.5	0.5	0.4	0.6	0.5	0.5	0.4
LL	0.4	0.4	0.4	0.4	0.4	0.3	0.4	0.3	0.5	0.4	0.4	0.3

Welfare (per cent changes)

		π_D^j		η		ω		ζ		σ		$\pi_D^{NA,OD} = 0.5$
Region	CC	L	H	L	H	L	H	L	H	L	H	$\pi_D^{LI} = 0.33$
NA	−1.1	−1.0	−1.1	−1.1	−1.1	−1.1	−1.1	−1.0	−1.1	−1.1	−1.1	−1.1
OD	−2.6	−2.4	−2.6	−2.6	−2.6	−2.6	−2.6	−2.5	−2.6	−2.6	−2.6	−2.6
LL	−1.6	−1.5	−1.6	−1.6	−1.6	−1.6	−1.6	−1.5	−1.6	−1.6	−1.6	−1.6

- *Parameters.* Our reading did not yield consensus values for a number of key parameters in the model, particularly those describing individual and social valuation of environmental quality, which crucially determine the size of the benefits of internalization.
- *Data.* Data on policy regimes, emissions and environmental quality are inadequate, particularly for the LI bloc.
- *Model structure.* Because of the static nature of our model, our results do not capture the potential effects of trade and environmental policies on industrial location and on technological change. The model is very highly aggregated.
- *Policy regime.* Both benchmark and counterfactual environmental policies are implemented as emission fees, which are at least cost effective and can be efficient. This regime contrasts with the actual policy regimes in many countries that employ inefficient regulatory schemes.

VI. SUMMARY AND CONCLUSION

The model developed in this paper represents an attempt to achieve a comprehensive treatment of local and global environmental externalities in a static framework and of their linkages with international trade. In spite of our efforts carefully to separate the various aspects of environmental externalities, our numerical findings must be viewed as exploratory, owing to our limited knowledge of precisely how environmental emissions impact on the environment. We also realize that two features of the model, perfect competition and capital immobility, are likely to dampen the impact of both trade and environmental policies. Even with these limitations, we believe that the results of our simulations shed some light on some fundamental questions concerning the linkages between environmental and trade policies.

Our results suggest that, although free trade may have a negative impact on environmental quality, its relative contribution to environmental degradation appears to be limited. Further, achieving significant environmental quality improvements via trade policy is likely to be extremely costly. This finding can be attributed to the following circumstances.

1. Trade accounts for a relatively small share of world production.
2. A large share of trade involves trade in environmentally 'clean' goods.
3. Estimates suggest that, even for 'dirty' traded goods, abatement costs account for a relatively modest share of total costs.

These facts contribute to our conclusion that trade restrictions are a very poor substitute for direct environmental protection.

Our experiments also indicate that the welfare gains from environmental protection are not significantly affected by changes in trade policies; at the same time, the size and distribution of the gains from trade liberalization are little affected by the presence of environmental externalities. These findings suggest that trade restrictions are not necessary companions to effective environmental policy, and that well-conceived environmental policies are unlikely to be disastrous in an open economy, as some appear to believe.

Protection of the environment is becoming a dominant concern in the design of economic policies, and our numerical results indeed suggest that the gains from increased environmental action may be very substantial. Nevertheless, the importance of coordinating trade and environmental policies should not be overstated. Even in the absence of international cooperation on environmental policies, the process of trade liberalization may promote a more efficient use of world resources.

REFERENCES

Ballard, Charles L., and Steven G. Medema 1988 (March) 'The efficiency effects of pigouvian taxes and subsidies: a computational general equilibrium approach. Paper presented at the NBER Applied General Equilibrium Workshop

Bhagwat, Jagdish (1981a) 'The generalized theory of distortions and welfare.' In Bhagwati (1981b)

— ed. (1981b) *International Trade: Selected Readings*, Second ed. (Cambridge, MA: MIT Press)

Blackhurst, Richard (1977) 'International trade and domestic environmental policies in a growing economy.' In *International Relations in a Changing World*, ed. R. Blackhurst et al. (Leiden: Sijthoff)

Braden, John B., and Charles D. Kolstad eds (1991) *Measuring the Demand for Environmental Quality* (New York: Elsevier Science Publishers)

Dewees, Donald N (1992) 'The efficiency of pursuing environmental quality objectives: the shape of damage functions.' Mimeo, Department of Economics, University of Toronto, June

Forster, B.A. (1981) Separability, functional structure and aggregation for a class of

models in environmental economics.' *Journal of Environmental Economics and Management* 8, 118–33
Jomini, Patrick, et al. (1991) *SALTER: A General Equilibrium Model of the World Economy – Volume 1: Model Structure, Database and Parameters.* Study undertaken by the Industry Commission for the Department of Foreign Affairs and Trade
Low, Patrick, ed. (1992a) *International Trade and the Environment* (Washington DC: International Bank for Reconstruction and Development)
— (1992b) 'Trade measures and environmental quality: the implications for Mexico's exports.' In Low (1992a)
Lucas, Robert E.B., David Wheeler, and Hemamala Hettig (1992) 'Economic development, environmental regulation and the international migration of toxic industrial pollution: 1960–88.' In Low (1992a)
Maloney, M.T., and B. Yandle (1984) 'Estimation of the cost of air pollution control regulation. *Journal of Environmental Economics and Management* 11, 244–63
Pethig, R. (1976) 'Pollution, welfare, and environmental policy in the theory of comparative advantage.' *Journal of Environmental Economics and Management 3*, 160–69
Radetzki, Marian (1992) 'Economic growth and the environment.' In Low (1992a)
Rutherford, Thomas Fox (1988) 'General equilibrium modelling with *MPS/GE*.' Paper, Department of Economics, University of Western Ontario
Shrybman, Steven (1990) 'International trade and the environment: an environmental assessment of the General Agreement on Tariffs and Trade.' *Ecologist* 20, 30–4
Siebert, Horst (1977) 'Environmental quality and the gains from trade.' *KYKLOS* 30, 657–73
Tietenberg, Tom (1991) *Environmental and Natural Resource Economics*, third ed. (Harper Collins)
Whalley, John (1991) 'The interface between environmental and trade policies.' *Economic Journal* 101, 180–9
World Resources Institute (1990) *World Resources, 1990–1991* (London: Oxford University Press)

[4]

The environment, international trade and competitiveness

Richard H. Snape

Interconnection between international trade issues and the environment is coming increasingly into focus. The Montreal Protocol (regarding the depletion of the ozone layer) and international conventions on whaling, hazardous wastes, and endangered species, relate to internationally traded products and provide for international trade measures to aid enforcement (Harris, 1991). International trade in rainforest and other products with world-wide environmental implications is receiving much attention and many calls are being made for its restriction. Meanwhile there is concern in industries in countries with tough environmental controls about competition from those without such controls.

A substantial and well-known literature has examined 'domestic distortions', including externalities from production and consumption, and the policy implications in an international trade context.[1] The environment as such has not featured strongly in these works explicitly, but adverse effects on the environment are leading examples of externalities. The chapter in this volume by Lloyd surveys more recent developments in the literature on the ranking of policy instruments in the context of pollution.

What this literature in the main has not addressed is internationally transmitted externalities. In one sense the international aspect is irrelevant. That is, if a particular policy is optimal from the efficiency perspective, then that policy will still be optimal whether or not the effects cross national borders.

However that is not the end of the internationality issue. As compared with economic activity and externalities which are wholly domestic, there are two extra dimensions in an international context. This is true whether it is the products which are traded internationally, or the externalities which are transmitted internationally, or both.

First, there is an additional set of policy instruments with which to address the problem, namely, international trade policies. Second, an additional jurisdiction is involved. The optimal intervention literature referred to above addresses the 'additional policy instrument' aspect and concludes that, from a first-best perspective, policies directed at international trade are not appropriate instruments with which to attack externalities. But when externalities are exported, the options available to those who are affected may be quite limited. This is one aspect of the jurisdiction question.

Another jurisdictional consideration is that of property rights and liability for damage. Which country has the right or obligation to regulate or tax economic activities which generate externalities when either the product or the externality is crossing international frontiers? Undefined property rights or liability for damage is inimical to economic efficiency, as is well known in the problem of the commons. It is usually more difficult to define and enforce property rights and liability internationally than nationally.

The 'polluter pays principle' is often advanced as a principle for liability, giving property rights for a clean environment to the polluted. Such a principle gives rights of compensation to the latter, or perhaps permits taxation or regulation of the polluter. The question has additional importance in an international context not only because of the possibility of clashes between legislatures and jurisdiction but because the tax revenues or the economic rents which arise from regulation can be substantial. The international distribution of who gains or loses from restricting pollution, for example, can hinge on who obtains these revenues.

The question and the analysis of who compensates whom was addressed by Coase in his celebrated paper (Coase, 1960). The international aspects parallel much of his analysis, which focused on localized nuisances, most of quite specific incidence. The jurisdictional relationships between governments considered here have much in common with his examples of relationships between individuals.

An objective of this chapter is to highlight and explore international aspects of environmental externalities using very simple models. The assumptions underlying the models presented have been chosen in such a way as to maximize the likelihood that trade will be an appropriate instrument of intervention. By then gradually relaxing these assumptions the analysis exposes the general inefficiency of trade policies in addressing environmental concerns. However, there may be situations in which, in the absence of the international definition of property rights and liability, trade policies are the only policy instruments available to a country to address a particular environmental problem. While there are some situations in which revenue from a pollution tax may provide the incentive for a government to take internationally beneficial action unilaterally (without the necessity for an international agreement), it is possible that in the absence of an international agreement a country may use the opportunity to move the terms of trade optimally in its favour (thus reducing world income, particularly if other countries retaliate).

Before summarizing and concluding the chapter, some 'competitiveness' problems associated with environmental controls and taxes are addressed as they are becoming of ever-greater concern to many industries and governments.

4.1 Trade policies and pollution

This section is concerned with internationally traded products which have environmental implications, and particularly with those resource and environmental problems which spill over from one country to another. The distinction in practice between national and international problems is not always clear, but the discussion concentrates mainly on those activities and policies which have identifiable effects on other countries. Thus acid rain, ozone depletion, whale extermination, nuclear fallout, rain-forest destruction, the use of pesticides in the production of products traded internationally or which pollute international waters, and carbon dioxide emissions which affect the world's climate, are all conceptually included, as are environmental policies affecting internationally traded goods. However, pollution of a local river from which internationally traded goods or services are not produced is not included.

In examining policies which may be adopted by governments for environmental or conservation reasons, it is important to identify the source of the problem. Is it the commonality of a resource which is the essence of a problem? Recognizing this commonality and dealing with it may provide the best approach from an international perspective, though not necessarily so from the perspective of every country. Is it the production of a product itself or its production processes which is of concern? If it is production itself which is the cause of the problem, reduction of production is appropriate. If it is a production process, then it is the process which needs to be addressed. If consumption of particular products is damaging the environment (e.g. some pressure-pack propellants), then consumption should be focus of attention for policy purposes.

As noted, while the division of the world into nations introduces the possibility of problems spilling over from one jurisdiction to another, it also provides another set of policy instruments: those associated with international trade. It also magnifies greatly income distribution problems associated with policies aimed at the efficient use of the world's resources. While within a country there are mechanisms for dealing with income distribution questions, any such mechanisms on the international arena are generally *ad hoc.*[2] Whalley and Wigle (1990) bring out the importance of the distribution question in a general equilibrium model in which they estimate that the tax revenue raised from carbon taxes designed to reduce world carbon emissions by 50 per cent would amount to 10 per cent of world gross product (see also Whalley, 1991).

To simplify the exposition the term 'pollution' is used to cover all external diseconomies referred to, and it is assumed that it is related to production, not consumption.[3] Thus 'pollution' is any activity which imposes costs on others in a manner which is not communicated efficiently by a market or a market substitute. (Such a market substitute may be a social norm – see Dasgupta, 1990). We assume that the pollution costs can be measured. This is an heroic assumption for it assumes not only that costs which one firm's activities impose on other firms, and which are not transmitted by the pricing mechanism, can be valued but also that the costs which are imposed on people generally (for example by the loss of a beautiful forest) also can be valued. Heroic or not, such valuations are made explicitly or implicitly all the time, for example, when it is decided to build a road in one location rather than another. For the purpose of analysis, these valuations must be made explicit though this should not blind one to the difficulty of placing even rough measures on the values in practice.

Initially it is assumed that the pollution is generated by production of a particular product and not by the use of a particular productive process. It is also assumed that property rights regarding the environment are not well defined or that transactions costs for those who have the rights are large enough to prevent them from being exercised. We also initially assume away 'government failure' problems in the levying of taxes or the imposition of restrictions.

In a closed economy, it is clear that either production or consumption of a product causing pollution could be restricted: the effects would be the same. The appropriate restriction will be one which brings into equality marginal social costs and marginal social valuation of the product, but the restriction (which could be induced through a tax) could be imposed on the producer or on the consumer. In practice it may be simpler administratively to impose it on one or the other, but that is a second-stage decision. Tax revenue would flow to the tax authority for use as the government saw fit. It may be most efficient to have marketable permits to pollute or to consume polluting products, so as to allow individual producers or consumers to evaluate the options.

Now turning to international trade and pollution, from a world efficiency perspective it is clear that it is again irrelevant whether the producers of the polluting production are induced to reduce production or the consumers of the polluting product are induced to reduce consumption. However, the incentive for a government to take such action in the interests of its nationals varies according to where the pollution 'falls' (meaning the location where the pollution costs are experienced) and which countries are producing and consuming the relevant product. This will now be explored in a series of very simple models. To anticipate a result which may appear paradoxical, it is shown that a country which is having pollution dumped on it by production abroad can be worse off if the global optimal tax on pollution is imposed by the polluting country, or by an international authority, than if no action were to be taken, even though world real income would be raised by such action. On the other hand it would be better off if it took the action itself. This result could also occur if it is a production process, including the use of a particular factor of production, which causes the pollution. Similarly, if importing countries restrict imports of products which pollute the exporting country (and this includes excessive felling of timber, for example), this may be judged harmful to the exporting country even if everyone is of one mind regarding the measurement of the environmental costs and agrees that it is in the world's interest that production be reduced.

When countries impose taxes or production restrictions on goods which are traded internationally, terms of trade changes bring gains or losses of real income to countries. To suppress as far as possible the terms of trade effects associated with changes in the level of production and consumption of the product in question in order to focus on pollution *per se*, constant costs of production are assumed initially. It is also assumed initially that the costs associated with a 'unit' of pollution are the same irrespective of the country in which the pollution falls and that is a constant cost of pollution per unit of output.[4] Competitive conditions are assumed in production and consumption. In all cases the relevant policies are applied so as to maximize global income.

4.1.1 *Constant costs of production and pollution*

4.1.1.1 Pollution falls only on the polluting country

Let us consider the optimum economic policy where a country A is producing, at constant cost, the polluting product (pollution being at a given rate per unit of output) and all the production is exported to country B and there are no other potential buyers. Country B does not produce the good nor does it import it from any other source. Assume also that all the pollution costs are contained within country A.

In Figure 4.1, $S(p)$ shows the private marginal and average costs of production and $S(s)$ shows the real or social costs of production, the difference between $S(p)$ and $S(s)$ being the costs of pollution. D is the demand curve in country B for the product. In the absence of any production, consumption or trade restrictions, OQ is the level of production, consumption and trade. While it is profitable for the producers in A to produce the good, for they earn a normal profit, A's real national product properly measured would be increased if production were to cease, for the revenue received by A does not cover real costs.[5] Despite the incentive for A to cease production, from an international point of view it may be desirable that A continues to produce it. This will be so as long as HBA (the consumers' surplus

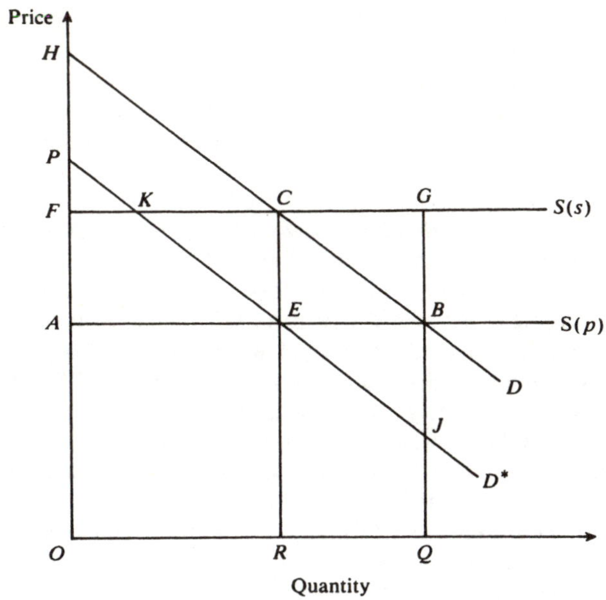

Figure 4.1 Effects of abating pollution from production with constant costs

in B) exceeds *FGBA* (the loss of real income in A arising from its production), that is, if *HCF* exceeds *CGB* (assuming equal welfare weights for residents of the two countries). But let us assume that pollution consciousness has not yet arisen and production exists. By not restricting exports A is effectively subsidizing production, for the benefit of B.

Now let us introduce pollution consciousness. The optimal policy from a world perspective would be for a restriction on production or consumption (or, in this case where all the production is traded internationally, on international trade) to a level *OR*. Should a tax be used to achieve that restriction it would be at a rate appropriate to the marginal generation of the pollution, *AF*/*OA*. Whichever country imposes the tax, the price of the product will increase in B by the full amount of the tax, to *OF*, while the price net of tax will remain constant in A. The incidence of the tax is thus wholly on B, due to the constant cost assumption. Production, consumption and international trade will be *RQ* units less than before. If A imposed the tax (on production or exports) it will gain by the tax revenue *FCEA* plus the reduction in production multiplied by the excess of social over private costs, *CGBE* (= *FGBA*). As there is no pollution in B, B loses by the new level of consumption multiplied by the price increase, *FCEA* (which is the tax revenue collected by A) plus the excess of consumers' valuation of the reduced consumption over its cost to B (that is, *CBE*). The world gain is *CGB*, the excess of the social (or real) cost of the quantity *RQ* over the valuation of it.

If B had imposed the tax (on consumption or imports) and retained the revenue then B would have borne only the *CBE* part of its cost and A would have gained only to the extent of the reduced production times the extent of the pollution, *CGBE*. However, now that pollution consciousness has arisen, A's government has an incentive to ban production unless it receives at least the price *OF*. Thus B would need to pay A the amount *FCEA* to produce the output *OR* if B imposed the tax. Whoever taxes, then, the outcome is the same: there is a loss of *FCBA* to B and a gain of *FGBA* to A, leaving a net world gain of *CGB*. While A might gain by restricting output (or exports) to a level below *OR*, this would not be optimal from a global viewpoint and thus is not considered further.

If an international authority had levied the tax (and retained it), A's gain would have been *CGBE* compared with no intervention, the same as if B had taxed. B's loss would be *FCBA*, the same as if A had taxed. But again A would have no incentive to produce unless it were to be compensated.

The situation would have been similar if quantitative controls had been used rather than taxes, except that the revenue associated with quantitative controls would not necessarily have passed to the governments of A or B: who received the benefit of the restrictions within countries would, as usual, depend on who received the entitlements to produce, trade, or consume under a regime of restriction. But then we have been implicitly assuming that tax revenues generate utility in the country receiving them; at this level of analysis one can make the same assumption regarding the economic rents arising from production restrictions, and assume also that real resources are not wasted in the pursuit of the economic rents or the benefits of the tariff revenues.

4.1.1.2 Pollution falls only on the consuming country

Assume now that the costs of the pollution associated with A's production of the commodity are felt entirely by B: the pollution falls entirely on B. Still using Figure 4.1, we now interpret $S(p)$ as the private and social cost of production to A and the private cost to purchasers in B of buying the product. D is the demand curve in B for the product, reflecting private valuations of the product. D^* is below D by the extent of the pollution costs to B from A's production, which is solely for B's consumption. (The assumption that the pollution externality is the same per unit irrespective of which country it falls in is a convenience but is of no other significance at this stage.) As B is the sole consumer, there is again, from a world efficiency point of view, no difference between A and B imposing taxes on consumption, production, or trade: the world efficiency gain will again be *CGB*, which is equal to *EBJ*.

If A levies the tax it gains by the tax revenue, *FCEA*, this being a net gain due to the assumption of constant costs. That is, it has obtained a terms of trade gain.[6] If A levies the tax, B gains *EBJ* (the excess of cost of the quantity *RQ* over the true valuation of it as shown by the curve D^*) but loses *FCEA*, the additional cost to it of the remaining consumption of *OR*, which equals the tax revenue in A. The net gain to B could be negative, even though A is taking the action to restrict the pollution which A is causing and which is all falling on B! However, as far as B is concerned it is possible that some tax by A is better than no tax, even though B might be worse off if the optimal tax from a world point of view were imposed. For world efficiency it does not matter who taxes. But if the polluter taxes according to the damage it is causing others, the others may be worse off. And, just as in the case in which A was receiving the pollution, it may be in A's interest to ban production even though the product is desirable from a global point of view and profitable for its producers, in this case it may in B's interest to ban consumption (or imports) if A receives the tax revenue, even though it is in the global interest for the product to exist. (This situation would exist if the tax revenue *FCEA* exceeded the true consumers' surplus, *PEA*; that is, if *KCE* exceeded *PKF*.) If A paid B at least the amount by which the tax revenue exceeded the true consumers' surplus, it would be worthwhile for B to continue consuming it.

If B levies the tax it has the efficiency gain in reducing consumption to the point at which the true marginal valuation of the product to it is equal to its cost, and it retains the tax revenue to balance against the additional cost to its consumers of the remaining consumption. Its net gain is *EBJ*. There is no gain or cost to A due to the constant cost assumption; A will receive the same net price but on a lower level of sales. But the government of A could now perceive an opportunity for gain: if it imposed the tax it would capture the tax revenue from B. Tax warfare could develop.

As before, if an international authority levies the tax and retains it, the situation for A is the same as if B levies it, and for B the same as if A levies it. And, as before, the analysis is essentially unchanged if quantitative barriers to production, consumption, or trade are imposed at the level *OR*: the outcome depends on which country imposes the restriction and who captures the revenue.

4.1.1.3 Pollution falls only on a third country

Consider a situation where A and B are as before but all the pollution falls on C who neither produces nor consumes the product. Again there are no other relevant countries. Only C has an incentive to seek a reduction of the pollution but C has no benefit from the product. C has an incentive to pay A to reduce production, and due to the constant cost assumption would be able to secure cessation of production at a very low cost. As A could obtain a terms of trade gain (at the expense of B) from reducing production, A may be very willing to use pollution as a justification to reduce (though not cease) production. But B would then have an incentive to pay A to raise (or continue) production. B would also have an incentive to compensate C for the pollution damage it suffers in order to discourage C from bribing A not to produce: such an arrangement would be Pareto-optimal. Interesting strategies could result.

4.1.2 *Increasing costs of production and pollution*

We now allow for increasing costs of production in country A and also for the pollution cost per unit of production to rise with the level of production. Other simplifying assumptions are retained, including that the cost of pollution is the same whichever country suffers the consequences of the pollution. Again it is irrelevant from the point of view of world efficiency whether consumption, production or trade is restricted. The terms of trade will change with the level of production this time, and there is scope for each country (and not just A) to impose traditional 'optimum' restrictions on international trade in order to secure the gains from trade restrictions. Such actions of course reduce world income, and we shall again assume that they are not adopted. Instead we focus only on the restriction of production, consumption, or trade which would correct the pollution distortion, and on the income distribution and incentive effects of this correction.

4.1.2.1 Pollution falls only on the polluting country

In Figure 4.2, $S(p)$ and $S(s)$ are private and social marginal costs of production, respectively, and $S(p)$ is also the supply curve to B, while the D and D^* curves are as in Figure 4.1. The optimum reduction of production is from OQ to OR. This will bring a world efficiency gain HGB, equal to the excess of the social cost of the production QR (in A) over the valuation of that quantity of product in B. This reduction can be achieved by a per unit tax of EA/OE yielding tax revenue of $ABCE$. To analyse the importance of the tax revenue in gains and costs, it is convenient to assume initially that a tax is levied by an international authority, and that the authority retains the tax revenue. We then can observe the difference that collection of the tax revenue would make to A or B.

With the pollution falling on A the net loss of consumers' surplus in B is $ABJF + BGJ$, while the real gain of producers' surplus to A is $HGJB$ (the excess of the social cost of production over revenue on the output RQ) minus $FJCE$ (the loss of revenue on the remaining output OR). The net overall gain for the two countries then is $BHG - ABCE$, the latter term being the tax revenue which we have assumed is held by an international authority. This shows that without the tax revenue, each country could be

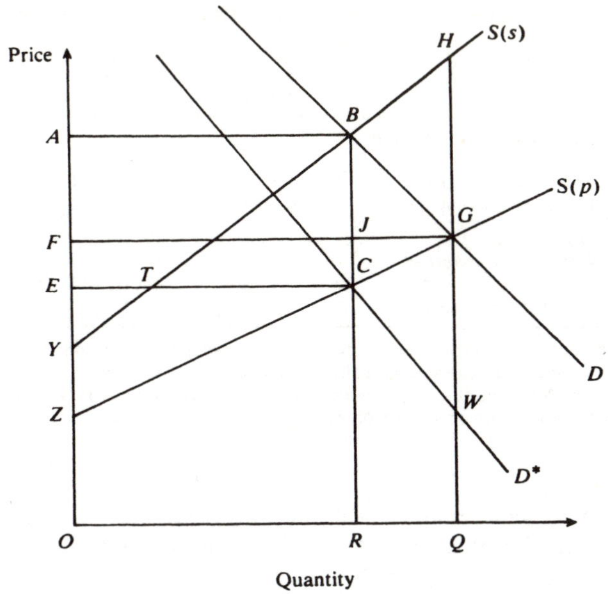

Figure 4.2 Effects of abating pollution from production with increasing costs

worse off: B certainly is and A may be. If B imposes the tax its loss is reduced to *BGJ* – *FJCE*, which could be negative (that is, a gain) though not necessarily so. That is, B may, as in the previous case, be worse off as compared with no tax whichever party imposes the tax, but will be better off if it imposes the tax than if A does.

While it is clearly desirable from a world point of view for the product to exist when the output is restricted to *OR* (the quantity at which the marginal social costs and valuations are equal) and it is profitable for A's producers to produce at this level (producers' surplus with respect to private costs is *ECZ*), again A may raise its real national income by not producing the good unless it receives the tax revenue. This is because the 'true' producers' surplus (that is, with respect to social costs of production) is *ETY* – *TBC*, which could be negative.[7] But it is no longer necessary for it to receive all the revenue to justify continuation of production.

4.1.2.2 Pollution falls only on the consuming country

When the pollution produced by A falls only on B, we can again use Figure 4.2. As in Figure 4.1 the D^* curve differs from the demand curve *D* by the pollution per unit of production (i.e. consumption) and D^* shows

Table 4.1 Summary of gains and losses from taxing polluting production

	A taxes production	B taxes consumption
(1) *Constant costs of production and pollution*:		
(a) Pollution falls on A	A+ B−	A+ B−
(b) Pollution falls on B	A+ B+/−	A0 B+
(2) *Increasing costs of production and pollution*:		
(a) Pollution falls on A	A+ B−	A+/− B+/−
(b) Pollution falls on B	A+/− B+/−	A+/− B+

Note: Country A produces the product and the associated pollution. The sign + indicates a real income gain for a country; − indicates a real income loss for a country; +/− indicates a real income gain or loss; and 0 indicates no change in real income.

the marginal social valuations of each level of consumption. $S(p)$ shows the marginal costs of producing in A and the supply curve to B. The world gain from the reduction of consumption, production, and trade to *OR* is again *HGB* and this is equal to the area *GCW*.[8]

Again assuming initially that the revenue is collected by an international authority, the gain of real consumers' surplus (that is with respect to the social valuation curve D^*) in B is $GWC - ABJF$ while the loss of producers' surplus in A is $FJCE + JGC$. And again without obtaining the tax revenue each country could be worse off as compared with no intervention, A necessarily being so in this situation. With the tax revenue B would be better off than with no intervention, while A may be if it receives the revenue. B has therefore an incentive to tax if it receives the revenue; A may not have such an incentive even if it receives the revenue, but will have an incentive if the alternative is for B to impose the tax or restriction.

4.1.2.3 Pollution falls only on a third country

Where the pollution falls on C, a non-producing, non-consuming country, the situation is very similar to the constant-cost case. C has an incentive to seek reduction of the polluting production, but no means to do it other than persuasion or payments to the others to do so. Because both A and B, in this case, would obtain a terms of trade gain from reducing trade below the free-trade level, they may be easily persuaded to do so, though the trade reduction which secured the optimum world output would only fortuitously be that which was, from a national point of view, also the income-maximizing trade reduction.

Table 4.1 summarizes the situations analysed above where there are two countries. In all situations it is important to note that world income increases, for we have assumed the optimum restrictions from a world efficiency point of view. Thus if one country loses the other must gain, and its gain exceeds the first country's loss.

4.1.3 *Property rights*

In this analysis there is a similarity with the property rights question as formulated by Coase (1960). As in Coase's analysis and with the absence of transaction costs, the efficiency question is independent of whether the polluter has the right to pollute, on the one hand, or whether the pollutee has a right not to be polluted, on the other. In the situations we have analysed above, there are two relevant property rights questions: whether polluters have the right to pollute internationally and which country has the right to tax or otherwise restrict ('tax', for short). But also important is which country has an incentive to tax. In each case above, and concentrating on pollution rather than conventional terms of trade considerations, it is only the polluted country which has a clear and general primary (rather than retaliatory, or defensive) reason to tax. If the polluted country is a producer or a consumer it has tax weapons available, but if it is neither it can only use bribery or persuasion. If the country producing or consuming the product is not being polluted, it only has a general incentive to tax if the alternative is that the other party, or an international authority will do so if it does not. (Again, this is setting on one side the terms of trade gains that exist quite separately from the pollution.)

It might seem reasonable through an international agreement to oblige polluters to restrict polluting production, that is, to give taxation property rights to them and oblige them to tax or otherwise restrict polluting production. But to do so could make countries which consume the product worse off than without restrictions, even if the pollution were all falling on the consuming countries. The incentives would be better in these simple cases if the taxation 'property rights' were to be allocated to the polluted, though this right could not be exercised where the pollution falls on countries which are neither significant producers nor consumers. An international agreement determining rights and liability could settle who has rights to compensation and tax.

It was noted earlier that marketable entitlements to pollute (or be polluted), or to consume polluting products, may be an efficient form of restriction. But where the pollution is international, which government has the right to issue licences? Agreement for an international authority to issue them could be warranted if an appropriate incentive mechanism could be devised.

As restriction of pollution to the appropriate level will increase world real income, those countries that gain from such restriction would in principle be able to compensate those that lose from it. Such compensation could involve those who are polluted paying those that pollute, even if the pollution all falls on other countries. The moral hazard incentives which such compensation may provide for the adoption of production processes which are not the most pollution-efficient from a world perspective, could argue against such international compensation.

4.2 Trade restrictions to protect the environment?

From the analysis above it appears that a case could be made for countries to restrict imports or exports of those products causing pollution. In all the cases considered, world real income would be increased by such actions, though the incentives to levy the taxes would depend on where the pollution fell. The analysis was set in a framework that incorporated assumptions most favourable to the use of import and export restrictions as policy options. As such assumptions are relaxed, import and export restrictions become less appropriate and/or more complicated to apply. We now examine some of the implications of relaxing the assumptions.

4.2.1 *Import restrictions*

First, the smaller the proportion of the polluting production which is imported by countries imposing import restrictions, the less effective will their import restrictions be and (while imports continue) the more costly to the importing country will be the restrictions on imports. If B and C are importing the product from A while all the pollution is falling on B, and B restricts its imports, then because the world price of the product will tend to fall as B reduces its imports, consumption in C will tend to rise (as it will in A also if A is consuming the product as well as producing it). Thus there is not a one-to-one relation between B's reduction in imports and the reduction of polluting production. Where there are many importing countries, even if all are bearing pollution costs, the relatively small importers will have an incentive to free-ride on the restrictions of the others. They will obtain lower import prices from the restrictions of others while their own import restrictions would have negligible effects on production and therefore on the pollution they are receiving.

Second, if importing countries on which pollution is falling also produce the product, and if their production pollutes themselves, then it is clear that restrictions on both imports and production (that is, on consumption) are appropriate. Restricting imports alone will stimulate domestic production and while there may be some pollution gain (for total consumption would fall with the higher domestic price) again the gain would be bought at a higher price than in the cases covered in the previous section. On the other hand if the pollution from importing countries' production falls on other countries, the importing countries do not bear the pollution cost of extra production and have an incentive to restrict imports but not production.

Third, we need to consider the case where production in all countries is not equally polluting. For world efficiency, production should be located so that the marginal cost (including in this the global pollution cost) is equalized in all the locations. This would require restrictions on imports (if import restriction is to be the policy instrument – though as already noted, it is production restriction which would be more appropriate) which differentiate according to source. But importing countries would have an incentive to differentiate according to the effects of pollution on themselves, not on the world as a whole. The problem becomes more complex when we allow that not all locations, producers, or production processes within a country may be equally polluting, so that import restrictions would have to differentiate between all of these. If it is a particular production process rather than production *per se* which causes pollution, neither trade nor production restrictions will address the real problem and provide the right incentives: it is the process itself or the pollution itself which needs to be addressed.

It is well known by economists that an import restriction is not an optimal policy instrument to use against production-generated pollution and that the incentives for countries to use them to combat pollution are haphazardly associated with the true costs and sources of pollution. But what weapons does a country have available to it, if it is being polluted by other countries? Paying others not to pollute is one, but we have already noted the moral hazard problems associated with this. So in the absence of international agreements with effective compliance (which generally means effective enforcement mechanisms), measures against imports comprise about the only economic instrument available to countries being polluted by others. (Measures against imports other than those which cause the pollution are a possibility also.) So in some situations import restrictions may be the only instrument available to increase national, and world, income.

4.2.2 *Export restrictions*

The situation is somewhat simpler with respect to export restrictions, whether the pollution falls on the polluting country or on others. Here it is obvious that it is production restrictions rather than export restrictions which are really appropriate, or restrictions on particular production processes or on production in particular areas, depending on the source of the problem. Restricting exports when there is domestic consumption (including processing) of the product will have a cushioned effect on production in that it will stimulate domestic consumption.

4.3 Competitiveness

The analysis in the previous two sections looked at the correction of the effects of external diseconomies in a manner designed to raise real world income. It also examined the international income distribution implications of these actions, and the consequential incentive effects for governments which were attempting to increase their own countries' real incomes. Individual firms do not see matters from this perspective. They see taxes on polluting production and requirements to satisfy environmental regulations as affecting their ability to compete on the world stage, and naturally are likely to attempt to influence policy. Partly under this influence and partly for mercantilist and 'strategic' trade policy reasons (including the moving of the terms of trade favourably for their own countries), governments also are much concerned for the competitiveness of their countries' industries on world markets.

It is clear that taxation or other restrictions on a polluting industry which is engaged in international trade will make it more difficult for that industry to compete. One view of the matter is expressed in Shrybman (1990):

> For a country wanting to maintain stringent environmental standards, while not undermining the competitiveness of its domestic industry, the choices are simple: (a) Establish import tariffs to offset pollution costs so that domestic producers will not be at a disadvantage when competing with imports from jurisdictions without similar environmental regulation, or: (b) Subsidize the cost of environmental protection with general revenues by underwriting pollution control costs.

In looking at this we need to distinguish between production- and consumption-generated pollution. If the pollution arises from *consumption* then domestically produced and imported products should be treated equally. An appropriate policy would be a consumption tax on the product or on the component generating the pollution, and this could be imposed directly on consumption or by means of matching taxes on production and imports.

It is more likely, however, that it is *production*-generated pollution which is of concern. In this case, the general concern is to compensate domestic producers for costs which they are required to bear but which their foreign competitors are not. This principle could have very widespread implications. On the one hand, different countries have different 'absorptive capacities' for pollution, and the real impacts of effluent on the environment, for example, vary greatly between countries. The absorptive capacity of the local environment is a resource in the production process similar to the amount of sunlight, the quality of labour, and the fertility and abundance of the local soil. If firms are compensated for different costs relating to the absorptive capacity of the environment, should they also be compensated for other natural disadvantages? Secondly, demand for environmental protection varies greatly between countries and typically grows with income (Pearce *et al.*, 1989). Thirdly, environmental control is one of many forms of legislation which differs across countries and for which producers may seek compensation. Minimum wages, labour laws, industrial health practices, and maternity, paternity and military leave, are examples of others. Application of the principle could easily explode into a proliferation of barriers to counter every sort of legislative and natural resource advantage.

If the objective is to secure efficient levels of output with all production costs taken into account, property rights can be with polluters or the polluted (assuming no transaction costs), as Coase (1960) established. But offsetting the costs by means of tariffs or by subsidies will sustain the level of output even though it may be efficient to curtail it. The line of argument usually followed by economists is that environmental costs are real costs incurred by firms in the productive process and that to increase real income these external costs should be brought to bear on those activities which generate them. (One form in which costs can be brought to bear is the opportunity cost of refusing to abate pollution when compensation is offered for this abatement.) The allocation of property rights can determine who should pay whom but it does not change the existence of these costs. While the costs would impair the firm's ability to compete on international markets, so be it: the costs are just as much real costs as those of labour and raw materials. Bringing the pollution costs to bear on the production activity which generates them will discourage production of those products in which a country does not have a true comparative advantage and thereby encourage production of those things in which it does have such an advantage.

There is thus an essential difference between (a) requiring pollution abatement and compensating for it, and (b) polluters compensating the polluted or the polluted offering payment to stop pollution. Under the alternatives in (b) the costs are brought to bear on the decision of whether or not to pollute. Under (a) the costs are not brought to bear on the production and pollution decision: there is no incentive to adjust production and pollution in the light of all the costs. Of course if it is consumption which generates pollution it is the consumption decision on which, for efficiency, the full costs should be brought to bear.

Compensation to producers for required environmental protection costs can be viewed as a payment from the polluted – society at large – to the polluter to reduce pollution. In the common situation in which the property rights regarding the rights to pollute or not-to-be-polluted have not been well defined in the past, polluters may very well argue that they purchased the right to discharge in an area when they purchased the property, or at least that they have as much right to discharge as other people have the right not to be discharged upon. Such arguments may lead to society at large bearing at least some of the cost of pollution reduction, but efficiency requires that the full costs be brought to bear on the production decision. Within a society, whether or not to offer compensation is a question of the internal distribution of income and wealth, not a question of international trade – except to the extent that the pollution spills abroad, or that other governments react to these subsidies through countervailing import duties, for example.[9]

Should this principle be applied internationally? It would imply that those countries receiving pollution should pay others to desist or to install abatement equipment. Again there are moral hazard problems, together with what could be an extraordinarily complex system of payments.

4.4 Summary and conclusions

This chapter has emphasized the international income distribution implications of controlling the environmental effects of economic activities, a matter that intertwines with, though is conceptually distinct from, the traditional national terms of trade gains achievable when trade is restricted. In restricting adverse environmental effects world welfare can be increased, but in doing so significant redistributions of income may occur according to which country(-ies) introduces the policies to contain environmental damage. (In contrast, trade restrictions to obtain traditional terms of trade gains lower world real income as well as redistributing it.)

It is shown that it is quite possible for a country which is inflicting environmental damage on other countries to reduce welfare in those other countries when it restricts this damage, even though this restriction raises world welfare. This arises from a terms of trade effect and is reflected in the collection of the tax revenue (or economic rent) by the country causing the damage. It is a result which underscores the importance of the question of who is collecting the environmental tax revenue.

If those countries which are suffering environmental damage are able to secure optimal (from a world point of view) production reductions of the activities causing the damage, they will gain from taking this action provided there is a close relation between the policy instrument they are using to achieve this reduction and the resulting production reduction. Where this damage is being inflicted by their own producers, a tax on production would be an appropriate policy. But where producers are inflicting damage on other countries, import or consumption restrictions by the latter countries on the product causing the damage may have little impact on the activity which is damaging their environment, yet the restrictions will have costs for the country imposing them. If there is a one-to-one relation between import or consumption restrictions on the one hand, and production of the product which is damaging the environment on the other hand, import or consumption restrictions (at an appropriate level) will be beneficial to those imposing them. The looser is this connection, however, the less likely that such restrictions will raise real income.

International trade policies thus are not appropriate instruments to use for countering those who exploit the world's resources, including environmental resources, inefficiently. Using them for this purpose will nearly always reduce global welfare. But, in some limited circumstances, such policies could bring a gain for a country which is being polluted from abroad, and may be the only policy option available.

The effects of these environmental policies on world income distribution are linked with the incentives which governments of various countries would have to introduce these policies. The receipt of the tax revenue (or the economic rent associated with other forms of restrictions) is a crucial element in providing incentives. Since the world real income will be raised by appropriate restrictions of activities which damage the environment, those countries which gain from these restrictions could always be able to compensate those who lose. Those who have the clearest incentive to intervene will be those whose environment is being damaged, while those inflicting the damage (on others) may lose unless it is they who are imposing the restriction and unless they are compensated by the others. Compensation paid from those damaged to those who inflict the damage provides an incentive to undertake damaging activity and raises a moral hazard question. It also raises the question of whether polluters have the right to pollute or whether those who are polluted have the right not to be polluted: this can only be settled through a determination of where the property rights lie.

Discouragement of polluting activities will affect international competitiveness. But pollution is a real cost of production. Attempting to counter the effects on competitiveness will tend to support an inefficient level of production, when all costs – including pollution costs – are taken into account.

Notes

Much of the work on this paper was undertaken when the author was Visiting Professor at the Graduate Institute of International Studies in Geneva. An earlier version of some sections was presented at the Troisième Cycle Romand en Economie Politique Conference 'Le Commerce International', at Champéry, Switzerland in March 1991. The author is grateful for discussions and comments to Kym Anderson, Richard Blackhurst, Bernard Hoekman, Michael Leidy, Gary Sampson and John Whalley. They are not responsible for any errors or opinions in the paper, and nothing in it should be attributed to them or to any institutions with which they are associated.

1. Examples of contributions in this area include Meade (1955), Johnson (1965), Corden (1974) and Bhagwati and Ramaswami (1963).
2. There are some provisions for re-distribution under international agreements. For example the GATT allows for compensation to injured countries as one of

a number of possible actions, when safeguard measures against imports are taken under Article XIX. International agreements themselves are a form of settling the international distribution of costs and benefits of actions which have cross-border effects.

3. There could be by-product benefits of the atmospheric kind which extend across international borders, just as there are by-product costs. Discouraging production which yields such consumptive benefits would raise real global income.
4. Some of the points which follow were addressed by Baumol (1971). He does not suppress the terms of trade effect, but rather examines the optimum tariff in the presence of externalities and monopoly power. Markusen (1975) explores tax structures to maximize national income, also in the presence of international externalities and monopoly power.
5. There would be some levels of output between zero and *OQ* at which it would be profitable to produce if A's government were to act as a monopolist exporter and could raise the export price above *OF*.
6. This is not the optimum tax from an income maximization point of view for A which would be such as to equate marginal revenue on the B market to A's marginal costs. We are assuming a tax which is at an optimum with respect to curing the effects of the pollution and thereby maximizing world income, the pollution being the only inefficiency from a world point of view, and are not examining the tax which would maximize the income of either A or B.
7. Note again the point made in note 5, that in the presence of monopolistic exporting, a non-zero level of output could be socially profitable.
8. The two triangles have equal height, defined by the change of quantity *RQ*, and equal bases, *HG* and *GW*, this because of the assumption that the pollution causes the same cost wherever it falls.
9. Foreign producers are likely, of course, to claim that such assistance for pollution abatement is 'unfair' competition if they are required to bear the costs themselves of such abatement in their own countries or if they are taxed for polluting.

References

Baumol, W. J. (1971), *Environmental Protection, International Spillovers and Trade*, Stockolm: Almqvist & Wiksell.

Bhagwati, J. and V. K. Ramaswami (1963), 'Domestic Distortions, Tariffs and the Theory of Optimum Subsidy', *Journal of Political Economy* **71**: 44–50.

Coase, R. H. (1960), 'The Problem of Social Cost', *Journal of Law and Economics* **3**: 1–44.

Corden, W. M. (1974), *Trade Policy and Economic Welfare*, London: Oxford University Press.

Dasgupta, P. (1990), 'The Environment as a Commodity', *Oxford Review of Economic Policy* **6**: 51–67.

Harris, S. (1991), 'International Trade, Ecologically Sustainable Development and the GATT', mimeo, Australian National University, Canberra, January.

Johnson, H. G. (1965), 'Optimal Trade Intervention in the Presence of Domestic Distortions', in *Trade, Growth and the Balance of Payments: Essays in Honor of Gottfried Haberler*, edited by R. E. Baldwin *et al.*, Amsterdam: North-Holland.

Markusen, J. R. (1975), 'International Externalities and Optimum Tax Structures', *Journal of International Economics* **5**: 15–29.

Meade, J. E. (1955), *Trade and Welfare: The Theory of International Economic Policy*, Volume 2, London: Oxford University Press.
Pearce, D. W., A. Markandya and E. B. Barbier (1989), *Blueprint for a Green Economy*, London: Earthscan Publications.
Shrybman, S. (1990), 'International Trade and the Environment: An Environmental Assessment of the General Agreement on Tariffs and Trade'. *The Ecologist* **20**: 30–4.
Whalley, J. (1991), 'The Interface between Environmental and Trade Policies'. *The Economic Journal* **101**: 180–9.
Whalley, J. and R. Wigle (1991), 'The International Incidence of Carbon Taxes'. in *Economic Policy Responses to Global Warming*, edited by R. Dornbusch and J. Poterba, Cambridge, MA: MIT Press.

[5]
Trade Measures for Environment: A Nearly Empty Box?

Arvind Subramanian

1. INTRODUCTION

EVENTS in recent months have appeared to pitch trade and environment as antagonists in mutually destructive competition for the attention of policy makers. Of the forty-eight bills on environmental matters introduced in the 101st Congress in the United States, thirty-three contained provisions affecting international trade of which thirty-one took the form of restrictive trade measures, the implication clearly being that trade contraction rather than expansion is the appropriate means of advancing environmental objectives.[1]

With hindsight, however, the confluence of these twin concerns seems to have been inevitable. On the one hand, multilateral efforts at cooperation and negotiation have progressively embraced a number of internal (or non-border) policy instruments, which were hitherto regarded as somehow outside the purview of international trade policy. In the last ten years, for example, the GATT has gone much beyond addressing tariffs, quotas and other border measures to internal instruments such as standards, intellectual property rights, production subsidies, investment measures, etc.[2] Globalisation and the concomitant concern with international competitiveness, especially with the loss of it from allegedly unfair practices, have motivated this search for cooperative

ARVIND SUBRAMANIAN is an Economic Affairs Officer in the GATT Secretariat in Geneva. The views expressed in this paper are those of the author and should not be attributed to his employing organisation. This paper has benefited from discussions with Kym Anderson, Richard Blackhurst, Vijay Kelkar, Patrick Low, Adrian Otten and especially David Hartridge and Aaditya Mattoo.

[1] The perceived unfriendliness of freer trade to the cause of the environment is also reflected in proposals calling for a re-writing of GATT rules. See Shrybman (1989) and Arden-Clarke (1991).

[2] Strictly speaking the view that internal instruments are not regulated by the GATT is fallacious. Under the national treatment obligation — possibly the most important aspect of the 'non-discrimination principle' — every conceivable policy instrument is constrained so as to prevent protection from being accorded to domestically produced goods. What has not been regulated, but progressively being done is the *level* at which these instruments can be set — levels of production subsidies, of intellectual property protection, of standards etc.

solutions encompassing a wider range of policy instruments.[3] It was inevitable that environmental issues, given their intrinsically emotive nature, would be a prime candidate for espousal by the practitioners of the unfair trade rhetoric.

On the other hand, increasing scientific work brought squarely into the popular domain awareness of certain environmental problems which were truly global in nature and potentially far-reaching, even catastrophic, in their consequences. It was also inevitable that the search for multilateral solutions in the environmental area would rely on the use of trade measures as an inducement mechanism, given the track record of their effectiveness in areas ranging from human rights, workers' rights and arms control to services, intellectual property and competition policy. Thus the internationalisation of the environmental agenda and 'greenification' of the trade agenda have been parallel, though intimately related processes, where denouement will be the focus of attention in the years to come.

The purposes of this paper is two-fold. First, to ouline an exhaustive taxonomy of the interactions between trade policy and environmental problems; and second, on the basis of this taxonomy, to analyse the role that trade measures can play. The analysis will be both positive and normative.

2. TRADE AND ENVIRONMENT: A TAXONOMY

It is imperative to make the distinction, even though it may be impractical to operationalise it in all instances, between environmental problems whose effects are localised within the country where they arise — domestic environmental problems (DEPs), and others whose effects cross national boundaries — transborder environmental problems (TEPs).[4] The distinction is important to make because, as will become evident below, it will enable the protectionist use of environmental arguments to be distinguished from their more legitimate use. In other words, the distinction facilitates the identification and analysis of two distinct categories of issues — those related to competitiveness and others related to the environment *per se*.

The distinction between purely domestic environmental problems and those with cross-border effects can be attacked on at least two levels. First, it is argued that even physical pollution is never confined to one country, since the biosphere is an individual whole — an argument for which, in the moral sphere, John

[3] See Bhagwati (1990) for an analysis in relation to United States trade policy.

[4] The latter can in turn be bilateral (Mexican pollution spilling over into the United States), regional (the acid rain problem) or global (ozone layer, global warming). See Mäler (1990) for a taxonomy of transborder environmental problems. The discussion below suggests that this category encompasses the majority of problems currently being discussed.

Donne provides high authority but which offers a dangerously tenuous basis for intervention by a foreign government. A more powerful objection is that even where there is no physical spillover onto other countries, environmental problems or policies often have non-physical spillover effects, giving rise to aesthetic, ethical or moral concerns strong enough to compel attention and response from governments. Examples include destruction of animal species and perceived cruelty to animals. Nevertheless, I believe there is a valid distinction between problems which impact on other countries' environment and those which do not.

Table 1 summarises the various interactions between trade and environment in terms of the *types* of trade measures that can be taken. These are described under each of the two categories identified above and examples are provided for each situation. Trade measures broadly fall under three categories which are called *direct trade interventions*, *supporting trade provisions*, and *trade inducements* respectively. In turn, actions taken under each of these categories can be unilateral or multilateral. Although these categories are not always mutually exclusive and overlap in terms of the effect of trade measures, it is nevertheless useful to make the distinction for analytical purposes.[5]

a. Direct Trade Interventions

I have chosen to characterise as 'direct trade interventions' trade measures which impact directly on the perceived environmental problem. In TEP situations such measures are taken to correct environmental externalities, which may be non-physical; examples would be the anticipated trade restrictions against fur and related products caught in leghold traps (unilateral action) and the ban on ivory trade under the CITES Convention (multilateral action). In DEP situations such measures may be taken to compensate for loss of competitiveness caused, for example, by lower environmental standards in an exporting country. Examples of trade interventions to correct for environment-related competitiveness effects include the Boren proposal[6] for the automatic levying of countervailing duties on imports from countries with allegedly low pollution standards (alleged to be *de facto* subsidies) (unilateral action) and the border tax adjustment rules (multilateral action) under the GATT permitting the levying of tariffs on products on the domestic production of which an environment tax has been levied. Trade interventions will also have sanctions-like effects and often these might be important as they will be directed at the very actions which create the externality (see Section 4 below).

[5] See Blackhurst and Subramanian (1991) for an earlier attempt at a similar taxonomy.

[6] See Senator Boren's proposed Pollution Deterrence Act of 1991.

TABLE I

Type of measure	Features	Transborder	Domestic
1. *Direct Trade Interventions*			
(a) Unilateral	Aimed to impact directly on the substantive problem: either the loss in competitiveness or the environmental externality; restrictive action will have penalising effects (incidental or otherwise) on actions creating the pollution.	(a) US import ban on Mexican Tuna, EC's threatened ban against exports of tropical timber and against fur products produced from animals caught in leghold traps.	(a) Countervailing duty against products produced under alleged 'low standards' (e.g. Boren Initiative). Export subsidies for pollution equipment.
(b) Multilateral		(b) Trade ban on Ivory and on several other endangered species under the CITES Convention. Trade restrictions in Basel Convention on Hazardous Wastes.	(b) Proposals in the Uruguay Round to exempt certain kinds of production subsidies for pollution abatement from countervailing action. Multilaterally sanctioned use of trade measures to offset production taxes imposed on environmental grounds as in the Superfund Panel Case.
2. *Supporting Trade Provisions*			
(a) Unilateral	Intended to enforce *other* actions or interventions, which address the substantive problem or externality; action by its nature will be in the related area and could have incidental penalising effects.	(a) Circle of Poison Act intended to stop exports of harmful pesticides on the grounds that they may be used in products which are reimported; import ban to enforce domestic consumption ban or domestic standards (e.g. Danish beer beer bottles case).	
(b) Multilateral		(b) Trade restrictions against non-signatories of Montreal Protocol. National actions that are sanctioned multilaterally.	
Trade Inducements			
3A. *Sanctions*:			
(a) Unilateral	Actions intended to change environmental behaviour and taken in *unrelated* areas: hence substitutable in principle by equivalent actions, e.g. financial sanctions for trade sanctions and technology transfer for trade incentives. Often sanctions will only be threatened and, if credible and effective, need not be taken.	(a) Pelly Amendment to US Fisherman's Protective Act of 1967 and Packward-Magnuson Amendment to the US Fisherman's Protective Act of 1967 under which imports of fish products in general can be restricted or prohibited. (e.g. Recent US action against Japan for policies endangering the sea turtle.)	(a) Use of trade restrictions to *raise* pollution standards abroad; use of trade restrictions to *lower* standards, e.g. threatened US action in Beef Hormone case.
(b) Multilateral		(b) None so far.	
3B. *Incentives*			
(a) Unilateral			
(b) Multilateral		(b) US-Mexico NAFTA negotiations for of market access in return for reduced transborder pollution.	(b) US-Mexico NAFTA negotiations for provision of market access in return for higher standards.

b. Supporting Trade Provisions

A trade measure can be characterised as a supporting trade provision when its function is to enforce another action, which is itself the substantive intervention; or in other words a trade provision is itself not the substantive intervention. A good example in the TEP category is the Montreal Protocol which provides for trade restrictions on CFC-related products against non-signatories. The substantive obligations or policy interventions envisaged under the Protocol are production and/or consumption related. The monitoring and restriction of trade with non-signatories ensures that the objectives of the agreement, namely the production and consumption obligations on signatories, are not circumvented or undermined.[7]

An example of a unilateral trade provision is the use of an import ban in order to enforce a domestic consumption ban. The law adopted by Denmark banning imports of soft drink bottled in non-reusable containers would thus be a trade provision used to enforce a domestic consumption ban. Similarly, the 'Circle of Poison Prevention Act', a proposal seeking to block exports of domestically banned pesticides on the grounds that they would be used on food grown abroad and re-imported, would also constitute a trade provision.

c. Trade Inducements (Carrot and Stick)

In their function as means, trade measures serve merely as instruments to induce (in a positive) (carrot) or negative (stick) sense) changes in environmental behaviour of other countries. In this role, trade actions are taken in *unrelated* products. By definition trade action under the other two categories has to be directed at the product in question. Here trade measures serve as punishments and/or rewards to induce others to participate in and subsequently comply with international environmental agreements or to change their environmental standards on competitiveness grounds. What is often not sufficiently recognised (or at least not translated into practice) is that in their role as inducements, trade measures are in principle substitutable by other measures — financial, technological, diplomatic, military etc. and it is not always evident as to why one form ought to be preferred to another. Another feature of trade

[7] The distinction between trade provisions and interventions is highlighted if we consider the trade ban on ivory. Several authors have argued that the optimal policy intervention to preserve the elephant population is a series of measures by ivory producing countries including the formation of a producers' cartel combined with better design of property rights to create the right incentives to invest in the maintenance of elephants as an asset. They envisage, however, that consuming countries would not import from those producers which did not follow the policy interventions envisaged. Such import restrictions would constitute trade provisions as their primary role would be to enforce other optimal policy interventions; the current ban on ivory trade is, however, seen by some as the optimal intervention. See Barbier et al. (1990).

inducments is that they need not always be used: often the *threatened* use of sanctions is sufficient to alter behaviour if this is seen as credible, and effective in the sense that it would impose costs on the victim which are sufficiently high to induce the desired change in behaviour.

Trade inducements can be further divided into trade *sanctions* and trade *incentives*. An example of trade sanctions under the TEP category is the Pelly Amendment which authorises trade restrictions in a whole range of unrelated products for failure by a country to observe United States' standards for tuna fishing methods. Similarly, the United States' threat to impose trade restrictions against Japan for its over-use of hawksbill sea turtles is another example of the role of trade sanctions. Sanctions could equally be used in cases not involving transborder spillovers. Countries might use sanctions to change the pollution standards of others because they are considered to be too low thus conferring competitive advantage. Alternatively, sanctions might be used on grounds that standards are too high as happened when the United States threatened to withdraw concessions against the EC for its standards on hormone in beef products which the United States alleged to be a non-tariff barrier to trade.[8]

However, inducements to change behaviur could also take the form of *trade incentives*: although few examples spring to mind, it could plausibly be argued that the NAFTA exercise involves, albeit implicitly, the use of incentives in the form of increased market access to Mexico in return for raising its environmental standards.[9]

A final distinction, one that will not be discussed, is worth bearing in mind in relation to the category of trade inducements. Trade sanctions can be used to *induce* participation in multilateral rule-making, but they could also be used to *sustain* it in the event of deviation from the agreed rules. Where incentives are used to secure cooperation, sanctions would consist of the withdrawal of such incentives. Under the GATT the possibility of retaliation in the form of withdrawal of existing concessions might be thought of as a means of sustaining cooperation by penalising defectors from the agreement. However, examples of

---

[8] Supporting trade provisions (category 2 above) may also have a sanctions-like effect. The trade restrictions against non-signatories envisaged by the Montreal Protocol have a penalising function. Non-signatories are worse off as a result of the trade restrictions because as importers and exporters of CFC products they are denied respectively, access to cheapest sources of supplies and to markets. However, the trade restrictions in the original protocol were not strong enough as sanctions to induce participation by at least two of the major consumers of CFC products; other inducements (in the form of the technology transfer fund) were required to achieve this objective.

[9] There are more examples of non-trade incentives being used in the environment area. An example of the provision of multilateral financial incentives is the creation in 1990 of the United Nations Environmental Fund through which certain international agencies would ensure that globally appropriate environmental policies would be pursued in developing countries. Similarly, the technology fund in the Montreal Protocol is an incentive mechanism.

trade sanctions to sustain cooperation in the environment area are more difficult to come by.[10]

3. DOMESTIC ENVIRONMENTAL PROBLEMS

As argued earlier, it was inevitable that differences in standards of pollution and pollution control or rate of exploitation of environmental resources would become causes for remedial trade action on grounds of unfair competition. As the taxonomy shows there are several possible trade responses to this 'problem'. However, before examining each it is worth asking what the alleged problem is which needs action. Comparative advantage is predicated on the existence of *differences* between countries — differences in factor endowments, preferences and technology. The familiar gains from trade or from international specialisation derive from this difference. In this picture the environment is one element of possible difference between countries. A country could have a greater endowment of environmental resources or a greater pollution assimilation capacity than another. Equally its social preferences could be different from the others leading to a lower valuation of environmental goods (including for example through high rates of time preference) or even of human resources (in the form of lower health and safety standards). In the eyes of the proponents of unfair trade these differences constitute 'problems' because they give rise to differences in competitiveness and far from being celebrated as creating opportunities for international specialisation are sought to be nullified through remedial action. The logical culmination of this line of thought would be to attack *any* difference in endowment, technology or preference as being symptomatic of unfair competitive advantage and to eradicate any trade created therefrom.[11]

Apart from being protectionist *per se*, it is also vulnerable to the slippery slope argument: with equal consistency arguments could be advanced for remedial action against lax population policy (as this might be seen as leading to low wages and increased competitiveness), differing standards on workers' rights, education and health. The more disconcerting question that is not posed, but which ought to be, is whether, on this line of reasoning, technological advantage should not also be seen as conferring unfair competitive advantage thus warranting trade action by the technological laggards? The risks and the costs in national and global welfare terms of going down this path are immense.

---

[10] However, non-trade punishment mechanisms can be found in some international environmental agreements such as the North Pacific Fur Seal Treaty under which deviation by one signatory can elicit withdrawal by another leading to the eventual termination of the agreement.

[11] A recent safeguard action was justified with appealing frankness on the grounds that the price of imports was lower than that of domestic competitors!

Thus where there are no physical spillovers, and this is an important caveat, there ought to be a serious presumption against the use of trade restrictive action — be it in the form of contingent protection action (e.g. countervailing or anti-dumping duty), competitive subsidisation *or* attempts to harmonise pollution standards.

However, even if it were admitted that differential environmental policies were a source of unfair competitive advantage, the empirical picture is not very supportive of the need for trade action. A number of studies show that even in the most pollution intensive industries, pollution abatement costs constitute a very small fraction (between one and three per cent) of total industry costs — hardly the sort of margin by which competitive advantage is conferred or 'injury' caused.[12]

Table 1 shows that there are several ways in which action on environment-related competitiveness grounds can be taken: first, to impose countervailing duties on products alleged to have been subsidised abroad either directly through the provision of environment-related subsidies or through the institution of a regime of low environmental standards or to provide offsetting environment-related subsidies to domestic producers in competition with such products: second, to change the other country's standard through the use of sanctions; and finally, where environmental action in one's own country is being taken, trade action to offset any consequent loss in competitiveness in the home market or in third country markets.

In terms of attaining the 'desired' objective of nullifying loss in competitiveness, a welfare ranking of the alternative instruments is possible: countervailing action is likely to be most distortionary as it raises domestic prices and does not help domestic producers in third country markets. Production subsidies would avoid these problems but would entail budgetary costs. From a national welfare viewpoint a first-best situation would result if the other country changed its standards especially if this can be accomplished costlessly, without resource transfers. But, from a global welfare point of view the main question is whether the *objectives* of such actions are justifiable given that they are predicated on notions of unfairness which are questionable and whose logical extension would lead to the negation of the very basis of international trade.

One of the ironies in the current view that existing trade arrangements somehow impede the pursuit of sensible environmental policies is that a closer

[12] Tobey (1990) finds, for example, that strict environmental regulations imposed in the 1960s and 1970s by industrialised countries have not measurably affected trade patterns in the *most polluting industries*, which are defined as those for which direct and indirect abatement costs account for greater than 1.85 per cent of total costs. The most polluting industry — chemicals — faced abatement costs equal to 2.89 per cent of total costs. For similar results in the case of Mexico, see Low (1991).

scrutiny might well point to the opposite conclusion. This is illustrated in the ruling of the GATT Superfund dispute which sanctioned the levying of an equivalent border tax on products the domestic production of which had been subject to a tax on environmental grounds. The implications of this ruling are two-fold. First, it suggests that any purely domestic objectives, in this instance an environmental objective, can be pursued without having to suffer the adverse international competitiveness implications because the latter can be neutralised, at least partially by an equivalent tax on the imported product. The important condition for access to the border-tax instrument is that the domestic tax be on a *product*. A second implication is that if the pollution is caused by a process rather than a product, domestic industry would lobby in favour of a *product* tax because of the attractiveness that it would offer in blunting the adverse competitiveness consequences. An inefficiency results, namely that of the choice of the second-best instrument — product rather than process tax — in relation to the given environmental externality.[13]

4. TRANSBORDER ENVIRONMENTAL PROBLEMS

In this section it will be argued that allegations regarding the incompatibility of freer trade and desirable environmental outcomes are misplaced. To anticipate the arguments, trade interventions especially when taken unilaterally are *inefficient* in attaining globally superior environmental outcomes; to put it another way, there are more efficient ways of achieving the same result. Furthermore, the use of unilateral trade sanctions is an *inequitable* way of pursuing what may well be desirable outcomes. Their availability might militate against the search for cooperative solutions, and also bias the nature of such solutions in terms of adversely affecting resource flows to low-income countries. Here again the opposition between trade and environment is a false one. The distinction is rather between unilateral and cooperative approaches to solving environmental problems. There might be a role for trade measures but only in the context of sustaining cooperative outcomes.

a. Trade Interventions and Environmental Externalities

All environmental externalities be they domestic or transborder arise from some kind of market failure which includes imperfectly functioning markets or their very absence.[14] The choice of appropriate policy instruments to correct externalities in a domestic context is the subject of a growing body of

---

[13] See also Sorsa in this issue.

[14] See Dasgupta (1990).

literature.[15] The relevant instruments range from Pigouvian taxes and subsidies, to assignment of property rights, regulatory instruments and emissions trading.

From the point of view of *global efficiency*, and leaving aside equity considerations, optimum intervention or the choice of appropriate intervention to correct the market failure is independent of whether the problem is domestic or transborder. The intuition underlying the theory of domestic distortions is that, in the absence of other distortions, the further removed the intervening instrument is from the source of the distortion the less efficient it is likely to be. Thus trade-based interventions are generally likely to be second-best instruments to correct the market failure relative to the production and consumption-based instruments mentioned above. (See Anderson, 1991; and Snape, 1991.)

The *extent* of the inappropriateness of trade interventions, i.e. the extent to which they are removed from the source of market failure arising in the context of environmental problems can be gauged from the following examples. Where the cause of the pollution is a process, a trade tax is at least twice removed from the optimum intervention. In the case of pollution stemming from carbon emissions a trade intervention is even further removed (a trade tax on carbon-containing products would be dominated by a production or consumption tax on such products; in turn this would be inferior to a tax on carbon emissions from factories, with the optimum instrument being a tax on the carbon content of fuel). Similarly, problems relating to *stocks* require intervention which corrects the relevant intertemporal externalities — imperfect or incorrect assignment of property rights, high rates of time preference leading to excessive depletion.[16] For some resources the problem may be a lack of markets. Existence value, the value attached by consumers to the knowledge that certain species exist even though they may never see them, is often not marketable. Over-exploitation, therefore, results because resource owners are not remunerated for some of the benefits they confer on others. Here too, trade actions will be an inappropriate instrument. Finally, in relation to environmental resources such as species of plants whose future value is unknown and which once destroyed cannot be recovered (irreversible), optimal intervention would require a mixture of proper assignment of property rights and even macroeconomic policy.[17] In the absence of a common identification or recognition of a problem, either because of conflicting social preferences or of lack of agreement on the scientific evidence,

[15] See Muzando, Miranda and Bovenberg (1990).

[16] See Barbier et al. (1990) for an analysis of the problem of depletion of elephant stocks in which the case against the desirability of trade interventions in an intertemporal context is argued.

[17] See Binswanger (1991) who argues that Brazilian deforestation is attributable largely to bad macroeconomic policy.

unilateral trade actions notably in relation to the more complex problems are likely to have very uncertain effects.[18]

The foregoing analysis has assumed away what might be seen as the key problem in relation to transborder externalities, namely that of distinct sovereignties trying to gain advantage, through the use of trade actions, at the expense of others. In other words, a concern with global efficiency or welfare neglects the fact that the allocation of that welfare amongst countries might lead to a situation less advantageous for some than what might be achieved through the use of trade actions. It is in relation to this question that trade sanctions play a key role.

b. Trade Sanctions

It has been one of the singular features of recent trade policy that the threatened or actual use of trade sanctions has been an important instrument to secure bilateral or multilateral cooperation in several areas of international policy making — in services, intellectual property, competition policy etc. At the outset a clear distinction needs to be made between trade sanctions used to induce cooperation, where such cooperation in the form of multilateral agreements governing environmental action does not already exist (*unilateral* trade sanctions — the main focus of this section) and sanctions which are needed to sustain such agreements and serve the role of securing compliance with actions agreed upon (*multilateral* trade sanctions).

With increasing evidence and recognition that environmental problems involve more than one country, attention is turning to finding cooperative solutions to these problems. The absence of a supranational enforcement authority implies that national jurisdiction and sovereignty must be respected. Consequently, any mechanism for securing cooperation must be self-enforcing in the sense that compliance with rules must be forthcoming voluntarily. This, however, may not always be easy, as there may be inherent contradictions between the individual (national) good and the collective (international) good exemplified in the famous prisoner's dilemma.[19]

In general, there are two ways of improving the incentives for countries to cooperate on international environmental issues. The first is by providing compensation to countries for their cooperation, and the second by threatening

[18] If the assumption that there are no other distortions does not hold, the inappropriateness of trade intervention cannot be presumed. A case-by-case determination would have to be made, but even then, given the enormous complexity of many environmental problems, trade interventions are unlikely to be the most appropriate instruments. See Anderson (1991). As Low and Safadi (1991) point out, in the hasty search for 'new' trade-based solutions, the environmental unfriendliness of prior non-trade interventions is inadequately examined.

[19] See Dasgupta (1990). The discussion in this section draws on the analysis in Blackhurst and Subramanian (1991).

coercive action in the event of non-cooperation — the sanctions approach.[20] The most important difference between these two is the effect on the distribution of welfare. The compensation route results in a higher level of welfare for the country whose cooperation is sought (and secured) than the level which would have prevailed had cooperation been secured through the threat of sanctions. Mcmillan (1990) shows that in a bargaining game a bargainer's payoff is higher, *ceteris paribus*, the worse is the opponent's alternative in the event of a breakdown in the bargain (formally described as the 'outside option'). The threat of sanctions affects the terms of agreement by worsening the opponent's payoffs in the event of non-cooperation rendering him in a 'weaker' bargaining position and allowing the user of the threat to appropriate a larger share of the cake. The import of this result is that if *unilateral* trade sanctions were permitted as a legitimate response to TEPs, in the subsequent *multilateral bargain*, their user could appropriate a larger share of the cake from, or alternatively could transfer a lower amount of resources to, the country whose cooperation is being secured. Therefore the greatest fear of unilateral trade sanctions is not necessarily that it would lead to protectionism (often it does not as sanctions are more often threatened than used), but that it might affect significantly the flow of resources especially to those developing countries whose cooperation would be important in securing viable and efficient multilateral environmental agreements.[21]

These two approaches seem, at first glance, to have analogies in the literature on the environment in terms of the polluter pays principle (PPP) and the victim pays principle (VPP). In an international context they imply respectively that the polluting and polluted (victim) nation should bear the costs of controlling or preventing the transborder pollution.

But the PPP/VPP distinction is very problematic to apply at the multilateral level. In relation to environmental flow problems such as the pollution of a river crossing borders it might be easy to distinguish the polluter and the victim. But in relation to several environmental problems such as the depletion of the ozone layer and greenhouse gas build up, which involve stocks, and those involving non-physical spillovers such as species preservation, 'cruelty' to animals, the very determination of polluter and victim becomes difficult. Indeed, the search for cooperative solutions through international negotiations involves decisions

[20] It is somewhat surprising to see that the environmental literature appears to take for granted that cooperation would require the payment of compensation (see e.g. Mäler, 1990; and Barrett, 1990) to polluting countries while appearing to ignore the recent history (which trade policy analysts are more aware of) of the use of sanctions to promote cooperation. On the latter, see Mcmillan (1990).

[21] This ignores the adverse effects of threatened sanctions on the *efficiency* of bargaining outcomes which could include counter-retaliation and the breakdown of cooperative bargaining and the weaker incentives that a country would have in abiding by the bargain if it feels that its cooperation has been secured through coercive means. See Bhagwati (1990) and Mcmillan (1990).

regarding the appropriate allocation of the costs of pollution abatement between countries based in part on a prior collective determination as to who is the polluter and who the victim and who should be accorded property rights.

A look at the current controversy in relation to the greenhouse gas problem clarifies this point. Alternative proposals have been put forward for the obligations — in terms of carbon emission reductions — that countries should be expected to assume.[22] On a static, marginal view of net carbon emissions, China and India would rank high among the category of polluters and an application of PPP might require greater reduction by these countries (or alternatively a smaller initial allocation of tradeable carbon permits). On the other hand, in the same situation, an application of VPP would require either lower levels of environmental obligations or greater levels of net resource flows to these countries. Here the application of VPP would stem from extraneous considerations, i.e. *despite* their being deemed to be polluters, global equity or population considerations might justify such resource flows.

However, if an intertemporal view were taken of the carbon emission problem, i.e. viewing the pollution of the atmosphere as a *stock* problem due to the emission of greenhouse gases over several hundred years, an application of PPP itself would necessitate net resource flows accruing to the countries mentioned above. In other words, compensation need not always reflect VPP: it might equally reflect PPP depending on the definition of polluter.[23]

A similar problem arises as regards flows of environmental services from certain environmental resources located within national boundaries, on which there are differences of opinion about the obligations of the rest of the world to pay for those services. A good example is the Amazon forest, which Brazil views as a national resource rendering environmental services to the rest of the world in the form of carbon absorption and species variety. Accordingly, Brazil could ask to be paid by the rest of the world for these international flows of services (or, in what amounts to the same thing, it could ask for compensation for the preservation of the forest). The other view is that these services of the

[22] In the context of the possible institution of a system of internationally tradable permits for carbon emissions, for example, it has been suggested that such permits be allocated on a *per capita* basis. Another approach advocated by some countries is that the allocation of future property rights in the context of the global warming problem should be inversely related to a country's cumulative contribution to the stock of greenhouse gases over the last hundred or more years. The argument in this case is that there should be some intertemporal equity in the right to emit sustainable amounts of waste into the atmosphere and hence in the right to future growth opportunities. A third option would be for each country to reduce current carbon emissions by an equal percentage — a proposal which implicitly allocates rights to discharge carbon into the atmosphere on a first come, first served basis. The income distributional implications of these various proposals — between different groups within a country, as well as between countries — are sizeable and thus could be expected to have a major impact on the willingness of particular countries to participate in an agreement to reduce the emission of greenhouse gases.

[23] Mäler (1990) and Low and Safadi (1991) for example tend to equate compensation with VPP.

Amazon forest are a universal resource. On this view, the world has a right to the forest's preservation and conversely its destruction should result in the rest of the world being compensated by Brazil.

Species preservation and allegations of cruelty to animals raise conflicts arising from differing societal valuations and preferences. Here too, international cooperation is meant to address the question of property rights. Is there a right to kill or not to kill dolphins, a right to catch animals in leghold traps or not? Should Mexican fisherman be penalised or threatened with penalties for *purse seine* net fishing or be compensated for having to desist from the activity or to use more expensive alternative technologies? The magnitude and direction of resource flows depends crucially on answers to these questions.

What the foregoing has illustrated is that in relation to transborder problems: (a) the use of sanctions or compensation determines crucially the resource flows or the share of the global welfare cake accruing to different countries; (b) this share depends on resolving questions relating to who is the polluter or victim or free-rider and as to who should have the property rights? This latter should be determined through cooperative means. Legitimising unilateral sanctions would amount to allowing unilateral determination as to who is the polluter and also as to who should have the property rights.

An important point which should not be overlooked is the effect that resource transfers themselves will have on global environmental quality. Evidence suggests that environmental quality and income levels are highly correlated; poverty and low incomes have been shown to crucially determine environmental degradation especially in relation to forest resources. The sanctions route thus carries with it the heavy cost that smaller resource transfers to low income developing countries would lead to further environmental degradation.

There is a parallel between the role of ecological arguments in relation to DEPs and to TEPs. In the former, several coalitions, including domestic industries and labour groups, are likely to hitch their wagon to the ecological star to secure or legitimise protectionist outcomes. In the case of TEPs, ecological arguments by tending to elevate the sanctity of certain outcomes — not to kill dolphins, not to burn forests — implicitly shape the determination of the international allocation of property rights by deeming the perpetrators of these acts as polluters. This favours the use of the sanctions rather than the compensation route to securing cooperation, adversely affecting the flow of resources to certain low-income environmentally abundant countries.[24] The risk of protectionism in relation to DEPs thus has a counterpart in eco-imperialism in relation to TEPs. In the former, groups with economic interests capture ecological arguments and in the latter, groups with environmental interests

[24] Thus, even if greater resources are transferred, it is seen as happening *despite* 'bad' environmental behaviour.

capture (the phenomenon of 'reverse capture') trade instruments to secure their objectives.

However, the foregoing discussion should not be interpreted as ruling out the use of sanctions altogether. There are, at least, two examples of situations where the use of trade sanctions might be appropriate. First, to induce cooperation where it has been established in the course of multilateral efforts to attain such cooperation that some countries are 'genuinely' free-riding. Establishing who is a true free-rider would probably be difficult, given the necessarily subjective nature of such judgements,[25] but a stronger case can be made for such an evaluation if the cooperative route has been explored than if it has not. Second, sanctions are probably necessary to enforce or sustain multilateral agreements — a credible threat of punishment (which would take the form of the withdrawal of the benefits of cooperation) would be effective in securing compliance with any agreement.

Nothing in the foregoing discussion has suggested that the threat of sanctions to induce changes in environmental behaviour should necessarily take the form of *trade* sanctions. And yet recent history shows that trade sanctions are the most often used instruments. The attractiveness of directed trade sanctions in the form of restrictions on the very product that creates the externality (import restrictions in tuna, import restrictions on tropical timber), is easy to see. They can be directed at the very economic agents who are responsible for creating the externality and the larger the import market the greater the magnitude of the penalty faced by such agents. The country taking the action does not have to rely on the intermediary services of the other government to influence the externality-creating agents as it would if financial sanctions were to be used.

But often trade sanctions take the form of restrictions on unrelated products which are therefore no different from, say, financial sanctions in terms of their effect. Indeed, in a welfare comparison between the use of financial sanctions and trade sanctions on unrelated products, the former may well be superior as they would not create the by-product distortions that trade sanctions would.[26] The revealed attractiveness of trade sanctions reflects, therefore, political economy according disproportionate influence to the pressure of sectional interests. In other words, the supply of trade sanctions is only too readily forthcoming and the threat of their use is seen to be credible despite its welfare consequences. This facilitates 'reverse' capture: the very ease of supply of trade

[25] This is related to the point about how 'multilateral' participation in an agreement should be, in order to decide whether non-participants are 'free-riding'. Sanctions against non-participants must always be somewhat arbitrary but are more defensible if membership is wide enough to establish a credible international consensus.

[26] More recently, there have been signs of use of the aid mechanism as sanctions: for example, Japan has begun to attach environmental guidelines to aid-funded projects. Similarly, a World Bank loan to Brazil in 1985 was interrupted because of fears expressed by environmental groups that it might aggravate deforestation.

sanctions leads to their use in furthering environmental objectives and creates a bias against the search for other forms (including through compensation) of securing cooperation.

On the other hand, it has to be admitted that if the success of trade sanctions or other forms of unilateralism diminishes interest in reaching negotiated solutions on the part of countries able to use them, they have been effective in bringing other countries to the negotiating table, even though, as suggested above, the results of such negotiations under the threat of sanctions may be less than optimal in equity terms.

c. Supporting Trade Provisions

As defined above, trade provisions serve the purpose of enforcing rules — national or multilateral, and are not intrinsic to correcting the given environmental externality. At the national level, import restrictions are often used to enforce domestic consumption bans or domestic standards.[27] For example, it is clear that a ban on domestic smoking would require the prohibition of imported cigarettes and that compliance with domestic emission standards would require a ban on cars not fitted with the appropriate catalytic convertor. But such unilateral actions are permitted under existing trading rules because they would meet the national treatment standard requiring equivalent treatment of domestic and imported products.[28] Similarly, trade provisions in multilateral agreements serve the function of ensuring their effectiveness as has been argued in the case of the Montreal Protocol. As long as the substantive

[27] Of course, there are cases, arising notably in relation to packaging requirements, where there might be concerns regarding standards becoming *de facto* restrictions despite their consonance with the non-discrimination principle.

[28] At the national level, measures that attempt to enforce domestic *process* standards by action against imported goods produced abroad under similar conditions might run foul of trading rules as the recent case between the United States and Mexico on the use of 'purse seine nets' has shown. However, it could be contended that there is a grey area of uncertainty arising in connection with certain kinds of trade provisions used to enforce domestic process standards. Consider the case where certain processes for the killing of animals in the production of meat for consumption (clearly therefore production methods) are disallowed domestically on grounds that they offend religious sentiments. A prohibition on the import of such meat might well be defended on the grounds that it is necessary to protect public morals in the country of importation and Article XX(a) of the General Agreement (a much overlooked provision) could be invoked. A case could be made that the logic of this example should be extended to other activities — chicken rearing, methods of catching animals or preparing products — that similarly offended aesthetic, ethical or religious sentiments. In such cases the problem arises as to how to circumscribe the domain of what constitutes legitimate grounds for offence. The slippery slope argument looms in the background — another country's health and labour standards might also be argued as offending a society's morals or sentiments and safeguards against the protectionist abuse of these arguments might be difficult to specify. A less contentious approach to these problems might be the use of labelling requirements which would allow consumers the freedom to exercise their preference against eco-unfriendly products or processes if they so wished.

interventions designed to correct the externality are appropriate and collectively agreed upon, the use of supporting trade provisions might have a useful role to play.

5. CONCLUSION

This paper has characterised the nature of trade policy measures which can be employed in relation to environmental problems. The conclusions that might be derived are the following. First, in relation to domestic environmental problems (i.e. where there are no spillovers across countries) the use of trade measures is flawed because it is largely protectionist in intent. They are aimed at negating the very source of comparative advantage which could legitimately be conferred by differences in environmental endowments, pollution assimilation capacities or social preferences regarding environmental outcomes. There is also the attendant risk captured in the 'slippery slope' argument: what source of comparative advantage is legitimate and not actionable under the garb of unfair trade? Would any outcome other than the eradication of trade or managed trade be immune to the accusation of unfairness?

Second, in relation to transborder environmental problems it was seen that trade interventions were *inefficient* instruments in correcting the market failures creating the environmental problem. Production or consumption interventions, creation of markets and proper assignment of property rights are likely to be more appropriate instruments of corrective action. It was also seen that unilateral trade sanctions were *inequitable* when used in the context of transborder problems as they permit unilateral determination of the international allocation of property rights and hence of the magnitude and direction of resource flows in a manner which is likely to be adverse for low-income countries. Insofar as there are strong and proven links between levels of income and environmental quality, the use of sanctions to secure cooperation may have further undesirable effects on environmental quality. However, the use of trade restrictive measures need not be entirely precluded: they might serve a useful role in securing compliance with multilateral agreements or even in inducing 'true' free-riders to assume greater obligations. Thus the opposition is not between freer trade and desirable environmental outcomes, but rather between unilateralism and multilateralism. Trade restrictions can be necessary or even desirable but only in the latter context, which allows truly cooperative solutions to be explored and secured.

REFERENCES

Anderson, K. (1991), 'Effects of Trade and Environmental Policies on the Environment and Welfare' in K. Anderson and R. Blackhurst (ed.), *The Greening of World Trade Issues* (Harvester-Wheatsheaf).

Arden-Clarke, C. (1991), 'The General Agreement on Tariffs and Trade, Environmental Protection and Sustainable Development', *World Wildlife Fund Discussion Paper*.

Barbier, E., J. Burgess, T. Swanson and D. Pearce (1990), *Elephants, Economies and Ivory* (London).

Barrett, S. (1990), 'The Problem of Global Environmental Protection', *Oxford Review of Economic Policy* 6, 68-79.

Barrett, S. (1991), 'The Paradox of International Environmental Agreements', mimeo (London Business School, January).

Bhagwati, J.N. (1990), 'Aggressive Unilateralism: An Overview', *Aggressive Unilateralism: America's 301 Trade Policy and the World Trading System*, J.N. Bhagwati and H.T. Patrick (eds.) (London: Harvester-Wheatsheaf).

Binswanger, H.P. (1991), 'Brazilian Policies that Encourage Deforestation in the Amazon', *World Development*, 19, 7, 821-830.

Blackhurst, R. and A. Subramanian (1991), 'Promoting Multilateral Cooperation on the Environment' in *The Greening of World Trade Issues*, K. Anderson and R. Blackhurst (eds.) (Harvester-Wheatsheaf).

Dasgupta, P.S. (1990), 'The Environment as a Commodity', *Oxford Review of Economic Policy* 6, 51-67.

GATT (1986), *The Text of The General Agreement on Tariffs and Trade* (Geneva).

Low, P. (1991), 'Trade Measures and Environmental Quality: The Implications for Mexico's Exports', mimeo (World Bank).

Low, P. and R. Safadi (1991), 'Trade Policy and Pollution', mimeo (World Bank, Washington DC).

Mäler, K.-G. (1990), 'International Environmental Problems', *Oxford Review of Economic Policy* 6, 80-108.

Mcmillan, J. (1990), 'Strategic Bargaining and Section 301' in *Aggressive Unilateralism: America's 301 Trade Policy and the World Trading System*, J.N. Bhagwati and H.T. Patrick (eds.) (London, Harvester-Wheatsheaf).

Muzando, T.R., K.M. Miranda and A.L. Bovenberg (1990), 'Public Policy and the Environment: A Survey of the Literature', *IMF Fiscal Affairs Department Working Paper 56*.

Shrybman, S. (1989), 'International Trade and the Environment: An Environmental Assessment of Present GATT Negotiations', Canadian *Environmental Law Association* (October).

Snape, R. (1991), 'The Environment, International Trade, and Competitiveness', forthcoming in K. Anderson and R. Blackhurst (ed.) *The Greening of World Trade Issues*, Harvester-Wheatsheaf.

Sorsa, P. (1992), 'GATT and Environment', *The World Economy*, 15, 1,

Tobey, J.A. (1990), 'The Effects of Domestic Environmental Policies on Patterns of World Trade: An Empirical Test', *Kyklos*, 43, 2, 191-210.

[6]

KYKLOS, Vol. 43, Fasc. 2, 191–209

The Effects of Domestic Environmental Policies on Patterns of World Trade: An Empirical Test

JAMES A. TOBEY *

I. INTRODUCTION

In theory, environmental control costs encourage reduced specialization in the production of polluting outputs in countries with stringent environmental regulations [PETHIG, 1976; SIEBERT, 1977; MCGUIRE, 1982]. In contrast, countries that fail to undertake an environmental protection program presumably increase their comparative advantage in the production of items that damage the environment. This relationship between trade and environmental policy receives considerable attention whenever countries are in the process of passing new pollution control measures. Groups who oppose existing measures, or the implementation of stiffer measures, argue that they reduce the ability of polluting industries to compete internationally [1]. With foreign trade an increasingly important sector in many of the world's economies, the arguments of such groups are now frequently weighted very heavily.

The premise that trade suffers from the imposition of environmental policy has a strong element of a priori plausibility but, surprisingly, has little empirical support. Several macroeconometric models [D'ARGE, 1974; ROBISON, 1986; OECD, 1985] have predicted that

* Affiliated with the United States Department of Agriculture, Economic Research Service, Research and Technology Division. This paper does not necessarily represent the views of the Department of Agriculture. I am very grateful for the thoughtful comments of Professors PETER MURRELL and WALLACE OATES, and the support of the Bureau of Business and Economic Research, University of Maryland.

1. In addition, the imposition of environmental regulations has often been suggested as a partial explanation for inflation in the U.S. and declines in productivity growth experienced by most industrialized countries in the 1970s.

pollution control measures should lead to a small but discernible effect on the balance of trade, but there are few studies to confirm this prediction.

The location-of-industry studies [LEONARD, 1988; PEARSON, 1987, 1985; WALTER, 1985] have explored the related ideas that stringent pollution control measures push industries out of the U.S. (the 'industrial-flight' hypothesis), and that less-developed countries compete to attract multinational industries by minimizing their own environmental policies (the 'pollution-haven' hypothesis). Their investigations, however, have been unable to find evidence in support of either hypothesis.

The present paper complements the results of the less rigorous location of industry studies by providing an empirical test of the hypothesis that stringent environmental policy has caused trade patterns to deviate in commodities produced by the world's 'dirty' industries.

The empirical tests are conducted using the cross-section Heckscher-Ohlin-Vanek (HOV) model of international trade. LEAMER [1984], BOWEN [1983] and others [MURRELL, 1990 and RYTERMAN, 1988] have popularized the application of this model to empirical tests of the sources of international comparative advantage. The basic HOV model is extended, in addition, to allow for non-homothetic preferences (NHP) and scale economies/product differentiation (EOS). Under all three specifications, two different approaches are taken to conduct the empirical tests. The first involves inclusion of a qualitative variable in the estimated equation to represent the stringency of pollution control measures. The second examines the signs of the estimated error terms when the variable measuring the stringency of a country's environmental policy is not included in the estimated equation.

It is found that the stringent environmental regulations imposed on industries in the late 1960s and early 1970s by most industrialized countries have not measurably affected international trade patterns in the most polluting industries. This result is consistent with and reinforces the results of the location-of-industry studies which use a very different empirical approach, but it may nevertheless be intuitively surprising to those who still fear the undesirable competitive effects of environmental policy.

THE EFFECTS OF DOMESTIC ENVIRONMENTAL POLICIES

Before proceeding with the empirical test, commodities whose production draws heavily on environmental resources – termed 'pollution-intensive' commodities – are defined.

II. DEFINITION OF POLLUTION-INTENSIVE COMMODITIES

A commodity's relative pollution intensity is defined in this study by the pollution-abatement costs incurred in its production in the

Table 1

I–O Industry	SITC	Description	Pollution Abatement Costs as Percentage of Total Costs
	Mining		
5	281	Iron ore, concentrates	2.03
6	283	Ores of nonferrous base metals	1.92
	Primary Nonferrous Metals		
38	681	Silver, platinum, etc.	2.05
38	682	Copper	2.05
38	683	Nickel	2.05
38	685	Lead	2.05
38	686	Zinc	2.05
38	687	Tin	2.05
38	689	Nonferrous base metals, n.e.s.	2.05
	Paper and Pulp		
24	251	Pulp and waste paper	2.40
24	641	Paper and paperboard	2.40
24	642	Articles of paper	2.40
	Primary Iron and Steel		
37	671	Pig iron	2.38
37	672	Ingots	2.38
37	673	Iron and steel bars	2.38
37	674	Universals, plates	2.38
37	675	Hoops and strips	2.38
37	676	Railway material	2.38
37	677	Iron and steel wire	2.38
37	678	Tubes and fittings	2.38
37	679	Iron, steel castings	2.38
	Chemicals		
27	513	Inorganic elements	2.89
27	514	Other inorganic chemicals	2.89
28	581	Plastic materials	2.36

United States. Such costs are reported by the U.S. Department of Commerce [1975] and the Environmental Protection Agency [1984]. KALT [1985] has taken these data for 1977 and matched them to sixty-four agricultural and manufacturing 2-digit I-O industries. These direct pollution abatement costs are then multiplied by the 1977 total expenditures I-O table to generate an estimate of total (direct and indirect) PACs per dollar of industrial output.

Commodities termed pollution-intensive are defined as the products of those industries whose direct and indirect abatement costs in the U.S. are equal to or greater than 1.85 percent of total costs. The cut-off of 1.85 percent is chosen because it results in a set of industries that are generally considered the most polluting (metals, chemicals, and paper industries) throughout the world[2]. Moreover, there is a considerable difference between the pollution-abatement costs in these industries and in those of the remaining group of industries.

In *Table 1*, these input-output industries which I have defined as pollution-intensive are matched to 3-digit SITC commodities and aggregated into five commodity groups including paper and pulp products (paper), mining of ores (mining), primary iron and steel (steel), primary nonferrous metals (nfmetals), and chemicals (chems). It is interesting to note at the outset the relatively small size of pollution abatement costs as a percentage of total costs in even the most highly regulated industries.

III. HECKSCHER-OHLIN-VANEK MODEL OF INTERNATIONAL TRADE

The HOV equations are a multi-factor, multi-commodity extension of the Heckscher-Ohlin (H-O) model of international trade. They have been used in three different ways. The factor content studies and cross-commodity regressions use measures of factor intensities and trade to infer factor endowments. The third methodology and the approach taken in this study, regresses trade in a specific commodity across countries on country characteristics, i.e., resource endow-

2. This cut-off does not include the petroleum industry. Petroleum is excluded because it is believed that the dynamics of this industry during this time (1975) were heavily influenced by extraordinary circumstances affecting the availability and processing of crude oil. LEONARD [1988] supports this view.

ments. In that resource endowments are the explanatory variables, such regressions reveal the direct influence of resources on trade in a specific commodity. Since this study seeks to reveal information on the most pollution-intensive commodities across countries, the cross-country analysis is chosen as the most appropriate approach.

A set of eleven resource endowments for the year 1975 is used to explain net exports of the most polluting industries under the HOV model[3]. These endowments are provided by LEAMER [1984] and include:

1. CAPITAL (CAP) Accumulated and discounted gross domestic investment flows since 1948, assuming an average life of 15 years.
2. LABOR 1 (LAB1) Number of workers classified as professional or technical.
3. LABOR 2 (LAB2) Number of literate nonprofessional workers.
4. LABOR 3 (LAB3) Number of illiterate workers.
5. LAND 1 (LND1) Land area in tropical rainy climate zone.
6. LAND 2 (LND2) Land area in dry climate zone.
7. LAND 3 (LND3) Land area in humid mesothermal climate zone (for example, California).
8. LAND 4 (LND4) Land area in humid microthermal climate (for example, Michigan).
9. COAL (COAL) Value of production of primary solid fuels (coal, lignite, and brown coal).
10. MINERALS (MINLS) Value of production of minerals: bauxite, copper, flourspar, ironore, lead, manganese, nickel, potash, pyrite, salt, tin, and zinc.
11. OIL (OIL) Value of oil and gas production.

The HOV model can be summarized by the following equations which explicitly incorporate this list of endowments:

$$N_{it} = CST_{i0} + b_{i1}V_{1t} + b_{i2}V_{2t} + \ldots + b_{i11}V_{11t} + \mu_{it} \quad (1)$$

where N_{it} are net exports of commodity i by country t; V_{kt} are endowments of resource k ($k = 1 \ldots 11$) in country t; b_{ik} are the coefficients which indicate the total effect (production and consump-

3. Trade data for 1975 comes from United Nations' trade tapes.

tion) of an increase in a resource on net trade of a specific commodity; μ_{it} is the disturbance term, and; CST_{i0} is the equation's constant term. The constant term embodies one resource endowment or country characteristic, which all countries are assumed to possess identically and which has a non-zero mean value.

If the environmental endowment, measured by the stringency of environmental regulations[4], has an effect on trade patterns then the set of eleven endowments in equation (1) is incomplete. In this case, estimation of the HOV trade equations implies a specification error involving an omitted variable. Two approaches are taken to test the effect of the environmental endowment on trade patterns under the HOV model when cross-country quantitative data on the environmental endowment are not available. In the first, a qualitative variable is included in equation (1) to represent the omitted variable, and, in the second an omitted variable test is conducted.

IV.

1. The HOV Model with Environmental Stringency

To test the pollution-haven hypothesis under the first approach, the following equation is estimated under ordinary least squares (OLS):

$$N_{it} = CST_{i0} + b_{i1}V_{1t} + b_{i2}V_{2t} + \dots + b_{i11}V_{11t} + b_{iE}D_{Et} + \mu_{it} \qquad (2)$$

where D_{Et} is a qualitative variable measuring the stringency of pollution control measures in country t based on a 1976 UNCTAD survey [Walter and Ugelow, 1979].

The degree of environmental stringency is measured on a scale from one (tolerant) to seven (strict); the mean score for developed

4. Although pollution emissions are a joint product of the production process, they can also be interpreted as an input in the production function because they can be viewed as one of the various uses of the environment [Baumol and Oates, 1988]. Since use of the environment is typically a public good, the environmental endowment has no price attached to it and will be used freely by industries until pollution control measures are instituted. Thus, in this study, a country's environmental endowment is measured by their stringency of pollution control measures.

THE EFFECTS OF DOMESTIC ENVIRONMENTAL POLICIES

Table 2

Index of the degree of Stringency of Environmental Policy
(7 = strict, 1 = tolerant)

Group A	Index	Group B	Index	Group C	Index
1 Austria	4	1 Chile	4	1 Colombia	5
2 Australia	5	2 Cyprus	1	2 Liberia	1
3 Belux	3	3 Israel	4	3 Nigeria	2
4 Denmark	5	4 Malta	1		
5 Finland	6	5 Singapore	6		
6 Germany	5	6 Spain	4		
7 Japan	7	7 Panama	4		
8 New Zeal.	5				
9 Nether.	5				
10 Norway	6				
11 Sweden	7				
12 UK	4				
13 USA	7				

Source: WALTER and UGELOW [1979].

countries is 6.1, while for developing countries it is 3.1. There are observations for 23 countries: 13 industrialized and 10 developing countries (see *Table 2*).

The results are presented in *Table 3* (absolute value of the t radio shown in parentheses beside the estimated regression coefficient). In no instance is the t ratio found to be statistically significant on the measure for the stringency of environmental policy in the five regressions of net exports of polluting industries.

2. *Omitted Variable Test*

A second approach to testing the effect of pollution control measures on trade patterns investigates the bias in the regression residuals when the variable representing countries' environmental endowments are not included in the HOV equations[5].

5. The idea for this methodology is attributable to RYTERMAN [1988]. RYTERMAN was able to show that technological flexibility is a significant variable in determining trade patterns between market economies and centrally planned economies.

Table 3

Variable Name	Equations (D. F. = 10) Mining (R^2=0.99)	Paper (R^2=0.96)	Chems (R^2=0.93)	Steel (R^2=0.89)	NFMetals (R^2=0.92)
CAP	−192 (2.4)	177 (1.6)	583 (5.6)	1537 (2.6)	−89 (1.0)
LAB1	735 (1.9)	−267 (0.5)	981 (1.9)	−1434 (0.5)	−550 (1.2)
LAB2	−111 (3.2)	−25 (0.5)	−154 (3.5)	54 (0.2)	44 (1.1)
LAB3	−15 (0.6)	50 (1.5)	−49 (1.6)	84 (0.5)	69 (2.5)
LND1	385 (1.5)	278 (0.8)	521 (1.6)	237 (0.1)	−254 (0.9)
LND2	−104 (0.7)	−192 (1.0)	−31 (0.2)	503 (0.5)	−247 (1.5)
LND3	1295 (2.8)	100 (0.2)	−268 (0.5)	−2898 (0.9)	−414 (0.8)
LND4	435 (0.9)	6089 (9.2)	−2003 (3.2)	−1374 (0.4)	−589 (1.1)
COAL	−78 (0.6)	−110 (0.6)	−283 (1.6)	−83 (0.1)	88 (0.6)
MINLS	338 (2.0)	330 (1.4)	88 (0.4)	26 (0.1)	715 (3.7)
OIL	−30 (1.6)	−110 (4.3)	−20 (0.8)	−142 (1.0)	17 (0.8)
D	−10314 (0.3)	2454 (0.1)	−1531 (0.1)	98844 0.4)	48658 (1.3)
CST	−5669 (0.1)	−168370 (1.0)	−107110 (0.7)	−697020 (0.8)	−122980 (0.9)

Consider first a simple HOV equation with one known and one unknown independent variable. Let x_{t2} represent a factor endowment for country t. Under the null hypothesis that the environmental factor (x_{t3}) has no effect on the pattern of trade, the equation specifying net exports (N_t) may be written as:

$$N_t = \beta_1 + \beta_2 x_{t2} + \tilde{\mu}_t \tag{3}$$

The alternative to the null hypothesis is represented by the following equation:

$$N_t = \beta_1 + \beta_2 x_{t2} + \beta_3 x_{t3} + \mu_t \tag{4}$$

If equation (3) is correct, the least squares estimators of β_1 and β_2 using equation (3) will be unbiased and efficient for all sample sizes. If equation (4) is correct, then estimation of equation (3) will still generate an unbiased estimator of β_2 given the following assumption[6]:

6. KMENTA [1971] shows that while $\hat{\beta}_2$ is unbiased, var($\hat{\beta}_2$) is positively biased. Therefore, the usual tests of significance concerning β_2 are not valid since they will tend to accept the null hypothesis more frequently than is justified by the given level of significance.

THE EFFECTS OF DOMESTIC ENVIRONMENTAL POLICIES

A1: The omitted variable is not correlated with any of the included independent variables.

Given assumption A1, estimation of equation (3) when the omitted variable (x_{t3}) does not equal zero will not affect $\hat{\beta}_2$. Its presence will, however, be embodied in the constant and disturbance term. Solving for $\tilde{\mu}_t$, the following equation can be derived:

$$= \beta_3(x_{t3} - \bar{X}_3) + \mu_t \quad (5)$$

Under the null hypothesis that x_{t3} has no effect on the pattern of trade so that $\beta_3 = 0$, $\tilde{\mu}_t$ is a consistent estimator of μ_t. Under the alternative case where pollution control measures are expected to have an effect on the pattern of trade, so that $\beta_3 \neq 0$, then (given assumption A1) $\tilde{\mu}_t$ provides a consistent estimate of equation (5).

A methodology to test the effect of pollution control measures on the pattern of trade may now be presented. Under the alternative hypothesis that equation (4) is correctly specified and assuming it also has all the properties of the classical regression model, then the sign of μ_t is expected to be random. Therefore, the expected sign of $\tilde{\mu}_t$ in equation (5) is the same as that of $\beta_3(x_{t3}-\bar{X}_3)$. β_3 is expected to be negative if pollution control measures reduce net exports of pollution-intensive commodities. To determine the sign of $(x_{t3}-\bar{X}_3)$, consider the distribution of the stringency of environmental regulations, x_{t3}, over the world. Industrialized, high-income countries have environmental endowments greater than the population mean $\bar{X}_3$, and less-developed countries have environmental endowments less than the population mean. Thus, the pattern of signs of $\tilde{\mu}_t$ under the alternative hypothesis depends on the distribution of x_{t3} over countries. Given the distribution above, the proportion of error terms that are postive for developing countries is expected to be significantly greater than the proportion of error terms that are positive for industrialized countries.

Let T_n represent the true proportion of errors for countries in group n (where $n=1$ corresponds to industrialized countries and $n=2$ corresponds to developing countries). The null hypothesis (H_0) states that the proportion of errors that are positive is the same for both industrialized and developing countries. The alternative hypothesis (H_1) states that the proportion of such errors is greater for developing countries than for industrialized countries.

$$H_0 : T_2 = T_1$$
$$H_1 : T_2 > T_1$$

A nonparametric statistical procedure was chosen to conduct the statistical test because it requires few assumptions regarding the distribution of the error terms. Under the null hypothesis, the test statistic may be given as[7]:

$$A = \frac{R_2 - R_1}{[\hat{T} \times (1 - \hat{T})[(1/I \times J_2) + (1/I \times J_1)]]^{1/2}}$$

where $R_n = S_n/(i \times J_n)$ represents the proportion of estimated errors that are positive; 'I' equals the total number of commodity groups (= 5), J_n equals the total number of countries in country group n; and S_n equals the number of estimated error terms for countries in group n that are positive.

$\hat{T}$ is an estimate of the true proportion under the null hypothesis. The best estimate of the true population proportion is constructed by combining the observations for both industrialized and developing countries as follows:

$$\hat{T} = (S_1 + S_2)/(I \times (J_1 + J_2))$$

To perform the omitted variable test a set of 58 countries is arranged in three groups (see TAble 4). Group one consists of industrialized, high-income countries. Environmental regulatory costs in this group are predicted to generate a comparative disadvantage in the production of polluting commodities. Group two is composed of upper-income developing countries and semi-industrialized nations without a stringent environmental program in 1975[8]. Group three is composed of middle to low-income developing countries.

A summary of information on the estimated residuals when equation (1) is estimated using this set of 58 countries is shown in Table 5. It is not possible to reject the null hypothesis that $T_2 = T_1$ in the comparison of industrialized countries with any combination of the

7. See YAMANE [1967].

8. A review of international environmental policy [TOBEY, 1989] is used to specify those countries with and without enforced pollution control measures as of the mid 1970s.

THE EFFECTS OF DOMESTIC ENVIRONMENTAL POLICIES

Table 4

Country Observations

Country	GDP per capita[1]	Country	GDP per capita[1] (1975 constant U.S. $)	Country	GDP per capita[1]
Group One		Group Two		Group Three	
Australia	5919	Argentina	3159	Afghanistan	380
Austria	4994	Brazil	1978	Burma	312
Belux	5569	Chile	1834	Colombia	1596
Canada	6788	Costa Rica	1835	Dom Rep	1443
Denmark	5969	Cyprus	1811	Ecuador	1300
Finland	5192	Greece	3360	Egypt	929
France	5864	Hong Kong	2559	El Salvador	1005
Germany	5758	Ireland	3067	Ghana	952
Iceland	5201	Israel	4154	Honduras	871
Japan	4904	Italy	3870	India	472
Netherlands	5321	Malta	2154	Indonesia	536
New Zealand	4769	Mexico	2276	Jamaica	1763
Norway	5419	Panama	2026	Korea	1530
Sweden	6749	Peru	1860	Liberia	830
Switzerland	6082	Portugal	2397	Lybia	6680[2]
UK	4601	Singapore	2875	Malaysia	1532
USA	7132	Spain	4032	Mauritius	1260
AVERAGE	5661	Turkey	1738	Nigeria	1179
		Yugoslavia	1960[2]	Paraguay	1186
		AVERAGE	2567	Philippines	912
				Sri Lanka	661
				Thailand	930
				AVERAGE	1002[3]

[1] HESTON and SUMMERS [1984].
[2] 1977 GNP per capita, from World Bank [1979], *World Development Report*.
[3] Excluding Libya.

developing country groups. These results reinforce the earlier finding which used a qualitative variable to represent the environmental endowment and which also found no effect of pollution control measures on HOV trade patterns.

IV. EXTENSIONS TO THE HOV MODEL

This section specifies alternative trade models when two of the HOV assumptions are relaxed (see LEAMER s[1984] for a complete list of

JAMES A. TOBEY

Table 5

Positive Residuals

Country Group	Paper	Steel	Chems	NFMetals	Mining	S_n[1]	J_n[2]	R_n[3]	A[4]
One	7	9	5	8	11	40	17	0.47	–
Two	5	10	9	5	6	35	19	0.37	–1.32
Three	10	18	15	5	11	59	22	0.54	0.96
2 + 3	15	28	24	10	17	94	41	0.45	–0.15

[1] S_n is the number of errors for group n that are positive.
[2] J_n is the number of countries in group n.
[3] $R_n = S_n/(I \times J_n)$.
[4] 'A' is the test statistic computed using group one as the sample of industrialized countries compared against groups of developing countries (T = 0.46). An absolute value of 1.65 for the test statistic in the normal distribution corresponds to a probability of 95 percent.

necessary assumptions) and reports the empirical results when the above empirical tests are again performed on these models.

The first exension of the HOV model allows for non-homothetic preferences. The HOV model assumes identical homnothetic tates – meaning that individuals facing identical commodity prices will consume commodities in the same proportions. In this cross-section study, with countries at various levels of development, this assumption may not be completely reasonable. To allow for NHP I assume that consumption across countries is a linear function of population and national income. When the HOV model is modified to incorporate this assumption, per capita net exports (n_{it}) become a linear function of per capita resource endowments (v_{kt}) as given by the following equation:

$$n_{it} = b^*_{i0} + \left(\sum_{k=1}^{K} b_{ik} v_{kt}\right) \tag{6}$$

where $b^*_{iO} = -c_{iO}$, and c_{iO} is a parameter that relates consumption of commodity i in country t to country t's population. As before, b_{ik} indicates the total effect of an increase in a resource on net trade of a specific commodity.

The same set of empirical tests are conducted using this equation.

Without burdening the reader with additional tables, I simply report that WALTER and UGELOW's variable is not significant in any of the OLS regressions. Similarly, the statistical comparison of error terms under the omitted variable test does not support the hypothesis being tested.

The second extension of the HOV model emphasizes scale economies and product differentiation. All of the pollution-intensive commodity groups are associated with what are generally considered very large-scale production processes. Moreover, HUFBAUER [1970] has found the production of paper products to be subject to large economies of scale and the production of nonferrous metals to be subject to diseconomies of scale. Scale economies may therefore be important in determining international comparative advantage for these goods. If this is the case, developing countries, with small economies and limited infrastructure outside of major cities may be at a disadvantage in the production of these commodities. A model which allows for the fact that the production function for polluting commodities exhibits economies of scale is therefore tested.

I use a model which MURRELL [1990] derives and which follows HELPMAN and KRUGMAN [1985] closely. The set of assumptions used to generate this model are essentially the same as those of the previous HOV model except that product differentiation and economies of scale are introduced. Specifically, it is assumed that each good can be produced in an infinite nujmber of varieties. Each variety of a single good has the same production function, but such functions vary between goods. Furthermore, the production function for each variety exhibits economies of scale, at least at low levels of output.

With the introduction of economies of scale and product differentiation, the export of good i by country t, x_{it}, are specified as follows [MURRELL, 1990]:

$$x_{it} = \sum_{k=1}^{K} b^*_{ik} V_{kt}(1 - G_t/G_w) \quad (7)$$

where G_t is the national income of country t and G_w is total world income.

Equation (7) cannot be derived from the H-O theory and and the asterisks on the coefficients of the equation are a reminder that these coefficients are not equivalent to b_{ik} in the previous two models.

Again, the same set of empirical tests are conducted, this time using equation (7). Once again, WALTER and UGELOW's variable is not found significant in any of the five OLS regressions. In contrast, the test statistics comparing the sign of the estimated residuals of industrialized and developing countries are significant at the 95 percent level of confidence, but, because they are negative, they also fail to support the hypothesis being tested.

V. A FIXED-EFFECTS EMPIRICAL TEST

A reasonable explanation for the empirical results above may be that the magnitude of environmental expenditures incurred by the industrialized countries in the late 1960s and early 1970s were not sufficiently large to cause a noticeable effect on trade patterns between countries with and without environmental protection programs. The cross-section HOV model may not be sufficiently precise to identify these small changes in factor abundances and comparative advantage. Thus, the effect of domestic environmental policy on trade may be getting lost in the 'noise'. By examining the change in trade patterns before and after te introduction of environmental measures in the industrialized countries, one might be able to detect the hypothesized shifts in trade patterns in response to environmental policies that don't show up in the equations using data from a specific point in time. Such a methodology would also be effective in capturing the effect of environmental policy even if there was a significant lag in the impact of pollution controls on international competitiveness.

Although endowment data are only available fo the year 1975, most resource endowments change little over time. At least for the most polluting industries, one might argue that the most important endowment change over the period 1970 to 1984 was the increase in environmental regulations. Consider then a HOV model where the change in net exports over 1970–84 is linearly related to the change in factor endowments over the same period. Under a 'fixed-effects' specification, assume tht, except for the environmental endowment, the change in factor endowments equals zero. In this case, one is left with the following equations:

$$\Delta N_{it} = E_t + \mu_{it}$$

THE EFFECTS OF DOMESTIC ENVIRONMENTAL POLICIES

Table 6

Variable Name	Equations (D. F. = 22) Mining ($R^2=0.03$)	Paper ($R^2=0.0+$)	Chems ($R^2=0.05$)	Steel ($R^2=0.0+$)	NFMetals ($R^2=0.04$)
E	−54155 (1.1)	−2298 (0.1)	78007 (1.9)	49437 (0.4)	−65593 (1.1)

where ΔN_{it} are 1984 minus 1970 net exports of commodity i by country t. E_t is the WALTER and UGELOW [1979] measure of the degree of the stringency of environmental policy in 23 countries in 1977. Since these countries generally did not have enforced environmental programs in place by 1970, the level of environmental policy given by this index is a reasonable proxy for the change in environmental policy. Finally, μ_{it} are the random error terms.

The results of the OLS estimation of this model are shown in *Table 6*. If environmental policies reduce countries' international comparative advantage in the most pollution-intensive commodities, then the sign on the environmental endowment coefficient should be negative and significant. Only in the chemicals group does the significance of the coefficient approach a conventionally accepted level of confidence. The sign, however, is positive, and once again does not support the hypothesized impact of pollution control measures on trade patterns.

VI. CONCLUDING REMARKS

Several tests are undertaken under a variety of specifications, but in no case is there any evidence that the introduction of environmental control measures has caused trade patterns to deviate from the HOV predictions. This result is important in that it casts serious doubt on the 'balance-of-trade' argument against environmental control which, as mentioned above, can be a strong deterrent to the implementation of new or stronger pollution control measures. the test results also lend support to the less empirically rigorous location-of-industry studies which maintain that the world distribution of 'dirty' industries has not been affected by differing country levels of environmental stringency.

As already noted, a reasonable explanation fo' these empirical results may simply be that the magnitude of environmental expenditures in countries with stringent environmental policies are not sufficiently large to cause a noticeable effect. This seems like the most likely explanation. Other explanations can, however, be postulated and I offer two possibilities below.

The first relates to the validity of the HOV equations themselves. The accuracy of the cross-section HOV model was recently questioned by BOWEN et al. [1987] who shows that since this model makes no reference to factor input intensities, it is only a weak test of the H-O hypothesis. The stricter H-O hypothesis requires that factor supplies, magnitude of the difference in robustness and accuracy of the weak version vis-à-vis the strict version is not clear.

The second observation relates to the nature of the pollution-intensive commodity groups and violations of the assumptions of the HOV model. this model assumes that commodities move inernationally at zero cost of tansportation, and that there are no other impediments to trade. However, transportation costs, tariffs, and subsidies[9] are important considerations in these industries and may affect a country's composition of trade. These trade impediments are difficult to deal with at an empirical level since they are very difficult to measure for large sets of countries. However, if they are distributed across countries in the same pattern as environmental controls then they would interfere with the ability of the HOV model to pick up the effect of environmental policy.

9. Many countries with stringent pollution control measures have offered various subsidies to polluting industries which lessen the impact of pollution control measures on world trade patterns in these industries.

THE EFFECTS OF DOMESTIC ENVIRONMENTAL POLICIES

REFERENCES

BAUMOL, W. and OATES, W.: *The Theory of Environmental Policy,* Second Edition, NY: Cambridge University Press, 1988.

BOWEN, H.: 'Changes in the International Distribution of Resources and their Impact on U.S. Comparative Advantages', *Review of Economics and Statistics,* Vol. 65 (1983), pp. 402–414.

BOWEN, H.; LEAMER, E. and SVEIKAUSKAS, L.: 'Multicountry, Multifactor Tests of the Factor Abundance Theorem', *American Economic Review,* Vol. 77 (1987), pp. 791–809.

D'ARGE, R.: 'International Trade, Domestic Income, and Environmental Controls: Some Empirical Estimates', in: KNEESE, A. (ed.), *Managing the Environment: International Economic Cooperation for Pollution Control,* New York: Praeger, 1974, pp. 289–315.

KRUGMAN, P. and HELPMAN, E.: *Market Structure and Foreign Trade,* Cambridge: MIT Press, 1986.

HESTON, A. and SUMMERS, R.: 'Improved International Comparisons of Real Product and its Composition: 1950–1980', *Review of Income and Wealth,* Vol. 30 (1984), pp. 207–262.

HUFBAUER, G.C.: 'The Impact of National Characteristics and Technology on the Commodity Composition of Trade in Manufactured Goods', in: VERNON, RAYMOND (ed.), *The Technological Factor in International Trade,* NY: Columbia University Press, 1970.

KALT, J.P.: 'The Impact of Domestic Environmental Regulatory Policies on U.S. International Competitiveness', Energy and Environmental Policy Center, Discussion Paper Series, John F. Kennedy School of Government, Harvard University, 1985.

LEAMER, E.E.: *Sources of International Comparative Advantage: Theory and Evidence,* Cambridge: MIT Press, 1984.

LEONARD, H.J.: *Pollution and the Struggle for World Product,* Cambridge: Cambridge University Press, 1988.

MCGUIRE, M.: 'Regulation, Factor Rewards, and International Trade', *Journal of Public Economics,* Vol. 17 (1982), pp. 335–354.

MURRELL, P.: *The Nature of Socialist Economies: Lessons from East European Foreign Trade,* Princeton University Press, 1990.

OECD: *The Macro-Economic Impact of Environmental Expenditures,* Organization for Economic Cooperation and Development, Paris, 1985.

PEARSON, C.: *Down to Business: Multinational Corporations, the Environment and Development,* Washington, D.C.: World Resources Institute, 1985.

PEARSON, C. (ed.): *Multinational Corporation, the Environment and Development,* Washington, D.C.: World Resources Institute, 1987.

PETHIG, R.: 'Pollution, Welfare, and Environmental Policy in the Theory of Comparative Advantage', *Journal of Environmental Economics and Management,* Vol. 2 (1976), pp. 160–169.

ROBISON, D. H.: 'Industrial Pollution Abatement: The Impact on Balance of Trade', Unpublished manuscript, University of Maryland, 1986.

RYTERMAN, R.: *Technological Flexibility and the Pattern of East-West Trade*, Ph. D. Thesis, University of Maryland, 1988.

SIEBERT, H.: 'Environmental Quality and the Gains from Trade', *Kyklos*, Vol. 30 (1977), pp. 657–673.

TOBEY, J.: *The Impact of Domestic Environmental Policies on International Trade*, Ph. D. Dissertation, University of Maryland, 1989.

U. S. Department of Commerce, Bureau of the Census: 'Pollution Abatement Costs and Expenditures', Current Industrial Reports, Washington, D. C., 1975.

WALTER, I.: 'Environmentally Induced Industrial Relocation to Developing Countries', in: RUBIN, S. J. and GRAHAM, T. R. (eds.), *Environment and Trade*, Allanheld, Osmum, and Publishers, 1982, pp. 67–101.

WALTER, I. and UGELOW, J.: 'Environmental Policies in Developing Countries', *Ambio*, Vol. 8 (1979), pp. 102–109.

YAMANE, T.: *Statistics: An Introductory Analysis*, NY: Harper and Row, 1967, pp. 584–585.

SUMMARY

The premise that trade suffers from the imposition of environmental policy has a strong element of a priori plausibility, but, surprisingly, has little empirical support. The present paper provides an empirical test of the hypothesis that stringent environmental policy has caused trade patterns to deviate in commodities produced by the world's 'dirty' industries. The empirical tests are conducted using the cross-section Heckscher-Ohlin-Vanek (HOV) model of international trade. It is not found that the introduction of stringent environmental control measures has caused trade patterns to deviate from the HOV predictions. This result casts serious doubt on the balance of trade argument against the imposition of stronger environmental control.

[7]

Trade and Environment Beyond Singapore

John Whalley

I. INTRODUCTION

Much, if not most, of the substantial recent literature on trade and environment (see Anderson and Blackhurst (1992), Beghin *et al.* (1994), Dean (1992), Esty (1994), Runge (1994), Ulph (1994) and Whalley (1991)) has largely concerned itself with the issue of whether policy linkage between trade and the environment can, in some sense, be justified. Is there a rationale for special trade rules to reflect environmental concerns? When does more trade help or hurt the environment? Should countries be allowed to use protection to achieve environmental goals? Should trade provisions in global environmental treaties be agreed to, even if they override provisions of trade treaties?

In contrast, this paper accepts that trade-environment linkage has entered the trading system, if for no other reason than that a natural instrument linkage exists, since (actual or threatened) trade measures can support transnational environmental objectives of importing countries and (although little discussed) environmental actions can, in principle, also support trade objectives of exporting countries (see Copeland and Taylor (1995)). Such linkage was implicitly accepted at the 1994 Marrakesh meeting that concluded the Uruguay Round, when a GATT/WTO Committee on Trade and Environment (CTE) was established. This Committee is to present its initial report at the first WTO ministerial meeting to be held in Singapore, December 9-13th 1996, and how this linkage will be reflected in the wider post Singapore trading system now seems a more pertinent issue rather than whether a justification for linkage exists.

The paper makes a number of points. Both because of the technical problems and wider precedents involved with any modifications to the GATT/WTO for environmental considerations, and the North-South divisions generated by the issue, progress within the GATT/WTO on this issue looks likely to be slow and painfully incremental rather than bold as environmental groups would wish to see. The mandate of the Committee on Trade and Environment for its Singapore report is largely limited to exploring what are the important environmental trade linkages. Little by way of new substantive proposals can be expected from it in Singapore.

Indeed, even taken largely as a GATT/WTO issue, there seem to be no widely agreed upon feasible options as ways to proceed; all proposals for ways forward to GATT/WTO trade and environment reform offered thus far seem to encounter problems. Advocacy that a future WTO Trade Round should be lead by the trade and environment issue (as a 'Green Round') seems not to reflect a realistic assessment both of where things stand in GATT/WTO on the issue, and the elements of reciprocity needed to drive a new Round forward.

The paper also argues that despite (and beyond) Singapore, one also has to go further than the GATT/WTO to see the potential evolution of the trade and environment issue. Developments on the trade and environment issue seem likely to be driven in the next few years as much by factors outside the GATT/WTO as well as within it, as new global environmental arrangements, some with potentially large trade implications (such as carbon emission limitation agreements), emerge. This has already arisen in the CTE with discussion of how to treat trade provisions of existing and new multilateral environmental agreements (MEA)s, such as the Montreal protocol, under the GATT/WTO. A credible argument is that the focus thus far on trade and environment issues of symbolic but limited quantitative significance in the trade and environment debate seems poised to change as discussion (outside of GATT/WTO) of a possible global environmental measures with potentially large trade effects accelerates.

The paper concludes by reemphasizing the potential the trade and environment issue has revealed for reigniting the recently dormant North-South divide on trade. Developing countries see trade and environment as a discussion of how trade barriers might go up against them and slow their growth and development, all in the name of meeting environmental objectives espoused by vocal NGOs in the developed world. Some of them use language such as 'green' or 'eco' imperialism, and argue that they should instead be compensated for showing environmental restraint. In contrast, environmental groups in the developed world argue that environmental issues are so serious that these should be the dominant considerations in the setting of the global policy framework, rather than trade concerns. This is a conflict that seems likely to intensify.

In summary, trade and environment remains an issue in flux, and one which is unlikely to be resolved quickly either in Singapore or through subsequent GATT/WTO negotiation. Also to treat trade and environment as solely a GATT/WTO issue risks missing the wider potential significance of environmental policy issues for the trading system; and its ability to resurrect North-South divisions in the trading system. This is especially the case given the complicating precedents the issue raises for other types of future negotiable trade linkages (such as labour standards).

II. THE TRADE AND ENVIRONMENT ISSUE, THE WTO, AND THE URUGUAY ROUND

General Considerations

The trade and environment issue is one that has come to have high profile in both the trade and the environment communities in recent years. In reality, there is no single issue, but instead a series of inter-related subissues which have agglomerated to fuel an ongoing debate as to what should be done about trade and environment linkage both within the framework of the WTO and more broadly.

At one level, consensus over possible trade and environment linkage derives from the argument, made early on in the debate, that increased trade inevitably implies increased consumption and production, and hence, lowered environmental quality. This theme was reflected in Congressional debates in 1991 and 1992 on NAFTA as it went through its various stages, where extreme environmental problems in the Maquiladora zone, including large untreated discharges into rivers, high infection rates in US border communities attributed to shared US-Mexican aquifers, and other related problems, were seen as inevitably worsening under a NAFTA with yet more US-Mexican trade.[1]

This view that environmental worsening necessarily follows from increased trade is, however, now widely seen as overly simplistic[2]. In the last few decades, developing countries who have been more outward-oriented in their trade policies (such as Korea

[1] Leonard and Christensen (1991) strongly made these arguments.

[2] However, Copeland and Taylor (1994) show how a simple static model of North-South trade can be used to examine linkages between national income, pollution, and international trade and produce results along these lines. Two countries produce a continuum of goods, each differing in pollution intensity. They show that the higher income country chooses stronger environmental protection and specializes in relatively clean goods. By isolating the scale, composition, and technique effects of international trade on pollution, they also show that free trade increases world pollution. An increase in the Rich North's production possibilities increases pollution, while a similar growth in the poor South lowers pollution; and unilateral transfers from North to South reduce worldwide pollution.

compared to, say, India up to the late 1980s) seem to have achieved higher rather than lower environmental standards. In part, this is due to their need to sell into higher income markets with higher environmental standards, which has required them to produce higher environmental standard products. In achieving high growth rates for significant periods of time, and hence higher living standards, these same countries also seem to have witnessed a clear positive impact on environmental quality, reflecting, in part, the income elasticity of their own demand for environmental quality. OECD countries' standards for air and water quality are also considerably higher today than they were 50 years ago (again due to higher incomes, and a positive income elasticity of demand for environmental quality), even though these same economies now trade considerably more as a percentage of GDP than formerly. The GATT (1992a) Annual Report built on these observations to argue, that, firstly, because gains are achievable through trade, real incomes will rise with increased trade; and, secondly, that if these income gains are spent on environmental protection, higher rather than lower environmental quality will result

At quite another level, debate on trade and environment linkage centres on the claim that environmental problems are now so serious that new and much needed environmental policy cannot be allowed to be thwarted by concerns over trade policy[3]. The argument is that the use of trade-restricting measures on environmental grounds should be allowed, even if presently not sanctioned by GATT/WTO. Thus, special trade promotion devices related to environmental objectives (such as export subsidies for pollution control equipment) should be allowed; trade restrictions which offset the effect of low environmental standards are justifiable; and provisions contained in

[3] See Shrybman (1989, 1990).

6

existing trade treaties (such as GATT/WTO, or the Treaty of Rome) should not preclude the use of new environmental arrangements, simply on grounds of precedent. The line of argument is that what is needed is to develop appropriate global management strategies for scarce environmental resources, and that trade policy is a key supporting mechanism to implement such resource management, rather than a policy to be decided upon solely on trade considerations.

The counter arguments to this reflect the contention that the benefits of an open trading system in the form of gains from trade have been slowly built up over 50 years of multilateral negotiation, and should not be easily surrendered to new protectionism sanctioned by environmental concerns[4]. Any special treatment for the environment under existing trade rules is also seen as setting a dangerous precedent. A domino theory of the trading system is sometimes raised; i.e., that special treatment for one issue will lead to special treatment for other issues, with, eventually, a disappearance in generality of the rule regime in the trading system as we know it today. Reinforcing these concerns is the risk of environmental capture; i.e. that trade policy could become more protectionist, not due to genuine environmental considerations motivating trade policy, but rather from protectionist interests using environmental arguments for their own ends and legitimizing their narrow sectional interests by appeal to environmental rationales[5].

---

[4] See, for instance, Bhagwati (1993).

[5] See the analytical discussions of this new political economy dimension to trade policy in Hillman and Ursprung (1994).

The WTO

Within the GATT/WTO, the trade and environment issue has also steadily grown in profile in recent years with the development of the wider trade and environment debate outlined above[6]. In its first forty years relatively few environmental cases came before GATT dispute settlement, and the only (somewhat oblique) environmental content of GATT contained in Article XX remained little clarified by dispute case resolution[7].

A central event in changing this situation was the report of the 1991 GATT panel requested by Mexico following US trade actions based on the practices of tuna fishermen off the Mexican west coast, and which subsequently ruled in Mexico's favour. The issue was that tuna were being caught in nets which incidentally entangled dolphins, causing some of the dolphins to be killed. The United States had made repeated representations to Mexico to reduce the number of dolphins killed in these tuna catches. Appealing to US legislation under the Marine Mammal Protection Act, Earth Island Institute, a California nonprofit group, moved in 1990 to ban the importation of canned, frozen and fresh tuna into the US from 5 countries (Mexico, Panama, Venezuela, Ecuador and Vanuatu). The US also implemented a labelling requirement under this law that set out the conditions under which canned tuna sold in the United States could be described as caught in a dolphin-friendly manner.

---

[6] See Charnovitz (1992).

[7] Appendix C of Esty (1994) outlines both previous GATT cases, and relevant US and EU case law. Some of the earlier GATT cases which touched on environmental issues involved excise duties on imported petroleum and products in the US to fund environmental clean up (the 1971 Superfund case); Canadian restrictions on export of unprocessed fish products from the West Coast fishery (1988), and import bans on cigarettes in Thailand (1990).

8

The request for a panel by Mexico and the subsequent panel decision in Mexico's favour attracted widespread attention because it was the first time that a GATT panel was asked to rule on an environmental issue in this way. There were public representations made in Geneva from environmental groups protesting the case and emphasizing what they saw as the anti-environment nature of the GATT. In their view concern for dolphins, not profit, should have been the driving force behind trade policy in the case.

Mexico based its case on two separate arguments. The first was that the US had no rights under GATT to impose such a trade ban. The United States argued that under Article XX(b) of the GATT it had rights to use trade bans to protect endangered species. The Mexican argument was that were no endangered species at issue; in this case the only point of contention was the nature of the fishing methods used. The Mexicans also appealed the US labelling condition as to when canned tuna could be displayed with a logo indicating that dolphin-friendly methods were used to catch the tuna, on the grounds that this would involve a violation of the mark-of-origin provisions of the GATT under Article IV, which only requires an indication of country of origin.

Following the tuna-dolphin panel report in favour of Mexico[8], dissatisfaction grew on GATT's position on trade and environment issues on several fronts. Environment groups saw GATT as anti-environment since it did not uphold the use of a trade

[8] The panel finding on behalf of Mexico ruled that the US ban was a violation of GATT Article III, and that the Article XX exceptions in GATT could not be applied on an extraterritorial basis ruling them inapplicable in this case. However, the panel report ruled in favour of the US on the labelling issue. The panel report was not pushed forward to adoption by the GATT Council for a variety of reasons, including Mexico's then emerging NAFTA negotiation; so the EC subsequently brought a second complaint on tuna-dolphin dealing with import bans in the US Marine Mammal Protection Act from third countries who trade with countries against whom primary actions are taken. The panel report (Tuna-Dolphin II) in 1994 ruled against the US, but on somewhat different grounds. See Esty (1994) pp.268-269.

restricting measure to limit incidental dolphin kills. The US Congress saw GATT as overriding the content of domestic US legislation to protect mammals; and more broadly the environmental content of GATT was seen as vague, weak, and in need of clarification and repair. The extremely limited environmental content of the Uruguay Round decisions (reflecting the 1986 negotiating mandate) intensified these concerns, as did the absence of any reference to the environment in the founding charter of the WTO.

The Uruguay Round

Despite the profile of the trade and environment issue in the mid to late stages of the Uruguay Round[9], the decisions from the Round do not deal directly with trade and environment issues since they were not formally part of the negotiating mandate. Much was made by environmental groups of the observation that the word 'environment' did not appear in the Draft Final Act from the Round (the Dunkel Text), which, including tariff schedules, ran to some 26,000 pages of text[10]. Also, the failure of the decisions establishing the WTO to set out future environmental objectives was seen as a chance squandered, and maybe lost for decades, to centrally address the trade and environment issue and establish broad principles in this area to guide the WTO in its future work.

Nonetheless, trade and environment issues were important in developments running parallel to the negotiations themselves, and in particular played a role in defining the

[9] A number of events contributed to raising the profile of trade and environment (virtually unheard of at its launch in Punta del Este in 1986) during the later part of the Uruguay Round besides the tuna/dolphin dispute. These included the Earth Summit at Rio in June 1992; the vocal opposition of environmentalists to the NAFTA, and the efforts of environmental groups to block adoption of both the NAFTA and the Uruguay Round decisions in the US.

[10] For a summary of the Uruguay Round agreements, see Whalley and Hamilton (1996).

work program for the WTO following the Round. Also, as Uimonen (1995) argues, it is not the case that the Uruguay Round decisions are free of environmental implications The Round includes agreements which discipline the trade restricting effects of standards and regulations which have environmental implications, and the agreements on subsidies, countervailing duties and intellectual property rights all have implications for environmental issues.

At a more technical level, the sanitary and phytosanitary measures and technical barriers to trade (TBT) agreements address problems raised by a number of contentious environmental and trade cases[11]. Their objective was to minimize the extent to which standards and regulations can have negative effects on trade, or act as disguised trade barriers, while still permitting GATT contracting parties to adopt or maintain standards that are necessary for the protection of human, plant, and animal life and health.

In the technical barriers to trade agreement, measures include those for environmental protection, as well as those regulations which apply to production and process methods (PPMs.) Each of these agreements defines a national treatment obligation as well as a necessity test, with the aim of minimizing adverse effects of measures taken, much like in GATT Article XX, with loose harmonization agreements for each of the two.

As Uimonen notes, the TBT agreement could prove a catalyst for future environmental trade because the Uruguay Round disciplines in this area seemingly restrict domestic policies rather than border measures. European countries, for instance, have been playing a leading role in developing new regulations covering waste

[11] Including the Canadian beer can case which involved a new environmental levy on beer packaged in cans. For details, see GATT (1992b) Focus 91, p.2

11

production and recycling, which include waste take-back schemes requiring producers to either take back their packaging waste for disposal or recycling, or pay fees to local authorities to accomplish the same objective, and these could be affected.

The Uruguay Round Subsidies Agreement makes several changes to earlier trade rules, and with potentially significant implications for environmental issues. The approach is one of recognizing the rights of contracting parties to protect themselves through the use of PPMs and related subsidies, while avoiding misuse of countervailing measures of protection. The Agreement offers a definition of subsidy, previously not contained in the GATT, in the form 'specific'[12] subsidies, and classifies them according to three categories. The Agreement also lists general subsidies characterized by government financial contributions as nonspecific and nonactionable subsidies; thus nonspecific environmental subsidies are now permitted.

On other environmentally related matters, the Uruguay Round generated results with varying degrees of ambiguity. In the area of standards, the thrust of the agreements from the Round is to discipline trade barriers, while allowing for differences in non-border measures. Exactly how much discipline will be exerted on national regulations, especially in the case of sanitary and phytosanitary standards, and what will constitute sufficient scientific justification for high standards remains unclear. Under the subsidies agreement, however, the use of countervailing measures to deal with unfair trade practices in the form of lax environmental standards is not permitted. But the agreement does imply that subsidies that take the form of foregone revenue for environmental taxes can be countervailable if they are specific.

[12] A 'specific' subsidy is one considered only available to 'an enterprise or industry or group of enterprises or industries within the jurisdiction of the authority granting the subsidy', GATT (1994). The definition of a subsidy also rests on whether there is a financial contribution by a government or any public body.

12

Post Uruguay Round[13]

At the ministerial meeting which concluded the Uruguay Round at Marrakesh in April 1994, the contracting parties agreed both that trade and environment should be on the future agenda for the WTO, and that a new Committee on Trade and the Environment (CTE) should be formed to assess trade and environment linkages. This Committee is to give its first report in Singapore in December 1996.

It was agreed that the agenda for the CTE work on trade and environment would cover (i) the relationship between multilateral environmental arrangements and the GATT/WTO, (ii) how environmental policies with significant trade effects impact the trading system (iii) how environmental taxes and charges interact with trade rules (iv) eco-labelling issues (v) WTO dispute settlement and MEAs (vi) environmental policy measures and market access and (vii) domestically prohibited goods. Progress on most of these issues has been slow. In essence, developed countries, and especially the EU, have argued for modifications to GATT/WTO disciplines for environmental reasons; while developing countries, fearful of legitimizing protection against their exports have taken a more cautious stance. Little of substance in any of these areas is expected to be concluded at Singapore.

On production and processing methods, proposals have been made to modify the present GATT principle of national treatment contained in Article III, and more specifically, the concept of like products, which presently disallows any distinction in trade policy treatment between products made in a clean' and 'dirty' manner. Present

[13] Also see the description of the wider post Uruguay Round agenda covering environmental and non-environmental issues in Woolcock (1996).

GATT/WTO rules are seen as inconsistent with activist domestic environmental policies, since they inevitably imply a competitive disadvantage to domestic industries, if exporting countries have lower standards. On MEAs, the aim has been to secure a GATT/WTO accommodation of the trade provisions of their agreements before any GATT/WTO inconsistent measures are taken under the Montreal protocol. Proposals include expanding the scope of GATT Article XX exceptions to explicitly cover MEA trade measures; the granting of GATT/WTO Waivers for such trade measures; and the grant of limited (contained) waivers which would condition the use of MEA trade measures. On other less significant issues, accommodation may be possible; joint Codes of Conduct for eco-labelling schemes is one. But in general, the picture is one of limited movement on the trade and environment issues in the CTE agenda pre Singapore.

At a less technical level, however, trade and environment continues to be repeatedly cited as a major component of the likely future focus for global trade policy negotiation and debate. Renato Ruggiero, Director General of the WTO, has identified trade and environment as one of four issues (along with competitive policy, labour standards, and investment) which will shape the future work programme of the WTO, and eventually form the lead issues of a future multilateral negotiating Round. Immediately after the Uruguay Round, there were several calls for a new negotiating Round to be a 'Green Round', and such calls, while less frequent, are still heard.

This profile for trade and environment as a lead issue within GATT/WTO thus seemingly coexists with difficulties in making much progress in Singapore, and clear divisions between developed and developing countries on the issue. The trade and environment component of any future negotiation would also be a rule writing rather than traditional reciprocity based negotiation, and one with precedents for other potential rule writing exercises (such as labour standards). While the Uruguay Round established precedents for rule writing concessions (for instance, in Intellectual Property by the developing countries) it further complicates any leading role to be played by the issue in a future multilateral negotiating Round.

III. THE ENVIRONMENTAL AGENDA FOR GATT/WTO AFTER SINGAPORE[14]

Given both the limited concrete progress on the trade and environment issue that seems likely in Singapore and its likely continued high profile as a potential lead issue for a future negotiating Round, it seems useful to speculate how the debate on the issue may develop within the WTO after Singapore, out into the medium term. I would argue both that the technical problems and worries over precedent will complicate any accommodation within the WTO on the trade and environment issue and cleavage between developed and developing countries on trade and environment will be likely remain and even intensify after Singapore. Also, increasingly it will be the case that developments outside the GATT/WTO, such as the potential trade effects of new global environmental agreements, and, to a lesser extent, environmental arrangements concluded in regional agreements, will enter and drive the debate.

Thus, the talk of either a separate environmental negotiation - a 'Green Round' of negotiations, or an environment-lead new wider Round - talk that was heard even before the conclusion of the Uruguay Round, may well continue. The pressures which have been building for changes to be made within the GATT/WTO to accommodate environmental concerns may also remain as the focus for GATT/WTO debate on trade and environment after Singapore, but with growing frustration both from advocates and opponents of change. Concerns of environmental groups over what they see as secretive GATT/WTO processes, in which they have no rights to appear or appeal will persist. Linkage not only of GATT/WTO arrangements to multilateral environmental

[14] This section draws heavily on the discussion in Uimonen and Whalley (1996), Ch.6).

agreements but also to new MEAs and onto trade patterns will become an evermore a key issue.

None of this indicates that nothing can be done in GATT/WTO post Singapore on trade and environment, as those who saw the seemingly deep divide on services pre Uruguay Round (in early 1986) will recall. But exactly how trade and environment would eventually be accommodated in GATT/WTO at this stage is unclear, both technically and politically; and what the GATT/WTO response would be, if there were one, to the wider impacts of environmental policies is at this stage unknown.

Broad GATT/WTO Modification

A variety of proposals have been offered as to how environmental considerations could be taken into account in future GATT/WTO agreements. One might be to more fully utilize what is presently available in the GATT, including the Article XXV waiver mechanism to allow for the use of otherwise GATT-inconsistent measures on evnironmental grounds. Another would be to seek changes to the GATT/WTO rules so as to allow for wide-ranging exceptions on environmental grounds. There could also be more narrowly focused elaborations and clarifications to the GATT agreements now in the WTO, aiming to deal centrally with environment and trade issues.

Waivers for individual Contracting Parties under Article XXV could be used for environmentally related trade restricting measures that would otherwise violate present GATT/WTO arrangements. Approval of a waiver requires a three-quarters majority.. Environmental waivers could possibly take on more general forms than those which have been seen in the GATT thus far, which are usually narrowly focused and granted to only one Contracting Party at a time. There could be bloc waivers, given simultaneously to subgroups (or even all) Contracting Parties, and allowing them to use specific trade-restricting measures for environmental purposes. There could even be broad-ranging waivers setting out general conditions under which environmental exceptions would be allowed.

Waivers have the attraction of addressing environmental concerns while leaving the existing structure of GATT/WTO disciplines unchanged, thus avoiding any need for a potentially complex and divisive rule rewriting negotiation. However, a series of waivers granted on a case-by-case basis runs the risk of yielding a chaotic and inconsistent outcome. Each waiver request would have to go through a separate waiver approval process, repeatedly raising potential problems in reaching agreement. Also, more widespread use of waivers in the environmental area seems to go against the current GATT/WTO trend of downplaying the use of waivers in other areas (such as agriculture).

Another way to bring environmental considerations more fully into the GATT/WTO would be to directly amend the General Agreement to allow for more explicit environmental exceptions than it now contains, although the requirements are stringent. Some key GATT articles (including Articles I and III) require acceptance by all members, while others require a two-thirds majority. Furthermore, amendments must pass national treaty ratification procedures, which further reduces the potential for success.

Table 1 reproduces a list of the main GATT articles that could potentially be involved in such a negotiation given in Uimonen and Whalley (1996) [15]. The scope of the possible changes to the GATT/WTO is immediately striking. Central to any such

[15] See also Arden-Clarke (1991), and Patterson (1991).

negotiation would be an attempt to clarify or change the language of XX(b) and XX(g). But other articles, including MFN and national treatment (Articles I and III) - the cornerstones of the GATT - might also be subjected to environmental review, as might a number of other key articles (VI, XI, XIII, XIV, XVI, XIX, XX) and trade provisions explicitly applying to developing countries (XVIII, and Part IV). Such a wide ranging negotiation on rule rewriting covering many GATT Articles would almost certainlyprove difficult to conclude, especially as many non environmental issues would likely be raised by individual countries. Alternatively, narrowing such a negotiation to only a few Articles makes it difficult to launch, because individual countries would want to see issues of particular importance to them dealt with.

An alternative but related approach might be to negotiate a side agreement on trade and the environment to so as to supplement and clarify the meaning of existing Articles of the General Agreement and other agreements in the WTO as they relate to environmental issues. For example, rules ranging from subsidy and competitiveness issues to procedures for the application of unilateral measures for environmental protection could be subject to clarification and elaboration. In addition, following GATT tradition since the Kennedy Round, 'special and differential treatment' on environmental issues could be granted to less-developed countries, perhaps in the form of longer time periods to implement environmentally related decisions.

19

Potential Environmentally Motivated Changes in Selected GATT/WTO Articles*

Article	Rule	Environmental Issues
I. Most-Favoured-Nation	The most favourable treatment for exports and imports must be granted to 'like' products of all countries.	Distinguishing products on the basis of environmental impact of products and/or PPMs.
II. Schedule of Concessions	Negotiated tariff bindings. An exception to tariff bindings allows for border tax adjustments on imports equivalent to domestic charges on like products consistent with Article III.	Allow for border adjustments on products using environmentally damaging PPMs. Disallow adjustments when imports have no cross-border environmental effects.
III. National Treatment	Once they have cleared customs and border procedures, imported goods are to be treated no less favourably than like domestic products with respect to domestic taxes and regulations.	Distinguishing products on basis of environmental impact of products and/or PPMs.
VI. Anti-dumping and Countervailing Duties	Allow ADDs on imports equal to the dumping margin when there is material injury as a result of dumping. Allow CVDs on subsidized imports when there is material injury.	Margins of dumping and subsidy to include marginal social costs of environmental damage. Countervailability of pollution abatement subsidies, 'lax standard'subsidies.
IX. Marks of Origin	Provides for MFN with regard to labelling requirements; countries should minimize adverse trade effects of marks of origin regulations.	Treatment of 'ecolabelling' laws.
X. Public and Administration of Trade Regulations	Countries should maximize transparency of regulations affecting trade.	Extension of transparency requirements to environmental measures and their scientific justification.
XI. Quantitative Restrictions	Prohibits quantitative restraints on imports and exports subject to certain exceptions.	Elaborate on or clarify environmentally based exceptions.
XII and XIV. Non-discrimination in QRs and exceptions	Allowable QRs to be applied similarly to all countries and exceptions to this rule	Allowable QRs to be applied similarly to all countries and exceptions to this rule

*This is reproduced here with slight modification from Table 6.01 in Uimonen and Whalley (1996)

20

XVI. Export Subsidies	Export subsidies for primary products should not result in a more than equitable share of world trade. Conditional prohibition of export subsidies to non-primary products. Tokyo Round Code prohibited these subsidies, increased discipline on domestic subsidies. Uruguay Round prohibits non-agricultural export subsidies, further increases disciplines on domestic subsidies	Further disciplines on environmentally damaging domestic subsidies. Allowances for CVDs against countries with 'lax'standards on some margin reflecting social cost.
XVI. Border Adjustment	Rebate of indirect taxes on products or inputs contained in products upon export is permitted. Uruguay Round allows for rebate of indirect taxes on enrgy used in production.	Disallow rebates for environmental taxes, energy taxes on exported goods.
XVIII. Developing Country Tariff Protection	Allows developing countries to give tariff and other assistance for purpose of economic development and to improve standards of living.	Allowances for environmentally based measures for developing countries.
XIX. Safeguards	Allows countries to take otherwise GATT-inconsistent measures temporarily when imports harm a competing domestic industry.	Allowances for trade measures to deal with sudden environmental problems associated with imports or exports.
XX. General Exceptions	Allows measures 'necessary' for protection of health and safety 'relating to' protection of exhaustible natural resources.	Loosening of 'necessity' test. Allowances for second-best measures. Allowances for extra-jurisdictional application of measures. Allowances for sanctions.
XXIV. Free Trade Areas and Customs Unions	Criteria for regional trading arrangements to be GATT-consistent.	Require EIAs in evaluating RTAs and consistency of environmentally related provisions of such agreements.

*This is reproduced here with slight modification from Table 6.01 in Uimonen and Whalley (1996)

21

Part IV. Special and Differential Treatment		Exceptions or easements for developing countries from any new environmental disciplines. Exceptions for developing countries to allow for otherwise GATT-inconsistent measures related to environmental protection.

*This is reproduced here with slight modification from Table 6.01 in Uimonen and Whalley (1996)

However, in the short run, it seems likely that the only practical mechanism available for fundamental environmental rule modification in the GATT/WTO fundamentally will be waivers, and these seem likely to yield an unsatisfactory conclusion. Even over a longer period, it remains unlikely that the GATT/WTO would be fundamentally amended, given both the scope of change and the practical difficulties involved. If, at some future date, the Contracting Parties attempt to agree on new trade/environment rules, it would most likely be in the form of a side agreement supplementing and interpreting existing rules.

Article XX Reform

At the forefront of any effort to change GATT rules as they apply to the environment would be both clarification and reconsideration of Article XX exceptions[16]. The issue here is as much one of determining what the current rules actually imply, as it is one of changing existing rules.

There is currently substantial confusion about the precise meaning of Article XX exceptions. Previous Article XX panels appear to have reached a consensus, that measures must be 'necessary' for health and safety or 'primarily aimed at' the conservation of an exhaustible resource. But confusion remains over whether exceptions should be narrowly defined to prevent their abuse, and the justification for such a narrow definition. For instance, the first[17] tuna-dolphin panel restricted the scope of Article XX by limiting its jurisdictional application. The second panel backtracked from the first panel on this point, and it substituted a criterion whereby a

[16] See the extensive discussion of Article XX issues in Charnovitz (1992), and Esty (1994, Ch.9)..

[17] See the earlier discussion in footnote 8, p.8, on the two tuna-dolphin panels.

23

country could not impose trade restrictions for environmental or other reasons, if the only way it could achieve its objective was by forcing the affected country to change its domestic policies.

There have been proposals for wide-ranging amendments to Article XX, to the effect that nothing in the GATT/WTO would prevent any Contracting Party from taking any action 'which it may deem necessary to protect the environment, including the establishment of import or export restrictions, and the use of subsidies ...' (Shrybman, 1989). These have been linked to provisions that, in any GATT/WTO dispute regarding actions taken to protect the environment (domestic or otherwise) the onus should be on the complainant to prove that the measure 'was not taken in good faith and that it was unreasonable' (Shrybman, 1989)[18]. A precedent for such proposals appears to be GATT Article XX(h) which provides exemptions for signatories to international commodity agreements along related lines. The obvious weakness is that such exemptions would provide open-ended cover for protection, as well as promote inefficient environmental policy. Under the cover of such an exemption any trade actions could, in principle, be taken in the name of environmental concerns[19]. Because of this, opposition to such proposals is especially strong, particularly from developing countries.

Trade restrictions on products with PPMs that cause environmental damage in the importing country are also an Article XX issue (as well as an Article III (MFN) issue) since they were called into question in the second tuna-dolphin panel report. The panel report asserted that the trade restrictions at issue could not, by themselves, achieve their

---

[18] Similar proposals for broad-ranging exceptions from GATT obligations for environmental purposes may be found in Arden-Clarke (1991).

[19] This obviously raises the political economy issues discussed in Hillmand and Ursprung (1994).

environmental objective; and so, if allowance is to be made for such second-best policies, the circumstances under which they would be permitted need to be addressed. This raises once again the issues implicit in the tuna-dolphin panel reports concerning 'necessity' tests; whether extrajurisdictional measures should be disciplined more severely, and how measures taken in the context of international environmental agreements should be dealt with.

One possible change might be to permit trade measures for extrajurisdictional environmental protection, but require that they be 'necessary' in a stricter sense than for measures to protect domestic health, safety, or environment. Such additional criteria might include demonstration of prior attempts to negotiate an international agreement under the auspices of an agreed upon international body, such as UNEP; and a 'good faith' estimate and offer of resource transfers, or even trade compensation.

Future reconsideration of the use of trade measures under Article XX may also draw on the results of UNCED, which reiterated the need to avoid arbitrary discrimination and disguised trading barriers, as with existing GATT rules. The Rio Declaration called on countries to avoid unilateral attempts to address environmental problems which originate outside a country's territorial jurisdiction. Furthermore, it called on countries to base their solutions on international consensus as far as possible.

If there is a general approach to rewriting Article XX so as to clarify general exceptions from GATT/WTO disciplines for environmental trade measures emerging from these documents, it is to avoid unilateralism and new forms of protectionism as far as possible. However, there is widespread disagreement as to exactly how to circumscribe future allowances for environmentally motivated trade measures in elaborating on these general principles.

Environmental Regulation

An equally central GATT/WTO issue beyond Singapore will be the interaction of environmental regulation and trade policy. The national treatment obligation under GATT/WTO in Article III requires Contracting Parties not use internal taxes or regulations in ways which give domestic protection, and requires domestic policies to treat imports no less favourably than 'like' domestic products. The GATT has interpreted this provision as requiring Contracting Parties not to use measures to discriminate in favour of products. The concept of 'like' product has been widely interpreted as prohibiting trade restrictions based on the processes and methods (PPMs) used to produce imported goods. PPM-based trade restrictions become prima facie violations of national treatment, which then must be justified under Article XX if they are to be allowed.

There are a variety of ways in which these disciplines might be relaxed. One approach might be to allow any measures which do not violate MFN and national treatment obligations. This would clearly be inadequate to discipline the protectionist use of such measures. Another might be to change the wording in Article XX(b) from 'necessary' to 'relating to' as in Article XX(g), with the aim of weakening the requirement that has evolved in past panel disputes, that a measure must be the least GATT-inconsistent measure reasonably available[20]. New language might require measures to be 'consistent with, and a part of, the framework of environmental policies of the nation imposing the measure' (Patterson, 1992, 107). Thus, rather than considering trade-restrictive measures within the set of all possible policies to achieve a given objective with a view toward identifying a less GATT-inconsistent measure, this

[20] See Patterson (1992).

approach might allow trade-distorting measures related to a nation's domestic environmental policies, as long as they avoid (in some sense) in protectionist abuse.

Dispute settlement panels have already examined whether regulatory or tax distinctions used for non-trade objectives are allowable in determining whether 'like' products are treated in accordance with Article III. The task for the WTO dispute settlement process on these matters has been to walk a line restricting national policy-making that inevitably entails incidental trade effects, and permitting the use of ostensibly domestic taxes and regulations for protectionist purposes.

Even if domestic taxes or regulations violate the national treatment obligation under Article III, they may still be justified under Article XX. This will raise further questions post Singapore as to how stringent such exceptions might be. The GATT approach to trade measures taken to protect domestic health, safety and environment under Article XX(b) thus far has been to permit them as long as they can be shown to be 'necessary' for the purpose, i.e. that they are the least GATT-inconsistent, or trade-distorting, measures available. For example, the Uruguay Round discisions discipline standards that are more stringent than international norms, to ensure that they are the 'least trade-distortionary' measures available. Whether this approach prevails will be an issue.

Transparency

Concerns have been frequently expressed in the environmental community over the seemingly closed procedures used in GATT/WTO negotiations and dispute settlement of environmental cases. These issues seem likely to persist post Singapore[21]. The most

[21] See also Arden-Clarke (1991) and Jackson (1992).

significant concerns have focused on the seeming secrecy of the dispute settlement process since most domestic legal systems define rights to appear before administrative tribunals, and also give rights to interested parties to appeal decisions. The absence of such rights in GATT disputes involving environmental issues has concerned many environmentalists.

The response from the trade community is usually to argue first, that panel procedures represent efforts to depoliticise political conflicts involving national governments, and that a more open process would undermine these efforts. They argue, second, that if such rights are granted to environmental groups, similar rights would have to be granted to other political groups in both environmental and other cases, potentially derailing the process.

Another transparency issue involves the provision of information to judge the environmental effects of proposed policy changes, including the outcome of any future multilateral negotiation.. In the US, federal policies often require environmental impact statements (EISs), under the 1969 National Environmental Policy Act. An unsuccessful attempt was made in the US courts to force compliance with this act arguing that the NAFTA and Uruguay Round agreements should be subject to its requirements. While there may be justification for assessments where narrowly focused trade policy changes with a significant environmental link are at issue, a requirement for entire trade agreements where most elements have no direct environmental relationship immediately apparent, runs the risk of significantly complicating the negotiation and ratification processes.

While an open process for trade negotiations, such as the Uruguay Round, may make exchanges of concessions more difficult, a more transparent set of procedures for dispute settlement would seem to be an improvement, especially for disputes arising over the trade effects of domestic policies, such as those under the S&P and TBT agreements. Under these agreements, either party to a dispute can request the formation of a technical expert group to examine the scientific merits of standards that appear stricter than international norms. The work of the expert group is then used by the panel; such panels may, but are not required to, seek information from outside sources. Some have suggested that a special category of cases be established for environmentally-related disputes, before which expert opinion can also be placed.

Subsidies and Competitiveness Issues

Questions will also arise post Singapore about the relationship between to environment, subsidies and competitiveness. These include whether to change current trade rules that restrict export and domestic subsidies, even if used for environmental protection; whether relatively lower environmental standards should be countervailable; and whether trade discipline on the use of subsidies might be environmentally beneficial.

The Uruguay Round increased restraints on the use of export subsidies, and these new rules apply equally to pollution abatement and other non-primary product industries. The idea behind limiting the use of export subsidies is to both prevent an 'unfair' trade advantage accruing to exporters receiving such subsidies, and to achieve neutrality with respect to trade policies (i.e., tariffs and export subsidies).

Export subsidies for environmentally friendly products are seen as a mechanism through which environmental protection technology could be transferred to developing countries, even though cash transfers to developing countries adopting appropriate environmental policies and not tied to purchase of particular products, would be more

29

efficient. However, there is a general reluctance to allow the use of such subsidies in light of experience in agriculture where subsidy wars have occurred. Furthermore, if not carefully designed, such special exceptions for export subsidies could lead to incentives to adopt end-of-pipe clean-up technologies as opposed to products and processes that pollute less and are inherently cleaner. Also, any use of such subsidies should be approached with caution because they can stimulate entry into polluting industries. Allowance for domestic environmental subsidies not 'generally available' would also need to be carefully designed to prevent abuse.

Thus, while environmental allowances for export and domestic subsidies will likely be explored post Singapore, particularly with respect to increasing access for less-developed countries to environmental protection technology, this will probably be done cautiously so that incentives to use subsidies (as opposed to 'polluter-pays' policies) do not grow.

Other GATT Articles

Post Singapore there will also likely be a discussion of environmental issues with other GATT Articles outside of Article XX. Table 1 earlier gives a list of GATT articles which could potentially come under scrutiny in any attempt to rewrite the GATT/WTO in the light of environmental concerns.

Articles I and III, the non-discrimination and national treatment cornerstones of the GATT, could be an initial focal point for such efforts. The objective would be that they be modified so as to allow discriminatory trade actions on environmental grounds. While Article XX is the natural route for countries seeking to use such measures, this will likely not preclude such changes being sought in the future. Under Article IX, various ecolabelling issues such as those implied by recent EU policy may be raised. At issue is the extent to which such measures represent non-transparent trade discrimination, or impose added costs on foreign producers.

Possible issues with Articles XI and XIII could be discriminatory import bans similar to those under dispute in the tuna-dolphin case. Pressures could be exerted here for special environmental exceptions to these two Articles, without the need to argue cases under the general exceptions of Article XX.

Article XVIII, which implies less stringent discipline on less-developed countries' use of tariffs and trade restrictions either to promote infant industries or for balance-of-payments reasons, could be a further focal point. Arguments could be made here either to grant further special rights to developing countries to allow use of trade restrictions which are, in some way, environmentally enhancing. Alternatively, existing special provisions could be restricted to make them conditional on the environment impacts of the policies used.

With Article XIX, which deals with safeguards, (circumstances under which countries can use trade-restricting measures to deal with import surges into their markets), an argument that has surfaced is the need for special rules to deal with surges from countries with environmentally lax standards or to deal with imports of products from areas of recently determined environmental damage. A requirement for environmental impact statements to be added into Article XXIV, which deals with free trade areas, is one possible direction that discussion could take.

Finally, Part IV of the GATT (Articles XXVV-XXXVIII), which both details the special and differential treatment developing countries are to receive in the trading system, could still be an important element in a future trade and environment negotiation, because of the basic commitment it gives to developing countries to open trade and, hence, compensation for environmental restraint.

Environment in a New Trade Round

As noted above, we are still some considerable way from the launch of a new trade round in the WTO, and some have even suggested that with ongoing 2-yearly ministerial meetings, a form of permanent negotiation might replace the GATT Rounds of the past. As I have indicated in a recent piece with Colleen Hamilton (Whalley and Hamilton, 1996), I would see this as unlikely for a number of reasons; deadlines to terminate force decisions; initial agenda forming negotiations define the bargaining set; and they also focus the reciprocal dealing to follow. Also, the 10-year implementation period for the Uruguay Round makes the launch of a new Round quickly unlikely. Nonethelesss, even for Singapore there have been calls for a commitment to be made to Global Free Trade by 2015 to lead the way to new multilateral negotiations to counterbalance regional initiatives such as APEC and FTAA.

Where then does trade and environment fit into all this? I suggested above that trade and environment seemingly is in the odd position of having enormous political momentum behind it as a lead issue for a future negotiation, while at technical and negotiating level seemingly being boxed in by problems of precedent and difficulties of counteracting the intent of established trade rules. These problems are greatly compounded by the North-South divide which seems to face any proposed significant change in the area.

Trade and environment will in my view remain a lead symbolic issue to the WTO work programme, but several developments could serve to slowly downplay its significance in a future Round. One would be a future Round more heavily focused on traditional reciprocity than rule writing (exchanges of concessions involving the new (post Uruguay Round) tariffs in agriculture, post MFA elimination tariffs in apparel, bound tariffs in developing countries). Another would be fragmentation of the current four "new-new"[22] key issues of environment, labour standards, competition policy and investment into separate negotiating boxes, which could happen with competition policy and investment. Yet another would be the continued non emergence of an issue on which developing countries could be given something in return for concessions by them on environment.

Thus, the post Singapore scenario I see is a continued high political profile for the trade and environment issue in the GATT/WTO, but with little substantive agreement either before or during a subsequent negotiating Round.

[22] In contrast to the "new" issues in the Uruguay Round of services, TRIPs and TRIMs.

IV. WIDER DIMENSIONS OF TRADE AND ENVIRONMENT LINKAGE POST SINGAPORE

Because of the arguments I make above regarding the prospects for progress post Singapore in the GATT/WTO on future trade and environment linkage, it should be no surprise that I also argue that the way that the trade and environment issue evolves post Singapore will reflect a range of factors beyond the technicalities of the GATT. These include the likely quantitative importance of what is at stake, the political divisions the issue creates and environmental provisions of regional trade arrangements (not discussed here in any detail)[23].

Implications of Quantification of Trade and Environment Linkages[24]

The preliminary indications now beginning to emerge from model based quantitative analyses of trade and environment interactions is that those that have been the subject of most debate and discussion in the GATT and other fora thus far may be of largely symbolic importance, with only limited consequences for global economic performance. On the other hand, the trade consequences of major environmental interventions not yet figuring prominently in the trade and environment debate, such as those that would follow from a possible global carbon tax, could seemingly be more substantial. In an extreme case, they might even reverse the growth in world trade in manufactures that we have seen in the last four decades of GATT-based trade liberalization. These studies typically involve calibration of models to various

[23] However, see the discussion in Esty (1994) and in Uimonen and Whalley (1996).

[24] This subsection draws on the discussion in Whalley (1996b).

benchmark or base case data sets, followed by counterfactual analysis around base cases.

One study suggesting small effects from those trade and environment policy linkages discussed thus far is Perroni and Wigle (1994) whose model covers six goods and sectors chosen to allow a separation between industries with more emissions and those with less, and to also allow separation of higher technology from lower technology industries. They calibrate their model to a 1986 global data set covering 3 major regions, (North America, Other Developed and Low and Middle Income countries), and a variety of pollutant activities. Emissions generated by industrial activity interact with various natural and geographical processes, including absorption and transmission of particulates via the atmosphere and oceans, impacting global environmental standards, and hence environmental quality for consumers. Having calibrated their model to a 1986 benchmark data set, Perroni and Wigle are able to analyze the effects of increased trade on environmental quality by alternative trade policy scenarios, including removal of all global trade barriers in their model. They directly capture the welfare effects of changes in environmental standards in the form of damage functions in explicit utility evaluations.

Their model results suggest that increased international trade generally has little impact on environmental quality. They also conclude that the magnitude of welfare effects of environmental policies are not significantly affected by simultaneous changes in trade policies when new environmental policies are introduced. Furthermore, the size and regional distribution of the gains from trade liberalization appears to be little affected by environmental policies. Their tentative conclusion is that the extent of trade and environment interactions seem smaller than might have beeen suggested by the intensity of debate on trade and environment up to the time of their writing (1993).

Another model based piece examining more conventional trade and environment linkages is Low (1992), which attracted substantial attention when published because of the similar conclusion that the trade impacts of environmentally oriented trade policies seem small[25]. Low reports a model based calculation of the effects of possible trade barriers being adopted in the United States to countervail perceived lax standards in key trading partners, including Mexico, and reports their impacts on trade. He uses data on pollution abatement costs by type of expenditure and by sector for the United States, which are, in turn, used to infer at what level trade barriers could be introduced in the US to counteract competitive disadvantages under an assumption of zero costs being incurred by firms in Mexico. The effects of such trade barriers on trade are then analyzed, using a model structure which captures relevant demand and supply elasticities.

Low identifies pollution intensive, or 'dirty' industries, as those with the highest pollution abatement expenditures. These industries are evaluated as to their contribution to Mexico's exports, and a simulation used to assess the effects on the exports of a special US import tax along the lines outlined above. In Low's data, such expenditures currently represented only a small part of total costs incurred by US

[25] Low's conclusion is also consistent with that reached by Tobey (1990) who uses an econometric approach to test the significance of pollution effects in a Heksher-Ohlin-Vanek model. A commodity's relative pollution intensity is defined in terms of pollution abatement costs incurred in production compared to similar US data, with endowment data from Leamer (1984), and trade data from UN trade statistics. Tobey's conclusion is that stringent environmental regulations imposed on industries in the late 1960s and early 1970s by most industrial countries have not affected trade patterns to any measurable extent in the most heavily polluting industries. A more recent piece by Levinsohn (1994) concludes that differing environmental regulations across states have little effect on location decisions; in part because, once again, the cost shares involved are small.

industries, with only 18 out of 123 industries incurring more than 1% of the value of their output in pollution abatement costs. On this basis alone, the impact of a special import tax, while still dependent on assumed values of elasticities, would thus be likely to be small.

Using a simple elasticity-based approach and 1986 data, Low's results suggest that the imposition of such a tax would cause a reduction of less than 2% in Mexico's exports. This compares with an approximate doubling in real terms for Mexico's trade with the United States between 1985 and 1992, suggesting that, if actually implemented, such environmentally based trade measures would have only a small effect on direct trade flows, because the cost components involved are themselves small.

However, a further set of model based analyses, analyzing the effects of major global environmental initiatives due to Whalley and Wigle (1991) and Piggott, Whalley and Wigle (1993) in two interrelated modelling papers, suggest that much larger trade effects would follow from new global arrangements designed to deal with major environmental problems, such as carbon emissions. The purpose of these two papers is to analyze the effects such as a possible carbon tax set at levels designed to stabilize global carbon emissions at early 1990s levels (the so-called 'Toronto call', after the setting of such an objective at a 1989 global scientific conference in Toronto)[26]. In both models, there is a production and demand structure in each region, with CES production functions defined over primary factors and other inputs. Primary factors, in turn, are broken down into energy and non-energy inputs, which cover greenhouse and

[26] Also see the recent renewed call for stringent emission targets by the International Panel on Climate Change (IPRC); "Tough Targets on Greenhouse Gases Urged", *Financial Times*, Friday 19th July 1996.

non-greenhouse, and carbon and non-carbon products. This leads to production of composite energy and, in turn, the eventual production of energy intensive and non-energy intensive products. International trade then takes place in energy-intensive and other goods, and carbon based products.

In the first piece, the possible international impacts of carbon tax options are evaluated. In the second the extent of sub-regional or unilateral country reduction in carbon emissions which would be undertaken to deal with global warming are analyzed, using a model extension with an explicit parameterization of preferences towards climate change. Results from these models suggest large effects on international trade flows from major environmental policy interventions, such as a carbon tax. The published papers do not directly report trade impacts since this was not their major focus, but in the presence of large carbon taxes which apply to a significant input component for manufacturing (and where the tax rates required range as high as 800% in order to generate reductions in carbon emissions to stabilize globally at 1990 levels) the cost component feeding through to manufactures is large. The result is a potentially major impact on international trade in manufactures, and resulting changes in global trade patterns. Global consumption of energy intensive manufactures falls sharply, and with it global trade. Some model scenarios suggest that taxes at such high levels as these could have more major consequences for trade in the global economy as developments under GATT the post-war years.

Thus, for example, in Whalley and Wigle (1991) there are major changes in net trade patterns between energy intensive goods and other goods for major regions. Japan, for instance, changes from net exporter of energy intensive manufacturers to a net importer. Other Europe, including eastern Europe, changes from a net importer to a net exporter, and the EU also changes from a net exporter to a net importer. In some results in Piggott, Whalley and Wigle (1993, p.127) there are further reductions in trade in the order of 50% from large global carbon taxes.

The implication is that major environmental policy initiatives in the post Singapore trading system may have more significant impacts on trade pattern, than initiatives undertaken within the GATT/WTO framework to more directly address the trade and environment issue. The GATT/WTO has little to say about such initiatives, and yet their implications for trade could overwhelm the trade impacts of anything done directly in the WTO on the trade and environment issue. While a carbon agreement may still be some years (or even decades) away, its significance for the trade and environment debate seems clear.

Developing Countries, Property Rights and Trade and Environment

A further important factor to take into account in charting the future of the trade and environment debate post Singapore involves the developing countries, who see linkage of trade to environmental quality as being driven largely by environmental interests in the higher rather than the lower income countries.[27] Their implicit argument is that environmental quality is a luxury good, and see consumer preferences of the higher income countries, not the lower income countries, as behind proposed rules linking trade and environment. From their perspective, these rules largely involve threats of trade restrictions being placed on their exports to pressure them to change their environmental policies, while richer industrialized countries seem not to be

[27] See the more extensive discussion of the developing country position on these issues in Whalley (1994).

targeted. The outcome they fear is that their growth and development is truncated by policies targeted at environmental conservation objectives set for their economies from outside. Developing countries, therefore, talk of 'green' or 'eco' imperialism, arguing that if the trading system continues to develop in this way, in the long run it can only be disadvantageous to them.

The tension is between the objectives of environmental advocates in industrial countries, and the strongly stated interest of developing countries in being able to pursue trade-led developmental strategies free from trade restrictions, including those motivated by environmental concerns. The developing countries also emphasize the extensive unilateral liberalization that has taken place in the developing world in the late 1980s and early 1990s, the trade gains which have flowed from this, and the industrial countries who have strongly supported it. Trade restrictions against developing countries in the name of environmental concerns of the wealthy in the developed world seem, to developing countries, to run counter to what they have been encouraged to do in recent years within the trading system.

Developing countries thus argue their property rights as far as any future trade and environment linkage is concerned. On issues such as deforestation,[28] they argue that the developed countries industrialized two hundred years ago and largely deforested during the process. They question the grounds on which the developed countries now assert rights over management of forests in developing countries, when their own deforestation was so clearly unrestrained in earlier years. Some developing countries go even further and argue that they should be compensated for showing environmental

[28] See Barbier *et al.* (1991) who analyze the environmental implications of trade in forestry products.

restraint, rather than being penalized if they fail to adopt environmental policies advocated by industrial countries.

These issues were strongly in evidence at the 'Earth Summit' in 1993 at Rio de Janiero. The Summit was held as part of the United Nations Conference on Environment and Development (UNDED), and the North-South tensions over the property rights issues discussed above were clearly evident. Three agreements resulted from the Rio meeting; the Rio Declaration on Environment and Development; Agenda 21; and the Forest Principles. Two further agreements were separately negotiated but signed at Rio; the UN Framework Convention on Climate Change, and the UN Convention on Biological Diversity.

The Rio Declaration states (in Principle 12) that trade policy measures used for environmental purposes should not involve arbitrary discrimination or be disguised trade restrictions, and that unilateral actions should be avoided. Chapter 2 of Agenda 21 stresses that all countries should benefit from an open trading system. While in no way representing binding and enforceable commitments, these statements nonetheless add political support to developing country positions on trade and environment issues, and threaten to fuel whatever post Singapore divisions emerge on the issue.

Post-Singapore, trade and environment is also one of several elements of trade policy linkage to non trade objectives which threatens to revive North-South tensions in the trading system (trade and labour standards is another). These were pronounced in the 1970s and early 1980s, but began to ebb in the mid 1980s when many developing countries abandoned import substitution protection, liberalised unilaterally, and then participated much more actively than before in the Uruguay Round. Having been assured that the trading system would be structured to speed their growth and development, finding in the mid 1990s that trade barriers against them may go up because of environmental concerns can only serve to unify developing countries in a rediscovered common cause. After moving away from the perceived blocwide interest of special and differential treatment towards pursuit of country interest, trade and environment post Singapore could well be the key to reviving the pursuit of a common Southern interest.

The trade and environment issue is thus seen by several developing countries in negative, and even hostile, terms. To them environmental pressure groups in wealthy countries in the developed world want to set global standards for environmental quality which meet their preferences, not those of the developing world. The ability of developing countries to provide environmental quality at these levels, and in ways which do not jeopardize their ability to achieve growth and development, is the issue.

Their rallying cry is one of compensation for environmental restraint, rather than legimitization of trade-based retaliation against environmental practices through trade rules. If developed countries are concerned about forest cover, they have the option of replanting trees in their own countries which they deforested centuries earlier even though to the more vocal environmental groups in developed countries such trees represent the lungs of the earth, a communally owned resource to be managed on a global basis. Developing countries thus see a policy agenda emerging in the developed world in which trade and environment plays a major role which seeks to define the parameters of a global resource management regime, independently of their growth and development aspirations.

V. CONCLUSIONS

This paper seeks to map out how the trade and environment issue may play out after the Singapore WTO ministerial meeting in December 1996, where the WTO Committee on Trade and Environment (CTE) is scheduled to offer its first report.

The paper first discusses trade and environment narrowly as a GATT/WTO issue arguing both that relatively little is expected to be concluded in Singapore, and that change post Singapore looks equally difficult to achieve. All ways forward to change; waivers, general GATT/WTO exceptions, rewriting GATT Articles, seem to encounter problems.

The paper then argues that wider developments outside GATT/WTO are likely to prove equally if not more important to the future evolution of the trade and environment issue. These include the trade impacts of new major environmental arrangements, such as global carbon taxes; and the hardening position on these issues in the developing world. When taken together with other factors, such as the environmental provisions of regional trade agreements, the post Singapore prospects for trade and environment seem likely to be shaped as much by developments outside the GATT/WTO as within it.

43

BIBLIOGRAPHY

ANDERSON, K. and R. BLACKHURST (eds.)(1993). *The Greening of World Trade Issues*, Harvester Wheatsheaf for the GATT.

ARDEN-CLARKE, C. (1991). *The General Agreement on Tariffs and Trade, Environmental Protection and Sustainable DevelopmentI.* World Wildlife Fund Discussion Paper.

BARBIER, E., B. AYLWARD, J. BURGESS and J. BISHOP (1991). "Environmental Effects of Trade in the Forestry Sector". International Institute for Environment and Development: London, mimeo.

BEGHIN, J.D., R. HOLST and D. VAN-DER-MENSBRUGGHE (1994). "A Survey of the Trade and Environment Nexus: Global Dimensions". *OECD Economic Studies*, Winter, pp.167-92.

BHAGWATI, J. (1993). "Trade and the Environment: The False Conflict"in Zaelke, D., P. Orbach, and R. Houseman (eds), *Trade and the Environment, Law, Economics, and Policy.* Washington: Island Press.

CHARNOVITZ, S.(1992). "GATT and the Environment: Examining the issues". *International Environmental Affairs*, Vol.4, No.3, pp.203-33.

CHARNOVITZ, S. (1991). "Exploring the Environmental Exceptions in GATT Article XX". *Journal of World Trade*, Vol 25, No.5, pp.37-55.

COPELAND, B.R.and M. SCOTT-TAYLOR (1995). "Trade and Transboundary Pollution". *American Economic Review*, Vol.85, No.4., pp.716-937.

COPELAND, B.R. and M. SCOTT TAYLOR (1994). "North South and the Environment". *Quarterly Journal of Economics*, Vol.109, No.3, pp.755-87.

DEAN, J.M. (1992). "Trade and the Environment: A Survey of the Literature", in Low and Patrick (eds,), *International Trade and the Environment.* World Bank Discussion Papers, No.159: Washington: DC

ESTY, D.C. (1994). *Greening the GATT: Trade, Environment, and the Future.* Washington: Institute for International Economics.

GATT (1994). *The Final Act of the Uruguay Round.* Marrakesh, 1994.

GATT (1992a). "Trade and the Environment" in *International Trade 90-91.* Vol. 1 (Part III). Geneva: GATT.

GATT (1992b). *Focus 91.* Geneva.

44

HILLMANN, A. and H. URSPRUNG (1994). "Greens, Supergreens, and International Trade Policy: Environmental Concerns and Protectionism", in *Trade, Innovation and Environment*. Dordrecht: Kluwer Academic Publishers.

JACKSON, J. (1992). "World Trade Rules and Environmental Policies: Congruence or Conflict?". *Washington and Lee Law Review*, Vol.49, No.4, Fall.

LEAMER, E. (1984). *Sources of International Comparative Advantage: Theory and Evidence*. Cambridge: Cambridge University Press.

LEONARD, R. and E. CHRISTENSEN (1991). "Testimony on Behalf of the Community Nutrition Institute Before the International Trade Commission Hearing on Economic Effects of a Free Trade Agreement Between Mexico and the United States". April 12, 1991.

LEVINSOHN, A. (1994). "Environmental Regulations and Manufacturer's Location Choices: Systematic Evidence from the Census of Manufactures", mimeo, presented at the Transatlantic Public Economics Conference on Market Failures and Public Policy, Turin, May 19-21, 1994.

LOW, P. (1992). "Trade Measures and Environmental Quality: The Implications for Mexico's Exports", P. Low (ed.), *International Trade and Environment*. World Bank Discussion Paper 159. The World Bank: Washington, D.C. 105-120.

PATTERSON, E. (1992). "GATT and the Environment- Rules Changes to Minimize Adverse Trade and Environmental Effects". *Journal of World Trade*, Vol.26, No.8, June, pp.99-109.

PERRONI, C. and R. WIGLE (1994). "International Trade and Environment Quality: How Important are the Linkages?". *Canadian Journal of Economics*, Vol.27, No.3, pp.551-67.

PIGGOTT, J., J.WHALLEY, and R.WIGLE (1993). "How Large are the Incentives to Join Sub Global Carbon Reduction Initiatives?". *Journal of Policy Modelling*, September.

RUNGE, C.F. (1994). *Freer Trade, Protected Environment. Balancing Trade Liberalization and Environmental Interests*. New York: Council of Foreign Relations Press.

SHRYBMAN, S. (1989). *International Trade and the Environment*. Toronto: Canadian Environmental Law Association.

SHRYBMAN, S. (1990). *International Trade and the Environment: An Environmental Assessment of Present GATT Negotiations*. Toronto: Canadian Environmental Law Association.

UIMONEN, P. (1995). "Trade Rules and Environmental Controversies". *The World Economy*, Vol.118, No.1, January, pp.71-86.

45

UIMONEN, P.and J. WHALLEY (1996). *The Trade and Environment Issue After the Uruguay Road* Macmillan: xxxx.

ULPH, A. (1994). "Environmental Policy and International Trade: A Survey of Recent Economic Analysis". *Noti di Lavoro* 53.94. Milan: Foundazione Eni Enrico Mattei.

TOBEY, J.A. (1990). "The Effects of Domestic Environmental Policies on Patterns of World Trade". *Kyklos*, Vol.43.

WHALLEY, J. (1996a). "Trade and environment, the WTO and Developing Countries", in R. Lawrence (ed), *Emerging New Issues in Global Trade*. Overseas Development Council: Washington, DC.

WHALLEY, J. (1996b). "Quantifying Trade and Environment Linkages Through Economywide Modeling:. In M.E. Bredahl, N. Ballenger, J.C. Dunmore and J.L. Roe (eds.), *Agriculture, Trade, and the Environment* Westview Press: Colorado.

WHALLEY, J. (1994). "Compensation or Retaliation: Developed and Developing Countries and the Growing Conflict Over Global Environmental Conservation", Institute for Policy Reform, May 1994.

WHALLEY, J. (1991). "The Interface Between Environmental and Trade Policies". *Economic Journal*, Vol. 01, No 405, 180-189.

WHALLEY, J. and C. HAMILTON (1996). *The Trading System After the Uruguay Round*. Washington: Institute for International Economics.

WHALLEY, J. and R. WIGLE (1991). "The International Incidence of Carbon Taxes", in R. Dornbusch and J.M. Poterba (eds.) *Economic Policy Responses to Global Warming*. Cambridge, USA:MIT Press.

WOOLCOCK, S. (1996). "An Agenda for the WTO: Strengthening or Overburdening the System?". Paper presented at a joint LSE/RIIA conference at Chatham House, London, May 30th 1996.

Part II
Quantifying the Dimensions of Linkage

[8]

Review of International Economics, 9(3), 414–428, 2001

Trade and Environment: Bargaining Outcomes from Linked Negotiations

*Lisandro Abrego, Carlo Perroni, John Whalley, and Randall M. Wigle**

Abstract

Some recent literature has explored physical and policy linkages between trade and the environment. This paper explores linkage through leverage in bargaining, whereby developed countries can use trade threats to achieve improved developing-country environmental management, while developing countries can use environmental concessions to achieve trade discipline in developed countries. A global numerical simulation model is used to compute bargaining outcomes from linked trade and environment negotiations. Results indicate joint gains from expanding the trade bargaining set to include the environment. However, compared with bargaining with cash side-payments, linked negotiations on policy instruments provide significantly inferior outcomes for developing countries.

1. Introduction

Since the early 1990s, trade and the environment has been a high-profile issue, with environmental groups arguing that restrictions are needed on certain types of trade (e.g., species, tropical lumber, pollution-intensive manufactures), and less-developed countries (LDCs) opposing what they see as a new threat of trade restrictions against their exports. Where countries fail to institute policies which internalize global or cross-border environmental externalities, environmental groups argue that appropriate trade restrictions can improve resource allocation. Trade liberalization advocates, on the other hand, see trade measures as very much second-best environmental policy, and worry over new trade restrictions.

This paper discusses possible LDC participation in linked trade and environment negotiations in the World Trade Organization (WTO), which we suggest would largely break down on North–South lines. The South we see as the custodian of environmental assets yet to be used (such as forests) and the North as having a high dependence on the use of these assets.

Whether or not environmental issues should be part of any future (post-Uruguay Round) trade negotiations is now central to the debate. Developed countries (DCs), responding to pressures from their own nongovernmental environmental organizations, have supported their inclusion, while LDCs have appeared more reluctant to do so. They instead seek direct compensation for implementing growth-slowing policies.

We argue here that global (and cross-border) environmental externalities provide LDCs with strategic leverage over the use of trade restrictions by DCs. Although

*Abrego and Perroni: University of Warwick, Coventry CV4 7AL, UK. Tel: +44 (1203) 523055; Fax: +44 (1203) 523032. Whalley: Universities of Warwick and Western Ontario, London, Ontario, Canada N6A 5C2. Tel: (519) 661-3509; Fax: (519) 661-3064; E-mail: lisandro.abrego@warwick.ac.uk. Wigle: Wilfrid Laurier University, 75 University Ave W., Waterloo, Ontario, Canada N2L 3C5. Tel: (519) 884-0710 X2438; Fax: (519) 888-1015. We acknowledge comments, advice, and suggestions from Don Fullerton, Larry Goulder, Geoff Heal, Bill Nordhaus, and V. Kerry Smith, and from an anonymous referee. We are grateful to the ESRC for financial support under an award on fiscal policies and the environment. Concluding stages of the work have drawn on support from the John D. and Catherine T. MacArthur Foundation.

GATT/WTO tariff barriers in OECD countries are now low, sectoral barriers in textiles, apparel, footwear, steel, and other areas are still significant, as are voluntary export restraints, regulatory restrictions in services, and the use of antidumping and countervailing-duty measures. Linking environmental and trade negotiations thus gives developing countries opportunities to restrain adverse trade policies in DCs, with environmental concessions being available to bargain for lower trade barriers. Linkage expands the bargaining set, which can result in more trade and lowered barriers. Seemingly, negotiations that link trade and the environment should be embraced by both the developing and developed world.

The literature on this has focused primarily on two related questions: whether international trade contributes to lowered environmental quality (e.g., Anderson, 1992a,b; Dean, 1992; Rauscher, 1992); and whether trade liberalization is desirable, both in terms of global efficiency and individual-country interest, when environmental emissions are not internalized (e.g., Dean, 1992; Pearce, 1992). The policy debate has also often been interpreted as reflecting concerns over these forms of linkage. There seems to be a presumption that linkage between trade and environmental policies is weak, and that trade policies are ineffective instruments of environmental protection—a conjecture confirmed by model-based estimates (Perroni and Wigle, 1994). As Blackhurst and Subramanian (1992) have pointed out, there are also strategic reasons for linking trade and environmental policies in multilateral negotiations; global cooperation should be easier to sustain when pursued through linked negotiations.

However, this strategic linkage does not seem to have been addressed directly in the literature. Barrett (1994) and Ulph (1996a,b), among others, have studied the matter theoretically, but define the strategic element from the standpoint of the market structure in which firms operate. Copeland and Taylor (1995) examine environmental policy games between open economies; they mention the possibility of a linkage between North–South trade and environmental policies, but do not explore it in detail. The papers that are most closely related to the analysis we present here are Cesar and Zeeuw (1994), Spagnolo (1996), Ludema and Wooton (1994), and Nordhaus and Yang (1996). The first of these builds a general framework linking environmental cooperation with cooperation in some other, nonspecified area, and shows that cooperation in both areas is sustainable provided that the two games roughly offset each other. Spagnolo's paper models linked international negotiations within a repeated-game framework. In both these papers, however, the policy games examined are fully independent, which is not the case for trade and environmental policies. Ludema and Wooton use a partial-equilibrium model to examine a non-cooperative policy game between two countries in the presence of a cross-border externality, but do not explore the possibility of environmental policy cooperation; although they point out that a linkage between trade and the environment could be implicitly present in some free trade agreements involving countries of different size. Nordhaus and Yang use a multi-region dynamic general-equilibrium model to compute non-cooperative Nash equilibria in environmental policies as well as cooperative equilibria where countries adopt globally efficient policies to reduce emissions. In their model, however, bargaining solutions are not examined and no interaction between trade and the environment is considered.

Here, we explore this negotiation linkage using a two-region (North–South) numerical simulation model of world trade and the environment, benchmarked to 1990 data and projected over a 100-year time horizon. We compute non-cooperative Nash equilibria (disagreement outcomes for bargaining), and bargaining outcomes (Nash bargaining) for trade negotiations only and joint negotiations over trade and the environment. The trade side of the model is a conventional heterogeneous-products (Armington) model, in which trade elasticities play a key role. The environmental structure of the model involves environmental assets in the South which are depleted more rapidly when used in trade-related production activities, and whose existence value enters North's preferences considerably more strongly than is the case for Southern preferences. The calibration of the model involves some strong assumptions and adjustments of data for model admissibility, but generates a specification with sharply asymmetric North–South preference weightings on environmental asset depletion.

The central case results we generate show that, relative to free trade, the South (as the smaller region) loses in a trade war. A trade-only negotiation helps both the North and South in lowering trade barriers, but leaves large barriers in the North. A joint trade and environment negotiation allows the North to generate welfare gains from Southern environmental management and the South to lower Northern trade barriers. The main theme is that LDCs should embrace a trade and environment negotiation as it provides them with more leverage over trade. However, in a negotiation with side-payments the South does considerably better than in a constrained negotiation, suggesting that a trade–environmental policy negotiation may be an inferior option; that is, a negotiation of cash compensation is better for them.

In our concluding section, we also note that bargaining that is constrained by trade rules—in which existing rules (such as MFN) are taken to imply restrictions on the bargaining set—may yield a different picture. If we consider a trade and environment linkage as a proposal under which MFN trade rules would also be relaxed where environmental effects are an issue, and if an initial weakening of MFN could lead to further system-wide weakening in other areas, then LDCs' concerns over a trade and environment negotiation may be more firmly based. In such cases, gains from expanded bargaining could be more than offset by losses from the weakening of prior agreed restraints on trade policy.

2. A Two-Region North–South Trade and Environment Model

We consider a world consisting of two regions, which we refer to as "North" (N) and "South" (S). Focusing on a two-region structure avoids the numerical complexities associated with computation of non-cooperative equilibria in higher dimensions, and allows us to focus on two-player cooperative solution concepts. Computational limitations in working with non-cooperative and cooperative game-theoretic solution concepts, rather than more traditional competitive equilibria, thus severely restrict dimensionality in the numerical analysis.

We consider an environmental asset, E, which is entirely owned by the South, and can be viewed as a stock reflecting available tropical habitat. Each region produces two goods, a tradeable good X and a nontradeable good Y. Region S uses two factors in production, value-added V, and the natural resource asset. Production in region N only uses value-added. Each region views tradeables produced domestically and abroad as imperfect substitutes, and consumes both domestic and imported traded goods, along with own-region nontradeables. The environment is depleted by its use in production, and enters the utility function of each region. Depletion occurs more heavily from use in production of the traded good. The endowment of value-added is constant in each region, and equal to G^i ($i = N, S$).

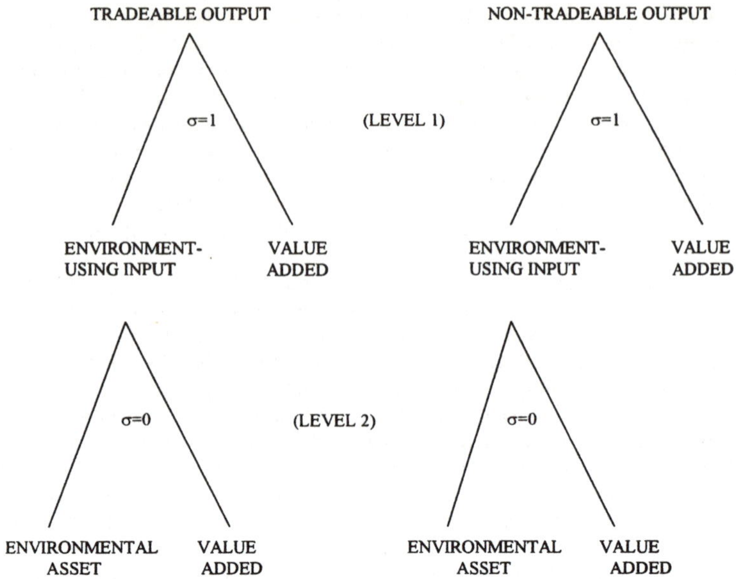

Figure 1. CES Production Structure in the Model (South Region)

Production

The structure of production in the model is set out in Figure 1. CES functions are used, in which value-added and the environmental asset can be transformed into an environment-using input at the lower level of nesting. At the higher level of nesting, the environment-using input and value-added are transformed into tradeable and non-tradeable output. We use substitution elasticities of zero at the lower level, and of unity at the higher level. Value-added used in the two levels of nest can be transformed at a constant marginal rate of transformation, which, for simplicity, we assume to be equal to unity. The rationale for using this construction is that it implies a nonzero cost for the environment-using input even when pollution taxes are zero; this, in turn, prevents infinite substitution away from other inputs. The main difference between the tradeable and nontradeable goods sectors lies in the share parameters on the environment-using input.

Prices and Environmental Taxes

Net-of-tax prices for value-added and the environment-using input are denoted as p^i ($i = N, S$) and are the same within each region. Each unit of environment-using input employed in production in region S reduces global environmental quality by an amount ε. We consider taxes on the use of the environmental asset at rate τ^S, and hence the gross-of-tax price of the environment-using input in the South is

$$p_E^S = p^S + \varepsilon\tau^S. \tag{1}$$

Value-added and the environment-using input are both used in the production of tradeables and nontradeables through unitary substitution elasticity, constant-returns-to-scale technologies. Thus, domestic prices of domestically produced goods are equal to unit costs:

$$p_j^N = c_j^N(p^N); \quad p_j^S = c_j^S(p^S, p_E^S); \quad j = X, Y. \tag{2}$$

For given output levels $L_j^i(i = N, S, j = X, Y)$, we can write aggregate domestic demands for the environment-using input (using Shephard's lemma) as

$$D_E^S = \sum_j L_j^S \frac{\partial c_j^S}{\partial p_E^S}, \quad j = X, Y. \tag{3}$$

Environmental Quality

Environmental quality enters the preferences of both the North and the South, but with a substantially higher share parameter in the North, reflecting the differential existence value placed on environmental assets by region. The quantity of environmental assets entering preferences as existence value equals the initial stock of assets less that amount used up in production (through deforestation, for instance). The period used for the model is a number of years or decades, during which significant depletion can occur depending upon the policy regime. For given demands for the environment-using input, environmental quality is then given as

$$Q = \overline{Q} - \varepsilon(D_E^S), \tag{4}$$

where $\overline{Q}$ denotes the initial endowment of the environmental asset (before use in production).

Trade and Demand

Each region levies *ad valorem* import tariffs at rates t^i, where superscripts refer to the importing region. The gross-of-tariff price of imported tradeables is thus

$$q^N = (1 + t^N)p_X^S; \quad q^S = (1 + t^S)p_X^N. \tag{5}$$

Given preferences, a level of environmental quality Q, commodity prices p_j^i, q^i, and incomes I^i, utility maximization yields uncompensated demands for domestic goods, D_j^i, and uncompensated import demands, M^i. The marginal valuation for environmental quality in each country, v^i, is also a function of the same variables.

Expanded income in each region is written as the value of resource endowments, plus tariff revenue, plus revenues from environmental levies, plus the (shadow) value of environmental quality (note that the latter is a function of income itself, which makes the definition of I^i implicit):[1]

$$I^N = p^N G^N + t^N p_X^S M^N + v^N Q; \tag{6}$$

$$I^S = p^S G^S + t^S p_X^N M^S + \tau^S \varepsilon D_E^S + v^S Q. \tag{7}$$

Market Equilibrium

Market clearing for competitive equilibrium in which use of the environmental asset is charged only through environmental levies requires the following:

$$L_X^N = D_X^N + M^S; \quad L_X^S = D_X^S + M^N; \tag{8}$$

$$L_Y^i = D_Y^i; \quad i = N, S \tag{9}$$

$$D_E^i + \sum_j L_j^i \frac{\partial c_j^i}{\partial p^i} = G^i; \quad i = N, S, \quad j = X, Y \tag{10}$$

where $D_E^N = 0$.

Choice of Functional Form

In the numerical implementation of the model, unit cost functions for tradeables and nontradeables production are a constant-elasticity-of-substitution (CES) aggregation of the environment-using input and value-added prices in the South region:

$$c_j^S(p^S, p_E^S) \equiv \left[(1-\alpha_j^S)(p^S)^{1-\beta^S} + \alpha_j^S(p_E^S)^{1-\beta^S}\right]^{\frac{1}{1-\beta^S}}; \quad j = X, Y \tag{11}$$

where the β are the elasticities of substitution between the environment-using input and value-added, and the α are share parameters. Note that, since the environment-using input is not utilized by the North, the corresponding cost function is simply

$c_j^N = p^N, j = X, Y.$

Preferences for domestic goods and imports in each region are represented by a two-level nested Cobb–Douglas/CES aggregation of the form

$$H^i(D_Y^i, D_X^i, M_A^i, M_B^i) \equiv (D_Y^i)^{\theta^i}\left[\delta^i(D_X^i)^{\frac{\sigma^i-1}{\sigma^i}} + (1-\delta^i)(M^i)^{\frac{\sigma^i-1}{\sigma^i}}\right]^{\frac{(1-\theta^i)\sigma^i}{\sigma^i-1}}; \quad i = N, S \tag{12}$$

where θ^i is a share parameter for nontradeables demand; δ^i refers to the share of domestic goods in total tradeables demand; and σ^i is the elasticity of substitution between same-region tradeables and tradeables produced in the other region.

Preferences for consumption and environmental quality are represented by a Cobb–Douglas utility function:[2]

$$U^i(Q, H^i) \equiv Q^{\eta^i}(H^i)^{1-\eta^i}; \quad i = N, S \tag{13}$$

where η^i is the Cobb–Douglas share parameter on environmental quality.

Policy Games in the Model

The model incorporates trade policy parameters in the form of tariffs, and environmental policy parameters in the form of environmental charges. A traditional tariff game can be analyzed (as in Johnson, 1953–4) in which regions play strategically against one another in tariffs. With the North being large and the South small, the presumption is that the North will gain from such a retaliatory game while the South will gain little, or more likely lose. There is also an environmental game that can be analyzed in terms of environmental charges associated with the use of the environmental asset. Since the South owns the environmental asset and the North places a high existence value on it, the South can use a policy instrument jointly with trade policy in a linked trade and environment game which can result in lower Northern trade protection.[3]

In using the model, therefore, we go beyond conventional numerical simulation work which mainly focuses on Walrasian competitive equilibria, by computing non-cooperative equilibria and bargaining outcomes. To do this, we iterate over calculations of optimal policy responses by individual regions, subject to a full set of general equilibrium constraints (as set out above) until convergence to a Nash equilibrium is achieved. We are able to do this separately for the tariff game and for the linked trade and environment game. We also compute cooperative bargaining solutions associated with these games, adopting Nash's (1950) bargaining solution. This is the most widely used cooperative solution concept in the literature, although others, such as Kalai-Smorodinsky (1975), could alternatively be used. In computing bargaining solutions, we take the non-cooperative Nash equilibrium solution utilities as representing the disagreement point, simulate the utilities possibilities frontier under cooperation, and apply the Nash criterion to the product of the differences in region utilities along the frontier and disagreement utilities.

In our central case, with trade or trade and environment games, no side-payments are considered, and thus the resulting outcomes remain second-best allocations. Typically in such equilibria there will be less than full internalization of the environmental externality. We also compute bargaining with side-payments. This realizes a full Pareto-optimal allocation, and allows us to assess how far towards Pareto optimality a joint trade and environment policy-based negotiation could move.[4] Note that side-payments should not be interpreted as implying lack of negotiation linkage: if there were no environmental agreement, zero tariffs would not be optimal even with side-payments. Thus, the side-payments we compute here represent net compensation for environmental restraint by the South *in conjunction with* trade policy cooperation.

3. Data and Model Parameterization

We have calibrated the model to a 1990 base case projected forward over a period of 100 years. The economies of the North and the South are both assumed to lie on a growth path on which value-added, production, and consumption grow at a constant rate, reflecting average growth rates over the period 1985–93. Data for this period imply rates of growth of 2.5% and 4% for the North and South, respectively. We assume a discount rate of 5%.

The production and consumption (and hence trade) data we use are based on information taken from World Bank (1992), World Bank (1995), and IMF (1995). Production activities are disaggregated into two parts: traded and nontraded production.[5] This implies a very high degree of aggregation, but, as indicated earlier, limitations associated with the computation of non-cooperative and cooperative equilibria severely restricts numerical analysis dimensionality. Furthermore, given the highly conjectural nature of some of the environment data we use, moving to a more detailed sectoral disaggregation would not significantly improve the reliability of numerical estimates obtained from the model.

In representing the regions, we include countries for the South which account for a significant portion of key global environmental assets, such as tropical forest and biological diversity. Table 1 identifies these countries and illustrates their importance in the ownership of the tropical rain forest asset. The countries included in the South region jointly control more than 80% of tropical forest and provide habitat for an unknown but presumed considerable proportion of species.[6] The North we take to be represented by OECD countries—who jointly reflect the environmental concern over

Table 1. Countries in the 'S' Region in the Model and Their Tropical Forest Cover

	Hectares 1990 (thousands)	*Proportion of world tropical forests (%)*
Angola	24,074	1.37
Bolivia	49,317	2.81
Brazil	561,107	31.95
Cameroon	20,350	1.16
Central African Republic	30,562	1.74
Colombia	54,064	3.08
Congo	19,865	1.13
Gabon	18,235	1.04
Guyana	18,416	1.05
India	51,729	2.95
Indonesia	109,549	6.24
Malaysia	17,583	1.00
Mexico	48,586	2.77
Mozambique	17,329	0.99
Myanmar	28,856	1.64
Papua New Guinea	36,000	2.05
Peru	67,906	3.87
Tanzania	33,555	1.91
Sudan	42,976	2.45
Venezuela	45,690	2.60
Zaïre	113,275	6.45
Zambia	32,301	1.84
Total "S" region	1,441,325	82.07
World	1,756,299	100.00

Source: World Resources Institute (1994).

Table 2. Production Data Used in the Model

	North	*South*
1990 GDP (billion US dollars)	20,942	1,387
Discounted 1990–2090 GDP (billion US dollars)	800,551	92,954

depletion of environmental assets and would be the lead players in any eventual trade and environment negotiation in the WTO—and the rest of the world.

Table 2 reports the base-year 1990 data on production by region and the corresponding 1990–2090 discounted data. Table 3 gives share, elasticity, and other parameters. In calibrating the model, we select a value of 2 for Armington substitution elasticities, a choice which is consistent with most model-based studies (e.g., Perroni and Wigle, 1994); we subsequently vary this value for sensitivity analysis.

Parameters for the environmental portion of the model are obtained as follows. The environment-using input coefficients by region have been computed from

Table 3. Model Parameters

	North	South
Goods submodel		
Calibrated share parameters		
Imports in tradeables demand	0.037	0.246
Nontradeables in aggregate demand	0.681	0.473
Intraregional trade in total trade	0.941	0.046
Substitution elasticities		
Armington trade elasticities (σ)	2.0	2.0
Tradeables–nontradeables substitution in consumption	1.0	1.0
Environment-using input-value-added substitution	1.0	1.0
Environment submodel		
Overall environmental damage[a]	NA[b]	0.10
Damage coefficients		
Tradeables	NA	0.22
Nontradeables	NA	0.06
Elasticity of marginal valuation with respect to income	1.25	1.25

[a] As a proportion of North's GDP. [b] NA, not applicable.

input–output data for selected OECD countries.[7] We make the strong assumption that LDCs use the environment-using input in the two sectors in the same ratio as they are used in OECD countries. We consider the following sectors as providing environment-using inputs: agriculture, forestry and fishing, mining and quarrying; petroleum and coal products; electricity, gas and water; and construction.

The initial (1990) endowment of the environmental assets in the South, relative to which depletion occurs, is set to be half of the North's GDP.[8] The value of base-case environmental damage, in terms of depletion of the endowment of the South's environmental asset, as valued by the North, is set to be equal to 10% of income in discounted value terms. This is admittedly highly conjectural, but could be rationalized as follows. The annual average depletion rate of tropical forests during the period 1981–90 was 0.6% (World Resources Institute, 1994). Assuming that this depletion rate remains constant throughout a 100-year period and assuming a quadratic damage function, the estimate of physical damage for our period of analysis would amount to approximately a 60% depletion of Southern environmental assets.

To impute a valuation for this damage, we can take Kramer and Mercer's (1997) estimate for the US of willingness to pay (WTP) to avoid the destruction of a certain area of tropical rainforest. We assume that this WTP changes with income growth (assumed to be 2.5% a year) throughout our period, and use an income elasticity of 1.25 (consistent with estimates obtained by Kramer and Mercer), to obtain an estimate for the stream of environmental damage for the 100-year period. Using a 5% discount rate, the present value of this stream is just above 10% of the North's GDP. These calculations are sensitive to parameter assumptions and in particular to the assumed damage function; at the same time, there exist other important aspects of environmental damage (such as loss of biodiversity) which are omitted from the calculation.

By choice of units we are able to set the marginal existence value of the North (v^N) equal to unity. The South's existence value of the environmental asset is calculated on the basis of the difference of per capita income between the two regions and using again an elasticity of marginal valuation with respect to income of 1.25 (again, consistently with Kramer and Mercer's findings). This gives an estimate of approximately 0.04 (relative to the North) for v^S.

We stress the fact that the calibration of the environmental side of the model relies on very strong assumptions on some key parameters. This is especially the case with the initial value for the environmental asset and the shape of the damage function, which crucially affects the elasticity of marginal valuation with respect to damage and the share of the environmental asset in preferences. Although we carry out sensitivity analyses on some key parameters—including the size of both the environmental asset and damage—we emphasize that our data constraints necessarily give our calculations a highly conjectural and illustrative nature, at least from a quantitative standpoint.

4. Simulations and Results

Our parameterized model has been used to analyze the implications for LDCs of a linked trade and environment negotiation. We employ this structure to first compute non-cooperative Nash equilibria of a tariff game (the disagreement point). Because of their relatively small size, LDCs are at disadvantage relative to the North in this non-cooperative equilibrium. A bargained trade outcome improves the developing country situation a little relative to the disagreement point, but significant trade barriers remain against LDCs. In contrast, a linked trade and environment bargained outcome, where bargaining involves both trade and environmental policies, helps LDCs since they can use their leverage in environmental policy (given the relatively high existence value in the North) to help reduce Northern trade barriers against them. These features emerge strongly from our central-case set of model results summarized in Table 4.[9] Here we have taken the central-case model specification summarized above and computed non-cooperative Nash equilibria in tariffs, bargained outcomes in trade (tariffs), and joint bargained outcomes covering both trade and environment policies. Trade elasticities are critical parameters in determining outcomes, and in this specification we have used a value of 2 for both North and South. As is well known, as these values approach unity, in a symmetric case both regions' optimal tariffs would become large, and values significantly in excess of unity need to be used to avoid numerical problems. Because the asymmetries in size in our model can lead to large tariffs and associated numerical problems, we use an upper bound of 500% for tariffs in both regions in computing model solutions.[10] However, this is not of great importance since, well before tariffs reach such a high level, trade between the two regions has virtually ceased.

In the central-case non-cooperative equilibrium (first column of Table 4), the South's internalization rate is close to zero, consistent with most of the utility loss from lowered environmental quality being borne by the North. The North's trade barriers reach the upper bound of 500%, while the South's non-cooperative tariff rate is around 100%. This difference in non-cooperative tariff levels reflects both differences in country size and the fact that, under zero environmental internalization in the South, the North employs tariffs as a second-best environmental policy instrument.[11]

The South's loss from a trade war is close to 9% of GDP, whereas the North gains a little relative to a free-trade zero-internalization scenario.

Table 4. Central-Case Model Results

	Non-cooperative equilibrium	*Bargaining over trade*	*Bargaining over trade and environment*
Tariff rates (%)			
North	500.00	253.63	0.0
South	101.03	0.0	47.68
Environmental internalization rate (%)[a]			
North	0.0	0.0	0.0
South	0.41	0.41	54.10
Hicksian equivalent variation (% of GDP)			
A. With respect to disagreement point			
North	0.0	0.57	6.53
South	0.0	2.54	6.87
B. With respect to zero taxes and tariffs			
North	0.27	0.84	6.79
South	–8.89	–6.35	–2.02

[a] Ratio of emission tax to marginal emission damage.

Bargaining over trade policies in the absence of side-payments (column two of Table 4) leads to an elimination of tariffs in the South and lowers tariffs in the North to around 250%. This generates substantial gains in the South (2.54% of GDP), which are significantly smaller than the almost 9.0% loss experienced by the South under tariff retaliation.[12]

In contrast, combining trade and environmental policies in a joint negotiation makes it possible to sustain a level of internalization in excess of 50%, and leads to the total elimination of tariffs in the North. Some trade barriers remain in the South, as a "concession" by the North in exchange for the higher internalization rate. In this outcome the South's gains in relation to a non-cooperative outcome are considerable—almost 7% of GDP—and a linked trade and environment negotiation is an attractive proposition to them.

As pointed out earlier, we can alternatively think of cooperation as reflecting tacit collusion in an infinitely repeated game,[13] where players maintain a cooperative stance if the gains from unilateral defection are less than the discounted gains from cooperation. By computing payoffs for the various players under cooperation, non-cooperation, and for unilateral deviations from cooperation, we could characterize the maximum discount rate for which the threat of future punishment is effective as an inducement to cooperate. To explore how linkage of trade and environment dimensions affects the viability of cooperation, we could compare the maximum discount values obtained for scenarios where dimensions of strategic interaction are considered in isolation and where they are examined jointly. Given the regional asymmetries in trade and environmental costs and benefits, without side payments it would never be possible to sustain any form of cooperation in this model that is consistent with Pareto optimality, either in environmental policies or in trade policies, independently of whether they are combined.

With explicit bargaining and lump-sum side-payments (Table 5), on the other hand, it is possible to achieve a first-best outcome with zero tariffs and 100% internalization.

Table 5. Trade and Environment Bargaining With and Without Side-Payments

	Hicksian equivalent variations relative to zero taxes and tariffs (% of GDP)	
	Central case	*Bargaining with side-payments*[a]
North	6.79	6.89
South	−2.02	5.11

[a] With side payments, tariff rates are equal to zero, and the environmental internalization rate is equal to 100%.

Introducing side-payments overwhelmingly benefits the South, whose gains more than double as a result. Compared with a situation with no intervention, with cash transfers the South ends up with welfare gains which are high and not much different from those of the North, even though Southern preferences for environmental quality are much weaker than Northern ones. Thus, compared to a negotiation involving cash compensation for environmental restraint, the South gains far less from a linked trade and environment negotiation. A linked trade and environment negotiation with no side-payments may be preferred to a trade-only negotiation, but may still be the wrong negotiation so far as the South is concerned. In reality, side-payments are not often used; and without side payments it could be difficult to achieve free trade even abstracting from environmental concerns. Thus, one might interpret our results as showing that linkage can induce freer trade by providing an imperfect substitute for income transfers.

We have performed sensitivity analysis of our central-case results to the Armington elasticities, the size of damage, the North's existence value, and the size of the environmental asset. This shows that varying key parameters have mainly quantitative effects, leaving most of our results qualitatively unaltered. Increasing trade elasticities weakens opportunities for negotiation linkage, resulting in a lower level of internalization through linkage. It can also make the linked negotiation outcome for the South inferior to the trade policy-only bargained outcome—a finding not inconsistent with the comparative statics properties of Nash bargaining solutions: a change which makes the utilities possibilities frontier more "skewed" in favor of one region, can benefit both parties, but it can conceivably also result in a lower level of utility for the other party. Intuitively, if there is more to be gained by one party from moving policies in the direction it favors, the affected party will become a "more concerned" negotiator.

A reduction in trade elasticities strengthens the potential for linked negotiations and makes it possible to achieve a level of internalization close to 100% even in the absence of side payments. On the other hand, decreasing (increasing) the level of damage reduces (increases) the non-cooperative level of tariffs in the North since the presence of environmental externalities in tradeables production in the South generates an additional incentive for the North to curtail trade beyond the standard terms-of-trade large-country motive. Negotiation linkage, however, becomes weaker (stronger). Lowering the Northern existence value has effects qualitatively similar to those of reducing the assumed level of damage. Finally, reducing the size of the environmental asset lowers non-cooperative tariffs, raises internalization levels, and makes the negotiation linkage weaker.

5. Concluding Remarks

This paper has addressed the issue of whether LDCs should participate in linked trade and environment negotiations in the WTO over the next few decades. We have developed a small-dimensional global simulation model capturing both North–South trade, and Southern use of environmental assets in trade-related production when there is a high Northern existence value on such assets. We calibrated our model to data over a projected 100-year period from 1990 to 2090, in which Southern countries are identified as those accounting for 80% of tropical assets (forest, species). We computed various model solutions for alternative scenarios, principally non-cooperative Nash equilibria for tariff games which serve as threat points for cooperative bargaining (Nash) solutions, and similar solutions for linked trade (tariffs) and environmental (taxes) policy games.

In our central-case analysis, linking trade and environmental policies in a joint negotiation expands the bargaining set and offers Southern LDCs an opportunity to exert discipline over Northern trade measures by making environmental concessions. The South thus benefits from a linked negotiation compared with a stand-alone trade negotiation. However, in a negotiation with side-payments, the South gains considerably more, suggesting that LDCs should negotiate over cash for environmental restraint rather than indirectly on trade and environmental policy instruments. Sensitivity analysis suggests that as trade elasticities increase, and optimal stand-alone tariffs fall, the benefits of linkage fall to the point that Southern countries benefit from being shielded from a trade and environment negotiation. Indeed, we report cases where linked negotiations can be detrimental to the South, but this is crucially dependent on the (axiomatic) bargaining solution concept adopted and is not true in our central case.

While model results are suggestive, our model parameterization is heroic, and there are missing features, reflecting developing country concerns over trade and environment linkage, which are not captured here. Trade and environment linkage could become the precedent for further wider linkage in trade negotiations, should developing countries agree to participate (trade and employment standards, for instance). Agreeing to the use of trade measures on environmental grounds would weaken the MFN principle in GATT/WTO, so central to developing-country interests. There is also ambiguity as to whether a cohesive Southern coalition can really be formed to participate in such a negotiation. Furthermore, cooperation in the GATT/WTO may not reflect a bargained agreement (which in the absence of a supranational authority would effectively not be enforceable) but rather a non-cooperative equilibrium supported by implicit triggered retaliation threats, which the agreement only serves to ratify *ex post*. Under this interpretation, introducing an environmental dimension alongside trade negotiations may inject instability into the system, especially if policies are not observable (Riezman, 1991), and make retaliatory episodes more likely.

References

Anderson, K., "The Standard Welfare Economics of Policies Affecting Trade and the Environment," in Kym Anderson and Richard Blackhurst (eds.), *The Greening of World Trade Issues*, London: Harvester-Wheatsheaf (1992a).

———, "Effects on the Environment and Welfare of Liberalizing World Trade: The Cases of Coal and Food," in Anderson and Blackhurst, *op. cit.* (1992b).
Bagwell, K. and R. W. Staiger, "Multilateral Tariff Cooperation during the Formation of Regional Free Trade Areas," NBER Working Paper 4364 (1993).
Barrett, S., "Strategic Environmental Policy and International Trade," *Journal of Public Economics* 54 (1994):325–38.
Blackhurst, R. and A. Subramanian, "Promoting Multilateral Cooperation on the Environment," in Kym Anderson and Richard Blackhurst (eds.), *The Greening of World Trade Issues*, London: Harvester-Wheatsheaf (1992).
Cesar, H. and A. de Zeeuw, "Issue Linkage in Global Environmental Problems," *Nota di Lavoro* 56.94, Fondazione ENI Enrico Mattei (1994).
Copeland, B. and M. S. Taylor, "Trade and Transboundary Pollution," *American Economic Review* 85 (1995):716–37.
Dean, J., "Trade and Environment: A Survey of the Literature," in P. Low (ed.), *International Trade and the Environment*, Washington, DC: World Bank (1992).
International Monetary Fund, *Direction of Trade Statistics Yearbook 1995*, Washington: IMF (1995).
Johnson, H. G., "Optimum Tariffs and Retaliation," *Review of Economic Studies* 21 (1953–54):142–53.
Kalai, E. and M. Smorodinsky, "Other Solutions to Bargaining Situations: Interpersonal Utility Comparison," *Econometrica* 43 (1975):513–18.
Ludema, R. and I. Wooton, "Cross-Border Externalities and Trade Liberalization: The Strategic Control of Pollution," *Canadian Journal of Economics* 27 (1994):950–66.
Nash, J., "The Bargaining Problem," *Econometrica* 18 (1950):298–346.
Nordhaus, W. and Z. Yang, "A Regional Dynamic General-Equilibrium Model of Alternative Climate-Change Strategies," *American Economic Review* 86 (1996):741–65.
OECD, *The OECD Input–Output Database*, Paris: OECD (1995).
Pearce, D., "Should the GATT Be Reformed for Environmental Reasons?" CSERGE Working Paper GEC 92-06 (1992).
Perroni, C. and R. M. Wigle, "International Trade and Environmental Quality: How Important are the Linkages," *Canadian Journal of Economics* 27 (1994):551–67.
Rauscher, M., "International Economic Integration and the Environment: The Case of Europe," in Kym Anderson and Richard Blackhurst (eds.), *The Greening of World Trade Issues*, London: Harvester-Wheatsheaf (1992).
Riezman, R. G., "Dynamic Tariffs with Asymmetric Information," *Journal of International Economics* 30 (1991):267–83.
Spagnolo, G., "Issue Linkage, Delegation and International Policy Cooperation, *Nota di Lavoro* 49–96, Fondazione ENI Enrico Mattei (1996).
Ulph, A. "Strategic Environmental Policy and International Trade," in C. Carraro, M. Hoel, A. Ulph, and A. Ingham (eds.), *Environmental Policy, International Agreements and International Trade* Cheltenham: Elgar (1996a).
———, "Environmental Policy and International Trade when Governments and Producers Act Strategically," in C. Carraro *et al.*, *op. cit.* (1996b).
World Bank, *World Development Report 1992: Development and the Environment*, New York: Oxford University Press (1992).
———, *World Tables 1995*, Baltimore: Johns Hopkins University Press (1995).
World Resources Institute, *World Resources 1994–95*, New York: Oxford University Press (1994).

Notes

1. This is added to income since environmental quality is purchased at its shadow price, but this price is not actually paid between countries; i.e., the North makes no actual payment to the South for the existence value of environmental quality they enjoy.

2. For this specification, the marginal valuation for environmental quality is proportional to (nonexpanded) income.
3. Throughout our analysis we maintain the assumption that countries in each bloc are able to coordinate policies among themselves in an interbloc non-cooperative equilibrium. Even though the necessary environmental institutional arrangements are not currently in place for such interbloc coordination to take place, they could well emerge in the future as has been the case in the trade arena. In UNCTAD, for instance, the G77 emerged as the common developing-country demand for special and differential treatment in GATT gained momentum in the 1970s.
4. Alternatively, one could view cooperation as reflecting a subgame-perfect equilibrium of an infinitely repeated game, supported by the threat of future punishment in response to unilateral deviations from a coordinated strategy (trigger strategies). In such a formulation, it would be possible to explore whether a linked trade–environmental policy game makes cooperation in both areas easier to sustain in comparison with a scenario where the trade and environment dimensions of strategic interaction are examined in isolation.
5. The nontraded-goods sector contains all distribution, transportation, construction, utilities, and government services. This corresponds roughly to 68% and 47% of GDP for the North and South, respectively.
6. As is well known, tropical ecosystems have a higher and more diverse number of species in a given area than temperate ecosystems. It is estimated that between 40% and 90% of all species live in tropical region habitats (World Resources Institute, 1994).
7. The countries are Germany, United Kingdom, and United States. The input–output data are taken from OECD (1995).
8. Although this assumption is largely arbitrary, it has only second-order implications for the behavior of the model; specifically, it affects only the *elasticity* of the marginal valuation of environmental quality, not its level (i.e., the model's behavior for marginal policy changes is unaffected). Nevertheless, we perform sensitivity analysis on this parameter
9. In our tables, we adopt the zero tariffs and taxes scenario as a benchmark, with which all other simulation results are compared. The idea is that such a scenario reflects the state of affairs at the beginning of the 1990s, when significant trade cooperation had been achieved but tensions over global environmental problems were relatively new. One could argue that a scenario featuring optimal taxes from the South's point of view would provide a more natural benchmark; however, since non-cooperative taxes are close to zero on our simulations, the difference between the two scenarios is negligible.
10. We also rule out negative tariffs which, given our model structure, would never be used as an optimal response.
11. This also contributes to the high level of tariffs, although the finding of high non-cooperative tariffs is, more fundamentally, a feature of Armington models featuring constant substitution elasticities.
12. Although we allow the non-cooperative level of internalization to adjust endogenously, it remains effectively unchanged (to the second decimal digit).
13. For an application of this approach to trade cooperation, see, for example, Bagwell and Staiger (1993).

[9]

General Equilibrium Effects of Environmental Policy: A CGE-Modeling Approach

LARS BERGMAN
Stockholm School of Economics, Box 6501, S-113 83 Stockholm, Sweden

Abstract. Estimation of emission control cost functions is often carried out in a partial equilibrium framework, i.e., under the assumption that emission control measures have negligible effects on input and output prices. In this paper a computable general equilibrium model is used for simulation of the impact on factor prices and resource allocation of reductions of SO_x-, NO_x- and CO_2-emissions. Thus the model includes markets for tradable emission permits, and the equilibrium prices of permits reflect the marginal costs of emission control. The results suggest that major emission reductions are likely to have general equilibrium effects, and thus that emission control cost functions that fail to take these effects into account may give a distorted picture of the economic impact of emission control.

Key words: Carbon taxation, environmental control cost function, computable general equilibrium.

1. Introduction

Estimation of emission control costs is often carried out in a partial equilibrium framework, i.e., under the assumption that the emission control measures have negligible effects on input and output prices and the allocation of resources in the economy. In a wide range of cases this is a perfectly reasonable assumption; the implementation of emission control measures only requires a small fraction of the economy's resources. However, in the case of emission control programmes aimed at significantly reducing the emissions of major pollutants such as SO_x, NO_x and CO_2, general equilibrium effects cannot be ruled out. Consequently the estimation of emission control costs should incorporate such general equilibrium effects.

The purpose of this paper is twofold. The first is to present a computable general equilibrium (CGE) model with markets for emission permits and technologies for emission control. The second is to investigate to what extent emission reduction policies are likely to have general equilibrium effects.

The model is implemented on Swedish data, and the analysis is inspired by the current policy goals to keep the Swedish CO_2 emissions constant at the 1988 level. More precisely, the model is used for computation of the marginal cost of reducing CO_2 emissions. The results suggest that far-reaching emission reductions do have non-negligible general equilibrium effects, and that emission control cost functions that fail to take these effects into account give a distorted picture of the economic impact of emission control.

Environmental and Resource Economics **1**: 43—61, 1991.

2. General Features of the Model and the Benchmark Data

The model is a static CGE model of an open economy. In some respects it differs from the standard approach in CGE-modeling. First, it includes emissions and emission control activities, as well as markets, and market prices, for tradable emission permits. The treatment of emission control is inspired by Görling (1988). Second, there is a distinction between old and new production units in some of the production sectors. This part of the model is inspired by Haaland *et al.* (1987), Bergman (1986) and Lundgren (1985). Third, some of the tradables producing sectors are treated as price-takers on international markets in the standard Heckscher—Ohlin fashion, while others to some extent are price-makers in accordance with the so-called Armington assumption generally adopted in open-economy CGE models.

The last feature of the model is related to the definition of production sectors. Thus, in general, there are three types of sectors in the model economy. The first are the so-called *T*-sectors. These sectors produce tradables and are price-takers on international markets. It is only among the *T*-sectors that a distinction between old and new production units is made. In the empirically implemented version of the model used in this study there are two *T*-sectors: An aggregate of forestry and the pulp and paper industries and an aggregate of the steel and chemical industries. These sectors are denoted FOREST and STEELCH, respectively.

The second type of sectors are called *M*-sectors. These are tradables producing sectors in which the domestic producers, as a group, have some influence on export prices. That is, the Armington assumption applies for the *M*-sectors. However, like in other Armington types of CGE models each individual producer in the *M*-sectors acts as a price-taker. Thus there is no monopolistic pricing in the *M*-sectors. In this study there are three *M*-sectors: An aggregate of export-oriented manufacturing industries[1] (MANUF), an aggregate of industries with a relatively high degree of protection[2] (SHELT), and an aggregate of low-trade, net importing industries[3] and private service sectors (NIMP).

The third type of sector are the non-tradables producing or *N*-sectors. There are two *N*-sectors in the model: The production of public services (PUBL) and the production of district heating (HEAT). In addition, electricity (ELEC) is a non-traded good, but as the production of electricity is treated in a special way, it is convenient not to treat electricity production as an *N*-sector. In addition to the domestically produced goods there is import of fuels, mainly oil, used both as an input in production and as a good for final use.

On the demand side domestic private and public consumption as well as domestic gross investments are aggregated into one single domestic end use sector. In addition to the demand of this sector there is net export demand in the *T*- and *M*-sectors, and an exogenously determined demand component in all sectors. In the case of HEAT this demand component actually reflects exogenously given domestic demand, while it simply reflects accounting errors in the other sectors.

There are four types of domestic intersectorially mobile factors of production in the model economy: Capital (CAPITAL), labor (LABOR), electricity generated in existing hydro and nuclear power plants (ELEC) and roundwood (NATRES), i.e., the natural resource base of the production sector FOREST. In addition, the base year (1985) capital stocks in FOREST and STEELCH are treated as sector-specific resources.

The benchmark data are an input-output table constructed on the basis of a 45-sector SAM for 1985. It should be noted that all flows, including the flows of capital and labor services and electricity, are measured as values in 1985 prices. As the underlying SAM has no disaggregation of imports into different commodity groups, the imports to a given sector is an aggregate of many different types of imported goods and services.

There are significant differences between the sectors in several respects. First, there are differences in factor proportions, both in terms of capital-labor ratios and electricity intensities. The sectors FOREST and STEELCH are both the most capital intensive and the most electricity intensive production sectors. Second, the electricity intensive sectors FOREST and STEELCH are quite big in terms of net export earnings, but small in terms of value added and employment. Except for the sector HEAT the electricity intensive sectors FOREST and STEELCH are also the most "emission intensive" production sectors. Thus both increasing scarcity of electricity and constraints on the emissions of SO_x, NO_x and CO_2 are likely to particularly affect these two sectors. This is one reason for the distinction between "old" and "new" capital in these sectors.

3. Assumptions about Technology

The technology of production is represented by a nested CES-Leontief production function in each production sector. The structure of the production function is the same for all sectors, but the elasticities of substitution between various inputs may differ across sectors. However, in the Base case simulations presented later on in this paper the elasticities of substitution are taken to be the same in all sectors. Starting from the "bottom", the structure of the production functions is the following.

The input of energy in sector j is denoted by Q_j, where Q_j is a CES aggregate of electricity (E) and fuels (F). Thus $Q_j = Q_j(E_j, F_j)$. The composite energy input is then combined with capital (K) into another CES aggregate, U_j, so that $U_j = U_j(Q_j, K_j)$. On the next level the composite input U_j is combined with natural resources (N) into a third CES aggregate H_j. That is, $H_j = H_j(U_j, N_j)$. However, as FOREST is the only sector using the particular type of natural resource dealt with here, i.e., roundwood, H_j and U_j are identical in all sectors except FOREST.

On the next level the composite input H_j, again by means of a CES aggregation function, is combined with labor into the composite input Y_j. Gross output in sector j, X_j, is then determined by the input in sector j of Y, i.e., Y_j, and intermediate inputs produced by the other sectors, X_{ij}, in accordance with a Leontief production function.

In "old" production units in FOREST and STEELCH all elasticities of substitution are assumed to be zero, i.e., all input-output coefficients are fixed, and total output is constrained by the exogenously given amount of sector-specific capital. The elasticities of substitution in "new" production units are all "guesstimates", although the guesstimating has been done with an eye on the results obtained by Walfridsson (1987) in a study of factor demand in a number of Swedish industries.

The general impression from Walfridsson's study is that electricity and fuels are relatively close substitutes in most sectors, while the substitutability of capital and electricity, like the substitutability of capital and fuels, is relatively low. In fact Walfridsson's results suggest that capital and energy are complements in some sectors. Labor and capital seem to be relatively close substitutes, but the estimated elasticity of substitution is well below unity in most sectors. To be more specific, the base case elasticities of substitution are assumed to be 0.8 in the Q_j- and Y_j-functions in all sectors, and 0.3 in the U_j-function of all sectors. The elasticity of substitution between U_j and N_j in FOREST is assumed to be 0.5.

The emission of various pollutants is the other feature of the production technology. Clearly the possibility of discharging production residuals into the environment can be seen as a factor of production, and one can envisage an elasticity of substitution between this factor of production and capital, labor, materials and energy. However, so far there is no empirical ground for making assumptions about such elasticities of substitution. Instead it has been assumed that emissions from combustion are proportional to the use of fuel and that emissions from industrial processes are proportional to gross output in each sector. Moreover, total emissions can be reduced by means of separate cleaning activities that are available to all sectors. The emission data are summarized in Table I and Table II.

4. Formal Description of the Model

a. TECHNOLOGY AND COSTS

To begin with, four types of implicit prices have to be defined. The first is the implicit price of composite energy, i.e. the CES-aggregate of electricity and

Table I. Total emissions of SO_x, NO_x and CO_2 in 1985 by sector (1000 tonnes)

	FOREST	STEELCH	MANUF	SHELT	NIMP	HEAT
From combustion						
SO_x	13.98	19.44	2.27	3.44	24.83	63.00
NO_x	23.48	17.01	1.93	2.69	112.42	28.00
CO_2*	28.28	69.60	10.56	13.09	211.63	112.85
From industr. proc.						
SO_x	37.00	52.00	0.00	0.00	1.00	0.00

*10^5 tonnes.

Table II. Emissions of SO_x, NO_x and CO_2 per unit of output (1000 ton per 10^9 SEK)

	FOREST	STEELCH	MANUF	SHELT	NIMP	HEAT
From combustion						
SO_x	0.2080	0.1497	0.0099	0.0112	0.0599	2.2317
NO_x	0.3494	0.1310	0.0084	0.0087	0.2710	0.9919
CO_2*	0.4208	0.5360	0.0459	0.0425	0.5101	3.9975
From industr. proc.						
SO_x	0.5505	0.4005	0.0000	0.0000	0.0024	0.0000

*10^5 tonnes per 10^9 SEK.

fuels. As the technology differs across sectors, the sectoral implicit prices of composite energy, P_{Qj}, differ across sectors as well. The definition of P_{Qj} is

$$P_{Qj} = \{\delta_{Qj} P_E^{1-\sigma_{Qj}} + (1-\delta_{Qj}) P_{Fj}^{1-\sigma_{Qj}}\}^{1/1-\sigma_{Qj}}; \quad j \in T, M, N, \tag{1}$$

where P_E is the price of electricity, P_{Fj} the price of imported fuels used in section j, σ_{Qj} the elasticity of substitution between electricity and fuels in the "production" of composite energy, and δ_{Qj} is a distribution parameter. The sector index on the fuel price is due to intersectoral differences with respect to the emissions associated with fuel use. In connection with the discussion later on of emissions and the prices of emission permits the variables P_{F_j} will be defined.

The next implicit price is the price of composite capital-energy, U. Again technological differences across sectors imply sectoral differences in terms of the price of this composite input, P_{Uj}. The definition of P_{Uj} is

$$P_{Uj} = \{\delta_{Uj} P_K^{1-\sigma_{Uj}} + (1-\delta_{Uj}) P_{Qj}^{1-\sigma_{Uj}}\}^{1/1-\sigma_{Uj}}; \quad j \in T, M, N, \qquad (2)$$

where thus P_K is the price of capital services and σ_{Uj} is the elasticity of substitution between capital and composite energy.

On the next level of input aggregation we have to define the price of composite input H, i.e., the capital-energy-roundwood composite. As roundwood is used only in FOREST the inputs H_j and U_j are identical in all other sectors, and consequently $P_{Uj} = P_{Hj}$ for all sectors except FOREST. For that sector the implicit price of composite input H is given by

$$P_{Hj} = \{\delta_{Hj} P_N^{1-\sigma_{Hj}} + (1-\delta_{Hj}) P_{Uj}^{1-\sigma_{Hj}}\}^{1/1-\sigma_{Hj}}; \quad j = \text{FOREST}, \qquad (3)$$

where P_N is the price of roundwood and σ_{Hj} is the elasticity of substitution between roundwood and capital-energy.

On the highest level of input aggregation we have to define the implicit price of Y, i.e. the capital-energy-(roundwood)-labor composite input, P_{Yj}. It is defined by

$$P_{Yj} = \{\delta_{Yj} P_L^{1-\sigma_{Yj}} + (1-\delta_{Yj}) P_{Hj}^{1-\sigma_{Yj}}\}^{1/1-\sigma_{Yj}}; \quad j \in T, M, N, \qquad (4)$$

where P_L is the price of labor services and σ_{Yj} is the elasticity of substitution between labor and the composite input H.

As was mentioned in the preceding section, the relation between inputs and output is given by sectoral production functions of the following type

$$X_j = \min\left\{\frac{Y_j}{A_j}, \frac{X_{ij}}{a_{ij}}, \frac{M_j}{m_j}\right\}; \quad i, j \in T, M, N,$$

where thus X_j is gross output in sector j, X_{ij} is input of sector i output in sector j, M_j is use of imported inputs in sector j and A_j, a_{ij} and m_j are Leontief input-output coefficients. As the technology is specified to exhibit constant returns to scale, the marginal and average cost of production in sector j can be written

$$C_j = P_{Yj} A_j e^{-\lambda_j t} + \sum_i P_i^D a_{ij} + P^M m_j + b_j + V_j; \quad j \in T, M, N, \qquad (5)$$

where C_j is the marginal (and average) cost of production in sector j, P_i^D is the domestic user price of sector i output and a_{ij} is the use of sector i output per unit of sector j output. P^M is the price of imports and m_j is the input of imports per unit of sector j output. The parameter b_j is the indirect tax per unit of sector j output and $\lambda_j t$ is an exogenously given productivity index. The parameter λ_j can be regarded as a measure of the annual rate of total productivity change, while t is the number of years from the benchmark year. The variable V_j is the total cost for sector j of holding a sufficient amount of emission permits. (More about that later on.)

In accordance with the assumption about fixed input-output coefficients in old production units in FOREST and STEELCH, the marginal and average cost of production in these units is given by

$$C_j^0 = R_j^0 k_j^0 + P_L l_j^0 + P_N n_j^0 + P_E e_j^0 + P_{Fj} f_j^0 + \sum_i P_j^D a_{ij}$$

$$+ P^M m_j + b_j + V_j^0; \quad j = \text{FOREST, STEELCH}, \qquad (5')$$

where the superscripts denote "old production unit", i.e., the production units existing at the benchmark year, and small letters denote input coefficients of sector-specific capital, labor, roundwood (in the case of FOREST), electricity and fuels. Observe that the coefficients a_{ij} and m_j are the same for "old" and "new" production units. The variable R_j^0 is rent on sector-specific capital.

b. PRICES AND DOMESTIC DEMAND

As was indicated above, the price of good i for domestic users is denoted by P_i^D. The corresponding producer price is denoted by P_i and the world market price for similar or identical goods is denoted P_i^W. The relation between these prices is the following:

The goods produced in the domestic price-taking sectors is, by definition, identical to goods with the same classification produced by foreign producers. Consequently it holds that

$$P_i^D = P_i^W = (1 + \tau_i)P_i; \quad i \in T, \qquad (6)$$

where τ_i is an *ad valorem* tax rate (initially equal to zero) on sector i output. From equation (6) it also follows that the exchange rate is taken to be the numéraire of the price system and set equal to unity.

For the price-making sectors the corresponding relation is

$$P_i^D = (1 + \tau_i)P_i; \quad i \in M, \qquad (7)$$

i.e., there is no direct relation between domestic and world market prices.

The domestic final demand for good i is denoted D_i, while exogenous demand is denoted G_i. Intermediate demand is given by the technology assumptions. Domestic final demand is given by a linear expenditure system so that

$$D_i = \bar{D}_i + \frac{\beta_i}{P_i^D}\left\{I - \sum_{i \in T,M} P_i^D \bar{D}_i - P_E \bar{D}_E - P_{FD} \bar{D}_F - P^M \bar{D}_M\right\};$$

$$i = T, M, N \tag{8}$$

$$D_E = \bar{D}_E + \frac{\beta_E}{P_E}\left\{I - \sum_{i \in T,M} P_i^D \bar{D}_i - P_E \bar{D}_E - P_{FD} \bar{D}_F - P^M \bar{D}_M\right\}; \tag{9}$$

$$D_F = \bar{D}_F + \frac{\beta_F}{P_{FD}}\left\{I - \sum_{i \in T,M} P_i^D \bar{D}_i - P_E \bar{D}_E - P_{FD} \bar{D}_F - P^M \bar{D}_M\right\}; \tag{10}$$

$$D_M = \bar{D}_M + \frac{\beta_M}{P^M}\left\{I - \sum_{i \in T,M} P_i^D \bar{D}_i - P_E \bar{D}_E - P_{FD} \bar{D}_F - P^M \bar{D}_M\right\}; \tag{11}$$

where I is the disposable income for domestic end use purposes less savings and D_E, D_F and D_m are the final use demands for electricity, fuels and imports, respectively.

c. FOREIGN TRADE AND MARKET CLEARING FOR *T*-, *M*- AND *N*-SECTORS

Given the production sector definitions no econometrically estimated domestic final demand model was available for this study. Instead the simplest possible demand model has been imposed. Thus it is assumed that household demand can be described by a linear expenditure system in which the constants are equal to 50% of the base year (1985) consumption levels, and the marginal expenditure shares are equal to base year average expenditure shares. In principle this is of course very unsatisfactory. However, as a result of the high level of aggregation and the sector definitions the supply of goods for private domestic final use is to a large extent dominated by the two sectors SHELT and NIMP. In view of this, the ad hoc assumptions about domestic final demand may not, after all, affect the results to any significant degree.

In the *M*-sectors the demand for export is given by

$$Z_i = Z_i^0 \left[\frac{P_i}{P_i^W}\right]^{\varepsilon_i} \cdot e^{\gamma t};, \quad i \in M, \tag{12}$$

where thus Z_i is the quantity of goods exported, ε_i is the price elasticity of export demand, γt is an exogenous measure of the "size" of the international market and Z_i^0 a constant. In the *T*-sectors, on the other hand, the net export is determined as the difference between domestic supply and demand.

The total demand for imports can be written

$$M = \sum_{j \in T,M,N} m_j X_j + D_M; \tag{13}$$

where thus M is the level of import.

The market equilibrium conditions for the T-, M- and N-sectors can now be written

$$X_i^0 + X_i = \sum_{i \in T,M,N} a_{ij} X_j + \sum_{j \in T} a_{ij} X_j^0 + D_i + G_i + Z_i; \quad i \in T \tag{14}$$

$$X_i = \sum_{j \in T,M,N} a_{ij} X_j + \sum_{j \in T} a_{ij} X_j^0 + D_i + G_i + Z_i; \quad i \in M \tag{15}$$

$$X_i = \sum_{j \in T,M,N} a_{ij} X_j + \sum_{j \in T} a_{ij} X_j^0 + D_i + G_i; \quad i \in N. \tag{16}$$

d. PRODUCER BEHAVIOUR IN T-, M- AND N-SECTORS

Producer behaviour is modeled on the basis of the standard assumption about profit maximization. Applied on "new" production units in the T-sectors, where thus producer prices of output are given by world market prices, this assumption implies the following constraints

$$P_i - C_i \leqslant 0; \qquad i \in T \tag{17}$$

$$(P_i - C_i)X_i = 0; \qquad i \in T \tag{18}$$

$$X_i \geqslant 0; \qquad i \in T, \tag{19}$$

i.e., pure profits are non-positive, output is non-negative and output is positive only if pure profits are equal to zero.

For the "old" production units in the T-sectors the corresponding condition is formulated in a slightly different way. The reason is that, to some extent, the rent on sector-specific capital is endogenously adjusted so that the equality between price and marginal cost can be maintained. Thus the profit maximization condition simply becomes

$$P_i = C_i^0; \, i \in T \tag{20}$$

and the same type of condition applies for the N-sectors, i.e.,

$$P_i = C_i; \, i \in N. \tag{21}$$

For the M-sectors the usual assumption in Armington CGE-models, that the group of domestic producers is unaware of its market power, is adopted. Thus, the producer prices of M-goods are required to be equal to the corresponding marginal costs, i.e.,

$$P_i = C_i;\ i \in \mathrm{M}. \tag{22}$$

This means that the unexploited market power of the producers to some extent can be exploited in other ways. In particular taxes or scarcity rents on domestic electricity resources can be a means to secure welfare gains at the expense of agents in the rest of the world. The size of these welfare gains, however, depends on the magnitude of the parameters ε_i. As these parameters were somewhat arbitrarily set equal to −5.0 in all net exporting M-sectors, the potential gains from direct or indirect export taxation are not significant.

e. PRODUCER BEHAVIOR IN THE ELECTRICITY SECTOR

Electricity generated in existing hydro and nuclear power plants is treated as a primary resource. However, electricity can also be produced in fossil fuelled plants. This type of electricity is called "substitute electricity". The supply of substitute electricity is denoted X_E. The production of substitute electricity is assumed to be based on a constant returns to scale technology. The particular features of this technology, i.e., whether it should be based on coal, natural gas or some other fuel, is assumed to be an exogenous political decision. The same applies to the emission properties of substitute electricity production.

The marginal cost of substitute electricity can be written

$$C_E = P_{FE}a_{FE} + P_K k_E + V_E; \tag{23}$$

where a_{FE} is the input of imported fuels per unit of output of substitute electricity and P_{FE} is the price of the particular fuel mix used in substitute electricity production. The parameters of this cost function are estimated by means of a data set compiled for a model of the Swedish energy markets (Carlsson, 1988).

Given the cost function, profit maximization implies

$$P_E - C_E \leqslant 0; \tag{24}$$

$$(P_E - C_E)X_E = 0; \tag{25}$$

$$X_E \geqslant 0. \tag{26}$$

f. FACTOR MARKET EQUILIBRIUM AND MACROECONOMIC CLOSURE

The supply of capital (K), labor (L) and electricity from existing hydro and nuclear power plants is exogenously given. The supply of roundwood is given by

$$N = [P_N]^{\rho_N}\overline{N}; \tag{27}$$

where $\overline{N}$ is an exogenous constant and ρ_N the elasticity of supply.

On the basis of Shephard's lemma the market equilibrium conditions for (intersectorially mobile) capital, labor, electricity and roundwood, respectively, can be written

$$K = \sum_{j \in T,M} \frac{\partial C_j}{\partial P_K} X_j + k_E X_E + \sum_e k_{Ce} X_{Ce}; \tag{28}$$

$$L = \sum_{j \in T,M} \frac{\partial C_j}{\partial P_L} X_j; \tag{29}$$

$$E = \sum_{j \in T,M,N} \frac{\partial C_j}{\partial P_E} X_j + D_E - X_E; \tag{30}$$

$$N = \frac{\partial C_j}{\partial P_N} X_j; \quad j = \text{FOREST}, \tag{31}$$

where X_E is the output of substitute electricity, i.e., electricity from other than hydro or nuclear power plants, and k_E is the input of capital services per unit of substitute electricity output. The last term in equation (28) is the demand for capital for emission reduction purposes. Thus, X_{Ce} is the amount of cleaning of pollutant e and k_{Ce} is the input of capital per unit of such "cleaning services".

Production in "old" units in the T-sectors is constrained by the availability of sector-specific capital in these sectors. However, it is reasonable to assume that the amount of capacity that is maintained depends on the level of profitability. Thus the equilibrium conditions for "old" capital are written

$$k_j^0 X_j^0 = (R_j^0)^{\rho j} K_j^0; \tag{32}$$

where ρ_j is a positive constant. Thus, the available capacity is an increasing function of R_j^0.

The total expenditure for domestic consumption and investment purposes, i.e., the variable I in equations (8)—(11), is indirectly determined by the current account constraint

$$\sum_{i \in T} P_i^W Z_i + \sum_{i \in M} P_i Z_i - P^M M - P_F F - P_{FE} F_E = S; \tag{33}$$

where S represents exogenously given flows on current account, and the total imports of fuels are given by

$$F = \sum_{j \in T,M,N} \frac{\partial C_j}{\partial P_F} X_j + D_F; \tag{34}$$

and

$$F_E = a_{FE} X_E,$$

where F_E is the fuel used for substitute electricity.

g. EMISSIONS AND EMISSION CONTROL

In the model there is a distinction between emissions from combustion and emissions from industrial processes, where the former are assumed to be proportional to fuel use, and the latter proportional to gross output. Thus the total emissions of pollutant *e*, T_e, are given by

$$T_e = \sum_i f_{ei} \frac{\partial C_i}{\partial P_{F_i}} X_i + f_{eD} D_F + p_{eE} a_{FE} X_E + \sum_i p_{ei} X_i,$$

$$e = SO_x, NO_x, CO_2, \quad (35)$$

where f_{ei}, f_{eE}, f_{cD}, and p_{ei} are the emissions per unit of fuel use or output (or consumption) of pollutant *e*.

However, for SO_x and NO_x there are possibilities to reduce the emissions by means of direct control measures. Technically this is modeled as a central abatement unit selling cleaning services to the different sectors. The price of these services is equal to the marginal cost of abatement so that

$$P_{Ce} = P_k k_{Ce}; \quad e = SO_x, NO_x, \quad (36)$$

where k_{Ce} is the use of capital services per unit of abatement. The total amount of cleaning services is denoted X_{Ce}, so that the total amount of capital services used for emission abatement purposes is equal to $k_{Ce} X_{Ce}$.

The marginal cost of cleaning is estimated primarily on the basis of data from the energy sector. This among other things means that for every set of environmental constraints and exogenous development of the sector HEAT, a set of marginal abatement costs for the energy sector is estimated by means of the above-mentioned model of the Swedish energy markets. These marginal cost estimates are then assumed to apply to the other sectors as well.

As was mentioned in the introduction, the environmental policy goals are expressed as upper limits on the total emissions. In the model this means that the total emissions of pollutant *e* must be lower than or equal to an upper limit $\overline{T}_e$. However, in a market economy like the Swedish the government has no direct control over total emissions. In practice a limit on the total emission of a given pollutant would be attained by means of a battery of regulations and charges, and through a trial and error process.

In the model, however, the government is assumed to make use of so-called emissions trading (see Tietenberg, 1985). This means that emission permits, corresponding to maximum allowed total emission, are given or sold to the emitters of the pollutant in question. For each source of emissions a sufficient amount of emission permits must be held. As the emission permits can be traded this means that a market for emission permits will be established. If the market for emission permits is perfectly competitive, a single market price is established. This means that the marginal cost of abatement at each individual source of emission can be compared with a unique market price of emission permits. Thus emissions trading is a way of equalizing the marginal cost of abatement across all emission sources.

In the model the upper emission limit $\overline{T}_e$ can be interpreted as the total supply of emission permits for pollutant e. If the price of such emission permits is denoted Π_e, the equilibrium conditions for the emission permits markets can be written

$$T_e - X_{Ce} - \overline{T}_e \leqslant 0; \tag{37}$$

$$\Pi_e(T_e - X_{Ce} - \overline{T}_e) = 0; \quad e = SO_x, NO_x \tag{38}$$

$$\Pi_e \geqslant 0. \tag{39}$$

That is, the non-negative price of emission permits is positive only if the constraint on total emissions is binding. Morever, cleaning services will be demanded only if the marginal cost of abatement is less than or equal to the market price of emission permits. Observe that there are no cleaning services for CO_2. Formally the equilibrium condition for SO_x and NO_x cleaning can be written

$$\Pi_e - P_k k_{Ce} \leqslant 0; \tag{40}$$

$$X_{Ce}(\Pi_e - P_k k_{Ce}) = 0; \quad e = SO_x, NO_x \tag{41}$$

$$X_{Ce} \geqslant 0. \tag{42}$$

h. USER-PRICES OF FUELS

Now when the prices of emission permits have been defined, it is possible to define the sector-specific fuel prices and the V-variables. Thus, the sector-specific fuel prices differ from the import price of fuel by the cost for the emission permits per unit of fuel use that the user need to have. Formally this can be written

$$P_{Fj} = P_F + \sum_e \Pi_e f_{ej}; \qquad e = SO_x, NO_x, CO_2 \tag{43}$$

$$P_{FD} = P_F + \sum_e \Pi_e f_{eD}; \quad e = SO_x, NO_x, CO_2. \tag{44}$$

This means that the price of composite energy, i.e. P_{Qj}, includes the cost of permits for fuel combustion related emissions. Consequently the variables V_j and V_E reflect the cost of permits for process related emissions. Formally this becomes

$$V_j = \sum_e \Pi_e p_{ei}; \qquad e = SO_x, NO_x, CO_2 \tag{45}$$

$$V_E = \sum_e \Pi_e p_{eE} a_{FE}; \qquad e = SO_x, NO_x, SO_2, \tag{46}$$

where thus the emissions from substitute electricity production are regarded as process related emissions.

i. DEFINITION OF GNP

This completes the description of the model. However, it might be useful to define the GNP measure that will be used for the presentation of simulation results later on. Thus, in terms of the variables of the model the economy's GNP can be written

$$\text{GNP} = P_K K + P_L L + P_E E + P_N N + \sum_{j \in T} R_j^0 K_j^0 + \sum_e \Pi_e \overline{T}_e + \sum_{j \in T, M, N} b_j X_j. \qquad (47)$$

5. Some Results

Most of the model's parameters are estimated by means of a simple benchmarking procedure on the basis of a SAM and emission data for 1985. In order to analyze the impact of environmental constraints, some kind of "base case" for the development of the economy over the simulation period 1985—2000 is needed. As the model is entirely static this means that it was solved for the year 2000 on the basis of assumptions about the values of the model's exogenous variables at that point in time. For convenience both these assumptions and the results can be presented in terms of average annual rates of change between 1985 and 2000.

The assumptions about exogenous variables are based on the corresponding assumptions in a recent long-term economic survey by the Ministry of Finance. Thus, it is assumed that the economy's stock of capital, and thus the supply of capital services, on the average grows by 2.0% per annum between 1985 and 2000, while the supply of labor is assumed to grow by 0.4% per annum during that period. In addition, sector specific factor productivity increases in the range 0.5—2.0% per annum are assumed.

The import price of fuels is assumed to increase by, on the average, 1% per year, while the relative prices of other traded goods are assumed to remain constant. The constants in the *M*-sector export functions are assumed to shift by 2.5% per annum, reflecting income growth in the relevant export markets.

The main results of the Base case simulation are summarized in Tables III and IV. In the Base case there are no constraints on the emissions of SO_x, NO_x and CO_2. It is also assumed that ten of the existing twelve nuclear power plants will be in operation during the entire simulation period. That is, the current plan to phase out two nuclear reactors in the middle of the 1990's is assumed to be implemented.

Table III. Calculated change of selected economic variables between 1985 and 2000

	1985	2000	1985—2000**
GNP*	920.7	1247.4	2.0
Electricity consumption*	29.6	32.3	0.6
Fuel consumption*	23.8	34.9	2.6
Output in			
FOREST	67.7	62.2	−0.6
STEELCH	129.9	127.4	−0.1
MANUF	229.9	400.9	3.7
SHELT	307.9	433.1	2.3
NIMP	414.9	539.7	1.8
PUBL	388.3	465.3	1.2
Price index of			
Capital	1.00	1.01	0.0
Labor	1.00	1.33	1.9
Electricity	1.00	1.58	3.1
Roundwood	1.00	0.89	−0.8

* In 10^9 SEK, 1985 prices.
** % per year.

Table IV. Calculated change of emissions between 1985 and 2000

	SO_x*	NO_x*	CO_2**
Actual emissions 1985	270	315	59
Calculated emissions 2000	300	377	88
Target emissions 2000	169	164	63

* 10^3 tonnes.
** 10^6 tonnes.

In the Base case it is assumed that "substitute electricity" is produced by means of coal-fired condensing power plants with advanced emission control equipment. As the 1985 electricity price level in Sweden was very low, reflecting both a certain degree of "normal year" overcapacity and an unusually big supply of hydro power, the marginal cost of substitute electricity is around 60% higher than the 1985 electricity price level. As a result, electricity demand growth is very slow, while the demand for imported fuels, i.e. oil, grows faster than GNP. This in turn means that emissions of SO_x,

NO_x and CO_2 increase in a way that is not consistent with the current environment policy goals (see Table IV).

In order to analyze the sensitivity of the Base case solution with respect to environmental constraints an alternative case, denoted the "Policy case" was constructed. In this case it was assumed that the emissions of SO_x, NO_x and CO_2 were constrained in accordance with current policy goals. The target emission levels at the turn of the century are indicated in Table IV together with the calculated unconstrained emission levels at that point in time. Clearly the emission constraints imposed in the Policy case are quite stringent, and it is likely that these constraints will have general equilibrium effects.

This hypothesis is confirmed by the model simulation. The differences between the Base case and the Policy case are summarized in Table V. The results suggest that the emission constraints will reduce GNP by 4.5% compared to the Base case. In terms of annual GNP growth rates between 1985 and 2000 the Policy case represents a reduction from 2.0% to 1.7%. Needless to say, the environmental benefits resulting from the emission reduction are not included in the GNP measure. Thus the numbers in Table V only say something about the costs of emission control.

The results in Table V also suggest that emission constraints of the type

Table V. Calculated impact of emission constraints on selected economic variables

	(1) Base case value 2000	(2) Policy case value 2000	(3) (2):(1)
GNP*	1247.4	1191.7	0.955
Electricity consumption*	32.3	32.3	1.000
Fuel consumption*	34.9	25.4	0.728
*Output in**			
FOREST	62.2	56.9	0.915
STEELCH	127.4	54.9	0.431
MANUF	400.9	441.4	1.101
SHELT	433.1	443.9	1.025
NIMP	539.7	534.5	0.990
PUBL	465.3	459.7	0.988
Price index of			
Capital	1.01	0.97	0.960
Labor	1.33	1.24	0.932
Electricity	1.58	1.58	1.000
Roundwood	0.89	0.81	0.910

* In 10^9 SEK, 1985 prices.

discussed here will have quite a significant impact on relative factor prices and the sectoral allocation of resources. It is also clear that the positive prices of CO_2 emission permits increase the user prices of fuels, and thus reduce the demand for fuels.

It follows from the construction of the model that the marginal cost of emission control is equal to the equilibrium price of the corresponding emission permits. In the model economy there are no direct technical measures, i.e., no "cleaning services", that can reduce the emissions of CO_2. This means that the price of CO_2 emission permits, and thus the marginal cost of reducing CO_2 emissions, only reflects factor substitutions in the production sectors and changes in the output composition of the economy as a whole.

By "general equilibrium marginal cost of emission control" is meant the marginal cost of emission control when all agents are fully adjusted to the resulting relative prices and all product and factor markets clear. The next set of experiments were aimed at calculating the general equilibrium marginal cost of CO_2 emission control as a function of the CO_2 emission level. Thus a series of model simulations were carried out and for each simulation more stringent constraints on CO_2 emissions were imposed. The results are summarized in Table VI.

The results speak for themselves. When CO_2 emissions are reduced by 10% compared to the Base case, there are essentially no general equilibrium effects. Electricity prices are somewhat higher than in the Base case, and the other factor prices are marginally different. GNP is practically unaffected.

Table VI. The calculated marginal cost of CO_2 emission control and selected economic variables at different CO_2 emission levels

	Emission reduction compared to Base case				
	0%	10%	20%	30%	40%
Marginal cost of CO_2 emission control*	0	0.073	0.158	0.319	0.547
Price index of					
Capital	1.010	1.002	0.977	0.955	0.938
Labor	1.325	1.320	1.295	1.272	1.239
Electricity	1.576	1.676	1.680	1.695	1.688
Roundwood	0.888	0.894	0.889	0.912	0.952
GNP**	1247.4	1247.4	1229.5	1215.3	1199.2

* SEK per kg CO_2.
** 10^9 SEK in 1985 prices.

However, when the CO_2 emissions are reduced by 20% or more there are significant general equilibrium effects, and the impact on GNP is non-negligible.

A government committee in Sweden has recently proposed that a CO_2 emission tax should be imposed. The proposed tax was 0.25 SEK per kg CO_2 in the 1985 price level.

Thus, under the conditions of the model experiment and on the basis of the results presented in Table VI the proposed tax would reduce CO_2 emissions by more than 20% but less than 30%. However, a constant CO_2 emission level would require around 30% lower CO_2 emissions than in the Base case.

Additional experiments indicated that the calculated marginal cost was quite sensitive to some of the underlying assumptions. For instance, an increase in the world market prices of the output of STEELCH would improve the economy's terms of trade and thus increase the national income. However, it would also increase output in the STEELCH sector, and thus increase the demand for CO_2 emission permits. As a result, the price of CO_2 emission permits increased from 0.319 in the 30% reduction case to 0.478 SEK per kg CO_2. Thus it seems to be difficult to draw conclusions about the likely impact of specific emission taxes unless the exogenous conditions are specified in detail.

Concluding Remarks

The results presented in the preceding section suggest that under certain conditions environmental policy measures have general equilibrium effects. Unless these general equilibrium effects are taken into account, policy analyses might give a distorted picture of a set of proposed environmental policies. The reported results also suggest that the implementation of reasonably large computable general equilibrium models is a feasible undertaking, and that models of this type can be useful as a device for ex ante policy evaluation.

Acknowledgement

Financial support from the Energy Research and Development Council and the Nordic Council of Ministers is gratefully acknowledged.

Notes

1 Food industry exposed to competition, printing industry, rubber goods industry, machine industry, means of transport industry, instrument/optics industry, electrical equipment industry, shipyards, other manufacturing industry.

[2] Agriculture, fishery, sheltered food industry, beverage and tobacco industry, textile and clothing industry, sawmills, timbered house industry and carpentry, gasworks, water purification works, goods trade, commissioned work.
[3] Mining and stone industry, constructing, hotels and restaurants, communications, post and tele, banking and insurances, housing management, other real-estate management, repair of vehicles, other private services.

References

Bergman, L. (1986), 'ELIAS — A Model of Multisectoral Economic Growth in a Small Open Economy', in B.-C. Ysander, ed., *Two Models of an Open Economy*, Stockholm: The Industrial Institute for Economic and Social Research.

Carlsson, A. (1988), Estimates of the Costs of Emission Control in the Swedish Energy Sector, Stockholm School of Economics.

Görling, A. (1988), Economic Growth and the Environment. Pollution Structure and Economic Effects of Some Environmental Programs (in Swedish), University of Gothenburg.

Haaland, J. I., V. D. Norman, T. Wergeland, and T. Rutherford (1987), 'VEMOD: A Ricardo—Heckscher—Ohlin—Jones Model of World Trade', *Scandinavian Journal of Economics* **89** (3), 251—270.

Lundgren, S. (1985), Model Integration and the Economics of Nuclear Power, Stockholm School of Economics, The Economic Research Institute.

Tietenberg, T. H. (1985), *Emissions Trading: An Exercise in Reforming Pollution Policy*, Washington D.C.: Resources for the Future.

Walfridsson, B. (1987), *Dynamic Models of Factor Demand.* An application to Swedish industry, University of Gothenburg.

[10]

ELSEVIER Journal of International Economics 47 (1999) 137–168

Journal of INTERNATIONAL ECONOMICS

Trade, spatial separation, and the environment

Brian R. Copeland*, M. Scott Taylor

Department of Economics, University of British Columbia, 997-1873 East Mall, Vancouver, B.C., Canada, V6T 1Z1

Received 18 March 1996; received in revised form 13 June 1997; accepted 8 September 1997

Abstract

We develop a simple two-sector dynamic model to show how pollution can provide a motive for trade by spatially separating incompatible industries. We assume that the production of "Smokestack" manufactures generates pollution, which lowers the productivity of an environmentally sensitive sector ("Farming"). Two identical, unregulated countries will gain from trade if the share of world income spent on Smokestack goods is *high*. In contrast, when the share of world income spent on the dirty good is *low*, trade can usher in a negatively reinforcing process of environmental degradation and real income loss for the exporter of Smokestack goods. © 1999 Elsevier Science B.V. All rights reserved.

Keywords: Two-sector dynamic model; Pollution; Production externality

JEL classification: F10; Q20

1. Introduction

In the last few years economists and environmentalists have engaged in a lively debate over the possible effects of international trade on the environment.[1] Perhaps one of the most serious limitations of much of the recent theoretical work by

*Corresponding author. Tel.: +1 604 822 8215; fax: +1 604 822 5915; e-mail: copeland@econ.ubc.ca

[1]See Grossman and Krueger (1993) and Selden and Song (1994) for empirical work. For theory, see Baumol and Oates (1971); Markusen (1975), (1976); Copeland and Taylor (1994), (1995), and Rauscher (1991). Dean (1992) and Beghin et al. (1994) are useful surveys of the trade and environment literature. Lopez (1994) and Smulders (1994) examine growth and environment issues.

PII: S0022-1996(98)00020-8

economists is that it ignores the long run effects of industrial pollution on productivity in environmentally sensitive sectors. Most of the existing work assumes that pollution is harmful only because consumers suffer a disutility cost from pollution. But if pollution also affects productivity, then it can jeopardize long run sustainability and lower the competitiveness of environmentally sensitive industries. And hence if trade affects pollution, then it may also affect long run income as well as amenity values. For many environmentalists, the neglect of these feedback effects is a key weakness of the standard economic approach to trade and the environment.

There is already ample empirical evidence linking industrial pollution to reduced fishing and agricultural yields, to negative effects on the value of standing forests, and to beach closures that hurt tourism. Current estimates of environmental damage suggest that such external effects are not negligible. Pearce and Warford (1993), (p. 28) report damage estimates from a low of 0.5–0.8% of GNP for the Netherlands, to 4.6–4.9% of GNP for Germany, to a high of 10% of GNP for Poland. Specific industry studies are also available.[2]

Despite the apparent link between the output of heavy industry and damage to environmentally sensitive sectors, economists are often sceptical of the potential for international trade to play a significant role in reinforcing or reversing current trends. In this paper we show that when production externalities are important, trade may in fact play a key role in determining environmental outcomes by spatially separating incompatible industries.

The intuition for many of our results is straightforward. Without trade, a country or region has to produce what it consumes and so environmentally sensitive industries may have their productivity impaired by pollution from other sectors of the economy. Trade can play a useful role in allowing incompatible industries to move away from each other. By separating incompatible industries, trade can reduce the damage from cross-sectoral production externalities and can generate productivity gains for the world as a whole. The benefits of higher global productivity may not be shared across all countries, however, because the productivity changes also bring forth terms of trade changes. We show that in some cases, the country that ends up with the polluting industry may suffer not only from reduced productivity in environmentally sensitive sectors, but also from a terms of trade deterioration that is brought on by its own environmental degradation.

We construct a very simple dynamic model to make transparent the role trade can play in separating incompatible industries. There are only two industries: a smokestack manufacturing industry which we denote by M, and an environmental-

---

[2]A recent comprehensive study of European Forests by the International Institute for Applied Systems concludes that sulphur emissions alone cost Europe $30 billion per year in forest losses (for a review of this research see Carrier and Krippi (1990)). Other supporting evidence can be found in the U.N. Environmental Data Report (1993) and FAO (1977).

ly sensitive industry such as agriculture, fishing or forestry denoted by A. For simplicity we refer to A as Farming output, but it should be thought of as a generic output from any environmentally sensitive sector.

We define a stock variable, "environmental capital", which is meant to capture the productivity-relevant aspects of environmental quality. The Smokestack industry emits pollution, and over time the flow of these pollutants degrades the nation's environmental capital. Since we assume that the free flow of services from the environment are inputs into farming, a lower stock of environmental capital necessarily lowers the productivity of other primary inputs in the farming sector. Throughout we assume that pollution stays within the country of origin, that there is no regulation of emissions from Smokestack, and that emissions do not create a direct utility cost to consumers. This simple framework isolates the impact of free trade when industrial pollution creates a negative cross-industry externality.

Within this framework we derive several surprising results. First, we show that opening a country to trade at world prices that are arbitrarily close to autarky prices can lead to a very large discrete change in environmental quality. As Baumol and Bradford (1972) showed, a country's long run production possibility set may be nonconvex when there are cross-sectoral production externalities. With nonconvexities in the production set, an open economy has a tendency to specialize in production, and there is the potential for a small price change to result in a large expansion of the pollution-intensive sector.

Second, we find that two identical countries can gain from trade. The standard explanation for trade between similar countries rests on the benefits of concentrating industries with increasing returns to scale. Here we find that the benefits of separating incompatible industries provides an alternative mechanism through which identical countries can gain from trade. As the environmental literature has pointed out (e.g., Helfand and Rubin, 1994) the presence of nonconvexities suggests that policy in many cases should encourage environmental damage to be spatially concentrated: if one industry harms another, then one solution is to separate them. We find that such spatial separation must occur as a result of trade: Endogenously evolving productivity differences will provide market incentives for the two countries to specialize in production. Thus, in some cases, an efficient allocation of production across countries can occur without the need for any environmental policy.

Third, the welfare implications of trade are quite surprising. We find that if the share of world income spent on the dirty product is large, then free trade must be welfare-enhancing for two identical countries. Conversely, if the share of world income spent on clean products is large, then one of the two countries must lose from trade. Moreover, losses are more likely the faster is the environment's regeneration rate and the smaller is the negative externality!

Lastly, once we introduce nonidentical countries we show that free trade can lock in the wrong (inefficient) pattern of specialization across countries. Trade can leave the country with the most resilient environment specialized in the clean good, while its trading partner produces all of the dirty good. Similarly, trade can leave the most populous country diversified in production, when production efficiency requires just the opposite.

This paper integrates two strands of the literature, one from environmental economics, and the other from international trade. Our model can be interpreted as an open economy and dynamic extension of the Baumol and Bradford (1972) model of pollution. It also bears a strong family resemblance to the open economy models that Melvin (1969), Panagariya (1981), and Ethier (1982) developed to analyze external economies of scale.

In the environment literature, it is well known that pollution externalities can lead to nonconvexities in the production set (Baumol and Bradford, 1972). While this result is well known, it has had relatively little impact on the mainstream of the environment literature. In part, this seemingly benign neglect has arisen because much of the relevant policy analysis has been carried out in a partial equilibrium framework; and in part, because some authors, such as Burrows (1986) have argued that the theoretical difficulties that nonconvexities create are of little practical significance for pollution policy. In contrast, we show that nonconvexities generated by pollution externalities can play a critical role in determining the pattern of trade, the gains from trade, and the environmental consequences of free trade.

In the international trade literature, nonconvexities play a central role. During the past twenty years, much of the new trade theory has examined increasing returns to scale as a determinant of trade. Many authors have modelled increasing returns as a positive externality external to firms, but internal to an industry (see Helpman, 1984, for a review). This generates potential gains from trade from concentrating industries with external economies in one location. In this paper, we consider the implications of a negative cross-industry externality.[3] Here the motive for trade is to spatially separate industries. In what follows we uncover a number of interesting parallels and contrasts between the implications of these two different, but similar, motives for trade.

In many ways our analysis continues a line of research originating with Frank Graham in the 1920's. Graham's argument was simply that free trade can create losses if trade changes the composition of national output in such a way as to reduce overall productivity. These trade-induced productivity losses then need to be weighed against terms of trade gains to determine the overall welfare consequence of international trade. As Ethier (1982) so clearly showed, Graham was right—free trade can create losses if there are external economies in one sector—although the conditions under which his hypothesis held were quite surprising and at odds with conventional wisdom. Here we identify another

[3]Panagariya considered negative externalities that were internal to an industry, and Ethier also briefly considered this case. This type of externality, however, tends to make the production frontier concave, and hence has much different effects.

channel through which overall productivity can fall (or rise!) when a country enters into international trade. And, like Ethier (1982), we provide results that were initially at odds with our own intuition regarding the welfare (and environmental) consequences of free trade.

The structure of the paper is as follows. We set up a simple dynamic model in Section 2 and study autarky in Section 3. In Sections 4–6, we consider the effects of trade. In Section 7, we briefly discuss possible extensions. Section 8 concludes.

2. The model

There are two primary factors: Labor (L) and the stock of environmental capital (K). The level of K is given at any moment in time, but may be degraded or enhanced over time, depending on the flow of pollution and nature's regenerative capacity. We assume that K evolves according to:[4]

$$\mathrm{d}K/\mathrm{d}t = g(\bar{K} - K) - Z \tag{1}$$

where $\bar{K}$ is the "natural" level of environmental capital, Z is the flow of pollutants, and $g>0$ measures the recovery rate of the environment.[5] Absent any pollution, in the long run environmental capital would gravitate towards its natural steady state at the pristine level $\bar{K}$. For example, we may think of Z as the average flow of sulphur oxides emitted per year, and K as a measure of average ambient air quality.

There are two industries denoted M and A. M, or Smokestack manufacturing, is a dirty industry that uses labor as an input and emits pollution as a joint product of output. We assume that one unit of labour can produce one unit of manufactures, and generates λ units of pollution:

$$M = L_{\mathrm{M}} \tag{2}$$

$$Z = \lambda L_{\mathrm{M}} \tag{3}$$

Our other industry, denoted by A, is an environmentally sensitive industry that

[4]We omit time subscripts to economize on notation. All variables refer to current period values unless indicated otherwise.

[5]Admittedly our pollution dynamics are quite rudimentary. Nature's regeneration function is linear and purely compensatory with reductions in K bringing about compensating increases in nature's rate of regeneration $(\mathrm{d}K/\mathrm{d}t)/K$. In addition, our regeneration function assumes that there is no minimum viable level of the environment's capital stock since $\mathrm{d}K/\mathrm{d}t$ is still positive at $K=0$. Moreover, since the flow of pollution emissions, Z, enters Eq. (1) linearly, the marginal physical damage of pollution to the environment is constant. These assumptions were chosen primarily to simplify the analysis and in Section 7 we consider the implications of two alternative specifications.

may be thought of as Farming.[6] Production of A uses labor as an input, but production is also dependent on the free flow of services (sun, rain, clean air and water, etc.) provided by the stock of environmental capital. Hence:

$$A = F(K)L_A \tag{4}$$

where L_A is labor allocated to agriculture and $F(K)$ is the flow of services arising from an environmental capital stock of K. For simplicity, we let $F(K)=K^{\varepsilon}$, with $0<\varepsilon<1$.[7]

Labour markets are competitive and labourers are freely and costlessly mobile across sectors. As a result, labour reallocates itself across sectors instantaneously ensuring that within a country, wages and marginal value products are always equalized when both sectors are active. This instantaneous adjustment in labour markets, coupled with our assumption of gradual adjustment of the environment's capital stock, simplifies the dynamic analysis considerably. Together these two assumptions primarily reflect our view that the speed of adjustment of the environmental processes involved are slow in relation to the usual equilibrating forces at work in market economies.

We assume a representative consumer with current period utility given by:

$$U = b_m \ln(M) + b_a \ln(A) \tag{5}$$

where b_m and b_a are the shares of spending on M and A. As noted above, to highlight the role of production externalities, we assume that environmental quality does not directly affect utility. Our main results do not require constant budget shares, nor homotheticity. The Mill–Graham assumption of constant budget shares has a long history in the trade and external economies literature (see Melvin, 1969; Ethier, 1982; Panagariya, 1981, etc.). Its primary usefulness lies in the ability to link primitives to the existence of certain types of Pareto ranked equilibria.

3. Autarky

We begin by considering the steady state properties of the model in autarky. Our primary motivation for considering autarky is to establish a benchmark showing

---

[6]Our analysis applies to any two industries where one inflicts a negative production externality on the other. Farming may be a bit of a misnomer, because agriculture is a major source of nonpoint source pollution.

[7] Eq. (1) assumes that pollution creates a constant marginal physical damage to the stock of environmental capital K, but our assumption of $\varepsilon<1$ in (4) ensures that equal reductions in K create increasingly large decreases in the productivity of clean good production. Holding prices and labour allocations fixed, our specification yields a typical increasing and convex marginal (economic) damage function.

that under our specification, the autarky equilibrium is unique and stable even though our economy's steady state production possibility frontier is strictly convex. Although multiple equilibria and instability are endemic to models where production externalities lead to nonconvexities, our assumptions rule out these complications in autarky. As a result, we are able to very clearly link free trade per se to the introduction of these complications.[8]

As a first step, we construct the economy's steady state production frontier to demonstrate that it is strictly convex throughout. Using (2) and (4), full employment of labor requires that at every point in time:

$$L = L_M + L_A = M + \frac{A}{K^{\varepsilon}} \tag{6}$$

This gives us an expression for the economy's short run production frontier. It is linear, reflecting the Ricardian structure of the economy in the short run. Points along such a frontier are not necessarily sustainable, however, since the environmental capital stock K in (6) is dependent on the economy's history of pollution discharge. Changes in M induce changes in pollution which in turn affect K. To obtain the steady state or sustainable production frontier, we use (3) and (2) in (1), and find that K evolves according to

$$\mathrm{d}K/\mathrm{d}t = g(\bar{K} - K) - \lambda M \tag{7}$$

A steady state corresponds to $\mathrm{d}K/\mathrm{d}t = 0$ in (7). Provided specialization in M will not result in destruction of the entire capital stock,[9] the steady state relationship between Smokestack output and environmental capital is then given by

$$K = \bar{K} - \lambda_M M \tag{8}$$

where $\lambda_M \equiv \lambda / g$. Using (8) to eliminate K in (6) and rearranging yields the steady state production frontier:

$$A = (L - M)(\bar{K} - \lambda_M M)^{\varepsilon} \tag{9}$$

This function is strictly convex.

Not surprisingly, given our convex production frontier, the steady state supply curve for Smokestack output is negatively sloped over some range. To construct this supply curve consider first the conditions under which both sectors are active in steady state. For manufacturing, the zero profit condition requires, using (2):

$$p_M = w \tag{10}$$

[8]This is a common practice. Ethier (1982) imposes sufficient structure on preferences and technologies to render autarky a unique and stable equilibria for exactly these same reasons.

[9]That is, we assume that $\bar{K} - \lambda L/g > 0$. This will not affect the qualitative results.

Agricultural firms maximize profits, treating the environmental capital stock as given, and thus using (4), we must have:

$$p_a K^{\varepsilon} = w \tag{11}$$

Dividing (10) by (11) yields

$$\frac{p_M}{p_a} = K^{\varepsilon} \tag{12}$$

which tells us that at a point in time relative prices are determined by the environmental capital stock. Consequently, if both industries are active in steady state, then using (8) in (12), we have

$$p \equiv \frac{p_M}{p_a} = (\bar{K} - \lambda_M M)^{\varepsilon} \tag{13}$$

which is a decreasing function of M. If $p_M/p_a < (\bar{K} - \lambda_M M)^{\varepsilon}$, for any M, it is profitable to shift labor out of M and into A, and conversely, if $p_M/p_a > (\bar{K} - \lambda_M M)^{\varepsilon}$, the M industry expands and A contracts.

The supply curve for M is illustrated in Fig. 1 (and denoted "S"). Along the locus of points described by (13), the economy produces both M and A. Notice

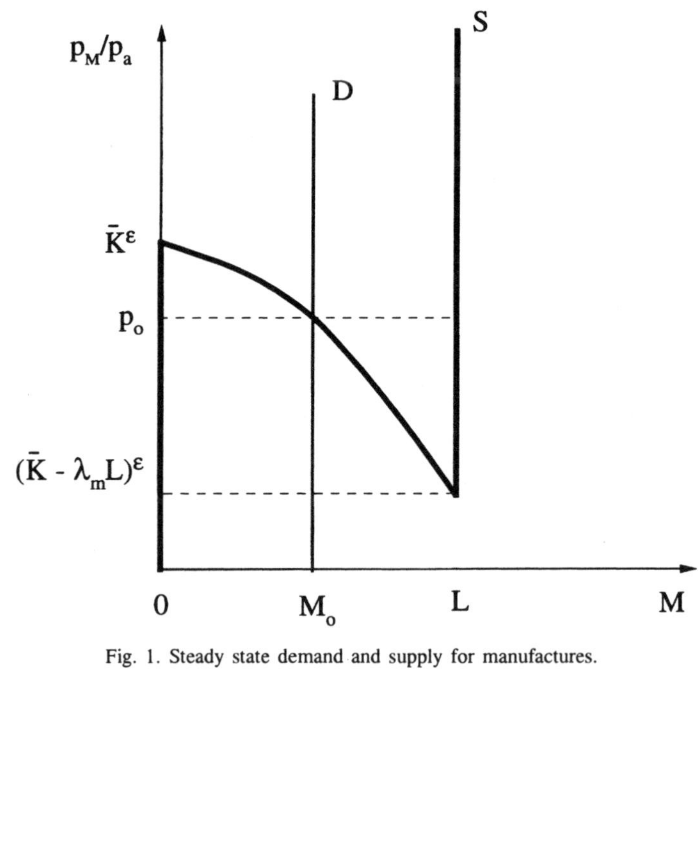

Fig. 1. Steady state demand and supply for manufactures.

that the supply curve slopes downward in this range: an increase in M results in a lower steady state environmental capital stock and lower productivity in agriculture. This reduces the demand for labor in agriculture and hence lowers the minimum price required to support the increased supply. The supply curve contains two other segments, corresponding to specialization in either M or A. For $p_M/p_a<\bar{K}^{\varepsilon}$, then for $M=0$, (13) is violated, it is profitable for A to expand, and the economy can specialize in A. Hence the vertical segment $[0, \bar{K}^{\varepsilon}]$ at $M=0$ lies on the supply curve. Finally, at $M=L$, the economy specializes in M. For $p_M/p_a>(\bar{K}-\lambda_M L)^{\varepsilon}$, it is profitable for M to expand, and consequently, the economy can specialize in M for any such price. This leads to the right hand vertical segment of the supply curve.

As is standard in models with convex production frontiers, supply is not unique over a range of prices and there may be multiple equilibria in autarky. Nevertheless, with sufficient restrictions on demand there is a unique equilibrium. With our Mill–Graham preferences, the demand for M is given by

$$D_M=\frac{b_M wL}{p_M}=b_M L \tag{14}$$

using (10). Hence the demand curve in autarky is vertical and we have:

Proposition 1. *A globally stable, unique steady state equilibrium exists in autarky.*

Proof. See Appendix A.

An alternative graphical method of proof is given in Fig. 2 (ignore for the moment the bold line labelled "Free trade pollution function"). If we measure pollution flows and environmental cleansing on the vertical axis and K on the horizontal axis, then the environment's cleansing function, $g(\bar{K}-K)$, can be illustrated by the downward sloping line in Fig. 2. As well, from (14) we know that the level of pollution emissions is independent of K and given by the "Autarky pollution function" $Z=\lambda M=\lambda b_M L$ shown in the figure. By construction a positive (negative) vertical distance between the cleansing function and the autarky pollution function implies that the stock of environmental capital must be growing (shrinking), and hence the unique steady state level of environmental capital is at $K=K_0$. Moreover as Fig. 2 makes clear, the unique steady state is globally stable and the adjustment of K towards its steady state value must be monotonic.

4. Free trade in a small open economy

We now consider trade. In autarky, domestic market conditions constrain the amount of pollution that the economy generates, and this in turn stabilizes the level of environmental capital. If Smokestack expands too much, farming output

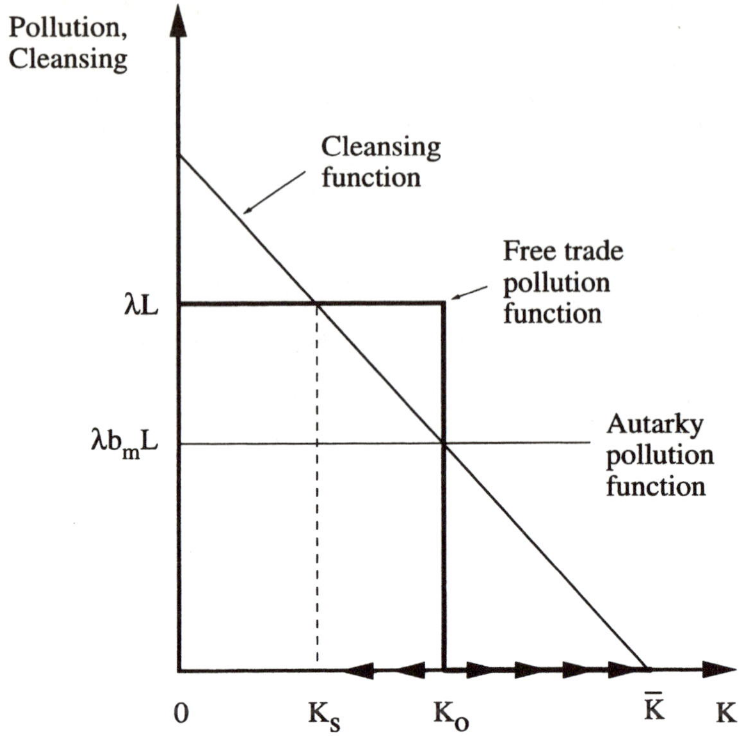

Fig. 2. Free trade for a small open economy.

becomes scarce, relative prices adjust, and market forces encourage smokestack to contract, thereby reducing pollution. Although there is still too much pollution because of the externality, the market for farming output acts as a restraint on pollution in autarky.

Trade can eliminate this market-driven check on the level of pollution. This is illustrated most effectively by considering a small price-taking economy that faces a world relative price p* equal to its autarky price p_o. The demand curve facing this small open economy is now perfectly elastic as shown by the dashed line at p_o in Fig. 1, and there are now three possible steady state equilibria in trade. These are illustrated in Fig. 1 and consist of the original autarky diversified equilibrium at M_o (with no trade) plus two additional equilibria where the economy is specialized in either *A* or *M* (with trade).

More significantly, the opportunity to trade has rendered the autarky equilibrium unstable. This can be illustrated with the aid of Fig. 3, which depicts a series of short run equilibria of the economy. The short run production frontier corresponding to the autarky steady state capital stock K_o is labelled in the figure as

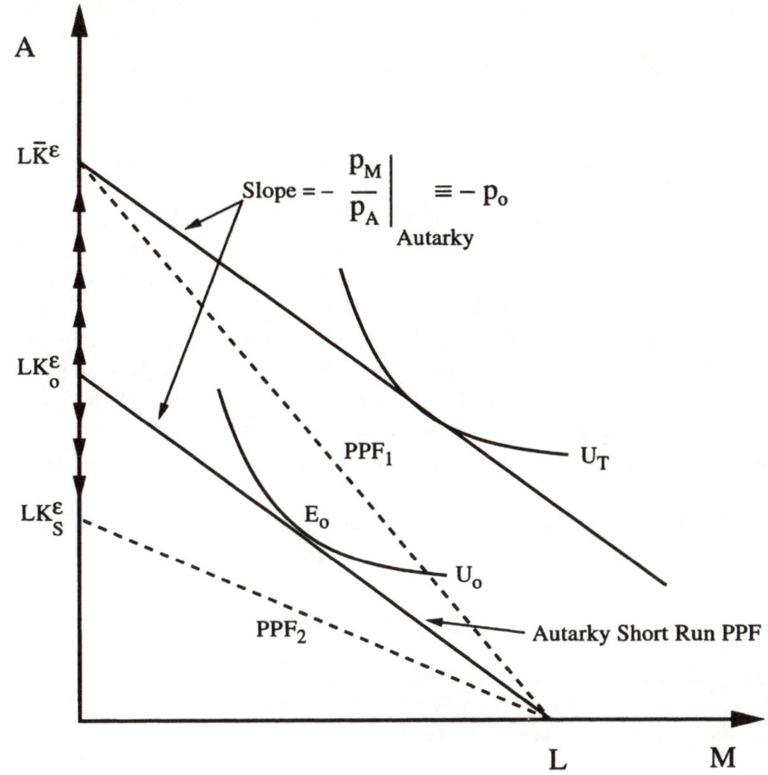

Fig. 3. Response of the short run production frontier to trade.

"Autarky Short Run PPF". For a given level of K, the production frontier is linear, and so in the short run, the model behaves like the simple Ricardian model. The autarky equilibrium is at point E_o, utility is U_o, and the autarky price ratio is p_o. Now suppose that the economy opens up to trade at a fixed world price equal to the autarky price ratio. To see that the autarky equilibrium is unstable, suppose that the economy deviates slightly away from point E_o and that production of M increases. This will lead to more pollution, and hence from Fig. 2, we know that environmental capital K will start to fall. But as K falls, productivity in sector A is reduced, and so the short production frontier starts to rotate downward (as indicated by the arrows on the A axis in Fig. 3). In autarky, prices would adjust, pollution would drop, and the economy would gradually return to point E_o. But in free trade, prices do not adjust, since they are now fixed in world markets. Consequently, as the PPF rotates downward, it becomes flatter than the world price ratio, and so the economy develops a comparative advantage in Manufacturing.

With a linear production frontier, this leads the economy to specialize in M, and so pollution rises. But this reinforces the initial movement away from point E_o, as K falls even more, causing a further flattening of the production frontier, and a strengthening of the comparative advantage in the polluting industry. A similar argument can be used to show that a slight *increase* in K will also be reinforced, leading the economy to specialize in sector A. Consequently, the autarky equilibrium is unstable in free trade.

The new possible steady states can be determined by constructing the free trade pollution function as illustrated in Fig. 2. As discussed above, in free trade (with $p^*=p_o$), a slight drop in K leads the economy to specialize in M. Consequently from Eq. (3), pollution rises to $Z=\lambda L$ for all $K<K_o$. This is illustrated by the left half of the heavy dark line in Fig. 2. On the other hand, if K rises above K_o, then the economy specializes in A, with pollution dropping to zero. Thus the free trade pollution function steps down to $Z=0$ for $K>K_o$ (the right half of the heavy dark line in Fig. 3). Finally, at $K=K_o$, production is indeterminate, since the short run production frontier has the same slope as the world price ratio. Consequently, the free trade pollution function is vertical at $K=K_o$.

Combining the free trade pollution function with the environment's cleansing function, we can see from Fig. 2 that the three possible steady states are at K_s, K_o, or $\bar{K}$, with K_o being unstable. With this construct in hand, it is straightforward to prove:

Proposition 2. *If trade occurs at fixed world prices equal to autarky prices, there are three possible steady state equilibria. Only the two specialized equilibria are stable; the diversified autarky equilibrium is unstable.*

Proof. See Appendix A.

Proposition 2 bears a strong resemblance to similar results in the trade and increasing returns literature. Its importance lies not in illustrating the theoretical possibility of instability, but rather in linking free trade with a cumulative process of environmental change begetting industrial restructuring that in turn begets further environmental change. A slight expansion in Manufacturing output creates a comparative advantage in M, which increases the output of M. This generates yet more pollution, which further degrades K, and reinforces the newly-created comparative advantage in M. This process of cumulative causation locks the country into a high-pollution, low-environmental-capital steady state. Conversely, if manufacturing output were to decline slightly below M_o, then the relative productivity of A rises, and a similar process would lead the economy to specialize in farming.

While trade at autarky prices leaves us with two possible trading equilibria, trade at just above or below autarky prices leaves us with more determinate results. If the world relative price of M is slightly below the autarky price, then at the outset of trade, the economy will unambiguously specialize in farming even at the initial level of $K=K_o$. In terms of Fig. 2, the vertical segment of the free trade pollution function is to the left of the one shown in Fig. 2. Consequently, the economy will evolve towards the steady state $K=\bar{K}$. Alternatively, if the price of M is slightly above the autarky price, then at the outset of trade the economy will specialize in smokestack. The vertical segment of the free trade pollution function will be to the right of the one shown in Fig. 2, and the steady state equilibrium will be at K_s.

Trade occurs in this model because it leads to a separation between the location of consumption and the location of production. With cross-industry externalities, such separation affects relative productivities and creates comparative advantage. Environmentalists have often made the point that trade can be harmful for the environment precisely because it separates the location of consumption from the location of production (see Daly, 1993, p. 57). The argument is that trade allows consumers of pollution intensive goods to escape the direct negative environmental consequences of their consumption. However, in a world with pure production externalities, the concentration of environmental destruction may well be desirable. In fact, with no direct disutility cost of pollution, free trade is always welfare improving in our small open economy model, despite the absence of pollution policy.

Proposition 3. *Free trade is welfare improving for a small open economy.*

Proof. See Appendix A.

This result can be illustrated with the aid of Fig. 3 for the case where the free trade price ratio is equal to autarky prices. If the economy specializes in farming, then trade leads to a regeneration of the stock of environmental capital, causing the short run production frontier to rotate upward to PPF_1. Consequently, free trade utility U_T is clearly above autarky utility U_0. Note that there are no static gains from trade, but there are dynamic gains. On the other hand, if the economy specializes in manufacturing, then the production point moves to L. Although the production frontier rotates downward, this does not reduce utility, because environmental capital is not used in the production of M. In this case, free trade utility is the same as in autarky. Finally, note that if the world price ratio is different than the autarky price ratio, then the gains from trade would be larger, as there would be standard static gains from trade in addition to the dynamic effects discussed above.

Once we introduce some complexities into the model, the benefits of separating industries must be weighed against potentially offsetting factors. For example, if relative prices can adjust along the transition path, then a country may end up "trapped" in an industry that at current world prices leaves it with lower real income than before trade.[10] We consider this and related issues in the following sections.

5. Trade in a two country world

We now consider trade between two countries, Home and Foreign. Foreign variables are denoted with an asterisk ("*"). To abstract from all other motives for trade, we start by assuming the countries are identical prior to trade: they have the same technology, labour supplies and environmental cleansing functions. Identical countries have identical stocks of environmental capital and identical relative prices in autarky. Consequently, autarky is a free trade equilibrium. This equilibrium is unstable, however, since any increase in Smokestack output by one country initiates a self-reinforcing cycle of pollution-induced declines in agricultural productivity, and increased comparative advantage in the Smokestack industry. Thus trade can emerge between two identical countries.

The standard explanation for trade between similar countries is based on increasing returns to scale. With increasing returns, there is an incentive for an industry to concentrate in one location to reap the benefits of positive external economies. Negative externalities across sectors provide an alternative, but closely related, motive for trade arising from the beneficial separation of incompatible industries. The analytics are closely related because of a symmetry imposed by general equilibrium resource constraints.

To see how this symmetry between external increasing returns in one sector and a cross-industry negative externality arises, suppose primary factors move into Farming. Moving factors into Farming means drawing them from Smokestack. Smokestack pollution falls, the environment improves, and this increases the productivity of primary factors in Farming. Note that the same beneficial increase in Farming's productivity could have arisen had we assumed Farming had external increasing returns linked to its output level. A consequence of this symmetry is that some of the intuition for our results is similar to Ethier (1982), but the parallels are not exact as we show in Section 6.

Given the Ricardian structure of the model there are three possible types of trading steady states. We consider each in turn below. In addition since we are starting with identical countries, there are always two symmetric equilibria of each type. For concreteness, in the following we will always associate Home with the

[10]As well, if the short run production frontier is concave, then the economy will not specialize completely in free trade, and so when the economy has a comparative advantage in M, the deterioration of environmental capital will be welfare-relevant. And if environmental quality enters directly into the utility function, then the welfare results must also be modified in an obvious way.

country that produces farm output and can in some cases be entirely specialized in farming.

5.1. High demand for the dirty good

Provided the demand for smokestack output is "high", both countries must produce Smokestack in any trading equilibrium. In our model a "high" demand corresponds to $b_m > 1/2$. This ensures that Foreign specializes in M, while Home produces both goods. In this case, wages must be equal across countries, and both countries will gain from trade.

The transition from autarky to the trading steady state is illustrated in Fig. 4. In autarky, both countries have K_o units of environmental capital and produce both goods. With the opening of trade, this no-trade equilibrium becomes unstable. Suppose Foreign output of M rises. This increases pollution, lowers K^*, and gives Foreign a comparative advantage in M. If the demand for Smokestack is high, then

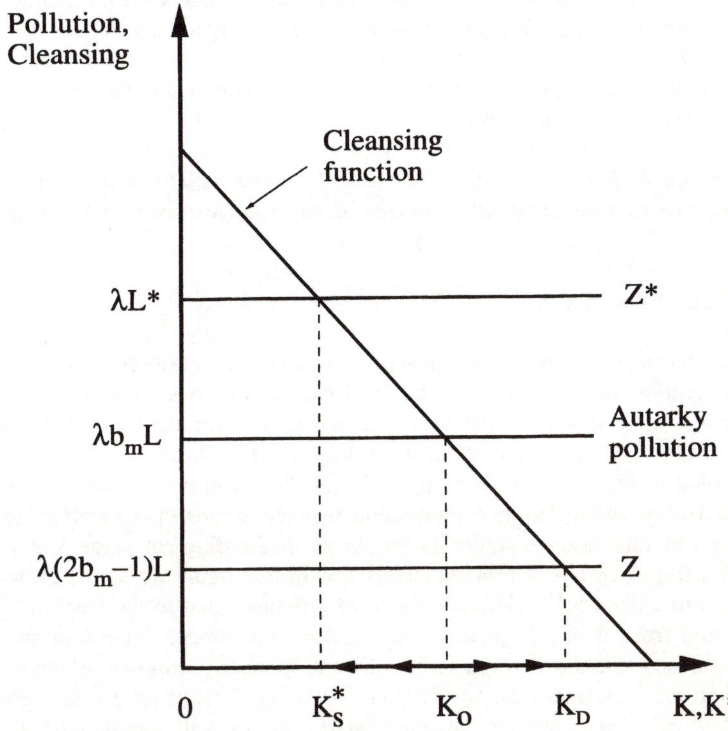

Fig. 4. High demand for Smokestack: Transition dynamics to a diversified steady state.

Foreign must specialize in M. Foreign's pollution level shifts up to $Z^*=\lambda L^*$ as shown, and its stock of environmental capital falls toward K_s^*, reinforcing its comparative advantage in M. Moreover, it is apparent from the figure that the adjustment of K towards its steady state is monotonic and that the steady state at K_s^* is stable.

At the same time, when Home begins to import Smokestack its output of M falls. As long as Smokestack is produced in both countries, wages must be equalized across countries ($w=w^*=p_m$), and recalling (14), the world demand for M is given by

$$M^w = b_m(wL + w^*L^*)/p_m = b_m(L + L^*)$$

Because Foreign produces L^* units of Smokestack when specialized, Home produces $M=M^w-L^*$ units. As a result, Home's flow of pollution in trade becomes

$$Z = \lambda M = \lambda[M^w - L^*] = \lambda[b_m(L + L^*) - L^*] = \lambda(2b_m - 1)L$$

since $L=L^*$. This new pollution level is shown in Fig. 4, and is positive if $b_m>1/2$. Since this flow of pollution is less than its autarky level, Home's stock of environmental capital begins to recover and it gradually moves toward its diversified steady state value at K_D. Moreover, it is apparent from the figure that the adjustment of K^* towards its steady state is monotonic and that the steady state at K_D is stable. More formally,

Proposition 4. *If $b_m>1/2$, then in the only stable steady state, trade emerges between two ex ante identical countries. Both countries produce Smokestack but only one country produces Farm output. Both countries gain from trade.*

Proof. See Appendix A.

While the effects of trade on the environment are very different across countries, both countries must gain from trade. Home gains from the increase in its production possibilities created by its improving environment, and Foreign gains from the terms of trade improvement brought about as the relative price of A falls in response to improved productivity in Home. This can be illustrated by referring to Fig. 3 once again. Home's production frontier rotates upward after free trade (although in this case not quite as far up as in the diagram since K evolves to $K_D<\bar{K}$). But since Home remains diversified in free trade, world prices must also adjust so that the world relative price of M remains equal to the slope of Home's production frontier. Consequently, p_M/p_A rises with trade. Since foreign exports M, this means that the Foreign terms of trade gradually improve as the economy adjusts to the new free trade steady state. Although foreign production remains at point L, it gains as its budget constraint rotates upward with the increase in p_M/p_A.

In this case, trade serves as an imperfect substitute for environmental policy.

B.R. Copeland, M. .S. Taylor / Journal of International Economics 47 (1999) 137–168 153

Because of the negative production externality, it is efficient to separate the two industries. International trade provides incentives for this separation to occur in a free market.[11] Separation per se is not, however, sufficient for trade to always benefit both countries. As we show below, when Smokestack is concentrated in one country alone, separation is almost complete, but the gains from this separation are not equally shared across countries. In fact, one country must lose from trade.

5.2. High demand for the clean good

Now consider the case where there is a relatively strong demand for the clean good ($b_a > 1/2$ or equivalently, $b_m < 1/2$). Two types of equilibria may emerge, depending on the strength of this demand. If b_a is sufficiently large, then both countries must produce A in the steady state. On the other hand, for intermediate values of b_a, both countries may be specialized in production. In either case, all of the manufacturing is concentrated in one country. As a result, wages need not be equalized across countries in free trade.

As before, the autarky allocation is an unstable free trade equilibrium, since any deviation in production patterns initiates a dynamic process that generates and reinforces comparative advantage. To analyze the adjustment path to the free trade steady state, suppose that Foreign deviates slightly from its autarky output levels and increases its output of M with the opening of trade. The ensuing pollution-created fall in K^* gives Foreign a comparative advantage in M and Home a comparative advantage in A. With a high demand for A, Home specializes in A. Foreign produces all of the world's M, but with K^* only marginally less than K, and with $b_a > 1/2$, Foreign must also produce some A.[12] Hence, at least in the early stages of adjustment, the Foreign country produces both goods, while Home is specialized in A. As we shall see, during the transition to the trading steady state Foreign could either remain diversified in production, or if the demand for Smokestack is sufficiently high, it may be driven to specialize. Home, on the other hand, must remain specialized.

Let us first consider the case where Foreign remains diversified in the steady state (b_a is large). The adjustment path is illustrated in Fig. 5(a), where we have plotted the regeneration function (1) and some pollution functions for the Foreign country, which we denote by Ω_i.[13]

---

[11] Notice, however, that the equilibrium is not Pareto efficient: because of the externality, there will still be excessive production of M in the country that produces both goods.

[12] To prove this result note that when $K = K^*$, world labour demand in M is $2b_m L < L$ since $b_m < 1/2$ (see $\Omega(K, K^*)$ below). Hence for K near K^*, Foreign must diversify.

[13] An equivalent, but quite cumbersome, analysis using phase plane techniques is available on request from the authors.

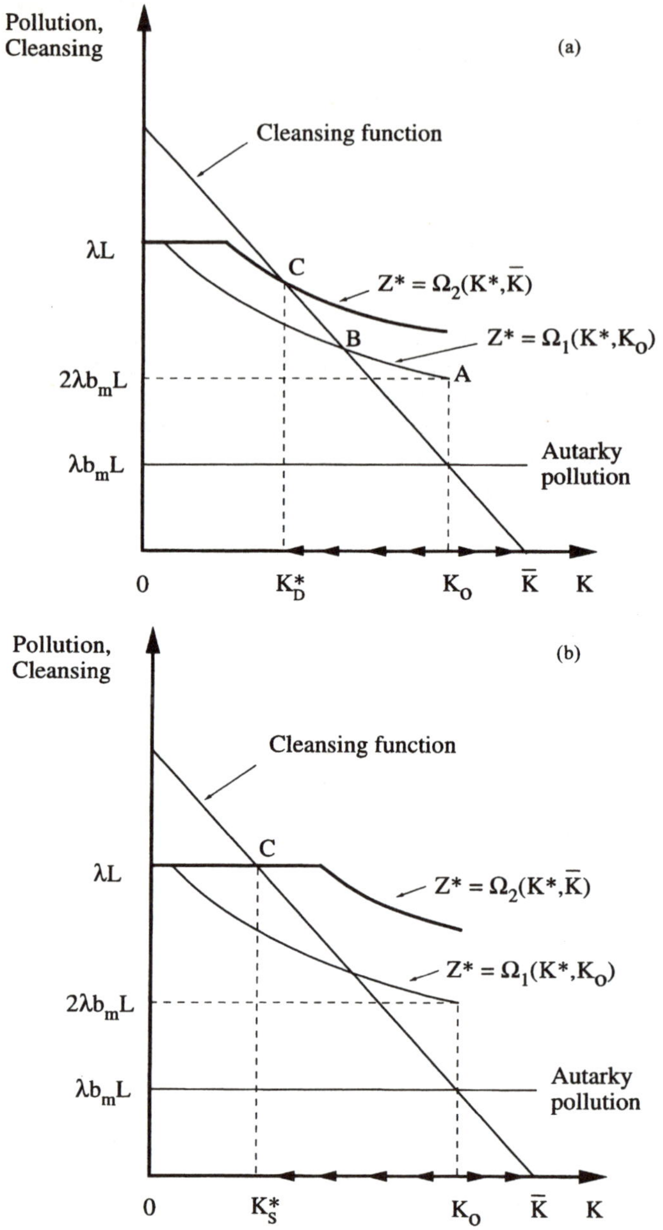

Fig. 5. (a) High demand for Agriculture: Transition dynamics to a diversified steady state. (b) High demand for Agriculture: Transition dynamics to a fully specialized steady state.

The pollution function Ω gives the level of pollution generated by Foreign as a function of the current level of K and K^*. Foreign pollution is a by-product of its manufacturing output, and since Home is specialized in A, Foreign must satisfy the world demand for M, which is

$$M^{W} = b_{m}(w^*L^* + wL)/w^* \tag{15}$$

To eliminate wages from (15), note that as long as both countries produce A, unit production costs must be equal across countries. This requires:

$$p_{a} = w/K^{\varepsilon} = w^*/K^{*\varepsilon} \tag{16}$$

Using (16) in (15), and recalling that pollution is $Z^* = \lambda M^*$, yields an expression for the foreign pollution function when production is diversified:

$$\Omega(K, K^*) = \lambda b_{m}(L^* + LK^{\varepsilon}/K^{*\varepsilon})$$

For given K, $\Omega(K^*; K)$ is a convex decreasing function of K^*. The intuition is straightforward. If K^* falls, Foreign productivity in A decreases. From (16), Home's wage (and hence the relative price of the clean good) must rise so that unit costs remain equal across countries. With a higher income created by a beneficial terms of trade effect, Home's demand for manufactures ($b_{m}wL/w^*$) must rise, thus increasing Foreign pollution. Foreign demand for manufactures, however, remains fixed at $b_{m}w^*L^*/w^* = b_{m}L^*$. Consequently, the world's derived demand for Foreign pollution rises as K^* falls.

On the other hand, Ω is *increasing* in K. As K rises, Home's real wage rises, thus increasing its demand for foreign-produced M. This stimulates the Smokestack industry and increases Foreign pollution. Thus an increase in K in the Home country shifts up the Ω curve in Fig. 5(a).

Finally, we must note that Foreign pollution is bounded above by the possibility that it may eventually specialize in M. If Foreign specializes in M, then its pollution is $Z^* = \lambda L^*$. Thus, taking this into account, Foreign pollution in trade is given by:

$$Z^* = \text{Min}[\lambda L^*, \Omega(K^*; K)]$$

One such pollution function is shown in Fig. 5(a) by the bold line.

With this apparatus in hand consider the transition to free trade. At the outset of trade Home specializes in A, Smokestack shuts down, and $Z = 0$. Home's pollution function becomes coincident with the horizontal axis in Fig. 5(a), and its environmental capital stock begins to recover. Over time it approaches $\bar{K}$. In contrast, when Home specializes in agriculture, Foreign initially doubles its manufacturing output. Consequently, foreign emissions jump to point A on $\Omega_1(K^*; K_o)$. Since foreign pollution is now higher than the natural regeneration rate, its environmental capital K^* starts to fall.

Over time, Foreign pollution rises for two reasons. First, as K^* falls, Home's terms of trade improve. This creates an increase in Home demand for Smokestack, while Foreign's own demand for Smokestack is fixed at $b_m L^*$ because Foreign is diversified during this process. Consequently, world demand for Smokestack rises, as does the world's derived demand for Foreign pollution. In Fig. 5(a), this corresponds to a movement along $Z^* = \Omega_1(K^*; K_o)$ towards point B. Second, Home's environmental capital K rises throughout the transition. This induces an increase in Home's real income that further raises Home's derived demand for Foreign pollution. In Fig. 5(a), this is captured by continual upward shifts of $\Omega(K^*; K)$ over time.

If the demand for the clean good is very strong, then Home cannot satisfy the entire world demand, and Foreign must remain diversified in the steady state. This is the case illustrated in Fig. 5(a). Foreign's steady state pollution function is $\Omega_2(K^*; \bar{K})$, and there is a stable steady state equilibrium at point C with $K^* = K^*_D$.[14] Foreign produces both goods, and Home is specialized in A. Although the two countries are initially identical, their welfare outcomes diverge with trade: Home must gain, and Foreign must lose.

Proposition 5. *There exists some* $\underline{b} < 1/2$ *such that if* $b_m < \underline{b}$, *then in free trade Home specializes in Agriculture and Foreign diversifies. There are no static gains from trade, but Home experiences dynamic gains from trade, while Foreign suffers dynamic losses.*

Proof. See Appendix A.

This can be illustrated with the aid of Fig. 3. Because Foreign output of M rises with trade, its production frontier begins to rotate downward. And because it is still producing some farm output, the fall in the production frontier reduces real foreign income for given prices. Moreover, since Foreign must remain diversified, the world relative price of M must adjust so that it remains equal to the slope of the foreign production frontier. Hence p_M/p_A must fall during the transition. Since Foreign exports M, this means that Foreign terms of trade deteriorate, further reinforcing its losses from trade. On the other hand, this terms of trade deterioration for Foreign is a terms of trade improvement for Home. This raises Home's demand for Foreign manufactures, leading to yet more foreign pollution. The foreign environment worsens, productivity in the clean sector falls, and the

[14] Since $\Omega_2(K^*; \bar{K})$ is convex, there could be multiple diversified equilibria in the Foreign country, but only the equilibrium with the largest K^* is stable. It is also possible that there may exist both diversified and specialized equilibria for Foreign for given b_a. However, during an adjustment from autarky to free trade as described above, the economy converges to the diversified equilibrium described above. For more details, see the unpublished notes referred to in footnote 13.

entire cycle of environmental degradation and terms of trade deterioration repeats and reinforces itself over time.

The contrast between Propositions 4 and 5 is striking. Trade is mutually beneficial only when the demand for the dirty good is sufficiently strong. With a strong demand for the clean good, one country must lose from trade even though trade still provides efficiency gains by separating incompatible industries. Foreign losses accrue from mutually reinforcing sources. Foreign loses because when it raises Smokestack output, it degrades its environment and lowers the world supply of Farm output (its import good). As a result, Foreign suffers from a deterioration in its terms of trade as a direct consequence of its own environmental degradation!

There are several important points to note about this possibility of losses from trade. First, the key to Foreign losing from trade is the negative terms of trade effect created by its own environmental degradation. Thus Propositions 3 and 5 are not inconsistent. If the terms of trade were held constant, Foreign would immediately specialize in Smokestack (and remain specialized) when it degrades its environment. As discussed in Section 4, depletion of its environmental capital in this case is essentially irrelevant to foreign welfare. Only when world prices adjust in response to changes in K and K^* does Foreign potentially lose from trade.

Second, it is striking that losses from trade only occur if the demand for the clean good is sufficiently high. As well, from our diagrammatic account it is apparent that losses from trade are more likely when the environment's regeneration rate, g, is high, and when the externality is relatively weak (ε is low). An increase in g shifts the cleansing function $g(\bar{K}-K^*)$ outwards making a diversified equilibria with losses from trade more likely. If ε is small, then Foreign's pollution function is almost a flat line for any given K; moreover, if ε is small then the shift upwards in the pollution function is smaller. Consequently, for both reasons, the smaller is ε the greater the possibility of diversification and losses.[15]

These seemingly inexplicable results are not without reason. When Foreign has a greater regeneration rate, any increase in Smokestack pollution leads to a smaller reduction in environmental capital. Consequently, Foreign's terms of trade deteriorate less from an increase in pollution, and Home gains less from the change in world relative prices brought about by Foreign's environmental degradation. As a result, Home's demand for Smokestack is less, and this makes diversification (and losses) more likely for Foreign.

As well, if e is small then the pollution-induced decline in the output of the clean good is relatively small. Again, the induced terms of trade effect is small,

[15]This does not imply that the losses from trade are greater when ε is small. We suspect that just the opposite is true: when ε is small a diversified equilibrium is more likely, but the losses from trade are smaller too. Note when $\varepsilon=0$ there can be no losses (or gains) from trade.

and the attendant increase in the demand for Smokestack by Home is smaller as well. Consequently, diversification and losses for Foreign are more likely again.

5.3. Both countries specialized

Finally, we consider the intermediate case where both countries specialize in the steady state. This occurs when $\underline{b}<b_m<1/2$: the demand for Smokestack is stronger than in the previous case, but not as strong as in part *A* of this section.

This possibility is illustrated in Fig. 5(b). In the steady state, Foreign's free trade pollution function is $\Omega_2(K^*;\ \bar{K})$ and the steady state equilibrium is at point C. Because of the relatively stronger demand for Smokestack during the transition, the foreign pollution function Ω eventually rises everywhere above the regeneration function. Consequently, Foreign specializes in Smokestack in the steady state.

The possibility of specialization has important welfare implications for the Foreign country. The time path of foreign welfare is not monotonic during the transition: it first falls, and later rises. In the early part of the transition, Foreign is diversified in production, and its welfare falls as shown above. But once Foreign specializes, further depletion of its own environmental capital becomes economically irrelevant, and moreover, Foreign (an importer of *A*) now benefits from a terms of trade improvement as Home's production of *A* rises over time.[16] A Foreign worker's real wage in terms of manufactures is constant throughout, but his or her real wage in terms of *A* starts to rise once the country specializes. To see this, note that once both are specialized, zero profits in each country requires $p_m=w^*$, and $p_A=w/K^\varepsilon$. Hence,

$$\frac{p_m}{p_A}=\frac{w^*K^\varepsilon}{w}=\frac{b_m LK^\varepsilon}{L^*(1-b_m)}$$

where the last step uses the market clearing condition for *M*.[17] Thus once Foreign is specialized, its terms of trade begins to improve as *K* continues to rise at home, and foreign welfare begins to rise. Whether or not Foreign experiences a net gain or loss from trade depends on its discount rate and on the speed with which it specializes in *M*.

On the other hand, Home must always gain from trade in this case. As shown above, it gains while Foreign is diversified. It must continue to gain when Foreign

[16]Home's environmental capital stock approaches its steady state value as t goes to infinity. Foreign specializes, if at all, in finite time. For more details, see the unpublished notes referred to in footnote 13.

[17]The market clearing condition for *M* when Foreign is specialized is just $b_m(wL+w^*L^*)/p_m=L^*$, which implies $w^*/w=b_mL/L^*(1-b_m)$.

specializes because its real wage in terms of Farm output continues to rise.[18] Summarizing,

Proposition 6. *If* $b_m < 1/2$, *and a diversified steady state does not exist (other than the unstable no-trade steady state), then both countries must specialize in production. Home (specialized in A) must gain from trade at every point during the transition. Foreign utility initially falls, and later rises during the transition from autarky to free trade.*

Proof. See Appendix A.

6. Comparative advantage and the allocation of activities across countries

Thus far we have abstracted from differences across countries that could create a comparative advantage basis for trade. Pollution-created nonconvexities will however interact with the more conventional determinants of trade in any world with nonidentical countries. We concentrate on two key differences that are prominent in the literature: differences in assimilative/regenerative capacity (g vs. g^*), and differences across countries in population density (L vs L^*). Apart from examining how other determinants of comparative advantage may interact in our setting, we will show that once we admit nonidentical countries free trade may now lock-in the "wrong" pattern of specialization across countries.

Suppose $g > g^*$, but countries are otherwise identical. Then the environment in Home has a uniformly faster rate of regeneration (perhaps because of prevailing weather patterns, proximity to oceans, or physical differences in the soil, etc.) In autarky, we have $K > K^*$ and Home has a lower relative price of the clean good. At the outset of trade Home will increase its output of A while Foreign increases its output of M. If $b_m > 1/2$, then both countries must produce manufactures in trade: Foreign specializes in M while Home produces both goods.[19] If $b_m < 1/2$, then Foreign produces Smokestack and perhaps some Farm output, Home specializes in Farming. Note that Home must always gain from trade, while Foreign could lose from trade when $b_m < 1/2$.

Because externalities are not internalized, allocations before and after free trade will not be Pareto efficient. Nevertheless, we can ask whether, given this market failure, the market-determined pattern of trade is the same as that which a global central planner would choose.

[18] From the zero profit condition at home, $w/p_a = K^\varepsilon$, which rises with K. For purchasing power in terms of M, note that from the previous footnote, $w/p_m = w/w^* = L^*(1-b_m)/Lb_m > 1$ since $b_m < 1/2$ and $L = L^*$. Recall that in autarky $w/p_m = 1$. Hence Home unambiguously gains from trade.

[19] The proof in footnote 12 also applies here because it does not rely on $g = g^*$.

In the present example, if one country must be diversified, a central planner would choose to locate the pollution intensive industry in the country with the higher environmental regeneration rate. This is because the higher "g" country can produce more Farm output for any given level of Smokestack since its regeneration rate is greater. If Smokestack demand is so high that it must be produced by both countries, then Foreign should specialize in Smokestack while Home diversifies. This is in fact the pattern of trade predicted when $b_m > 1/2$, and hence free trade allocates activities efficiently in this case.

But if $b_m < 1/2$, and full specialization does not occur, then Foreign is diversified while Home is specialized in A. The resulting pattern of trade is inefficient. If we forced Foreign to specialize in A and let Home diversify, then world output would be higher.[20] Consequently, we have shown:

Proposition 7. *The country with the faster rate of regeneration has the lowest autarky price of the clean good, exports the clean good in free trade, and always gains from trade. The direction of trade is efficient if* $b_m > 1/2$, *or if full specialization occurs. It will be inefficient for* b_m *sufficiently small.*

Now suppose $L^* > L$, but countries are otherwise identical. In autarky, we have $K > K^*$ and the less densely populated country has a comparative advantage in the clean good. At the outset of trade, Home increases its output of A while Foreign increases its output of M. If b_m is sufficiently large, then both countries must produce manufactures in trade: Foreign specializes in Smokestack while Home produces both goods. If b_m is sufficiently small, then both countries must produce A: Home specializes in A while Foreign diversifies. Home must always gain from trade, while Foreign can lose if b_m is sufficiently small.

For the direction of trade to be efficient, the smallest number of workers in the clean sector should be subject to the productivity-reducing effects of Smokestack pollution. Hence when the demand for Smokestack is high enough that both countries must produce it, a planner would choose Foreign (the more populated country) to specialize in Smokestack and Home to be diversified, since this minimizes the number of workers in the clean sector who have their productivity reduced. This is in fact the pattern of specialization created by trade.

When the demand for Smokestack is low (the demand for the clean good is high) it should only be produced in the less populated country (Home) to minimize the number of workers in the clean industry that are disadvantaged by Smokestack's productivity reducing effects. This is opposite to the pattern of trade that occurs in a free market. Hence we have:

Proposition 8. *The more densely populated country has the lowest autarky price*

[20] Note, however, that a transfer may be required to ensure a Pareto improvement.

of the dirty good and will export it in free trade. The less densely populated country always gains from trade, the more densely populated country can lose when b_m *is sufficiently low. The direction of trade is efficient if* $b_m > L^*/(L+L^*)$, *and will be inefficient if* b_m *is sufficiently low.*

Proof. See Appendix A.

Both Propositions 7 and 8 show that trade need not lead to an efficient trade pattern. This is in sharp contrast to Ethier (1982) where free trade leads to an efficient pattern of specialization across countries. The reason is straightforward: concentration and separation are not equivalent, except in the sole case where both countries specialize completely. If we concentrate all of Smokestack in one country, we have not completely separated Smokestack from the environmentally sensitive industry. Since the productivity effects induced by trade arise from separation in our case, (and not concentration as in Ethier, 1982), our results differ.

For example, in an external economies model like Ethier (1982), whenever the demand for the increasing returns (IRS) good is low so that the IRS industry can fit into the smallest country, then it doesn't matter whether the larger or smaller country produces all of the IRS good. The logic is simply that there are benefits to concentrating IRS production in one country, but the concentration is complete if either of the two countries produces all of the IRS good. In contrast, when the demand for Smokestack is low so that Smokestack can fit inside the smallest country, efficiency is not met by either country taking all of the dirty industry production. Alternatively, when the demand for Farm output is so low that Farming can fit inside the smallest country, efficiency is again not met by either country taking all of the clean industry production. In both cases, because Smokestack affects the productivity of those workers remaining in the clean industry, it now matters which country gets the Smokestack industry.

7. Extensions and qualifications

The model we constructed in Section 3 was designed to illustrate as cleanly as possible the role that cross-sectoral externalities can play in generating trade and the role of terms of trade effects in distributing the gains from such trade across countries. While this stripped down model was useful to illustrate our basic point, its simplicity may belie important qualifications. Here we briefly consider some limitations of our analysis and report on their likely significance to the main results.

A simplifying assumption of our model was that each country consisted of only one region so that Smokestack and the environmentally sensitive industry could not separate geographically within a country. Clearly for large countries this form of domestic separation is possible in practice, although its feasibility is dependent on both the exact form of pollution emitted by Smokestack and by the mobility of factors across regions. If we maintain our 1 factor model, assume perfect mobility of labour, and introduce two regions within a country (each with their own environmental sink), then industries will separate across regions in autarky and free trade will provide no additional service in separating incompatible industries. Free trade at autarky prices will be a stable equilibrium and no trade will occur at these prices.

Alternatively, if there is zero factor mobility and two regions within a country, then there will be some spatial separation across regions in autarky but it is now limited by the immobility of factors across regions. In this context, trade can again play a role in separating incompatible industries much as described in our earlier sections. Hence the degree of internal factor mobility is a key determinant of whether international trade can play a useful role in separating incompatible industries.

In reality many environmentally sensitive industries are likely to be tied geographically by the location of specific factors. Tourism is tied to lakes, trees and mountains; fishing to streams and coastal areas. Unfortunately perhaps, forestry, pulp and paper, electricity generation and many other heavy industries are also tied to these same specific factors (trees, streams, rivers and access to water). Since many of these specific factors are highly concentrated geographically, then so too will be incompatible industries. As a result, free trade can again provide for further spatial separation and the logic of our model follows as before.

Another simplifying assumption was our choice of a one-factor model. While the Ricardian nature of the model at each point in time brings strong tendencies towards specialization, it is important not to attribute too much to this assumption. Our results rely most heavily on the nonconvexity introduced by cross-industry externalities. If we were to add more factors and let the industries differ in factor intensities, then there would be two forces at work determining the steady state production possibility frontier. The cross-industry externality tends to make the frontier bowed in to the origin while differences in factor intensities work in just the opposite direction. Our very simple steady state production frontier that was uniformly convex to the origin would be replaced by one with alternating concave and convex segments. If the autarky equilibrium occurred in a region where marginal rates of transformation were declining, then free trade at autarky prices would again be an unstable equilibrium. Free trade at autarky prices would again bring very large environmental consequences, although it would not bring about full specialization as in our Ricardian formulation. Consequently, we view the 1 factor assumption as a useful vehicle for illustrating our main points, but it is not wholly responsible for our results.

Third, our specification of the accumulation equation for environmental capital is clearly quite restrictive. For example, nature's cleansing function exhibits the property that its rate of cleansing is higher the lower is the level of environmental capital. This type of "compensatory" growth function is often adopted in the renewable resources literature, but it rules out certain catastrophic outcomes that may arise when the quality of the environment falls below some minimum threshold. As well, our damage function is simply linear in the level of pollution emitted whereas the marginal physical damage from pollution may well be increasing in pollution levels. Burrows (1986) notes that the specification of the cross-sectoral externality will affect the likelihood of relevant nonconvexities in the production set. Here we consider two modifications to the accumulation equation.

First, if we replace our simple linear specification in Z with a convex and increasing damage function $h(Z)$ then very little of our analysis changes. In Fig. 2, the free trade and autarky pollution functions are still independent of the environment's capital stock and are just vertical translates of those shown. In the remaining figures similar adjustments need to be made, but since we only exploit the first derivative properties of our pollution functions the qualitative results of our analysis are unchanged by the monotonic transformation of Z to $h(Z)$.[21]

As second modification to the accumulation function, suppose that the cleansing function is logistic instead of linear. That is, let

$$dK/dt = gK(\bar{K} - K) - Z \tag{17}$$

and assume that $\bar{K}^2/4 - \lambda L/g > 0$, so that specialization in M need not lead to the complete destruction of K.[22] The cleansing function is now concave, first increasing in K from $K=0$, reaching a peak, and then decreasing. First note that the autarky pollution function is not affected by the change in the regeneration function (it will be a horizontal line as in Fig. 2). There are, however, now three potential steady state equilibria in autarky: $K=0$, $K=K_L$, and $K=K_H$, where K_L occurs on the upward sloping portion of the cleansing function, and K_H is on the downward sloping portion. The middle equilibrium, $K=K_L$, is unstable; the other two are stable. Let us consider an autarky economy that has not destroyed its environmental capital and is at the steady state $K=K_H$. Then because the regeneration function is downward sloping in the neighbourhood of K_H, the economy will respond to international trade in much the same way as in our previous analysis. The free trade pollution function also looks the same as before (it is a step function as in Fig. 2). For example in the case where free trade prices equal autarky prices, a slight drop in K leads to the development of a comparative advantage in M, and consequently specialization in M; while a slight increase in K leads to specialization in A and pollution falls to zero. Autarky is an unstable free

[21]The long run production frontier will no longer be strictly convex throughout. However, recall that private costs do not reflect true opportunity costs because of the externality. Long run behavior is represented by the long run supply curve, which continues to be downward sloping in the region where the economy is diversified.

[22]This is analogous to our assumption in footnote 9.

trade equilibrium, and the dynamics of adjustment to free trade follow much the same pattern as in Fig. 2. The analysis of the two country case is also qualitatively similar.

Finally, throughout we have ruled out pollution policy. We have adopted this assumption not because we believe that it is necessarily an accurate description of the real world, but because a serious consideration of policy would detract us from our main focus. If pollution policy was designed to correctly account for the negative long run consequences of Smokestack pollution, and if pollution policy was flexible and could respond to the changing conditions brought about by trade, then free trade could never lead to losses. Alternatively if we assume that pollution policy was a rigid technological standard on emissions (such as a restriction on an allowable λ), then our results carry through as before. As well, once we allow for active pollution policy it is necessary to ask whether such a policy may be used as disguised trade policy. In our two-country model several strategic issues arise, and a full examination of these issues must be left to further work.

8. Conclusion

Free trade may have little or no effect on a polluted small open economy, but it may also have some quite surprising and significant effects as well. When industrial pollutants lower the productivity in environmentally sensitive sectors, trade can play a useful role in spatially separating incompatible industries. And while many environmentalists are concerned that trade allows for the spatial separation of dirty product consumers and dirty product producers, we find that such separation can bring benefits in terms of production efficiency. However, while the separation of incompatible industries brings productivity gains to the world, the division of these gains may not be shared uniformly across countries. Accordingly, we find that the type of separation matters and several surprising results follow: two identical countries can engage in mutually beneficial trade; trade will be mutually beneficial if the demand for the dirty good (Smokestack) is high; one country must lose if the demand for the clean good (Farming) is high; and losses are more likely the less sensitive is Farming to industrial pollutants, and the faster is the environment's cleansing rate. These results seem at first inexplicable, but they are in fact by-products of the terms of trade effects created when the spatial separation of industries creates productivity changes across countries.

Acknowledgements

We are grateful to E. Helpman, A. Kotwal, C. McAusland, G. Tan, the referees, and participants in presentations at the NBER Summer Workshop, the Canadian

Institute for Advanced Research, UC Berkeley, UC Davis, Kobe University, Oregon State University, Simon Fraser University, and University of Washington for their comments on earlier versions of this paper. This research was supported by grants from the Social Sciences and Humanities Research Council of Canada.

Appendix A

Proof of Proposition 1. Using (14) to replace M in (7), we obtain a simple linear differential equation governing the evolution of the capital stock from any initial value. Solving this initial value problem yields $K(t)=K_0+[K(t=0)-K_0]e^{-gt}$ where K_0 is the steady state capital stock given in Eq. (8). $K'(t)<0$ if $K(t=0)>K_0$, and $K'(t)>0$ if $K(t=0)<K_0$. Therefore the steady state is unique, globally stable, and convergence to the steady state is monotonic.

Proof of Proposition 2. By hypothesis we have $p^*=K_o^{\varepsilon}$, which implies that labour's value of marginal product is equal in both industries and the temporary pattern of production is indeterminate. Suppose this economy produces a level of M slightly greater than M_o. Since M_o was the steady state level, Eq. (1) ensures $dK/dt<0$ at $K=K_o$. K drops below K_o, the economy immediately specializes in M and pollution rises to $Z=\lambda L$. As is apparent from Fig. 2, the economy converges to a stable steady state at K_s. Alternatively, if this economy produces a level of M slightly less than M_o then by parallel reasoning $dK/dt>0$. K rises above K_o, the economy immediately specializes in A and pollution falls to $Z=0$. The economy converges to the stable steady state at $\bar{K}$.

Proof of Proposition 3. Utility must rise if the value of national output rises since pollution has no direct disutility cost. At the outset of trade, $K=K_o$ and world prices may differ from autarky prices. Labourers move into the sector that at free trade prices maximizes (or leaves unchanged) national income. From Proposition 2 we know the dynamics of environmental change either monotonically increase labour productivity in farming if the economy specializes in farming, or leaves unchanged labour productivity in smokestack if the economy specializes in smokestack. As a result, national income cannot fall with trade (and must rise if autarky and free trade prices differ).

Proof of Proposition 4. Autarky is always an unstable trading equilibrium. When $b_m>1/2$ both countries must produce M since world demand is $b_m(wL+w^*L^*)/p_m=b_mL(w+w^*)/p_m$ and this always exceeds one country's maximum supply of L. Note that if $w=p_m$, then $w^*\geq w$; or if $w^*=p_m$, then $w\geq w^*$; in either case we have $b_m(wL+w^*L^*)/p_m>L$ as required. The analysis of Fig. 4 has shown each country moves towards its own stable steady state monotonically. To prove that each country gains recall that during the transition, relative prices adjust continuously to clear markets. Because both countries produce M, wages (and hence incomes) must always be equalized across countries. Purchasing power in terms of smokestack output is unaffected by trade ($w/p_M = 1$ before and after trade). Purchasing power in terms of Farm output is $w/p_a = K^{\varepsilon}$, and this must rise monotonically along the adjustment path.

Proof of Proposition 5. Since $b_m < 1/2$, one country must specialize in A; we have denoted this country "Home". Using an analysis similar to that in the proof of Proposition 2, a locally stable diversified equilibrium will exist in the Foreign country and be reached in the transition to free trade if

$$g(\bar{K} - K^*) = \lambda b_m L[1 + (\bar{K}/K^*)^{\varepsilon}] \equiv \Omega(K^*, \bar{K}) \qquad \text{(A1)}$$

has at least one positive solution $K^* = \hat{K}^*$ such that (1) $\hat{K}^* > K_s$, the environment's capital stock when all Foreign labor is allocated to Smokestack, and (2) the curve Ω is flatter than the regeneration function $g(\bar{K} - K^*)$ at $K^* = \hat{K}^*$. For b_m sufficiently small (i.e. b_a sufficiently large) we can guarantee at least one positive solution $\hat{K}^* > K_s^*$ because a fall in b_m shifts the entire family of curves $\Omega(K^*, \bar{K})$ in towards the origin. Moreover, we can ensure that condition (2) will hold for sufficiently small b_m because Ω is strictly convex and decreasing in K^*, and because at the initial point K_o^*, we have $\Omega = 2\lambda b_m L > \lambda b_m L = g(\bar{K} - K_o^*)$. Let $\underline{b}$ be the largest b_m such that condition (1) above is satisfied. Then for $b_m < \underline{b}$, the foreign country will approach a locally diversified steady state equilibrium in free trade. To prove the welfare results note that Foreign purchasing power in terms of M is unaffected throughout the transition since $w^*/p_m = 1$ before and after trade. However, Foreign's purchasing power in terms of A is $w^*/p_a = K^{*\varepsilon}$, which declines monotonically as K^* falls along the transition path. Home's purchasing power in terms of A is $w/p_a = K^{\varepsilon}$, which rises with K along the transition path. Its wage in terms of M is $w/p_m = w/w^* = w/p_a K^{*\varepsilon} = (K/K^*)^{\varepsilon}$. Since K rises and K^* falls, Home's purchasing power in terms of M must also rise along the transition path.

Proof of Proposition 6. Since $b_m < 1/2$, one country must specialize in A; we have denoted this country "Home". Referring to the proof of Proposition 5, suppose there exists b_m such that $\underline{b} < b_m < \frac{1}{2}$. Then (A1) does not have a solution in K^* that satisfies condition (1) in Proposition 5. Consequently, $\Omega(K^*, \bar{K}) \geq g(\bar{K} - K^*)$ for all K^* such that $K_s^* \geq K^* > K_o^*$ (as illustrated in Fig. 5(b)). Consequently, using an analysis similar to that in the proof of Proposition 2, the foreign economy will approach a steady state equilibrium in which it is specialized in M. The welfare results are proven in the text.

Proof of Proposition 8. The gains from trade and pattern of trade results are simple applications of earlier results. Here we prove the results on the efficiency of the direction of trade. First, we verify the claim that the direction of trade is efficient if $b_m > L^*/(L+L^*)$. Note that if $b_m(L+L^*) > L^* > L$, then both countries must produce Smokestack. World demand for M is then $b_m(L+L^*)$. When Foreign specializes in M, world farm output is $A^{*w} = (1-b_m)\{\bar{K} - (\lambda/g)[b_m(L^*+L) - L^*]\}^{\varepsilon}(L^*+L)$. Now reverse the pattern of specialization by assuming Home specializes in M, and denote world farm output in this case as A^w. Then $A^w = (1-b_m)\{\bar{K} - (\lambda/g)[b_m(L^*+L) - L]\}^{\varepsilon}(L^*+L)$. Comparing, we find that $A^{*w} > A^w$ if $L^* > L$, and hence Foreign specializing in farm output is efficient.

Next we show that the direction of trade is inefficient if b_m is sufficiently low. Suppose world demand for M is L^*_m units, and this is less than L. If Home specializes in A, we have $A^w = \bar{K}^{\varepsilon}L + [\bar{K} - (\lambda/g)L^*_m]^{\varepsilon}(L^* - L^*_m)$. If Foreign specializes in A, we have $A^{*w} = \bar{K}^{\varepsilon}L^* + [\bar{K} - (\lambda/g)L^*_m]^{\varepsilon}(L - L^*_m)$. Consequently, $A^{*w} > A^w$ if $L^* > L$.

References

Baumol and Bradford, 1972. Detrimental externalities and nonconvexity of the production set. Economica 39, 160–76.

Baumol and Oates, 1971. The theory of environmental policy. Cambridge University Press, Cambidge, UK.

Beghin, J., Roland-Holst, D., van der Mensbrugghe, D., 1994. A survey of the trade and environment nexus: Global dimensions. OECD Economic Studies 23, 167–192.

Burrows, P., 1986. Nonconvexity induced by external costs on production: Theoretical curio or policy dilemma. Journal of Environmental Economics and Management 13, 101–128.

Carrier, J., Krippi, E., 1990. Comprehensive study of European forests assesses damage and losses from air pollution. Environmental Conservation 17, 365–367.

Copeland, B.R., Taylor, M.S., 1994. North–South trade and the environment. Quarterly Journal of Economics 109, 755–787.

Copeland, B.R., Taylor, M.S., 1995. Trade and Transboundary Pollution. American Economic Review 85, 716–737.

Daly, H., 1993. The Perils of Free Trade. Scientific American, Nov. 50–57.

Dean, J.M., 1992. Trade and the environment: A survey of the literature. In: Low, P. (Ed.), International Trade and the Environment. World Bank discussion papers, World Bank, Washington, DC.

Ethier, W., 1982. Decreasing costs in international trade and Frank Graham's argument for protection. Econometrica 50, 1243–1268.

FAO, 1977. Economic impact of the effects of pollution on the coastal fisheries of the Atlantic and Gulf of Mexico regions of the US. Fisheries Technical Paper No. 172.

Grossman, G.M., Krueger, A.B., 1993. Environmental impacts of a North American free trade agreement. In: Garber, P. (Ed.), The Mexico–U.S. Free Trade Agreement. MIT Press, Cambridge MA, pp. 13–56.

Helpman, E., 1984. Increasing returns, imperfect markets, and trade theory. In: Jones, R.W., Kenen, P.B. (Eds.), Handbook of International Economics, Vol. 1. North Holland, Amsterdam.

Helfand, G.E., Rubin, J., 1994. Spreading versus concentrating damages. Journal of Environmental Economics and Management 27, 84–91.

Lopez, R., 1994. The environment as a factor of production: The effects of economic growth and trade liberalization. Journal of Environmental Economics and Management 27, 63–184.

Markusen, J.R., 1975. Cooperative control of international pollution and common property resources. Quarterly Journal of Economics 89, 618–632.

Markusen, J.R., 1976. International externalities and optimal tax structures. Journal of International Economics 5, 15–29.

Melvin, J., 1969. Increasing returns as a determinant of trade. Canadian Journal of Economics 2, 389–402.

Panagariya, A., 1981. Variable returns to scale in production and patterns of specialization. American Economic Review 71, 221–230.

Pearce, D.W., Warford, J.J., 1993. A World Without End: Economics, Environment, and Sustainable Development. Oxford University Press, Oxford.

Rauscher, M., 1991. National environmental policies and the effects of economic integration. European Journal of Political Economy 7, 313–329.

Selden, T.M., Song, D., 1994. Environmental quality and development: Is there a Kuznets curve for air pollution emissions? Journal of Environmental Economics and Management 27, 147–162.

Smulders, S., 1994. Market structure and the environment: Essays on the theory of endogenous growth. Mimeo, Hilvarenbeek.

U.N. Environment Programme, 1993. Environmental data report 1993–94. Blackwell, Oxford.

[11]

The Economic Journal, **101** (*March* 1991), 180–189
Printed in Great Britain

THE INTERFACE BETWEEN ENVIRONMENT AND TRADE POLICIES*

John Whalley

Last March I gave the Frank Paish Lecture to the Society under the title 'Economic Life in a Greenhouse'. In my lecture, I tried both to survey professional opinion as to some of the possible climatic implications of the greenhouse effect, and also to draw out the economic consequences which might follow.[1] Towards the end of my talk, I made reference to some preliminary joint work with Randy Wigle,[2] a colleague at Wilfrid Laurier University in Canada, on the global consequences of carbon tax schemes designed to limit and/or reduce the build-up of CO_2 emissions, a key element underlying the greenhouse effect.

The written version of the lecture consciously does not reproduce the survey material which made up the first part of the lecture. Instead, it elaborates on the issues raised towards the end. It incorporates the work by Randy Wigle and myself, and offers some thoughts on what seems to be a growing issue for the 1990s; namely, the consequences for the international trading system of interactions between trade issues and both future global and current national environmental policies.

What follows emphasises that, if they occur in the next few decades, global policy responses[3] (carbon taxes, tradeable permit schemes) to environmental concerns will almost certainly have large economic effects. Among these are likely to be significant effects on trade patterns and trade volumes. Large interregional effects will also accompany such policies, depending upon how such policies are implemented. Also, the 1990s may see a growing use of trade measures to achieve objectives set for environmental policies. Environmental policies towards such countries as Brazil, the Philippines and others where deforestation is a concern may increasingly take the form of threatened trade sanctions unless compliance with global environmental policy objectives occurs.[4]

* This paper is based on a broader talk 'Economic Life in a Greenhouse', given as the Frank Paish Lecture to the annual meetings of the Royal Economic Society held in Nottingham in March 1990. It draws heavily on joint work with Randy Wigle, to whom I am grateful for repeated discussion on the issues covered. I am indebted to Ngee-Choon Chia for research support.

[1] The discussion of the possible scientific dimensions of the greenhouse effect was, in part, based on Schneider (1989). A range of the economic consequences discussed are set out in Cline (1989).

[2] See Whalley and Wigle (1989).

[3] See Robertson (1990) for a recent discussion of negotiation and treaty aspects of such responses.

[4] While no formal trade sanctions linked to environmental objectives have yet been used against these countries, a regional development grant made by the World Bank to Brazil in 1985 was interrupted in 1985 because of concerns expressed by environmental groups in OECD countries that the loan to develop Northern Brazil would result in significant deforestation (see Le Prestre (1989, p. 181), and Repetto and Gillis (1988, p. 281)). The same policy approach is reflected through the recent creation of the UN Environmental Fund through which the World Bank, the UN Environmental Programme, and the UN Developmental Programme will jointly provide $1 billion to countries in Asia, Africa and Latin American

There may also be growing pressures to link fairness in trade to environmental policies. Thus, in countries where there are more stringent environmental standards than in neighbouring states, the argument will be that imports are relatively favourably treated by their neighbours' environmental policies because their production is not subject to the higher costs associated with stronger environmental regulation. The logical next step will be the argument that because such trade was unfair, protection should be granted to domestic producers.

The present structure of international trade arrangements seems neither to make allowance for such pressures, nor to indicate how they could be accommodated. The GATT, with its present thirty-eight articles, makes no explicit reference to environmental matters.[5] Thus, trade measures justified on arguments about unfair trade linked to environmental considerations are unlikely to have a foundation under GATT. They would almost certainly be ruled as GATT-incompatible by GATT panels if complaints were brought.

Threats of trade measures against countries who do not comply with global environmental policies would face much the same difficulty. No GATT justification for the use of such measures exists. Either increases would occur in remaining unbound tariffs, or other trade measures would come into play, such as anti-dumping and countervailing duties (with some reinterpretation). Either way, there would be yet further erosion in the global system of trade rules beyond that which has already occurred in the 1970s and 1980s.[6]

Given the quantitative orders of magnitude involved the argument made here is that the interaction of these two sets of policies made in the 1990s may well yield turbulence, conflict and confusion.[7]

I. POLICY RESPONSES TO GLOBAL ENVIRONMENTAL ISSUES

One key element of the emerging interface between environmental policies and trade is possibly policy responses to global warning. Some of the proposals made thus far (carbon taxes, tradeable permits) aim to reduce consumption of

to ensure 'that their development programs are undertaken in a manner which protects their global environment'. (See *Wall Street Journal*, Tuesday, September 18, 1990.)

[5] The coverage of environmental concerns in the GATT is both remote and tangential, and nowhere in the General Agreement is the word 'environment' used. Article 20-B which allows Contracting Parties to use import restrictions to protect human life and health, including measures against toxic substances (see GATT (1986) p. 37). The standards code which emerged from the Tokyo Round in 1979 directs Contracting Parties not to use product standards (including environmental standards) in such a way as to create unnecessary obstacles to trade. See Rubin and Graham (eds) (1982), p. 169. A new GATT working group has also been established on Domestically Prohibited Goods and Hazardous Substances (see Sankey (1989)). None of these, however, deals with environmental issues in a central way.

[6] The term 'erosion' of the global system of trade rules refers to unchecked deviations from the GATT principles of trade measures being non-discriminatory, transparent, and based on tariffs. Erosion of these principles was present in agriculture in the 1940s when the GATT was signed, spread to textiles and clothing in the early 1960s, spread further into steel and voluntary export restraint arrangements in the 1970s, and continued with increased use of contingent trade protection measures (anti-dumping and countervailing duties) and unilateral actions (Section 301 of the 1988 Trade Act in the United States) in the 1980s. For more discussion, see Low (1990) and Whalley (1989).

[7] Furthermore, as discussed in Leonard (1988), there are linkages between investment flows and environmental policies with certain inward investment to developing countries being driven, in part, by relatively lax environmental standards. These issues seem likely to also grow in prominence in the 1990s.

carbon-based energy products (oil, coal, natural gas) and thus slow (or even stabilise) the build-up of atmospheric carbon dioxide.[8]

The approach suggested here is to tax (or quota restrict) the carbon content of individual fuels; hence different tax rates would apply to coal, natural gas, and oil.[9] Such taxes are seen as meeting a specified target for global reduction in carbon emission levels. Targets commonly discussed lie between 20 and 50% of projected levels by some specified date.[10] Taxes are usually proposed as a fixed dollar (or currency) amount on a physical unit basis; say, $250 per ton of carbon embodied in each fuel.[11] Ad valorem equivalent carbon tax rates (which vary by fuel) are in the region of 50–100% (higher in some cases). The rate needed in any given carbon tax scheme is thus dependent on a variety of factors, including the target emission reduction and assumed elasticity values for energy demand and supply functions. The latter will, in part, determine how closely the emission reduction target will be met by any given tax rate.

As can be seen from Table 1, carbon use around the globe is highly concentrated, suggesting that significant intercountry effects may accompany the introduction of such a tax. Emissions per capita in developed countries are on average around 20–30 times those of developing countries; three countries (United States, U.S.S.R., and China) account for over 50% of emissions. On the other hand, carbon use per dollar of GNP is typically much higher in developing countries, reflecting the use of relatively inefficient energy conversion technologies.

It is the size of some of the potential inter-country effects which might accompany such taxes which I have tried to quantify in recent joint work with Randy Wigle (Whalley and Wigle, 1989, 1990). We use a global equilibrium model and produce a number of counterfactual calculations which provide an indication of what could happen to the global economy if carbon taxes of various kinds were introduced. The models we have used incorporate trade, production and consumption of both energy and non-energy products for a number of countries (or groups of countries). To keep the models manageable, we do not identify fuel types within the broader carbon-based energy category, even though the various elements within this category (oil, coal, natural gas) would, in practice, be taxed at different rates. The model also does not incorporate existing taxes on energy products (such as excise taxes on gasoline), even though these vary by region, and could also affect results.

[8] Those proposals have generated a number of country responses already in European countries. Although much smaller than the globally proposed taxes, taxes in Sweden, Finland and Denmark already exist, with planned taxes under way in Italy, the Netherlands and Norway (see *The Economist*, March 17, 1990, pp. 45–57).

[9] Edmunds and Reilly (1983), for instance, consider taxes at rates of 100% on coal, 78% on oil, 56% on gas, and 115% on shale oil. Flavin (1990, fn. 45) suggests tax rates proportional to the carbon content of fuels; with coal average 24·12 kilograms of carbon per gigajoule, oil 19·94 (82% of coal), and natural gas 13·78 (57% of coal).

[10] Manne and Richels (1990), for instance, consider a target of a 20% reduction from base line emission levels by 2020, with a stabilised level of emissions thereafter, until 2100. See also Nordhaus (1977, 1990).

[11] Tax rates of this order are considered by Manne and Richels (1990) and Nordhaus (1990). They imply more than a five fold increase in the price of coal, and a doubling or more in gasoline prices.

Table 1*

Country Characteristics of Fossil Fuel Carbon Emissions, 1987

	Emissions per capita in tons/year	Country emissions as % of world total	Grams of carbon per $ of GNP
U.S.	5·03	21·9	276
Canada	4·24	1·9	247
Australia	4·00	1·1	320
Soviet Union	3·68	18·5	436
Saudi Arabia	3·60	0·8	565
Poland	3·38	2·3	492
W. Germany	2·98	3·3	223
U.K.	2·73	2·8	224
Japan	2·12	4·5	156
Italy	1·78	1·8	147
France	1·70	1·7	133
S. Korea	1·14	0·8	347
Mexico	0·96	1·4	609
China	0·56	10·7	2,024
Egypt	0·41	0·4	801
Brazil	0·38	0·9	170
India	0·19	2·7	655
Indonesia	0·16	0·5	403
Nigeria	0·09	0·2	359
Zaire	0·03	0·01	183
Average for the world	1·08		327

* Information reported in this table has been extracted from table 2-1, p. 19 of Flavin (1990) who, in turn, uses a variety of primary sources in his calculations.

In the simpler of these two models (Whalley and Wigle, 1989), the world is divided into three regions. The first is the developed world (all countries with per capita income in 1986 above US$2,000 and with less than 25% of exports in fossil fuels). The second is the developing world (all countries with per capita income in 1986 below US$2,000, and with less than 25% of exports in fossil fuels). The third is oil exporters, which includes all OPEC countries and major non-OPEC energy exporters.

Nested CES functions are used in the model to represent production and demand in each region, as shown in Table 2. Each region is endowed with three non-traded primary factors: (i) primary factors, exclusive of energy resources, (ii) carbon-based energy resources (deposits of oil, gas and coal), and (iii) other energy resources (hydro-electric capacity and nuclear). Both energy resources are converted into the relevant energy products through a refining/extraction process, which uses other resources (primary factors). There are three internationally traded commodities: carbon-based energy products, energy-intensive goods, and other goods (all other GNP). Energy-intensive goods, other goods, and the composite energy product (carbon-based and non-carbon-based energy) are the commodities which enter final demands.

Carbon-based and non-carbon-based energy products use the respective energy resources and primary factors. Non-carbon-based energy products are

Table 2

Production and Demand Structures Used by Whalley and Wigle (1989) to Evaluate Carbon Tax Options to Achieve Reductions in CO_2 Emissions

A. Factors and goods

Endowments	Produced goods
Carbon-based energy resources (*CR*)	Carbon-based energy products (*CP*)
Non-carbon-based energy resources (*ER*)	Non-carbon-based energy products (*EP*)
Primary factors (*PF*)	Composite energy (*E*)
	Energy-intensive goods (*EI*)
	Non-energy-intensive goods (*NEI*)

B. Structure of production

Stage 1: Production of energy products

PF^i — CP — CR^i PF^i — EP^i — ER^i

Stage 2: Production of composite energy

CP — E^i — EP^i

Stage 3: Production of energy-intensive and other goods

E^i — EI — PF^i E^i — NEI — PF^i

C. Arguments in final demands

EI, NEI, E^i

i denotes good which is distinguished by country of production.

non-traded, since hydro-electric, solar and nuclear power are not traded in significant quantities between the regions they consider. A domestic energy composite is produced by a third (energy conversion) industry, using inputs of the two energy products. The two final-goods (energy-intensive goods, and other goods) use primary factors and the composite energy product as inputs. Perfect competition is assumed throughout for all sectors and in all regions.

Equilibrium in this model involves full global market clearing in all three traded goods (carbon-based energy products, energy-intensive manufactures, and other goods). For the two non-traded goods (non-carbon energy products, and composite energy) there is domestic market clearing within each economy. Since prices in this system are treated as completely flexible, they will adjust to the levels required to clear the relevant international and domestic markets.

Whalley and Wigle (1989) use their model in counterfactual mode[12] to evaluate international incidence effects of alternative carbon tax schemes for the three regions. This involves constructing base (or reference) case data for 1986 to which the equilibrium model is calibrated[13] (i.e., the parameters are chosen such that the model will reproduce the base case data as a full equilibrium solution prior to any policy change being introduced). The base case data thus fully describes a no-policy-change model solution. Different

[12] This is a technical term used in the applied general equilibrium modelling literature; see Shoven and Whalley (1984, and forthcoming) for more details.

[13] See Whalley and Wigle (1990) for a more complete discussion of data and elasticity parameters used in the model, and Mansur and Whalley (1984) for a discussion of calibration.

Table 3

Whalley and Wigle's (1989) Analyses of Carbon Tax Options

A. Target reduction in carbon use — 50% reduction in global carbon use relative to base case

B. Tax options considered:
1. National production based tax
2. National consumption based tax
3. Global tax

C. Carbon tax rates needed to meet emission reduction targets

Option	Tax rate/rates* (range by region)
1	80·42–80·78%
2	79·51 – 83·41%
3	80·59%

D. Gain or loss by region under each option (Hicksian EVs $billion 1986; figures in parentheses are % of GDP)

	Tax option		
Region	1	2	3
Developed countries	−179·7	−67·3	−252·92
	(−1·68)	(−0·63)	(−2·36)
Oil exporters	46·99	−108·13	−122·84
	(10·80)	(−24·85)	(−28·73)
Developing countries	−151·23	−120·60	+93·98
	(−4·76)	(−3·80)	(+2·96)
World	−283·94	−269·12	−281·78
	(−1·98)	(−2·07)	(−1·97)

* These are gross tax rates, i.e. an 80% tax rate means that for each $ spent by consumers, 80 cents is collected in tax. The equivalent net tax rate is 400% (i.e. 80/20%).

carbon tax schemes can then be introduced, with a new equilibrium (counterfactual equilibrium) solution computed for each. Using a pair-wise comparison (base case versus counterfactual), impacts on regions are calculated.

Table 3 reports Whalley and Wigle's (1989) central case results based on 1986 annual data. They consider three alternative forms of carbon tax: a national production-based tax, a national consumption-based tax, and a global tax. In each case, the target emission reduction is 50% relative to the base case model solution.

As Table 3 indicates, their central case estimates of the annual gains or losses for the regions identified in the model under each of the carbon tax options are large. In making these estimates, they calculate Hicksian equivalent variations (EVs) in $ billions (expressed in 1986 prices). These measures capture the combined gains or losses to regions from the production and sale of carbon-based products, as well as the consumption side gains associated with price changes. They also capture the economy-wide effects of energy price changes as they feed through the model. Their results suggest the global economic cost of carbon taxes to be in the range of $280 billion per year. This represents a cost in the region of 2% of world product.

Effects by region differ dramatically across the various tax options. Developed countries lose $250 billion per year, or approximately 2·4% of the value of income, under a global tax; whereas their loss under a national consumption-based carbon tax is substantially smaller, $67 billion or 0·6% of income. Developing countries lose over $150 billion (or 4% of income) under a national production-based carbon tax, whereas they gain $95 billion (or 3% of national income) under a global tax. Oil exporters gain substantially from a national production-based tax, while they lose from either a global tax or a national consumption-based tax.

These results, therefore, underline the point emphasised above; namely, that any carbon limitation initiatives will have major implications for the international economy. Under a national production-based tax, energy producers will collect tax revenues; hence oil exporters will gain. Under a national consumption tax, oil importers will collect revenues, and hence developed countries lose less. Under a global tax, the revenues are redistributed on a per capita basis and developing countries and centrally planned gain substantially. And effects on trade flows between regions (reported in Whalley and Wigle (1989) will be substantial).

II. TRADE POLICY AS AN INSTRUMENT OF ENVIRONMENTAL POLICY, AND ENVIRONMENTAL POLICY AS A SOURCE OF TRADE POLICY TENSIONS

A second element of the emerging interface between environmental and trade policies which seems likely to become more prominent in the 1990s is the use of trade policies as an enforcement machine for environmental policies, and the related issue of pressures on trade policies created by differing environmental regulation across countries.

The notion that trade policies may ultimately be used to enforce global environmental policies is something that has been little considered by those who have been active in debates on global environmental policy, but lurks as a major concern among trade policy practitioners.[14] It has commonly been assumed that what was necessary to deal with such problems as global warming, CFCs, and other matters was to negotiate an international treaty which would bind all signatories to reductions in levels of emissions. The assumption was that some form of enforcement procedure would automatically follow. Moral commitment to emission reduction would hopefully be sufficient to implement the treaty.

It has become apparent, however, that such an approach neglects many elements of interaction between environmental and other policies. Typically, global environmental action involves a large public good element, since one's country's decision to reduce emissions confers benefits on all other countries. To rely on sanctions within the environmental area as the enforcement device simply does not seem practicable. In theory, it is conceivable that a global

[14] See the recent discussion of possible levies on 'dirty trade' within the U.N. Environmental Program (see *The Economist*, pp. 24–25, Sept. 8–14, 1990).

treaty on carbon emission reduction could specify a penalty system which would allow other countries to deviate from carbon emission reduction targets if particular countries did not meet their own commitments. What seems more likely, however, is that large countries would use threats of actions in other non-environmental policy areas to enforce environmental treaty commitments.

The instrument which is most commonly suggested for this purpose is trade threats. Thus, it is not inconceivable in the next ten years that with concerns over deforestation in Brazil, the Philippines, Costa Rica, and elsewhere, commitments in these areas agreed upon either globally or by a subset of larger developed countries, may in part be policed through trade threats used against these countries. This would involve the use of threatened increases in trade barriers or actual trade retaliatory measures, until compliance with environmental goals occurred.

If growth should resume in China and continue through the 1990s and into the next century, given current emission levels in China, it is not inconceivable that trade policies in OECD countries might be linked to the adoption of more energy-efficient energy conversion technologies in China. The effect would be to use trade sanctions to encourage China to reduce coal burning and move to oil, gas, or even nuclear power. Even for localised problems, such as trans-border pollution problems between the United States and Mexico, or acid rain issues involving the European countries, trade threats could be part of the interaction of policies linking enforcement to environmental objectives.

The difficulty for the trading system in all of this is that the GATT has little to say about environmental policies and their impact on trade, and the potential further erosion of already frail trading rules through such actions is significant and by itself impedes economic performance. All that countries are entitled to do under GATT is ban imports of hazardous or toxic substances on health and safety grounds. Any use of trade threats seeking to achieve environmental objectives, would run full-square into the disciplines contained in the General Agreement. Environmentally motivated trade measures executed in a manner which was GATT-compatible could not involve complaint to a GATT panel, with a dispute settlement procedure ultimately sanctifying retaliatory measures. Any increase in barriers, to be GATT-compatible, would have to take the form of increases in GATT unbound tariffs.

In reality, environmentally motivated trade threats from larger countries would, in all probability, involve unilateral actions, such as we now see in Section 301 of the 1988 Trade Act, or threats of anti-dumping or other contingent trade-restricting measures. The severity of these would be likely to increase with concerns over environmental issues. The pressures such developments would create for the trading system are obvious, as are the new difficulties potentially facing global trade out into the 1990s and beyond.

Beyond the issues raised by enforcement of global environmental policies through trade sanctions come a further set of trade-related issues reflecting differing environmental regulations across countries and possible uses of trade remedy measures justified by such differences. North American economies and a number of the European countries have already adopted stringent environmental standards. Producers within these countries have long complained that they operate in a relatively unfair trade environment, since their costs are significantly higher than those of comparable producers in neighbouring countries.[15] The danger in the 1990s is that these political pressures may eventually be translated into more focused pressures for trade remedy actions justified on these grounds. This could involve attempts to reinterpret dumping law in such a way that they capture cost differences due to differing environmental standards, and possible attempts to reinterpret the definition of subsidy under countervailing duty law with a similar aim in mind.[16]

The GATT, as with environment-driven trade threats, has nothing to say on these matters. But to the extent that their severity increases in the decade of the 1990s, so the potential wider problems for the global trading system will also come to the fore. Attempts to introduce environmental considerations into future GATT rounds or other trade negotiating fora may occur. And the vocabulary within which trade policy is debated could well swing towards discussion of 'green' and 'dirty' trade.

III. SUMMARY AND CONCLUDING REMARKS

This paper suggests that in the 1990s we may well see an emerging interface between environmental and trade policies. I suggest in the paper that it may come more to the fore in the 1990s, and in ways which were little anticipated at the birth of the environmental movement in the 1960s and 70s. If indeed global policy responses to issues such as global warming are enacted, the consequences for both regional imbalances and the patterns of trade between regions, is likely to be severe. In addition, the pressures within the trading system which would accompany attempts to use trade policy as an instrument of enforcement of environmental policies, and the further pressures created by differing environmental policies in countries seem likely to be of substantial importance in the years ahead.

How all of this plays out remains to be seen. As the paper emphasises, our global trade institutions (especially the GATT) have evolved as if there were no environmental linkages to trade; and recent environmental arrangements (such as the Montreal Protocol on CFCs) seem, from a trade policy viewpoint, to have given little thought to implementation and enforcement, suggesting non-environmental instruments may be resorted to in order to achieve environmental objectives. Global institutional evolution to reflect these linkages thus seems to be in its infancy, and the 1990s may well see institutional adaptation in this area, in addition to simply a heightened focus on issues.

University of Western Ontario

[15] Rubin and Graham (1982), p. 174, for instance, report cost differentials across countries for compliance with air pollution standards in different countries. These are based on a U.S. Commerce Department study published in 1975. For wood pulp, costs per ton may range from $494 for U.S. firms, to $13 for Canadian firms, and zero for Finnish firms. For copper, smelting costs are 6·6¢ per pound in the United States, as against 0·5¢ per pound in Peru and Chile.

[16] See the discussion in Rubin and Graham (1982), p. 165.

References

Cline, W. R. (1989). 'Political economy of the greenhouse effect.' Mimeo, Institute for International Economics, Washington, D.C. August.

Economist, The. March 17, 1990, pp. 45–7.

Economist, The. September 8–14, 1990, pp. 24–5.

Edmunds, J. and Reilly, J. (1983). 'Global energy and CO_2 to the year 2050.' *The Energy Journal*, vol. 4, no. 3, pp. 21–47.

GATT (1986). *The Text of The General Agreement on Tariffs and Trade*, p. 37. July, Geneva.

Flavin, C. (1990). 'Slowing global warming.' In *State of the World* (ed. Lester R. Brown). New York: W. W. Norton.

Leonard, H. J. (1988). *Pollution and the Struggle for the World Product.* Cambridge: Cambridge University Press.

Le Prestre, Philippe (1989). *The World Bank and the Environmental Challenge*, p. 181. Cranbury, New Jersey: Associated University Presses, Inc.

Low, Patrick (1990). 'United States Trade Policy and the future of the multilateral trading system.' Mimeo (July).

Manne, A. S. and Richels, R. G. (1990). 'Global CO_2 emission reductions – the impacts of rising energy costs.' Revised version of a paper presented to the International Association of Energy Economics, New Delhi (February). Mimeo.

Mansur, A. and Whalley, J. (1984). 'Numerical specification of applied general equilibrium models: estimation, calibration and data.' In *Applied General Equilibrium Analysis* (ed. J. B. Shoven and H. Scarf), pp. 69–127. Cambridge: Cambridge University Press.

Nordhaus, W. D. (1977). 'Economic growth and climate: the carbon dioxide problem.' *American Economic Review*, Papers and Proceedings (February), pp. 341–6.

—— (1990). 'A survey of estimates of the cost of reduction of greenhouse gas emissions.' Mimeo.

—— and Yohe, G. W. (1983). 'Future paths of energy and carbon dioxide emissions.' In *Changing Climate: Report of the Carbon Dioxide Assessment Committee.* National Research Council. Washington: National Academy Press.

Repetto, Robert and Gillis, Malcolm (eds) (1988). *Public Policies and the Misuse of Forest Resources.* Cambridge: Cambridge University Press.

Robertson, D. (1990). 'The global environment: are international treaties a distraction?' *The World Economy*, vol. 13, no. 1.

Rubin, S. J. and Graham, T. R. (1982). 'Summary and conclusions.' In *Environment and Trade* (ed. S. J. Rubin and T. R. Graham), p. 169. New Jersey: Allanheld, Osmun and Co. Publishers Inc.

Sankey, John (1989). 'Domestically prohibited goods and hazardous substances – a new GATT working group is established.' *Journal of World Trade*, vol. 23, no. 6, pp. 99–108.

Schneider, Stephen (1989). 'The greenhouse effect: science and policy.' *Science*, vol. 243 (February), pp. 771–81.

Shoven, J. and Whalley, J. (1984). 'Applied general equilibrium models of taxation and international trade: an introduction and survey.' *Journal of Economic Literature* (September), pp. 1007–51.

—— and —— (forthcoming). *Applying General Equilibrium.* Cambridge: Cambridge University Press.

Whalley, J. (1989). *The Uraguay Round and Beyond: The Final Report from the Ford Foundation Project on Developing Countries and the Global Trading System.* London: Macmillan.

—— and Wigle, R. (1989). 'Cutting CO_2 emissions: the effects of alternative policy approaches.' A paper presented to a conference on Applied General Equilibrium Modelling in San Diego, on September 8–9, 1989.

—— and —— (1990). 'The international incidence of carbon taxes.' Paper prepared for a conference on Economic Policy Responses to Global Warming organised by the Istituto Bancario Sao Paolo di Torino, to be held at Palazzo Colonna, Rome, October 4–6, 1990.

Part III
Specific Studies of Linkage

[12]

Trade Liberalization and the Environment in the Pacific Basin: Coordinated Approaches to Mexican Trade and Environment Policy

John Beghin, David Roland-Holst, and Dominique van der Mensbrugghe

In this paper we analyze the environmental implications of growth and opening up of trade in Mexico based on an empirical economywide model. In particular, we study how tradeoffs between growth and environmental objectives can be minimized by using targeted policies on pollution emissions in coordination with outward-oriented trade strategies. Most economywide studies of trade and environment linkages rely on effluent intensities associated with output and do not allow for substitution between nonpolluting factors (labor and capital) and polluting intermediate consumption such as chemicals or energy (Lee and Roland-Holst). By contrast, pollution emissions in the present model are linked to using polluting inputs rather than directly to output levels. We also embed this analysis in a dynamic framework to take account of exogenous components of factor supply and productivity growth over the twenty-year period 1990 to 2010.

The analysis is presented in three stages. First, pollution abatement policies are considered alone and their effects on growth, sectoral allocation, and trade are evaluated. The next step is to consider trade liberalization alone. Trade distortions in place before the NAFTA and Uruguay Round accords are removed progressively over time, and results calibrate the expansionary effects of trade liberalization as well as its environmental implications. These include "win-win" cases such as in the fertilizer sector, as well as intensified environmental degradation arising from the transportation sector. In a third and last scenario, we combine environmental and trade policies and show how they interact. These results indicate that the combination of policies generally can mitigate the undesirable effects of each set of policies alone, such as trade-induced pollution growth and the real contractionary effects of environmental policy. Thus, it appears that more liberal and outward-oriented trade policy can coexist with more rigorous attention to environmental values.

The trade and environment debate has evolved considerably in recent years.[1] First, pressures to use trade instruments for environmental ends were debunked as a blunt and inefficient approach to environmental policy (Anderson and Blackhurst). Environmental degradation is increasingly recognized as a leading policy issue, however, and its links to economic policies are now being addressed more directly. Coordination of trade liberalization with the introduction of targeted environmental policies is being supported by analytical investigations of trade and environment linkages (Copeland; Beghin, Roland-Holst, and van der Mensbrugghe 1994b). In this paper we provide empirical evidence to substantiate recommendation for policy coordination.

J. Beghin is associate professor at North Carolina State University. D. Roland-Holst is senior economist and head of program, and D. van der Mensbrugghe is an economist, both at the OECD Development Centre, Paris, France. Senior authorship is not assigned.

The views expressed in this paper are those of the authors and should not be attributed to their affiliated institutions. This study is part of the OECD Development Centre research program on Sustainable Development: Environment, Resource Use, Technology, and Trade. The results presented here represent one of six developing country case studies now under way (Chile, China, Costa Rica, Indonesia, Mexico, and Vietnam). The authors thank Maurizio Bussolo and Sébastien Dessus for excellent research assistance.

[1] See Beghin, Roland-Holst, and van der Mensbrugghe (1994a) for an up-to-date survey.

Amer. J. Agr. Econ. 77 (August 1995): 778–785

Another important recent development in the same literature has been decomposition of pollution into three underlying components, attributable respectively to composition, technology, and scale (Grossman and Krueger; Copeland and Taylor). The composition component measures the change in pollution induced by a change in the commodity composition of aggregate production (more or less of dirty or clean goods). The technology element represents the change in pollution coming from evolving (usually cleaner) technologies (usually resulting in a change in input mix). The last aspect, the scale effect, measures the increase in pollution attributable to an increase in aggregate economic activity. Trade exerts important influences in all three of these dimensions. Efficiency gains induced by outward-oriented strategy lead to positive scale effects on pollution (i.e., more output and more pollution). The technology effect is also influenced by trade policy, as removal of trade distortions changes relative input prices, input mix, and hence the pollution intensity of production. In the context of trade liberalization, the composition effect reflects the realization of comparative advantages, which may be in either dirty or clean activities. We document the role of these three effects in our empirical study.

One major finding is that the growth-environment tradeoffs in Mexico are not debilitating to the economy. Only one pollutant category (bioaccumulative toxic substances in water) appears to have a high opportunity cost in terms of the contractionary effects of abatement. Growth with an outward-oriented trade strategy and pollution taxes in place is sustainable in the sense that pollution emissions can be mitigated significantly over time. From the opposite perspective, trade expansion alone occasions significant environmental damage in only a few sectors (e.g., energy). In fact, the composition of output becomes cleaner under free trade; hence, our evidence fails to support the hypothesis that Mexico would specialize in dirty industrial activities. Increasing outward orientation by Mexico induces a combination of contraction and expansion of polluting activities whose aggregate net effects are not particularly significant.

Another important finding is the variegated nature of abatement effects among industries, particularly with regard to different abatement policies. In the case of pollution taxes, the technological effect dominates in many sectors, except for the dirtiest ones where substitution away from pollution-intensive intermediates is difficult. The composition effect is dominant in this latter case. Trade liberalization tends to increase reliance on imports to substitute away from dirty domestic output without penalizing consumption. Hence, under combined reforms, the composition effect often is dominant because it represents the cheaper abatement method for the economy. For example, if a pollution tax was put on SO_2 emissions, Mexico would substantially increase its imports of cement and decrease its domestic cement production. Trade liberalization accentuates this role of imports substituting for pollution-intensive domestic production, as well as domestic specialization in cleaner activities that can be exported. In this manner, trading opportunities reduce the implicit growth costs of effluent taxation. One caveat here is that foreign producers may not appropriately price their environment; i.e., trade displaces the pollution externality abroad (see Lee and Roland-Holst for an example of this in a bilateral context). In the case of Mexico, however, this possibility is remote, since its NAFTA partners are at least as concerned with environmental degradation as Mexico.

Besides policy simulations, our investigation yields interesting stylized facts about pollution emission in Mexico. A few sectors are responsible for most of the pollution emission: energy sectors, petro-chemical, minerals and their transformation, and cement; agriculture is a major contributor to toxic water pollution. Many emission types are correlated (the same sectors are often intensive in several effluents) and there is relatively little substitution across discharge media (water, air, land), so limited analytical and administrative resources could profitably be focused on a subset of effluents and industries. The major policy implication that emerges from these stylized facts is the possibility of targeting a limited number of pollutants and industries with monitoring and regulation while achieving major environmental gains in the whole economy.

TEQUILA Model

The Trade and Environment equilibrium Analysis (TEQUILA[2]) Model has been adapted from the OECD Development Centre's prototype computable general equilibrium (CGE) model for its sustainable development program

[2] Thanks to Sébastien Dessus for the acronym.

(Beghin et al.). The model is (recursive) dynamic and multisectoral and we summarize its features in this subsection. Production is based on constant returns to scale technology and the structure of production consists of a series of nested CES functions. Final output is determined from the combination of (nonenergy) intermediate inputs and a composite bundle of energy and value added. Nonenergy intermediate inputs are assumed to be used in fixed proportions with respect to total nonenergy intermediate demand. The energy-value-added bundle is further decomposed into a labor aggregate on the one hand, and a capital-energy bundle on the other. Labor demand is further decomposed into eight occupational categories. The capital-energy bundle is in turn disaggregated into capital demand and demand for an energy aggregate. Finally, the energy bundle is decomposed into different base fuel components. One of the key advantages of this type of production structure is that emissions are linked to intermediate consumption rather than to final output. Depending on the degree of substitutability between intermediate goods and the other factors of production, sectors can substitute away into cleaner input mix if emission taxes are imposed. If one relies on output-based pollution coefficients or a pure Leontief technology, the only way to reduce emissions is to reduce output.[3]

Another key feature of the TEQUILA model is the vintage structure of capital. The model assumes a putty/semiputty production technology. It is normally assumed that the substitution possibilities of so-called old capital are smaller than the substitution possibilities of new capital, implying that acceleration of investment would allow producers more flexibility in reacting to emission taxes.

The TEQUILA model is calibrated to a detailed social accounting matrix (SAM) for Mexico, with eight labor categories and twenty households. The bulk of labor and capital income is distributed to the different households, and it is therefore possible to assess the distributional impacts of changes in both trade and environmental policies. Households are assumed to maximize utility using the extended linear expenditure system (ELES).

Labor is assumed to be perfectly mobile across sectors, while capital is only partially mobile, reflecting differences in the transferability of capital equipment across sectors. Both wages and capital returns are determined by economywide equilibrium conditions. However, the labor supply curve is differentiated by labor type and can generate either full or partial employment conditions. Trade is modeled assuming goods are differentiated with respect to region of origin and destination. On the import side, we use the CES specification attributed to Armington. Domestic output is treated symmetrically in a CET specification, where producers are assumed to differentiate between the domestic and export markets. The small-country assumption is maintained for the world prices of both Mexican imports and exports.

The model incorporates three closure rules. The government surplus/deficit is assumed to be fixed in real terms. Normally, some tax rate is endogenous to achieve this budget balance. If the household direct tax rate is endogenous, this closure rule can generate significant impacts on the distribution of income. The second closure rule is that investment is savings driven. Changes in savings levels—household, government, or foreign—will have a direct impact on the investment level. The final closure rule holds that the trade balance is fixed (in foreign currency terms). The impact of this closure rule is that trade liberalization typically leads to a real depreciation, as increasing import demand must be matched by rising exports at constant world prices.

Emissions are assumed to be generated by the consumption of goods, both in intermediate use and in final demand. (In certain sectors, there is an autonomous component of emissions that is directly linked to the level of output.) The data on effluents are estimated following the methodology of Dessus, Roland-Holst, and van der Mensbrugghe, which, in turn, is based on the World Bank database obtained from Martin et al. Excise/effluent taxes are used to achieve pollution abatement. These taxes are measured as unit of currency per unit of emissions and are tacked on to the producer price of the polluting commodity. Pollution itself is characterized by a vector of thirteen measures of various water, air, and soil effluents. These include toxic pollutants in water, air, and land (TOXAIR, TOXWAT, TOXSOL), bio-accumulative toxic metals in air, soil, and water (BIOAIR, BIOWAT, BIOSOL); air pollutants such as SO_2, NO_2, CO, volatile organic compounds (VOC), and particulate intensity (PART); and finally, water pollution [biological Oxygen Demand (BOD)], and total suspended solids (TSS).

[3] The conversion from output to input-based pollution statistics is explained in Dessus, Roland-Holst, and van der Mensbrugghe.

There are three essential dynamic components in the TEQUILA model. The first is factor accumulation. Labor supply is assumed to grow exogenously, while the capital stock evolves with investment activity. The second element is productivity growth. There are efficiency factors for capital, labor (by each occupation), and energy. The efficiency factors are normally exogenous, but the capital efficiency factor is imputed in the benchmark simulation to achieve a specified trajectory of real GDP growth. The third element is a vintage capital assumption. The composition of the capital stock, which will determine the degree of flexibility in production, is influenced by the time path of total and sectoral investment allocation.

Simulation Scenarios

We consider three basic scenarios in reference to a twenty-year (1990–2010) base trend. The latter determines the reference growth and pollution trajectory in absence of environmental, trade, or other policy reforms. The first reform scenario looks at the impact of piecemeal environmental policies, elucidating the extent of the growth-environment tradeoff in Mexico and how it is influenced by international trade. Specifically, the policy calls for phasing in a 25% emission reduction with respect to reference trends for one type of effluent at the time. The phasing entails sequential reductions of 10% in 1995, 15% in 2000, 20% in 2005, and 25% in 2010. The second scenario considers a piecemeal unilateral trade liberalization, along with a modest increase in export prices to mimic terms-of-trade effects that would follow from NAFTA, and increased access to North American markets. Trade distortions are expressed as ad valorem tariffs that will be eliminated progressively from their reference levels (1989); 90% of original tariffs in 1995, 60% in 2000, 30% in 2005, and no tariff in 2010. Terms-of-trade effects are assumed to be similarly progressive, increasing observed world prices by 2% in 1995, 4% in 2000, 7% in 2005, and 10% in 2010. The purpose of this scenario is less to estimate empirically the welfare gains of trade liberalization than to see how the environment is affected by an outward-oriented strategy. The change in sectoral composition of production and trade is also of interest, since it might reveal evidence of specialization in dirty production, with an implicit transfer of environmental services to countries buying Mexican exports or, conversely, of dirty industries contracting under world market discipline.

The last set of simulations combines the two types of reforms. Here the objective is to see to what extent free trade and environment policies combine their impacts on efficiency and the environment. For each simulation we report summary results, although the simulations have been carried out with the fully disaggregated model (ninety-four sectors). The more disaggregated results are available from the authors.

Results

Aggregate simulation results are presented in table 1 for the individual abatement taxes and for trade liberalization. Abatement taxes inducing 25% reductions in individual effluent categories are uniformly contractionary in terms of real GDP (row 4 of table 1). In light of the extent of pollution reduction, however, these negative growth effects are surprisingly small, ranging from –0.29% (NO_2 reduction) to –4.4% (BIOWAT reduction). The three toxic pollutant indices (TOXAIR, TOXWAT, and TOXSOL) are highly correlated. A few industries are responsible for most of the pollution emissions and typically discharge several types of pollutants simultaneously; the composition effect induced by a tax on a specific pollutant decreases other emissions because of low substitution between discharge media and high correlation between different types of emissions by medium.

Decomposition of pollution abatement[4] reveals that the composition effect is dominant in the most polluting industries such as petroleum refining or cement. By contrast, the technological effect, measured by the decrease in the pollution intensity per unit of output, is dominant for many sectors in which it is relatively inexpensive to abate pollution by substituting away from polluting inputs without reducing output. Scale effects are the least important source of abatement; hence, the tradeoff between environment and economic growth does not appear to be acute in Mexico.

Unilateral trade liberalization and better terms-of-trade occasion a 3.2% rise in real GDP, but also an increase in all major pollutants by about the same proportion (from 2.5% to 4.8%). In the absence of policies that alter the relative costs of polluting activities, the

[4] Detailed results are available from the authors.

Table 1. Aggregate and Sectoral Results of Individual Abatement and Trade Liberalization

	Aggregate Abatement of 25% by Type of Emission													Trade
	toxair	toxsol	toxwat	bioair	biosol	biowat	so2	no2	co	part	voc	tss	bod	Liberalization
Aggregates														
Toxic index	−19.41	−23.37	−16.19	−5.99	−6.07	−5.49	−2.92	−2.92	−10.42	−3.02	−15.70	−0.08	−12.26	2.50
Bio-accum index	−31.07	−23.20	−0.98	−24.57	−24.72	−9.10	−0.35	−0.34	−2.25	−1.00	−3.31	−0.41	−1.03	3.87
SO2–NO2–CO index	−12.67	−15.06	−20.25	−2.85	−1.38	−7.49	−14.68	−14.79	−16.18	−16.44	−17.46	−1.30	−5.49	4.84
Real GDP	−1.12	−1.31	−0.56	−0.66	−0.60	−4.39	−0.29	−0.29	−0.42	−0.39	−0.73	−0.04	−0.56	3.22
Labor supply	−0.15	−0.24	−0.42	−0.13	−0.11	−2.23	−0.01	−0.01	−0.03	−0.05	−0.15	−0.01	−0.24	0.16
Capital stock	−1.31	−1.52	−0.68	−0.83	−0.74	−5.76	−0.33	−0.32	−0.46	−0.46	−0.79	−0.06	−0.67	4.25
Total exports	−2.55	−2.79	−2.04	−1.11	−1.00	−4.20	−1.22	−1.25	−0.78	−1.32	−0.97	−0.05	−1.46	21.95
Total imports	−1.03	−1.01	−1.04	−0.47	−0.40	−3.36	−1.03	−1.06	0.01	−1.09	0.45	−0.02	−0.65	31.86
Sectoral Output														
Agriculture	−0.47	−1.30	−4.61	0.24	0.25	−2.37	−0.12	−0.11	−0.33	−0.15	−1.33	0.00	−2.14	−2.44
Mining	−23.35	−27.37	−20.49	−8.94	−7.99	−10.45	−5.77	−5.61	−5.12	−6.87	−5.18	−1.14	−20.26	12.80
Food processing	0.13	−0.28	−1.95	0.20	0.22	−1.99	−0.05	−0.06	−0.01	−0.07	−0.81	0.00	−1.09	2.02
Textiles	−1.69	−3.83	−1.01	0.48	0.46	−1.29	0.10	0.12	−3.61	0.11	−6.06	0.02	−0.55	0.37
Wood and paper prod	−1.26	−1.29	−1.98	−0.43	−0.38	−4.49	−0.30	−0.25	−1.22	−0.47	−4.21	−0.02	−0.96	−0.01
Petroleum	−16.28	−22.38	−28.43	0.59	0.32	−3.03	−19.72	−19.82	−20.04	−19.33	−27.70	0.17	−9.33	1.90
Chemicals	−10.88	−15.83	−7.39	−1.00	−1.03	−2.94	−0.41	−0.42	−13.46	−0.43	−21.76	−0.03	−4.52	−0.09
Processed minerals	−9.43	−9.54	−1.19	−9.51	−8.90	−13.32	−0.81	−1.01	−0.53	−1.71	−0.13	−0.51	−2.27	2.63
Other manufacturing	−3.62	0.23	4.55	−5.13	−4.64	−2.35	0.58	0.55	1.31	0.15	1.63	−0.27	3.58	14.94
Services	−0.09	−0.17	0.17	−0.26	−0.23	−5.66	−0.30	−0.28	0.01	−0.36	−0.06	−0.01	0.04	4.03

Note: All figures are percentage changes with respect to base trends in 2010.

scale effect is thus dominant for all pollutants and most sectors. There appears to be a positive abatement effect via a changing composition of output toward cleaner goods. However, dirty activities expand in a few sectors (e.g., energy sectors like oil, gas, and electricity). Examples of win-win cases are the staple agricultural activities that are responsible for toxic water pollution and the fertilizer industry, which also contracts under free trade. No noticeable technology effect occurs in the absence of incentives to shift the input mix to achieve abatement.

Naturally, an important element of the incidence of these reforms is the social costs and benefits of pollution reduction and the preservation of environmental assets. At the present time, we have made no attempt to incorporate this kind of valuation in the model, but it should be noted that the abatement levels achieved are one to two orders of magnitude larger than the economic costs in percentage terms.

To see the possible effects of coordinated reforms, we have reproduced analogous results (table 2) for trade liberalization combined with each of the individual abatement policies.[5] The main advantage of coordinated reforms is to combine efficiency gains from free trade with distortions implemented to achieve second-best environmental objectives. Real economic growth (real GDP in table 2) is positive for all but one environmental tax (BIOWAT). Food processing, services, and manufacturing other than chemicals and metals expand with the coordinated policies. The abatement multiplier effects vary little compared to their values under the first scenario. Aggregate trade expands by about 20% for exports, and 30% for imports, quite comparable to the expansion induced by trade liberalization alone. It is perhaps reasonable to conclude from this that domestic environmental policies in this country are relatively "transparent" with respect to the real and dynamic gains from trade. In other words, the effects of trade and environment policies generally are decomposable and, comparing tables 1 and 2, nearly additive.

In the combined scenarios, decomposition of abatement is quite different from what it was under the exclusive environmental reform, but again, nearly additive between pollution and trade reforms. The composition effect is significantly larger in the joint reform. Enhanced trading possibilities induced a stronger substitution of imports for dirty domestic output and a specialization in cleaner goods that can be exported. For most effluent abatement the scale effect contributes negatively. This is the generic effect of growth, which is offset primarily by the changing composition and, to a lesser extent, by cleaner technology (input mix) in production. In sum, trade has two effects: a pro-growth effect detrimental to the environment and a composition-substitution effect that mitigates environmental degradation. Trade has a secondary effect on the technology component. Imports are cheaper and cleaner from a domestic perspective, and this hinders the incentives to decrease emission intensities. This latter aspect generally has been overlooked; trade liberalization provides price discipline for pollution abatement achieved by modifying the input mix in domestic production.

[5] Note that abatement policies are not combined because the effluent categories are not mutually exclusive.

Concluding Remarks

Our empirical results support several findings. Economic integration of Mexico in the regional economy will not, as many fear, exacerbate environmental degradation. The pollution elasticity with respect to growth is very stable in Mexico (near unity) and trade orientation does not have much impact on that elasticity. Actually, the new patterns of resource allocation and output composition achieved under free trade are less pollution-intensive. Nevertheless, a strong scale effect dominates this, and economic growth increases total pollution in most categories. Environmental policy reforms that target emissions linked to the utilization of polluting goods (in either intermediate or final use) are the best ways to achieve pollution mitigation. Our results suggest that it would be appropriate to target a subset of sectors and pollutants further, achieving high abatement levels will lower administrative costs. Free trade and trade integration represent an important source of growth opportunities, and when combined with appropriate environmental policies can raise material living standards in Mexico while mitigating environmental degradation.

References

Anderson, K., and R. Blackhurst. *The Greening of World Trade Issues*. Ann Arbor MI: University of Michigan Press, 1992.

Beghin, J., S. Dessus, D. Roland-Holst, and D. van

Table 2. Aggregate and Sectoral Results of Individual Abatement Combined with Trade Liberalization

	Aggregate Abatement of 25% by Type of Emission												
	toxair	toxsol	toxwat	bioair	biosol	biowat	so2	no2	co	part	voc	tss	bod
Aggregates													
Toxic index	-19.69	-23.10	-14.78	-3.98	-4.10	-3.64	-1.37	-1.37	-8.50	-1.42	-13.99	2.43	-10.87
Bio-accum index	-31.10	-20.98	3.99	-24.66	-24.69	-6.35	3.63	3.65	1.67	2.72	0.83	3.35	3.84
SO2-NO2-CO index	-9.91	-11.71	-17.24	1.89	3.35	-3.52	-14.47	-14.65	-12.29	-16.36	-13.93	3.51	-1.29
Real GDP	2.02	1.89	2.65	2.54	2.61	-1.67	2.85	2.85	2.81	2.74	2.50	3.18	2.63
Labor supply	0.06	-0.03	-0.41	0.05	0.07	-2.31	0.15	0.16	0.14	0.11	0.01	0.15	-0.08
Capital stock	2.85	2.71	3.54	3.39	3.49	-2.21	3.83	3.84	3.80	3.68	3.45	4.19	3.56
Total exports	19.26	19.38	20.40	20.73	20.89	16.90	20.31	20.27	21.45	20.19	21.40	21.89	20.70
Total imports	30.67	31.01	31.28	31.22	31.35	27.29	30.31	30.27	32.13	30.23	32.75	31.83	31.42
Sectoral output													
Agriculture	-2.71	-3.53	-7.23	-2.08	-2.07	-5.08	-2.58	-2.57	-2.70	-2.61	-3.69	-2.43	-4.57
Mining	-16.31	-22.76	-15.12	6.31	6.95	0.71	4.13	4.42	8.34	3.33	8.29	11.77	-15.74
Food processing	2.55	2.17	0.41	2.36	2.36	-0.23	1.98	1.96	2.10	1.96	1.33	2.03	1.13
Textiles	-1.36	-3.44	-0.52	1.00	0.97	-0.92	0.53	0.56	-3.30	0.56	-5.89	0.40	-0.06
Wood and paper prod	-1.02	-0.79	-1.63	-0.41	-0.36	-4.80	-0.34	-0.28	-1.12	-0.55	-4.23	-0.03	-0.67
Petroleum	-16.97	-22.73	-28.88	3.13	2.75	-1.24	-23.58	-23.72	-19.29	-22.82	-27.60	2.14	-9.07
Chemicals	-12.74	-17.31	-7.74	-1.25	-1.30	-3.16	-0.53	-0.55	-14.74	-0.53	-23.61	-0.11	-4.87
Processed minerals	-8.00	-7.22	2.45	-8.87	-8.08	-12.28	1.73	1.40	2.31	0.49	3.06	1.98	1.22
Other manufacturing	12.69	18.72	23.34	8.20	8.97	12.66	16.32	16.25	17.50	15.59	18.26	14.56	21.93
Services	4.04	3.99	4.27	3.77	3.81	-2.35	3.63	3.65	4.02	3.56	3.95	4.02	4.15

Note: All figures are percentage changes with respect to base trends in 2010.

der Mensbrugghe. "Prototype CGE Model for the Trade and the Environment Programme." Unpublished, Paris, October 1994.

Beghin, J., D. Roland-Holst, and D. van der Mensbrugghe. "A Survey of the Trade and Environment Nexus: Global Dimensions." *OECD Econ. Stud.* 23(Fall 1994a), in press.

___. "Trade and Pollution Linkages: Piecemeal Reform and Optimal Intervention." OECD Development Centre Technical Papers No. 99. Paris, September 1994b.

Copeland, B.R. "International Trade and the Environment: Policy Reform in a Polluted Small Open Economy." *J. Environ. Econ. and Manage.* 20(1994):44–65.

Copeland, B.R., and S.M. Taylor. "North-South Trade and the Environment." *Quart. J. Econ.* 109(1994):755–87.

Dessus, S., D. Roland-Holst, and D. van der Mensbrugghe. "Input-Based Pollution Estimates for Environmental Assessment in Developing Countries." OECD Development Centre Technical Papers No. 101. Paris, October 1994.

Grossman, G.E., and A.B. Krueger. "Environmental Impacts of a NAFTA." CEPR Discussion Paper series No. 644. London, April 1992.

Lee, H., and D. Roland-Holst. "International Trade and the Transfer of Environment Cost and Benefits." J. Francois and K. Reinert, eds. *Applied Trade Policy Modeling.* Cambridge UK: Cambridge University Press, 1994.

Martin, P., D. Wheeler, M. Hettige, and R. Stengren. "The Industrial Pollution Projection System: Concept, Initial Development, and Critical Assessment." Unpublished, The World Bank, 1991.

[13]

Environmental Impacts of a North American Free Trade Agreement

Gene M. Grossman
and Alan B. Krueger

Environmental advocacy groups in the United States have voiced their concerns about a potential North American Free Trade Agreement (NAFTA). Some went so far as to oppose the congressional granting of fast-track negotiating authority to the president to enable American negotiators to enter into talks with their Mexican counterparts. The reservations of the lobbying groups mirror a growing perception on the part of environmentalists worldwide that an open world trading system may be inimical to the goal of preserving a clean, healthy, and sustainable global commons.

The arguments linking trade liberalization with environmental degradation have not been fully articulated.[1] With regard to a NAFTA, the environmentalists have expressed a number of reasons for fearing that freer trade and direct investment flows between the United States and Mexico may aggravate pollution problems in Mexico and in the border region.[2] At the least-discerning level, some have argued simply that any expansion of markets and economic activity inevitably leads to more pollution and faster depletion of scarce natural resources. A more pointed argument recognizes that pollution already is a severe problem in Mexico and that the country's weak regulatory infrastructure is strained to the breaking point. Under these conditions, it is feared that any further industrialization that results from the liberalization of trade and investment will exacerbate an already grave situation.

Other environmentalists draw their conclusions by extrapolating the experience of the maquiladora sector in Mexico. The maquiladoras are predominantly foreign-owned firms that produce largely for export to the United States under a Mexican policy that allows duty-free imports of foreign components for further processing and reexport. Originally, maquiladoras were required to locate within a 20-kilometer strip along the U.S.-Mexico border in order to qualify for special customs treatment. The sector grew rapidly and with little governmental oversight, and now is widely regarded as being a major contributor to the perilous environmental and social conditions in the border region. Environmental groups point to this sector as a prime example of how unregulated expansion in response to trade opportunities can create risks to worker safety and public health. They argue that investments in this sector have been encouraged by the lax enforcement of environment and labor protection laws in Mexico and fear that any further expansion in trade and investment flows between the United States and Mexico will be motivated by firms' desires to avoid the high costs of meeting U.S. regulations.

A further concern of some environmental groups is that a NAFTA may undercut regulatory standards in the United States. Spokespersons have made the political-economic argument that, with freer trade, industry groups in the United States will demand less stringent pollution controls in order to preserve their international competitiveness, so that environmental standards will tend toward a lowest common denominator. The environmentalists worry, moreover, that existing environmental protection laws in the United States may be seen as nontariff barriers to trade in the context of a regional trade agreement.

Although the environmental groups have raised a host of valid questions, they have so far been unable to provide convincing and well-supported answers to these questions. Many of their arguments fail to recognize all of the implications of trade liberalization for resource allocation and natural resource use in each of the trade-partner countries. Moreover, the empirical claims that have been made rely mostly on anecdotal evidence and on extrapolation of the experience in one region or industry to the entirety of economic activity in Mexico. Indeed, relatively little is known at any level of generality about the relationship between a country's trade regime and its rate of environmental degradation, or even about the relationship between a country's stage of economic development and its output of pollution. Theoretical investigation of these topics has been limited, and empirical studies are virtually nonexistent.

It is useful to distinguish three separate mechanisms by which a change in trade and foreign investment policy can affect the level of pollution and the rate of depletion of scarce environmental resources.[3] First, there is a *scale* effect, capturing the simple intuition espoused by the environmental advocates. That is, if trade and investment liberalization causes an expansion of economic activity, and if the nature of that activity remains unchanged, then the total amount of pollution generated must increase. The environmental groups point, for example, to the deleterious environmental consequences of the combustion of fossil fuels and to the air pollution that is generated by the trucking industry. To the extent that economic growth gives rise to an increased demand for energy, which then is generated by means similar to the prevailing methods, there will be an increased output of harmful pollutants that attends an increase in economic output. Similarly, to the extent that expanded trade gives rise to an increased demand for cross-border transportation services without there being any change in trucking practices, increased trade will contribute to a deterioration in air quality.

Second, there is a *composition* effect that results from any change in trade policy. When trade is liberalized, countries specialize to a greater extent in the sectors in which they enjoy competitive advantage. If competitive advantage derives largely from differences in environmental regulation, then the composition effect of trade liberalization will be damaging to the environment. Each country then will tend to specialize more completely in the activities that its government does not regulate strictly, and will shift out of production in industries where the local costs of pollution abatement are relatively great. On the other hand, if the sources of international comparative advantage are the more traditional ones, namely cross-country differences in factor abundance and technology, then the implications of the composition effect for the state of the environment are ambiguous. Trade liberalization will lead each country to shift resources into the sectors that make intensive use of its abundant factors. The net effect of this on the level of pollution in each location will depend upon whether pollution-intensive activities expand or contract in the country that on average has the more stringent pollution controls.

Finally, there is a *technique* effect. That is, output need not be produced by exactly the same methods subsequent to a liberalization of trade and foreign investment as it has been prior to the change in regime. In particular, the output of pollution per unit of economic product need not remain the same. There are at least two reasons to believe that pollution per unit of output might fall, especially in a less developed country. First, foreign producers may transfer modern technologies to the local economy when restrictions on foreign investment are relaxed. More modern technologies typically are cleaner than older technologies due to the growing global awareness of the urgency of environmental concerns. Second, and perhaps more important, if trade liberalization generates an increase in income levels, then the body politic may demand a cleaner environment as an expression of their increased national wealth. Thus, more stringent pollution standards and stricter enforcement of existing laws may be a natural political response to economic growth.

In this chapter we explore some of the empirical evidence that bears on the likely environmental impacts of a NAFTA. In section 1, we shed some light on the relative magnitudes of the scale and technique effects. We use a cross-country sample of comparable measures of pollution in various urban areas to explore the relationship between economic growth and air quality. After holding constant the identifiable geographic characteristics of different cities, a common global time trend in the levels of pollution, and the location and type of the pollution measurement device, we find that ambient levels of both sulfur dioxide and dark matter suspended in the air increase with per capita GDP at low levels of national income, but decrease with per capita GDP at higher levels of income. The turning point comes somewhere between $4,000 and $5,000, measured in 1985 U.S. dollars. For a third measure of air quality, namely the mass of suspended particles found in a given volume of air, the relationship between pollution and GDP is monotonically decreasing.

Sections 2 and 3 address different aspects of the composition effect. In section 2 we ask whether and to what extent the sectoral patterns of U.S. foreign investment in Mexico and of Mexican exports to the United States are affected by the laxity of environmental regulations in Mexico as compared to the stricter enforcement of controls in the United States. We relate the sectoral pattern of maquiladora activity, of U.S. imports from Mexico under the offshore assembly provisions of the U.S. tariff codes, and of total U.S. imports from Mexico to industry factor intensities, U.S. tariff rates, and the size of pollution abatement costs in the U.S. industry. We find that the traditional determinants of trade and investment patterns are significant here, but that the alleged competitive advantages created by lax pollution controls in Mexico play no substantial role in motivating trade and investment flows.

Finally, in section 3 we begin with the premise that resource allocations in the United States, Mexico, and Canada have been guided by competitive advantages generated by differences in factor endowments. We borrow from Brown, Deardorff, and Stern (1991) their estimates of the change in resource allocation that might result from a NAFTA, and discuss the implications of these predicted changes in the structure of production for levels of pollution in each country.

1 Economic Growth and Urban Air Pollution

As we noted above, economic growth has offsetting implications for the anthropogenic generation of air pollution. On one hand, some pollutants are a natural by-product of economic activities such as electricity generation and the operation of motor vehicles. As economic activity expands, emissions of these pollutants tend to grow. On the other hand, firms and households can control their pollution to some degree by their choice of technology. Cleaner technologies produce less pollution per unit of output. As a society becomes richer, its members may intensify their demands for a more healthy and sustainable environment, in which case the government may be called upon to impose more stringent environmental controls.

Little is known about the empirical relationship between national income and concentrations of various pollutants. Investigation of this issue has been hampered by the paucity of data on pollution that are available on a comparable basis for a representative sample of countries. However, since 1976 the World Health Organization (WHO) has collaborated with the United Nations Environment Programme in operating the Global Environmental Monitoring System (GEMS). The goal of this project has been to monitor closely the concentrations of several air pollutants in a cross-section of urban areas using standardized methods of measurement. This data set, which to our knowledge has not previously been analyzed by economists, provides us with an opportunity to examine how air quality is affected by economic growth.[4]

In the next subsection we describe the GEMS project, the types of pollution that it monitors, and the data that it has generated. Section 1.2 gives the details of the statistical analysis that we have performed. Our findings are presented in section 1.3 and the implications for Mexico are discussed in section 1.4.

1.1 The GEMS Data

The GEMS monitors air quality in urban areas throughout the world. Daily (or, in some cases, weekly) measurements are taken of concentrations of sulfur dioxide (SO_2) and suspended particulate matter.[5] Data on particulates, which are gases and liquids suspended in the air, are collected by different methods (described further below) that alternatively measure the mass of materials in a given volume of air and the concentration of finer, darker matter, sometimes referred to as "smoke."

Sulfur dioxide is a corrosive gas that has been linked to respiratory disease and other health problems.[6] It is emitted naturally by volcanoes, decaying organic matter, and sea spray. The major anthropogenic sources of SO_2 are the burning of fossil fuels in electricity generation and domestic heating, and the smelting of nonferrous ores (World Resources Institute,

1988). Other sources in some countries include automobile exhaust and the chemicals industry (Kormondy, 1989). Sulfur dioxide emissions can be controlled by the installation of flue gas desulfurization equipment (scrubbers) on polluting facilities, and by switching electricity-generating and home-heating capacity to lower sulfur grades of coal or away from coal altogether.

Particulates arise from dust, sea spray, forest fires, and volcanoes. Most of these naturally produced particles are relatively large. Finer particles are emitted by industry and from domestic fuel combustion (World Resources Institute, 1988). Larger particles reduce visibility but have a relatively minor health impact, whereas the finer particles can cause eye and lung damage and can aggravate existing respiratory conditions (U.S. EPA, 1982). Particulate emissions from anthropogenic processes can be reduced via the installation of control equipment and by switching to fuels that, when burned, emit fewer particles.

The GEMS sample of cities has been changing over time. Sulfur dioxide was monitored in 47 cities spread over 28 different countries in 1977, 52 cities in 32 countries in 1982, and 27 cities in 14 countries in 1988. Measurements of suspended particles were taken in 21 cities in 11 countries in 1977, 36 cities in 17 countries in 1982, and 26 cities in 13 countries in 1988, while data for darker matter (smoke) are available for 18 cities in 13 countries for 1977, 13 cities in 9 countries for 1982, and 7 cities in 4 countries for 1988. In all, there are 42 countries represented in our sample for SO_2, 19 countries in our sample for dark matter, and 29 countries in our sample for suspended particles. The participating cities (listed in the appendix) are located in a variety of developing and developed countries and have been chosen to be fairly representative of the geographic conditions that exist in different regions of the world (Bennett et al., 1985). In most of the cities included in the project, air quality measurements are taken at two or three different sites, which are classified either as center city or suburban, and as commercial, industrial, or residential. Multiple sites in the same city are monitored in recognition of the fact that pollutant concentrations can vary dramatically with local conditions that depend in part upon land use. Observations at most sites are made on a daily basis and the data set includes measures of the mean, median, 80th, 95th, and 98th percentile of daily observations in a given site for a given year.

Sulfur dioxide concentrations have been determined by a number of well-accepted methods (see WHO, 1984). The reliability of these methods has been checked in independent studies, and an intercomparison exercise was performed using one particular method as a reference point (Bennett et al., 1985). It was concluded that the measurements by alternative methods are roughly comparable, although particular meteorological conditions can affect the various methods differently. With these results in mind, we have chosen to pool our sample of observations of SO_2 concentration, but to allow for a dummy variable to reflect the method of measurement at each site.

Suspended particles are measured by two main methods. High volume gravimetric sampling determines the mass of particulates in a given volume of air, whereas the smoke-shade method assesses the reflectance of the stain left on a filter paper that ambient air has been drawn through. The former method measures the total weight of suspended particles, while the latter is predominantly an indication of dark material in the air. As the two methods yield incomparable measures that capture different aspects of particulate air pollution, we treat the data generated by gravimetric and smoke-shade methods separately in our analysis.[7]

Table 2.1 provides the mean, median, and standard deviation for the 50th and 95th percentiles of daily observations in our sample of cities for each of the three types of pollution. Figure 2.1 displays the corresponding histograms. The median of daily observations on SO_2 range from a minimum of zero to a maximum of 291 micrograms per cubic meter ($\mu g\ m^{-3}$) of air whereas the 95th percentile of daily measures range from 0 to 1,022

Table 2.1
Descriptive statistics on air pollution in urban areas

Pollutant	Mean	Standard deviation	Median	WHO standard
Sulphur dioxide 50th percentile	33.08	33.11	26.2	40–60
Sulphur dioxide 95th percentile	117.17	112.71	87.0	100–150
Dark matter 50th percentile	42.22	41.92	29.5	50–60
Dark matter 95th percentile	127.47	101.45	102.0	100–150
Suspended particles 50th percentile	146.62	126.79	91.0	60–90
Suspended particles 95th percentile	301.01	268.01	187.0	150–230

Notes: Pollutants are measured in μg per cubic meter. World Health Organization standards listed for the 50th percentile are for the annual average measure, and those listed for the 95th percentile are for the 98th percentile of daily measures. Sample size is 1,370 for sulphur dioxide, 1,021 for suspended particles, and 506 for dark matter.

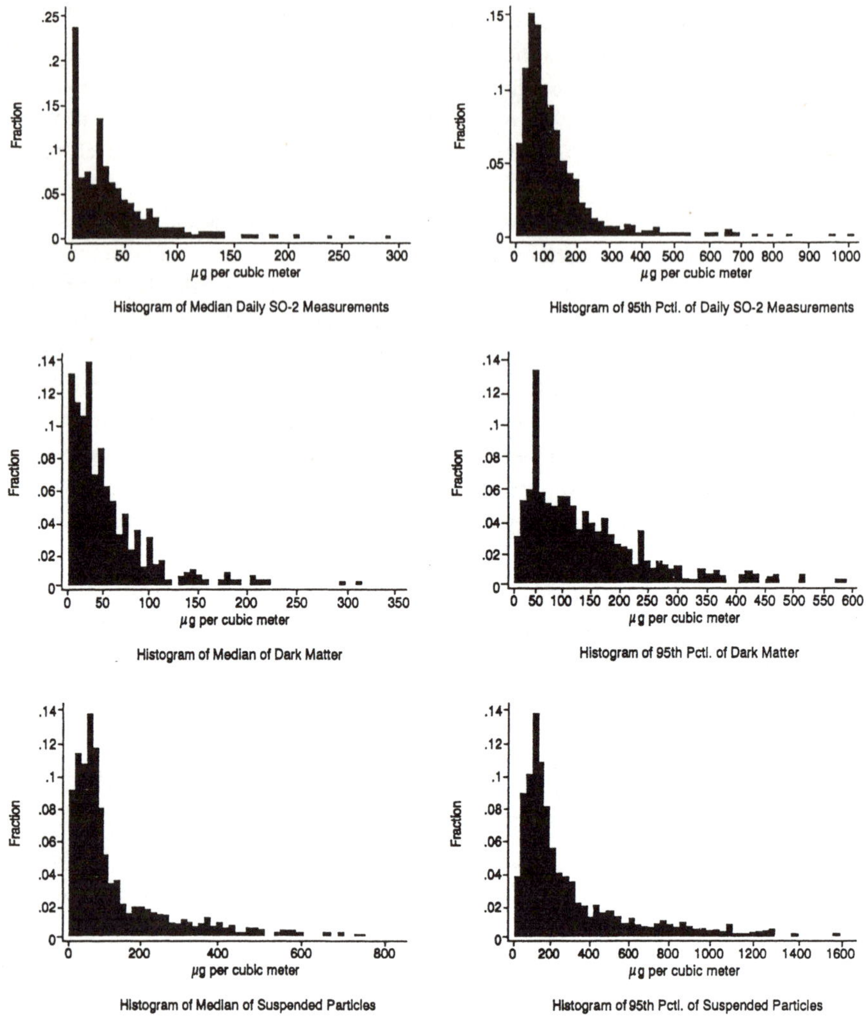

Figure 2.1
Histograms of air pollutants

$\mu g\ m^{-3}$.[8] These numbers can be compared with the World Health Organization recommendation that annual average SO_2 concentrations ought not to exceed 40–60 $\mu g\ m^{-3}$ and that 98th percentile concentrations ought not to exceed 100–150 $\mu g\ m^{-3}$. The median of daily observations for suspended particles varied from zero to 715 $\mu g\ m^{-3}$, while that for the 95th percentile observation ranged from 15 to 1,580 $\mu g\ m^{-3}$. The WHO guidelines for suspended particles list 60–90 $\mu g\ m^{-3}$ as the safe limit for the annual mean and 150–230 $\mu g\ m^{-3}$ as the safe limit for the 98th percentile. Finally the median of daily observations of dark matter (or smoke) in the sample of sites varied from zero to 312 $\mu g\ m^{-3}$, while the 95th percentile observation varied from 2 to 582 $\mu g\ m^{-3}$. The WHO recommends that dark matter not exceed 50–60 $\mu g\ m^{-3}$ in annual average and 100–150 $\mu g\ m^{-3}$ in the 98th percentile of daily observations.

1.2 Estimation

Concentrations of pollutants in the air depend upon the amounts that are emitted by natural and anthropogenic sources and on the ability of the atmosphere to absorb and disburse the gases or particles. Thus our analysis of the relationship between growth and air quality must allow for an influence of city and site characteristics on the observed concentrations of the various pollutants in addition to the dependence on national product.

We have sought to explain the median and 95th percentile of daily observations for SO_2, suspended particles, and dark matter. As explanatory variables, we have included functions of per capita GDP in the country where the site is located, characteristics of the site and city, and a time trend. We used the Summers and Heston (1991) data for per capita GDP, which attempt to measure output in relation to a common set of international prices. Initially we allowed the coefficient on per capita GDP to vary across income ranges by including a dummy variable in our regressions for each $2,000 interval of per capita GDP. These relatively unrestricted regressions suggested that a cubic function of per capita GDP would fit the data fairly well. The cubic equations are the main focus of our subsequent analysis.[9]

In the equation for concentrations of SO_2, we included dummy variables for the location within the city (central city or suburban) and for the land use of the area near the testing site (industrial, commercial, or residential). We also included a dummy variable for the method of measurement (gas bubbler or otherwise). Another dummy indicated whether the city was located along a coastline or not (reflecting the disbursement properties of the local atmosphere). We included a variable for the population density of the city and a dummy variable for whether the city was located in a country ruled by a communist government.[10] Finally, a linear time trend was included to allow for the possibility that pollution has been abating (or worsening) worldwide, in response to increased global awareness or for other reasons.[11]

The regressions for suspended particles and dark matter included a similar set of right-hand-side variables, except that we did not include a dummy variable for the method of monitoring dark matter, because all measurements were taken in the same way. Because dust is an important natural source of particulate matter, we included as an additional explanatory variable a dummy that indicates whether the measurement site is located within 100 miles of a desert.[12]

Some commentators have argued that a country's level of pollution might be directly related to its openness to international trade, perhaps because environmental regulations tend to a least common denominator. To test this hypothesis, we estimated one set of regressions in which we included the trade intensity of the country in which the site is located (ratio of the sum of exports and imports to GDP) as a separate determinant of the concentration of the air pollutants.[13]

For each pollutant, we estimated a random effects model, allowing for a component of the error term that is common to a given year's observations at different sites located in the same city.[14] We find that the variance of the common-to-the-city component of the estimated residuals is relatively large in comparison to the idiosyncratic (site-by-time) component, so that ordinary least squares would give inconsistent estimates of the standard errors of the regressions. We also calculated one set of estimates that allowed for fixed site effects. In other words, we included a separate dummy variable for each of the different sites in our various samples. The fixed effects were intended to capture the unobservable topographical and meteorological conditions at a site that might contribute to its ability to absorb or disburse pollution. Of course, when we included the fixed site effects, we dropped the dummy variables reflecting the location of the site within the city and the location of the city on a coastline or near a desert, as these influences were no longer separately identified. The model with fixed site effects provides an especially stringent test of the relationship between national income and pollution, inasmuch as it ignores all information contained in the cross-country variation in pollution levels and relies instead only on the variation in air quality that resulted at the various sites from changes in GDP during the twelve years of GEMS observations (and then only that part of the variation that cannot be explained by a common linear time trend).

1.3 Findings

The results of our various estimates of the random effects models for the three pollutants are given in tables 2.2–2.4. These regressions do not include the model with fixed site effects, which we discuss separately below.

Figure 2.2 displays, for the median of daily observations on each pollutant, the estimated coefficients on the dummy variables indicating whether a country's per capita GDP falls in the range from $2,000 to $3,999, from $4,000 to $5,999, and so on. The coefficient estimates have been plotted above the midpoint in the range, for example, above $3,000 for GDP in the range from $2,000 to $3,999. These coefficients should be interpreted as indicating the amount of extra pollution a country with a per capita GDP in a given range is likely to have, holding constant the values of other explanatory variables (site location, city population density, etc.), relative to a country with a per capita GDP in the range from zero to $2,000. The figure also shows the estimated amount of extra pollution that is associated with a given level of per capita GDP (relative to a country with a per capita GDP of $1,000) that comes from regressing the pollution concentrations on per capita GDP, per capita GDP-squared, per capita GDP-cubed, and the remaining explanatory variables. The figure shows that, in each case, the cubic functional form approximates well the shape of the relationship between pollution and GDP that is indicated by the less restrictive regressions.

Figure 2.3 depicts the estimated relationship between per capita GDP and SO_2, derived from the cubic equations, for both the 50th and 95th percentile of daily observations. For both measures, the concentration of SO_2 rises with per capita GDP at low levels of national income, falls with per capita GDP in the broad range between $5,000 and $14,000 (1985 U.S. dollars), and then levels off or perhaps begins to rise again.[15] The turning point in the predicted relationship for the median of daily observations comes at $4,107, while that for the 95th percentile observation occurs at $4,635. We estimate that a country with per capita GDP of $5,000 will have a 20 $\mu g\ m^{-3}$ greater concentration of SO_2 for the 95th percentile of its daily observations, as compared to a country with a per capita GDP of $1,000, all else equal. Table 2.2 indicates that the hypothesis that SO_2 pollution is unrelated to the level of GDP can be rejected at the .01% significance level in the regression for the median observation and at the

Table 2.2
The determinants of sulphur dioxide air pollution, random effects estimates (standard errors in parentheses)

	50th percentile			95th percentile		
Variable	(1)	(2)	(3)	(4)	(5)	(6)
Per capita GDP $2,000–$3,999	4.70 (3.94)	—	—	3.28 (13.67)	—	—
Per capita GDP $4,000–$5,999	6.43 (4.19)	—	—	23.45 (14.57)	—	—
Per capita GDP $6,000–$7,999	−4.15 (5.31)	—	—	−15.00 (18.42)	—	—
Per capita GDP $8,000–$9,999	3.91 (4.55)	—	—	20.80 (15.79)	—	—
Per capita GDP $10,000–$11,999	−9.33* (4.40)	—	—	−3.58 (15.26)	—	—
Per capita GDP $12,000–$13,999	−19.07* (5.74)	—	—	−3.58 (19.82)	—	—
Per capita GDP $14,000–15,999	−11.82* (5.11)	—	—	−24.62 (17.61)	—	—
Per capita GDP $16,000–$17,999	−10.28 (6.63)	—	—	−11.35 (22.34)	—	—
Per capita GDP ($1,000s)	—	7.14* (2.50)	11.22* (2.64)	—	12.02 (8.66)	22.18* (9.22)
Per capita GDP-squared	—	−1.12* (0.34)	−1.44* (0.34)	—	−1.68 (1.53)	−2.42* (1.18)
Per capita GDP-cubed	—	0.041* (0.013)	0.047* (0.013)	—	0.055 (0.043)	0.068 (0.044)
Coast	−8.68* (2.39)	−6.68* (2.32)	−5.73* (2.32)	−52.62* (8.17)	−46.79* (7.94)	−45.27* (8.03)

Central city	9.45*	8.94*	8.94*	35.42*	34.33*	35.31*
	(1.83)	(1.82)	(1.86)	(5.76)	(5.73)	(5.77)
Industrial	1.58	1.32	1.74	10.95	10.39	9.65
	(1.95)	(1.94)	(2.01)	(6.06)	(6.04)	(6.12)
Residential	−5.30*	−5.71*	−4.97*	−4.08	−5.45	−3.23
	(1.96)	(1.95)	(2.01)	(6.10)	(6.08)	(6.14)
Population density (10,000/sq. mi.)	5.54*	4.09	10.31*	41.74*	35.43*	49.81*
	(2.65)	(2.57)	(4.64)	(9.27)	(8.97)	(16.30)
Year	−1.69*	−1.79*	−1.77*	−5.38*	−5.32*	−5.12*
	(0.36)	(0.34)	(0.35)	(1.21)	(1.18)	(1.22)
Communist	11.59*	11.47*	12.64*	88.05*	88.04*	90.77*
	(3.88)	(3.83)	(3.86)	(13.47)	(13.32)	(13.61)
Trade intensity	—	—	−15.47*	—	—	−40.96*
			(4.38)			(15.36)
p-value for all GDP variables	.0001	.0001	.0001	.06	.07	.007
Per capita GDP at which pollution reaches peak	—	$4,107	$5,257	—	$4,635	$6,182
		(1,327)	(1,179)		(3,309)	(2,963)
σ_ε^2	556	554	579	5,593	5,575	5,555
σ_α^2	368	378	323	5,431	5,541	5,232
R^2	.158	.150	.166	.132	.125	.138

Notes: Equations also include an intercept, a dummy to indicate that the type of area is unknown, and a dummy to indicate that the measurement device is a gas bubbler. σ_α^2 is the estimated variance of the common-to city component of the residuals, and σ_ε^2 is the estimated variance of the idiosyncratic component of the residual. Sample size is 1,370 for columns 1, 2, 4, and 5; sample size is 1,301 for columns 3 and 6.

*Statistically significant at .05 level for a two-tailed t-test.

Table 2.3
The determinants of dark matter pollution, random effects estimates (standard errors in parentheses)

	50th percentile			95th percentile		
Variable	(1)	(2)	(3)	(4)	(5)	(6)
Per capita GDP $2,000–$3,999	50.50* (11.77)	—	—	99.21* (31.77)	—	—
Per capita GDP $4,000–$5,999	58.25* (12.63)	—	—	118.05* (33.99)	—	—
Per capita GDP $6,000–$7,999	43.49* (13.10)	—	—	111.74* (35.23)	—	—
Per capita GDP $8,000–$9,999	21.26 (13.07)	—	—	39.85 (35.12)	—	—
Per capita GDP $10,000–$11,999	22.27 (13.04)	—	—	30.27 (35.17)	—	—
Per capita GDP $12,000–$13,999	27.29 (28.64)	—	—	16.10 (74.95)	—	—
Per capita GDP ($1,000s)	—	79.33* (13.04)	30.52 (16.79)	—	173.84* (34.32)	113.19* (47.45)
Per capita GDP-squared	—	−12.38* (2.05)	−5.08* (2.54)	—	−25.62* (5.38)	−16.45* (7.16)
Per capita GDP-cubed	—	0.56* (0.10)	0.233 (0.121)	—	1.09* (0.26)	0.68* (0.34)
Desert	40.19* (8.61)	42.11* (8.49)	−10.12 (14.21)	113.03* (23.24)	118.14* (22.67)	44.27* (41.85)
Coast	−21.29 (4.94)	−21.75* (4.55)	−17.68* (4.52)	−35.85* (13.00)	−41.44* (11.87)	−33.46* (12.50)

Central city	9.55*	8.26*	10.95*	32.41*	20.32*	21.44*
	(4.05)	(3.96)	(3.86)	(9.38)	(9.18)	(9.50)
Industrial	0.25	−0.55	−0.13	−5.95	−6.37	−5.92
	(4.23)	(4.18)	(4.06)	(9.62)	(9.51)	(9.74)
Residential	−10.60*	−11.56*	−7.09*	−21.64*	−22.51*	−15.20
	(3.98)	(3.93)	(3.87)	(9.12)	(9.01)	(9.34)
Population density (10,000/sq. mi.)	1.32*	1.35*	2.92*	0.70	0.94	4.75
	(0.37)	(0.36)	(1.17)	(0.98)	(0.95)	(3.17)
Year	−0.26	−0.60	−0.59	0.41	−0.15	1.27
	(0.58)	(0.56)	(0.58)	(1.51)	(1.45)	(1.59)
Communist	−20.44*	−20.93*	−14.44	−0.98	−9.73	7.56
	(7.91)	(7.54)	(8.51)	(20.87)	(19.78)	(23.39)
Trade intensity	—	—	−6.57	—	—	−12.05
			(6.35)			(17.84)
p-value for all GDP variables	.0001	.0001	.0001	.0001	.0001	.0001
Per capita GDP at which pollution reaches peak	—	$4,721	$4,240	—	$4,970	$4.971
		(771)	(2,180)		(973)	(2,105)
σ_ε^2	598	953	864	4,865	4,828	4,772
σ_α^2	192	186	166	2,183	2,040	2,108
R^2	.345	.352	.210	.315	.315	.221

Notes: Equations also include an intercept and a dummy to indicate that the type of area is unknown. Sample size is 506 for columns 1, 2, 4, and 5; sample size is 457 for columns 3 and 6.

*Statistically significant at .05 level for a two-tailed t-test.

Table 2.4
The determinants for suspended particles pollution, random effects estimates (standard errors in parentheses)

	50th percentile			95th percentile		
Variable	(1)	(2)	(3)	(4)	(5)	(6)
Per capita GDP $2,000–$3,999	−102.4* (11.9)	—	—	−191.4* (25.4)	—	—
Per capita GDP $4,000–$5,999	−129.7* (13.5)	—	—	−247.4* (29.0)	—	—
Per capita GDP $6,000–$7,999	−101.9* (31.8)	—	—	−134.2 (69.2)	—	—
Per capita GDP $8,000–$9,999	−201.2* (22.4)	—	—	−348.8* (47.1)	—	—
Per capita GDP $10,000–$11,999	−221.1* (13.0)	—	—	−425.0* (27.7)	—	—
Per capita GDP $12,000–$13,999	−187.9* (14.6)	—	—	−368.1* (31.6)	—	—
Per capita GDP $14,000–15,999	−183.1* (12.5)	—	—	−366.2* (27.1)	—	—
Per capita GDP $16,000–$17,999	−184.5 (15.5)	—	—	−381.2* (32.9)	—	—
Per capita GDP ($1,000s)	—	−71.97* (8.02)	−72.54* (8.49)	—	−144.31* (17.81)	−146.48* (17.74)
Per capita GDP-squared	—	6.03* (1.08)	5.81* (1.10)	—	12.65* (2.28)	12.31* (2.28)
Per capita GDP-cubed	—	−0.157* (0.043)	−0.143* (0.040)	—	−0.353* (0.085)	−0.328* (0.084)
Desert	189.6* (19.0)	213.3* (18.6)	289.4* (34.3)	354.7* (40.7)	409.8* (39.6)	489.5* (68.9)

Coast	0.42	4.47	2.90	−9.78	0.22	−4.39
	(7.73)	(7.58)	(7.41)	(16.41)	(16.01)	(15.43)
Central city	11.11*	12.99*	14.76*	32.52*	36.31*	39.11*
	(5.24)	(5.20)	(4.28)	(10.47)	(10.40)	(10.46)
Industrial	13.73*	15.23*	11.15	44.28*	47.55*	40.48*
	(5.79)	(5.77)	(5.91)	(11.55)	(11.49)	(11.66)
Residential	−12.17*	−9.67*	−9.45	−1.19	3.83	2.02
	(5.83)	(4.78)	(5.90)	(11.62)	(11.51)	(11.66)
Population density	5.20	−4.64	−17.55	−41.38	−43.97*	−74.43*
(10,000/sq. mi.)	(9.99)	(9.64)	(12.63)	(21.84)	(20.95)	(26.92)
Year	−2.06	−2.27*	−2.26*	−1.41	−1.65	−1.27
	(1.20)	(1.14)	(1.15)	(2.58)	(2.43)	(2.41)
Communist	90.52*	108.37*	107.81*	221.51*	256.46*	251.12*
	(13.21)	(12.65)	(12.54)	(28.68)	(27.28)	(26.52)
Trade intensity	—	—	−12.39	—	—	6.49
			(15.17)			(31.23)
p-value for all GDP variables	.0001	.0001	.0001	.0001	.0001	.0001
σ_ε^2	3,379	3,350	3,482	12,950	12,793	13,085
σ_α^2	3,353	3,754	3,073	18,043	17,218	14,894
R^2	.581	.577	.574	.569	.582	.590

Notes: Equations also include an intercept, a dummy to indicate the type of area unknown, and two dummies to indicate the kind of instrument used to measure suspended particulate matter. Sample size is 1,021 for columns 1, 2, 4, and 5; sample size is 971 for columns 3 and 6.

*Statistically significant at .05 level for a two-tailed t-test.

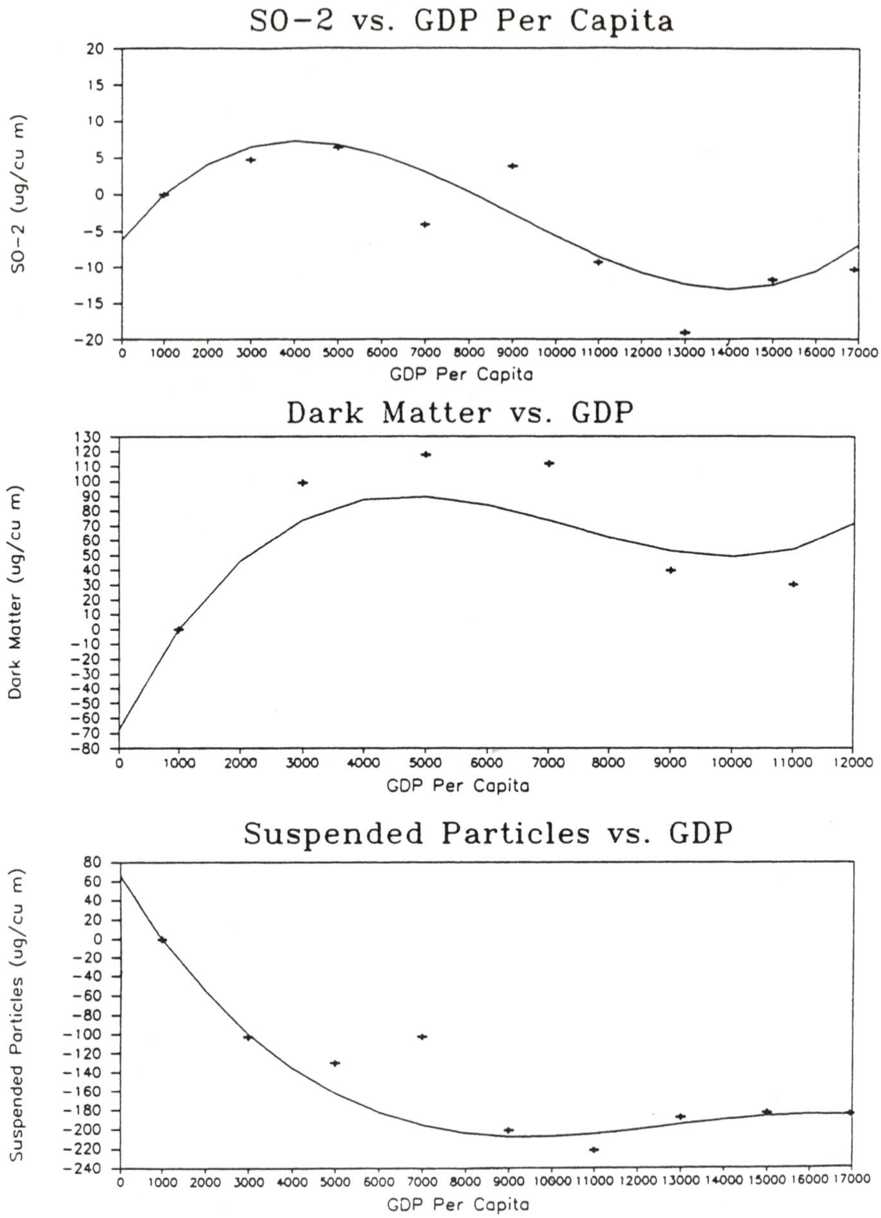

Figure 2.2
Fitted cubic and unrestricted dummies

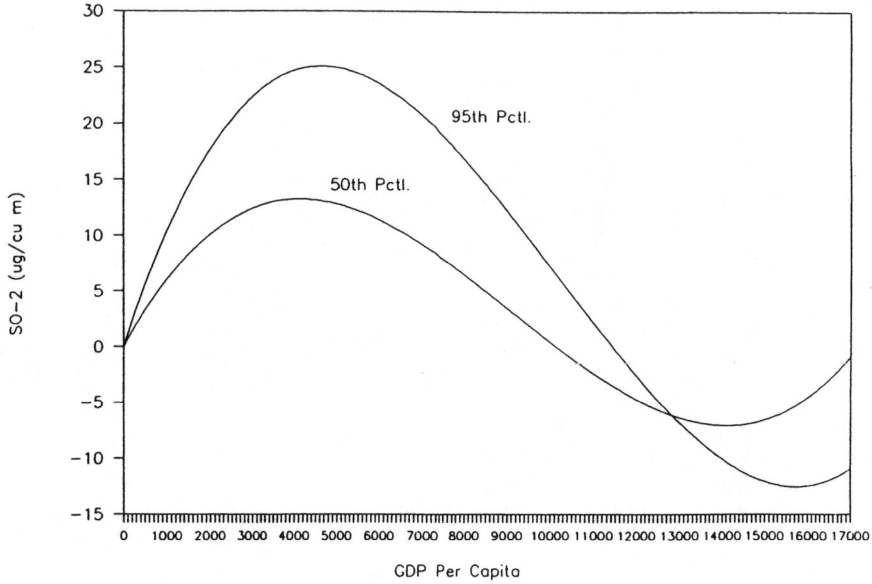

Figure 2.3
SO_2 vs. GDP per capita

7% level in the regression for the 95th percentile observation (see columns 2 and 5).

Table 2.2 reveals that several other variables contribute significantly to the cross-city variation in concentrations of SO_2. For example, cities located on a coastline are estimated to have lesser concentrations of SO_2: 6.68 $\mu g\ m^{-3}$ lower for the median of daily observations and 46.79 $\mu g\ m^{-3}$ lower for the 95th percentile observation. Concentrations of SO_2 are higher in the center city than in the suburbs, lower in residential areas than in commercial areas, and higher in industrial areas than in commercial areas (although this effect is not statistically significant at conventional significance levels). More densely populated cities suffer greater concentrations of SO_2, all else equal. We also find that SO_2 pollution has been significantly greater in cities located in communist-ruled countries. Finally, we note that SO_2 levels have been trending downward in our sample of cities even after controlling for the effects of income and other variables. The downward trend may reflect an increasing global awareness of the health problems associated with SO_2, and the expanding efforts that are being made worldwide to limit sulfur emissions.

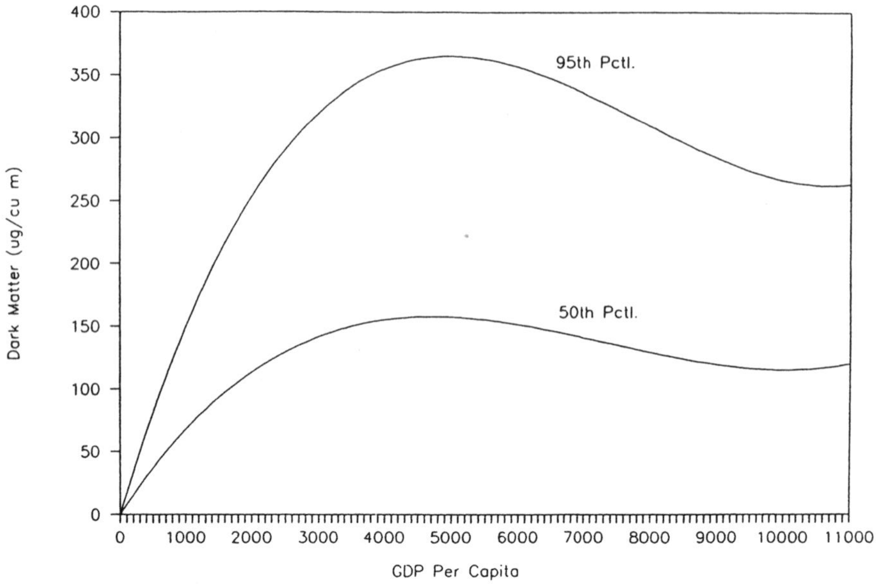

Figure 2.4
Dark matter vs. GDP per capita

Columns 3 and 6 of table 2.2 present estimates of a model for SO_2 determination that includes trade intensity as an additional explanatory variable. Contrary to the fears of some environmentalists, we find that SO_2 levels are significantly *lower* in cities located in countries that conduct a great deal of trade (relative to their GDP). We have no good economic explanation for this finding.

Figure 2.4 depicts the estimated (cubic) relationship between dark matter and per capita GDP for the median and 95th percentile of daily observations. Apparently the nature of the relationship is much the same as for SO_2. The concentration of smoke in the air rises with per capita GDP at low levels of income, peaks at around $5,000 (1985 U.S. dollars), and falls with GDP at higher income levels until it eventually levels off. We see in columns 2 and 5 of table 2.3 that the three GDP variables are jointly significant in the determination of dark matter pollution at the .01% significance level. Moreover, the size of the estimated effects are quite large. We estimate that a country with a per capita GDP of $5,000 will have a higher concentration of smoke by about 90 $\mu g\ m^{-3}$ in its median of daily observations and 220 $\mu g\ m^{-3}$ in its 95th percentile observation, compared to one with a per capita GDP of $1,000. Recall that the WHO recommends that

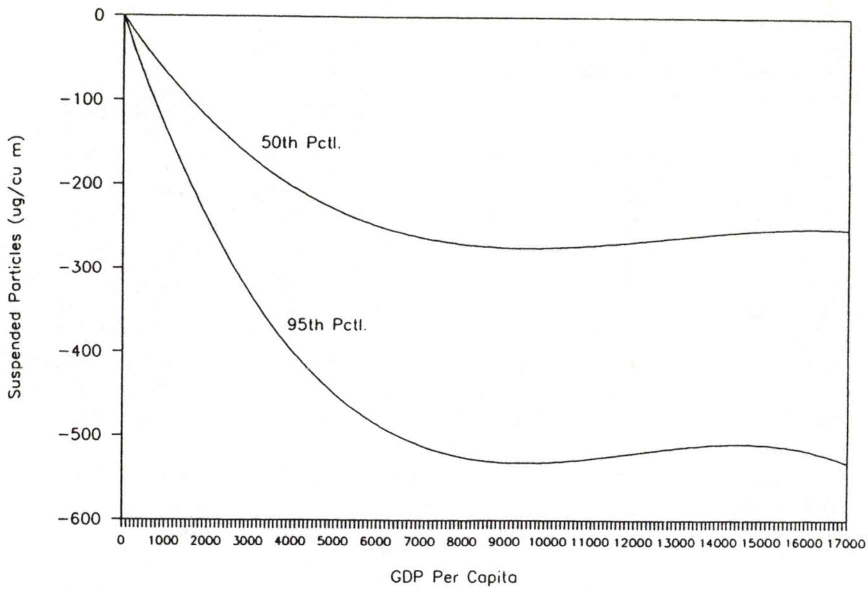

Figure 2.5
Suspended particles vs. GDP per capita

concentrations of smoke not exceed 50–60 $\mu g\ m^{-3}$ for the mean observation and 100–150 $\mu g\ m^{-3}$ for the 98th percentile observation.

Not surprisingly, the dummy variable indicating proximity to a desert has a positive and significant coefficient in the regressions explaining concentrations of dark matter. A location on a coast reduces a city's concentration of this type of pollution, and again the effect is statistically significant. We find that smoke pollution levels are greater in center cities than in suburbs, and smaller in residential areas than in commercial areas. Also, dark matter, like SO_2 rises with population density, although this effect is significant only in the regression for the median of daily observations. Finally, there appears to be neither a global trend in this type of pollution (once the upward movement in world incomes has been accounted for) nor a significant association with trade intensity.

Unlike the other two pollutants, the mass of suspended particles in the air appears to fall in response to increases in per capita GDP at low levels of economic development (see figure 2.5). This relationship continues until per capita GDP reaches about $9,000, whereupon economic growth has no further effect on the concentration of suspended particles. Again, the estimated effects are large in comparison to the WHO guidelines, and again

Table 2.5
Random effects estimates of the determinants of air pollution including fixed site effects (standard errors in parentheses)

	SO_2		Dark matter		Suspended particles	
Variable	50 pctl	95 pctl	50 pctl	95 pctl	50 pctl	95 pctl
Per capita GDP ($1,000s)	12.54* (4.69)	−8.28 (15.11)	24.35 (17.70)	77.89 (49.71)	63.44* (13.94)	142.18* (30.30)
Per capita GDP-squard	−1.74* (0.52)	0.10 (1.67)	−4.15 (2.73)	−12.10 (7.66)	−2.84 (1.49)	−6.21 (3.23)
Per capita GDP-cubed	0.05* (.02)	−0.00 (.06)	0.19 (0.13)	0.51 (0.36)	0.04 (0.05)	0.07 (0.11)
Year	−1.05* (0.28)	−3.51* (0.90)	−0.91* (0.42)	−1.12 (1.17)	−3.60* (0.82)	−5.58* (1.77)
Number of site dummies	239	239	87	87	161	161
p-value for GDP variables	0.0001	0.118	0.479	0.250	0.0001	0.0001
σ_ϵ^2	161	1,951	141	1,070	919	3679
σ_z^2	97	982	93	755	512	2473
R^2	0.76	0.77	0.87	0.82	0.91	0.91

Notes: Sample size is 1,370 for SO_2, 506 for dark matter and 1,021 for suspended particles. The SO_2 equations also include a dummy for the measuring device, and the suspended particles equations include two dummies for measuring device.
*Statistically significant at .05 level for a two-tailed t-test.

the three GDP variables are jointly significant in the determination of this measure of air quality.

As with dark matter, cities situated near to a desert are likely to experience higher concentrations of suspended particles than cities located elsewhere. This effect is both quantitatively large and highly significant. The coefficients on the communist dummy, the center-city dummy, and the industrial-area dummy all are positive and statistically significant in the regressions for both the median and 95th percentile of daily observations. The global trend in suspended particle pollution apparently has been downward, although the coefficient on the year variable is statistically significant only in the regressions for the median of daily observations. Finally, a country's trade intensity has a small and statistically insignificant effect on this form of pollution.

Table 2.5 reports the estimated coefficients from a random effects model for each type of pollutant that also allows for fixed site effects. The numbers of site dummy variables that were included in the various regressions are shown in the table. These estimates of the relationship between per

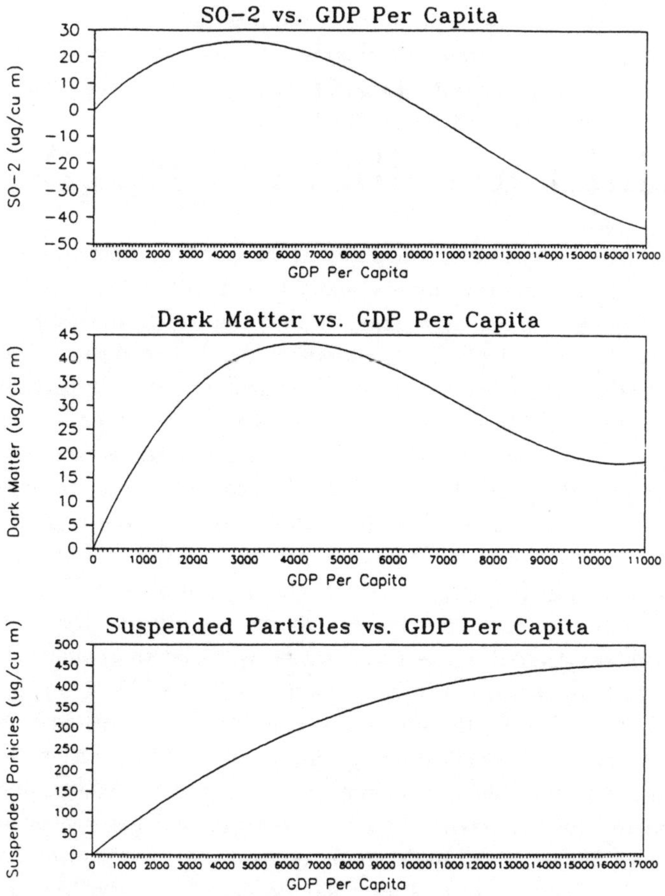

Figure 2.6
Fixed effects estimates—50th percentile

capita GDP and the various measures of air quality rely only on the covariation between GDP and concentrations of the pollutants over time within the individual sites, and not on the cross-country variation in pollution and GDP at a given moment in time. The estimated relationships for the median of daily observations of SO_2 and dark matter hold up remarkably well (see figure 2.6). In each case, the data continue to indicate an inverted U-shaped relationship between pollution and national income, with peak levels of pollution occurring for per capita incomes in the range from $4,000 to $5,000. Only the estimated coefficients from the fixed site effects model for suspended particles suggest a different relationship between per capita GDP and concentrations of the pollutant than is found in the regressions without site effects. In this case, the estimation indicates a monotonically increasing relationship between particulate pollution and national output in the sample range of output levels.

1.4 Implications for Mexico

Unfortunately, Mexico has not participated in the GEMS project and reliable measures of its air pollution are not available (U.S. GAO, 1991b). Thus predictions for Mexico must be inferred from relationships that hold in other countries at similar stages of development. Surely the available evidence suggests that air quality has deteriorated with economic growth in Mexico (U.S. GAO, 1991b). Our estimates indicate that this experience is common in poor countries, but that the positive association between two pollutants and economic output ceases when the typical country reaches a per capita income level of about $5,000 (1985 U.S. dollars). We note that Summers and Heston (1991) put Mexico's per capita GDP in 1988 (adjusted to reflect the purchasing power of its currency) at $4,996. Thus we might expect that further growth in Mexico, as may result from a free trade agreement with the United States and Canada, will lead the country to intensify its efforts to alleviate its environmental problems.

Recent measures taken by the government of Mexico suggest that the country already may have reached the turning point in terms of air pollution. In the last year, the Salinas government has reduced the lead content of petrol, ordered several power stations to burn natural gas instead of sulfur-generating fuel oil, and shut down oil refineries and private firms that were found to be major sources of air pollution (The *Economist*, May 18, 1991). Also, new cars are being fitted with catalytic convertors, a new fleet of cleaner buses has been introduced, and drivers have been banned from using their cars in Mexico City one day each week. To beef up enforcement, the budget of the environmental protection ministry has been increased sevenfold (*New York Times*, Sept. 22, 1991). Further growth may enable the government to implement fully its planned $2.5 billion, four-year program to clean up Mexico City.

2 Pollution Abatement Costs and the Pattern of U.S.-Mexico Investment and Trade

A main source of concern about a NAFTA is that it will enable firms to circumvent U.S. environmental protection laws. If the costs of meeting pollution controls are high in the United States and low or negligible in Mexico, then the asymmetry in standards or enforcement efforts can create a competitive advantage for Mexican producers and can motivate U.S. firms to relocate their production facilities south of the border. In these circumstances, liberalization of trade and investment flows can strengthen the incentives for "environmental dumping."

A number of authors, including Pethig (1976), Siebert (1977), Yohe (1979), and McGuire (1982), have studied the theoretical relationship between environmental regulations and the pattern of trade. They find that strict environmental standards or costly controls weaken a country's competitive position in pollution-intensive industries and diminish its exports (or increase its imports) of the product of such sectors. Countries that fail to regulate industrial pollution increase their specialization in activities that damage the environment. McGuire has extended these results to include direct foreign investment: controls cause firms active in the pollution-intensive industry to relocate their activities to the less regulated countries.

While these theoretical predictions are plausible and intuitive, they have found little support in previous empirical studies of trade and investment patterns. For example, Tobey (1990) has tested the hypothesis that environmental regulations have altered the pattern of trade in goods produced by "dirty" industries. He finds that a qualitative variable describing the stringency of environmental controls in twenty-three countries fails to contribute to the determination of their net exports of the five most pollution-intensive commodities. Similarly, Walter (1982) and Leonard (1988) conclude that there is little evidence that pollution abatement costs have influenced the location decisions of multinational firms. Apparently, the cross-country variation in the costs of meeting environmental controls is not so large as to be a major factor in the determination of nations' comparative advantages.

Our purpose in this section is to address this issue in connection with the pattern of U.S. imports from Mexico and the pattern of U.S. foreign investments in Mexico. There is some evidence from a GAO survey suggesting that a few American furniture manufacturers may have moved their operations to Mexico in response to the California's tightening of air pollution control standards for paint coatings and solvents (U.S. GAO, 1991c). But the question remains as to whether the overall sectoral pattern of U.S. economic relations with Mexico has been meaningfully affected by the higher cost of pollution abatement in the United States. If the pattern of specialization has been so influenced, then the composition effect of a further liberalization of trade and investment may be damaging to the environment.

Using data from the Bureau of Census's 1988 survey of pollution abatement costs in American industries (U.S. DOC, 1988), we have conducted three sets of tests. We have studied the 1987 pattern of U.S. imports from Mexico in three-digit SIC manufacturing industries, the pattern of 1987 U.S. imports from Mexico that have entered the country under the offshore assembly provisions (again at the three-digit SIC level), and the sectoral pattern of value added by maquiladora plants in (approximately) two-digit industry categories. In each case we have investigated whether pollution abatement costs in the United States help to explain the pattern of Mexican specialization and trade.

Our estimates of the determinants of the pattern of manufactured imports from Mexico are recorded in the first two columns of table 2.6. We use the ratio of 1987 U.S. imports from Mexico to total U.S. shipments in the same industry as the dependent variable. The explanatory variables include factor shares (reflecting the intensity of use of the various factors by the different industries; see Harkness [1978]), the U.S. effective tariff rate on imports of goods in the industry, and the ratio of pollution abatement costs (operating expenses) to total value added in the U.S. industry.[16,17] We also report another regression that includes the average injury rate in the industry as an additional independent variable. As firm outlays for worker compensation insurance are roughly proportional to injury rates (Krueger and Burton, 1990), the injury variable proxies for one (large) component of the cost to American manufacturing firms of U.S. labor protection laws.

We computed the factor shares as follows. We took the payroll expenses in an industry to represent a combined compensation for unskilled or "raw" labor and human capital. Payments to unskilled labor were defined as the product of the number of workers in the industry and the economywide average yearly income of workers in manufacturing with less than a high school education. We formed a share by dividing this amount by value added, and considered the remaining part of the total labor share to represent the payment to human capital.[18] Finally, we calculated the share of capital in value added as the difference between one and the total payroll share.[19]

Factor intensities figure prominently in the determination of the pattern of U.S. imports from Mexico. The ratio of imports to total U.S. shipments is smaller in industries that are highly intensive in their use of human or physical capital. This means, of course, that Mexico exports to the United

Table 2.6
The determinants of the pattern of U.S. imports from Mexico and of value added by maquiladora

Independent variables	Total U.S. imports from Mexico as fraction of U.S. shipments		Mexican value added in 807 imports as fraction of U.S. value added		Maquiladora value added as fraction of U.S. value added	
	(1)	(2)	(3)	(4)	(5)	(6)
Constant	.028*	−.027*	.019*	.021*	.010	.015*
	(.008)	(.009)	(.006)	(.007)	(.007)	(.007)
Human capital share	−.053*	−.053*	−.016	−.015	−.015	−.016
	(.016)	(.016)	(.010)	(.010)	(.012)	(.011)
Physical capital share	−.024*	−.023*	−.026*	−.027*	−.011	−.016
	(.010)	(.011)	(.009)	(.010)	(.010)	(.011)
Pollution abatement cost as fraction of U.S. industry value added	.014	.012	−.165*	−.151*	−.085	−.077
	(.060)	(.061)	(.073)	(.074)	(.098)	(.090)
Tariff rate	−.002	−.001	—	—	—	—
	(.028)	(.029)				
Injury rate	—	.005	—	−.001	—	−.028
		(.020)		(.016)		(.020)
R^2	.127	.127	.095	.095	.236	.392
Sample size	135	135	136	136	19	19
Mean of dependent variable	.0069	.0069	.0022	.0022	.0012	.0012

Notes: Standard errors are in parentheses. Columns (1) and (2) are OLS estimates. Columns (3), (4), (5), and (6) are maximum likely estimates of Tobit models. For the Tobit models, we calculated the reported values for R^2 as $1 - \sigma_\varepsilon^2/\sigma_0^2$, where σ_ε^2 denotes the estimated variance of the error from the Tobit model and σ_0^2 is the estimated variance of the residual from a Tobit estimation that includes only a constant on the right-hand side.
*Indicates statistically significant at .05 level.

States goods that have a relatively high share of unskilled labor in total factor cost. The coefficients on the physical and human capital variables both are statistically significant at the 5 percent level, but the latter coefficient is quantitatively much larger. We estimate that a 10 percentage point increase in the share of human capital reduces the ratio of imports to shipments by 0.52 percentage points, while a 10 percentage point increase in the share of physical capital lowers the import ratio by only 0.24 percentage points. Note that the mean ratio of imports to shipments across all manufacturing industries is 0.69%.

We estimate that the import ratio rises with the share of pollution abatement costs in U.S. industry value added, as would be predicted by a model of environmental dumping. However, the impact of these regulatory costs is both quantitatively small and statistically insignificant. Consider for example an industry that has the mean ratio of pollution abatement costs to industry value added and another that has a ratio that is two standard deviations higher. We estimate that the latter industry will have a greater ratio of imports to U.S. shipments by about 0.05%, which is less than .05 of a standard deviation in the import variable. This finding can be understood from the fact that pollution abatement costs average only 1.38% of value added across all manufacturing industries and rise to only 4.85% in an industry that is two standard deviations above the mean. The implied variation in competitiveness is small in comparison with that which arises from cross-industry variations in labor costs, for example.

We note that the injury rate has a positive coefficient when it is included in the import equation, but this variable too has a very small and statistically insignificant effect. Finally, the coefficient on the tariff variable has the theoretically predicted negative sign (imports are smaller in industries with high effective tariff rates), but also is not significant.[20]

We turn next to the determinants of the pattern of U.S. imports from Mexico under the offshore assembly provision (i.e., import category 807.00 in the old TSUSA tariff schedule). U.S. trade law provides for duty-free reentry of American-made components embodied in imported final goods. In cases where intermediate products are exported for further processing or assembly abroad, the applicable tariff rate applies only to the foreign value added. Nearly 44% of the value of Mexican exports to the United States qualified for this customs treatment in 1987 (Schoepfle, 1991). We study these imports separately, because much of the output by maquiladora plants enters the United States in this manner, and maquiladoras are the source of most of the item 807.00 U.S. imports from Mexico (Schoepfle,

1991). Thus the sectoral pattern of item 807.00 imports gives us an idea as to the pattern of maquiladora activity.

The middle two columns of table 2.6 report estimates of an equation for the ratio of the Mexican value added in imports entering under the 807.00 code in 1987 to the total value added by the U.S. industry. We would expect this variable to be high in industries where maquiladoras are especially active, that is those in which Mexico enjoys a competitive advantage. The independent variables in these equations are the same as before, namely the factor shares, the share of pollution abatement costs in U.S. industry value added, and in one set of estimates, the industry injury rate. The tariff variable was omitted from these regressions because our effective tariff rate applies to all imports from Mexico, and does not reflect the average tariff paid on imports that entered under the offshore assembly provision. We use a Tobit model to estimate these equations in view of the fact that item 807.00 imports are zero in 58 of the 136 industry categories. Because the import share cannot be negative, a censored regression model is appropriate.

The foreign content of U.S. item 807.00 imports from Mexico is highest in relation to total value added in the corresponding U.S. industry in sectors that make relatively intensive use of unskilled labor. This is not surprising, as many U.S. manufacturers attempt to outsource to maquiladora operations the most unskilled-labor-intensive phases of the production process. We find a negative association between the Mexican content of item 807.00 imports as a fraction of total U.S. industry value added and both the human capital share and the physical capital share in U.S. industry costs. The coefficient on the physical capital variable is estimated to be nearly twice as large in absolute value as that on the human capital variable (reversing the ordering found for total imports from Mexico), and the former coefficient is statistically significant at the 5% level, whereas the latter is statistically significant at only the 10% level.

Again, we fail to find a significant positive relationship between the size of pollution abatement costs (as a fraction of value added) in the U.S. manufacturing industry and the scale of sectoral activity in Mexico. In fact, the foreign content of item 807.00 imports from Mexico appears to be *lower* in relation to the size of the U.S. industry in sectors where U.S. pollution abatement costs are relatively high. The negative coefficient on the abatement cost variable is found to be statistically significant at the 5% level, although this may of course reflect a spurious correlation between these costs and some omitted variable. When the U.S. injury rate is included in the equation for item 807.00 imports, the estimated coefficient on this variable is also negative. This would imply that relatively little Mexican assembly activity takes place in those industries where the cost to U.S. employers of workers' compensation insurance and other accident-related costs are especially high. However, in this case, the estimated coefficient is not significantly different from zero, so we cannot reject the hypothesis that the association between injury rates and the pattern of Mexican assembly operations is nil.

The final set of estimates recorded in table 2.6 relate to the activity of Mexican maquiladoras. The Instituto Nacional de Estadistica Geografia E Informatica (INEGA) has surveyed all maquiladoras on the government's list of in-bond producers. Their publication, *Estadistica de la Industria Maquiladora de Exportacion, 1978–1988,* provides data on value added by maquiladoras in eleven different manufacturing industries. We developed a concordance of the available data to a two-digit SIC basis and sought to explain the ratio in 1987 of value added by maquiladoras to value added in the corresponding U.S. industry.[21] The explanatory variables are defined as before, except that now we calculate factor shares and pollution abatement costs as a fraction of value added at the two-digit SIC level.

The estimated coefficients from the models of maquiladora activity confirm our findings for total U.S. imports from Mexico and for imports under tariff item 807.00. Again we find that Mexican competitive advantage derives from an abundance of unskilled labor, and that value added by maquiladoras declines in relation to value added in the United States the greater are the shares of human and physical capital in industry cost. Although neither coefficient has been estimated precisely enough to allow for a clear rejection of the hypothesis that the associations are zero, the magnitudes of the coefficients are very much in line with what we have found before. Also, we find no evidence in support of the hypothesis that U.S. regulatory costs contribute to the explanation of the pattern of maquiladora activity. Neither the coefficient on the abatement cost variable nor that on the injury rate variable has the (positive) sign that one would expect if American firms are investing in maquiladora plants primarily to avoid the high costs of environmental and labor protection laws at home. Evidently, the costs involved in complying with these laws are small in relation to the other components of total cost that determine whether it is profitable to operate in the United States or Mexico.

3 Resource Reallocation: Implications for Pollution

Our findings in section 2 suggest that relative factor supplies govern the pattern of trade between Mexico and its neighbors to the North. We might expect, therefore, that trade liberalization will stimulate Mexican production in unskilled-labor-intensive industries, while the United States and Canada will shift resources into sectors that make relatively heavy use of capital and skilled labor. The removal by Mexico of barriers to direct foreign investment can have the opposite effect on international patterns of specialization, if foreign firms bring with them the factors that are scarce in Mexico. Then local production may expand in (moderately) capital and skilled-labor-intensive sectors. The question that arises is, what are the environmental implications of these potential resource reallocations?

To answer this question fully, we need several pieces of information. First, we need to know which sectors will expand in each country, and by how much. Second, we need to know the pollution intensities of the various industries. Finally, we must know how NAFTA will affect the production technologies used in each location, so as to gauge any changes in pollution generated per unit of output. Estimates of NAFTA impacts on the production structure in each country are available from computational modeling exercises. Brown, Deardorff, and Stern (1991), for example, have predicted resource movements for several different scenarios of policy change under a NAFTA. Unfortunately, the remaining informational requirements pose more serious difficulties. Concerning the pollution generated by different industries, the United States collects data only on releases of *toxic waste* (and that of questionable quality), while Mexico collects no such data whatsoever. And although our findings in section 1 suggest that production techniques might well change in response to a trade agreement that generates economic growth in Mexico, it is difficult to assess how these changes will be distributed across industries.

In this section we draw upon the detailed estimates of Brown, Deardorff, and Stern (BDS) to derive some possible environmental implications of the resource reallocations that would result from a NAFTA. After describing the BDS modeling exercise, we turn to two issues. First, we discuss the model's predictions about each country's demand for the services of utilities. Second, we use the information available in the U.S. EPA's *Toxic Resources Inventory* to analyze how a NAFTA might affect releases of hazardous waste by the manufacturing sectors in the three partner countries.

The BDS estimates are based on a computable general equilibrium model of the economic interactions between the United States, Canada, Mexico, a group of thirty-one other major trading nations, and an abbreviated fifth region comprising the rest of the world. The model aggregates production into twenty-three categories of tradable goods and six categories of non-tradable goods and services. The industries are treated either as perfectly competitive or monopolistically competitive, with the latter set exhibiting economies of scale. Output in each sector is produced from intermediate inputs and an aggregate of capital and labor. The authors allow for varying degrees of substitution between capital and labor in the different sectors, but treat labor as a homogeneous input. The latter assumption is unfortunate in view of our finding in section 2 that human capital endowments play a central role in determining the bilateral trade pattern between the United States and Mexico.

Since it is not clear what policy measures will be included in a NAFTA, BDS explore a number of alternatives. In one scenario they assume the removal of all bilateral tariffs between the United States, Canada, and Mexico, and an easing of U.S. quantitative restrictions that generates a 25% increase in U.S. imports of agricultural products, food, textiles, and apparel from Mexico. In a second scenario they allow for these same forms of trade liberalization and also a relaxation of restrictions on direct foreign investment in Mexico. The liberalization of investment is assumed to result in an (exogenous) 10% increase in Mexico's capital stock. It should be noted that in both of these cases, the estimated impacts include not only the removal of existing barriers between Mexico and its trade partners, but also the ultimate implementation of the policy changes that comprise the already concluded Canada-U.S. free trade agreement.

It is well known that many pollutants, such as sulfur dioxide, nitric oxide, nitrogen dioxide, and carbon dioxide, are by-products of electricity generation, especially when fossil fuels are burned. Thus an important determinant of the net effect of trade liberalization on air pollution will be the induced change in the demand for electricity. Unfortunately, the disaggregation in the BDS model does not allow us to identify the likely impacts of a NAFTA on electricity use, inasmuch as the model treats electricity as a component of the broader category of utilities. It is interesting to note, nonetheless, that BDS predict a *decline* of 0.56% in output by the Mexican utilities sector in response to a hypothetical agreement involving an elimination of tariffs and an increase in U.S. import quotas. This prediction can be understood from the fact that the scenario generates output contractions in ten of twenty-one Mexican manufacturing sectors, and expansions are anticipated primarily in labor-intensive industries such as food, textiles, apparel, leather products, and footwear, which presumably are not the sectors that use energy most intensively. But just as Mexico will shift resources into activities that require relatively little energy input, the United States and Canada may be expected to do the opposite. The model predicts modest increases of 0.07 percent and 0.09 percent, respectively, in production by utilities in the United States and Canada.

Quite different conclusions emerge from the scenario that attempts to capture the effects of a potential liberalization of investment flows. The exogenous 10% increase in the Mexican capital stock that is taken to be the outgrowth of an easing of restrictions on foreign investment effects an expansion of every manufacturing industry there, with the implication that demand for utilities must rise. The experiment generates an increase in utilities output in Mexico of 9.31%. Presumably, air quality would deteriorate in this case, unless the associated income growth gave rise to political demands for more stringent standards and tougher enforcement.

We turn next to toxic waste. Our focus on this form of pollution is primarily a reflection of data availability. As far as we know, this is the only type of pollution for which data on releases are collected at the firm level. U.S. law requires all manufacturing firms with ten or more employees that use at least 10,000 pounds of one or more of over 300 chemicals to report their annual chemical releases to the EPA. Lines of business are recorded along with information on releases, enabling aggregation of the data to the industry level.

Several pitfalls in the use of the data contained in the Toxic Release Inventory (TRI) should be noted.[22] First, since the report reflects releases rather than exposures, it cannot reflect the great differences that exist in the rates at which different chemicals are dispersed or transformed. Second, releases are measured only in terms of weight, and no effort is made to account for the fact that some high-volume releases are relatively benign, while other lower-volume releases may create great health risks. Third, many toxic chemicals are omitted entirely from the inventory. Fourth, the inventory does not reflect emissions by firms outside the manufacturing sector or by federal facilities. Fifth, the EPA conducts relatively little verification of the information it receives and makes relatively little effort to ensure compliance with the reporting requirements. Finally, there is no way to know whether the relationships between toxic waste and industry outputs in Canada and Mexico mirror those in the United States, or whether there are great differences across countries in the industry-specific relationships between hazardous waste and quantities of output.

We have used the predictions of the BDS model and the data on the industry breakdown of toxic releases by U.S. manufacturing firms contained in the TRI to generate table 2.7. The table contains estimated impacts on total toxic releases by the manufacturing industries of Mexico, the United States, and Canada in response to two scenarios for a NAFTA. As

Table 2.7
Estimated impacts of NAFTA on toxic releases by manufacturing enterprises (pounds in thousands)

	Trade liberalization only			Trade and investment liberalization		
Industry	Mexico	U.S.	Canada	Mexico	U.S.	Canada
Food and tobacco products	5	17	40	129	10	39
Textile products	22	499	39	169	487	42
Apparel	6	18	28	15	57	28
Lumber and wood products	−13	86	−88	76	74	−88
Furniture	128	210	176	257	148	178
Paper products	55	1,198	−953	611	1,198	−971
Printing and publishing	−10	52	−49	56	40	−48
Chemical products	−1,430	12,198	−1,178	4,047	12,408	−1,180
Petroleum and coal products	62	93	19	29	70	19
Rubber and plastic products	−484	693	2,072	289	636	2,062
Leather products	37	−26	181	158	−38	182
Stone, clay, glass, and concrete	0	124	152	107	112	152
Primary metals	−15	−1,591	5,437	2,166	−1,452	5,494
Fabricated metals	+1	558	254	259	530	254
Nonelectrical equipment	−61	587	−103	62	569	−104
Electrical equipment	1,445	−1,101	217	1,490	−1,091	217
Transportation equipment	−178	−594	1,435	354	−594	1,424
Miscellaneous manufacturing	171	32	338	192	97	332
Total	−261	13,053	8,017	10,466	13,261	8,032

before, the scenarios distinguish a NAFTA that effects only trade liberalization and one that also includes investment liberalization measures in Mexico. In constructing the table we have assumed that an industry-specific fixed coefficient characterizes the relationship between the amount of toxic release and the quantity of output produced. We have calculated this coefficient using output and total release data for the United States in 1989.[23] To the extent that releases per unit of output are *uniformly* higher or lower in Mexico or Canada than they are in the United States, the estimates in table 2.7 for these countries can be adjusted upward or downward to reflect these percentage differences. But lacking data for Canada and Mexico, we cannot address the possibility that these countries have higher or lower pollution coefficients than the United States in some industries but not in others.

The table tells a similar story to the one told by the utilities sector. A liberalization of trade in the absence of increased capital flows causes Mexico to shift resources toward industries that, on average, generate less pollution than its current producers. In particular, the BDS model predicts contraction by the industries producing chemical products and rubber and plastics products, both of which generate great quantities of waste per unit of output. The beneficial environmental effects of these resource flows are largely offset by an expansion of the electrical equipment industry, but a small positive net impact remains. The reallocation of resources in the United States and Canada differ from those in Mexico, as these countries enjoy comparative advantage in a complementary set of activities. The model predicts an expansion of the chemical products industry in the United States, and of the primary metals industry in Canada, with the implication that aggregate chemical releases by manufacturing enterprises will rise in both of these countries.

Again, the scenario that assumes a 10% increase in Mexico's capital stock has quite different implications for Mexico. As noted before, such growth in the capital stock causes output to expand in every Mexican manufacturing industry. If the relationship between waste and output remains unchanged, then total chemical releases must rise.

Although our estimates in this section must be taken with a large grain of salt, they suggest conclusions that accord well with intuition. Because Mexico enjoys comparative advantage in a set of activities (agriculture and labor-intensive manufactures) that on the whole are "cleaner" than the average, the composition effect of trade liberalization may well reduce pollution there. On the other hand, a NAFTA will cause the United States and Canada to specialize more in physical and human capital-intensive activities, to the possible (slight) detriment of their local environments. On the global level, a net benefit may derive from the movement of the dirtier economic activities to the more highly regulated production environments.

4 Conclusions

Environmental advocacy groups have pointed to several risks that might be associated with further liberalization of trade between the United States and Mexico. While they raise a number of valid concerns, our findings suggest that some potential benefits, especially for Mexico, may have been overlooked. First, a more liberal trade regime and greater access to the large U.S. market is likely to generate income growth in Mexico. Brown, Deardorff, and Stern (1991), for example, estimate potential short-run welfare gains to Mexico of between 0.6% and 1.9% of GDP. We have found, through an examination of air quality measures in a cross-section of countries, that economic growth tends to alleviate pollution problems once a country's per capita income reaches about, U.S. $4,000 to $5,000. Mexico, with a (purchasing-power adjusted) per capita GDP of $5,000, now is at the critical juncture in its development process where further growth should generate increased political pressures for environmental protection and perhaps a change in private consumption behavior. Second, trade liberalization may well increase Mexican specialization in sectors that cause less than average amounts of environmental damage. Our investigation of the determinants of Mexico's trade pattern strongly suggests that the country draws comparative advantage from its large number of relatively unskilled workers and that it imports goods whose production requires intensive use of physical and human capital. The asymmetries in environmental regulations and enforcement between the United States and Mexico play at most a minor role in guiding intersectoral resource allocations. But as it would appear that labor-intensive and agricultural activities require less energy input and generate less hazardous waste per unit of output than more capital- and human capital-intensive sectors, a reduction in pollution may well be a side benefit of increased Mexican specialization and trade.

Our findings must remain tentative until better data become available. We have been unable to use any information about the pollution situation as it currently stands in Mexico, since environmental monitoring there has been unsystematic at best. Furthermore, the kinds of pollutants that we can examine are limited by data availability (e.g., there are no reliable data on emissions of carbon dioxide in different countries). Still, one lesson from our study seems quite general and important. The environmental impacts of trade liberalization in any country will depend not only upon the effect of policy change on the overall scale of economic activity, but also upon the induced changes in the intersectoral composition of economic activity and in the technologies that are used to produce goods and services.

Appendix: Cities included in sample

Sulphur dioxide		Dark matter		Suspended particles	
City	Country	City	Country	City	Country
Accra	Ghana	Athens	Greece	Accra	Ghana
Amsterdam	New Zealand	Auckland	New Zealand	Athens	Greece
Athens	Greece	Bogota	Colombia	Azusa	United States
Auckland	New Zealand	Brussels	Belgium	Baghdad	Iraq
Azusa	United States	Cairo	Egypt	Bangkok	Thailand
Baghdad	Iraq	Cali	Colombia	Beijing	China
Bangkok	Thailand	Caracas	Venezuela	Birmingham	United States
Beijing	China	Christchurch	New Zealand	Bogota	Colombia
Birmingham	United States	Copenhagen	Denmark	Bombay	India
Bogota	Colombia	Dublin	Ireland	Brussels	Belgium
Bombay	India	Fray Louis Beltran	Argentina	Calcutta	India
Brussels	Belgium	Glasgow	United Kingdom	Cali	Colombia
Cairo	Egypt	Gourdon	France	Caracas	Venezuela
Calcutta	India	Hong Kong	Hong Kong	Chattanooga	United States
Cali	Colombia	Lima	Peru	Chicago	United States
Caracas	Venezuela	Lisbon	Portugal	Christchurch	New Zealand
Chicago	United States	London	United Kingdom	Copenhagen	Denmark
Christchurch	New Zealand	Madrid	Spain	Cordoba	Argentina
Copenhagen	Denmark	Medellin	Colombia	Davao	Philippines
Cordoba	Argentina	Mendoza	Argentina	Delhi	India
Davao	Philippines	Rio de Janeiro	Brazil	Fairfield	United States
Delhi	India	San Lorenzo	Argentina	Ferreyra	Argentina
Dublin	Ireland	Santa Fe	Argentina	Frankfurt	Germany
Fairfield	United States	Santiago	Chile	Guangzhou	China

Sulphur dioxide		Dark matter		Suspended particles	
City	Country	City	Country	City	Country
Frankfurt	Germany	Sao Paulo	Brazil	Hamilton	Canada
Fray Louis Beltran	Argentina	Tehran	Iran	Harris County	United States
Glasgow	United Kingdom	Toulouse	France	Helsinki	Finland
Gourdon	France	Tucuman	Argentina	Hong Kong	Hong Kong
Guangzhou	China	Warsaw	Poland	Houston	United States
Hamilton	Canada	Wroclaw	Poland	Iligan City	Philippines
Harris County	United States			Jakarta	India
Helsinki	Finland			Karachi	Pakistan
Hong Kong	Hong Kong			Kuala Lumpur	Malaysia
Houston	United States			La Plata	Argentina
Jakarta	India			Lahore	Pakistan
Kuala Lumpur	Malaysia			Lisbon	Portugal
Lahore	Pakistan			Los Angeles	United States
Lima	Peru			Manila	Philippines
Lisbon	Portugal			Medellin	Colombia
London	United Kingdom			Melbourne	Australia
Los Angeles	United States			Mendoza	Argentina
Madrid	Spain			Montreal	Canada
Manila	Philippines			Nairobi	Kenya
Medellin	Colombia			New Delhi	India
Melbourne	Australia			New York	United States
Mendoza	Argentina			Osaka	Japan
Milan	Italy			Palpala	Argentina
Montreal	Canada			Rio de Janeiro	Brazil
Munchen	Germany			Santa Fe	Argentina
Nairobi	Kenya			Sao Paulo	Brazil
New Delhi	India			Shanghai	China
New York	United States			Shenyang	China

Osaka	Japan	St. Ann	United States
Rio de Janeiro	Brazil	St. Louis	United States
San Lorenzo	Argentina	Sydney	Australia
Santa Fe	Argentina	Tehran	Iran
Santiago	Chile	Tel Aviv	Israel
Sao Paulo	Brazil	Tokyo	Japan
Seoul	Korea	Toronto	Canada
Shanghai	China	Vancouver	Canada
Shenyang	China	Xian	China
St. Ann	United States	Zagreb	Yugoslavia
St. Louis	United States		
Stockholm	Sweden		
Sydney	Australia		
Tehran	Iran		
Tel Aviv	Israel		
Tokyo	Japan		
Toronto	Canada		
Toulouse	France		
Tucuman	Argentina		
Vancouver	Canada		
Warsaw	Poland		
Wroclaw	Poland		
Xian	China		
Zagreb	Yugoslavia		
Zurich	Switzerland		

Notes

We are grateful to the Industrial Relations Section and International Finance Section of Princeton University, and the National Science Foundation for partial financial support. We thank Loren Baker, Kainan Tang, and Guillermo Frias for research assistance, and Drusilla Brown, Gardener Evans, and Greg Schoepfle for sharing their unpublished data. Joanne Gowa, Howard Gruenspecht, and Jeff Mackie-Mason provided helpful comments and discussion.

1. See Low and Safedi (1991), who cite several examples of writings that view open trade as detrimental to environmental protection.

2. See, for example, Gregory (1991), Kelly and Kamp (1991), National Wildlife Fedevation (1990), Leonard and Christensen (1991), and Ortman (1991).

3. A similar decomposition of the effects of economic growth on the output of pollution has been proposed by the Task Force on the Environment and the Internal Market (1990).

4. The GEMS data have been statistically analyzed by some environmental scientists (see World Health Organization [1984]), but they have neglected to use any economic variables in their exclusively bivariate analyses.

5. The GEMS data for 1977–1984 are published by the World Health Organization in the series *Air Quality in Selected Urban Areas*. Unpublished data for 1985–1988 have been kindly provided to us by Gardener Evans of the U.S. Environmental Protection Agency.

6. Lave and Seskin (1970) find, for example, that variation in SO_2 and population density together explain two-thirds of the variation in death from bronchitis in a sample of U.S. cities.

7. A few sites used nephelometric methods to measure suspended particles; i.e., they measured the light loss due to scattering when a light beam is passed through a sample of particle-laden air. This method gauges the mass of suspended particles, much as does the high-volume gravimetric method. Since the estimates are comparable in many cases, we pooled the observations from these two types of instruments, but included a dummy variable to allow for device-specific measurement differences.

8. Actually, SO_2 concentrations are never literally zero, but the machines are unable to detect very low levels of the gas.

9. We also estimated equations in which we entered per capita GDP in quadratic form. In general, the quadratic equations do not fit quite as well as the cubic equations, though in many cases the shape of the estimated relationship between income and pollution is found to be roughly the same.

10. Population densities were collected from several different sources. These sources and other details of our data set are available upon request.

11. We began our analysis with separate dummy variables for each year in our sample, but the estimates of thls model strongly suggested a simple, linear time trend.

12. However, we coded the desert dummy variable as zero for Cordoba, Argentina, in view of the fact that a mountain range lies between this city and the nearby desert. The regressions fit somewhat better with Cordoba treated this way, although none of our conclusions about the relationship of particulate pollution to GDP depends upon this designation.

13. The data on trade intensities were taken from the World Bank database.

14. That is, if μ_{ijt} is the total residual in the equation for some pollutant at site i in city j at time t, we assume that $\mu_{ijt} = \alpha_{jt} + \varepsilon_{ijt}$, where α_{jt} is the common-to-the-city component, ε_{ijt} is the idiosyncratic component, and $E(\alpha_{jt}\varepsilon_{ijt}) = 0$. Our estimation takes into account the unbalanced nature of this panel data set.

15. There are only two countries in our sample (the United States and Canada) with per capita incomes in excess of $16,000, so the fact that the estimated curves turn upward in this range probably should not be viewed as strong evidence for a renewed positive relationship between national product and SO_2 pollution at high income levels.

16. The Census survey did not include the apparel industry (SIC category 23). For these observations and four others with missing data, we inserted the average ratio of pollution abatement costs to value added for all manufacturing sectors included in the survey.

17. We note that the survey data on pollution abatement costs may give an underestimate of the average abatement cost in the U.S. industry. Absent from the survey are those firms that have exited the industry or moved their operations to Mexico or elsewhere. Conceivably, the potential (but not actual) producers that are missing from the survey sample may include some that ceased operations due to especially high, firm-specific costs of pollution abatement.

18. For twelve industries, this method gives a negative number as the estimate of the share of human capital. To ensure that our results were not sensitive to the choice of income for an unskilled worker, we also computed factor shares using the income level for unskilled workers ($10,819) that made the minimum share of human capital in our sample of industries equal to zero. The estimated import equations with these measures of factor shares look much the same as for our original measures.

19. The import figures and the effective tariff rates were provided to us by Greg Schoepfle of the U.S. Department of Labor. The tariff rates were estimated by dividing the total duties collected on imports from Mexico in a two-digit SIC industry by the total value of imports in the industry. Data on shipments, value added, employment, and payroll were taken from the N.B.E.R. trade and immigration data set (see Abowd, 1991). Since the trade data are classified according to the old (1972) SIC categories, we used manufacturing census data that were bridged to this classification scheme. The average income for a worker in the manufacturing sector with less than a high school education was calculated from the 1987 *Current Population Survey* by the authors. Injury rates by industry were taken from the Bureau of Labor Statistics publication, *Occupational Injuries and Illness in the United States by Industry*. In the few cases where an injury rate was not available for a

three-digit industry, we used instead the average injury rate for the applicable two-digit industry.

20. A simultaneity bias may exist here, insofar as many political-economic theories of tariff formation predict that high tariff rates will endogenously emerge in industries in which import penetration is great.

21. We note that INEGA withheld industry-level data for industries with sixteen or fewer maquiladora establishments. Thus our analysis treats as zero the maquiladora activity in sectors where some small amount of production may have taken place.

22. The following discussion is based on U.S. GAO (1991a).

23. The output data, which were provided to us by Drusilla Brown, are those that were used in the calibration of the BDS model. Since these data are reported on an ISIC basis, we were forced to reclassify some industries in order to make them compatible with the SIC-based TRI data.

References

Abowd, John M. 1991. "The NBER Immigration, Trade, and Labor Markets Data Files." In J. M. Abowd and R. B. Freeman, eds., *Immigration. Trade. and the Labor Market*. Chicago: The University of Chicago Press for the National Bureau of Economic Research.

Bennett, Burton G., Kretzschmar, Jan G., Akland, Gerald G., and de Koning, Henk W. 1985. "Urban Air Pollution Worldwide." *Environmental Science and Technology* 19:298–304.

Brown, Drusilla K., Deardorff, Alan V., and Stern, Robert M. 1991. "A North American Free Trade Agreement: Analytical Issues and a Computational Assessment." Mimeo. Institute of Public Policy Studies, University of Michigan.

Gregory, Michael. 1991. "Sustainable Development vs. Economic Growth: Environmental Protection as an Investment in the Future." Statement on Behalf of Arizona Toxics Information before the International Trade Commission, Hearing on Probable Economic Effect on U.S. Industries and Consumers of a Free Trade Agreement Between the United States and Mexico.

Harkness, Jon. 1978. "Factor Abundance and Comparative Advantage." *American Economic Review* 68:784–800.

Kelly, Mary E., and Kamp, Dick. 1991. "Mexico-U.S. Free Trade Negotiations and the Environment: Exploring the Issues." Mimeo. Texas Center for Policy Studies, Austin TX, and Border Ecology Project, Naco, AZ.

Kormondy, Edward J., ed. 1989. *International Handbook of Pollution Control*. New York and Westport, CT: Greenwood Press.

Krueger, Alan B., and Burton, John F., Jr. 1990. "The Employers' Costs of Workers' Compensation Insurance: Magnitudes, Determinants, and Public Policy." *Review of Economics and Statistics* 72:228–240.

Lave, Lester B., and Seskin, E. P. 1970. "Air Pollution and Human Health." *Science* 169:723–733.

Leonard, H. Jeffrey. 1988. *Pollution and the Struggle for World Product*. Cambridge: Cambridge University Press.

Leonard, Rodney E., and Christensen, Eric. 1991. "Economic Effects of a Free Trade Agreement between Mexico and the United States." Testimony on Behalf of Community Nutrition Institute before the International Trade Commission, Hearing on Docket No. 332–307.

Low, Patrick, and Safedi, Raed. 1991. "Trade Policy and Pollution." Mimeo. International Trade Division, World Bank.

McGuire, Martin C. 1982. "Regulation, Factor Rewards, and International Trade." *Journal of Public Economics* 17:335–354.

National Wildlife Federation. 1990. "Environmental Concerns Related to a United States-Mexico-Canada Free Trade Agreement." Mimeo. National Wildlife Federation, Washington, D.C.

New York Times. 1991. "Facing Environmental Issues." Sept. 22, Sec. 3:5.

Ortman, David E. 1991. "On a Comprehensive North American Trade Agreement." Testimony on Behalf of Friends of the Earth, National Wildlife Federation, and the Texas Center for Policy Studies before the Subcommittee on Trade, Committee on Ways and Means, U.S. House of Representatives.

Pethig, Rudiger. 1976. "Pollution, Welfare, and Environmental Policy in the Theory of Comparative Advantage." *Journal of Environmental Economics and Management* 2:160–169.

Schoepfle, Gregory K. 1991. "Implications for U.S. Employment of the Recent Growth in Mexican Maquiladoras." *Frontera Norte* 3:25–54.

Siebert, Horst. 1977. "Environmental Quality and the Gains from Trade." *Kyklos* 30:657–673.

Summers, Robert, and Heston, Alan. 1991. "The Penn World Table (Mark 5): An Expanded Set of International Comparisons, 1950–1988." *Quarterly Journal of Economics* 106:327–368.

Task Force on the Environment and the Internal Market. 1990. *1992: The Environmental Dimension*. Bonn: Economica Verlag.

The Economist. 1991. "Smog City." May 18:51.

Tobey, James A. 1990. "The Effects of Domestic Environmental Policies on Patterns of World Trade: An Empirical Test." *Kyklos* 43:191–209.

United States Department of Commerce. 1988. *Manufacturers' Pollution Abatement Capital Expenditures and Operating Costs*. Washington, D.C.: Bureau of the Census.

United States Environmental Protection Agency. 1982. *Air Quality Criteria for Particulate Matter and Sulfur Oxides*. Research Triangle Park, N.C.: U.S. EPA.

United States General Accounting Office. 1991a. "Toxic Chemicals: EPA's Toxic Release Inventory is Useful but Can be Improved." Report No. GAO/RCED-91-121, Washington, D.C.

United States General Accounting Office. 1991b. "U.S.-Mexico Trade: Information on Environmental Regulations and Enforcement." Report No. GAO/NSIAD-91-227, Washington, D.C.

United States General Accounting Office. 1991c. "U.S.-Mexico Trade: Some U.S. Wood Furniture Firms Relocated from Los Angeles Area to Mexico." Report No. GAO/NSIAD-91-191, Washington, D.C.

Walter, Ingo. 1982. "Environmentally Induced Industrial Relocation to Developing Countries." In S. J. Rubin and T. R. Graham, eds., *Environment and Trade*. New Jersey: Allanheld, Osmun, and Co.

World Health Organization. 1984. *Urban Air Pollution. 1973–1980*. Geneva: World Health Organization.

World Resources Institute. 1988. *World Resources: 1988–89*. New York: Basic Books.

Yohe, Gary W. 1979. "The Backward Incidence of Pollution Control—Some Comparative Statics in General Equilibrium." *Journal of Environmental and Economic Management* 6:187–198.

[14]

The Toxic Intensity of Industrial Production: Global Patterns, Trends, and Trade Policy

By HEMAMALA HETTIGE, ROBERT E. B. LUCAS, AND DAVID WHEELER*

This paper exploits a newly developed data set to investigate recent changes in the international distribution of industrial pollution. In particular, we examine three issues: (1) the relationship between the toxic intensity of industrial production and the level of economic development, (2) the impact of OECD environmental regulation on global changes in toxic intensity, and (3) the relationship between trade policy and the toxic intensity of industrial production in LDC's.

Our study uses measures of the toxic intensity of manufacturing in 80 countries from 1960 to 1988. For each country and year, we have used UN industrial data to calculate shares of total manufactured output for 37 sectors defined on the international standard industrial classification (ISIC). To obtain country-specific toxic-intensity indexes, we have multiplied these shares by U.S. sectoral toxic intensities, estimated as total pounds of toxic release per dollar's worth of output. The sectoral intensities have been calculated from a sample of 15,000 U.S. plants which we have obtained by merging data from two sources: the U.S. Environmental Protection Agency's (EPA's) 1987 Toxic Release Inventory, which provides plant-level release estimates for 320 toxic substances; and the 1987 Census of Manufactures, which provides plant-level data on output value.[1]

Our calculation of international toxic intensity indexes from constant U.S.-based sectoral intensities can only be defended as the best feasible procedure: actual toxic release data for other economies are unavailable. However, a detailed analysis of potential bias reported in Lucas et al. (1991) suggests that sectoral ranking by toxic intensity has remained approximately constant across the OECD economies during the past two decades. Moreover, it is not even clear that sectoral toxic intensities are higher in LDC's. Their lack of formal environmental regulation is often compensated for by the presence of imported industrial equipment whose vintage is, on average, newer than that of OECD facilities. Newer equipment imported from the OECD economies is generally less polluting as well.[2]

I. Economic Development, Environmental Regulation, and Toxic Intensity Change

We have pooled our country-specific toxic-intensity indexes with time-series estimates of income per capita to test two broad hypotheses: (1) industrial pollution intensity follows an inverse U-shaped pattern as development proceeds; and (2) OECD environmental regulation has significantly displaced toxic industrial production toward less-regulated LDC's. The rationale for the latter hypothesis is obviously founded on relative production cost. The former is based

*Hettige and Wheeler are, respectively, Consultant in the Industry and Energy Department and Senior Economist in the Environment Department, World Bank, 1818 H Street, N.W., Washington, DC 20433. They are also research associates at the Center for Economic Studies, U.S. Bureau of the Census, which cosponsored this research with the World Bank. Lucas is Professor of Economics, Boston University, 270 Bay State Road, Boston, MA 02215.

[1]For a detailed discussion, see Paul Martin et al. (1991). Toxic intensities have been calculated in both unweighted and risk-weighted form, with substance-specific risk weightings drawn from the EPA's Human Health and Ecotoxicity Database (HHED). Since risk-weighted and unweighted sectoral intensities are very highly correlated, we have employed only unweighted intensities for this analysis.

[2]For a detailed discussion, see Mainul Huq and Wheeler (1992), Wheeler and Martin (1991), and Wheeler and Huq (1992).

on the general notion of three stages of industrial development dominated by (i) agroprocessing and light assembly, which are (relatively) low in toxic intensity, (ii) heavy industry (e.g., metals, chemicals, paper), which has high toxic intensity, and (iii) high-technology industry (e.g., microelectronics, pharmaceuticals), which is again lower in toxic intensity. In part this is perceived as a natural evolution and in part a response (in the last stage) to growing pressure for environmental regulation at higher incomes.

In our econometric analysis, we distinguish between the pattern of change in pollutant intensity measured per unit of GDP and intensity measured per unit of industrial output. In all equations estimated the left-hand variable is the log of pollutant intensity. We allow for a direct quadratic effect of per capita income and include an interaction between per capita income and time to test for the impact of per capita income on the change in intensity.[3]

Our results indicate an inverse U-shaped pattern for intensity per unit of GDP, thus supporting the findings of other recent, more partial analyses such as the international study of urban air pollution by Gene M. Grossman and Alan B. Krueger (1991). However, we find no such pattern for intensity per unit of industrial output. In fact, our results suggest that the pollution intensity of manufacturing output rises steadily with income, at most tapering off somewhat at very high incomes. From this we conclude that the GDP-based intensity result is due solely to a broad shift from industry toward lower-polluting services as development proceeds.

We have tested the displacement hypothesis by dividing our pooled data into subsets for each decade since 1960. Our results are strongly consistent with the displacement hypothesis, since the estimated pattern for the 1960's is quite different from that for the latter decades. For the 1960's we find a positive interaction between income per capita and time: toxic intensity grew most quickly in high-income economies. During the 1970's and 1980's, after the advent of stricter OECD environmental regulation, this pattern was sharply reversed: toxic intensity in LDC manufacturing grew most quickly.

II. Toxic Intensity Change and Trade Policy

We have extended our analysis to investigate the possibility that toxic displacement has been affected by policies in LDC's as well. Specifically, we have considered the impact of trade policy on the sectoral composition of LDC manufacturing in two sets of regression experiments. In the first, we have tested the effect of trade protection for chemicals production, which is by a considerable margin the most toxic intensive manufacturing sector. Our estimates indicate that the toxic intensity of LDC manufacturing output rises with both a higher tariff on chemicals and greater nontariff barriers to the importing of chemicals (though the latter effect is statistically weaker).[4]

Of course, these simple protection measures are far from ideal. A higher absolute tariff on chemicals may not draw resources into this sector if even higher protection is offered in other activities. We have therefore examined the effect of a tariff on chemicals given (or relative to) average tariffs on all manufactured goods, again finding a positive association with overall toxic intensity.

Our second analysis examines whether the general orientation of trade policy has had a significant impact on industrial emissions intensity. Only a few international measures of overall trade orientation exist. We have chosen to focus on a recent index constructed by David Dollar (1990), in part because this index avoids the subjectivity of some other indexes, but also because it en-

[3]Space limitations have prevented us from including econometric results in tabular form. All results are available from the authors upon request.

[4]Tariff and nontariff barrier information have been drawn from UNCTAD (1987).

compasses a fairly large number of countries.[5] We have incorporated it into a cross-sectional analysis of toxic-intensity change for a large sample of LDC's in the 1970's and 1980's. Our estimating equations incorporate the effects of per capita income, growth in per capita income, and the interaction of the latter with Dollar's (1990) index. We find a significant interaction for the 1970's and an even greater effect for the 1980's: outward-oriented, high-growth LDC's have slow-growing or even declining toxic intensity of manufacturing, while toxic intensity increases more rapidly in inward-oriented economies.

Our findings on trade policy and toxic-intensity change suggest a revised view of the displacement phenomenon. Rapidly increasing toxic intensity does not seem to have characterized all LDC manufacturing in the wake of stricter OECD environmental regulation. Paradoxically, intensity has grown much more rapidly in economies that are relatively closed to international trade. This seems to reflect (as Grossman and Krueger [1991] also note) the workings of comparative advantage: more open economies have had higher growth rates of labor-intensive assembly activities which are also relatively low in toxic intensity. Highly protected economies have had more rapid growth of capital-intensive "smokestack" sectors.

III. Summary and Conclusions

Overall, our analysis indicates an upward long-term trend in industrial emissions, both relative to GDP and relative to manufacturing output, for the majority of countries. Moreover, these positive, long-term trends are clearly higher among the lower-income countries. This is consistent with an industrial displacement effect on the dirtier industries as a result of the tightening environmental regulations in the industrialized nations since 1970. However, it seems to conflict with prior evidence on the relatively small cost of environmental regulation for OECD firms (Judith M. Dean, 1991). One possibility is that the expected profitability of investment in pollution-intensive sectors has also been affected by growing concern over legal liability or reputational damage. Certainly our evidence suggests that another contributory factor has been import protection imposed by the developing countries. Higher tariffs and quotas on chemicals are found to be associated with an industrial base skewed toward toxic intensive activities. Moreover, countries that have pursued more outward-oriented strategies in trade are estimated to have suffered less from growth in toxicity of their industrial mix.

In closing, we should note some major limitations of our results. First, our analysis is only indirect: we examine changes in industry structure, inferring the toxic-intensity implications from our fixed U.S.-based intensity estimates. The full story cannot be told until much better data on technology and waste-treatment choices are available. In addition, our focus has been on local effects. Some emissions generate transnational or even global damage. For the latter, it is the world total emissions rather than their location that ultimately matters, though the two may not be independent when some countries are better able to regulate emissions. Our focus on manufacturing production alone is not meant to deny that mining, forestry and agriculture, as well as consumption of manufactured products, can have devastating ecological effects. For the present, our data simply do not encompass these other activities. Any more general statements about the effects of economic development, environmental regulation, and trade policy must await more complete data and analysis.

[5]Dollar's index uses the Summers/Heston price index (see Robert Summers and Alan Heston, 1988) for a constant basket of commodities across countries. Under free trade, such a basket of tradable goods ought to have the same price everywhere. Departures from unity may then be interpreted as a consequence of some form of trade barrier (though this may include transport costs). In practice some nontradables enter the basket of commodities. Dollar (1990) attempts to control for this difficulty by regressing the raw index on measures of factor endowments (presumed to affect relative prices of nontradables across countries). The residual from these regressions is then adopted as Dollar's measure of relative openness.

REFERENCES

Dean, Judith M., "Trade and the Environment: A Survey of the Literature," unpublished manuscript prepared for the 1992 World Development Report, 1991.

Dollar, David, "Outward Orientation and Growth: An Empirical Study Using a Price-Based Measure of Openness," unpublished manuscript prepared for the 1991 World Development Report, 1990.

Grossman, Gene M. and Krueger, Alan B., "Environmental Impacts of a North American Free Trade Agreement," unpublished manuscript prepared for the Conference on the U.S.-Mexico Free Trade Agreement, 1991.

Huq, Mainul and Wheeler, David, *Industrial Cleanup Without Regulation: Public Enterprises in Bangladesh*, Washington, DC: World Bank, 1992 (forthcoming).

Lucas, Robert E. B., Wheeler, David and Hettige, Hemamala, "Economic Development, Environmental Regulation and the International Migration of Toxic Industrial Pollution: 1960–1988," unpublished manuscript presented at the World Bank Symposium on International Trade and the Environment, Washington, DC, 1991.

Martin, Paul, Wheeler, David, Hettige, Hemamala and Stengren, Ralph, "The Industrial Pollution Projection System: Concept, Initial Development, and Critical Assessment," mimeo, Washington, DC: World Bank, 1991.

Summers, Robert and Heston, Alan, "A New Set of International Comparisons of Real Product and Price Levels: Estimates for 130 Countries, 1955–1985," *Review of Income and Wealth*, March 1988, *34*, 1–24.

Wheeler, David and Huq, Mainul, *Technical Change, International Diffusion, and Environmental Impact in the Steel Industry: 1960–1989*, Washington, DC: World Bank, 1992 (forthcoming).

Wheeler, David, and Martin, Paul, "Prices, Policies, and the International Diffusion of Clean Technology: The Case of Wood Pulp Production," unpublished manuscript presented at the World Bank Symposium on International Trade and the Environment, Washington, DC, 1991.

UNCTAD, *Handbook of Trade Control Measures of Developing Countries*, Geneva: United Nations Conference on Trade and Development, 1987.

[15]

Trade Measures and Environmental Quality: The Implications for Mexico's Exports

Patrick Low

Introduction

Public attention, particularly in the United States, is focused as never before on links between trade policy and the environment. The immediate explanation for this is the deliberations in Congress in early 1991 on the extension of executive trade negotiating authority. Although the renewal of this authority had been discussed for many months almost exclusively in terms of U.S. participation in the Uruguay Round, extension of the authority was also required for the proposed negotiation of a free trade agreement (FTA) with Mexico. With surprising suddenness, the locus of the debate shifted to the Mexico FTA issue.

A major reason why the FTA proposal moved to center-stage was that environmental groups mobilized and petitioned against the FTA negotiations on the grounds that free trade between the United States and Mexico would be damaging to the environment -- an environment which was seen as already seriously compromised through accumulated neglect. The premise underlying many of the environmentalists' arguments was simply that more open trade would mean accelerated environmental degradation. The success of environmental groups in capturing public attention was abetted by the fact that an anti-FTA stance dovetailed with the concerns of labor groups, whose argument against more open trade was a more familiar one, focusing on competitiveness and wage differentials between the United States and Mexico. For at least some of the environmentalist lobbies, however, it was merely coincidental that their demands appeared indistinguishable from those of labor and industry groups opposed to freer trade.

The absence of a solid coalition between environmental groups and labor/industry interests contributed to the success of the executive branch in convincing a part of the environmental lobby that a failure to establish closer trade and economic relations between Mexico and the United States would be more threatening to environmental quality than a free trade agreement. In securing enough votes to defeat legislative proposals against extended trade negotiating authority, however, the Bush Administration is committed to ensure that environmental concerns are accorded appropriate attention. More precisely, there will be parallel negotiations on the environment and a long-term Border Environmental Plan is to be drawn up by the end of 1991.[1]

Even though trade liberalization in the context of the North American FTA negotiations might not be hostage to explicit environmental conditionality, the issue is unlikely to disappear. There is still a widely held view that specialization through trade and economic growth are harbingers of environmental degradation. And there are still influential interest groups that would treat disparities in environmental standards, or even differences in the costs of pollution abatement and control, as justifying the application of unfair trade remedies.

---

[1]Report to the Congress by the President (1991).

This paper focuses on the implications for Mexico's exports of the imposition by the United States of a hypothetical "dirty" industry import tax that would equalize expenditures by U.S. and Mexican industries on pollution abatement and control. Although the justification for such a tax is extremely dubious on economic grounds, the idea has been promoted as a way of eradicating "unfairness" arising from differences in industry competitiveness among countries, attributable to differential environmental standards and compliance costs.

The paper contains four more sections. The next section presents data on dirty industries, based on differences in pollution abatement and control expenditures among industries in the United states. This is followed by an examination of the extent to which Mexico's exports comprise the output of dirty industries, and looks at the growth of these industries in terms of their exports during the 1980s. The paper then analyzes the current U.S. trade policy regime facing dirty industry exports from Mexico, and presents the results of a simple simulation designed to estimate the likely trade impact of a dirty industry import tax.

The Identification of Dirty Industries

There is no standard definition of dirty industries. Like previous studies of trade and environmental policy, notably by Tobey (1990) and Kalt (1985), this paper identifies dirty industries as those incurring the highest level of pollution abatement and control expenditures. Annex Table A lists 123 industries identified at the 3-digit SIC level in descending order of pollution intensity. The data are for the year 1988, and pertain to U.S. industry. Table 7-1 in the text summarizes the above information at the 2-digit SIC level, where gross costs of pollution abatement are expressed as a percentage of industry output to yield the unit cost of abatement expenditure (column 3). This table also shows how pollution abatement operating costs are divided up between payments to government (sewage and waste disposal services) and direct operating costs to firms for air and water pollution abatement and waste disposal. These operating costs include depreciation of abatement equipment, labor, materials and supplies, and services, equipment leasing, and other costs.

Industrial activities classified as the most pollution intensive on the basis of the abatement and control costs they incur tend to be concentrated in relatively few sectors, including cement, chemicals, pulp and paper production, certain wood industries, petroleum refining, and ferrous and nonferrous metal industries. The numbers given for pollution abatement and control expenditures should be treated as indicative.[2] Apart from limitations regarding the accuracy of the data, it should also be noted that only direct abatement costs have been included in the calculation of the degree of dirtiness.[3]

Perhaps the most interesting fact to emerge from these data is that pollution abatement and control expenditures are small in relation to total output for the great majority of industries. The maximum "charge" resulting from pollution abatement and control activities amounted to just over 3 percent of output for the dirtiest industry (cement), and only 18 out of 123 3-digit SIC industries incurred expenditures greater than 1 percent of output. The weighted average for all industries was 0.54 percent (See Annex Table A).

---

[2]See U.S. Department of Commerce (1988) which explains that the statistics were compiled from a probability sample and are subject to sampling variations. The final report on the 1986 data (not reported here) also discusses some other data limitations.

[3]An attempt could have been made to measure the pollution intensity of industries in terms of inputs as well as final output. Kalt (1985) did this using the technical coefficients from the U.S. input-output table. Although the procedure did result in some reordering of industries by degree of dirtiness, it did not make much difference in terms of which broad industry groups were classified as dirty and which were not. Moreover, expressed as a share of total output, pollution abatement expenditures remained modest.

107

Table 7-1: Pollution Abatement Operating Costs by Type of Expenditure, 1988
(Values in Millions of U.S. Dollars)

SIC No.		Total gross cost (1)	Total industry output (2)	Abatement costs as percentage of output (3)	Payments to government			Operating costs by form of pollutant abated				
											Solid waste	
					Total	Public sewage services	Solid collection and disposal	Total	Air	Water	Hazardous	Nonhazardous
20	Food and kindred products	1,160.1	351,514.9	0.33	398.6	347.8	50.8	761.5	157.8	325.6	13.2	264.9
21	Tobacco manufactures	37.6	23,831.8	0.16	6.1	5.3	0.8	31.5	12.4	9.5	0.6	9.0
22	Textile mill products	177.0	64,767.9	0.27	62.4	50.1	12.4	114.6	30.5	48.8	6.5	28.8
24	Lumber and wood products	236.1	72,065.4	0.33	20.2	10.1	10.1	215.9	84.0	47.5	16.8	67.6
25	Furniture and fixtures	118.4	39,226.1	0.30	11.1	5.8	5.3	107.3	33.8	6.6	37.4	29.5
26	Paper and allied products	1,343.3	122,556.2	1.10	141.6	107.8	33.8	1,201.7	372.4	520.0	32.5	276.9
27	Printing and publishing	206.4	143,906.8	0.14	41.8	24.7	17.1	164.6	72.0	9.5	22.4	60.8
28	Chemicals and allied products	3,074.9	259,699.1	1.18	181.8	154.4	27.4	2,893.1	706.4	1,274.1	467.1	445.5
29	Petroleum and coal products	2,005.5	131,414.8	1.53	30.5	14.6	15.9	1,975.0	1,175.8	547.1	142.8	109.3
30	Rubber and misc. plastics products	278.0	94,200.2	0.30	50.7	27.0	23.7	227.2	62.5	35.2	35.4	94.1
31	Leather and leather products	23.1	9,663.7	0.24	7.8	5.7	2.0	15.3	2.5	5.6	0.9	6.4
32	Stone, clay and glass products	438.5	63,059.4	0.70	27.7	17.1	10.6	410.7	247.7	50.6	25.8	86.8
33	Primary metal industries	1,809.0	149,079.8	1.21	63.4	47.5	15.9	1,745.6	965.8	468.5	136.2	175.0
34	Fabricated metal products	761.9	158,833.8	0.48	73.1	49.0	24.1	688.9	135.0	267.8	169.3	116.7
35	Machinery, except electrical	429.7	243,260.8	0.18	56.6	38.2	18.4	373.1	68.4	101.2	90.7	112.7
36	Electric and electrical equipment	659.3	186,950.8	0.35	86.0	62.6	23.5	573.2	92.2	189.9	163.1	128.0
37	Transportation equipment	974.5	354,047.8	0.28	82.6	60.2	22.3	891.9	215.7	239.0	267.8	169.3
38	Instruments and related products	197.7	114,528.4	0.17	23.1	18.2	4.9	174.6	21.7	61.7	49.0	42.3
39	Misc. manufacturing industries	76.7	34,869.4	0.22	12.7	6.0	6.7	64.0	10.1	14.9	9.5	29.5
	Total	14,008.6	2,617,476.9	0.54	1,378.7	1,052.9	325.8	12,629.9	4,466.5	4,223.1	1,687.0	2,253.2

Sources: U.S. Department of Commerce (1988).
U.S. Department of Commerce (1988).

Mexico's Exports of Dirty Industry Products

This section briefly examines Mexico's exports in terms of the products that would be vulnerable if measures were adopted by Mexico's trading partners to reduce or eliminate trade in pollution-intensive goods. The questions of whether such action could be justified, and what the actual trade effects might be, are taken up in due course.

Annex Tables B and C list Mexico's exports of pollution-intensive goods to the United States and to the world. Notwithstanding the difficulties of establishing a concordance between a classification system based on processes (SIC) and one based on products (SITC or TSUSA), these tables have attempted to identify dirty products in terms of pollution abatement and control expenditures in excess of 0.5 percent of output.

The 48 products identified in the tables at the SITC 3-digit level accounted for 11 percent and 12 percent respectively of Mexico's exports to the United States and to the world in 1989. The tables also record growth rates of exports between 1981 and 1989 in constant (1990) dollar terms. Exports of pollution-intensive products to the United States increased at an average rate of 9 percent per year during the 1980s, compared with 3 percent for all commodities. The growth rates for individual products varied widely. Similarly, exports of pollution-intensive products to the world grew by 5 percent over the same period, while the comparable figure for total exports was 1 percent.

In summary, the trade data show that Mexico's export earnings are not overly dependent on pollution-intensive products, which account for a little over one tenth of total exports. On the other hand, pollution-intensive exports have grown considerably faster than total exports during this period. A continuation of this trend could be at risk if Mexico's trading partners were to take trade measures against dirty products.

Pollution-Intensive Goods and Trade Policy

This section examines existing import measures applied on Mexico's exports to the United States and simulates the effects on those exports of the imposition of a "pollution abatement and control expenditure (PACE) equalization tax." Taking current trade measures first, Table 7-2 shows that the average applied U.S. tariff on Mexico's exports is 2.9 percent (1990 applied rates, including preferences). The comparable figure for the products reported in Table 7-2 as being most affected by a PACE equalization tax (see below) is 2.3 percent. The final column of the table lists nontariff barriers (NTBs) on the products identified, covering a textile item (of silk or man-made fibers), certain pigments, cement and various steel products. The trade coverage ratio of these NTBs is 3.6 percent in terms of 1986 trade flows, whereas Erzan and Yeats (1991) report higher frequency counts for Mexico's total exports to the United States.[4]

Since the products listed in Table 7-2 include both low volume pollution-intensive items and high volume "clean" items, the conclusion to be drawn here is that currently, U.S. trade policy is insensitive to the pollution intensity of imports, at least as far as Mexico is concerned.

Turning to the simulation exercise, whose results are reported in Table 7-2, it was assumed that following the removal of all U.S. tariffs on Mexican exports under an FTA, a PACE equalization tax was added back. The PACE equalization tax is equivalent to pollution abatement and control expenditures incurred

---

[4]This study reports a trade coverage ratio for all NTBs (as defined by the UNCTAD data base) of 39 per cent, and a 4 percent coverage ratio for "hard core" NTBs (quantitative restrictions -- quotas, prohibitions and VERs -- and flexible import fees).

Table 7-2: Simulation Results for Abatement Cost Equalization Tax on U.S. Imports from Mexico

TSUSA	Commodity	U.S. imports from Mexico 1986 (US$'000)	Current weighted MFN or preferential tariff	Cost equalization tax	Total trade creation and diversion effects (US$'000)	Current nontariff barriers (1989)
114	Canned and cured seafoods	357,683	-	0.3	2,867	
160	Coffee, processed	573,051	-	0.3	4,880	
167	Beverages (largely beer)	121,009	2.1	0.5	1,377	
252	Paper, not impregnated or coated	28,344	-	2.0	1,370	
256	Paper, paperboard, cut to size or shape	172,133	4.1	0.4	1,228	
389	Other articles of silk or man-made fibers, not ornamented	114,292	9.0	0.4	1,611	MFA restraints
416	Inorganic acids	58,870	-	2.2	3,396	
473	Pigments	25,654	0.5	2.0	1,428	Countervailing duties
475	Petroleum, crude and refined	3,601,596	0.5	1.6	167,863	
511	Cement	112,090	-	3.1	10,998	Countervailing duties
605	Silver	247,754	-	2.3	14,059	
606	Iron or steel products (containing other metallic minerals)	45,373	2.5	1.2	1,765	VERs
607	Hollow drill steel	42,202	6.2	1.4	1,999	VERs
608	Terneplate and terne-coated sheets	51,414	6.4	1.4	2,457	VERs
610	Rails, joint bars and tie plates, of steel	49,418	2.5	1.4	2,283	VERs
612	Copper, copper products	86,469	0.7	1.8	2,466	
626	Zinc, zinc products	40,934	1.5	2.3	2,324	
657	Articles of ferrous and nonferrous metals	41,404	-	1.0	1,608	Antidumping duties
660	Engine and engine parts	820,155	2.7	0.3	9,234	
661	Machinery and mechanical equipment	144,182	2.3	0.3	1,952	
664	Excavators, mechanical shovels, elevators hoists, cranes, etc.	88,982	1.6	0.3	1,248	
676	Office machines	327,962	1.9	0.4	6,225	
678	Other machines	259,855	3.6	0.3	4,055	
682	Electric motors	488,511	2.9	0.4	8,341	
683	Batteries, various electric machines	214,236	2.2	0.3	2,733	
684	Electrodomestic equipment, telephone apparatus, televisions	530,181	4.1	0.3	7,306	
685	Sound equipment	1,496,456	4.8	0.4	25,978	
686	Current regulators, circuit breakers	96,592	5.0	0.4	1,723	
687	Electric lamps, tubes	292,085	0.6	0.4	5,884	
688	Electrical conductors	917,923	4.8	0.3	12,107	
692	Motor vehicles (except motorcycles)	1,637,890	3.3	0.3	23,131	
727	Furniture	258,812	2.0	0.2	1,972	
	Sub-total	13,343,512	2.3	N/A	337,868	
	Other imports	5,367,826	N/A	N/A	37,795	
	Total imports	18,711,338	2.9	0.6	375,663	

110

by the relevant industries in the United States.[5] This procedure involves the simplifying and unrealistic assumption that the equalization of pollution control expenditures between Mexico and the United States requires the full allocation of U.S. expenditures on Mexico's exports, or in other words that Mexican industries spend nothing at all on pollution control. This assumption, together with the assignation of the highest possible PACE equalization tax in cases where more than one SIC number concorded to a single TSUSA number, imparts an upward bias to the estimates of the trade-reducing effects of a hypothetical PACE equalization tax reported in Table 7-2.

Even if a PACE equalization tax were to be adjusted by Mexico's own expenditures on pollution abatement and control, it is far from clear what the justification would be for an attempt to offset differences in these expenditure levels. In the first place, assimilative capacities between countries are likely to be different, so that the costs of attaining the same environmental standards would not be the same. Secondly, social preferences as to the acceptable level of environmental quality may well differ between countries, which would provide a further reason for expecting abatement and control costs to differ.

Cost equalization is even more difficult to justify when local pollution questions are at issue, as opposed to those involving transfrontier spillovers. Moreover, whatever the nature of the pollution problem, it is not obvious that the threat or the imposition of trade restrictions will have a positive effect on environmental quality. In this particular instance, the trade restrictions would amount to a resource transfer from Mexico to the United States. They would not reflect the kind of cooperative behavior that could lead to agreement on environmental standards, or on how to achieve them. In short, the underlying rationale for cost equalization proposals has more to do with competitive considerations than with environmental quality. The idea of simulating the trade effects of a cost equalization tax was initially provoked by a legislative proposal to this effect made recently in the U.S. Senate.[6] What would the effects be on Mexico's exports if a cost equalization tax were introduced following the establishment of an FTA?

The data presented in Table 7-2 suggest that the trade effects of a PACE equalization tax would be very modest, amounting at most to a 2 percent loss in export earnings for Mexico. In addition to the reasons given above as to why this estimate of a PACE equalization tax is biased upward (zero pollution abatement expenditure in Mexico and nomenclature concordance procedures), another significant source of upward bias should be noted. This arises from the assignation of the same PACE equalization tax to crude and refined petroleum (1.6 percent -- see Table 7-2), when in effect this comparatively high rate should properly be applied only to refining activities, representing just 5 percent of Mexico's fuel exports to the United States in 1989. Exports of crude petroleum to the United States far exceed those of refined products.

While these procedures will impost an upward bias to the calculation of the effects of a PACE equalization tax, it is worth noting certain factors that could make U.S. pollution abatement and control

---

[5]The point made earlier about the difficulty of concording production and trade data applies equally in this case.

[6]The proposed legislation is the International Pollution Deterrence Act of 1991 (S.984). Under the legislation, U.S. countervailing duty law would be modified so that the failure to maintain effective pollution controls and environmental safeguards would constitute a countervailable subsidy. The amount of the subsidy would be calculated as the cost that would have to be incurred by a foreign manufacturer or producer to comply with environmental standards imposed on U.S. producers of the same products. Although this proposal is not strictly designed to attain cost equalization, it would probably have a comparable effect. In any event, it is significant that the legislation is cast in terms of pollution abatement costs rather than environmental standards.

expenditures higher than the data suggest. First, it would appear that the capital expenditure information (in respect of which a depreciation figure is given in the recurrent cross data) refers only to "end-of-the-pipe" expenditures and not to overall capital costs related to environmental quality considerations.[7] Second, particular environmental policies (such as an outright prohibition on certain technologies or production processes) may raise industry costs, but not be reflected in the PACE data. It is difficult to gauge the likely magnitude of such considerations, but overall, abatement and control of expenditures cannot be said to represent an important cost item for most industries. On the other hand, stricter environmental standards in the future would undoubtedly raise these costs.

In general, it should be emphasized that these are approximate calculations, based on a number of simplifying assumptions. As noted earlier, it was assumed that all U.S. imports from Mexico were accorded duty-free treatment and that the PACE equalization tax, at an average rate of 0.6 percent (see Table 7-2), was then added back. The total trade effects of the PACE equalization tax were calculated using reduced form equations to measure trade creation and trade diversion.[8]

Several limitations of this approach to the calculation of the trade effects of a notional PACE equalization tax should be emphasized, including its static, short-term and partial nature. It should also be noted that for computational and data availability reasons, the trade data used in the simulation are quite old, relating to 1986. The trade creation and trade diversion equations require elasticity estimates for import demand, export supply and substitution (cross price elasticities). For the calculations in Table 7-2, the price elasticities of import demand were based on estimates that have been widely used in other studies.[9] The export supply elasticity was assumed to be infinite (with a computing value of 99), and the cross elasticity of substitution was assigned a uniform value of -1.5.

How realistic are these assumptions, or more precisely, how sensitive are the simulation results to the elasticity values? Some sensitivity analysis is reported in Annex Table D. This analysis suggests a significant degree of sensitivity to the elasticity estimates, leading to a range in the estimates of export contraction for Mexico of between 1.2 percent and 2.6 percent of total exports. However, even though the elasticity assumptions have a significant effect on the magnitude of estimated export losses, the importance of this is greatly reduced by the fact that the numbers are so small in relation to total exports.

Annex Table E summarizes some other variations made in the simulation to see whether the application of a PACE equalization tax on Mexican exports would have a significantly different impact if other countries were also subject to the tax.[10] As expected, the export contraction experienced by Mexico as a

---

[7]The author is grateful to David Wheeler for pointing this out.

[8]Trade creation is the increase in imports resulting from lower trade barriers, and trade diversion is the result of substitution among preferential and nonpreferential suppliers (with no increase in total trade). The magnitude of trade creation depends on the demand and supply elasticities of imports, and the degree of trade liberalization. The size of the trade diversion effect depends largely on the elasticity of substitution between preferential and nonpreferential suppliers, in relation to the price effects of the (preferential) trade liberalization. See Laird and Yeats (1990).

[9]See Cline et al. (1978), Stern et al. (1975) and Laird and Yeats (1990).

[10]It will be recalled that the simulation results reported in Table 7-2 assumed that Mexico went to free trade with the United States and then exclusively faced a PACE equalization tax.

result of the hypothetical tax becomes less the greater the number of affected countries. Once again, however, the modest magnitude of the numbers means that the overall effect is not very dramatic.

To sum up this section, it has been argued that current U.S. trade policy does not have any systematic differential effect on Mexican exports in terms of their pollution intensity. This applies both to variations in tariff levels and to the incidence of NTBs, with prevailing measures reflecting considerations other than environmental quality. Because pollution abatement and control costs are small in relation to industrial output in the United States, the effects on Mexico's exports of a PACE equalization tax are also small.

Conclusions

This paper has looked at one way -- the imposition of a hypothetical PACE equalization tax by the United States against Mexican exports -- in which trade policy might be used, at least ostensibly, to meet environmental objectives.[11] There are three main reasons why such a policy would be flawed.

First, and most importantly, a PACE equalization tax or some similar arrangement would have very uncertain environmental consequences. The resource transfer implied by a PACE equalization tax, even if it were significantly larger than this paper has estimated it to be, would hardly guarantee a modification in the environmental behavior of the country upon whose exports the tax was levied. In the final analysis, a policy of this kind would be driven by considerations of competitiveness, and not of environmental quality. It would be a response to the notion that differential environmental standards, or perhaps even differential compliance costs for the same standards, were a source of unfair competition. If variations in the environmental assimilative capacities of countries, differences in social preferences, and the local (as opposed to transfrontier) nature of many environmental problems were taken into account, then this "remedial" application of trade policy would be hard to justify.

Secondly, as a policy designed to secure a "level playing field," or in other words to protect domestic industry from a cost disadvantage arising from governmental regulation, a PACE equalization tax would be largely ineffectual. It would provide a minor margin of protection to domestic industry, simply because the costs of complying with environmental standards represent a relatively small element in total costs. It would have nuisance value. This nuisance value might assume greater significance over time, however, if levels of pollution abatement and control expenditure were to increase, or an exporting country developed greater reliance on pollution-intensive products.

Thirdly, the nuisance value of a PACE equalization tax would be increased by the fact that it could well fall foul of GATT obligations. A tax applied discriminately against one country, as simulated in this paper, would be in breach of the most-favored-nation rule of Article I of the GATT. A PACE equalization tax that raised the total level of import charges above the maximum "bound" level committed to in GATT would also constitute an infringement, unless negotiations were undertaken to make the necessary compensatory tariff reductions on other imports.

In sum, a PACE equalization tax or any similar intervention would amount to bad environmental policy and bad trade policy, and it would carry negative consequences for the GATT trading system.

---

[11]Environmental objectives may also be addressed through trade measures in order to enforce domestic product standards, to enforce international agreements and to persuade other countries, through encouragement or threat, to adopt a particular set of environmental standards.

Annex Table A: POLLUTION ABATEMENT OPERATING COSTS BY U.S. INDUSTRY, 1988
(In Millions of U.S. Dollars)

SIC	Industry	Pollution abatement operating cost	Industry output	Cost/ output	Share of total industry output
324	Cement, hydraulic	134.1	4,234.3	3.17	0.17
261	Pulp mills	127.5	5,260.1	2.42	0.20
245	Wood buildings/mobile homes	158.2	6,627.3	2.39	0.26
333	Primary nonferrous metals	373.5	15,918.4	2.35	0.62
281	Industrial inorganic chems	488.5	22,109.6	2.21	0.86
286	Industrial organic chems.	1,275.4	59,971.7	2.13	2.34
263	Paperboard mills	334.6	16,094.2	2.08	0.63
262	Paper mills	661.2	33,545.8	1.97	1.31
287	Agricultural chems.	312.6	16,077.1	1.94	0.63
332	Iron and steel foundries	220.4	12,066.4	1.83	0.47
291	Petroleum refining	1,919.3	118,829.5	1.62	4.63
331	Blast furnace/basic steel	893.5	64,058.6	1.39	2.50
329	Misc. nonmetallic min. prods.	140.5	10,991.9	1.28	0.43
347	Metal services nes	108.4	9,191.4	1.18	0.36
249	Misc. wood prods.	98.9	8,477.8	1.17	0.33
348	Ordnance and accessories	92.1	8,021.8	1.15	0.31
334	Secondary nonferrous metals	71.5	6,663.4	1.07	0.26
339	Misc. primary metal prods.	36.2	3,514.9	1.03	0.14
289	Misc. chem. prods.	169.2	17,778.1	0.95	0.69
282	Plastics and synthetics	456.4	48,388.2	0.94	1.89
345	Screw machine prods., bolts	68.1	8,642.5	0.79	0.34
295	Paving and roofing materials	57.7	7,929.7	0.73	0.31
226	Textiles finishing, exc. wool	45.1	6,603.2	0.68	0.26
375	Motorcycles/bicycles & parts	6.8	1,056.8	0.64	0.04
254	Partitions and fixtures	36.9	5,770.8	0.64	0.22
328	Cut stone & stone prods	5.6	890.1	0.63	0.03
322	Glass/ware pressed/blown	53.2	8,562.5	0.62	0.33
311	Leather tanning/finishing	15.4	2,487.8	0.62	0.10
299	Misc. petroleum/coal prods.	28.5	4,655.6	0.61	0.18
383	Optical instruments/lenses	12.1	2,001.4	0.60	0.08
214	Tobacco stemming/redrying	14.1	2,366.8	0.60	0.09
325	Structural clay prods.	17.4	3,010.4	0.58	0.12
341	Metal cans/shipping containers	72.5	12,555.6	0.58	0.49
342	Cutlery, handtools	80.6	14,109.4	0.57	0.55
321	Flat glass	13.8	2,442.2	0.57	0.10
396	Costume jewelry	11.5	2,087.5	0.55	0.08
336	Nonferrous foundries	38.6	7,257.2	0.53	0.28
283	Drugs	221.1	43,986.6	0.50	1.71
203	Pres. fruit & veg.	183.4	38,301.3	0.48	1.49
208	Beverages	235.4	49,722.2	0.47	1.94
386	Photographic equip./supplies	93.3	20,545.8	0.45	0.80
367	Electronic components/access.	258.6	56,999.4	0.45	2.22
207	Fats and oils	92.2	20,516.9	0.45	0.80
306	Fabricated rubber prods. nes	44.2	9,867.2	0.45	0.38
374	Railroad equip.	14.7	3,285.9	0.45	0.13
221	Weaving mills, cotton	25.3	5,664.5	0.45	0.22
373	Ship/boat building/repair	65.4	14,728.1	0.44	0.57
335	Nonferrous rolling/drawing	174.7	39,600.7	0.44	1.54
326	Pottery and related prods.	10.3	2,550.5	0.40	0.10
395	Pens/pencils/office & art supp	11.6	2,880.5	0.40	0.11
285	Paints and allied prods.	54.3	13,531.7	0.40	0.53
229	Misc. textiles	27.8	6,967.1	0.40	0.27
366	Communication equip.	140.1	36,092.7	0.39	1.41
206	sugar & confec. prods	70.2	19,640.9	0.36	0.77
385	Opthalmic goods	6.9	1,945.8	0.35	0.08
264	Misc. converted paper	137.3	39,462.6	0.35	1.54
301	Tires and inner tubes	38.9	11,240.1	0.35	0.44
343	Plumbing/heating exc. electric	19.8	5,729.9	0.35	0.22
356	General industrial machinery	93.3	27,198.3	0.34	1.06
209	Misc. foods	101.2	30,096.7	0.34	1.17
372	Aircraft & parts	265.1	79,552.5	0.33	3.10
344	Fab. structural metal prods.	144.1	43,389.6	0.33	1.69
361	Electric distributing equip.	30.1	9,097.2	0.33	0.35
346	Metal forgings/stampings	92.5	29,932.1	0.31	1.17
204	Grain mill prods	125.1	40,945.2	0.31	1.60
362	Elec. industrial appar.	51.1	16,818.8	0.30	0.66
243	Millwork. plywood etc.	69.1	22,858.5	0.30	0.89
252	Office furniture	23.1	7,778.9	0.30	0.30
364	Elec. lighting & wiring	55.9	19,236.3	0.29	0.75

114

Annex Table A cont'd.

SIC	Industry	Pollution abatement operating cost	Industry output	Cost/ output	Share of total industry output
369	Misc. elec. equip./supplies	66.6	23,013.6	0.29	0.90
363	Household appliances	49.6	17,332.4	0.29	0.68
351	Engines and turbines	45.7	16,223.1	0.28	0.63
202	Dairy products	130.1	46,994.3	0.28	1.83
307	Misc. plastics prods.	181.2	67,242.3	0.27	2.62
358	Refrigeration/service machinery	68.1	25,578.7	0.27	1.00
223	Weaving/finishing, wool	5.1	1,928.4	0.26	0.08
275	Commercial printing	122.3	47,459.5	0.26	1.85
284	Soaps, cleaners & toilet goods	97.4	37,856.2	0.26	1.48
251	Household furniture	48.1	19,130.8	0.25	0.75
393	Musical instruments	2.2	875.8	0.25	0.03
323	Prods. of purchased glass	14.5	5,800.8	0.25	0.23
371	Motor vehicles/equip	548.1	221,575.4	0.25	8.63
379	Misc. transport equip.	13.8	5,655.3	0.24	0.22
394	Toys/sporting goods	23.9	9,970.1	0.24	0.39
222	Weaving mills, synthetic	20.1	8,462.6	0.24	0.33
354	Metalworking machinery	55.2	24,365.5	0.23	0.95
376	Guided missiles/space vehicles	60.7	28,193.7	0.22	1.10
205	Bakery prods	51.8	24,156.8	0.21	0.94
201	Meat Products	170.8	81,188.7	0.21	3.16
304	Rubber/plastic hose/belting	10.7	5,268.1	0.20	0.21
242	Sawmills and planing	40.8	20,143.6	0.20	0.78
327	Concrete, gypsum & plaster	49.1	24,576.7	0.20	0.96
316	Luggage	1.9	956.7	0.20	0.04
352	Farm/garden machinery	26.7	13,560.1	0.20	0.53
278	Blankbooks/bookbinding	8.3	4,276.1	0.19	0.17
225	Knitting mills	25.1	13,223.7	0.19	0.52
399	Misc. manufactures	23.7	13,286.9	0.18	0.52
349	Misc. fabricated metal prods.	47.8	27,261.6	0.18	1.06
353	Construction/related machinery	48.1	27,749.4	0.17	1.08
359	Misc. mach., nonelectric	37.9	21,875.2	0.17	0.85
253	Public building furn.	4.5	2,660.8	0.17	0.10
259	Misc. furniture/fixtures	6.1	3,884.7	0.16	0.15
382	Measuring/controlling devices	41.7	26,813.9	0.16	1.04
276	Manifold business forms	11.6	7,781.4	0.15	0.30
244	Wood containers	3.4	2,294.4	0.15	0.09
387	Watches/clocks/watchcases	1.8	1,295.1	0.14	0.05
228	Yarn and thread mills	14.1	10,320.3	0.14	0.40
384	Medical instruments/supplies	34.3	25,329.9	0.14	0.99
227	Floor covering mills (textiles)	13.8	10,256.1	0.13	0.40
279	Printing trade services	5.5	4,478.5	0.12	0.17
314	Footwear, except rubber	4.7	4,258.1	0.11	0.17
211	Cigarettes	22.1	20,078.3	0.11	0.78
213	Chewing/smoking tobacco	1.3	1,185.1	0.11	0.05
273	Books	17.8	17,136.6	0.10	0.67
271	Newspapers	33.7	32,926.8	0.10	1.28
365	Radio/TV receiving equip.	7.1	8,360.4	0.08	0.33
277	Greeting card publishing	2.3	3,081.7	0.07	0.12
241	Logging	8.1	11,663.8	0.07	0.45
391	Jewelry/silverware/plated ware	3.8	5,768.7	0.07	0.22
357	Office & computing machines	27.6	67,643.9	0.04	2.64
381	Search/navigation equip.	7.6	36,596.5	0.02	1.43
272	Periodicals	3.8	18,611.8	0.02	0.73
274	Misc. publishing	1.1	8,154.4	0.01	0.32
All Industries		14,008.6	2,617,476.9	0.54	100.00

Sources: U.S. Department of Commerce, Bureau of Census, Manufacturers' Pollution Abatement Capital Expenditures and Operating Costs (1988).
U.S. Department of Commerce, Bureau of Census, Annual Survey of Manufacturers (1988).

Notes:

1. The data cover firms of 20 employees or more with pollution abatement costs in excess of US$1 million.
2. Major SIC Group 23 (Apparel and other textile products) are excluded from the survey.

Annex Table B: MEXICO'S EXPORTS TO THE UNITED STATES OF DIRTY INDUSTRY PRODUCTS, 1981-89
(In Thousands of U.S. Dollars)

SITC	1981		1982		1984		1986		1988		1989		Compound growth rate: 1981-1989 (1990 constant $)
	Value	Share	Value	Share	Value	Share	Value	Share	Value	Share	Value	Share	
25 PULP AND WASTE PAPER													
251 PULP AND WASTE PAPER	81	0.0	222	0.0	137	0.0	540	0.0	739	0.0	8,384	0.0	48%
33 PETROLEUM AND PRODUCTS													
334 PETROLEUM PRODUCTS,REFIN	329,577	2.4	262,797	1.7	894,102	4.9	414,200	2.4	374,827	1.6	218,358	0.8	-3%
335 RESIDUAL PETRLM PROD NES	7,370	0.1	12,064	0.1	43,889	0.2	22,007	0.1	7,058	0.0	7,138	0.0	-7%
51 ORGANIC CHEMICALS													
511 HYDROCARBONS NES,DERIVS	993	0.0	4,749	0.0	141,127	0.8	10,044	0.1	11,725	0.0	6,816	0.0	12%
512 ALCOHOLS,PHENOLS ETC	7,819	0.1	4,599	0.0	16,561	0.1	15,594	0.1	29,385	0.1	84,962	0.3	28%
513 CARBOXYLIC ACIDS ETC	1,333	0.0	7,286	0.0	21,916	0.1	13,804	0.1	54,839	0.2	31,248	0.1	29%
514 NITROGEN-FNCTN COMPOUNDS	2,581	0.0	2,762	0.0	681	0.0	1,155	0.0	4,682	0.0	15,303	0.1	14%
515 ORG-INORG COMPOUNDS ETC	188	0.0	40	0.0	1,395	0.0	6,482	0.0	4,646	0.0	6,702	0.0	58%
516 OTHER ORGANIC CHEMICALS	2,950	0.0	3,611	0.0	8,716	0.0	7,001	0.0	8,712	0.0	16,856	0.1	15%
52 INORGANIC CHEMICALS													
522 INORG ELEMNTS,OXIDES,ETC	167,831	1.2	168,631	1.1	153,097	0.8	96,831	0.6	154,312	0.7	159,580	0.6	-4%
523 OTHR INORG CHEMICALS ETC	12,015	0.1	10,065	0.1	24,677	0.1	27,870	0.2	46,491	0.2	55,633	0.2	17%
53 DYES,TANNING,COLOUR PROD													
532 DYES NES,TANNING PROD	65	0.0	74	0.0	7,087	0.0	5,141	0.0	18,712	0.1	16,337	0.1	93%
533 PIGMENTS,PAINTS,ETC	2,521	0.0	2,353	0.0	3,631	0.0	4,716	0.0	15,890	0.1	11,657	0.0	20%
54 MEDICINAL,PHARM PRODUCTS													
541 MEDICINAL,PHARM PRODUCTS	16,803	0.1	17,252	0.1	13,489	0.1	21,349	0.1	25,770	0.1	16,654	0.1	-1%
58 PLASTIC MATERIALS ETC													
582 PROD OF CONDENSATION ETC	602	0.0	1,124	0.0	8,183	0.0	60,961	0.3	63,191	0.3	9,344	0.0	54%
59 CHEMICAL MATERIALS NES													
591 PESTICIDES,DISINFECTANTS	2,632	0.0	773	0.0	2,141	0.0	3,131	0.0	13,164	0.1	1,087	0.0	16%
598 MISCEL CHEM PRODUCTS NES	4,323	0.0	5,240	0.0	61,456	0.3	7,232	0.0	8,686	0.0	23,105	0.1	12%
63 WOOD,CORK MANUFACTRS NES													
634 VENEERS,PLYWOOD,ETC	28,929	0.2	32,474	0.2	56,175	0.3	60,195	0.3	95,676	0.4	11,258	0.0	4%
635 WOOD MANUFACTURES NES	44,370	0.3	39,098	0.2	37,905	0.2	37,407	0.2	58,042	0.2	94,542	0.3	4%
64 PAPER,PAPERBOARD AND MFR													
641 PAPER AND PAPERBOARD	5,522	0.0	6,264	0.0	41,550	0.2	62,613	0.4	130,830	0.6	138,392	0.5	43%
642 PAPER,ETC,PRECUT,ARTS OF	83,519	0.6	96,537	0.6	109,201	0.6	161,756	0.9	227,806	1.0	250,682	0.9	9%
66 NONMETAL MINERAL MFS NES													
661 LIME,CEMENT,BLDG PRODS	10,657	0.1	12,576	0.1	86,748	0.5	142,853	0.8	166,600	0.7	167,459	0.6	35%
663 MINERAL MANUFCTURES NES	12,205	0.1	13,300	0.1	12,325	0.1	15,723	0.1	24,859	0.1	32,524	0.1	7%

Annex Table B cont'd.

SITC	1981 Value	1981 Share	1982 Value	1982 Share	1984 Value	1984 Share	1986 Value	1986 Share	1988 Value	1988 Share	1989 Value	1989 Share	Compound growth rate: 1981-1989 (1990 constant $)
664 GLASS	8,017	0.1	27,118	0.2	55,949	0.3	82,487	0.5	127,701	0.5	126,493	0.5	24%
665 GLASSWARE	14,830	0.1	16,613	0.1	32,707	0.2	42,032	0.2	57,671	0.2	69,962	0.3	15%
67 IRON AND STEEL													
671 PIG IRON ETC	19,518	0.1	14,014	0.1	18,295	0.1	18,024	0.1	38,929	0.2	54,604	0.2	10%
672 IRON,STEEL PRIMARY FORMS	21	0.0	47	0.0	12,621	0.1	11,411	0.1	17,118	0.1	23,736	0.1	115%
673 IRON,STEEL SHAPES ETC	2,340	0.0	13,147	0.1	61,390	0.3	27,312	0.2	38,896	0.2	22,019	0.1	15%
674 IRN,STL UNIV,PLATE,SHEET	404	0.0	5,744	0.0	71,245	0.4	68,469	0.4	99,708	0.4	112,871	0.4	51%
675 IRON,STEEL HOOP,STRIP	87	0.0	298	0.0	3,911	0.0	1,539	0.0	2,391	0.0	N.A.	0.0	21%
676 RAILWY RAILS ETC IRN,STL	0	0.0	1	0.0	0	0.0	0	0.0	22	0.0	76	0.0	72%
677 IRN,STL WIRE(EXCL W ROD)	160	0.0	191	0.0	606	0.0	1,308	0.0	1,342	0.0	934	0.0	22%
678 IRON,STL TUBES,PIPES,ETC	20,796	0.1	20,693	0.1	110,473	0.6	50,203	0.3	88,161	0.4	100,697	0.4	17%
679 IRN,STL CASTINGS UNWORKD	752	0.0	112	0.0	1,670	0.0	1,534	0.0	4,281	0.0	6,033	0.0	32%
68 NONFERROUS METALS													
681 SILVER,PLATINUM,ETC	207,463	1.5	189,969	1.2	310,741	1.7	238,173	1.4	244,014	1.0	320,487	1.2	1%
682 COPPER EXC CEMENT COPPER	41,004	0.3	23,690	0.2	40,675	0.2	85,008	0.5	268,311	1.1	204,418	0.7	24%
684 ALUMINIUM	648	0.0	367	0.0	4,807	0.0	4,622	0.0	33,155	0.1	16,607	0.1	57%
685 LEAD	25,386	0.2	12,494	0.1	20,061	0.1	11,786	0.1	23,937	0.1	19,864	0.1	-2%
686 ZINC	14,803	0.1	18,371	0.1	57,507	0.3	38,899	0.2	74,239	0.3	118,844	0.4	21%
689 NONFER BASE METALS NES	5,001	0.0	1,579	0.0	2,646	0.0	4,645	0.0	15,000	0.1	12,255	0.0	15%
69 METAL MANUFACTURES NES													
691 STRUCTURES AND PARTS NES	3,989	0.0	2,221	0.0	4,119	0.0	3,871	0.0	6,414	0.0	10,394	0.0	10%
692 METAL TANKS,BOXES,ETC	1,913	0.0	1,314	0.0	11,429	0.1	21,238	0.1	32,007	0.1	28,736	0.1	40%
693 WIRE PRODUCTS NON ELECTR	4,787	0.0	5,358	0.0	8,933	0.0	15,407	0.1	21,439	0.1	30,615	0.1	19%
694 STL,COPPR NAILS,NUTS,ETC	762	0.0	1,995	0.0	3,387	0.0	3,668	0.0	12,017	0.1	12,495	0.0	27%
695 TOOLS	17,023	0.1	9,305	0.1	15,672	0.1	23,049	0.1	29,603	0.1	33,398	0.1	8%
696 CUTLERY	175	0.0	207	0.0	627	0.0	454	0.0	4,403	0.0	4,278	0.0	43%
697 BASE MTL HOUSEHOLD EQUIP	8,354	0.1	6,996	0.0	10,428	0.1	15,524	0.1	47,206	0.2	31,475	0.1	19%
699 BASE METAL MFRS NES	55,646	0.4	67,539	0.4	98,821	0.5	134,628	0.8	232,564	1.0	297,958	1.1	16%
SUB-TOTAL	1,198,765	8.6	1,143,274	7.2	2,704,909	14.8	2,103,896	12.0	3,067,171	13.0	3,043,270	11.1	9%
OTHER COMMODITIES	12,814,511	91.4	14,626,833	92.8	15,561,959	85.2	15,442,595	88.0	20,477,330	87.0	24,496,793	88.9	3%
TOTAL ALL COMMODITIES	14,013,276	100.0	15,770,107	100.0	18,266,868	100.0	17,546,491	100.0	23,544,501	100.0	27,540,063	100.0	3%

Source: COMTRADE Data files.

Notes:

1. These are import statistics because Mexico's export statistics in COMTRADE do not report "maquila" output.
2. The compound growth rates in the final column were calculated on the basis of the average of 1981/82 and 1988/89 trade.
3. The deflator used is the Unit Value index in U.S. dollars terms of manufactures exported from the G-5 countries (France, Germany, Japan, United Kingdom and United States), weighted proportionately to the countries' exports to the developing countries.

Annex Table C: MEXICO'S EXPORTS TO THE WORLD OF DIRTY INDUSTRY PRODUCTS, 1981-89
(In Thousands of U.S. Dollars)

SITC	1981 Value	1981 Share	1982 Value	1982 Share	1984 Value	1984 Share	1986 Value	1986 Share	1988 Value	1988 Share	1989 Value	1989 Share	Compound growth rate: 1981-1989 (1990 constant $)
25 PULP AND WASTE PAPER													
251 PULP AND WASTE PAPER	454	0.0	1,370	0.0	1,395	0.0	807	0.0	34,804	0.1	29,719	0.1	51%
33 PETROLEUM AND PRODUCTS													
334 PETROLEUM PRODUCTS,REFIN	525,017	2.4	676,687	2.7	958,710	3.5	501,195	2.1	652,599	2.0	231,158	0.7	-7%
335 RESIDUAL PETRLM PROD NES	7,695	0.0	13,401	0.1	44,456	0.2	22,301	0.1	11,727	0.0	7,160	0.0	-5%
51 ORGANIC CHEMICALS													
511 HYDROCARBONS NES,DERIVS	10,031	0.0	6,264	0.0	165,252	0.6	24,230	0.1	40,379	0.1	36,823	0.1	17%
512 ALCOHOLS,PHENOLS ETC	15,887	0.1	14,697	0.1	31,662	0.1	25,784	0.1	58,476	0.2	92,321	0.3	18%
513 CARBOXYLIC ACIDS ETC	92,073	0.4	135,285	0.5	177,502	0.6	204,312	0.9	330,008	1.0	264,169	0.7	9%
514 NITROGEN-FNCTN COMPOUNDS	10,712	0.0	31,252	0.1	7,611	0.0	15,507	0.1	35,922	0.1	42,559	0.1	5%
515 ORG-INORG COMPOUNDS ETC	15,872	0.1	34,996	0.1	11,454	0.0	18,686	0.1	23,981	0.1	20,446	0.1	-5%
516 OTHER ORGANIC CHEMICALS	11,874	0.1	20,058	0.1	23,756	0.1	31,700	0.1	31,022	0.1	45,208	0.1	8%
52 INORGANIC CHEMICALS													
522 INORG ELEMNTS,OXIDES,ETC	293,468	1.3	225,089	0.9	191,545	0.7	127,886	0.5	204,345	0.6	194,853	0.6	-6%
523 OTHR INORG CHEMICALS ETC	50,126	0.2	26,634	0.1	37,103	0.1	59,678	0.2	91,028	0.3	97,808	0.3	8%
53 DYES,TANNING,COLOUR PROD													
532 DYES NES,TANNING PROD	2,522	0.0	2,938	0.0	9,391	0.0	9,570	0.0	28,308	0.1	26,420	0.1	29%
533 PIGMENTS,PAINTS,ETC	27,684	0.1	21,695	0.1	18,927	0.1	37,768	0.2	65,090	0.2	32,684	0.1	5%
54 MEDICINAL,PHARM PRODUCTS													
541 MEDICINAL,PHARM PRODUCTS	69,722	0.3	60,468	0.2	47,734	0.2	82,275	0.3	86,957	0.3	70,967	0.2	-1%
58 PLASTIC MATERIALS ETC													
582 PROD OF CONDENSATION ETC	15,277	0.1	16,325	0.1	31,448	0.1	75,507	0.3	88,574	0.3	29,689	0.1	14%
59 CHEMICAL MATERIALS NES													
591 PESTICIDES,DISINFECTANTS	3,745	0.0	5,972	0.0	4,545	0.0	12,989	0.1	24,731	0.1	3,762	0.0	11%
598 MISCEL CHEM PRODUCTS NES	26,841	0.1	23,426	0.1	76,412	0.3	34,270	0.1	44,865	0.1	39,038	0.1	3%
63 WOOD,CORK MANUFACTRS NES													
634 VENEERS,PLYWOOD,ETC	29,283	0.1	36,614	0.1	56,796	0.2	60,343	0.3	96,113	0.3	11,349	0.0	3%
635 WOOD MANUFACTURES NES	46,074	0.2	51,969	0.2	39,536	0.1	38,267	0.2	59,364	0.2	95,772	0.3	2%
64 PAPER,PAPERBOARD AND MFR													
641 PAPER AND PAPERBOARD	11,856	0.1	12,741	0.1	47,360	0.2	65,368	0.3	175,283	0.5	154,218	0.4	34%
642 PAPER,ETC,PRECUT,ARTS OF	85,670	0.4	112,949	0.4	111,004	0.4	163,550	0.7	231,146	0.7	253,490	0.7	8%
66 NONMETAL MINERAL MFS NES													
661 LIME,CEMENT,BLDG PRODS	12,748	0.1	20,614	0.1	88,764	0.3	143,715	0.6	174,276	0.5	169,500	0.5	29%
663 MINERAL MANUFCTURES NES	15,556	0.1	18,244	0.1	13,627	0.0	18,107	0.1	29,532	0.1	35,020	0.1	5%

continued overleaf

Annex Table C cont'd.

SITC	1981 Value	1981 Share	1982 Value	1982 Share	1984 Value	1984 Share	1986 Value	1986 Share	1988 Value	1988 Share	1989 Value	1989 Share	Compound growth rate: 1981-1989 (1990 constant $)
664 GLASS	11,761	0.1	37,341	0.1	73,839	0.3	94,262	0.4	144,214	0.4	146,965	0.4	21%
665 GLASSWARE	41,299	0.2	29,537	0.1	39,915	0.1	50,560	0.2	74,910	0.2	87,173	0.2	7%
67 IRON AND STEEL													
671 PIG IRON ETC	21,914	0.1	15,200	0.1	26,959	0.1	25,208	0.1	48,251	0.2	63,377	0.2	11%
672 IRON,STEEL PRIMARY FORMS	290	0.0	5,149	0.0	19,057	0.1	31,379	0.1	53,003	0.2	60,320	0.2	41%
673 IRON,STEEL SHAPES ETC	31,122	0.1	17,809	0.1	86,105	0.3	49,583	0.2	150,821	0.5	85,439	0.2	18%
674 IRN,STL UNIV,PLATE,SHEET	838	0.0	7,792	0.0	79,735	0.3	107,445	0.4	144,005	0.4	197,114	0.6	53%
675 IRON,STEEL HOOP,STRIP	213	0.0	423	0.0	4,176	0.0	1,680	0.0	2,866	0.0	153	0.0	17%
676 RAILWY RAILS ETC IRN,STL	11	0.0	608	0.0	59	0.0	45	0.0	2,528	0.0	76	0.0	16%
677 IRN,STL WIRE(EXCL W ROD)	758	0.0	452	0.0	1,709	0.0	3,805	0.0	3,259	0.0	1,157	0.0	14%
678 IRON,STL TUBES,PIPES,ETC	24,828	0.1	30,229	0.1	121,349	0.4	65,731	0.3	161,333	0.5	187,336	0.5	22%
679 IRN,STL CASTINGS UNWORKD	1,402	0.0	317	0.0	1,812	0.0	1,553	0.0	4,406	0.0	6,806	0.0	22%
68 NONFERROUS METALS													
681 SILVER,PLATINUM,ETC	433,161	2.0	339,314	1.3	442,087	1.6	311,142	1.3	423,913	1.3	506,637	1.4	-1%
682 COPPER EXC CEMENT COPPER	65,408	0.3	42,672	0.2	78,904	0.3	90,164	0.4	304,279	0.9	316,336	0.9	20%
684 ALUMINIUM	2,845	0.0	1,921	0.0	6,269	0.0	5,672	0.0	40,895	0.1	19,372	0.1	33%
685 LEAD	55,695	0.3	39,013	0.2	54,539	0.2	37,697	0.2	68,121	0.2	65,377	0.2	1%
686 ZINC	49,192	0.2	21,716	0.1	78,116	0.3	59,791	0.2	99,987	0.3	144,380	0.4	13%
689 NONFER BASE METALS NES	8,032	0.0	1,869	0.0	3,240	0.0	5,662	0.0	18,258	0.1	16,999	0.0	13%
69 METAL MANUFACTURES NES													
691 STRUCTURES AND PARTS NES	8,587	0.0	19,105	0.1	6,931	0.0	6,604	0.0	7,704	0.0	10,621	0.0	-8%
692 METAL TANKS,BOXES,ETC	4,978	0.0	8,542	0.0	11,985	0.0	22,136	0.1	35,463	0.1	29,380	0.1	18%
693 WIRE PRODUCTS NON ELECTR	6,637	0.0	7,649	0.0	9,959	0.0	16,623	0.1	26,146	0.1	34,383	0.1	16%
694 STL,COPPR NAILS,NUTS,ETC	2,475	0.0	3,483	0.0	3,896	0.0	4,488	0.0	15,066	0.0	14,386	0.0	18%
695 TOOLS	26,119	0.1	14,819	0.1	17,650	0.1	26,050	0.1	35,518	0.1	39,163	0.1	4%
696 CUTLERY	2,745	0.0	2,991	0.0	1,227	0.0	2,106	0.0	8,533	0.0	9,815	0.0	12%
697 BASE MTL HOUSEHOLD EQUIP	19,052	0.1	11,714	0.0	11,772	0.0	18,914	0.1	52,269	0.2	33,204	0.1	10%
699 BASE METAL MFRS NES	62,490	0.3	79,142	0.3	104,115	0.4	145,236	0.6	250,686	0.8	315,596	0.9	15%
SUB-TOTAL	2,262,039	10.3	2,308,495	9.1	3,481,395	12.6	2,957,351	12.3	4,794,964	14.9	4,375,698	12.4	5%
OTHER COMMODITIES	19,667,049	89.7	22,977,955	90.9	24,157,701	87.4	21,039,832	87.7	27,283,743	85.1	30,951,450	87.6	1%
TOTAL ALL COMMODITIES	21,929,088	100.0	25,286,450	100.0	27,639,096	100.0	23,997,183	100.0	32,078,707	100.0	35,327,148	100.0	1%

Source: COMTRADE Data files

Notes:

1. These are import statistics (expressed in current U.S. dollars) because Mexico's export statistics in COMTRADE do not report "maquila" output.
2. The compound growth rates in the final column were calculated on the basis of the average of 1981/82 and 1988/89 trade.
3. The deflator used is the Unit Value index in U.S. dollars terms of manufactures exported from the G-5 countries (France, Germany, Japan, United Kingdom and United States), weighted proportionately to the countries' exports to the developing countries.

119

Annex Table D: SENSITIVITY ANALYSIS ON ELASTICITY ESTIMATES
(In Thousands of U.S. Dollars)

Elasticity Assumptions	Trade Creation	Trade Diversion	Total Effect	Share of 1986 Exports (%)
"Best" estimates em = "best available" (BA) ex = 99 es = -1.5	-235,605	-140,059	-375,663	2.0
Changes in em				
Alternative 1 (em = 0.5 BA)	-115,204	-138,426	-253,630	1.4
Alternative 2 (em = 1.5 BA)	-361,201	-141,664	-502,866	2.6
Changes in ex				
Alternative 1 (ex = 1)	-74,235	-137,692	-211,927	1.2
Alternative 2 (ex = 3)	-134,198	-138,519	-272,717	1.5
Changes in es				
Alternative 1 (es = 0.75)	-233,531	-69,573	-303,103	1.6
Alternative 2 (es = -2.25)	-237,666	-211,444	-499,110	2.6

Key em = price elasticity of import demand
ex = elasticity of supply
es = cross price elasticity of substitution

Annex Table E: ALTERNATIVE ASSUMPTIONS ABOUT THE GEOGRAPHICAL INCIDENCE OF THE PAC EQUALIZATION TAX
(In Thousands of U.S. Dollars)

Alternative Scenarios	Trade Creation	Trade Diversion	Total Effect	Share of 1986 exports (%)
Basic Scenario Mexico to free trade with PAC equalization tax added back; regime unchanged for all other. U.S. imports				
Mexico	-235,605	-140,059	-375,663	2.0
Alternative 1 PAC equalization tax applied to all developing countries; regime unchanged for U.S. imports from industrial countries				
Mexico	-217,349	-64,549	-281,898	1.7
All developing countries	-1,389,662	-418,316	-1,807,978	1.5
Alternative 2 PAC equalization tax applied to all U.S. imports				
Mexico	-217,349	-	-217,349	1.3
All countries	-4,259,633	-	-4,259,633	1.2

References

Cline, William R., et al. 1978. *Trade Negotiations in the Tokyo Round.* Washington D.C.: Brookings Institution.

Erzan, Refik and Alexander Yeats. 1991. Prospects for United States–Latin America Free Trade Areas: Empirical Evidence Concerning the View from the South. Washington, D.C.: World Bank, mimeo.

Kalt, Joseph, P. 1985. 'The Impact of Domestic Regulatory Policies on International Competitiveness.' *Harvard Institute of Economic Research*, Discussion Paper No. 1411.

Laird, Samuel and Alexander Yeats. 1990. *Quantitative Methods for Trade Barrier Analysis.* New York: New York University Press.

Report to the Congress by the President. 1991. Response of the Administration to Issues Raised in Connection with the Negotiation of a North American Free Trade Agreement. (May).

Stern, Robert, et al. 1975. *Price Elasticities in International Trade.* London: Macmillan.

Tobey, J.1990. 'The Effects of Domestic Environmental Policies on Patterns of World Trade: an Empirical Test,' *Kyklos*, vol. 43, no. 2, pp. 191–209.

U.S. Department of Commerce. 1988a. *Annual Survey of Manufacturers.* Washington, D.C.: U.S. Government Printing Office.

———. 1988b. *Manufacturers' Pollution Abatement Capital Expenditures and Operating Costs.* Washington, D.C.: U.S. Government Printing Office.

[16]

Economic Development, Environmental Regulation and the International Migration of Toxic Industrial Pollution: 1960-88

Robert E.B. Lucas, David Wheeler and Hemamala Hettige

Introduction

This paper is largely empirical. It examines how the structure of manufacturing production varies, both across countries and through time, in relation to the toxic emissions of the component industries. Evidence is also presented on the connection between these variations and trade policy liberalization.

Industrial emissions may be thought of as output multiplied by the pollution intensity of that output. In turn the pollution intensity of output derives from the mix of industrial products, the processes used to produce each of these goods, and treatment of the resultant waste from these processes. It is important to establish at the outset that the present investigation addresses only the first of these elements in pollution intensity -- the effect of product (or industrial) mix. This scope of analysis is dictated by the nature of the data available, described later. Yet this evidence does offer some interesting insights, for little systematic prior evidence exists in this sphere.[1]

Meanwhile the next section discusses, in broad terms, some of the elements likely to affect the pollution intensity of industrial production, before turning to the results.

Sources of Change in Pollution Intensity

Development and Private Comparative Advantage

In the absence of any binding controls on the generation of environmental bads -- including failure of private contractual arrangements to contain damaging effects -- there will be over production and over consumption of environmentally harmful commodities. Free trade in such an unregulated context results in a distribution of production across countries founded on comparative private cost advantages without regard to environmental costs: the capacity or willingness of nations to withstand or accept environmental damage does not enter the trade calculus.

As nations develop, the range of commodities in which they have a private comparative cost advantage in trade obviously shifts. These shifts may arise from accumulating capital available per worker, from improvements in the state of know-how and worker skills, or from enhanced identification or ability to exploit natural resources. Even if there were no environmental regulation in wealthier economies, free trade under these conditions might well lead to disproportionately rapid growth of industrial pollution in developing countries. Rising manufacturing emission intensity with income might simply reflect a shift toward comparative advantage in manufacturing generally, and of more capital intensive (smokestack) industries, which also happen to be pollution intensive, in particular.

---

[1] See, however, Grossman and Krueger (1991).

68

Environmental Regulation

The standards required by environmental regulations vary substantially across countries for several reasons:

(a) *World income inequality*: The desire for a cleaner environment is presumably a normal good, in the sense that demands for tighter standards rise with income. The lower income countries would then be less concerned to avoid local environmental damage, as were the advanced nations at an earlier stage in their growth.

(b) *Environmental absorptive capacity*: Being able to locate industries with emissions harmful to humans far from densely populated areas presumably has its attractions. On the other hand, some sparsely populated regions exhibit particularly fragile ecosystems, diminishing their capacity to withstand toxic releases.

(c) *Regulatory capability*: Differences in the ability to enforce regulations may explain part of the observable gaps in legislated norms and in the strictness of enforcement.

Regulating environmental damage and taxing emissions can, in principle, be used to internalize the external costs stemming from various forms of pollution. Such instruments, if effective, must alter the costs of production and hence comparative cost advantage in trade. If the externalities inherent in environmental damage are appropriately contained then trade will take place according to the social comparative advantage of nations, an advantage defined by a balance of environmental and other costs. But since both private costs and environmental costs differ from country to country one would not expect to see an even spatial distribution of toxic emissions in an optimally regulated world. Indeed, rising incomes may well first give rise to worse emission levels, as cost advantage shifts toward pollution intensive industries. This trend may then be overtaken at higher income levels by electoral demands for a cleaner environment and perhaps enhanced capacity for enforcement.

Economic Policy Regime

Industrial development has traditionally been viewed as damaging to the environment. Since environmentalists have joined most economists in associating liberal economic regimes with more rapid industrial growth, they have tended to look askance at openness. However, this view neglects the possibility that more open economies follow a less pollution-intensive industrial development path. If openness decreases pollution intensity, then its negative environmental impact via aggregate growth is certainly mitigated and may even be reversed.

The labor cost advantage of developing economies, if allowed free rein in the market, will enhance the prospects of many light assembly activities whose environmental impact is modest. Protection, on the other hand, is often focused on relatively capital- and pollution-intensive sectors such as chemicals and steel.

Summing Up: Towards Testable Hypotheses

The previous discussion has identified three forces which may have significantly affected the worldwide incidence of industrial pollution: development-related changes in private comparative advantage; environmental regulation in the wealthier economies; and differences in economic policy regimes. From this we distill three lines of analysis to be pursued.

69

(i) ***Development and sectoral composition*:** The patterns of pollution intensity of manufacturing production in relation to level of economic development, as measured by income per capita, are explored. In particular, it is frequently asserted that pollution exhibits an inverse U-shaped relationship with per capita income: in other words, pollution is believed to first rise faster than output at low levels of income then to rise more slowly than output after some critical income threshold.[2]

(ii) ***OECD environmental regulation and displacement*:** Since it is difficult to proxy for the strictures and implementation of OECD environmental regulations, direct tests of any resultant production relocation are difficult to undertake. Nonetheless, at least broad differences in trends across differing time periods may be examined to ascertain whether production relocation of dirtier industries has been more rapid during episodes of enhanced OECD environmental regulation.

(iii) ***LDC economic policy and pollution intensity*:** Has actual import protection among the developing countries promoted or discouraged production of the dirtier industrial products? This is examined here by posing the question: Have periods of trade liberalization led to more or less rapid growth in the pollution-intensive industries among the LDCs?

Data: Sources and Issues

Data Sources

Three primary data sources are drawn upon to derive a measure of pollution intensity of manufacturing output in some 80 countries from 1960 to 1988 for the purposes of this study.[3]

The first data source is a sample of 15,000 plants, drawn from the U.S. Environmental Protection Agency's (EPA's) Toxic Release Inventory (TRI) for 1987. First mandated by amendments to U.S. Superfund legislation in 1986, the TRI records air, water, underground and solid waste releases of 320 toxic substances by each reporting plant.

As the second data source, the U.S. Census Bureau provided the output data, drawn from the 1987 Census of Manufactures, for each of the 15,000 EPA sample plants. After matching plant-level observations and translating from U.S. five digit SIC identifiers to the ISIC codes, the aggregate toxic releases per unit of output are calculated for each of 37 ISIC industry categories.

In fact, three toxic intensity measures per unit of output are considered in this analysis. The first is total pounds of all 320 toxic releases -- whether atmospheric, effluent or solid -- per dollar's worth of output. In Table 5-1, this measure is labeled Total Release Intensity. However, such a measure neglects the fact that some emissions are obviously of greater concern than others. However, the EPA's Human Health and Ecotoxity Database (HHED) contains several measures of toxicological and carcinogenic potency of specific emissions. Based upon these the EPA reports an ordinal measure of human toxicity risk associated with each chemical emitted, ranging from category 1 (mild) through 4 (very serious). The second measure of toxic

---

[2] Although there are many assertions that such a pattern prevails there is little systematic evidence either to support or refute this presumption. See, however, Grossman and Krueger (1991) who indeed find such an inverse-U pattern in a cross-country study of urban air pollution.

[3] For full technical details, see Martin, Wheeler, Hettige and Stengren (1991).

70

Table 5-1: Toxic Release Intensities by Manufacturing Industries

Industry	ISIC Code	Total lbs. per Million 1987 US Dollars	Risk Factor Weighted Linear	Risk Factor Weighted Exponential
Food Products	3110	781.6	1418.0	20776.7
Beverages	3130	205.1	387.1	4647.5
Tobacco	3140	489.0	977.9	5308.9
Other Textile Production	3210	3502.2	6289.7	51086.7
Spinning, Weaving	3211	3106.7	7400.0	154381.3
Wearing Apparel	3220	1744.8	3341.8	17515.8
Leather & Products	3230	15380.7	25762.0	268922.3
Footwear	3240	2277.7	3324.0	11695.0
Wood Products	3310	4399.4	9247.0	137294.6
Furniture, Fixtures	3320	5366.8	10056.8	61291.0
Other Paper Prods.	3410	8741.7	16897.6	98109.5
Pulp, Paper	3411	6225.9	11720.6	116899.8
Printing, Publishing	3420	7513.9	14931.6	109252.0
Other Industrial Chem.	3510	52260.3	105302.7	966600.0
Basic Ind. Chem.	3511	32254.6	54922.9	609770.9
Synthetic Resins	3513	14002.9	26436.7	544602.8
Other Chemical Prods.	3520	3563.8	6582.8	58049.0
Drugs and Medicines	3522	3966.7	7416.5	42819.7
Petroleum Refineries	3530	3757.9	7669.5	78634.6
Petroleum & Coal Prods.	3540	2544.1	4777.4	29444.3
Rubber Products	3550	2934.2	5385.5	26305.2
Plastic Products n.e.c.	3560	9335.0	17310.5	175559.9
Pottery, China, etc.	3610	3614.5	5479.4	29164.7
Glass & Products	3620	1481.2	2893.2	43583.8
Non-Metal Prods. n.e.c.	3690	3853.8	5920.2	44194.1
Iron and Steel	3710	7642.8	12931.9	349897.7
Non-Ferrous Metals	3720	9334.3	13234.7	151219.2
Metal Products	3810	4592.5	9103.6	166930.2
Other Machinery n.e.c.	3820	1596.2	2840.5	39165.8
Office & Computing Mach.	3825	303.3	452.4	3163.4
Other Electrical Mach.	3830	1797.3	3195.2	38967.4
Radio, Television, etc.	3832	1808.3	3137.4	29207.4
Transport Equipment	3840	1007.8	2085.8	28055.7
Shipbuilding, Repair	3841	2546.5	3743.2	17426.9
Motor Vehicles	3843	666.9	1188.4	15733.1
Professional goods	3850	887.6	1576.5	16127.0
Other Industries	3900	2706.8	4679.0	42682.7

intensity is then a linear weighted sum of toxic releases per dollar's worth of output, using these risk factors 1 through 4 as weights. The implicit assumption inherent in this second measure is that the HHED risk scale is inherently linear, with one pound of emission with risk factor 4 as damaging as four pounds of releases with risk factor 1. This may not be a reasonable approximation. In consequence a third measure of toxic intensity is derived, assuming that the HHED risk weights are exponential (1, 10, 100, 1000) instead of linear. In Table 5-1, the latter two measures are labeled Linear and Exponential Intensities.

One feature of the three intensity measures in Table 5-1 is particularly significant for our analysis: their simple (unweighted) correlation is very high across the 37 ISIC categories. (See Table 5-2). Little is thus lost by focusing on one index, and we have chosen to work with the total (unweighted) toxic intensity.

Table 5-2: Correlation Coefficients: Industry Toxic Intensity

	Linear Weights	Exponential Weights
Total	0.995	0.944
Linear Weights	0.941	

The third data source are the UN annual sectoral output data for each reporting country during the period 1960-1988.[4] To create annual toxic intensity estimates for each sample country, the Total Toxicity Intensity measures from Table 5-1 are applied to ISIC sector shares. These national intensity estimates form the basis for the analysis of the sources and probable environmental consequences of changing sectoral composition in the next section of this paper.

The Assumption of Constant Sectoral Intensities

As noted in the introduction, this paper does not attempt a comprehensive analysis of changes in international industrial pollution. Constant, U.S.-based, output intensities are adopted because there is no choice -- international data on within-sector process mix and abatement choices have not yet been collected. Nevertheless, the following estimates will have first-order validity if there is rough stability in the *relative* pollution intensity of sectors across countries and over time.

Such an assumption of fixed toxic intensity embodies at least three elements:

To apply observed U.S. emission intensities to other countries assumes similar technologies and enforcement standards across countries. For instance, to the extent that lower income countries have more pollution-intensive techniques for given industries than does the United States (whether because

[4] A part of these data are published in the United Nations Industrial Statistics Yearbook.

of the state of know-how, from differing regulations, of from greater difficulty in enforcement) the measures generated here would understate toxic outputs from the lower income nations. On the other hand, if emissions per unit of output are roughly similar no matter where the product is produced the measures here will provide a reasonable approximation.

Closely related to the first point is an issue arising from the level of disaggregation available in the industrial data. To apply the U.S. intensities to other countries requires an assumption either that the pollution intensity of various products within an industry group are not too dissimilar or that the mix of products within each industry is essentially the same across countries.

Third, there is an assumption that emissions are related to output by an industry rather than, for instance, to value added. It is not obvious that this is an unreasonable assumption, though limitations on international data on value added prevent exploring sensitivity with respect to this assumption.

In fact most existing empirical work assumes rough constancy in relative cross-sectoral pollution intensity, invariably identifying the same sets of "heavy polluters" (e.g. metals, cement, pulp and paper, chemicals) and "light polluters" (e.g. most light assembly, food products, instruments). This has been largely based on two sources: (a) case-oriented engineering estimates of intensities in the few air and water pollutants which have been conventionally regulated in the OECD economies since 1975; and (b) reported annual total output- or investment-based intensities of expenditure on pollution abatement and control. In an appendix to this paper some partial evidence is reviewed on the plausibility of rough constancy in sectoral intensities. This evidence suggests that this assumption may not be too misleading, at least as a first approximation, and so the following analysis retains the assumption of fixed toxicity intensity common to almost all prior work.

Toxic Intensity of Industrial Production

Economic Development, Time Trends and Trade Policies

In this section some proximate determinants of variations in industrial toxic intensity are explored. The results are presented in two parts, first looking at the pattern with respect to income per capita and through time, then turning to the role of trade policy.

Levels of Development and Time Trends

The visual evidence in Figures 1.A and 1.B brings out two important points:

(i) Across countries, an inverse U relationship does indeed hold between GDP per capita and the total estimated toxic releases from manufacturing relative to GDP. This is shown in Figure 1.A (and is confirmed in unreported regression analysis).[5] This does not, of course, necessarily imply that every country must follow a pattern of rising toxic intensity of production at first, as development proceeds, followed by declining intensity at more advanced stages of development: the time path for individual countries need not follow the cross-country pattern. It should also be emphasized that this pattern does not necessarily imply a decline in aggregate toxic releases at higher levels of GDP, only that toxic releases per unit of production fall among higher income countries.

[5] The measure on the vertical axis in Figure 1.A is pounds of toxic emissions per 1987 US$1000 of GDP in each country.

73

FIGURE 1.A

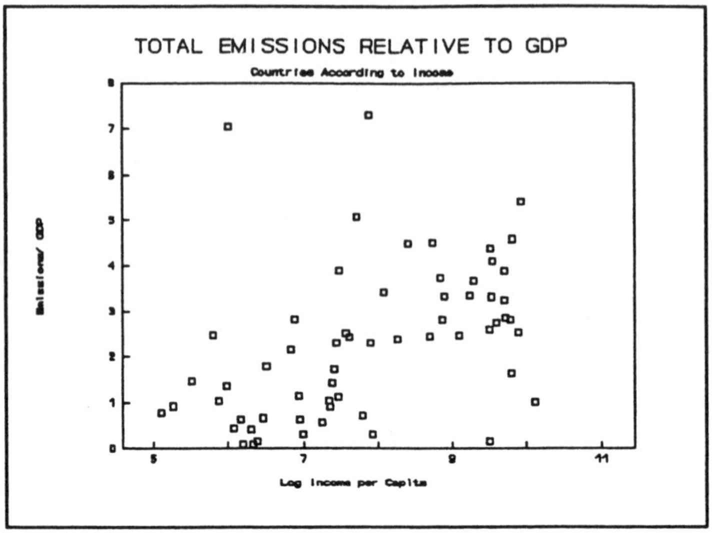

(ii) However, Figure 1.B exhibits no such tendency for intensity of manufacturing toxicity per unit of manufacturing output to decline among the high income countries. In other words, the declining portion in the inverse U relationship just noted is a result of the declining fraction of GDP accounted for by industrial output and not a result of any shift toward a less toxic mix of industries within manufacturing.

74

FIGURE 1.B

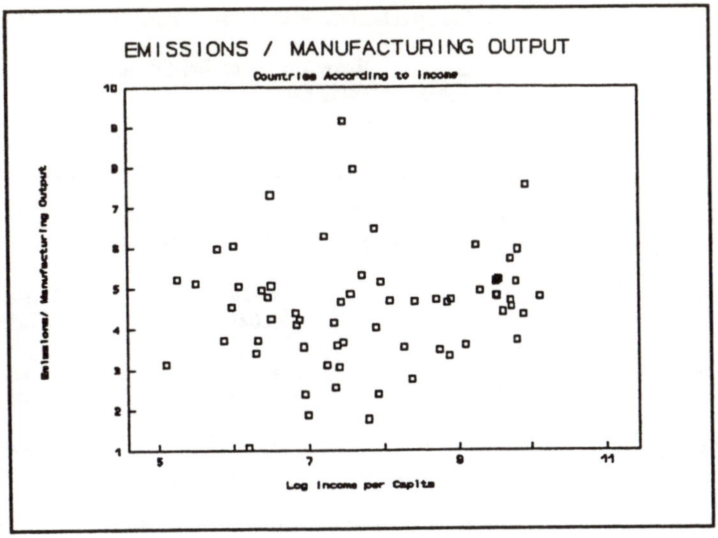

A more detailed regression analysis is also conducted for pooled cross-section time-series data, based on the following equation:

$$\ln N_{it} = a_0 + (b_1 + b_2 Y_{it})t + (b_3 + b_4 Y_{it}) Y_{it}$$

where N_{it} = Toxic Intensity (country i, period t)
Y_{it} = Real income per capita (US 1987$)
t = Time

This specification allows for possible variations of trend intensity growth (b_1), both with income (b_2) and over different periods: 1960-73; 1974-79; and 1980-88. The latter permits one test of the possibility that stricter OECD environmental regulation in the mid-late 1970's had a significant overall impact on the sectoral composition of international manufacturing. The responsiveness of toxic intensity with respect to income (b_3) is also permitted, in this specification, to vary with income itself (b_4).

Table 5-3 reports fixed-effects estimates of this equation for the period 1960-1988, with one dummy variable included per country. When intensity is defined as industrial emissions divided by GDP, the rise in intensity with respect to rising income at least tapers off at higher income levels. On the other hand, when intensity

75

Table 5-3: Pooled Annual Data Across Countries: Fixed Effects Regressions

	Dependent Variables: Logarithm (Toxic Emissions/Manufacturing Output or GDP)				
	Toxic Emissions Relative to				
	Manufacturing Output			GDP	
	(1)	(2)	(3)	(4)	(5)
Time trend	9.206	9.901		27.396	
	(12.15)	(12.21)		(17.94)	
Trend: 1960-73			4.598		17.895
			(3.04)		(6.03)
1974-79			4.629		17.982
			(3.07)		(6.08)
1980-88			4.637		17.973
			(3.09)		(6.10)
Income per capita	0.886	0.666	0.870	2.483	2.310
	(4.06)	(2.82)	(3.99)	(5.76)	(5.38)
Income squared		0.001		-0.001	-0.001
		(2.39)		(2.66)	(2.50)
Income* Trend	-0.450	-0.350	-0.442	-1.260	-1.173
	(4.11)	(2.98)	(4.03)	(5.89)	(5.51)
No. country dummies	80	80	80	73	73
No. observations	1517	1517	1517	1395	1395
R squared	0.79	0.79	0.80	0.93	0.93

Note: T-statistics in parentheses.

is defined as pollutants per unit of manufacturing output this is definitely not the case (indeed, the relationship in equation (2) goes the other way).

To summarize, these results imply:

- that there is no transition to lower toxic intensity in manufacturing at high incomes. The toxic intensity of GDP declines only because the manufacturing share in GDP declines beyond a certain level of income.

- that growth in toxic intensity has been far more rapid in the developing countries.

Trade Liberalization and Toxic Intensity of Manufacturing

In order to explore the consequences of alternative trade regimes upon local toxic intensity of manufacturing production, a price level distortion index, recently developed by David Dollar (1990) for the period 1973-1985, is adopted.[6] For present purposes, Dollar's sample of 95 developing countries is divided into seven rank groups: rank 1 LDCs exhibit the least distortion from international price norms; rank 7 are the most highly distorted. The OECD economies are not included in Dollar's sample. Two approaches are therefore adopted to the OECD countries: (a) assigning a Dollar rank of 0 to these cases; (b) omitting the OECD countries from the sample.

The average annual rate of growth in total toxic intensity relative to manufacturing output within each country is regressed upon Dollar's index of trade openness.[7] More precisely, the country growth rates in toxic intensity are regressed upon the growth rate in per capita income within the country over the relevant time interval, the logarithm of the initial per capita income at the beginning of each interval, and the Dollar index interacted with the growth in per capita income. The estimated equations also incorporated a measure of the share of export earnings derived from fuel exports (in an attempt to capture any impact of related toxic-intensive sectors) but in the balance this has no apparent effect.

One interpretation of any differences between the three decades is as follows: the 1960s provide a pre-environmentalist control, while the 1970s and 1980s may provide evidence about short- and long-run adjustments in the wake of stricter OECD regulation. The estimated results are presented for the three decades in Table 5-4.

---

[6] Briefly, Dollar's index uses the Summers and Heston price index for a constant basket of commodities across countries. Under free trade, such a basket of tradable goods ought to have the same price everywhere. Departures from unity may then be interpreted as a consequence of some form of trade barrier. In practice some nontradables enter the basket of commodities. Dollar attempts to control for this latter difficulty by regressing the raw index on measures of factor endowments (presumed to affect relative prices of nontradables across countries). The residual from these regressions is then adopted to form the purged index.

[7] The annual growth rates are first estimated by fitting a regression of intensity upon time within each of three time intervals: 1960-69; 1970-79; 1980-88. The trend growth rate is estimated this way only for countries with at least five observations available within each time period, so the sample size varies slightly from decade to decade.

77

Table 5-4: Impact of Income Growth, Level of Development Openness to Trade and Fuel Status on the Growth Rate of Toxic Intensity (by decade)

	Dependent Variable Growth Rate in Toxic Emissions/Manufacturing Output					
	Including OECD Countries			Excluding OECD Countries		
	60s	70s	80s	60s	70s	80s
Intercept	-0.071 (0.78)	0.053 (2.39)	-0.030 (1.19)	0.03 (0.19)	0.094 (2.39)	-0.067 (1.60)
Growth in per capita income	0.096 (0.19)	-0.596 (1.63)	-1.71 (2.72)	-0.008 (0.30)	-0.696 (1.57)	-1.96 (2.1)
Ln (initial per capita income)	0.008 (0.60)	-0.005 (1.80)	0.006 (1.65)	0.001 (0.01)	-0.012 (2.0)	0.012 (1.9)
Fuel share in exports	-0.046 (0.32)	-0.021 (0.834)	-0.003 (0.14)	-0.010 (0.06)	-0.031 (1.09)	-0.016 (0.51)
Dollar's index interacted with income growth	-	0.223 (1.92)	0.589 (3.10)	-	0.297 (2.10)	0.664 (2.37)
No. observations	25	56	55	19	44	39
R squared	0.03	0.18	0.19	.01	0.22	0.22

Note: T-statistics in parentheses

For the 1960s, when almost no environmental regulations had yet been imposed by the various countries, our regression has no explanatory power: from these data we are unable to detect any significant general trend in toxic intensity change; no impact for either initial income or income growth during the 1960s.

In the 1970s and 80s, however, the situation changes sharply. The implications of the results for these two decades are perhaps most readily seen from the tableau marked as Table 5-5. This tableau has three dimensions:

Three income levels are represented:
Low ($150)
Middle ($1,800)
High ($22,000)

Two annual growth rates are shown:
Slow (1%)
Fast (6%)

And two level's of Dollar's index are depicted:
Open (1)
Closed (6)

The fundamental importance of policy emerges strikingly in these results. Fast-growing closed economies had very rapid change toward toxic-intensive structures in both the 1970s and 1980s, with acceleration in the latter decade for both low- and middle-income developing countries. In contrast, fast-growing open economies had essentially toxic-neutral structural change in the 1970s and a strong shift toward less-toxic structure in the 1980s. The same trends are evident in slower-growing economies, but less pronounced.

This evidence leads us to a strong qualification of our earlier conclusions:

While developing countries as a whole had greater toxic intensity growth in the 1970s and 1980s, trends for individual countries depended heavily on the growth rate of income and the policy regime. The story of "toxic displacement" seems to have been focused in relatively closed, fast-growing economies.

Summary and Conclusions

Several previous studies have asked whether environmental controls imposed in the industrialized economies are diverting investments in pollution-intensive activities offshore.[8] In broad terms these studies reach a negative conclusion: direct investment does not appear to be stimulated by such regulations, in part because the cost of emission controls is generally a tiny fraction of operating costs. Yet direct investment reflects only a portion of what may be happening to world production patterns; technology transfers may occur with no simultaneous direct investment and production may readily shift toward a different global distribution without either direct investment or technology transfer.

[8] Dean (1991) offers a very useful survey of this material.

79

Table 5-5: Percent Change in Total Toxic Intensity Relative to Manufacturing Output

LOW INCOME COUNTRIES

	Policy Regime			
	Open		Closed	
Per Capita Income Growth	70s	80s	70s	80s
Slow	2.4	-1.2	3.5	1.8
Fast	0.6	-6.7	7.2	10.9

MIDDLE INCOME COUNTRIES

	Policy Regime			
	Open		Closed	
Per Capita Income Growth	70s	80s	70s	80s
Slow	1.2	0.4	2.3	3.3
Fast	-0.1	-5.2	6.0	12.4

HIGH INCOME COUNTRIES

Per Capita Income Growth	70s	80s
Slow	-0.1	1.9
Fast	-1.9	-3.7

In this paper, a very general test of the displacement hypothesis has been attempted. Time series estimates of manufacturing pollution intensity for a large sample of developed and developing countries during the period 1960-1988 have been developed. The results derived from these data may be summarized in terms of the three lines of analysis set out earlier in this paper.

Development and sectoral composition

(a) As a result of industrial composition shifts, total manufacturing emissions relative to GDP grow faster than GDP at lower levels of income per capita, then grow less quickly at higher levels of income. In other words an inverse U-shape is confirmed between industrial pollution intensity and income.

(b) The decline which is observed in total industrial emissions relative to GDP at higher income levels is a result of the declining share of manufacturing in GDP rather than a result of any shift toward a cleaner mix of manufacturing activities. The pooled cross-country time series estimates reveal no tendency for toxic intensity of manufacturing itself to exhibit an inverse U-shape. On the other hand, the data do indicate that the more rapidly-growing high income countries have actually enjoyed a negative growth in toxic intensity of their manufacturing mix. To what extent the latter result is a reflection of more rapid introduction of cleaner technologies in more rapidly-growing economies cannot be discerned, but it is certainly a potential explanation.

OECD environmental regulation and displacement

It is frequently asserted that stricter regulation of pollution-intensive production in the OECD countries has led to significant locational displacement, with consequent acceleration of industrial pollution intensity in developing countries. All our results are consistent with this hypothesis. Both sets of estimates suggest that the poorest economies have the highest toxic-intensity growth. The estimated toxic-intensity elasticity of income growth for a typical (midrange-distortion) LDC economy was apparently negligible in the 1960s, positive in the 1970s, and even higher in the 1980s. Of course, one cannot be certain of a causal connection between these decade patterns and the roughly concurrent shifts in OECD environmental policies. Yet the results are nonetheless suggestive of a potential contributory effect.

LDC economic policy and pollution intensity

Pollution intensity has grown most rapidly in developing economies which are relatively closed to world market forces. Relatively closed, fast-growing economies experienced very rapid structural transitions toward greater toxic-intensity. The opposite seems to have been true, however, for more open economies.

More work on this issue clearly needs to be done, but the results in this paper suggest that net toxic displacement toward the LDCs may not have been inevitable during the past two decades. Restrictive trade policies imposed by the developing countries themselves may even have been the main stimulus to toxic industrial migration, rather than regulatory cost differences between the North and South.

It is hoped that these results will prove suggestive for future directions for analysis: much remains to be done. For instance, although the present results suggest that more liberal trade policies among the developing countries have focused manufacturing production on a cleaner mix of industries, we still lack evidence on the effects of freer trade policies upon the choice of production technique, upon waste disposal, on toxicity of consumption activities and environmental harm from changes in agriculture. Moreover, this paper has focused upon the global distribution of toxic emissions rather than upon changes in the global aggregate. It is too early to draw any sweeping conclusions about the connections between protectionist trade policies and environmental effects, but it is hoped that this paper has shown that at least this debate can be enjoined founded upon empirical evidence.

81

APPENDIX

This appendix presents four types of evidence relating to the constancy of toxic intensity emissions for given industries.

1. Constancy Across Measures of Pollution Intensity

The analysis in the text uses the U.S. Environmental Protection Agency's Toxic Release Inventory (TRI) data. Since these data are not available before 1987 (and then only for the United States), no international or intertemporal series is available for cross checking. Useful indirect evidence can be obtained, however, by checking the intersectoral correlation between the TRI data and the U.S. data on Pollution Abatement and Control Expenditures (PACE). Figure A.1 shows the rank of 19 2-digit industries according to: (a) the percentage of new plant and equipment expenditures absorbed by pollution abatement and control; (b) the linear weighted toxic pollution intensity of the industry. In this graph there is a clear outlier -- SIC 27 (printing and publishing) -- which exhibits high emissions according to the TRI data but very low pollution abatement expenditures. If this exception is excluded, then pollution intensity (whether total, linear or exponentially weighted) is quite highly correlated with pollution abatement expenditures. (See Table A.1).

Table A.1

**Rank Correlations:
PACE Expenditure Intensity (1986)
and Measures of Toxic Pollution Intensity
(19 2-Digit SIC Sectors)**

	Printing and Publishing (SIC 27):	
Toxic Intensity	Excluded	Included
Unweighted	0.72	0.55
Linear Human	0.76	0.55
Exponential Human	0.74	0.64

Figure A.1

PACE Expenditure Intensity Rank (1986)
vs. Linear Weighted Toxic Pollution Intensity Rank (1987)
(19 2-Digit SIC Sectors)

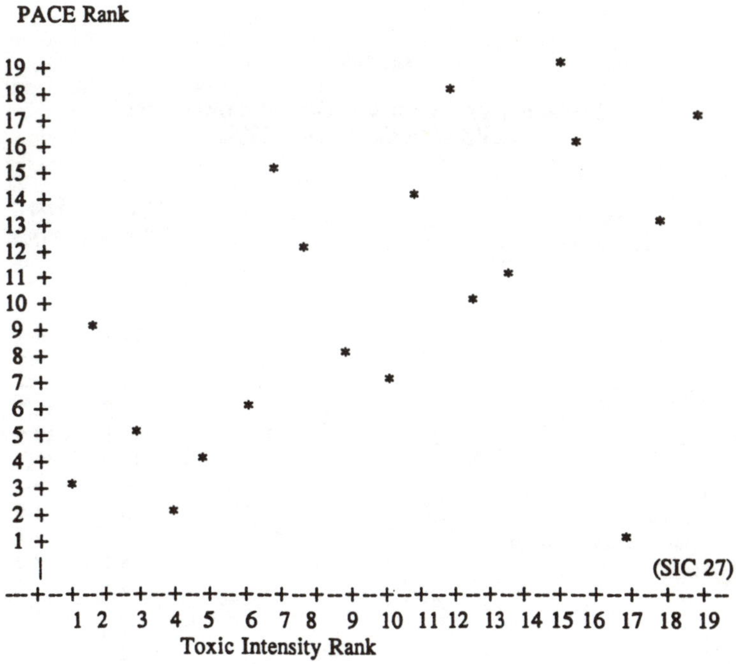

83

2. Constancy Across Countries in the OECD

Figure A.2 plots the rank of 13 industries in West Germany during the mid-1970s and the United States for 1975, according to pollution abatement expenditures relative to new investments in plant and equipment. The raw data underlying this graph are presented in Table A.2. There is a clear positive association in sectoral ranking across the two countries, and in fact the rank correlation is 0.8. Comparable data for other countries (and especially for the LDCs) are not available. However, this two- country comparison suggests that industries needing substantial abatement controls in one country also require expensive controls in another, despite differences in emphasis on the various pollutants and media of release in the two countries.

Table A.2

Percent of New Plant and Equipment Expenditures on Pollution Control, mid-1970s

	United States	West Germany*
Nonferrous metals	24.1	8.4
Paper	16.8	9.6
Stone, clay, glass	14.3	--
Iron, Steel	13.5	10.7
Petroleum	11.8	19.9
Chemicals	10.9	11.1
Electric power	9.7	--
Electrical machinery	5.8	1.9
Lumber, furniture, instruments, misc.	5.3	2.4
Food, beverages	5.2	3.2
Textiles	4.6	1.5
Rubber	4.0	1.9
Motor vehicles	3.9	2.0
Apparel, leather, tobacco, printing/publishing	2.8	1.5
Machinery, except electrical	1.8	1.3
Fabricated metals	--	0.5

*West German data are averages for the period 1971-77

Sources: Tietenberg (1988), U.S. Department of Commerce Survey of Current Business (various); OECD (1985).

84

Figure A.2

Sectoral Pollution Abatement Expenditure Intensity Rankings
West Germany vs. United States

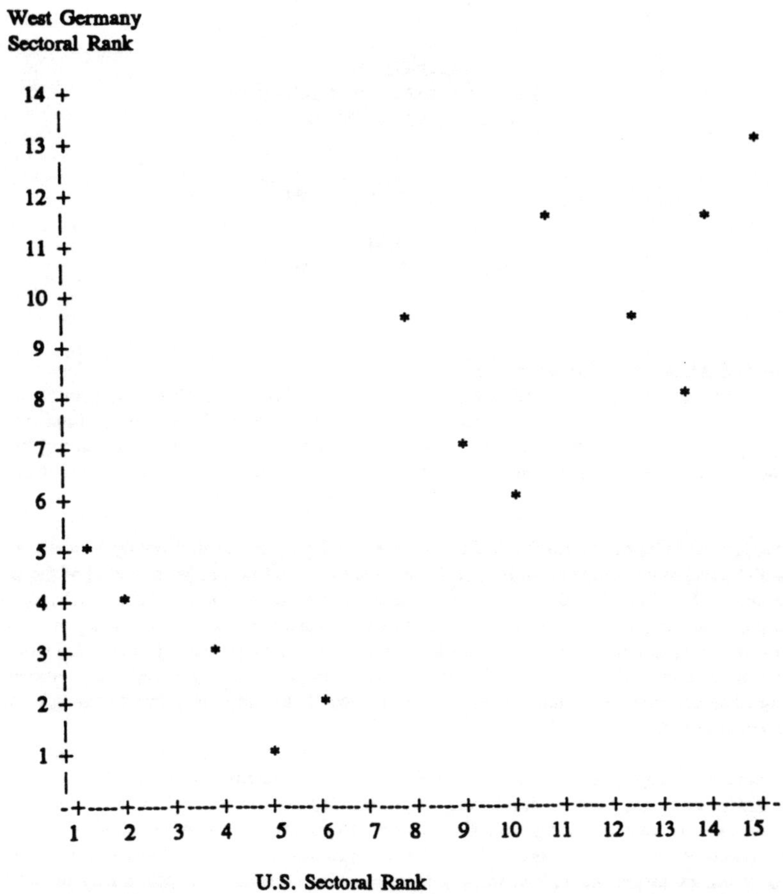

85

3. Constancy Over Time in the United States

In the United States, sectoral Pollution Abatement Control Expenditure data have been collected since the 1970s. Table A.3 presents correlations for PACE expenditure intensities (PACE divided by total shipment value) in 1974, 1980, and 1986.[9] The correlations are very high and show no sign of decreasing over time. We conclude that, in the United States at least, sectoral "heavy polluters" have retained their identity since 1970.

Table A.3
Correlations:
Sectoral PACE Expenditure Intensities
(19 2-Digit SIC Sectors)

	1974	1980
1980	0.94	
1986	0.94	0.94

4. Process and Abatement Considerations

Economists generally assume that sectoral technology mix will be different in developing countries, and that pollution abatement equipment will not be installed in the absence of formal regulation. Empirical work on the technology question from an environmental perspective has only recently begun, and survey evidence on abatement choices is practically nonexistent. A few recent studies, however, raise some doubts about the conventional wisdom.

A twenty-five year analysis of international diffusion for wood pulping technology by Wheeler and Martin (1991) finds that developing countries with open trade policies exhibit no lag in adoption of the newest and cleanest technology. Huq and Wheeler (1991, forthcoming) report survey results for a small sample of pulp and fertilizer plants in Bangladesh. The combination of public ownership and aid dependency in this extremely poor economy has led to technology adoption which is largely dictated by prevailing norms in donor countries. Although formal regulation is almost entirely lacking, many large, polluting Bangladeshi enterprises have already instituted monetary compensation and first-level effluent treatment in response to strong pressure from neighboring communities.

There is at present no strongly persuasive evidence about the environmentally relevant direction of departures from typical OECD technology mix in developing countries. Wheeler and Huq (1991, forthcoming) find rapid adoption of the newest, least polluting (electric arc) steel technology in many developing countries. This, coupled with newcomer avoidance of the highly-polluting open hearth process, which remained important in many OECD countries during the 1970s, implies average pollution intensities which may be quite close to typical OECD intensities, even allowing for significant differences in abatement. Thus Wheeler and Martin (1992, forthcoming) find that slower average adoption of new clean pulping technology by developing countries is almost exactly counterbalanced by slower average decline in the oldest technology (mechanical pulping), which is also quite clean.

---

[9] Our thanks to Hamid Alavi for generously making these data available to us.

86

5. Summing Up

This evidence, although admittedly sparse, nonetheless suggests that an assumption of constant relative toxic intensities within industries, both across countries and through time, may not be too egregious: the adopted measures of toxic intensity is highly correlated with PACE expenditure intensity; for the United States and West Germany aggregate sectoral PACE expenditure intensities are highly correlated; within the United States, PACE expenditure intensities have very high intertemporal correlations; and case study evidence suggests a number of reasons why LDC technologies are not necessarily more pollutant intensive as often presumed.

References

Dean, Judith. 1991. Trade and the Environment: A Survey of the Literature. Background paper for the *World Development Report 1992*. Washington, D.C.: World Bank.

Dollar, David. 1990. *Outward Orientation and Growth: An Empirical Study Using a Price-Based Measure of Openness*. Washington: World Bank.

Grossman, Gene M. and Alan B. Krueger. 1991. Environmental Impacts of a North American Free Trade Agreement. Paper prepared for the conference on the United States-Mexico Free Trade Agreement. (October). Huq, Mainul and David Wheeler. 1991. Industrial Cleanup Without Regulation: Public Enterprises in Bangladesh. Washington, D.C.: World Bank, mimeo.

Martin, Paul, David Wheeler, Mala Hettige, and Ralph Stengren. 1991. *The Industrial Pollution Projection System: Concept, Initial Development, and Critical Assessment*. Washington, D.C.: World Bank.

OECD. 1985. *Environmental Policy and Technical Change*. Paris.

Tietenberg, T. H. 1988. *Environmental and Natural Resource Economics*. Chicago: Scott Foresman.

United Nations. *Industrial Statistics Yearbook*. New York: United Nations.

U.S. Department of Commerce. Bureau of Census. *Survey of Current Business* (various).

Wheeler, David and Paul Martin. 1991. *Prices, Policies, and the International Diffusion of Clean Technology: The Case of Wood Pulp Production*. Washington, D.C.: World Bank.

———. 1992. Cross Country Projection of Pollution Intensity: A Test on Technology Mix in Wood Pulp. Washington: World Bank, mimeo, forthcoming.

——— and Mainul Huq. 1991. Technical Change, International Diffusion, and Environmental Impact in the Steel Industry: 1960–1989. Washington, D.C.: World Bank, mimeo.

Part IV
Institutional Background

[17]

Trade and the Environment: Does Environmental Diversity Detract from the Case for Free Trade?

Jagdish Bhagwati
T. N. Srinivasan

The potency of the contention that fair trade or level playing fields constitute a precondition for free trade and that, therefore, harmonization of domestic policies across trading countries is necessary before free trade can be embraced to one's advantage, should not be underestimated today. It is nowhere more manifest or more compelling in its policy appeal than in the area of environmental standards.

Both the *general* view that cross-country intra-industry (CCII) harmonization of environmental standards is required if free trade is to be implemented and the *specific* proposals currently in vogue to implement this view are therefore in need of analytical scrutiny.[1] This is the task that we undertake primarily in the present chapter.

Section 4.1 briefly reviews the factors that drive the demands for cross-country intra-industry harmonization of environmental standards and the specific proposals, in particular the countervailing of so-called "social dumping" when harmonization does not obtain but free trade does. Its main purpose, however, is to categorize the (four) main issues that arise as the "high-standard" and "low-standard" countries engage in freer trade and contemplate consequences of the differences in their environmental standards when the pollution involved is purely domestic.

Section 4.2 sets forth several basic theoretical propositions (derived from the theoretical Appendix), concerning optimal commercial and environmental policies under different circumstances when the environmental problem is purely domestic. In light thereof, the basic legitimacy and desirability of free trade with diversity of domestic environmental standards is established. Also, a detailed examination of two (of the four) issues distinguished in section 4.1 is offered: relating to the objections to diversity under free trade, reflecting fears of unfair trade and the loss of one's high standards.

Section 4.3 considers the related but distinct problems raised by concerns with ethical preferences or "values" that result in objections to free trade with diverse standards.

Section 4.4 addresses the concern that current institutional mechanisms for overseeing free trade, chiefly the GATT and its successor the World Trade Organization (WTO), threaten high standards by permitting successful challenges by low-standard countries on diverse grounds reflecting mainly their market-disruption potential.

While these analyses concern the issues arising from purely domestic environmental problems, section 4.5 concludes by sketching the trade problems that differentially arise when the environmental problems are international (or "global"), that is, when they involve transborder externalities.

4.1 Demands for Cross-Country Intra-Industry Harmonization of Environmental Standards: Categorizing the Issues for Purely Domestic Environmental Problems

In reviewing and assessing the demands for CCII harmonization of environmental standards, it is customary now to make a distinction of analytical importance between (1) environmental problems that are intrinsically *domestic* in nature (though they may be "internationalized" for reasons we will discuss); and (2) those that are intrinsically *international* in nature because they inherently involve "physical" spillovers across national borders.

Thus, if India pollutes a lake that is wholly within its borders, the pollution is an intrinsically domestic question. If, however, India pollutes a river that flows into Bangladesh, the pollution is an intrinsically international question. So are the well-known problems of acid rain, ozone-layer depletion, and global warming. These intrinsically international problems of the environment raise questions that interface with the trade questions both in common and in different ways from the intrinsically domestic problems.

It has become commonplace among some environmentalists to assert that this distinction is of no consequence because the intrinsically domestic environmental problems are increasingly seen to have transnational impacts. Science has shown, for instance, that aerosol sprays are not just an environmental nuisance where used; they endanger the planet! But the fact that science seems occasionally to turn local (and partial-equilibrium) environmental impacts into transnational (and general-equilibrium) impacts is no proof that the former are an empty set. We should not be deterred, therefore, from using this important conceptual distinction.

4.1.1 Objections to Diversity of Standards

It would seem, at first glance, that at least the intrinsically domestic environmental problems should be matters best left by governments to domestic solutions and within domestic jurisdiction (although transnational, global "educational", and lobbying activities by environmental nongovernmental organizations, the NGOs, are compatible with this solution). Why should anyone object to the conduct of free trade with any country on the ground that its preferred environmental choices and solutions (by way of setting pollution standards and taxes) to intrinsically domestic questions are unacceptable because they are incompatible with the case for (gains from) free trade? Yet, the fact is that they do.

And the objections are directed, not merely at free trade, but also at the institutional safeguards and practices, as at the GATT, which are designed to ensure the proper functioning of an open, multilateral trading system that embodies the principles of free trade. These objections take mainly four forms:

1. *Unfair Trade.* If you do something different, and especially if you do what appears to be less, concerning environment than I do in the same industry or sector, this difference is considered to be tantamount to lack of "level playing fields" and therefore amounts to "unfair trade" by you. Free trade, according to this doctrine, is then unacceptable because it requires, as a precondition, "fair trade."[2]

2. *Losing Higher Standards.* Then again, the flip side of the "fair trade" argument is the environmentalists' fear that if free trade occurs with countries having "lower" environmental standards, no matter what the justification for this situation, the effect will be to lower their own standards. This will follow from the political pressure brought to bear on governments to lower standards to ensure the survival of their industry.

An associated argument is that capital will move to countries with lower standards, so that countries will engage in a "race to the bottom," each winding up with lower standards than desired because standards are lowered to attract capital from each other.

3. *Conflicting Ethical Preferences.* Environmentalists also often worry about the compatibility of ethical preferences and free trade among trading nations who do not share the same ethical preferences. Free trade in products that offend one's moral sense (either in themselves, or because of the way in which they are produced, as in the use of purse seines in catching tuna or leghold traps in hunting for fur) is then considered

objectionable because *either* trade in such products should be withheld so as to induce or coerce acceptance of such preferences *or* such trade should be abandoned, even if it has no effective consequence and might even hurt only oneself, simply because "one should have no truck with the devil,"[3] *or* one's labor or industry "should not have to compete" with others who do not uphold the ethical standards that one considers important.

The first argument presumes higher morality in one's behalf, which should be spread to other nations with lower morality (and with corresponding lack of standards/laws therefore to reflect the higher morality). The other arguments seek no such morally imperial outreach; one simply wants no part in complicity with lower morality elsewhere via participating in gainful free trade with nations guilty of tolerating such lower morality while the other rejects these gains from trade somewhat differently as imposing an "unfair" burden on one's producers who conform to the higher ethical standards. In each case, the diversity of standards is considered then to be incompatible with the pursuit of free trade.

4. *Institutional Vulnerability of High Standards to Countries with Low Standards Fearing Protectionism.* Then, finally, the environmentalists fear that they will lose their high standards, not because market forces under free trade bias the *domestic* political equilibrium in favor of lower standards or generate a race to the bottom,[4] but because the current "institutional" arrangements, at the GATT in particular, enable the low-standards countries to object to, and threaten, the high standards in other countries by claiming protectionist intent or consequences, for instance.[5]

4.1.2 The Political Salience of These Objections

Thus, just consider why the first argument concerning the *unfair trade* of lower CCII standards elsewhere has become such a politically salient issue today. Though we will turn to this argument in greater depth in section 4.2, it should suffice to note here that the fear is that competition will be greater if a rival abroad faces lower burdens of environmental regulations, and hence the argument follows that this competitive advantage enjoyed by one's foreign rivals is *illegitimate* and must be countervailed, much as dumping or subsidization is, or must be eliminated at the source.

Thus, Senator David Boren, who introduced legislation in the U.S. Congress to countervail the "social dumping" allegedly resulting from lower standards abroad, proposed such a measure on the ground that[6] we can no longer stand idly by while some US manufacturers, such as the US carbon and steel alloy industry, spend as much as 250 percent more on environmental controls as a percentage of gross domestic product than do other countries.... I see the *unfair advantage enjoyed by other nations exploiting the environment* and public health for economic gain when I look at many industries important to my own state of Oklahoma.

We will argue, in section 4.2, that environmental diversity is, contrary to these statements, perfectly legitimate, that it can arise not merely because the environment is differently valued between countries in the sense that the utility function defined on income and pollution is not identical and homothetic, but also because of differences in endowments and technology across countries. Hence, the common presumption driving harmonization and (alternatively) "social-dumping"-countervailing demands, that others with different CCII standards are illegitimately and unfairly reducing their costs, is untenable.[7]

Nonetheless, these demands are part of a general shift to demands to harmonize a great, and possibly increasing, number of domestic policies: in labor standards, in technology policy, and so on. Why?[8]

With industries everywhere increasingly open to competition, thanks precisely to our postwar success in dismantling trade barriers, with multinationals spreading technology freely across countries through direct investments, and with capital more free than ever to move across countries, producers face now the prospect that their competitive advantage is fragile and that more industries than ever before are "footloose." There is, therefore, much more sensitivity to *any* advantage that one's rivals abroad may enjoy in world competition, and a propensity for the rivals to look over their shoulders to find reasons why their advantage is "unfair."

The notion of unfairness is also attractive to those who seek relief from international competition. If you go to your congresswoman and ask for protection because the competition is tough, it is going to be difficult to get it. After all, many of them have been sufficiently educated, or perhaps brainwashed (depending on your point of view), into thinking that protection, while not a four-letter word, is not something you want to embrace if you aspire to anything like statesmanship. But if you go to her and say that your successful rival is playing by "unfair" rules, you are going to do better. In the United States, in particular, the "unfairness" notion can take you really far, since the economic and social ethos reflects notions of fairness and equality of access (rather than success) more than anywhere else.

The fact that the United States also went through the "diminished giant" syndrome vis-à-vis the Pacific nations, which fed its fear of consequent deindustrialization, also made the American politicians more susceptible during the 1980s to these "unfair trade" arguments from interested lobbies. The continuing dominance of the United States in setting the world's trading agenda powerfully reinforces, in turn, the trend toward "fair trade" and "level playing fields."

While the "unfair trade" argument for rejecting free trade with countries with different environmental standards is therefore part of the generic and more general demands for harmonization and level playing fields in world trade, environment (whose protection is legitimately a virtue in itself) brings to this trend yet added arguments with perhaps even more powerful appeal. Chief among them is the fear, leading to the second argument in the list, that competition with the imports and exports in third markets from countries with lower standards will put pressure on domestic industries, triggering political action by them to lower standards *down* to the levels abroad.

Believing (possibly with justification) that U.S. Vice President Dan Quayle's Competitiveness Council was doing precisely this under the administration of President George Bush, the environmental NGOs in the United States, and their friends in the European Community and elsewhere, came to see this lowering of standards as a real threat to their goals if free trade were embraced and if harmonization *up* were not imposed simultaneously by coercion on foreign countries, especially the poor ones. As Walter Russell Mead put it in a much cited article in *Harper's Magazine*:[9]

> Either the progressive systems of the advanced industrial countries will spread into the developing world or the Third World will move north. Either Mexican wages will move up or American wages will move down. Environmentalists, labor unions, consumer groups, and human-rights groups must go global—just as corporations have done.

This concern reflects at the global level the debate within the EC: the fear that the Common Market's free trade and free capital flows will lead to harmonization *down* of standards "from below" and the efforts by many in consequence to impose harmonization at a *higher* level of standards "from the top."

Finally, the demands for CCII harmonization are fed also by the feared adverse effects of free trade and capital flows on the real wages of workers: an issue that became important in the 1992 presidential election in the

United States. The Bill Clinton campaign did not just focus on the failure of the Bush administration to revive the economy. It also made much of the so-called structural problem that is defined by the stagnation of real wages of the unskilled workers during the 1980s. At least one of the candidates for explaining this phenomenon has been the integration of the world economy and the competition in consequence with poor countries with abundant unskilled labor.

We doubt the importance of this explanation,[10] but it has powerful appeal. The attempts at globalizing the higher environmental and labor standards, with the latter coming uncomfortably close to attempts at also raising wages in the industrial sectors of the poor countries on human-rights and labor-rights grounds, can be seen in fact as indirect ways of trying to reduce the perceived threat to real wages of the unskilled in rich countries from free trade with (and capital outflows to) the poor countries.

We may remark that, if the argument about the adverse effect of trade on wages of the unskilled is really bought, we are back to the old concerns that free trade with the poor countries will truly act like free immigration from them: the immigration would directly depress workers' wages; free trade would indirectly do so. Interestingly, in the animated British debate prior to the passage of the 1905 Immigration Act, the free traders were also free immigrationists, and the protectionists were also for restrictions on immigration. Immigration was even described as free trade in paupers![11]

Hence, the growing sentiment that free trade with the poor countries will increasingly depress rich countries' real wages should eventually lead to, not just palliatives like the imposition of environmental and labor standards that are harmonized upward, and attempts at restricting capital outflows (synonymous in politics with "losing jobs") to them by way of direct foreign investment. We predict that we will also witness increasing attempts at encouraging population control in these countries.[12]

4.2 The Case for Free Trade with Diversity of Environmental Standards

We now argue (based on the theoretical analysis in the Appendix) that the case for free trade, with diversity of environmental standards across countries, is essentially robust. We then proceed to address specifically the two issues distinguished at the beginning of this chapter: unfair trade and fear of loss of higher standards.

At the outset, note that "standards" may refer to general principles such as the "polluter pays" principle, or they may be defined as the precise tax rates that are levied on the polluter. In the political debate over differential standards, along with demands for CCII harmonization or for "eco-dumping" duties when harmonization does not obtain, the complaints are evidently against lower pollution tax rates or charges—for example, that widget manufacturers are taxed, for the effluents that they discharge, at lower rates in Mexico than in the United States. These definitions, therefore, indicate the sense in which we will discuss CCII harmonization in this chapter, unless otherwise specified.

4.2.1 The Basic Theoretical Presumptions

Distinguish again between the two major cases: where the pollution is domestic and where it is global (and spills over across national borders). Then the following basic theoretical conclusions follow (Appendix), defining welfare in the conventional economic sense:

Domestic Pollution

1. For a small country (with no influence on its terms of trade), free trade remains the best policy, with its own pollution being taxed as required and regardless of whether the other country fixes its own pollution.[13] Where abatement is feasible with spending, there is no case for a subsidy.[14]

2. For a small country, if its own pollution is not taxed optimally, free trade will generally cease to be optimal. Also, it follows equally from the postwar theory of commercial policy under distortions that free trade, with domestic distortions, can immiserize.[15]

3. For a large country, free trade is not an optimal policy, but an optimal tariff is (on the assumption that there is no retaliation), while its domestic pollution is directly fixed through a pollution tax. As is well known, such an optimal solution for the large country is not Pareto optimal for the world economy.[16]

4. With free trade between two countries (small or large) and optimal pollution taxes within each country, global Pareto optimality will follow.

5. However, generally speaking, the optimal pollution taxes (in a globally Pareto optimal solution) will *not* be equal across the countries: *diversity in these tax rates will be both natural and appropriate, hence also "legitimate."*

6. Imposing one country's pollution tax rates on another will then create an *inefficient*, globally Pareto suboptimal solution.

7. Such harmonization, or "straitjacketing" to be more accurate, of the other country's standards toward one's own will also necessarily harm the

other country. Thus a lower-standard country, forced to "harmonize up," will be harmed.

8. Whether such "harmonization up" will benefit the higher-standard country is, however, problematic: it may help or harm.[17] The presumption that it will necessarily help is false.

Global Pollution

1. When global pollution occurs, the globally Pareto optimal solution will be characterized by free trade and by pollution taxes in each country producing the pollution, these taxes being different except in singular circumstances.[18]

2. The globally Pareto optimal solution is not necessarily equitable. To be equitable as well, the market solution must be generally supplemented by (lump-sum) transfers.[19]

3. A small country, taking the foreign terms of trade, tariffs, and pollution abatement as given, will continue to find free trade to be its optimal policy. It will combine this with optimal pollution taxes and abatement addressed to its own pollution.[20] But such Cournot behavior makes little sense: it is more likely that each small country will "free ride" on pollution taxes and abatement and reproduce the "tragedy of the commons" in the use of the common property resource (i.e., the target of the pollution).

4. A large country, indulging in Cournot behavior with respect to the foreign tariffs and pollution abatement expenditures, will use an optimal tariff, not free trade, to maximize its welfare. The Cournot behavior, however, will yield a Nash equilibrium that is not Pareto optimal.[21]

4.2.2 Examining the Objections: Unfair Trade and Feared Loss of High Standards

In light of these propositions, we can now proceed to examine the four issues distinguished in section 4.1, especially the first one relating to "unfair trade" and the associated agitation for countervailing duties against "eco-dumping" in the absence of CCII harmonization.

Does Diversity of Environmental Standards Imply That Low-Standard Countries Are Indulging in "Unfair Trade"?

The theoretical analysis clearly shows that the basic presumption is that different countries will have *legitimate diversity of CCII environmental taxes and standards*. This diversity will arise even if they share the same "utility function" with associated trade-offs between income and different types of pollution: the diverse tax rates can come from differences in technology and in endowments in the broadest sense (so as to include weather, demography, geography, inherited abatement policies, etc.).[22]

As it happens, there is also no compelling reason to think that every society must share the same utility function. It is perfectly appropriate, and not an indulgence of willful "sovereignty," for Mexico to value clean water higher than clean air, compared to the United States, because a dollar expended on the former instead of the latter will produce greater health gains for Mexicans, whereas the situation would be the reverse for the United States.

The overall trade-off between income and (some generalized index of) pollution will also be different between societies: income may be more valuable at the margin when societies are poor and poverty takes people close to malnutrition than when societies are rich and malnutrition results from overindulgence rather than deprivation. A clear example again is the emphasis on saving dolphins rather than increasing productivity in tuna fishing in the United States and the contrasting emphasis on ameliorating poverty instead in Mexico by using purse seines that kill dolphins while fishing for tuna.

The notion, therefore, that the diversity of CCII pollution standards and taxes is illegitimate and constitutes "unfair trade" or "unfair competition" is itself illegitimate. So is the consequent demand, following from this notion, that CCII harmonization is necessary for "free and fair trade,"[23] in the absence of which CCII differences must be treated as eco-dumping and be countervailed.

In fact, since the effect of such policies would be to force (at least some) countries to harmonize up their preferred lower CCII standards, the consequence would equally be to inflict a welfare loss on them. We might even argue that, while we advocate free trade traditionally, with diversity of domestic standards, on the presumption that voluntary trade is beneficial (relative to autarky) for every trading nation, and hence it is a mutual-gain policy prescription, the opposite is true for CCII harmonization to be superimposed on free trade:[24] it will amount to immiserization of the trading nation whose standards are being "distorted" up.

This basic case against CCII harmonization can be challenged on grounds that we now examine and mainly find unpersuasive.

Objection 1: Competing with Foreign Firms That Do Not Bear Equal Burdens Is Unfair This competitiveness argument is common, especially on the part of some business groups and also some unions. As notions of unfairness are expressed by them, and as implied by proposed legislation to equalize burdens, this is certainly a strongly felt belief. Underlying it is the sense of outrage that one's ability to hold on to an industry is compromised by the fact that one's rivals abroad do not carry the same burdens.

The contrary arguments, which reject this competitiveness argument, are as follows:

(a) The fact that others abroad do not carry the same burdens is symmetric with the fact that these countries have different wages, capital costs, skills, infrastructure, weather, and what have you: all of which lead to differential advantages of production and trade competitiveness. Diversity of environmental tax burdens is thus no ground for complaints of unfairness.

(b) Losing competitive advantage because we put a larger negative value on a certain kind of pollution than others do is simply the flip side of the differential valuations. To object to that implication of the differential valuation is to object to the differential valuation itself, and hence to our own larger negative valuation. To see this clearly, think only of a closed economy without trade. If we were to tax pollution by an industry in such an economy, its implication would be precisely that this industry would shrink: it loses competitive advantage vis-à-vis other industries in our own country. To object to that shrinking is to object to the negative valuation being put on the pollution. There is, therefore, nothing "unfair" from this perspective, if our industry shrinks because we put higher standards on our industry and others, who mind the pollution less, choose lower standards.

(c) Besides, attributing competitive disadvantage to differential pollution tax burdens in the fashion of CCII comparisons for individual industries confuses absolute with comparative advantage. Thus, for example, in a two-industry world, if both industries abroad have lower pollution tax rates than at home, both will not contract at home. Rather, the industry with the *comparatively* higher tax rate will.

Objection 2: Others' Lower Standards Do Not Reflect Their Citizens' Preferences Correctly In turn, some environmentalist critics argue that the foreign governments do not reflect their citizens' "true preferences," and therefore in relation to these true preferences that would lead to higher valuation of pollution, the governments have unduly low standards, implying "unfair" competition.

There are counterarguments, in turn:

(a) Similar arguments, about failure of "political markets," apply to most countries, including high-standard countries, and to many areas of governmental regulation. It is commonly argued that the earliest legislations mandated "too-high" environmental standards that went beyond the "optimal" levels because costs were ignored and virtually limitless gains were assumed from the regulations. Now, in the United States for sure, cost-benefit considerations are steadily being introduced into the legislative process; and even the judiciary seems to have turned increasingly to this type of analysis, which then tends to weaken the bite of the standards legislatively laid down.[25]

Since arguments can be made persuasively that all legislation strays from the optimal because of political market failures endemic to any political system, however democratic, objecting only to lower environmental standards as reflecting such political market failure is to be arbitrary. It is also to open a Pandora's box, in favor of the more powerful countries that can then throw stones at others' glass houses while building a fortress around their own.

(b) Again, even if one argues that the decisions made undemocratically by a dictatorship or an oligarchy are vitiated, there is no reason to believe that the higher standards being pursued by a foreign country representing the competitive interests of a foreign industry or labor union in an industry are what a more democratic process would yield. The correct approach should rather be to encourage a shift to more democratic procedures in arriving at social and economic legislation, including environmental policy. Process, not outcomes (especially outcomes sought by self-serving groups elsewhere), is what we should aim at in countries that lack democratic ways.[26]

Should High-Standards Countries Force Low-Standards Countries into Upward Harmonization to Preserve Their High Standards?

In political-economy theory there are two forms of argument for CCII harmonization that take the high standards themselves to be at risk under free trade. Consider each, in turn.

(1) The less common argument is simply that, under pressure of competition from the low-standard countries, the political equilibrium will shift in favor of those who oppose high standards.

But this argument suffers from the fallacy of misplaced concreteness. Intensified international competition, *no matter why it arises,* will put such pressure on governments to reduce business costs. Why pick on lower standards elsewhere, even assuming that they are contributing to the problem?

(2) Far more worrisome to environmentalists than the simple effects of trade competition are the fears that "capital and jobs" will move to countries with lower standards, triggering a "race to the bottom" (or, as John Wilson has remarked, more accurately a race *toward* the bottom) where countries lower their standards in an interjurisdictional contest, below a level that some or all would like, in order to attract capital and jobs. So, a cooperative solution that would *coordinate* the setting of standards would, generally speaking, be a better solution. This coordinated solution, however, need not be characterized by harmonization at the level of the standards in the high-standard country or, in fact, by harmonization at all.

What we have here is a valid theoretical argument.[27] It is stated with analytical rigor as follows: independent governments (or jurisdictions), setting public policy for environmental protection (via taxes and abatement) and competing for investment by reducing environmental standards in a world of mobile and scarce capital, will set these standards at levels that are "too low," that is, that are inefficient for the world economy (composed of the nations whose governments compete in this way). The inefficiency is to be construed as usual: alternative policies exist that make at least one jurisdiction better off and no other jurisdiction worse off. In short, we have nonPareto-optimal Cournot-Nash equilibria (as we have already stated in earlier analysis in this chapter), characterized by lower environmental standards than in the cooperative equilibrium.

To see the matter more clearly, consider the following analysis based on arbitrarily specified, conventional payoff matrices reflecting the incomes yielded (in brackets) when different pollution abatement expenditures are undertaken at levels 0 and A (i.e., zero and a finite amount) by the two countries, home and foreign. The abatement expenditures are assumed to be a monotonic and increasing function of environmental standards.

There are thus four possible combinations of home and foreign expenditures on abatement. The payoffs associated with each combination with the first (resp. second) component being the payoff of the home (resp. foreign) jurisdiction are given by the following payoff matrix:

		Foreign expenditure	
		0	A
Home expenditure	0	$(-2, -2)$	$(2, -3)$
	A	$(-3, \ 2)$	$(1, \ 1)$

It is easily seen that each jurisdiction has a *dominant* strategy, namely, to spend nothing, because by doing so it maximizes its payoff whether the other jurisdiction spends nothing or A. Yet, compared to this *individually* rational dominant-strategy Nash equilibrium with both jurisdictions spending nothing on abatement, the *collectively* rational strategy of each spending A will yield a *higher* payoff for *both*.

Of course jurisdictional competition need not necessarily lead to such a "prisoner's dilemma" type of Nash equilibrium. For example, if the payoff matrix is as follows,

(−4, −4)	(2, −3)
(−3, 2)	(1, 1)

so that one jurisdiction spends nothing while the other spends A, $(0, A)$ and $(A, 0)$ are "pure strategy" Nash equilibria.

In both these cases the Nash equilibrium is characterized by a "race to the bottom" in the sense that the pollution abatement expenditure is zero for at least one jurisdiction. But this result need not occur, as consideration of the following payoff matrix shows. Thus, consider

(−2, −2)	(2, −3)
(−3, 2)	(3, 3)

and it is readily seen that we have a unique Nash equilibrium where each jurisdiction spends A on abatement.

Of course, these are arbitrarily constructed payoff matrices, and we need to ground them in underlying models of economies to see whether such outcomes are sensible within them. As argued by John Wilson, this can indeed be done to show that the "race to the bottom" need not occur, and that even a "race to the top" might.[28]

The question that now arises is whether this theoretical possibility of the "race to the bottom" is an empirical possibility of any significance. Leaving out the question as to whether the parametric evidence shows that the noncooperative Nash equilibrium, including the special case of the prisoner's dilemma, will be characterized by significantly lower environmental standards relative to the cooperative equilibrium, we may ask whether there is any empirical support anyway for the propositions that (1) capital is in fact responsive to the differences in environmental standards and (2) different countries and jurisdictions actually play the game then of competitive lowering of standards to attract capital. Without both these phenomena holding in a significant fashion in reality, the "race to the bottom" could be a theoretical curiosity.

As it happens, systematic evidence is available for the former proposition alone, but the finding is that the proposition is not supported by the studies to date: at best, there is very weak evidence in favor of inter-jurisdictional mobility in response to CCII differences in environmental standards. Arik Levinson, who has reviewed the available evidence thoroughly, concludes:[29]

> The conclusion of the literature on domestic location decisions, like that on international locations, is that there is not a lot of evidence that environmental regulations deter investment. In fact, most authors are careful to note the limitations of their research, and to place caveats on their counterintuitive conclusions that stringent regulations do not deter plants nor do lax regulations attract them. But the literature as a whole presents fairly compelling evidence that this is true.

Of course, there are many ways to interpret this finding of an extremely weak effect of CCII differences in environmental standards on industry location. There are three classes of explanation for the finding: (1) that the differences in standards are not significant and are outweighed by other factors that affect locational decisions; (2) that exploiting differences in standards is not a good strategy relative to not exploiting them; and (3) that lower standards may paradoxically even repel, instead of attracting, direct foreign investment.

Explanation 1

a. The obvious, and most cited, explanation is that the standards differences are a small factor in the location decision because they are dominated by other more important factors such as tax breaks, infrastructure facilities, and proximity to markets.[30]

b. Industry location may be seen to be more sensitive to CCII differences in standards if executive enforcement and voters-cum-NGO activism are taken into account as well. The de facto differences in standards may then be more acute than assumed in many studies.[31]

Explanation 2

c. Another (static) explanation is that when multiplant firms, such as most multinationals, invest in different locations, they tend to work uniformly with the most stringent standards they face among these locations, to reduce the transaction costs involved in making diverse choices.[32]

d. Another (dynamic) explanation is that, faced with divergent standards, firms extrapolate that all countries are on an escalator to similar higher standards and therefore decide that it is best to be "ahead of the curve" in the countries that currently have lower standards and to conform to higher standards even though not required. In this case, again, convergence of standards adhered to will emerge, as in the preceding (static) argument, and differences in (required) standards across different jurisdictions will become moot, showing little relationship in practice between such differences and industry-location choices.[33]

e. Another (dynamic) explanation is that firms may argue that the higher-standard countries are the ones that innovate, that many innovations lead to embodied technical change, that such innovations are likely to be embodied (only) in recent vintages of capital goods that already meet the higher standards, and therefore the important benefit of significant technical change will accrue to a firm only insofar as processes and capital goods using higher-standard technology at present are being used by it.

Explanation 3

f. An ingenious explanation of a different analytical variety is that multinationals are discouraged from investing in low-standard countries because local firms have comparative advantage in using pollution-intensive technology that conforms to lower standards. Hence, direct foreign investment (DFI) is likely to be less, not more, when CCII differences in standards are greater between countries![34]

A possible underlying explanation is that firms in the higher-standard countries are likely to scrap their earlier-vintage lower-standard equipment and sell it to the lower-standard countries for the local firms to use, instead of undertaking DFI themselves with such discontinued technology. In short, arm's-length sale of lower-standard equipment to local manufacturers may be preferred to DFI with such equipment, because the local firms are more likely to be able to work with this technology than the multinationals that have moved on to higher-standard, newer-vintage technology—engineering and maintenance know-how tend to be specific to the technology one is working with.

Most of these suggested explanations only reinforce the view that CCII differences in standards, as a factor prompting a "race to the bottom," should not be a source of concern.[35] And this conclusion is further reinforced when one contemplates the fact that there is almost no evidence for the proposition that, regardless of the capital-sensitivity to CCII differences in environmental standards, different countries and jurisdictions nonetheless actually compete for capital by sacrificing environmental standards[36] (as against doing so via tax breaks, infrastructure construction, tariff policy, preferential trading arrangements such as NAFTA where Mexico sought DFI-diversion toward itself through preferential access to the U.S. market, etc.).

The fuss that is made nonetheless over the "race to the bottom" in the political arena, as happened in the NAFTA negotiations, may then be explained either as a reaction to ill-founded fears or as a cynical ploy to advance environmental or protectionist lobbying interests.

Other Arguments and an Alternative Proposal

Therefore, neither the concern with "unfair trade" nor the concern with "threats to high standards," as the reason to push for CCII harmonization as a precondition for free trade or alternatively to invoke eco-dumping duties to countervail CCII differences in pollution tax burdens, is compelling. It is best to take, as a general policy, the option of *mutual recognition* of standards, recognizing the fact that diversity of CCII standards is basically a natural and appropriate phenomenon, consistent with free trade and the consequent gains from trade for all.

Protectionist Capture The wisdom of the policy conclusion of the preceding paragraph is reinforced by contemplating the certain protectionist consequences of doing otherwise. Thus, consider what an eco-dumping procedure, supplementing our normal antidumping (AD) procedure, would do. We presume that the eco-dumping procedure would calculate the subsidy implied by lower standards and proceed to levy a countervailing duty unless the foreign costs were raised by the estimated amount, with the option that the duty would be lifted when foreign standards were suitably raised and the costs of foreign firms demonstrably raised by the calculated amount.

It is well known that AD actions have become the favored policy instrument of protectionists today. Their desirability from the viewpoint of protectionists derives form the fact that, unlike safeguard actions (under Section 201 of U.S. law and Article XIX of the GATT), AD actions are *selective*: they can target down to the level of the firm, not just a specific foreign country! Besides, compared to preset tariffs, they are also *elastic*: the duties will be set at rates that are decided during litigation and therefore are a function of litigation expenditure, impartiality of the procedures governing the litigation, and the bilateral game played between the complainants and their targets.

Furthermore, in playing the game, the rules are set in favor of litigants, relative to what the rules would be if the objective of AD actions were truly to avoid economically defined predation. In particular, the usual game of reconstructing true costs, against which prices charged are compared to determine dumping margins, has been played to the hilt to get these margins to be as high as possible in litigation. But, as was the case with the former centrally planned economies whose own prices and costs were dismissed as illegitimate, these reconstructed "true" costs can be arbitrary, leading the procedure to effective protectionist capture.

Such capture would surely be the case also with eco-dumping duties, since the eco-dumping margins would have to be *necessarily* estimated on the basis of reconstructed costs of meeting the pollution standards of the complainant country. The U.S. Environmental Protection Agency, for example, would be estimating the cost of implementing U.S. standards in Rio or in Jakarta, so as to arrive at the implicit (*not* actual and observable) subsidy that must be countervailed through an eco-dumping duty by the United States, just as the Department of Commerce does for conventional dumping. There is no reason to doubt that the inherently arbitrary outcomes would be similarly obliging to local lobbies.[37]

Infinite Shadow Prices? Thus we conclude that the demands for eco-dumping duties to countervail CCII differences in environmental standards and pollution tax and abatement burdens are both illogical (in denying the legitimacy of such diversity) and unwise (in being inherently susceptible to protectionist capture). We have considered, at different stages of our analysis, several reasons why these demands nonetheless appear reasonable and why they have political salience. We must conclude, however, by adding one more reason, which probably has a counterpart also in the case of labor standards and which springs from the nature of our basic argument for the legitimacy of diversity in CCII standards.

Recall our argument that the different shadow prices for pollution that can, and generally will, emerge among different countries, implying differential rather than harmonized environmental taxes and standards, are "natural" for us to contemplate and accept. But suppose that we were putting an infinite price on any and every specific pollution, regardless of its level, small or large. Then these differences would disappear. We believe that many environmentalists have tended to approach their specific environmental concerns with an implicit infinite shadow price, thus leading to demands for harmonization, though this tendency is declining. This fact is well-illustrated by the following remarks in Cropper and Oates' excellent recent review of environmental economics:[38]

The economist's view had—to the dismay of the profession—little impact on the initial surge of legislation for the control of pollution. In fact, the cornerstones of federal environmental policy in the United States, the Amendments to the Clean Air Act in 1970 and to the Clean Water Act in 1972, explicitly prohibited the weighing of benefits against costs in the setting of environmental standards. The former directed the Environmental Protection Agency to set maximum limitations on pollutant concentrations in the atmosphere "to protect the public health": the latter set as an objective the "elimination of the discharge of *all* [our emphasis] pollutants into the navigable waters by 1985." [Although standards were to be set solely on the basis of health criteria, the 1970 Amendments to the Clean Air Act did include economic feasibility among its guidelines for setting source-specific standards. Roger Noll has suggested that the later 1977 Amendments were, in fact, more "antieconomic" than any that went before. See Matthew McCubbins, Roger Noll, and Barry Weingast (1989) for a careful analysis of this legislation.]

The evolution of environmental policy, both in the U.S. and elsewhere, has inevitably brought economic issues to the fore: environmental regulation has necessarily involved costs—and the question of how far and how fast to push for pollution control in light of these costs has entered into the public debate. Under Executive Order 12291 issued in 1981, many proposed environmental measures have been subjected to a benefit-cost test. In addition, some more recent pieces of environmental legislation, notably the Toxic Substances Control Act (TSCA) and the Federal Insecticide, Fungicide, and Rodenticide Act (FI-FRA), call for weighing benefits against costs in the setting of standards.

Once, therefore, we get away from the limited, perhaps almost empty, set of infinite-shadow-price environmental objectives, we are then back also to the legitimacy of diversity of standards among trading nations as the natural and reasonable way to look at the issue.[39]

An Alternative Proposal We should thus reject the calls for "CCII harmonization or countervailing duties on eco-dumping." But the political salience of such calls remains a major problem. One may well ask then, Are there any "second-best" approaches, short of the eco-dumping and CCII harmonization proposals, that may address some of the political concerns at least economic cost? In that spirit, we would suggest the following proposal for consideration.

Proposal: Extend the Domestic Standards of High-Standard Countries to Their Firms in Low-Standard Countries, Unilaterally or through an OECD Code

In our view, the political salience of the harmful demands for eco-dumping duties and CCII harmonization is greatest when plants are closed by one's own multinationals and shifted to other countries. The actual shifting of location, and the associated loss of jobs in that plant, magnify greatly the fear of the "race to the bottom" and of the "impossibility" of competing against low-standard countries. Similarly, when investment by one's own firms is seen to go to specific countries that happen to have lower standards, resentment is readily focused against those countries and their standards. However, when jobs are lost simply because of *trade* competition, it is much harder to locate one's resentment and fear on one specific foreign country and its policies as a source of unfair competition.[40] Hence, a second-best proposal could well be to address this particular fear, however unfounded and often illogical, of outmigration of plants and investment by one's firms abroad in low-standard countries.

The proposal is to adapt the Sullivan Principles approach to the problem at hand. Under Sullivan, U.S. firms in South Africa were urged to adopt U.S. practices, not the South African apartheid ways, in their operations. If this principle that U.S. firms in Mexico be subject to U.S. environmental policies (choosing the desired ones from the many that obtain across different states in the federal United States) were adopted by U.S. legislation, it would automatically remove whatever incentive there was to move because of environmental burden differences.[41]

This proposal that one's firms abroad behave as if they were at home—do in Rome as you do in New York, not as Romans do—can be either legislated unilaterally by one high-standard country or by a multilateral binding treaty among different high-standard countries. Again, it may be reduced to an exhortation, just as the Sullivan Principles were, by single countries in isolation or by several as through a nonbinding but ethos-defining and policy-encouraging OECD Code.

The disadvantage of this proposal, of course, is that it does violate the diversity-is-legitimate rule whose desirability was discussed earlier. Investment flows, like investment of one's own funds and production and trade therefrom, should reflect this diversity. The proposal, therefore, reduces the efficiency gains from a freer flow of cross-country investments today. But if environmental tax burdens are not very different or do not figure prominently in firms' locational decisions, as the empirical literature seems to stress,[42] the efficiency costs of this proposal could also be minimal while the gains in allaying fears and therefore moderating the demand for bad proposals could be very large indeed.

Yet another objection may focus on intra-OECD differences in high standards. Since there are differences among the OECD countries in CCII environmental tax burdens in specific industries for specific pollutions, this proposal would lead to "horizontal inequity" among the OECD firms in third countries. If the British burden is higher than the French, British firms would face a bigger burden in Mexico than the French firms. But then such differences already exist among firms abroad, since tax practices among the OECD countries on taxation of firms abroad are not harmonized in many respects.[43] Interestingly, the problem of horizontal equity has come up in relation also to the demands of the poor countries (which often find it difficult to enforce import restrictions effectively) that the domestic restrictions on hazardous products be automatically extended to exports by every country. Such a practice would put firms in the countries with greater restrictions at an economic disadvantage. But agreement has now been reached to disregard the problem.

Other problems may arise: (1) monitoring of one's firms in a foreign country may be difficult; and (2) the countries with lower standards may object on grounds of "national sovereignty." Neither argument may be compelling. It is unlikely that a developing country would object to foreign firms doing better by its citizens in regard to environmental standards (which it cannot afford to impose, given its own priorities, on its own firms). Equally, it would then assist in monitoring the foreign firms.

4.3 The Question of Ethical Preferences

So far, we have considered only those demands for harmonization of cross-country intra-industry standards that arise because of considerations centered on "unfair trade" and the fear that one's standards would be endangered if competitiveness were reduced because of lower standards abroad.

However, we must recognize that, for some environmentalists, the desire to spread one's ethical values to others also leads to demands for harmonization, especially of production processes. Thus, opponents in the United States of purse-seine fishing of tuna, which cruelly kills dolphins along with the tuna, would like to see the suspension of trade in Mexican tuna so as to get the Mexicans to accept the U.S. restrictions on such fishing. Of course, some of the agitation proceeds from environmentalists who would find it morally reprehensible to trade in products whose harvesting has cruelly abused nature or a preferred species. But a main impulse is simply the old, morality-driven desire to spread the values to which one subscribes, suspension of access to one's market being justified by a consequentialist ethic rather than a categorical imperative. Consider these two arguments in reverse order.

4.3.1 Spreading Ethical Preferences to Others

We think that GATT sanctioning of the use of unilateral *state* action to suspend other countries' trade access, or (in GATT-defined parlance) their trading rights under the GATT "treaty," unless one's choice of ethical concerns is adopted by others through implicit harmonization in one's direction, is inappropriate for several reasons.[44]

(1) The values sought to be imposed are often not at the level of "human rights" violations such as the massacres perpetuated on one's population or apartheid. They are "lesser" values and are idiosyncratic in the sense of being closely culture-bound rather than reflective of basic and universal aspects of human nature. Thus Americans are particularly touched by dolphins being caught cruelly in purse seines in tuna fishing. But we wonder when we see on television an interview with the man who brought this practice to national attention by filming the dolphins in distress: he is, we think, eating fish in the wilds. If Americans have their dolphins, the Indians have their sacred cows. Animal-rights activists object to slaughterhouses. Others may see the fishing scenes in Robert Redford's *A River Runs through It*, not as magical moments of rapport with nature, but as violation of it with cruelty to a fish that twists and turns, writhing in agony.

The culture specificity of these values, and hence their lack of salience to other economically weaker nations on whom they are sought to be imposed, creates then the inevitable sense that the use of trade sanctions to impose them is simply an act of unjustified moral militancy that is itself ethically offensive. This view gains further credibility when the "values" being pushed on others are actually at the expense of more fundamental values. For example, Americans would prefer to protect dolphins at the expense of Mexican prosperity. The use of purse seines, which are more productive than other nets, would reduce Mexican poverty, but Americans put dolphins ahead of Mexicans. The Mexican reaction may then well be similar to the way American liberals would react if they had to confront the moral militancy of Pat Robertson allied with Genghis Khan.

(2) And then there is the objection that comes from the lack of symmetry in imposing one's idiosyncratic moral preferences on others, as between the strong and the weak nations. Thus, even some NGOs in poor countries, whose natural tendency would be to ally with NGOs in rich countries, have expressed resentment and opposition to the "eco-imperialism" implied when the strong nations use trade power to force their preferred values on the weaker nations but the equally autonomous values of the weaker nations cannot be forced upon the stronger nations in the same way.[45] These NGOs deny that the NGOs of the strong nations have a monopoly on virtue.

Thus we may quote the most radical of today's proenvironment NGOs in India on this issue, in an editorial, "Trade Control Is Not a Fair Instrument," in the country's leading environmental magazine, *Down to Earth*:[46]

In the current world reality trade is used as an instrument entirely by northern countries to discipline environmentally errant nations. Surely, if India or Kenya were to threaten to stop trade with USA, it would hardly affect the latter. But the fact of the matter is that it is the northern countries that have the greatest impact on the world's environment and yet, their past record in their own countries ... is nothing to be proud of.... the instruments that need to be devised for ... a system of global discipline must be fair and equally accessible to all. Reinforcing [through unilateral muscle-flexing by rich-country NGOs and their governments via trade sanctions] the power that already flows in a northern direction cannot improve the world.

(3) The 1991 GATT report *Trade and the Environment* drew attention, not to this disturbing asymmetry of effective enforceability of the "values" of the North versus the equally autonomous "values" of the South owing to differential power. Rather, eschewing the problem of asymmetric power and instead assuming that each nation can play the same game with equal effectiveness, it advanced the "slippery slope" scenario: if any country could suspend another's trading access in products produced in an "unacceptable" fashion (when no international physical spillovers could be cited as a possible justification and only "values" were at stake), the result was likely to be a proliferation of trade restrictions without any discipline or restraint:[47]

It is difficult to think of a way to effectively contain the cross-border assertion of priorities. If governments suspend the trading rights of other nations because they unilaterally assert that their environmental priorities [i.e., "values"] are superior to those of others, then the same approach can be employed on any number of grounds. Protectionists would welcome such unilateralism. They could exploit it to create embargoes, special import duties and quotas against rivals by enacting national legislation that unilaterally defines environmental agendas that other countries [with different "values"] are likely to find unacceptable.

Changing the world trading rules so as to permit the suspension of trading rights of others by individual contracting parties, based simply on the unilateral and extra-territorial assertion of their environmental priorities, undoubtedly would be difficult because many countries would consider such a change to be a big step down a slippery slope.

(4) These views concerning unilateralism to impose one's values on others acquire yet greater cogency when we recognize that there are alternative ways in which one's values can be indulged and propagated.

(a) Most important, if your values are good, as with human rights values that are now widely shared, they will spread because of their intrinsic appeal. Mahatma Gandhi's idea of nonviolence spread far and wide, not because India had economic power to force it on others or because Western NGOs urged trade sanctions against their own nations to canvass its adoption. It spread because of its inherent and powerful moral attractiveness. The Spanish Inquisition should not be necessary to spread Christianity; quite appropriately, the pope has no troops.

Thus consider the following argument, advanced by one of the ablest advocates of environmentalist causes, Steve Charnovitz, in defense of biodiversity:

There are important medical reasons to preserve biodiversity. But there are also important moral reasons. Geopolitical boundaries should not override the word of God who directed Noah to take two of every living creature into the Ark "to keep them alive with you."[48]

We must confess that, as two Hindus among nearly 900 million on this planet, we find this moral argument culture-specific rather than universal in its appeal. It is unlikely that it can spread because of its intrinsic moral merit; should it then be forced on others anyway?

(b) Moreover, alternative private options are often available to propagate your particular ethical preferences if greater activism is desired. Nothing today proscribes NGOs in United States, for example, from financing NGOs in Mexico that bring pressure on *their* government to change its attitude on purse seines, thus changing the balance of forces in Mexico away from more productive tuna fishing that benefits Mexico economically and toward "dolphin-safe" fishing that benefits the dolphins in the Eastern Pacific instead.

(c) Then again, voluntary private boycotts can be a potent instrument as well. A long-standing tradition permits such private boycotts in pluralistic democracies. Provided that labeling requirements provide an opportunity for consumers to make choices in the marketplace between, say, "dolphin-safe" and "dolphin-unsafe" tuna, these boycotts will provide an option to "dolphin-agitated" activists.[49]

This option is not the same as proscription, of course. Environmentalists will thus note that labeling may be ineffective because "consumers may act *rationally* in calculating that their individual purchase of environmentally unfriendly products ... would have only a negligible effect" and that "consumers may act *irrationally*" by not appreciating the ecological importance of avoiding the consumption of the offending product.[50]

Then again, there are bound to be substantive disagreements about the nature and extent of labeling: "dolphin-unsafe" labeling may be objected to as too pejorative and "tuna from Mexico" may be considered too weak. The problems that have plagued the labeling issue for a variety of reasons within the United States itself, both in terms of its design and its uniformity versus diversity among the different states of the union, will not go away at the international level: if anything, they will be more fiercely debated.[51]

But, against these factors that weaken the efficacy of the voluntary-boycott prescription, we must put contrary arguments. Indeed, one might argue that, if enough people desire to attach opprobrium to "dolphin-unsafe" tuna, then "dolphin-safe" tuna producers can use their own "dolphin-safe" labels, requiring only state monitoring and prosecution of false labeling by the dolphin-unsafe tuna producers. After all, the Body Shop has done pretty well in this way.

Moreover, boycotts in rich countries with big markets, even when leaky, can carry disproportionate clout, and the funds at the disposal of some of the environmental NGOs and certainly in their aggregate (as demonstrated when they carry enormously expensive full-page ads simultaneously in newspapers such as the *New York Times*, *Washington Post*, and *The Financial Times*) are evidently large relative to what the poor countries they occasionally target can muster in defense of their own practices and preferences.[52]

One might also add that the passionate zeal with which these boycotts are advocated, and the occasional willingness to portray those that disagree as morally defective, add to their potency as weapons.

A critic may well suggest that we contradict ourselves if we allow private boycotts but would disallow governmental prohibitions, since governments are only "agents" of the citizens. Strictly speaking, this criticism is not true: there is considerable debate in the social science literature on the "principal-agent" relationship and on how poor an agent the government can be. But, that complexity aside, we do distinguish all the time in democracies between state and private actions, permitting far greater latitude to the latter. Thus, when the Harvard lawyer Alan Dershowitz agitated successfully to have the Boston Symphony Orchestra cancel Vanessa Redgrave's appearance because of her politically incorrect views, he was considered well within his rights to disgrace himself; but the U.S. government proscribing her appearance would have been a disgrace to the nation and in violation of national tradition and would surely have been struck down by our courts. And this asymmetry between what private parties and public governments may do is likely to be accepted by most democratic governments today.

(5) So far, we have proceeded on the assumption that unilateral suspension of trade access to spread one's ethical preferences is effective and have argued essentially that it is unwise and undesirable. But a legitimate critique may well be that such action is likely to be ineffective in its objective, thus disrupting trade to no advantage.

It is hard to settle this question on theoretical grounds alone. The cost imposed on the nation whose offending trade is suspended may or may not be significant enough to matter in its calculation; the cost itself will reflect the importance of the embargoed market relative to others, ability to evade, and so on. But it is surely improbable that this cost in any specific instance will be compelling.[53]

The matter becomes less problematic if the cost is greatly increased by other punishments and inducements: Mexican compliance with nonuse of purse seines, despite the favorable Tuna-Dolphin Panel ruling, was secured by convincing President Carlos Salinas de Gortari that it would be hard to pass NAFTA in Congress otherwise. These added instruments, however, will be available only to large and powerful nations, chiefly the United States, making the argument's relevance fairly negligible for most nations.

The sanctioning, as WTO-consistent, of unilateral, governmental withdrawal of market access from other nations for their offending products simply with a view to coercing them into accepting one's idiosyncratic "value" preferences seems, therefore, to be undesirable on several grounds, chiefly these:

- It is essentially intransitive, with each nation able to say its specific values are better than another's; it thus creates the potential for chaotic spread of trade restrictions based on self-righteousness, compounded by a likely encouragement of the process by protectionists.

- In its reliance on force rather than persuasion, it is inherently asymmetric toward poor nations with less economic clout, implying that the economically strong nations are also morally superior and their governments must not be constrained by multilateral rules from coercing others into conversion.
- There are alternative private options that can be used to create a multilateral consensus of shared values based not on the sword but on precept, example, and even pressure through boycotts.[54]

Even though some of the environmental NGOs in the United States, in particular, and perhaps elsewhere too, are skeptical or scornful of them, it is noteworthy that these arguments are spreading within the international community. Thus, Steve Charnovitz has recently complained:[55]

> The GATT's campaign against unilateralism is having some impact. Earlier this year, the UN Conference on Trade and Development adopted a resolution stating that "Unilateral actions to deal with environmental challenges outside the jurisdiction of the importing country should be avoided." The Rio Declaration repeats this statement.

We have little doubt, however, that unilateral actions designed simply to spread "lesser values" to others through the use of suspension of trading access are unwise. We are, therefore, only delighted that this view is gaining ground.

4.3.2 Rejecting Trade in "Defiled" Products

Suppose, however, that your intention in unilaterally denying Mexico access to the U.S. market is not to change Mexican fishing of tuna in a "dolphin-safe" direction, but simply to avoid eating a "defiled" product that offends your moral values.[56] Should you then be forced into consuming Mexican tuna? That would seem a tall order to many.

But there is an answer to this objection. Nothing in current or prospective GATT rules forces you (quite correctly) into this offensive option. For, you could certainly compensate the country whose trading rights (i.e., access to your market) are being denied or suspended by *either* offering other concessions, *or* (in the odd manner of GATT procedures) having the other country withdraw some "equivalent" concessions of its own to you.

Confronted by this argument, some environmentalists are offended: why should we have to pay for our principles? The answer is that it is a small price to pay if the alternative (of unilateralism) has the many drawbacks that we have noted already. If it is right in the Christian tradition to buy indulgences to pay for one's vice, perhaps one should not object to a proposal to pay for one's virtue: at least, the former is for personal gain, the latter (if you accept our arguments) for social gain.[57] Besides, the "payment" is not in cash but in compensation in the form of reductions of other trade barriers against the foreign country to offset the enactment of the trade barrier against its offending export (or a retaliatory raising of trade barriers by the foreign country). Such payment, in fact, should work in the direction of moving resources away from the offending foreign activity, thus reinforcing the case for using such a policy option.

Charnovitz also appeals to "original intent" to argue that the original signatories to the GATT, and earlier practice in some cases, permitted exceptions to market access based on extrajurisdictional exercise of "values" in cases such as the prohibited U.S. landing and sale of U.S. sponges from the Gulf of Mexico gathered by "certain harmful methods [such as] diving or using a diving apparatus."[58] We are assured by academic legal experts on the GATT, however, that the GATT's "original intent" is not unambiguously inferred in this as in many other instances.

John Jackson, one of the leading authorities on GATT law, has thus argued:[59]

> It has been argued [by Charnovitz] that the drafting history of the GATT would lead to an interpretation of Article XX that would permit governments to take a variety of environmental measures and justify them under the general exceptions of GATT. While this view is interesting, and the research is apparently thorough, it is not entirely persuasive and overlooks important issues of treaty interpretation. Under typical international law, elaborated by the Vienna Convention on the Law of Treaties, preparatory work history is an ancillary means of interpreting treaties. In the context of interpreting the GATT, we have more than forty years of practice since the origin of GATT, and we also have some very important policy questions.... Thus, unlike certain schools of thought concerning United States Supreme Court interpretation of the United States Constitution, it is this author's view that one cannot rely too heavily on the original drafting history.

In any event, the liberal environmentalists who would ordinarily oppose the appointments of "original intent" judges on the Supreme Court should not endorse this juridical approach in seeking to prevent the GATT from pursuing (what we have argued are) sensible interpretations of its laws on environmental issues.

4.3.3 Dealing with Ethical Preferences

Where does this analysis leave us? Based on it, as also on arguments in the discussion that follows immediately concerning the way GATT deals with objections by contracting parties to processes of production (as distinct from products themselves) used by other contracting parties, we think that the following recommendations have merit in case of ethics-based objections to providing market access:

Unilateralism

• Unilateral suspension of trading access for reasons based on ethical preference should not be sanctioned by the WTO.

• Such unilateral suspensions, where desired, should be "paid for" by other, equivalent trade concessions.

Plurilateralism and Multilateralism

Where the ethical preference is embodied in a plurilateral (i.e., multination) treaty signed by many nations, we need to distinguish between two major cases:

1. Plurilateral treaties concerning an ethical preference, as on preventing the production of chickens in batteries or injecting cattle with hormones, for instance, may be signed by enough nations to enable a WTO waiver; in this case, the compatibility of the plurilateral treaty and the WTO is assured.

2. When the number of nations signing the ethical-preference-embodying treaty falls short of the required WTO waiver majority, then the conflict can lead to problems. In particular:

• *Products*: Where the plurilateral treaty simply provides for *suspension of trade access* for the offending products—such as ivory or tigers or whales—there is no difficulty in enforcing such a ban as long, of course, as the ban extends in a nondiscriminatory fashion to both foreign and domestic supply.[60]

Where, however, the signatory nations seek to impose *trade sanctions* (i.e., trade disruption of products other than the one in dispute), as a punishment aimed at securing compliance, the consensus appears to be that such sanctions would be GATT-inconsistent.[61] In that case, our solution would be to treat these sanctions as indeed so and instead to encourage nations to use other instrumentalities (of the kind discussed earlier, e.g., suasion, NGO activities) to secure the necessary acceptance of the ideas by a plurality of WTO contracting parties sufficient to obtain a waiver. This is indeed the procedure that has been used to undertake trade embargoes in matters such as apartheid where South Africa, despite being a GATT member, was embargoed under multilateralism-based UN procedures that would equally have procured a GATT waiver.

• *Processes*: The GATT would appear to proscribe the suspension of market access to other contracting parties in products whose manufacture or production is objected to by the importing contracting party. In our view, as developed in the next section, this is a desirable proscription. If, therefore, it is desired that such suspension of market access be undertaken in any event—as was the case with the proscription of hormone-fed beef by the EC—then we would recommend that the suspension be "paid for" by compensatory trade concessions elsewhere, exactly as in the case of unilateral trade access suspensions discussed previously.

4.4 Institutional Vulnerability of High Standards to Objections by Low-Standard Countries: GATT's Threat to Environmental Autonomy

We turn finally to the question of the threats seen by many environmentalists to their high standards (aimed at domestic regulation) by GATT procedures that enable low-standard countries to question, and (if successful) to undermine, these high standards. We must ask, Are the environmentalists legitimately worried about the roadblocks that current and prospective GATT rules can pose for environmental regulations and standards aimed entirely at domestic production and consumption, matters that are conventionally and properly within domestic jurisdiction?

Now, as long as these rules are applied without discrimination between domestic and foreign suppliers and among different foreign suppliers, there is really little that GATT rules can do to prevent a country from doing anything that it wants to do. For domestic conservation, safety, and health reasons, a contracting party of the GATT can even undertake discriminatory, selectively targeted trade-restraining action, subject to safeguards, under Articles XX(b) and XX(g).[62]

Thus, if you insist on safety belts or air bags in cars, you can impose them on cars as long as both imports from all sources and domestic production are symmetrically treated. So also for requiring catalytic converters to reduce environmentally harmful emissions.

4.4.1 The Problem of Processes

The most significant and contentious conceptual question arises when you have a rule that says that consumption (from both domestic and foreign sources) of a product will be restricted if the product is produced, *using a process you disapprove of*. Objecting to a process used in a foreign (or, strictly, nondomestic) jurisdiction is, under GATT rulings, not acceptable. There are two types of such process-related problems that we might distinguish:

1. Where the process used is objected to because of "values": e.g., purse seines or leghold traps.

2. Where the process used is objected to because it creates cross-border physical spillovers and hence a global pollution problem: e.g., acid rain or global warming.[63]

GATT law, as currently interpreted, forbids the use of trade restrictions for *both* classes of objections. For the first class of actions, this proscription seems to us justified, in light of our discussion in section 4.3.

The presence of cross-border physical spillovers, whose analysis we sketch only briefly in section 4.5, raises more legitimate worries about altogether ruling out process-related trade restraints, and appropriate changes in GATT law will be necessary in this class of cases where it seems evidently inappropriate to prevent nations from *any* use of trade restraints to limit the physical harm being imposed on them by other nations whose trade accentuates this harm. Such use must, however, be regulated in a way that ensures symmetry of rights, equity, and efficiency. Devising appropriate procedures and rules to regulate the use of such trade restraints in the context of global environmental problems is a challenge for the architects of the new GATT system.

4.4.2 Products

It would appear, however, that the GATT rules should cause no problems for the environmentalists (except for the process-related issues) when only purely domestic environmental problems are at issue. Thus, the GATT report argues:[64]

> Under GATT's rules, governments can employ many different measures to protect and improve the local environment. Thus, sales taxes on products that can create pollution (those containing chloroflurocarbons, for example), deposit refund schemes for recyclable waste (bottles, scrap cars), or favourable tax treatment of environmentally friendly products (lead-free gasoline, solar panels for home heating) and other non-discriminatory measures ensuring a pattern of domestic consumption that minimizes pollution would not normally be open to challenge.

There is also nothing in the GATT that prevents contracting parties from taxing or regulating domestic producers who engage in polluting activities—even to the extent of prohibiting the production and sale of particular goods. For instance, ceilings on air pollution levels, and levies on companies that discharge pollutants into lakes and rivers, are fully consistent with GATT rules.

In certain cases, even a measure taken for environmental protection purposes which would otherwise violate GATT obligations not to discriminate may be permitted under Article XX of the GATT. The narrowly-defined exceptions in Article XX permit a contracting party to place health, safety or domestic resource conservation goals ahead of non-discrimination, but only when certain conditions are fulfilled. In general, these conditions ensure that a trade measure is necessary for the achievement of such goals—and that these goals are not used as a pretext for reducing competition from imports.

GATT rules, therefore, place essentially no constraints on a country's right to protect its own environment against damage from either domestic production or the consumption of domestically produced or imported products. Generally speaking, a country can do anything to imports or exports that it does to its own products, and it can do anything it considers necessary to its own production processes.

Alas, that is not the end of the matter for the environmentalists. For, as the GATT report suggests, even if a regulation or a standard were set in an apparently nondiscriminatory fashion, it is perfectly possible that

- in reality, its intention is to discriminate against imports rather than to reach the stated (environmental or other) objective; and
- in practice, even if the intention is truly to reach the stated goal, the choice from different ways to reach that goal may have been in favor of a regulation or standard that effectively discriminates most, rather than least, against imports.

Then again, especially when safety and health standards are set (as with phytosanitary standards), there have been increasing demands for "scientific tests" as a precondition for the imposition of such standards, so as again to make these palatable to other trading nations who might see their resulting loss of markets as otherwise unreasonable.

These are perhaps the most contentious issues today where the trading interests see the reasonableness of current and prospective GATT procedures designed to ensure as much freedom of access to markets as possible, whereas the environmental interests see in the same procedures an unreasonable bias against themselves. In all these areas, the GATT permits challenges to be mounted by contracting parties to be mediated by dispute settlement panels and for codes and rules that define how the panels might adjudicate these disputes. We will say a little about each of these issues.[65]

The Intention Issue

Economists have long recognized the intention issue. Thus the classic instance we regale our students with relates to Gottfried Haberler's example of the provision in the German tariff, dating from 1902 and valid decades later, which was clearly meant to apply to Switzerland and Austria, relating to "brown or dappled cows reared at a level of at least 300 meters above the sea and passing at least one month in every summer at a height of at least 800 meters."[66]

Within the environmental field, a fine example where the United States was the aggrieved party is provided by the Canadian province Ontario's 10 percent tax on beer cans but not bottles, on environmental grounds. Even if the United States authorities did not challenge the objective of restricting the use of cans,[67] they could legitimately note that the law was likely to have been motivated by the desire to discriminate against foreign beer supplies who (unlike local rivals) predominantly used cans rather than bottles, combined tellingly with the fact that the use of cans for other products such as soups and juices (where Ontario producers would have been affected) was not proscribed.[68]

It is hard to see how a good, open trading system cannot permit member countries to examine the bona fides of environmental (and other) regulations in this way. Surely, given the ease with which regulations and standards can be misused for protectionist purposes, *some* mechanism must exist for grievances to be aired and adjudicated. The GATT dispute settlement mechanism, improved after the Uruguay Round and further changed in the direction of greater transparency, is sufficiently objective and neutral between contracting parties to provide a better method for dealing with the problem than national procedures that would always be suspect as having been influenced by national political considerations.

The Alternative-Measures Issue

There are more difficult issues, however, when the question of the use of alternative ways of reaching an environmental objective is raised.

It seems totally sensible that, if alternative ways of meeting an environmental objective exist, a contracting party should be asked to choose one that infringes least on another's trading rights. In fact, this view seems embodied in GATT's Article XX(b), which allows even discriminatory trade restrictions against another contracting party if the measures are deemed "necessary" to protect human, animal, or plant life or health.

Two different views of the matter, however, can be taken in interpreting what is "necessary." Thus, in the case of Thailand's restrictions on importation and internal taxes on cigarettes, the GATT panel decided that Thailand should use the "least GATT-inconsistent" measure to achieve its domestic objective. Then again, one could consider a "least-trade-restrictiveness" test which, of course, will not necessarily coincide with the "least-GATT-inconsistency" test.[69]

Aside from the greater difficulty of determining ordinally what greater and lesser GATT-consistency means, the economic superiority of the test that requires least damage to trade is manifest. In fact, the December 1991 Dunkel Draft of the proposed Uruguay Round treaty adopted the latter test: it is built into the Standards Code and also into the Sanitary and Phytosanitary Decision. It is also the test used in the GATT panel decision in 1992 on the alcoholic beverages case where the United States lost. The laws in five states that required a common carrier to enforce their tax and alcohol policies were held to be unacceptable because

> the United States has not demonstrated that the common carrier requirement is the least trade restrictive enforcement measure available to the various states and that less restrictive measures, e.g. record-keeping requirements of retailers and importers, are not sufficient for tax administration purposes.[70]

This test seems reasonable, of course. The objections to it amount mainly to objections to the methods by which the Beverage Panel arrived at the judgment that less-trade-restrictive measures to achieve the same objectives were available in that instance. But there are indeed inherent difficulties in defining the set of alternative policies that, with differential trade impact, would achieve identical environmental (or other domestic) objectives. It is hard to imagine *identical* results on these objectives from alternative policies, though *similar* results can sometimes be deemed possible (though, here too, judgments will differ in many cases).

In the end, any practical enforcement of the "least-trade-restrictive" test for evaluating the acceptability of an environmental regulation or standard will likely force the adjudicating panel into evaluating, implicitly or explicitly, *trade-offs* between the cost in trade disruption and the cost in reaching the environmental objective: a phenomenon and a problem that economists, who accept free lunches but do not believe in them, have no difficulty recognizing.

The jurisprudence, by necessity if not by choice, will have to move in the direction of evaluating and deciding upon the solution to such trade-offs. Thus, in the case of EC law, in the case involving Denmark's laws concerning disposable beer cans, the European Court of Justice seems to have explicitly considered such a trade-off between the interests of "free movement of goods" (and consequent trade benefits) and "environmental protection."[71]

It is natural, therefore, that environmentalists and trade experts who seem occasionally to attach opposing weights to the environmental and the trade benefits of any regulation or standard will worry about what weights the adjudicating panels would choose in reaching their decisions. If, therefore, disputes are to arise between nations, and tests of "necessity" that imply weighing alternative policies leading to different trade-offs are to be utilized, it is certainly proper for the environmentalists to seek improvements in the dispute settlement process that would give them greater access in terms of the ability to file written friend-of-the-court briefs and also make the panel procedures more transparent than hitherto at the GATT.

A complementary policy of prevention rather than cure would also be useful as we move increasingly into this difficult and contentious area. The input of "principally affected" trading countries into the setting of domestic environmental and other regulatory standards, such that the policy alternatives are discussed and adopted in light of such input, would help to reduce conflict to an irreducible minimum that the judicial process must address and resolve. Instances of such international input into domestic setting of standards are not lacking: the United States, worried by the trade-restrictive implications of EC standards-setting procedures, has indeed gained some access to the EC processes. But clearly more institutionalized and satisfactory procedures for doing so, available to weak and not just to strong nations, would appear to be a most useful innovation.

The Scientific-Test Issue

The use of scientific tests to determine whether a product can be proscribed, even on a nondiscriminatory basis between imports and domestic production, creates yet another important source of disagreement. Suppose that the United States uses Alar to spray apples and that the EC does not. Suppose then that, faced with agitation from consumers who consider Alar-sprayed apples to be a hazard to their health, the EC bans their sale. The U.S. industry and government can then be expected to demand that the EC justify, through the use of a scientific test, its fear that Alar-sprayed apples are a hazard.

Although this case is hypothetical, the EC-U.S. conflict on the EC's proscription of hormone-fed beef is not. In this instance, the U.S. beef producers that used hormones and the biotech industry that invented and produced the hormones were pitted against what they considered to be a wholly unscientific fear of hormone-fed beef. The United States went to the length of trade retaliation under Section 301; the EC in the end did not counterretaliate; and the matter was not taken to the GATT dispute settlement process for adjudication, with both the EC ban and the U.S. retaliation continuing in place. Given the high probability that a scientific test criterion would have been required by a GATT dispute settlement panel, it is likely that the EC would have lost the case.

But the case was an early warning sign of the tension between commercial and environmental interests on this issue. Admittedly, even hard science is not hard enough most of the time. The many who are convinced of a hazard to their health, no matter what the *current* preponderance of scientific opinion, might well turn out to be right after all. Then again, even if scientists were agreed on measuring the risk from any event or act of consumption or production, the subjective reaction of different people to the objective risk may vary greatly and, in fact, does.

It is tempting then to say, Let any regulation pass, regardless of the scientific test, no matter that it reduces another's access to one's market. But we are back then to the "slippery slope" scenario. Without the restraining hand of current science, the itch to indulge one's fears could be overwhelming.

The solution may then well be to institutionalize what in effect happened with the hormone-fed beef case: have the scientific test; if you lose, "pay up" (as the EC did) if you do not wish to change your regulation or standard; or settle by shifting your regulation or standard so as to broadly move in the direction of achieving your objective by alternative policies (e.g., by labeling hormone-fed beef rather than proscribing it altogether, and then undertaking education, propaganda, and boycotts against its use).

Again, if the notion of "paying up" appears offensive to the environmentalists because science should not stand in the way of our deeply held concerns, we would just urge them to undertake one thought experiment. We all know from science today that AIDS does not spread through simple contact. Suppose that our immigration policy nonetheless rules out HIV-infected immigrants, even when refugees and family reunification are involved, because large numbers of Americans are sure (unscientifically) that such admissions will spread AIDS to them. Would a typically liberal, activist environmentalist agree to such a policy?

The Circumventing-Democracy Issue

We would be remiss if we did not also note the increasing appeal to some environmentalists of the notion that "the process of negotiating international agreements [like the GATT's Uruguay Round] is less subject to public scrutiny, and therefore a threat to democratic accountability,"[72] and that "faceless" and unelected bureaucrats at the GATT will overrule democratically enacted environmental and other social regulations. Leaving aside the question whether such regulations will be overturned—an issue that we just discussed at length—the question regarding democratic process is far more complex than the simplistic denunciations that find their way into anti-GATT propaganda. In particular, we would argue the following:

1. It is inconsistent to hold simultaneously, as many do, that the low standards of other countries should be countervailed by foreign NGOs and governments that are "unelected" and "faceless" as far as these low-standard countries are concerned, while condemning the GATT panel members, chosen by democratic procedures multilaterally agreed among the contracting parties, as "faceless" and "unelected."

2. Is it really correct to hold that one level of governance is more "democratic" than another? After all, it is the contracting parties that have chosen the GATT panel procedures democratically.

3. Moreover, it is not necessarily correct to argue that the closer the level of governance to the ground, the better the decision. If local governance were dominant, Al Capone could flourish without the Feds, capital punishment would thrive, land reforms in developing countries (legislated and enforced from the top when grassroots activism is frustrated by the local power structure) might go slower, and so on.

4. There is no reason to think that the GATT works any worse than the national or local legislatures in these matters. Contrast the contribution of the GATT, including its panels, with the gift that the U.S. Congress gave to the world in 1934 with the Smoot-Hawley Tariff and is currently giving us with its 301 and Super 301–style championing of aggressive unilateralism.

5. The current U.S. position, opposed effectively by other contracting parties, that environmental NGOs be allowed to participate in GATT Council deliberations on panel rulings is couched in terms of transparency and democracy. But it raises compelling objections that presumably emerged during this debate:

a. The NGOs should be able to participate through their own governments, which represent them *and* other constituents in democratic governments; there is no reason to think that their added participation is any

more desirable than that of consumer groups, protectionist lobbies, unions, and the like, all of whom can and do compete for influence in national politics and hence on international policy deliberations.
b. The environmental NGOs are not necessarily handicapped financially vis-à-vis the other groups, and their organization and clout are disproportionately greater than their finances, since they can often successfully claim the higher moral ground (e.g., we are "rescuing the dolphins" from the rapacious multinationals; we are "saving the planet"), so they certainly do not need a "second voice," when others are denied it, at the GATT Council.
c. While there are indeed NGOs in the developing countries, the heavily financed ones are in the rich countries and will reflect *their* concerns, priorities, and views (e.g., protecting dolphins rather than aiding Mexico's tuna industry to help Mexico's development and removal of poverty); the rich countries would then have a double voice, when they can often drown out the voice of the poor countries with just one voice, thus undermining the notion of democracy at the *international* level.

4.5 Concluding Observations: Environmental Problems with Transborder Externalities and Trade Questions

We conclude our exhaustive analysis of the case of purely domestic environmental problems, and the associated demands for CCII harmonization and eco-dumping countervailing duties and so on, with a sketch of the policy problems that arise in the context of transborder externalities. These are generally more complex in character than the ones that arise with purely domestic pollution[73] and more compelling as well. It may be useful, from a policy viewpoint, to distinguish between two cases: (1) a special case where the problem is simplified by assuming a single country that pollutes the other, raising questions of response such as the use of trade barriers by the other; and (2) a general case where the problem is truly global in character. A good example of the former is U.S. transmission of acid rain to Canada; an excellent example of the latter is global warming, to which many countries contribute while all are affected by it (though each in a different degree, and not all negatively).

4.5.1 One-Way Transmission of Pollution and Two Countries

The case of pollution transmitted from one country to another is helpful because it illustrates in a simple way the problem raised by transborder externalities concerning the use of second-best trade instruments by the injured country when the offending country does not implement a first-best solution and uses its jurisdictional autonomy in the spirit of malign neglect. The principal question, then, is whether a country that is being damaged by pollution from another has the right to impose a trade restraint to affect the exports, and hence production, and hence the pollution, of the other country that comes into one's area.[74]

Thus, suppose that the United States is transmitting acid rain to Canada, thanks to its CO_2-producing processes used in producing electricity in a CO_2-intensive way, since U.S. generation of electricity uses fossil fuel (whereas the Canadian industry uses cleaner, hydroelectric processes). If the United States refuses to tax its electricity producers for the SO_2 pollution they generate, or refuses to compensate Canada for the damage that is inflicted by the acid rain that is transmitted to Canada by wind drift, then should Canada have the right to tax its import of U.S. electricity (and even of other U.S. exports that are produced using the electricity that produces the acid rain and then transmits a fraction of it to Canada)?

Modifying the GATT rules to explicitly allow for such a possibility would make sense as a "second-best" solution, since the offending party (the United States in the example) refuses to undertake a "first-best" solution. That also seemed to be, as Charnowitz has noted, the position taken in some early and unofficial thinking by the GATT Secretariat. Of course, the usual caveats about satisfying scientific tests and the like would have to be noted and codified.[75]

The problem, of course, is that this type of trade remedy is generally likely to be so weak for problems like acid rain that one may ask, Is it worth modifying the GATT/WTO to legitimate such trade actions? Thus, take the example of acid rain itself. The generation of acid rain in the United States, a fraction of which comes across to Canada, is geographically concentrated, of course, at the border whereas the import tariff would affect all electricity generation in the United States; moreover, the effect on SO_2 generation would be indirect, not direct through tax on the process itself; then again, only a fraction of the acid rain generation effect would get into the transmission. The tariff instrument would then be extremely weak, and the Canadian gain from its use in reducing the loss from the acid rain would be outweighed by the reduced gains from trade, that is, the gains from importing cheaper electricity from the United States.[76]

4.5.2 Global Transborder Externalities

The chief policy questions concerning trade when global pollution problems are involved, as with ozone-layer depletion and global warming, take a different turn related to the cooperative-solution-oriented multilateral treaties that are sought to address them.[77] They are essentially tied into noncompliance ("defection") by members and "free riding" by nonmembers. Because any action by a member of a treaty relates to targeted actions (such as reducing CFCs or CO_2 emissions) that are a public good (in particular, that the benefits are nonexcludable, so that if I incur the cost and do something, I cannot exclude you from benefiting from it), the use of trade sanctions to secure and enforce compliance automatically turns up on the agenda.

At the same time, the problem is compounded because the agreement itself has to be *legitimate* in the eyes of those accused of free riding or noncompliance. Before those pejorative epithets are applied and punishment prescribed in form of trade sanctions legitimated at the GATT/WTO, these nations have to be satisfied that the agreement being pressed on them is efficient and, especially, that it is equitable in burden sharing.[78] Otherwise, nothing prevents the politically powerful (i.e., the rich nations) from devising a treaty that puts an inequitable burden on the politically weak (i.e., the poor nations) and then using the cloak of a "multilateral" agreement and a new GATT/WTO legitimacy to impose that burden with the aid of trade sanctions with a clear conscience, invoking the "white man's burden" to secure the "white man's gain".

As a result, the policy demand, often made, to alter the GATT/WTO to legitimate trade sanctions on contracting parties who remain outside of a treaty, whenever a plurilateral treaty on a global environmental problem dictates it, is unlikely to be accepted by the poor nations without safeguards to prevent unjust impositions. The spokesmen of the poor countries have been more or less explicit on this issue, with justification. These concerns have been recognized by the rich nations.

Thus, at the Rio Conference in 1992, the Framework Convention on Climate Change set explicit goals under which several rich nations agreed to emission-level-reduction targets (returning, more or less, to 1990 levels), whereas the commitments of the poor countries were contingent on the rich nations footing the bill.

Ultimately, burden sharing by different formulas related to past emissions, current income, current population, and so on is inherently arbitrary; such formulas also distribute burdens without regard to efficiency. Economists will argue for burden sharing dictated by cost minimization across countries, for the earth as a whole: if Brazilian rain forests must be saved to minimize the cost of a targeted reduction in CO_2 emissions in the world, while the United States keeps guzzling gas because it is too expensive to cut down, then so be it. But then this efficient "cooperative" solution must not leave Brazil footing the bill! Efficient solutions, with compensation and equitable distribution of the gains from the efficient solution, make economic sense.

A step toward them is the idea of having a market in permits again, at the world level: no country may emit CO_2 without having bought the necessary permit from a worldwide quota. That system would ensure efficiency,[79] whereas the distribution of the proceeds from the sold permits would require a decision reflecting multilaterally agreed ethical or equity criteria (e.g., the proceeds may be used for refugee resettlement, UN peacekeeping operations, aid dispensed to poor nations by UNDP, the WHO fight against AIDS, and so on). This type of agreement would have the legitimacy that could then provide the legitimacy in turn for a GATT/WTO rule that permits the use of trade sanctions against free riders.

(Please see the original article for the relevant appendices)

NOTES

We have profited from the comments on an earlier draft by several project participants, especially Ken Abbott, Christopher Bliss, Drusilla Brown, Alessandra Casella, Alan Deardorff, Robert Hudec, Al Klevorick, Brian Langille, Virginia Leary, Andre Sapir, and John Wilson, at a conference at the Minnesota Law School in July 1993 and at a Washington, DC, conference in October 1994. The comments of Claude Barfield, Steve Charnowitz, Dan Esty, William Nordhaus, Susan Rose-Ackerman, and Karl-Göran Mäler have been very helpful. While we take joint responsibility for the entire chapter, the blame for any errors in the text must be assigned to Bhagwati and in the Appendix to Srinivasan!

1. By CCII, we mean harmonization of standards within the *same* industry across different trading countries.

2. This, of course, is the central issue addressed later in this chapter.

3. The suspension of trade generally, i.e., the use of trade "sanctions" (to promote human rights, for instance) is a related but different issue that we do not discuss in this chapter in depth.

4. As in argument 2.

5. The difficulties posed by the GATT, and now the WTO, for the environmentalists extend to GATT law (i.e., Dispute Settlement Panel findings) in regard to the ethical-preference issue as well. The general issue of GATT law on the entire range of relevant questions concerning the environment is addressed by Frieder Roessler in Chapter 2 in Volume 2 of this work.

6. *International Pollution Deterrence Act of 1991*, Statement of Senator David L. Boren, Senate Finance Committee, October 25, 1991.

7. We will be considering several objections to this view, of course, before reaching this conclusion.

8. The entire range of the factors (philosophical, economic, and political) that are currently prompting the drive toward CCII harmonization is reviewed and synthesized by Bhagwati

in Chapter 1. See also the discussion in Daniel Esty, *Greening the GATT* (Washington, DC: Institute for International Economics, 1994), pp. 108–114, 156–167.

9. "Bushism, Found: A Second-Term Agenda Hidden in Trade Agreements," *Harper's Magazine*, September 1992, p. 44.

10. Cf. J. Bhagwati and M. Kosters, eds., *Trade and Wages* (Washington, DC: American Enterprise Institute, 1994). Several trade economists share this skeptical view; see the most recent review in Jagdish Bhagwati, "Trade and wages: Choosing among alternative explanations," *Federal Reserve Bank of New York Economic Policy Review*, January 1995.

11. Cf. J. Bhagwati, "Free traders and free immigrationists: Friends or foes?" (mimeo) (New York: Russell Sage Foundation, 1992).

12. The prominent U.S. role in the UN Conference on Population in Cairo in September 1994 may be explained, at least in part, in this fashion.

13. Cf. Appendix, section A4.1.1.

14. Cf. Appendix, section A4.1.2.

15. Thus, any unfixed domestic distortion, such as failure to have optimal pollution taxes or adequate institutional arrangements to prevent the overuse of commons, for instance, can lead to immiserization under free trade vis-à-vis autarky. Cf. the review in Bhagwati (1971). Also see the recent writings of Graciela Chichilinsky, Peter Lloyd, and others on this question.

16. Cf. Appendix, section A4.1.3.

17. Cf. the contribution of D. Brown, A. Deardorff, and R. Stern (Chapter 5). The answer eventually depends on how the offer curve of the lower-standard country shifts with the harmonization up.

18. The conditions under which tax harmonization will occur in a globally Pareto optimal solution are discussed in section A4.2.3 of the Appendix.

19. Cf. Appendix, section A4.2.4.

20. Cf. Appendix, section A4.2.1.

21. Cf. Appendix, section A4.2.2.

22. We should also state the related but distinct proposition that diversity of standards across countries will be observed as the norm in competitive equilibrium and, besides, will change with trade and hence income (as implicit, of course, in our preceding analysis and in the Appendix). This proposition is also derived, in the context of a model where standards are characterized as having some of the characteristics of "public goods" in each of two trading countries and enter directly the utility functions in these countries, by Alessandra Casella in Chapter 3. The focus of our analysis instead is on the issue of CCII harmonization and on the question of standards diversity when welfare maximization is being pursued (and may require departure from a laissez-faire competitive equilibrium).

23. This phrase has passed even into the latest annual report of the Council of Economic Advisers as part of a definition of "competitiveness" that Paul Krugman has castigated in a recent article in *Foreign Affairs*.

24. If the country is large, then we must substitute an optimal tariff for free trade in this sentence.

25. Thus recent judicial determinations in the United States have undermined the public law that had grown up earlier with strong support for environmentalism, not reflective of costs and benefits, for the possibility of "takings" in the public environmental interest and in regard to standing and judicial review. The earlier public law literature is well represented by Abram Chayes, "The role of the judge in public law litigation," *Harvard Law Review*, 89 (1976), and Ronald Dworkin, *Law's empire*, 1986; and it is also well developed in India, in regard to standing (for NGOs etc.) in particular, in the public interest litigation developed in the Supreme Court. The reverse movement in the United States can be seen from cases such as *Lucas* v. *South Carolina Coastal Council* and *Nollan* v. *California Coastal Commission* on takings, *Lujan* v. *National Wildlife Federation and Lujan* v. *Defenders of Wildlife* on standing, and *Competitive Enterprise Institute* v. *National Highway Traffic Safety Administration* and *Corrosion Proof Fittings* v. *EPA* on judicial review. The last area has, in particular, seen the increased judicial scrutiny of the cost-benefit aspects of executive actions implementing legislated regulation. The U.S. Congress is itself currently in the midst of an intense battle over precisely this question, with the New Democrat Clinton administration much more open to cost-benefit analysis than the older Democrats.

26. The question of democracy is addressed, from a different perspective, in section 4.4.3.

27. An in-depth review and synthesis of the theoretical literature on this question is provided by John Wilson in his chapter for the project, "Capital mobility and environmental standards: Is there a theoretical basis for a race to the bottom?" (Chapter 10 of this volume). We therefore only sketch the nature of the argument here.

28. Wilson, Chapter 10.

29. Cf. Arik Levinson's chapter for the project, "Environmental regulation and industry location: International and domestic evidence" (Chapter 11 of this volume). Levinson looks at both the international and the domestic evidence (e.g., interstate locational decisions in the United States, since states have different standards), having himself produced first-rate work in the latter genre.

30. Cf. Levinson, Chapter 11, citing, for instance, work by Baumol and Oates, Low, etc.

31. Levinson, Chapter 11, cites work by Hamilton, Baldwin, and Welles, and Walter on voter participation, in particular.

32. Levinson, Chapter 11, cites this explanation from the work of Gladwin and Welles, and Knögden. The argument requires that the transaction costs of diverse choices are large enough to offset the forgone advantage of meeting each standard only as necessary and not beyond. Besides, it does not apply to single-plant firms or to subsidiaries that act as more or less independent decision makers.

33. Again, the argument requires that the advantages of being "ahead of the curve" offset the advantages of conforming to lower standards now and adapting or retooling later when the higher standards emerge.

34. Cf. Levinson, Chapter 11, citing Pearson.

35. E.g., the (static and dynamic) arguments underlying Explanation 2 imply that CCII differences will be disregarded by multinationals in any event, with their plant-design choice gravitating toward the higher-standard technology everywhere and therefore locational choices becoming independent of CCII differences in standards.

36. Cf. Levinson, Chapter 11.

37. To our knowledge, the countervailing of *implicit* subsidies would be a novel principle in GATT law on subsidies as well, and is not to be contemplated with equanimity in view of its explosive potential; it is probably for this reason that the concept of remedy used by the proponents of harmonization of standards is that of AD rather than of CVD (countervailing duties on foreign subsidies).

38. Cropper and Oates (1992, pp. 675–676).

39. Questions raised by "values"-related differences in CCII standards are considered separately later in this chapter.

40. This statement, of course, does not apply equally to trade in highly differentiated products like autos where one can get fixated on specific countries, e.g., Japan.

41. See Bhagwati, "American Rules, Mexican Jobs," *New York Times*, March 24, 1993.

42. Recall our analysis, based on Arik Levinson's review, Chapter 11.

43. One of the important reasons for such nonharmonization (documented by Joel Slemrod in Chapter 6) is that horizontal equity among firms from different countries abroad can conflict with the desire to have horizontal equity among one's firms at home and one's firms abroad. This problem comes up quite directly in regard to personal income taxation where the U.S. practice is to tax on basis of citizenship while the practice elsewhere is to tax on basis of residence. The former ensures horizontal equity between U.S. citizens at home and abroad but, given the residence-based taxation practice of other nations, leads to lack of horizontal equity between, say, U.S. and French citizens in Manila or New Delhi where U.S. citizens must continue to pay U.S. income taxes (subject to some exemptions) while the French citizens do not have to pay French income taxes. The questions raised by the U.S. practice of exercising income tax jurisdiction on its citizens abroad, through the citizenship rather than residence nexus, have been extensively studied by modern economists cognizant of the extensive international personal mobility today. Cf. Jagdish Bhagwati and John Wilson, eds., *Income taxation and international personal mobility* (Cambridge, MA: MIT Press, 1991).

44. Insofar as it involves suspension of trade access by a country for products that are produced by processes that are disapproved of, it is also GATT-*illegal* as per the first Tuna-Dolphin Panel finding, and as discussed in section 4.4.

45. This "break in the ranks" occurs when there are diverse priorities at stake. Among single-issue NGOs, as on child labor, we can expect more international solidarity, of course.

46. August 15, 1992, p. 4. The magazine is published in New Delhi and enjoys a large circulation.

47. GATT, *Annual Report* (Geneva, Switzerland, 1991), pp. 33–34.

48. Steve Charnovitz, "GATT and the environment: Examining the issues," *International Environment Affairs*, 4(3), Summer 1992, p. 211. This is an interesting, thought-provoking, and lucidly argued but ultimately unpersuasive critique of the GATT report (note 47) and of the Dolphin-Tuna Panel Report.

49. Cf. GATT, *Annual Report* (1991), pp. 33–34.

50. Cf. Charnovitz, "GATT and the environment," p. 213.

51. The recently activated GATT Group on Environment Measures and International Trade has among its tasks the examination of the trade effects of packaging and labeling requirements intended to protect the environment. It has been examining the packaging and labeling questions in depth.

52. It is not just that the budgets of the poor countries are financially strapped. It is also that few parliaments would sanction expenditure of the huge amounts of money that are needed to take out ads in the Western papers and to hire lobbyists in Washington. The only democratic exception seems to be Mexico, which had, at the end of 1991, as many as 71 lobbying firms in the United States registered as "foreign agents" acting on behalf of NAFTA.

53. We are talking here of unilateral actions. Where a substantial plurilateral or multilateral consensus is achieved on a suspension of trade access, the cost imposed will generally be higher.

54. Jessica Matthews has argued that sometimes unilateralism has enabled the United States to provide leadership on important issues. But, even if this were true, it would not justify unilateralism. After all, just because dictatorships may sometimes be beneficial, we would not permit them and renounce our loyalty to democracy.

55. Charnovitz, "GATT and the environment," pp. 206–207.

56. So, you are not a "consequentialist" but one who has an "absolute" moral value. You may not expect to change Mexican behavior; you may even be hurting only yourself. But you may be doing what you think duty or virtue compels. It is worth noting, however, that one does not have to deny Mexico access to the U.S. market to avoid eating a "defiled product." After all, by not eating any tuna whatsoever and by directing political action at boycotts or education instead of seeking official embargoes, one can hurt the market for Mexican tuna as well. As noted earlier, the market pressure induced by such an action could also lead Mexican fishermen to abandon dolphin-unsafe fishing methods in order to regain lost markets.

57. There is, of course, a "moral hazard" problem: countries may become deliberately sinful to be bribed into virtue. But we doubt this is likely to be a serious problem, since the compensation in practice is likely to continue to be in form of other trade concessions in lieu of the one withdrawn.

58. Ibid., pp. 204–205.

59. Cf. Jackson, (1992), pp. 1241–42.

60. This point is argued in section 4.4. It may, however, be useful to clarify the matter so as to eliminate any ambiguities and doubts in the matter.

61. Section 301 actions aimed at securing new trade concessions, rather than at securing compliance with treaty-defined trade objections, fall into this class of problems, of course. On their GATT-inconsistency, see Jagdish Bhagwati and Hugh Patrick, eds., *Aggressive unilateralism* (Ann Arbor: Michigan University Press, 1991), especially the contributions by Hudec and Bhagwati.

62. These questions are addressed with far greater authority by Frieder Roessler, legal counselor to the GATT, in Chapter 1 of Volume 2 of this work. Also see Chapters 2 and 3 by Robert Hudec and Daniel Farber.

63. Nearly all cases can be fitted into one or both of these categories. Thus producing chickens in batteries may be objected to as cruel, fitting it into category 1. Overfishing in the commons to which I have access fits into category 2. If you use your forests in an "unsustainable" way, I may object to it because I think that is bad per se, i.e., category 1, or because it affects global warming and hence me, i.e., category 2, or because of both reasons.

64. GATT, *Annual Report* (1991), pp. 22–23.

65. The GATT law on this general question, and its relatively more environmentally friendly nature relative to the interstate "Dormant Clause" doctrine in the United States, are the subject of the penetrating analysis by Daniel Farber and Robert Hudec in their chapter for this project (Chapter 2 in Volume 2). They distinguish between the "facially discriminatory" and the "facially neutral" (but nonetheless discriminatory, whether "indirectly" and "incidentally" or otherwise) regulations, analyzing how GATT and U.S. jurisprudence apply to each of these in regard to their implications for trade that lead to litigation.

That the GATT law is essentially more environmentally friendly was borne out also by the GATT panel finding in the EU versus the United States case on U.S. fuel conservation measures in September 1994, which upheld much of the U.S. law as consistent with the GATT, even when the conflict seemed compelling prima facie.

66. Gottfried Haberler, *Theory of international trade* (London: William Hodge, 1936), p. 339. Haberler cited this amusing case as an instance of the manner in which countries evaded the obligation of the most favored nation clause.

67. As we will argue, a challenge to recycling and packaging requirements cannot be ruled out on the ground that alternative, less-trade-restricting measures are possible and should be undertaken.

68. From the economic perspective, a domestic firm acting strategically may also be able to persuade its government to enact higher standards whose effect is to make the cost of entry by foreign rivals, which must tool up to meet these higher standards, disproportionately higher (since the domestic firm has a significantly higher proportion of its sales in its own market). Higher standards in this case would then be in reality a protectionist technique for making market access by foreign firms more expensive.

69. Cf. Charnovitz., "GATT and the environment," pp. 213–214. For the Thailand case, see GATT, *Basic Instruments and Selected Documents*, 375/200 (Geneva, Switzerland). Also see Esty, *Greening the GATT*, p. 48.

70. Cited in Charnovitz, "GATT and the environment," p. 214.

71. Cf. ibid., p. 215. Charnovitz calls this the "proportionality" issue, but it is really a "trade-off" issue.

72. This was the issue addressed to a panel of trade and legal scholars at the Conference on the Morality of Protectionism at the New York University Law School in November 1992. It is quoted in Robert Hudec's excellent contribution, "'Circumventing' Democracy: The Political Morality of Trade Negotiations," New York University *Journal of International Law and Politics*, vol. 25. 1993, pp. 311–322.

73. Some issues are, of course, similar to those raised in the case of domestic environmental problems. Thus, we must ask again, How convincing is the science being invoked to spur action? Ironically, some of those who attack the use of science to attack environmental regulations in challenging phytosanitary standards defend the use of science in urging action on global problems. The fickle nature of science in these matters is evident from the

history of the ozone problem. Scientists in the United States were in the forefront in suggesting the link between CFCs and ozone depletion, leading in 1978 to the prohibition of the use of CFCs in aerosol spray cans. The Europeans were skeptical; so was the Reagan administration. The discovery of the big hole in the ozone layer in Antarctica in 1984 turned almost everyone around, leading to the Montreal Protocol in 1987 and the further change therein in 1990 to eliminate CFCs by A.D. 2000.

74. The theoretical analysis of this instrument is in the Appendix, section A4.1.3, and, more fully, in Markusen (1975).

75. This would clearly be a case where the process that generates the *physical* transborder externality is being objected to and a trade measure against it is being legitimated, as distinct from the "*values*" objection to a process as discussed earlier.

76. This is the conclusion reached by Aparna Guha in a dissertation at Columbia University, examining the options before Canada in relation to the acid rain from the United States. She is currently studying the possibility of a market in permits to use fossil fuels in U.S. electricity generation where Canada could bid and pay herself to reduce the acid rain being generated in the United States. This approach would require, of course, that the permits be segmented by the states that generate the acid rain that comes across to Canada, else the cost to Canada could become prohibitive. There is much excellent work on the acid rain problem, including by Karl-Göran Mäler and his associates in Stockholm.

77. Of course, the question of single-country use of a second-best tariff policy can be raised here just as well as in the preceding case, but this question has raised no interest in the global-pollution context.

78. Cf. Appendix, section A4.2.6 on this question.

79. This efficiency is only in the sense of cost minimization when pollution anywhere equally affects a single target such as CO_2. The number of permits may, however, be too small or too large, and getting it right by letting nonusers also bid (and then destroy permits) is bedeviled by free rider problems.

80. In this appendix, unless otherwise stated, we will simply *assume* that the relevant set of first-order conditions indeed characterize a unique solution to the optimization problem under consideration. We do not go into the assumptions on the production, utility, and pollution functions that will ensure that this will be the case.

81. Cf. Srinivasan (1987) and Bhagwati (1971).

82. Note also that we do not have a reason to subsidize the use of abatement technology.

83. Of course, the precise values of the optimum tariff and subsidy would in general differ depending on whether or not abatement is feasible.

84. Even though the trade flows of a small economy by definition have no influence on the terms at which the flows take place, such flows could influence the output in the rest of the world. This is best seen in a Ricardian model in which the small open economy specializes in producing its exportable good while the rest of the world (ROW) is incompletely specialized and the equilibrium world prices are the autarky prices of the ROW. With the opening of trade with the small economy, ROW still consumes its autarky consumption bundle while its production adjusts to accommodate the trade flows from the small economy. Although policy-induced changes in the trade flows of the small economy do not affect equilibrium world prices, they do affect the production in ROW and, hence, pollution, if pollution is a by-product of production.

85. Since the home (resp. foreign) country takes the foreign (resp. home) country's outputs and resources allocated for abatement as given, each country's reaction function with respect to the variables it chooses (X_2, K_a, and L_a for the home country and X_2^*, K_a^*, and L_a^* for the foreign country) are functions of the values of the variables for the other country taken as given. Nash equilibrium is a mutually consistent set in the sense that each country's choices as obtained by substituting the other country's choices in its reaction function, when substituted into the latter's reaction functions, yield the latter's choices. Thus $X_2(X_1^{*N}, X_2^{*N}, T^{*N}, K_a^{*N}, L_a^{*N})$ etc. when substituted in the reaction function $X_2^*(\ )$ will yield back X_2^{*N} and vice versa. We are assuming that such Nash equilibria exist. The existence issue is a complex one.

86. The variables λ_1 and λ_2 are the Lagrangean multipliers associated with the constraints of equations 17 and 18, respectively; these are shadow prices in global welfare units of good 1 and 2, respectively.

87. It is assumed that the parameters and endowments are such that the feasibility constraints $X_1 \leq \bar{H}$ and $X_2^* \leq \bar{H}^*$ hold.

88. The more general case of different tastes is briefly discussed on page 212, however.

89. Its efficiency can be demonstrated by showing that this solution satisfies the conditions for Pareto optimality subject to the requirements that pollution does not exceed $\hat{P}$ and there are no transfers. In particular, we can show that shadow cost of pollution in global welfare units will be the same in the two countries, though higher than its value at the no-transfer Pareto optimum without a binding upper-bound constraint on pollution.

91. Among the important contributions, aside from those reviewed in the Appendix, are Lloyd (1992), Snape (1992), and Baumol and Oates (1988). There are many others on issues such as the "race to the bottom" that are not addressed intensively in this chapter but are the foci of other authors in this project.

REFERENCES

Baumol, William, and Wallace Oates. 1988. *The theory of environmental policy*, 2nd ed. Cambridge, England: Cambridge University Press.

Bhagwati, Jagdish, N. 1971. "The generalized theory of distortions and welfare." In J. Bhagwati, R. Jones, R. Mundell, and J. Vanek, eds., *Trade, balance of payments, and growth: Papers in international economics in honor of Charles P. Kindleberger*. Amsterdam: North Holland.

Cropper, Maureen, and Wallace Oates. 1992. "Environmental economics: A survey." *Journal of Economic Literature*, 20 (June): 675–740.

Johnson, Harry. 1954. "Optimum tariffs and retaliation." *Review of Economic Studies*, 21 (55): 152–153. Reprinted in H. G. Johnson, *International trade and economic growth* (London: Allen and Unwin, 1958).

Lloyd, Peter. 1992. "The problem of optimal environmental policy choice." In Kym Anderson and Richard Blackhurst, eds., *The greening of world trade issues*. New York: Harvester/Wheatsheaf.

Markusen, James. 1975. "International externalities and optimal tax structures." *Journal of International Economics*, 5:15–29.

Markusen, James. 1976. "Cooperative control of international pollution and common property resources." *Quarterly Journal of Economics*, 90:618–631.

Snape, Richard. 1992. "The environment, international trade and competitiveness." In Kym Anderson and Richard Blackhurst, eds., *The greening of world trade issues*. New York: Harvester/Wheatsheaf.

Srinivasan, T. N. 1987. "Distortions." In J. Eatwell, M. Newgate, and P. Newman, eds., *The new Palgrave*, 865–867. London: Macmillan.

[18]

The World Trade Organization and the Environment

Steve Charnovitz

I. INTRODUCTION

In celebrating the fiftieth anniversary of the General Agreement on Tariffs and Trade (GATT), we should be proud of the accomplishments of the individuals of past generations who established the world trading system.[1] Although the history of the GATT has played out more circuitously than was intended when it came into effect in 1948, the GATT eventually has achieved much of what its founders envisioned. The waste from protectionism has been diminished. Trade has become an engine of economic growth. National trade policy is governed by a web of international legal obligations. In addition, a respected international organization for trade oversees the process from Geneva.

1. The Challenge of Sustainability

The World Trade Organization (WTO), however, must not rest on its laurels. Unlike some scourges, such as smallpox, which can be eradicated, protectionism will be with us as long as there are nation states. So the WTO must maintain the fight against protectionism, but even this is not sufficient. The WTO needs to help governments deal with the side effects of trade, such as its impact on people and nature. There is an obvious political rationale for this: the trading system depends upon continued public support. However, there is an equally important economic rationale. Without the correct government policies on the environment, free trade may not produce an optimal outcome.[2] Indeed, it may not even produce a positive outcome.

What is the impact of trade on the environment? The extreme critics of the WTO suggest that international trade itself is unsustainable.[3] Other

This article is based on a chapter written in FRA GATT TIL WTO, a volume published by the Norwegian Institute of International Affairs in honour of the fiftieth anniversary of the GATT.

[1] General Agreement on Tariffs and Trade, 30 Oct. 1947, 55 U.N.T.S. 194 [hereinafter GATT]; the current version is available in GATT, THE TEXT OF THE GENERAL AGREEMENT ON TARIFFS AND TRADE (1986).

[2] FORD RUNGE, FREER TRADE, PROTECTED ENVIRONMENT 23 (1994).

[3] Herman E. Daly, *Against Free Trade: Neoclassical and Steady-State Perspectives* (Publication of the Pacific Basin Research Center, Harvard University) 32–52 (1994).

individuals in the ecological economics school ponder whether certain trade flows are predicated on unsustainable production or consumption.[4] Even mainstream economists admit that market prices may undervalue the environment and fail to reflect significant spillovers.[5] Although this critique has implications for domestic commerce as well as for international trade, there is reason to believe that transborder trade and investment may be particularly oblivious to environmental implications. For instance, hazardous waste trade might be profitable only because exporters do not take into account the burdens on importing communities.

Sustainability is being promoted by a new set of global actors making demands that were not heard five decades ago. Environment, development, grass-roots, and human rights non-governmental organizations (NGOs) want to have input into the economic decisions being made at the WTO, the World Bank, and the OECD. This development has been a particularly difficult challenge for the GATT/WTO, which has had a tradition of parochialism and secrecy.[6] The WTO, however, has begun to crack open its doors to NGOs.

2. Visions of the Future

It is difficult to predict the future, but analysts can lay out scenarios of the way events may unfold.[7] These scenarios can help the public choose policies (and politicians) that are more likely to lead to the most desirable future. Broadly speaking, there are two possible scenarios for how the WTO can address the environment. Let us call one the segregative approach and the other the integrative approach.

The segregative approach would continue the mindset that has characterized the trading system during most of the past fifty years. In this framework, the agreements of the GATT and WTO are viewed solely as contracts among parties that should be interpreted narrowly in order to guarantee predictable commercial relations.[8] The WTO persists in maintaining its exclusive

[4] See *generally* CARL FOLKE, ed., INTERNATIONAL TRADE AND THE ENVIRONMENT, SPECIAL EDITION OF ECOLOGICAL ECONOMICS, 9 ECOLOGICAL ECON. no. 1 (1994).

[5] *Trade, the Environment and Public Policy, in* THE GREENING OF WORLD TRADE ISSUES 19 (Kym Anderson & Richard Blackhurst, eds., 1992); *see also* RUNGE *supra* note 2, at 24–8.

[6] Steve Charnovitz, *Participation of Nongovernmental Organizations in the World Trade Organization,* 17 U. PA. J. INT'L ECON. L. 331 (1997).

[7] *See* HAROLD D. LASSWELL & MYRES S. MCDOUGAL, JURISPRUDENCE FOR A FREE SOCIETY 973–86 (1992).

[8] For example, in April 1998, the WTO panel adjudicating the shrimp-turtle dispute held:

> In our view, if an interpretation of the chapeau of Article XX were to be followed which would allow a Member to adopt measures conditioning access to its market for a given product upon the adoption by the exporting Members of certain policies, including conservation policies, [then] GATT 1994 and the WTO Agreement could no longer serve as a multilateral framework for trade among Members, as security and predictability of trade relations under those agreements would be threatened.

United States—Import Prohibition of Certain Shrimp and Shrimp Products, 6 Apr. 1998, WTO Doc. WT/DS58/R, para. 7.45.

membership policy. Applicants such as China or Russia—no matter how many people they represent—are kept out of the club.[9] In addition, the WTO remains separate from the UN and, indeed, considers this separation a virtue. Similarly, the WTO perceives no obligation to coordinate policies with UN agencies such as UNEP.

By contrast, the integrative scenario anticipates major change. The WTO would seek to harmonize international trade law with international law generally and would take seriously the goal in the WTO preamble that allows "for the optimal use of the world's resources in accordance with the objective of sustainable development, seeking both to protect and preserve the environment . . ."[10] The WTO would not forget its core mission to prevent protectionism, but it would pursue this mission with an eye towards the imperative of sustainable development. To that end, the WTO would become a more open institution and would welcome input by civil society.

Which of these scenarios will characterize the WTO in the twenty-first century? It probably will be the integrative approach—although that outcome is by no means certain. Advocates of a more outward-looking trading system need to continue pushing the WTO to change.

This article consists of three parts. First, it looks back at the creation of the GATT and at the discussions of trade and the environment that took place in the early 1970s. Second, the article provides a retrospective analysis of the "trade and environment" debate during the 1990s. Third, it looks ahead to what the trade regime should do now to improve its interaction with the environment regime.

II. THE EARLY YEARS OF GATT AND THE ENVIRONMENT

It has often been said that the GATT was written at a time before policymakers thought about the environment.[11] This was a convenient story for trade officials who were trying to explain why various (usually hypothetical) environmental laws would violate trade rules. It was also a convenient story for reform-minded NGOs seeking to "green" the GATT by adding new provisions. The story, however, is untrue.

The GATT was written at a time of revived interest in international environmental challenges. This is reflected most clearly in the environmental

[9] *See, e.g., Barshefsky, Chinese Ambassador Offers Different Views of WTO Entry*, INSIDE U.S. TRADE, 8 May 1998, at 9.

[10] Marrakech Agreement Establishing the World Trade Organization, 15 Apr. 1994, Preamble, 33 I.L.M. 15 (1994) [hereinafter WTO Agreement].

[11] Steven Shyrbman, *International Trade and the Environment: An Environmental Assessment of the General Agreement on Tariffs and Trade,* 20 THE ECOLOGIST 30, 33 (1990); William Prince and David Nelson, *Developing an Environmental Model: Piecing Together the Growing Diversity of International Environmental Standards and Agendas Affecting Mining Companies,* 7 COLO. J. INT'L ENVTL. L. & POL'Y 247, 256 (1996).

treaties of that era. In 1946, several governments finalized a Convention for the Regulation of the Meshes of Fishing Nets and the Size Limits of Fish.[12] Later that year, the International Convention for the Regulation of Whaling was approved.[13] The parties noted that "it is essential to protect all species of whales from further overfishing."[14] In 1949, two important fisheries agreements were consummated: the International Convention for the Northwest Atlantic Fisheries and the Convention for the Establishment of an Inter-American Tropical Tuna Commission.[15] In 1950, the International Convention for the Protection of Birds was approved to replace the International Convention for the Protection of Birds Useful to Agriculture, which had been written five decades earlier.[16]

There were several international conferences that laid the groundwork for a post-war conservation policy. In 1947-8, a group of governments and NGOs established the International Union for the Conservation of Nature and Natural Resources, which is now known as the World Conservation Union (IUCN).[17] In 1948, there was an Inter-American Conference on Conservation of Renewable Natural Resources.[18] One of the conference papers pointed out the potential for using traditional commodity agreements to promote the conservation of "fugitive" renewable resources, such as fisheries and migratory birds.[19] In 1949, UNESCO held an International Technical Conference on the Protection of Nature.[20] Also in that year, the UN held a Scientific Conference on the Conservation and Utilization of Resources.[21]

From the documentary history of the UN Conference on Trade and Employment, we know that the drafters of the Havana Charter for an International Trade Organization (ITO) (ITO Charter) were aware of the

[12] Apr. 1946, 231 U.N.T.S. 200. There is a trade provision in art. 9.

[13] International Convention for the Regulation of Whaling with Schedule of Whaling Regulations, 2 Dec. 1946, 161 U.N.T.S. 72.

[14] *Id.* Preamble.

[15] Fisheries, 8 Feb. 1949, 1 U.S.T. 477; Tuna, 31 May 1949, 80 U.N.T.S. 3.

[16] 18 Oct. 1950, 638 U.N.T.S. 185. There are trade provisions in arts. 3–4.

[17] Lynton Keith Caldwell, International Environmental Policy 50, 144 (1996); Leif E. Christoffersen, *IUCN: A Bridge-Builder for Nature Conservation*, *in* Green Globe Y.B. 59 (1997).

[18] Proceedings of the Inter-American Conference on Conservation of Renewable Natural Resources (U.S. Dep't of State, 1948).

[19] S.V. Ciriacy-Wantrup, *Conservation of Renewable Natural Resources in Relation to Economic Instability, in id.*, 222, 228–9. He notes two instruments that can be used: regulation of capture and establishment of a limited geographic monopoly.

[20] International Technical Conference on the Protection of Nature: Proceedings and Papers (1950).

[21] Proceedings of the United Nations Scientific Conference on the Conservation and Utilization of Resources (1949), UN Doc. E/Conf. 7/7 Vol. 1. It is interesting to note that several environmental NGOs attended this conference, such as the Wild Life Protection Society of South Africa, the American Fisheries Society, the (US) National Wildlife Federation, and the Society of American Foresters. *Id.* at lii–liv.

exigencies of nature protection. Although the ITO Charter did not enter into force, there is a vital connection between it and the GATT.[22] First, the GATT was drafted by the same delegates working on the ITO Charter. Second, the commercial chapter of the draft ITO Charter was used as the template for the GATT. Third, the ITO interim commission evolved into the GATT Secretariat.

In late 1946, the drafters discussed the way in which the new commodities disciplines would interact with "conservation agreements, such as international fisheries conventions" which would "have to regulate production or trade in order to achieve their object."[23] At the formal session a few months later, the drafting committee added an exception to the commodities chapter for "international fisheries or wildlife conservation agreements with the sole objective of conserving and developing these resources."[24] During subsequent drafting sessions, however, this provision was watered down.

In December 1947, at the UN Conference on Trade and Employment in Havana, Cuba, the delegate from Norway sought to reinvigorate the exception. He noted that fishery and wildlife agreements were entered into by nations "on the basis of biological and oceanographical evidence that the resources were declining."[25] Norway's proposal was supported by the delegate from France, who recalled that numerous international conferences had attempted to craft measures for the protection of fisheries, including whales.[26] Eventually, it was agreed to include a broader conservation exception in the commodities chapter. The delegates also decided to copy this same exception into the commercial chapter to cover trade measures "taken in pursuance of any inter-governmental agreement which relates solely to the conservation of fisheries resources, migratory birds or wild animals . . ."[27]

While the GATT's drafters did not pursue positive linkages regarding the environment, they were not pro-segregation.[28] The documentary history shows that some environmental issues were considered, and the exceptions in

[22] World Trade Organization, Guide to GATT Law and Practice 3–7 (1995).

[23] Memorandum from R.B. Schwenger to John Leddy, 16 Jan. 1947, US National Archives, Box 122.

[24] *Report of the Drafting Committee of the Preparatory Committee of the UN Conference on Trade and Employment*, 5 Mar. 1947, UN Doc. E/PC/T/34, at 43–4.

[25] UN Doc. E/Conf.2/C.5/SR.7, 12 Dec. 1947, at 2–3.

[26] *Id.* at 3.

[27] Havana Charter for an International Trade Organization, 24 Mar. 1948, art. 45(1)(a)(x) (not in force), Can. T.S.1948:32 [hereinafter ITO Charter]. .

[28] By contrast, the urge for integration is clearer in the way that the ITO Charter dealt with the problem of unemployment. For example, art. 2 states that "[t]he Members recognize that the avoidance of unemployment . . . is not of domestic concern alone, but is also a necessary condition for the achievement of the general purpose . . . [of the ITO]." Art. 5(2) states that the ITO "shall, if it considers that the urgency of the situation so requires, initiate consultations among Members with a view to their taking appropriate measures against the international spread of a decline in employment, production or demand." Art. 7(3) states that "in all matters relating to labour standards . . . [the ITO] shall consult and cooperate with the International Labour Organization." *Id.*

GATT were designed to cover them.[29] Due to the fact that the drafters viewed environmental regulation through the paradigm of conservation, accommodating such regulation would have seemed perfectly consistent with the GATT's overall purpose of boosting economic efficiency. Indeed, GATT itself points to the "desirability of assuring an economic employment of productive resources."[30]

Over twenty years passed before the GATT began to consider explicitly environmental issues. In 1971, the GATT Council established a Group on Environmental Measures and International Trade to examine upon request "any specific matters relevant to the trade policy aspects of measures to control pollution and protect human environment . . ."[31] Unfortunately, it took another twenty years for the group to hold its first meeting.[32] Yet the GATT did make one significant contribution to understanding "trade and the environment." In 1971, Jan Tumlir of the GATT Secretariat prepared a report for submission to the UN (Stockholm) Conference on the Human Environment.[33] Tumlir's study was more thoroughly reasoned than the more publicized Secretariat study of 1992.[34] His study was particularly perceptive in pointing out how trade measures might be useful in addressing transborder environmental problems.[35]

At around the same time, the IUCN was drafting what became the Convention on International Trade in Endangered Species of Wild Fauna and Flora (CITES).[36] Since import restrictions on foreign wildlife were contemplated, the IUCN sought the advice of the GATT Secretariat in regard to any conflict with GATT rules.[37] Gardner Patterson, who was then GATT's

[29] Steve Charnovitz, *Exploring the Environmental Exceptions in GATT Article XX*, 25 J. WORLD TRADE 37 (October 1991).

[30] GATT, *supra* note 1, at art. XVIII:11.

[31] GUIDE TO GATT LAW AND PRACTICE, *supra* note 22 at 1114.

[32] It is interesting to recall that in 1987, the GATT panel examining the complaint against the U.S. Superfund law suggested that the European Commission (the plaintiff) might take its concern about the Polluter Pays Principle to the GATT Group. The commission had argued that the U.S. import tax violated trade rules and was inconsistent with the Polluter Pays Principle. *See* Taxes on Petroleum and Certain Imported Substances, GATT, B.I.S.D. (34th Supp.) at 136, 162, para. 5.2.6. The commission did not follow this suggestion.

[33] INDUSTRIAL POLLUTION CONTROL AND INTERNATIONAL TRADE (GATT Studies in International Trade, No. 1) (1971).

[34] *Cf. Trade and the Environment, in* 1 INTERNATIONAL TRADE 90-1 (GATT, ed., 1992), at 19. For an analysis of the 1992 study, *see* Steve Charnovitz, *GATT and the Environment: Examining the Issues*, 4 INT'L ENVTL. AFF. 203 (1992).

[35] INDUSTRIAL POLLUTION CONTROL AND INTERNATIONAL TRADE, *supra* note 33, at 16. The Secretariat's 1992 report makes no mention of Tumlir's 1971 study.

[36] 3 Mar. 1973, 993 U.N.T.S. 243. *See Experience with the Use of Trade Measures in the Convention on International Trade in Endangered Species (CITES)*, OECD Working Papers, No. 47, (1997).

[37] The records do not show any correspondence from the GATT to the IUCN asking whether the contemplated Tokyo Round trade agreements would conflict with environmental treaties.

assistant director-general, replied that the draft treaty seemed consistent with GATT Article XX.[38]

In summary, contrary to the way some commentators portray it, the GATT was born during a period of growing interest in international environmental policy. The GATT's drafters were aware of these events and took steps to keep trade rules from interfering with them. At the advent of the UN Conference on the Human Environment, the GATT sought to make a substantive contribution. It was not until the late 1980s and early 1990s, however, that the GATT began to see a divergence between trade and environmental goals.

III. THE TRADE AND ENVIRONMENT DEBATE FROM 1990 TO 1998

The current trade and environment debate began at the GATT's Brussels Conference in December 1990 when countries of the European Free Trade Association (EFTA) proposed a ministerial statement on trade and the environment.[39] Following this unsuccessful conference, the EFTA countries sought to convene the GATT Group on Environmental Measures and International Trade.[40] Yet this request met opposition from several developing countries.[41] It took almost the entire year to convene the first meeting.

Contemporaneously, environmental groups were beginning to look closely at the GATT. There was a growing recognition that trade and trade policy interacted with environmental policymaking. Rather than welcome their interest, however, the GATT projected hostility towards environmentalists and other public interest groups.[42] At this time, many key GATT documents were deemed confidential and were not made available to the public. The GATT Secretariat did release dispute panel reports but not until after they were adopted by the GATT Council.[43] Thus, environmental groups, who wanted to be in a position to influence the GATT Council's review of a report, were being told that GATT rules prevented them from seeing a report in time to have any impact on its disposition. This denial of access was particularly grating because the GATT trumpeted "transparency" as a principle of trade policy. The long delay in setting up the Group on Environmental Measures and International Trade was taken as yet another sign of the GATT's antipathy for the environment.

[38] Letter from Gardner Patterson to F.G. Nicholls, IUCN, 24 Feb. 1991 (on file at IUCN).

[39] Minutes of the 46th Session of the GATT Contracting Parties, 12–13 Dec. 1990, GATT Doc. SR.46/2, at 5–9.

[40] JOHN CROOME, RESHAPING THE WORLD TRADING SYSTEM: A HISTORY OF THE URUGUAY ROUND 276–84 (1995).

[41] *See* Minutes of Meeting of the GATT Council, 28 June 1991, GATT Doc. C/M/250, at 2–22.

[42] *See, e.g.*, Frances Williams, *GATT Shuts Door on Environmentalists*, FIN. TIMES, 21 July 1994, at 6.

[43] Patti A. Goldman, *Resolving the Trade and Environment Debate: In Search of a Neutral Forum and Neutral Principles*, 49 WASH. & LEE L. REV. 1279, 1285 (1992).

This climate of distrust was the backdrop for the first GATT Tuna-Dolphin decision in 1991.[44] The case involved a complaint by Mexico that the US government's tuna import ban violated GATT rules. Under US law, tuna is banned from any country whose fishing practices do not meet specified criteria for dolphin safety.[45] The panel found in favour of Mexico and declared the US law to be GATT-illegal.[46] This decision came as a shock to environmental groups around the world. The more radical environmental groups were able to capitalize on the decision by launching a vituperative anti-GATT campaign. Yet even the mainstream environmental groups were deeply troubled. It was not that the US law was GATT-consistent. Almost everyone conceded that the law was too arbitrary to meet GATT rules. The problem was that the panel issued a broad, rather careless, decision whose logic seemed to question the validity of scores of environmental laws and treaties.

Although there was clear evidence from the preparatory history of the GATT that its drafters realized the need for a GATT environmental exception, the panel took a very narrow view of the scope of GATT Article XX. According to the panel, GATT Article XX(b) applied only to import measures "to safeguard life or health of humans, animals or plants *within* the jurisdiction of the importing country [emphasis added]."[47] Similarly, Article XX(g) applied only to measures conserving natural resources that were "primarily aimed at rendering effective restrictions on production or consumption within their [the importing party's] jurisdiction."[48]

This decision alarmed environmentalists because of its far-reaching implications.[49] Unlike trade policy, which is narrowly focused on a company or on an industry within a country, environmental policy typically has a wide scope. Ecosystems will often transcend political borders. Thus, in saying that environmental trade instruments had to be limited to a government's domestic territory, the panel seemed to be denying the basic principles of environmental policy. For example, throughout the twentieth century, governments have banned imports of endangered species as a means of thwarting this deleterious traffic.[50] The campaign against trade in bird plumage was one of the first

[44] *See generally* Steve Charnovitz, *The Environment vs. Trade Rules: Defogging the Debate*, 23 ENVTL. L. 475 (1993); Benedict Kingsbury, *The Tuna-Dolphin Controversy, the World Trade Organization, and the Liberal Project to Reconceptualize International Law*, 5 YBIEL 1 (1994).

[45] 16 U.S.C. para. 1371(a)(2).

[46] *United States Restrictions on Imports of Tuna*, GATT B.I.S.D. (39th Supp.) at 155. The original caption of the case (and its current designation as "Tuna I" by the trade community) reflects the view that the *real* issue is trade in tuna, not protection of dolphins.

[47] *Id.* at para. 5.26.

[48] *Id.* at para. 5.31.

[49] William J. Snape, III & Naomi B. Lefkovitz, *Searching for GATT's Environmental Miranda: Are Process Standards Getting "Due Process?"* 27 CORNELL INT'L L.J. 777, 785 (1994) (stating that at best the panel demonstrated the GATT's insensitivity toward hard-fought conservation victories and at worst revealed GATT's insidious desire to exempt international commerce from any legitimate or reasonable regulatory oversight).

[50] *See* Steve Charnovitz, *A Taxonomy of Environmental Trade Measures*, 6 GEO. INT'L ENVTL. L. REV.1 (1993).

international conservation efforts. Was the panel implying that all such import bans were GATT-illegal? It was unclear.

What was even more troubling was that the panel made no distinction between areas of national jurisdiction and areas in the global commons. That is, the panel seemed to be saying that no state could use trade measures to protect ocean resources or the atmosphere since those resources lay outside the jurisdiction of all states. The panel's hard line against the legal protection for dolphins seemed hypocritical to environmentalists as they learned more about how the GATT tolerated economic protection for automobiles, textiles, agriculture, and tuna.

Environmentalists were still reeling from the Tuna-Dolphin decision when the GATT struck again six months later with the release of the new Secretariat report on trade and the environment. Given that the Tuna-Dolphin ruling was still pending before the GATT Council, it was inappropriate for the Secretariat to take a position on the legal issues involved. Nevertheless, the Secretariat declared that "it is not possible under GATT rules to make access to one's own market dependent on the domestic environmental policies or practices of the exporting country."[51] The report also cast doubt on the GATT-legality of the trade measures used in the Montreal Protocol on Substances That Deplete the Ozone Layer.[52]

The GATT Group on Environmental Measures and International Trade started meeting in late 1991, and many observers hoped that the group could bridge the gap between environmentalists and the GATT. Unfortunately, the group made no progress.[53] The simplest problems went unsolved. For example, environmentalists yearned for a clear statement that the GATT would not stand in the way of multilateral environmental agreements. Yet even that minimal objective was unattainable.

At the Ministerial Meeting, which was held in Marrakech in 1994, the GATT agreed to charter a new Committee on Trade and Environment (CTE). The CTE was asked to look at most of the key trade and environment issues, but no effort was made to broaden participation beyond that in the previous GATT Group.[54] For example, governments were not asked to send

[51] *Trade and the Environment*, *supra* note 34, at 23.

[52] *Id.* at 21, 25, 36. For a discussion of the trade measures in the Montreal Protocol, see OECD, *Experience with the Use of Trade Measures in the Montreal Protocol on Substances That Deplete the Ozone Layer*, OECD/GD(97)230 (1997). For text of the Montreal Protocol, *see* 26 I.L.M. 1550 (1987).

[53] *See Report by the Chairman of the Group on Environmental Measures and International Trade*, GATT B.I.S.D. (40th Supp.) at 75.

[54] The need for broadening was clear from some statements made in the GATT Council that seemed to reflect the position of trade bureaucrats rather than governments more generally. For example, in June 1991, the Swedish representative—speaking for all of the Nordic countries—declared that the manner in which products were produced abroad did not affect the domestic environment. Minutes of Meeting of the GATT Council, *supra* note 41, at 13. One wonders what the reaction would have been if this statement had been reported in the Swedish press.

environment ministry officials (although some countries did). Representatives from international organizations—such as UNEP—were allowed to attend CTE meetings, but they were not allowed to speak. The most serious deficiency, however, was the unwillingness of the WTO to allow input from NGOs. NGO participation might have helped to lubricate the North-South friction that paralyzed the CTE.

The CTE met for over two years, but, in the end, it produced few results of any substance.[55] For example, one of the most important issues to be discussed by the CTE was the environmental benefit of removing trade restrictions and distortions. Many observers had marked this as one area in which the trade and environment regimes could be integrative. Economists talked about "win-win" scenarios where wider market access could make it possible for developing countries to increase economic growth through trade and then channel some of the higher national income into environmental investment. Another constructive proposal was the removal of subsidies that are bad for both the economy and the environment. Agricultural, fishery, energy, and mining subsidies are often pointed to as most in need of reform.[56]

Several governments presented thoughtful papers (or "non-papers" as they were called) to the CTE on this issue. For instance, the government of Norway suggested that the CTE identify sectors where trade liberalization could be conducted in such a way as to generate both economic and environmental gains.[57] The energy sector was pinpointed as one example in which trade liberalization might result in such a "double dividend." Norway's paper also suggested that the trading system offer incentives for the use of environmentally friendly products.

Despite the constructive proposals on the table, the only policy conclusion that was reached by the CTE was that further work was needed. The CTE did not recommend specific actions by governments to open their markets nor did it recommend specific actions by the WTO to review harmful subsidies. The CTE's analytical output was also weak. For example, the CTE offered no estimates of the environmental or economic benefits that would be achieved from reducing subsidies in particular sectors. Almost perversely, in view of its

[55] *See* Steve Charnovitz, *A Critical Guide to the WTO's Report on Trade and Environment*, 14 ARIZ. J. INT'L & COMP. L. 341 (1997); Andrew Griffith, *Market Access and Environmental Protection: A Negotiator's Point of View*, Canada Department of Foreign Affairs and International Trade (1997); Winfried Lang, *Trade and Environment: Progress in the World Trade Organization?* 27 ENVTL. POL. & L. 275 (1997); Michael Reiterer, *The WTO Ministerial Conference—The Committee on Trade and Environment: Highlights of the Report to Ministers and Outlook on Future Work*, 2 AUSTRIAN REV. INT'L & EUR. L. 107 (1997).

[56] *See, e.g.*, the papers by Mark Ritchie, Christopher Stone, and Kazuhiro Ueta in *Final Report: Japan—United States Collaboration on Trade and Environment between the Global Environment and Trade Study and the Global Industrial and Social Progress Research Institute* (Feb. 1998); World Bank, *Subsidies and the Environment: A Televised Dialogue* (1997).

[57] WTO, *Report (1996) of the Committee on Trade and Environment*, WT/CTE/1 (7 Nov. 1996) para. 121.

failure, the CTE's main recommendation was that its charter be extended. The WTO members readily agreed to do so at the Ministerial Meeting held in Singapore in December 1996.[58]

Once the WTO got started, the first dispute it considered was an environmental case.[59] The governments of Venezuela and Brazil complained that a US regulation pursuant to the Clean Air Act made it difficult for them to export reformulated gasoline to the United States. In its first decision, the WTO Appellate Body ruled that the US domestic environmental regulation violated GATT rules.[60] Although this decision was yet another example of how difficult it is for environmental measures to qualify under GATT Article XX, the decision was notable because it was the first time that an environmental measure had come close to fitting under one of the Article XX exceptions. But what the Appellate Body gave with one hand, it took away with the other. Although the US regulation met the Article XX(g) subsection, the regulation was still deemed a GATT-violation because it did not meet the terms of the Article XX headnote. According to the Appellate Body, the regulation was "unjustifiable discrimination" and a "disguised barrier to trade."[61]

The CTE met only three times in 1997 and failed to produce any substantive output.[62] It will meet three times in 1998.[63] Although the CTE's performance has been disappointing, the WTO has taken other steps in a positive direction to improve its relationship with civil society. The most significant advance has been a new disclosure policy that releases many more documents to the public.[64] The WTO also set up a web site for easy access to documentation.[65] In order to improve the flow of information to, and from, NGOs, the WTO Secretariat started holding symposia on sustainable development. A two-day symposium in March 1998 provided opportunities for about 150 NGOs to discuss issues with experts, government delegates, and WTO staff.[66] This symposium was a cutting-edge civil society consultation that included

[58] *Ministers Adopt Trade/Environment Report, Renew Committee Created to Look at Issues,* 20 INT'L ENV'T REP. 3 (8 Jan. 1997).

[59] Steve Charnovitz, *New WTO Adjudication and its Implications for the Environment,* 19 INT'L ENV'T REP. 851 (1996).

[60] United States—Standards for Reformulated and Conventional Gasoline, *Report of the Appellate Body*, 35 I.L.M. 603 (1996).

[61] *Report of the Appellate Body*, *id.*, at 632–3.

[62] WTO, *Report (1997) of the Committee on Trade and Environment*, WTO Press Release (3 Dec. 1997) para. 3.

[63] *The WTO Committee on Trade and Environment Adopts its Work Programme and Schedule of Meetings for 1998*, WTO Press Release (20 Mar. 1998).

[64] JOHN BARLOW WEINER & BRENNAN VAN DYKE, A HANDBOOK FOR OBTAINING DOCUMENTS FROM THE WORLD TRADE ORGANIZATION (International Centre for Trade and Sustainable Development, 1997).

[65] <http://www.wto.org>.

[66] WTO, *Background Document for World Trade Organization Symposium of Non-Governmental Organizations on Trade, Environment and Sustainable Development* (March 1998). For information on the symposium, *see* <http://www.iisd.ca/sd/wtosymp/sdvol12no1e.html>.

individuals from NGOs, corporations, law firms, and universities. In addition, the WTO gave NGOs observer status at the Ministerial Conference in 1996 and 1998.

During the past few years, there have been several private initiatives to increase mutual understanding of the trade and environmental regimes. These international study groups comprised participants from around the world. The most notable of these initiatives were the Winnipeg Group (sponsored by the International Institute for Sustainable Development), the "Talloires Group," the Asser Instituut conferences, and the Expert Panel on Trade and Sustainable Development (sponsored by Worldwide Fund for Nature (WWF)).[67] In addition, several NGOs founded the International Centre for Trade and Sustainable Development, which is located in Geneva.[68] The centre, which receives financial support from governments, seeks to facilitate access to the WTO, promote understanding of current policy issues, and disseminate information in all directions.

While the trade and environment debate has not yet "greened" the WTO, the debate has had one very fortunate consequence of improving the coordination of national policymaking. Since governments have needed to attend CTE meetings (and also meetings held by the OECD), national trade ministries have begun talking regularly with national environment ministries. A lot of good may come from this.

Coordination of international policymaking has improved, but it has still not improved enough. Although the trade and environment issue has been considered at several meetings of the Commission on Sustainable Development, there is still no ongoing cooperation between the WTO and other international agencies with environmental mandates, such as UNEP, the Global Environment Facility, and the International Labour Organization. Recently, the CTE acted to grant observer status to the Secretariats of CITES and the Convention on Biological Diversity (CBD).[69] But there has been no effort to formulate common goals—for example, the suppression of illegal traffic—for joint implementation by the WTO and appropriate international environmental organizations. In summary, the WTO has begun to grow out of the segregative tendencies that it manifested during the early 1990s. The greatest progress has occurred on institutional

[67] *See, e.g.*, INTERNATIONAL INSTITUTE FOR SUSTAINABLE DEVELOPMENT, TRADE AND SUSTAINABLE DEVELOPMENT PRINCIPLES (1994); Abram Chayes, Jan Martinez, & Lawrence Susskind, *Parallel Informal Negotiation: A New Kind of International Dialogue*, 12 NEGOTIATION J. 19 (Jan. 1996); ASSER INSTITUUT, THE RELATIONSHIP BETWEEN THE MULTILATERAL TRADING SYSTEM AND THE USE OF TRADE MEASURES IN MULTILATERAL ENVIRONMENTAL AGREEMENTS—SYNERGY OR FRICTION? (1996); WWF, Expert Panel on Trade and Sustainable Development, *Report of the 3rd Meeting* (Nov. 1997).

[68] <http://www.ictsd.org>.

[69] *Report (1996) of the Committee on Trade and Environment*, *supra* note 57, para. 6. For text of the Convention on Biological Diversity *see* 31 I.L.M. 818 (1992).

issues, such as the release of documents. The least progress has occurred in dispute settlement.[70]

IV. IMPROVING TRADE AND THE ENVIRONMENT

The trade and environment debate has been very useful in highlighting the limited perspectives of both sets of policymakers. Ideally, one could use the same framework for setting both economic and environmental policies. Elsewhere, I have suggested the need for a new paradigm of an "ecolonomy" that merges economic and ecological analysis.[71] But at the present time, we do not have such a paradigm. Our best analytic approach, therefore, is probably to weigh trade values in making environmental policy and to weigh environmental values in making trade policy.

The trade regime has offered some well-reasoned advice to environmentalists,[72] including the insights that increased trade can enable greater environmental protection and that trade measures are blunt environmental tools. The trade regime has also offered some advice that is not so well reasoned. The greatest error has been the failure to apply the political economy insights from trade theory to environmental theory. To start with the basics, why should states cooperate on trade policy? The standard answer is that governments systematically get trade policy wrong (that is, they are too protectionist) because they try to satisfy special interest groups.[73] Once governments recognize this weakness, they solve it through a "constitutional" mechanism, such as the GATT, to restrain themselves from adopting protectionist policies.[74] This theory is a coherent and sensible explanation of how the GATT operates. Governments agree to a set of trade rules and to the international enforcement of these rules in order to prevent non-cooperation. When a group of countries wants to liberalize faster than the GATT/WTO membership as a whole, they do so through preferential (often regional) trade agreements. Such agreements discriminate against non-members, but do so in order to thwart free riders who want to gain the benefits of liberalization elsewhere without agreeing to liberalization themselves.

[70] *See* Steve Charnovitz, *Environment and Health under WTO Dispute Settlement*, 32 INT'L LAW (forthcoming 1998).

[71] Steve Charnovitz, *Improving Environmental and Trade Governance*, 7 INT'L ENVTL. AFF. 59, 60 (1995). *See also* JOZO TOMASEVICH, INTERNATIONAL AGREEMENTS ON CONSERVATION OF MARINE RESOURCES 42 (1943) (noting that the theory of conservation is closely related to the theory of international economic relations).

[72] *See, e.g.*, THE GREENING OF WORLD TRADE ISSUES, *supra* note 5.

[73] There are two variants of this. One is a pure government failure—that is, protectionism is wrong for the country doing it. The other is that protectionism is okay for the country doing it because it shifts costs to others, but fails as a strategy because other countries shift costs back.

[74] The most prolific spokesman for this view is E.U. Petersmann. *See, e.g.*, E.U. PETERSMANN, CONSTITUTIONAL FUNCTIONS AND CONSTITUTIONAL PROBLEMS OF INTERNATIONAL ECONOMIC LAW (1991).

When trade theorists look at environmental policymaking, however, they apply an entirely different analysis. Instead of seeing government failure, they perceive government success. That is, trade analysts assume that the low environmental standard in country A is a rational for country A. Sometimes this rationality is said to be objectively based—for example, country A can assimilate a lot more pollution than country B. Alternatively, it is said that country A's citizens consciously choose low environmental standards. For example, the GATT Secretariat has opined that differences in environmental policies "are properly regarded as domestic choices reflecting, among other factors, the domestic trade-offs between income and environment" and that such differences "can well be an additional source of gainful trade among these nations . . ."[75]

In assuming that governments set their environmental policies correctly, the trade regime can logically claim that there is little need for a government to try to influence another country's domestic environmental policy. Thus, efforts to harmonize environmental standards are suspect.[76] The fallacy of this assumption, however, is that we are talking about the same governments. Can it really be true that governments systematically get trade policy wrong—thus justifying trade rules—and yet systematically get environmental policy right—thus negating the case for harmonization? If anything, one would anticipate the opposite situation. That is, governments are much more likely to set improper environmental policy than to set improper trade policy. Trade policy is, after all, conceptually easy; the case against protectionism is overwhelming.[77] By contrast, environmental policy is difficult. A society can suffer high costs by making regulations too tough as well as too lenient.

Thus, if trade analysts looked more realistically at environmental policy, they would see that many of the techniques that are used by the trade regime would also be useful for the environment regime.[78] One technique is to maintain a set of rules in order to keep countries from trying to externalize burdens onto other countries. Another technique is to create a dispute settlement mechanism to enforce these rules. A third technique is to develop a method for dealing with free riders. Although the preferential trading arrangement would probably not be useful for environmental management, the technique itself—that is, discrimination against non-cooperators—is transferable to the environmental regime.

[75] *Trade and the Environment*, *supra* note 34, at 29.

[76] Jagdish Bhagwati & T.N. Srinivasan, *Trade and the Environment: Does Environmental Diversity Detract from the Case for Free Trade?*, *in* 1 FAIR TRADE AND HARMONIZATION 159 (Jagdish Bhagwati & Robert E. Hudec eds., 1996) (arguing against harmonization).

[77] *See, e.g.*, JAGDISH BHAGWATI, PROTECTIONISM (1988).

[78] *See* DANIEL C. ESTY, GREENING THE GATT 73–98 (1994); Steve Charnovitz, *Book Review*, 5 YBIEL 633 (1994) (reviewing Esty's book).

1. New Directions for the WTO

The GATT of 1947 was a deregulatory agreement designed to address government failure. The WTO of the future needs to be more prescriptive. US Trade Representative Charlene Barshefsky put it well when she said: "Sustainable development is not only beneficial to world trade, it has got to be a basic principle of world trade."[79]

A focus on sustainability must examine both production and consumption.[80] Many trade policy analysts prefer trade rules that treat "like" products equivalently regardless of their method of production. For example, solar energy would be treated in the same way as coal-based energy; sustainably produced timber would be treated in the same way as unsustainably produced timber. The integrative scenario would require the WTO to rethink the line that exists between product and process.[81]

To promote sustainability, the WTO should become a world competition agency, regulating in some areas and deregulating in others. Already, we see the rudiments of this new approach. For example, the WTO Agreement on Technical Barriers to Trade (TBT Agreement) calls on governments to use international standards (except when such standards would be ineffective or inappropriate).[82] This agreement does not reflect a hands-off attitude; it is proactive. The TBT Agreement promotes common standards as a way of preventing trade barriers that impede competition. Another example is the Agreement on Trade-Related Aspects of Intellectual Property Rights (TRIPS), which incorporates the rules of intellectual property treaties.[83] TRIPS seeks to upgrade national laws in order to promote innovation and fair competition. Innovation policy is necessitated by market failure, not by government failure. Yet another example is the Agreement on Pre-Shipment Inspection, which directs governments to regulate private inspection activities to assure that they are non-discriminatory and "objective."[84] Clearly, this agreement is not GATT-like because it calls for an interventionist government policy.

An institution that concerns itself with market failure, that seeks to harmonize standards, and that sets rules for private entities is an institution positioned to respond to the challenges of sustainable development. Whether the

[79] Remarks by U.S Trade Representative Charlene Barshefsky at the Institute of International Economics, 15 Apr. 1998, available in LEXIS, News, Federal News Service.

[80] *See, e.g.*, James Salzman, *Sustainable Consumption and the Law*, 27 ENVTL. L. 1243 (1997).

[81] *See* Steve Charnovitz, *Green Roots, Bad Pruning: GATT Rules and their Application to Environmental Trade Measures*, 7 TUL. ENVTL. L. J. 299–30 (1994) (discussing the fuzzy line between product and process).

[82] Agreement on Technical Barriers to Trade, Art. 2.4, 15 Apr. 1994 [hereinafter TBT Agreement], WTO Agreement, *supra* note 10, Annex 1A.

[83] Agreement on Trade-Related Aspects of Intellectual Property Rights, Art. 1.3, 15 Apr. 1994, WTO Agreement, *supra* note 10, Annex 1C.

[84] Agreement on Preshipment Inspection, Art. 2.1, 15 Apr. 1994, WTO Agreement, *supra* note 10, Annex 1A.

WTO will do so is up to the governments that comprise it. But those who doubt that the trading system is institutionally capable of promoting sustainable development have missed key facets of the transformation of the GATT into the WTO.

In the early 1990s, the director of the GATT, Arthur Dunkel, predicted that the next multilateral trade negotiation would be a "Green Round."[85] This does not seem likely to occur now. Even when Dunkel made this statement, many analysts doubted that the trade regime would ever negotiate environmental policy. But while the WTO of 1998 is not directly setting environmental policy, it does try to shape such policymaking indirectly by promoting conformity with WTO rules.

The debate over multilateral environmental agreements (MEAs) is one example of the way in which the WTO is silently influencing environmental policy.[86] Technically, nothing emerged from the consideration of MEAs in the CTE. Moreover, no government has lodged a WTO complaint against a MEA. More realistically, however, the emanations from the CTE's discussion of criteria for using trade measures in MEAs will surely make it more difficult for environmental negotiators to draw upon such trade measures. Several months ago, the WTO director-general said publicly that "a number of the most important Multilateral Environmental Agreements contain trade measures whose consistency with WTO rules might be open to question."[87] Such warnings can only be intended to signal environmental negotiators to cease using trade measures.

2. Specific Proposals

The simplest pro-environment action for the WTO would be to stop giving false prescriptions to the environment regime. However, there are also positive steps that the WTO can take to move towards the integrative scenario. Here are five suggestions:

1. Market-Based Environmentalism: The WTO should promote market based solutions to environmental problems.[88] One way to do this is to improve information that is communicated to consumers about the environmental footprints of particular products. Labels, product seals, and

[85] *See* Senator Bill Bradley, Floor Statement, 1 Dec. 1994, available in LEXIS, Federal Document Clearing House.

[86] For elaboration on the MEA issue, see Richard G. Tarasofsky, *Ensuring Compatibility between Multilateral Agreements and the GATT/WTO*, 7 YBIEL 52 (1996).

[87] "A Shared Responsibility: Global Policy Coherence for Our Global Age." Address by Renato Ruggiero to the Conference entitled "Globalization as a Challenge for German Business: Export Opportunities for Small and Medium-Sized Companies in the Environmental Field," 9 Dec. 1997, at 6.

[88] Sanford E. Gaines, *Rethinking Environmental Protection, Competitiveness, and International Trade*, U. Chi. Legal F. 231 (1997); Thailand Environment Institute, The Compatibility of Trade and Environmental Regulation 18–20 (1997).

producer certifications are examples of effective methods of providing such information. Despite the informational value of labels (or perhaps because of it), some groups want to use the WTO to suppress eco-labels on the grounds that they create unnecessary obstacles to international trade in violation of the TBT Agreement.[89] A lot of criticism has been aimed at labels specifying the production process, but even purely descriptive labels—for example, that timber is tropical—have been opposed. At the very least, the WTO should not let the TBT Agreement be used to thwart eco-labels. But the WTO can also take positive steps to promote eco-labeling by providing a clearinghouse for the best certification and inspection techniques. In addition, the WTO can promote the environmental efforts of the International Organization for Standardization (for example, ISO 14001) by encouraging the use of these standards.[90]

2. Environmental Assessments: The WTO should carry out an environmental impact assessment of any new trade round.[91] This action was not done during the Uruguay Round and, as a result, claims by government officials that the round would have benign environmental results were not credible. From its report, it appears that the CTE did not even discuss this option.[92] There was a discussion of assessments done by national governments, but such assessments are likely to be too narrow and too politicized to be of use to the global community.
3. Developing Countries: The WTO should do more to provide economic opportunities for developing countries.[93] The political strength of Northern environmental NGOs needs to be harnessed in favour of greater trade liberalization so that developing countries can expand exports. One strategy is to push the WTO to use its anti-subsidy disciplines to attack subsidies that harm the environment.[94]
4. Plurilateral Agreements: Although most of the WTO agreements are part of a unified set of obligations, the WTO provides for "plurilateral" agreements on an à-la-carte basis (for example, the Agreement on Government

[89] For a good discussion of the legal issues, see Halina Ward, *Trade and Environment Issues in Voluntary Eco-Labelling and Life Cycle Analysis*, 6 REV. EUR. COMM. & INT'L ENVTL. L. 139 (1997).

[90] TBT Agreement, Art. 2.4 provides that where relevant international standards exist, governments shall use them as a basis for their technical regulations, except when such standards would be an ineffective or inappropriate means for the fulfillment of the legitimate objectives pursued, *supra* note 82.

[91] Assessments might also be done of new free trade zones. *See Rise in Free-Trade Zones Posing Major Threat to Soil, Water, Air, Environment Group Warns,* 20 INT'L ENV'T REP. 1132 (10 Dec. 1997).

[92] *Report (1996) of the Committee on Trade and Environment*, *supra* note 57, at paras. 47 and 181.

[93] *See, e.g.*, J. Michael Finger & L. Alan Winters, *What Can the WTO Do for Developing Countries?*, *in* THE WTO AS AN INTERNATIONAL INSTITUTION 365 (Anne O. Krueger, ed., 1998).

[94] JOHN WHALLEY & PETER UIMONEN, ENVIRONMENTAL ISSUES IN THE NEW WORLD TRADING SYSTEM 126 (1997).

Procurement).[95] It is easy to imagine adding trade-related environmental agreements in order to improve their coordination with the WTO. One could start with the Basel Convention on the Control of Transboundary Movements of Hazardous Waste and Their Disposal.[96]

5. Cooperation: The WTO should improve its policy cooperation with allied organizations. The clear benefits of functional international organization in the post-war period have caused some analysts to forget that the fruits of functionalism depend upon cooperation among institutions. WTO Article V(1) authorizes cooperation with intergovernmental agencies, but the WTO has not yet responded favourably to overtures by UNEP. It is interesting to note that the UN Conference on Trade and Development (UNCTAD) and the CBD Secretariat recently signed a cooperative agreement.[97] WTO Article V(2) authorizes cooperation with NGOs, but the WTO has done so only with two NGOs.[98] It is time to do so with environmental NGOs, perhaps starting with the IUCN. Initiating formal cooperation with UNEP and the IUCN would send a signal around the world that the WTO takes sustainable development seriously.

V. CONCLUSION

The fiftieth anniversary of the GATT is a proper cause for satisfaction. Trade liberalization has contributed to peace and prosperity. Yet, in addition to celebrating the past, we must plan for the future. This article lays out two scenarios for the WTO. The integrative scenario is obviously the preferable one. It would make the WTO more responsive to world needs. It would broaden the WTO's goals to embrace sustainable development. Several of the agreements of the Uruguay Round point the way towards initiating these fundamental changes.

The first part of this article reviewed the founding of the post-war trading system. It showed that the authors of the GATT were aware of ecological challenges and that they sought to allow space within the GATT for multilateral environmental agreements. When trade and the environment first became an issue in the early 1970s, the GATT adopted a constructive approach. The second part of the article examined the trade and environment debate of the 1990s. It showed how the GATT became less tolerant of environmental values. A difficult case—the Tuna-Dolphin dispute—became the

[95] WTO Agreement, *supra* note 10, at art. X:9 and Annex 4. Agreement on Government Procurement, available in LEXIS, ITrade library, GATT file.

[96] For the text of the convention, *see* 28 I.L.M. 657 (1989).

[97] *UNCTAD, Biodiversity Treaty Sign Secretariat Accord*, 20 INT'L ENV'T REP. 1162 (1997).

[98] *See* Daniel C. Esty, *Non-Governmental Organizations at the World Trade Organization: Cooperation, Competition, or Exclusion*, 1 J. INT'L ECON. L.123 (1998); Richard Blackhurst, *The Capacity of the WTO to Fulfill its Mandate, in* THE WTO AS AN INTERNATIONAL INSTITUTION, *supra* note 93 at 43–4.

vehicle for defining when individual governments could use (or rather not use) trade measures to protect marine life in the global commons. The GATT/WTO is still trying to (un)paint its way out of this corner. Finally, the third part looked at how we might improve the environmental dimension of the trade regime. It began by showing how trade analysts misunderstand environmental policymaking and consequently prescribe the wrong solutions. Next, it made five specific recommendations on the topics of: market-based environmentalism, environmental assessments, developing countries, new plurilateral agreements, and WTO cooperation.

Although few of the feared collisions between trade and environment have occurred, the tension between the two regimes has not subsided. The GATT/WTO legal regime is perhaps stronger than ever, but, eerily, public skepticism about economic globalization is also stronger than ever.[99] The WTO of the future must make sure that nature is not just another commodity. It is only by building environmental safeguards into the trading system that the public can gain the confidence that it needs to support free trade.

[99] Guy de Jonquières, *Network Guerrillas*, FINANCIAL TIMES, 30 April 1998, at 20; Bhushan Bahree, *As WTO Marks 50th Birthday, Event Attracts Opponents to Globalization*, WALL STREET JOURNAL, 18 May 1998, at B6B.

[19]

Trade and the Environment

Interaction between international trade and the environment is as old as trade itself. Awareness that the interaction has implications in public policy terms is more recent. Nevertheless, it dates back at least to the trade provisions in the 1933 convention on fauna and flora.[25] In the late 1960s, environmental problems caused by the discharge of waste and other pollutants into the natural environment emerged seriously; and so did concerns over the implications for international competitiveness.

Over the past two decades, producers in countries with stricter environmental standards have worried increasingly about the impact of those standards on their competitiveness in world markets. At the same time, governments and firms in other countries have expressed concern about new barriers being erected against imports produced under less strict standards.

Most recently, there has been growing public concern with issues related to the pollution of the global commons (for example, ozone depletion and climate change), as well as with species diversity and the treatment of animals. This has raised important questions about the use of trade policies to influence environmental measures in other countries.

The objective of this chapter is to provide an initial analysis of these and other interactions between trade and the environment, especially as they affect the multilateral trading system.[26] Part 1 provides, for easy reference, an overview of the main issues and a summary of the principal conclusions. Part 2 explains, on the basis of existing experience and judgement, which environmentally-motivated trade policy actions are permitted by GATT rules, and which are not. This is done with the understanding that the authority to interpret the rules of the General Agreement ultimately rests with GATT's contracting parties, that is, with its member countries. Part 3 examines issues which arise when environmental effects are wholly domestic. Issues which arise when there are transborder physical spillovers into another country or into the global commons are covered in Part 4. The focus shifts in Part 5 to the risk that environmental concerns and policies could lead, wittingly or unwittingly, to inappropriate or even counter-productive restrictions on international trade.

1. Overview and summary

The main issues and principal conclusions can be grouped under five headings: the contribution of trade to a better environment, the need for multilateral cooperation, the role of trade policies, the political economy challenge, and risks and opportunities for the trading system.

The contribution of trade to a better environment

Views differ regarding the impact of international trade on the quality of the natural environment. For some, expanding trade is a source of increased wealth and diffusion of technology, both of which enhance societies' ability to protect and up-grade their environments. Others argue that unrestricted trade can be harmful to the environment, especially when a country's environmental policies are weak or nonexistent.

While the latter view does draw attention to certain trade-related environmental risks, there is no reason to assume that growth of per capita income necessarily, or even on average, damages the environment. To begin with, the increases in per capita income – which are boosted by increased market access and expanding trade – provide more resources to contain environmental damage, helping to

[25] The full title of the convention, which is still in force, is the Convention Relative to the Preservation of Fauna and Flora in their Natural State. See Appendix I for a summary of multilateral environmental treaties containing trade provisions.

[26] There is no generally agreed definition of «environment». The moderately broad definition used in this report – which includes the full range of pollution-related problems, plus soil erosion and loss of fertility, deforestation, product safety (food, hazardous wastes), endangered species and the treatment of animals – reflects the range of environmental issues that have been raised in discussions of the linkages between trade and the environment. The inclusion of a particular environmental issue in the analysis reflects not a judgement about the actual or potential seriousness of the problem, but rather only that it is being widely debated and therefore that there is an interest in exploring its possible implications for trade and the trading system.

finance pollution control and remedial clean-up. A country with a stagnant economy, by contrast, will be under greater pressure to stint on improving the environment.

Furthermore, if the average citizen is convinced of the need to devote more material and human resources to achieve a better environment as his or her income rises, the growth of per capita income ultimately will lead to increased expenditure on the environment. The available evidence suggests that this is indeed happening.

The opportunity for countries to trade in world markets for goods and technology facilitates the implementation of needed environment-improving processes at home. These processes often first appear in countries at the frontier of environmental regulation, and products embodying them must be exported if other countries are to catch up. Similarly, trade can help consumers make environmentally beneficial choices – for instance, imports of low-sulphur coal can encourage them to abandon the use of polluting high-sulphur coal. Trade in recycled inputs can help countries economize on resource use.

While trade liberalization is likely to reduce some protectionist barriers which are encouraging environmentally harmful activities, it is also possible that trade liberalization could worsen particular environmental problems in the absence of appropriate domestic environmental policies. Conceivably, an expansion of trade could produce negative environmental effects so large that they outweigh the conventional benefits from open markets (increased specialization, more competition and so forth), resulting in an overall decline in national welfare. However, this is possible only if a country lacks a domestic environmental policy that reflects its environmental values and priorities.[27] If that is the case, the most effective action is to concentrate on introducing appropriate environmental policies rather than trying to work around bad ones by foregoing trade liberalization or attempting to fine-tune interventionist trade policies. A lack of appropriate environmental policies creates problems not just in the trade sector, but throughout every facet of a country's economic life. Manipulating trade policies is not only costly – in terms of a less efficient international division of labour – but also ineffective in dealing with the negative consequences elsewhere in the economy caused by the absence of appropriate environmental policies.

This is evident, for example, in efforts to promote sustainable development. Although that term means different things to different people, most definitions encompass two basic notions.[28] First, there is a need to place much greater emphasis on assigning values or prices to environmental resources, with a view to identifying and valuing the environmental effects of economic activity. Second is the idea that each generation should pass on to the next at least as much capital - environmental and man-made – as it inherited.

Neither aspect of sustainable development is intrinsically linked to international trade. A failure to place a value on environmental resources would undermine sustainable development even in a completely closed economy. Trade is seen, rather, as a «magnifier». If the policies necessary for sustainable development are in place, trade promotes development that is sustainable. Alternatively, if such policies are lacking, the country's international trade may contribute to a skewing of the country's development in an environmentally damaging direction, but then so will most of the other economic activities in the country. Clearly the correct action in such cases is to work for the adoption of an appropriate overall domestic environmental policy, rather than focusing attention on problems that are allegedly trade-related.

The need for multilateral cooperation

Environmental issues can become internationalized in at least one of three ways. The first two, which can occur even when the issues are in principle purely domestic, are through concerns over the impact of environmental policies on international competitiveness, and through the assertion of jurisdiction over other nations' environmental priorities and practices. The third and most obvious way is through the transborder spillover of pollution into another country or the global commons (primarily the upper atmosphere and the oceans). Although current concerns with the environment encompass a wide range of issues, from water pollution to ozone depletion, and the treatment of animals to standards for pesticide residues in food, they all share a common need for multilateral cooperation, not only to minimize potential trade frictions, but especially to identify and implement workable and effective solutions to regional and global environmental problems.

As a result, it is no longer possible for a country to create an appropriate environmental policy entirely on its own. Even when environmental problems are domestic (in the sense that no pollution is escaping across the border), an attempt by countries to go it alone on environmental policies would sooner or later lead to frictions with trading partners and most likely to unilateral trade actions. What is needed is multilateral rules to guide countries in formulating their own environmental policies and in responding to domestic complaints about

[27] This proposition is demonstrated in Anderson (1992c). *Note:* the full details of the references are provided in the list of references at the end of this chapter.

[28] The Annex in Pearce, Barbier and Markandya (1989) contains a compendium of definitions employed by different authors. See also Dasgupta and Mäler (1990).

the impact of their own and other countries' policies on international competitiveness. To back up the rules, a dispute settlement procedure is necessary for handling conflicts that cannot be resolved among the countries concerned. If existing rules and procedures are judged to be adequate for the task, fine. If not, some negotiated changes will be necessary.

When an environmental problem involves a transborder physical spillover, the only alternative to unilateral actions based on economic and political power is for countries to cooperate in the design, implementation and enforcement of an appropriate multilateral agreement for dealing with the problem at hand. This will often also be the case with assertions of jurisdiction over other countries' practices and policies, including the treatment of animals and endangered species.

Regardless of the nature of an environmental problem, the contribution of multilateral cooperation is to reduce the possibility that solutions are affected by differences in the economic and political strengths of the parties involved. Given the justifiable basis for a diversity of environmental standards among countries, it is important to minimize the risk of solutions being imposed by the larger or richer countries.

Negative incentives – in particular, the use of discriminatory trade restrictions on products unrelated to the environmental issue at hand – are not an effective way to promote multilateral cooperation. Alternatively, the use of positive incentives coupled with peer pressure can be a viable option – and all the more so since the likelihood of negative incentives being a workable and sustainable approach in the medium-term and across a range of issues is open to serious doubt.

The role of trade policy

This chapter argues, and there is much support for this view, that unilateral restrictions on trade would never be the most efficient instrument for dealing with an environmental problem. Of course it is always possible to find an example, hypothetical or taken from the real world, which appears to contradict that conclusion. But always at the base of such an example would be a national environmental policy that is considered inappropriate.

If all countries participated in all international environmental agreements, there would be nothing more to add. However, it is often a challenge just to get a critical mass of countries – let alone all countries – to participate in an international environmental agreement. As soon as participation is less than universal, trade policy re-enters the picture, albeit in a different role. Trade measures could be used as one type of «carrot» – or, despite the arguments noted above, as one type of «stick» – to encourage participation.

Past experience suggests that the organizers of an environmental agreement are also likely to consider including trade provisions – that is, measures affecting trade only in the product or products covered by the agreement – designed to minimize the extent to which trade between participants and non-participants could undermine the agreement. Recalling that a country's trade in a particular product is nothing more than the difference between production and consumption, there is also the option of controlling both production and consumption in the participating countries. In this case there would be no need to have separate controls on trade flows.

The risk of protectionist responses

There is much evidence which points to a serious risk of environmental issues and concerns being exploited by protectionists for their own benefit. This can occur at any of several stages: by promoting policies that discriminate against imports as part of the solution to environmental problems, by biasing the choice between positive and negative incentives in favour of trade sanctions, by pushing for the inclusion of unnecessary trade provisions in multilateral agreements, or by deliberately promoting product standards that place a proportionately greater cost burden on foreign producers. These concerns are heightened by the efforts of protectionist groups to draw environmental groups into implicit or explicit alliances.

If the use of inefficient policies to achieve environmental goals were costless for environmental interests, then practical politics might argue for embracing such coalitions whenever possible. But it is not likely to be costless, and certainly not in the medium and long term. Biases that protectionist interests introduce into the environmental policy package increase the costs of environmental improvements. In the longer term, this can only reduce the amount of improvement the society will be willing to undertake. When that happens, the protectionist interests gain not only at the expense of the rest of the economy, but also at the expense of the natural environment.

Risks and opportunities for the trading system

There is a serious risk that the trading system could get badly bruised by a rush to deal with environmental issues which are viewed as urgent by important segments of the population in an increasing number of countries. To someone unfamiliar with, or indifferent to, the contribution of economic efficiency and the trading system to postwar economic prosperity, trade measures can too easily seem to be low cost and readily available tools for pursuing environmental goals.

As regards the design and implementation of environmental policies, GATT rules place essentially no constraints on the ability of countries to use appropriate policies to protect their environment from damage from domestic production activities or from the consumption of domestically produced or imported products. Concern over the possibility that technical or other kinds of regulations could create unnecessary obstacles to trade has led, it is true, to certain multilateral disciplines. But those disciplines contain qualified exceptions for actions related to protecting or improving the environment.

When the environmental problem is due to production or consumption activities in another country, the GATT rules are more of a constraint, since they prohibit making market access dependent on changes in the domestic policies or practices of the exporting country. The rationale for this is that to do otherwise would invite a flood of import restrictions as countries (especially those with large markets) either attempted to impose their own domestic environmental, economic and social policies on other countries, or used such an attempt as a pretext for reducing competition from imports.

Furthermore, the fact that GATT rules block the unilateral use of trade measures to dictate changes in the environmental policies of other nations does not mean that governments are powerless. They still have the possibility of negotiating a multilateral solution or, failing that, of requesting a GATT waiver. These options offer the prospect of resolving environmental problems and conflicts, while at the same time effectively guarding against the excesses that would result from unilateralism.

In other words, GATT rules could never block the adoption of environmental policies which have broad support in the world community. This is because in most instances the support of two-thirds of GATT's membership – currently 69 out of 103 countries – is sufficient to amend the rules or grant a waiver. What the rules do constrain is attempts by one or a small number of countries to influence environmental policies in other countries not by persuasion and negotiation, but by unilateral reductions in access to their markets.

The real risk, therefore, is not that trade policies will be used, but that they will be used unilaterally. If the door were opened to use trade policies unilaterally to offset the competitiveness effects of different environmental standards, or to attempt to force other countries to adopt domestically-favoured practices and policies, the trading system would start down a very slippery slope. Countries are not clones of one another, and will not wish to become so – certainly not under the threat of unilateral trade measures.

The opportunities presented to the trading system consist mainly in exploiting the various ways in which open international trade can contribute, in conjunction with appropriate national environmental policies, to the improvement and protection of the environment. From an institutional standpoint there is a need for a careful examination of the existing rules to be certain that they do not hinder multilateral efforts to deal with environmental problems. This will be one of the important tasks of GATT's recently activated Group on Environmental Measures and International Trade.

More broadly, the economic growth stimulated by open trade policies increases wealth and spreads knowledge and information, which in turn increase the range of choices available to consumers, including the option of choosing to enjoy the services of a higher quality environment.

2. GATT law and the environment

Within any nation the judicial system spends a good part of its time interpreting the country's laws. Experts can also differ on the applicability of certain laws to particular situations, over what is and is not permitted. It is not surprising, therefore, that GATT's rules and disciplines give rise to issues of interpretation, especially in a relatively new area of concern such as the interaction between trade policy and the environment.

It is possible, nonetheless, to be reasonably precise about what current GATT rules say regarding the use of trade policies to further environmental goals. The first point to stress is the central role of non-discrimination in GATT law.

The rules of the General Agreement are concerned primarily with preventing discrimination, that is, with limiting the extent to which countries can discriminate between home products and imports, between imports from different countries, and between goods sold in the home market and those exported. It is reasonable to conclude, therefore, that even though the General Agreement does not mention the environment explicitly, non-discriminatory environmental policies ordinarily would not be subject to any GATT constraints.

Protecting the nation's own environment

Under GATT's rules, governments can employ many different measures to protect and improve the local environment. Thus, sales taxes on products that can create pollution (those containing chloroflurocarbons, for example), deposit refund schemes for recyclable waste (bottles, scrap cars), or favourable tax treatment of environmentally friendly products (lead-free gasoline, solar panels for home heating) and other non-discriminatory measures ensuring a pattern of domestic consumption that minimizes pollution would not normally be open to challenge.

There is also nothing in the GATT that prevents contracting parties from taxing or regulating domestic producers who engage in polluting activities – even to the extent of prohibiting the production and sale of particular goods. For instance, ceilings on air pollution levels, and levies on companies that discharge pollutants into lakes and rivers, are fully consistent with GATT rules.

In certain cases, even a measure taken for environmental protection purposes which would otherwise violate GATT obligations not to discriminate may be permitted under Article XX of the GATT. The narrowly-defined exceptions in Article XX permit a contracting party to place health, safety or domestic resource conservation goals ahead of non-discrimination, but only when certain conditions are fulfilled.[29] In general, these conditions ensure that a trade measure is necessary for the achievement of such goals - and that these goals are not used as a pretext for reducing competition from imports.[30]

GATT rules, therefore, place essentially no constraints on a country's right to protect its own environment against damage from either domestic production or the consumption of domestically produced or imported products. Generally speaking, a country can do anything to imports or exports that it does to its own products, and it can do anything it considers necessary to its own production processes.

There are, nevertheless, some points to add. It is accepted among GATT's member countries that technical regulations should not be formulated in such a way as to constitute unnecessary obstacles to trade. Among the agreements signed at the end of the Tokyo Round (which supplement the General Agreement) is the Agreement on Technical Barriers to Trade, whose rules oblige its Parties to use international standards whenever possible. However, it also explicitly allows its Parties to deviate from such standards if they «are inappropriate for the Parties concerned, for inter alia such reasons as ... protection for human health or safety, animal or plant life or health, or the environment; fundamental climatic or other geographical factors; ....» At the same time, any such derogation would be subject to the basic obligation that it does not result in an unnecessary obstacle to trade.

Under this same Agreement, it is also possible for an exporting country to challenge another country's ban on the sale of a particular product on the grounds that the ban is not based on scientific criteria and is thus an unnecessary obstacle to trade.

In a similar manner, the Subsidies Agreement (also from the Tokyo Round) discourages the use of trade-distorting subsidies, but then explicitly recognizes the right of signatories to use subsidies for «the redeployment of industry in order to avoid ... environmental problems».

These various provisions are an attempt to find a reasonable, good-faith balance between the desire to avoid distortions to competition and the desire to allow each country sovereignty over measures affecting its natural environment and the health and safety of its residents. This is not an easy task. The issues are among the most sensitive in any society, and the scientific understanding often is such that it comes down to a matter of subjective risk management (Box 2). Well-informed and fair-minded individuals can differ – sometimes substantially – on where to strike the balance.

When one country seeks to change another's environmental behaviour

Production and consumption activities in other countries can also be a source of domestic environmental concern. Pollution may be spilling over borders and harming either the regional environment (acid rain) or the global commons (ozone depletion). Or land development projects may be threatening the extinction of animal or plant species and uncontrolled fishing may be depleting fish stocks in the high seas. It is not unreasonable that the government of a country concerned by such practices would seek to see them changed – and that it would find it difficult to accept that this would not be possible.

There are various options for attempting to induce changes in the production or consumption behaviour of another country. However, unilateral increases in import barriers are not, prima facie, among them.

In principle, it is not possible under GATT's rules to make access to one's own market dependent on the domestic environmental policies or practices of the exporting country.

The requirement not to discriminate between different sources of imports – which of course applies to a much broader range of issues than just those related to the environment – is intended not only to prevent trade distortions. It exists also to protect each member of GATT from the unilateral imposition of domestic standards or policies by

[29] Article XX also contains the exception which allows countries to discriminate against imports produced by prison labour.

[30] Answering the question of whether a particular trade measure is «necessary» involves one or both of two considerations: whether other measures consistent with the General Agreement are reasonably available to achieve the goal and, if not, whether it is the least trade distorting way of achieving the goal. For a more general discussion see, for example, Charnovitz (1991), McDorman (1991) and Petersmann (1991).

Box 2 – Sanitary and phytosanitary risk management

Countries often have elaborate programs for the assessment and management of risk to determine the measures needed to ensure safe food supplies for humans and animals, to protect plants and animals from pests or diseases, and to protect humans from diseases which may be carried by animals or by plants. The GATT recognizes the right of countries to maintain such measures subject to the requirement that the measures do not arbitrarily or unjustifiably discriminate between countries where the same conditions prevail, or are not a disguised restriction on international trade (Article XXb).

There are three principal steps in sanitary and phytosanitary risk management which give rise to opportunities for introducing restrictions on trade, inadvertantly or otherwise.

First, *risk assessment* involves evaluation of either:

– the likelihood of a pest or disease becoming established or spreading and its potential consequences, or

– the potential adverse effects on human or animal health as a consequence of additives, contaminants or toxins in foods, feedstuffs or beverages.

The evaluation of plant and animal pests or diseases must be based not only on information about the pest or disease itself and its means of reproduction or contamination, but also on the ecological conditions (that is, climate, geography, and associated biota) which may foster or limit its spread, and the susceptibility of animal or plant populations (the zoosanitary and phytosanitary conditions). The evaluation of contaminants in foods requires information on chemical properties such as acute and chronic toxicity, carcinogenecity, and teratogenecity. Sanitary and phytosanitary measures are not limited to the protection of commercial species, but are applied also for the protection of wild flora and fauna. For pesticides, evaluation of the ways in which the pesticide affects the environment, particularly ground water, is also often required. Clearly, an improper assessment of risk, for example because of lack of information, misrepresentation of facts or the inclusion of inappropriate factors, may result in unwarranted barriers to trade.

Second, determining the *acceptable level of risk* – the appropriate level of health or sanitary protection – requires a judgement that reflects, among other things, a society's values. Uncontrollable and unknown factors often make it prohibitively expensive or impossible fully to guarantee safety. More generally, government authorities seek instead to determine levels of «no unreasonable risk» or «negligible risk» because of the excessive costs of approaching «zero risk» relative to other competing objectives such as ensuring adequate food production, efficient use of resources, and the economic benefits of production and trade. «Tolerance» levels may be set which indicate, for example, the maximum amount of a contaminant which will be permitted. In certain cases, where the consequences of acting otherwise could be severe, a zero tolerance, or no measurable level, may be set.

Third, perhaps the greatest potential for disruption of international trade occurs in the selection and application of health and sanitary *risk management measures.* Government authorities make risk management decisions which specify conditions or levels of use of particular products in order to limit associated risks to acceptable levels. These measures may include quarantine requirements, chemical use restrictions, vaccination policies, processing regulations, testing, inspection and certification requirements. Various measures may achieve equivalent results in terms of health protection, but have very different consequences with regard to trade. Where importing countries insist on their own testing or certification procedures, delays and uncertainty about results present further costs to traders. The manner by which requirements are administered may also pose unnecessary burdens on imported goods.

The degree of complexity in risk assessment, flexibility in setting the level of acceptable risk, and discretion in determining risk management measures all imply that countries may occasionally, perhaps under interest-group prodding, impose unwarranted, trade-inhibiting restrictions. One of the objectives of the Uruguay Round negotiations is to establish disciplines that will permit governments to provide the necessary protection for humans, animals and plants while minimizing the adverse effects that such measures may have on international trade.

importing countries through the threat of market access restrictions. It protects trade relations from degenerating into anarchy through unilateral actions in pursuit of unilaterally-defined objectives, however valid they may appear.

If the goal is to influence environmental policies and practices in other countries, the option which is most consistent with orderly international relations is inter-governmental cooperation leading to a multilateral agreement (see Part 4 below). By offering each country the opportunity to explain and defend its view of the problem, the negotiating process increases the chances of uncovering solutions acceptable to all the affected parties. Cooperative efforts also offer the best chance of ensuring that the policy changes deal directly with the problem at hand and that they provide minimum scope for protectionist abuses.

Trade provisions in multilateral environmental agreements

One of the first tasks of the recently activated GATT Group on Environmental Measures and International Trade is to consider the trade provisions in environmental agreements vis-a-vis the obligations of contracting parties under the GATT.[31] Of the 127 multilateral agreements in the area of the environment, 17 have trade provisions (Table 14).

The majority of environmental agreements with trade provisions are those concerned with the protection of fauna

[31] The Group has also been asked to examine the transparency of national environmental regulations which are likely to affect trade, and the trade effects of packaging and labelling requirements intended to protect the environment.

and flora. For example, the parties to the Convention on International Trade in Endangered Species of Wild Fauna and Flora (CITES), including the producing states, have agreed to a ban on trade in ivory. Import bans are also applied by certain countries to whales, flying foxes, polar bears, North Pacific fur seals, migratory birds, and many other species.

The goals of such environmental agreements can probably be best achieved if the participating countries ban all sales of the endangered animals or plants, not just their importation or exportation. The GATT permits its contracting parties to ban the domestic sale of a product and to enforce such a ban at the point of importation or exportation provided, of course, that the ban applies regardless of the origin or destination of the product. The most effective way of applying these environmental agreements is therefore likely to be also the one that would ensure consistency with the GATT.[32]

When foreign products are subjected to a more stringent treatment than domestic products, there is a potential source of conflict with the GATT's national treatment provision. As noted earlier, the GATT does, however, permit a difference in treatment as an exception under Article XX(b) for measures necessary to protect human, animal or plant health or life in the importing country. For example, phytosanitary regulations deal with the spread of pests and disease across borders through international trade in plant material. Various plant protection agreements permit rigorous inspection and even prohibition of imports.

Another possible source of conflict with the GATT rules occurs when an environmental agreement specifies a difference in the trade measures affecting parties and non-parties. For example, the trade provisions of the Montreal Protocol, the Basel Convention, and CITES (for those species in which managed trade is permitted) require parties to apply more restrictive trade provisions to non-parties than to parties. GATT's member countries have not as yet been required to take a decision on whether such departures from the non-discrimination principle can be justified under Article XX.

Table 14
Multilateral environmental agreements by subject, 1933-90

(Number of agreements)

	Total	With trade provisions
Marine pollution	41	0
Marine fishing and whaling	25	0
Protection of fauna and flora	19	10
Nuclear and air pollution	13	1
Antarctica	6	0
Phytosanitary regulation	5	4
Locust control	4	0
Boundary waters	4	0
Animal cruelty	3	1
Hazardous wastes	1	1
Other	6	0
Total	127	17

It is not clear that such departures from the non-discrimination principle are always necessary to achieve the environmental goal of the environmental agreement. For example, the parties to the Montreal Protocol on chloroflurocarbons (CFCs) could have structured the Protocol in such a way that it reduced consumption of CFCs in the participating countries by the target amount, without the necessity of including provisions for special restrictions on trade with non-parties.[33] Since, however, the drafters had other goals as well, including that of providing compensation to CFC producers in the participating countries (by allowing them to receive extra profits from selling the diminishing quantity of CFCs), trade provisions which discriminate against non-participants were included in the Protocol.[34]

Changing GATT's rules

Provided there was broad support for the idea, GATT's member countries could decide to allow the imposition of import restrictions on exports from countries whose environmental regulations were considered to be «inadequate». This could be done by amending or supplementing the provisions of the General Agreement, or by the granting of a waiver. Regardless of the way in which the change was made, it would be necessary to define inadequate environmental regulation and to develop procedures and criteria that would minimize the chances of abuse.

Under Article XXV, waivers of specific GATT obligations may be granted to individual contracting parties or to all contracting parties. They are adopted by a two-thirds majority of the votes cast, with the added requirement that the majority must comprise more than half of the contracting

[32] It should be noted that import duties and export taxes are consistent with the rules of the General Agreement, provided they do not exceed the bindings set out in a country's schedule of concessions. While most of the major trading nations as well as an increasing number of developing countries have bound nearly all of their import duties, they have not negotiated bindings on export taxes.

[33] One way would be to impose taxes on the consumption of CFCs, or a quota on domestic consumption implemented by a system of auctioned domestic sales licenses which permitted the license holder to buy from all potential suppliers, regardless of whether they are in a participating country. In either case, the scarcity value of the reduced amount of CFCs would accrue to the government (in the form of tax or auction receipts). Production of CFCs in participating countries could then be regulated by quotas set at the projected level of consumption in those countries.

[34] See Enders and Porges (1992).

parties. Waivers are granted subject to conditions ensuring that the privileges accorded are used for the intended purpose.

If most of GATT's contracting parties agree to participate in a particular multilateral environmental agreement, the consistency of its trade provisions with GATT is not likely to be a problem since there would be enough votes to secure a waiver, if necessary. In situations where the environmental objective for which the agreement is to be negotiated is of interest to only a few countries, it would also be possible for the interested countries to request a waiver if the trade measures which they propose to adopt are not consistent with their GATT obligations. The success of their request would depend on their ability to convince enough contracting parties of the wisdom of granting the waiver.

In dealing with transborder environmental issues, use of the waiver approach would ensure that the proposed trade policy actions would be focused on the environmental problem in question, and that they would be transparent, multilaterally negotiated, have broad support among the GATT membership, and be subject to conditions designed to avoid abuse.

This is not to imply that waivers offer a ready way around GATT obligations. The prevailing view is that waivers are to be granted only exceptionally and for a limited period of time, and that they are not a substitute for revisions of the rules.

Experience with the GATT dispute settlement process

The ways in which GATT rules operate in the environment area, including their role in preventing protectionist abuses and attempts to impose standards unilaterally on other countries, become more tangible in actual trade disputes. In the past decade, the GATT dispute settlement process has produced five panel reports that include relevant interpretations of GATT rules in the environmental area.[35]

In two of those disputes a contracting party had banned imports or exports, and claimed the ban was justified under Article XX(g) as a measure relating to the conservation of exhaustible natural resources. One involved a United States ban on imports of tuna and tuna products from Canada. In 1982 the GATT Council adopted the panel's recommendations, which rejected the United States' claim that its embargo was justified on conservation grounds, the main basis for the rejection being that the United States had no catch limits for its own fishing fleets on most of the species of tuna it was embargoing.[36] In the second case, involving a Canadian ban on exports of unprocessed herring and salmon, the panel report adopted in 1988 found that because there were no limits on Canadian consumption of herring and salmon, there was no link between conservation of those species and the export prohibition.[37]

As the panel in the Canadian herring and salmon case said, the purpose of including Article XX(g) in the General Agreement was not to create a loophole for discriminatory or protectionist trade policy measures, but to ensure that GATT rules would not hinder conservation policies.

In a third case, Thailand sought to justify a virtual ban on imported cigarettes under Article XX(b) as a measure «necessary to protect human, animal or plant life or health». The panel's report, adopted in 1990, accepted that smoking endangers human health and that measures to reduce cigarette consumption were permissible.[38] It agreed that Article XX(b) permitted a contracting party to put health goals above its trade obligations, but that the discrimination against imported cigarettes had to be «necessary». The panel did not see any reason why it was necessary to ban cigarette imports while leaving domestic production and sales of cigarettes unrestricted. The panel found that other, non-discriminatory measures could meet the health goal.

A panel report adopted in 1987 dealt with a complaint brought by Canada, the European Communities and Mexico against United States taxes on petroleum and certain imported substances, the proceeds of which were used to help finance a «Superfund» for cleaning up toxic waste sites.[39] The European Communities had argued with respect to one of those taxes that special rules, including the OECD's «polluter pays principle» (PPP), had to be applied because the tax concerned pollution. The panel found, however, that the GATT rules on border tax adjustments apply regardless of the purpose of a tax, that the PPP had never been adopted by the GATT, and that the tax in question was a legitimate border tax adjustment. On the other hand, the panel found that another tax, imposed on imported petroleum at a higher rate than domestic petroleum, was inconsistent with GATT rules on national treatment.

The most recent environment-related dispute involved Mexico's challenge to a United States embargo, under the Marine Mammal Protection Act, of imports of yellowfin tuna

[35] The dispute between the United States and the European Communities over the use of growth hormones in beef production is not on this list because it has not entered the formal GATT dispute settlement process.

[36] See GATT, *Basic Instruments and Selected Documents*, Twenty-ninth Supplement, p. 91.

[37] See GATT, *Basic Instruments and Selected Documents*, Thirty-fifth Supplement, p. 98.

[38] See GATT, *Basic Instruments and Selected Documents*, Thirty-seventh Supplement, p. 200.

[39] See GATT, *Basic Instruments and Selected Documents*, Thirty-fourth Supplement, p. 136.

Box 3 – Tuna and dolphins

Schools of yellowfin tuna often swim beneath schools of dolphins in the eastern tropical Pacific Ocean. As a result, when tuna are fished with purse seine nets, dolphins can be trapped in the nets and will die unless released. The United States' Marine Mammal Protection Act (MMPA) sets dolphin protection standards – involving a ceiling limit on dolphin catches – for the domestic fishing fleet and for countries whose fishing boats harvest yellowfin tuna in the eastern tropical Pacific Ocean. If a country exporting such tuna to the United States cannot prove to the United States authorities that its tuna fleets meet the dolphin protection standards set out in the law, the United States government must embargo all imports of yellowfin tuna and tuna products from that country and from «intermediary» countries that purchase tuna from the country subject to the direct embargo. Under this law, the United States government has prohibited imports of yellowfin tuna and tuna products from Mexico, Venezuela and Vanuatu, and from the intermediary countries of Costa Rica, France, Italy, Japan and Panama.

In February 1991, Mexico asked for a GATT dispute settlement panel, arguing that the United States' embargo on yellowfin tuna and tuna products was inconsistent with GATT provisions. The United States argued that the GATT's national treatment provision (Article III) permitted the enforcement at the border of dolphin protection standards set out in the MMPA. The Panel found that the standard of Article III – namely, that imported products be accorded no less favourable treatment than domestic products – required a comparison between products of the exporting and importing countries, and not a comparison between production regulations of the exporting and importing countries that had no effect on the product as such. Therefore, the United States could not embargo imports of tuna products from Mexico simply because Mexico's regulations affecting the production of tuna did not satisfy United States regulations.

The United States also argued that the import embargo could be justified under the Article XX exceptions clauses for measures otherwise inconsistent with GATT obligations, which protect animal health or exhaustible natural resources. However, the Panel found that Article XX does not permit a contracting party to take trade measures to enforce its own laws regarding animals or exhaustible natural resources outside its jurisdiction.

The reasoning behind these findings was as follows. If the United States' arguments were accepted, then any country could ban imports of a product from a country merely because the exporting country pursues environmental or health policies different from its own. This would create a very large loophole in the GATT for any country unilaterally to apply trade restrictions not for the purpose of enforcing its own laws within its jurisdiction, but to impose the standards set out in its laws on other countries. In such a situation, the potential for protectionist abuses would be very great. It would certainly work against the main objective of the multilateral trading system – to provide stable and predictable market access opportunities through agreed rules and disciplines.

The Panel's task was limited to examination of this matter in the light of existing GATT obligations. It was not asked whether either party's environmental policies as such were appropriate. In finding that a country may not restrict imports of a product solely because it originates in a country whose environmental policies are different, the Panel stressed the all-or-nothing choice which Article XX presents. If the GATT contracting parties wished to permit environmental trade restrictions such as those under the United States dolphin protection law, they would need to agree on limits to prevent abuse. Since Article XX does not provide such limits, the Panel stated that it would be better to amend or supplement the provisions of the General Agreement or to provide a waiver, since each of these alternatives would provide an opportunity for the contracting parties to develop and negotiate provisions to minimize the risk of excessive use and abuse.

Another issue Mexico had raised before the Panel concerned the United States' Dolphin Protection Consumer Information Act, which requires that if tuna products are labeled «Dolphin safe», they must meet certain dolphin protection standards. The Panel found that this labelling practice was not inconsistent with GATT provisions, because it was designed to prevent deceptive advertising practices on all tuna products, whether imported or domestically produced.

Copies of the panel report are available on request from the GATT Secretariat.

and tuna products from Mexico, and a United States law regulating labelling of tuna products as «Dolphin Safe», which Mexico claimed discriminated against its products. The dispute settlement panel found in Mexico's favour on the embargo, but upheld the United States labelling law (Box 3). This case differs, it should be added, from the other four cases in that the GATT Council has deferred consideration of the panel's report for formal adoption (this was done on the basis of a joint request from Mexico and the United States, which are trying bilaterally to resolve the dispute).

3. «Domestic » environmental issues and world trade

In principle, domestic environmental problems – that is, those which do not involve physical transborder spillovers – can be resolved by purely domestic policy choices. Such choices are made on the basis of various considerations. For instance, a government evaluates the costs of immediate environmental damage prevention as against the longer-term costs of eventual clean-up if prevention is foregone. And it assesses, by whatever measures are available, the nation's own priorities regarding the trade-off between income and environmental quality.[40] These decisions are, of course, taken within the framework of the international environmental conventions to which it is a signatory.

[40] The absence of official (written) environmental regulations is not evidence of a lack of national environmental standards. As long as the quality of the environment has not fallen below the society's implicit environmental standards, the society is not likely to feel a compelling need to make its standards explicit through formal legislated regulations.

This holds for pollution caused both by production activities (such as the dumping of waste by-products into a lake or river) and by consumption activities (for example, the disposal of household waste or smog caused by automobile emissions). Governments also set health and safety standards for goods and services consumed in the domestic economy, reflecting their own evaluation of the risks and the correct approach to risk management (Box 2 above), as well as domestic regulations regarding the humane treatment of animals and procedures to follow in situations in which a species is threatened with extinction.

Economic analysis strongly supports the view that effective solutions to problems involving purely domestic environmental problems are not likely to involve trade policies that discriminate against imports. That is, judged on the basis of economic efficiency, there are almost no practical circumstances in which such a trade policy measure would be the «first best» tool for dealing with such problems.[41] There would appear to be, therefore, no implications for trade policy in general, or for the GATT in particular.

Nevertheless, despite the intrinsically domestic character of the problems and the policy choices to be made when pollution remains within borders, these issues have become internationalized. This has happened in two ways: one stems from a concern with the implications for firms' competitiveness, the other from attempts to assert jurisdiction over the environmental priorities of other countries.

The competitiveness issue

In discussions about international competitiveness a catching metaphor from sports is often used: is there a «level playing field»? The change in the world economy that propels most forcefully the unfair trade crusade is the rise in the trade-to-GNP ratios of many countries and the associated dramatic increase in the criss-crossing of foreign investments. As the globalization process has reduced the «economic distance» between countries, everyone tends to be in everyone else's backyard. This has led to more intense import competition in domestic markets and ever-fiercer export competition in third markets.[42]

While these trends are signs of success for the international trading system they are also fertile ground for allegations that unfair advantages are accruing to rivals – especially so given the subjectivity of «fairness», as that term relates to international competition. Firms which find their market shares and profits under competitive pressure are prone to label as unfair any source of cost advantage enjoyed by their foreign rivals.

Environment enters the picture

When it comes to the impact of environmental policies on production costs, demands by domestic producers for a «level playing field» often find support among environmental groups. One reason is their fear that if «lower» standards abroad regarding industrial pollution are perceived at home to be detrimental to competitiveness, they could give rise to political pressures to lower the standards at home. The competitiveness argument thus tends to bring industry and environmental lobbies together in attacking lower standards abroad. One notion is that the lower standards lead to «ecological dumping» – a choice of words which evidently seeks to forge a link between environmental policies and the «fair trade» debate.

In practice, if a lowering of domestic environmental standards is ruled out, demands for a level playing field take one or more of three forms:

– that the countries with lower environmental standards harmonise up to the higher standards in the importing country;

– that the imports of foreign products considered to be produced in «environmentally dirty ways» be subjected to special duties designed to offset the «unfair cost advantage» from the less strict standards;[43] or

– that the domestic industries be given subsidies to cover the added costs of meeting the higher standards.

[41] See, for example, Anderson (1992c), Lloyd (1992) and Snape (1992), as well as Bhagwati (1971) and Corden (1974). This conclusion rests on a general approach based on the fact that the policy instruments available to achieve a particular goal generally can be ranked from the most efficient to the least efficient, with the most efficient policy instrument being the one which operates directly on the source of the problem. Instruments further down the list – and trade policy is typically far down it – are more costly for two related reasons: first, because they are further removed from the source of the problem, and second, because they generally create undesirable «by-product distortions» in other areas of the economy.

[42] See, for example, Bhagwati (1991) and Porter (1990).

[43] On 25 April 1991 legislation was introduced in the United States Senate which would allow the imposition of special duties on imports produced under environmental standards that are less strict than those in the United States (*International Trade Reporter, 1.5.91*). More recently, the Chairman of the Finance Committee's International Trade Subcommittee proposed negotiating multilateral rules that would allow countries with high environmental standards to impose special tariffs on goods coming from countries with lower standards, in order to offset any unfair lower production costs (*Inside U.S. Trade,* 20.9.91).

Under existing GATT rules, to increase a country's tariffs on products originating in countries with less strict environmental policies is very difficult, for two reasons. First, if the tariffs in question are «bound» under the GATT – as is the case with nearly all tariffs of the industrial countries and with an increasing number of tariffs in developing countries – they cannot be raised except through an elaborate re-negotiation process. Second, and much more to the point, such tariff increases would violate GATT's «most favoured nation» (MFN) principle.

There are objective considerations which suggest that countries near the top of the development ladder are likely to have different priorities from countries further down the ladder, and that as a result they are likely to have and enforce stricter environmental standards. This appears to be borne out quite well in practical experience (see Box 4 for a specific example involving air pollution).[44]

The existence of less strict environmental standards in a lower income country, therefore, is not a sufficient basis for claiming that the environmental standards are «too low» or that the country is manipulating its environmental standards in order to improve the competitiveness of its producers. To substantiate such a claim, it would be necessary at the very least to demonstrate that the standards are even lower than would be expected on the basis of such factors as the level of per capita income and the characteristics of the physical environment.

Clearly, that would be very difficult to do. Moreover, the charge might also be aimed at highly developed countries in which stringent environmental standards may have been adopted in some areas but where, because of competitiveness considerations, governments have shied away from high standards in others.[45] In short, any move to impose unilaterally special duties on imports of goods and services produced in countries with less strict environmental standards is likely to be very divisive for the multilateral trading system in particular and international relations in general.

There are other problems with proposals to neutralize the effects of environmental policies on competitiveness. When the environmental problems are strictly domestic (do not involve physical spillovers onto other nations), the differences in policies are properly regarded as domestic choices reflecting, among other factors, the domestic trade-offs between income and environment. Seen thus, the differences in costs of production due to differences in standards can well be an additional source of gainful trade among these nations – as are any number of other natural advantages.[46]

It is also important to recognize that in principle there is no difference between the competitive implications of the type raised by different environmental standards and the competitive consequences of many other policy differences between countries. Differences between countries in tax and other policies toward savings and investment affect the capital stock, which means that countries encouraging capital formation may be enhancing their competitive advantage in capital-intensive industries. Large expenditures on education, and immigration policies which selectively encourage the immigration of skilled labour, will encourage competitive advantage in skill-intensive industries vis-à-vis countries whose policies do not favour the skilled. The extent of government support for science education can influence competitive advantage in high-tech industries.

The list is almost endless. Where is the line to be drawn if the competitive implications of differences in so many government policies are to become a source of demands for the neutralization of the consequences for trade?

It is time to look beyond the immediate context of each such demand – and environment is only the latest example – and to see the danger looming. Inevitably differences exist between countries stemming from their varying histories, social aspirations, political objectives and constraints, and

[44] See, for example, Baumol and Oates (1979, pp. 176-80; 1988, Chapter 15), Thompson (1973, p. 73), Tucker (1982, Chapter 1), Bernstam (1991) and Anderson (1992 a,b). A 1978 study by Walter and Ugelow, based on questionnaires sent to national officials in developed and developing countries, found that while the strictness of environmental policies varied within each group, the level of strictness was nonetheless higher on average in the developed countries.

Judging from reports in the press, it is in the rapidly growing economies – such as the Republic of Korea, and Taiwan – that environmental awareness and concern is the greatest among developing economies. In a recent paper, Chung (1991) summarizes the results of surveys taken in the 1980s by the Republic of Korea's Ministry of Environment. These record a sharp increase in public concern with environmental quality, and Chung concludes that the «data suggest that the income elasticity of demand for environmental preservation is quite high in Korea».

This is not to say that the average person with a lower income is less sensitive to environmental pollution than the average person with a higher income, but simply that the evidence suggests his or her spending priorities are different. Nor does it mean that the level of per capita income is the only factor that matters. It seems plausible that the demand for a cleaner environment could also be stimulated by such factors as increases in education and information (both positively correlated with per capita income), as well as reductions in the cost of pollution control. Ideas and information can spread quickly and diffusion is not always fastest in countries with high per capita incomes (see, for example, Weiner (1990) on compulsory primary education and banning child labour). Moreover, the declining cost of information on health and environmental effects of economic activities by itself is contributing to the adoption of stricter environmental standards by an ever-larger number of countries.

[45] For example, a recent article in the European edition of the *Wall Street Journal* (8 July 1991) described the concern among some United States legislators regarding the activities of the White House Council on Competitiveness in the environment area. According to the article,

> Among other things, the council has been instrumental – either directly or through informal talks within the executive branch – in blocking a proposal to require recycling at municipal incinerators; putting off a plan to discourage the incineration of lead batteries, a source of toxic pollution; and softening a proposal to improve visibility in the Grand Canyon by sharply reducing sulphur-dioxide emissions from a nearby power plant.

The article also quotes the chairman of the House Environment Subcommittee as stating that «The Council on Competitiveness has taken on the task of helping polluters block (the) EPA's efforts to write clean-air regulations with the unabashed purpose of protecting industry from the cost of regulation.» Other legislators, it should be added, strongly defended the activities of the Council.

[46] For more on the economics of this issue, see for example Anderson (1992c) and Bhagwati (1992).

Box 4 – Income and pollution

On *a priori* logic, economic growth need not worsen pollution. But, empirical evidence to prove the point is not always easy to find. A recent study suggests, however, that income growth has been associated with reduced pollution over significant ranges of per capita income.*

The study is based on data collected by the Global Environmental Monitoring System (GEMS). The GEMS project – a joint venture of the World Health Organization and the United Nations Environmental Programme – has monitored air quality in urban areas throughout the developed and developing world since 1976. Concentrations of sulphur dioxide and suspended particles are measured frequently by comparable methods in several different locations in each of the participating cities.

Analysis of the data related the levels of pollutants to various characteristics of the sites and cities (whether the site was situated in the city-centre or suburbs, whether the city was situated on a coast or not, its population density, and so forth) and to the level of per capita GDP in the country in which the city was located.

The chart below – depicting the variation in sulphur dioxide pollution attributable to variation in per capita income across countries and time – is typical of the study's findings. Concentrations of SO_2 have risen with income at low levels of per capita GDP, fallen with income at higher levels of per capita GDP, and eventually leveled off in the most advanced economies. The estimated turning point comes at about $5,000 (1988 US dollars). The conclusions for smoke pollution are much the same as those for SO_2 pollution.

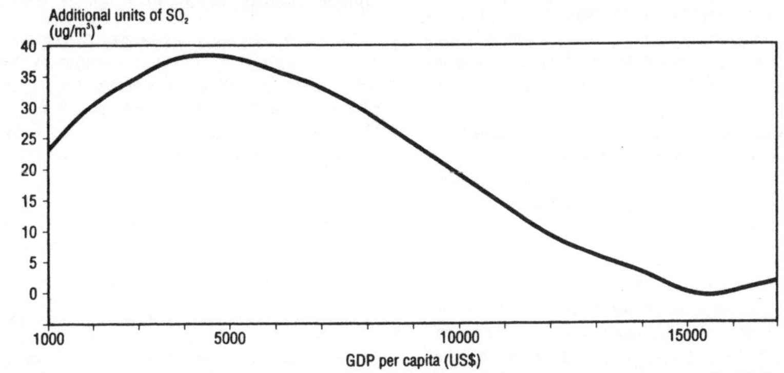

* Grossman and Krueger (1991). The numbers on the vertical scale indicate the amount of *additional* SO_2 pollution a city located in a country with a given level of per capita GDP is likely to have *relative to* a city in a country with a per capita GDP of $15,000-$16,000 (holding constant the values of the other explanatory variables, such as population density). Noting that there are only two countries in the sample with per capita incomes in excess of $16,000 (the United States and Canada), the authors observe that while the curve turns upward in this range, «this probably should not be viewed as strong evidence for a renewed positive relationship between national product and SO_2 pollution at high levels». (p. 15) The curve is based on 95th percentile figures (that is, 95 per cent of the observations during the year at each site recorded a lower level of SO_2 concentration, and 5 per cent a higher level of SO_2 concentration).

economic circumstances. These are differences that cannot simply be ironed out to produce a generalized policy structure that is a clone of policies favoured by other countries. To allow each contracting party unilaterally to impose special duties against whatever it objects to among the domestic policies of other contracting parties would risk an eventual descent into chaotic trade conditions similar to those that plagued the 1930s.

Competitiveness has always been a major concern of the GATT. The rules and disciplines regarding non-discrimination and national treatment are part of a broader concern with the stability and predictability of market access and with the need to ensure that trade can take place in an undistorted manner. At the same time, the contracting parties have been careful to consider as trade distorting only a limited range of measures. The fact that most policies and regulations differ from country to country has not been considered trade distorting, even though it is recognized that those differences can affect international competitiveness. To do otherwise would most likely bring chaos to the conduct of international trade.

Keeping the competitiveness issue in perspective

Empirical studies generally suggest caution in asserting that cost differences due to differences in environmental regulations are substantial, or that the trade and investment effects within particular industries are large.[47] There is, it is true, limited evidence of cross-border relocation by business firms in response to national differences in environmental policy climates.[48] A number of copper smelters, petroleum refineries, and asbestos, ferroalloy, and vinyl chloride plants reportedly were constructed abroad rather than in the United States for environmental reasons in the 1970s and early 1980s. Similarly, a number of petrochemical complexes and chemical plants originally slated for Germany and the Netherlands were evidently re-sited in Belgium, France, and Spain.[49] And some Japanese pollution-intensive investments were reportedly channelled to developing nations in Southeast Asia and Latin America. But the evidence, viewed on a world scale, certainly does not suggest massive relocation of investment.

Several factors may help explain why a significant redirection of foreign investment and trade in response to variations in environmental standards has not been observed. For example, site-shifting within countries was feasible and considered preferable in a number of instances. More importantly, reduced environmental costs from investing abroad almost certainly were often counterbalanced by other considerations, such as labour availability and quality, wage rates, supporting infrastructure, tax incentives, market size, transport costs, and country risk.

[47] See, for example, Siebert (1977), McGuire (1982), Walter (1982), Tobey (1990), Grossman and Krueger (1991) and Low (1991). When considering the impact of pollution controls on firms' production and investment decisions, two points need to be kept in mind: first, recalling the insights offered by the «effective rate of protection of value added» approach to the analysis of trade barriers, the pollution control costs should be related – data permitting – to value added rather than to total output or sales; and second, because the products of polluting industries tend to be highly standardized intermediate goods which are purchased in bulk by other industries, the price elasticity of demand as between different sources is likely to be high.

[48] Gladwin and Walter (1976), and Gray and Walter (1984).

[49] See Rauscher (1992) for a general analysis of the impact of regional trade liberalization on the environment and welfare of countries within and outside the region. Environmental aspects of the proposed North American free trade agreement are examined in Chapter 7 of Hufbauer and Schott (1992).

Firms are also finding that marketing their products to environmentally-conscious consumers as environmentally «safer» or «cleaner» can offset the impact of higher pollution abatement expenditures. The evident international diffusion of environment-consciousness suggests a ladder where those who incur the pollution abatement costs now are likely to be followed later by others. In turn, this means that investment expenditures in abating pollution, and technical changes and innovations induced by environmental policies (more stringent than elsewhere at any point of time), will position the leaders to compete more effectively in the future even if they reduce competitiveness now. In other words, for many sectors there is almost certainly a «J-curve» at work here: competitiveness declines initially but rises soon thereafter.[50]

Competitiveness: objecting to higher standards

So far the discussion has focused on competitiveness concerns triggered by measures designed to deal with production-related pollution. Competitiveness concerns of a different kind arise in connection with measures in the areas of consumption pollution and health and safety standards. Here the issue takes the form of complaints by foreign

[50] Environmental policies clearly stimulate trade in new goods, services and technology. For example, a sample of titles of recent press articles includes: «IBM to Become Green Consultants», «U.S. Environmental Firms Expected to Prosper», «New Dutch Muckrakers Aim to Make Profit Not Pollution» and «Growing Array of Firms in Europe Are Starting to Play the Green Card: Even Arms Manufacturers See Profit in Goods and Services With Environmental Angle». (*Financial Times*, 6.2.91; *Journal of Commerce*, 27.5.91; *International Herald Tribune*, 2.7.91; and the European edition of the *Wall Street Journal*, 12.7.91, respectively). See also Cairncross (1991). This view receives strong support from Michael Porter in his recent book *The Competitive Advantage of Nations* (1990, pp. 647-48):

> »Stringent standards for product performance, product safety, and environmental impact contribute to creating and upgrading competitive advantage. They pressure firms to improve quality, upgrade technology, and provide features in areas of important customer (and social) concern. ... Particularly beneficial are stringent regulations that anticipate standards that will spread internationally.»

Although this reasoning suggests that low income countries with less strict environmental standards are not likely to claim a big share of the expanding market for environmentally-related goods and services, firms in those countries could have an edge in developing new goods and services geared to the environmental needs of low income countries. For example, the private Brazilian firm Heliodinamica S.A. is currently engaged in the development of solar energy, as well as participating in the growth of the microelectronic industry by producing monocrystalline silicon electronic grade wafers. It also has the capability to design complete photovoltaic as well as solar energy hot water generation systems for industrial, commercial and residential applications. The company is presently exporting to India and other developing countries (as well as to Australia, Spain, the United Kingdom and the United States) and has been approached by other developing nations, including India, Argentina, Kenya, Pakistan, Nigeria, Peru and Bangladesh, with the aim of acquiring photovoltaic know-how (in 1990 Heliodinamica was chosen by the International Trade Center (UNCTAD/GATT), to receive ITC export development support).

Box 5 – Notifications related to the environment under the Agreement on Technical Barriers to Trade

Signatories to the Tokyo Round Agreement on Technical Barriers to Trade are required to notify other Parties through the GATT Secretariat of products to be covered by their proposed technical regulations. Each notification includes a brief indication of its objective and rationale if the regulation differs from international standards (or where international standards do not exist), whenever the regulations are expected to have a significant effect on the trade of other Parties. The protection of human health or safety, animal or plant life or health, or the environment are among the reasons foreseen in the Agreement for which Parties may find it appropriate to adopt technical regulations or standards which differ from international standards (where they exist).

Since the middle of the 1980s, protection of the environment has become more widely cited as an objective and rationale for applying technical regulations. Indeed, from 1980 to 1990, 211 notifications of this nature were made. A further 168 similar notifications were made, but citing grounds of public health and safety.

These notifications can be sorted into the following nine broad categories according to areas of environmental concern and the product(s) to which the technical regulations apply.

Area of environmental concern	Objective/Rationale	
	Protection of the environment	Public health and safety
1. Air pollution, particularly by exhaust emissions, including use of unleaded gasoline and alternative fuels for motor vehicles	71	9
2. Noise emissions: motor vehicles, boats, aircraft, tools and machinery, household appliances	20	24
3. Water pollution, particularly by detergents, marine paints and chemicals, feedstuffs for marine fish farming	12	0
4. Hazardous substances:	87	94
(a) General	5	1
(b) Ozone-depleting substances, particularly CFCs and halons, including implementation of the Montreal Protocol	16	0
(c) Polychlorinated phenyls (PCPs, PCBs and PCTs)	6	3
(d) Fertilizers, pesticides, insecticides, fumigants, and equipment for their application	20	51
(e) PVC, chlorine	3	0
(f) Heavy metals, particularly mercury and cadmium	3	6
(g) Other chemicals, toxic products and dangerous preparations	32	20
(h) Asbestos and related products	2	13
5. Waste: recycling and disposal, including batteries and accumulators	8	2
6. Transport of dangerous products	5	11
7. Radiation	3	6
8. Conservation of endangered species	3	0
9. Energy conservation	2	22
Total	211	168

producers that the importing country's regulations or standards are too strict, rather than – as with controls on production pollution – complaints by domestic producers that foreign standards are too lax.

Consumption pollution. Many countries have strict controls on pollution associated with consumption. Examples include emission control equipment on automobiles, packaging requirements to reduce solid waste, and limitations on the phosphate content of detergents. If any of the products which are causing pollution are imported, it is only reasonable that they be subjected to the same taxes or regulations as the domestic versions since the pollution stems from the consumption of the products (rather than their production) and therefore is independent of where they were produced.

In contrast to the production pollution case, where some producers have to comply with stricter environmental standards than others, in this case the domestic and foreign producers are on essentially equal footing - all of them have to equip their automobiles with catalytic converters, or supply their products in environmentally friendly packaging, or find benign alternatives to phosphates. The equality of treatment inherent in controls on consumption pollution substantially reduces, but does not eliminate, the potential for frictions over the impact on competitiveness.[51]

Health and safety standards. As environmental awareness has increased, the use of health and safety standards has become more common (Box 5). From the viewpoint of competitiveness, health and safety standards for domestically consumed goods and services have much in common with policies for reducing consumption pollution. In both cases, for example, there is no dispute over the need for the standards to apply equally to domestic and imported versions.

There are, however, important differences that make trade disputes over health and safety standards more likely and more intense than disputes over policies dealing with consumption pollution. These include the inherent uncertainty stemming from consumers' perceptions and psychology, the subjectivity of many standards stemming from the inexact nature of their scientific basis, differences between countries in their attitudes toward risk, and the keen sense of national sovereignty over health and safety issues. Nowhere has this been more evident than in the long-running dispute between the United States and the European Communities over the use of growth hormones in beef production. Precisely because of these unavoidable differences in the views of countries on the reasonableness, scientific or otherwise, of even nondiscriminatory trade restrictions imposed because of safety and health concerns, it is important to have available both multilateral disciplines and an impartial dispute settlement mechanism.[52]

The assertion of jurisdiction over environmental priorities in other countries

The internationalization of otherwise purely domestic environmental issues can come from an altogether different source, namely the assertion of a right to have a voice in determining production processes in other countries. This assertion of jurisdiction can be based on a variety of grounds: the preservation of endangered species that belong to a foreign habitat; an objection to foreign production processes which are considered cruel and inhumane to animals, such as the incidental killing of dolphins in purse seine nets or the use of leghold traps in fur trapping; or a general objection to the pollution of the natural environment in other countries even though the pollution remains entirely within their borders.[53]

Demands for suspending the trading rights of other nations when they do not comply with the expectations of external groups seeking to assert their own environmental priorities over others are often the consequence of these pressures. One recent example is the dispute over imports of Mexican tuna into the United States (see Box 3 above). In another, involving Japan's imports of the shells of hawksbill sea turtles (which are on the endangered species list), the United States threatened to ban imports from Japan of all animal products, including more than $300 million in fish, plus pearls. Japan responded by agreeing to ban importation of the shells by the end of 1992. It is doubtful, however, that such unilateral approaches can be generalized or sustained over a long period.

Just as it would be difficult to contain the competitiveness argument, it is difficult to think of a way to effectively contain the cross-border assertion of priorities. If governments suspend the trading rights of other nations because they unilaterally assert that their environmental priorities are superior to those of others, then the same approach can be employed on any number of grounds. Protectionists would welcome such unilateralism. They could exploit it to create embargoes, special import duties and quotas against rivals by enacting national legislation that unilaterally defines environmental agendas that other countries are likely to find unacceptable.

Changing the world trading rules so as to permit the suspension of trading rights of others by individual contracting parties, based simply on the unilateral and extra-territorial assertion of their environmental priorities, undoubtedly would be difficult because many countries would consider such a change to be a big step down a slippery slope. But this does not mean that alternative policy options are unavailable. There are always alternative means of influencing environmental objectives and practices in other nations' jurisdictions, short of using the unilateral trade weapon.

[51] A recent issue which has caused trade frictions involves the requirement that certain liquids – such as mineral water, soft drinks and beer – be retailed in returnable bottles. Foreign bottlers claim that such a requirement adds much more to their costs than it does to the costs of local bottlers. Other aspects of environmentally-motivated packaging regulations are also receiving increased attention (see, for example, the December 6, 1991 issue of the *Financial Times*).

[52] For more on this issue, see for example, Kozloff and Runge (1991).

[53] In cases where a domestic environmental issue is internationalized because jurisdiction over others' environmental practices and policies is being asserted, there is a formal similarity to the class of cases - examined in Part 4 below – where there are physical spillover effects across nations. For want of a better term, such cases could be described as involving psychological – as distinct from physical – transborder spillover effects. The «pain» from such spillovers can be as real as that from physical spillovers such as acid rain. On the other hand, there is an important difference as well. Such spillovers risk becoming, in practice, open-ended (a characteristic they share with demands for global harmonization of standards to avoid competitiveness effects). On the other hand, the number of potentially harmful physical spillovers is inherently more limited and hence they are far less likely to open up a Pandora's box of demands ranging well beyond environmental concerns.

One example is consumer-based actions, including the promotion of environmental labelling so that consumers can easily concentrate their purchases on products produced in what they consider to be environmentally safe ways.[54]

Again, there is nothing under customary international law and practices that would prevent nongovernmental organisations in one country from actively diffusing their environmental ideas to residents of other countries, so as to create popular support for changes in environmental policies. This would open the door, in turn, to inter-governmental cooperation and the creation of a multilateral agreement to set standards for the activity in question – surely a realistic option considering the 127 multilateral environmental agreements noted in Table 14.

A role for trade policies?

At the beginning of the analysis of «domestic» environmental issues, it was noted that it is very unlikely that using a trade measure would be the most efficient way of dealing with a domestic environmental problem. Is this conclusion altered by the evident internationalization of such problems?

When competitiveness concerns are at work, the answer is no. To use trade policies in this case (to neutralize the trade and investment effects of different national pollution standards) would be inefficient for a number of reasons. First, it would block an opportunity for a mutually beneficial expansion of trade. Second, it would not necessarily cause the other countries to alter their environmental policies. An added drawback is the fact that it could be the exports of the lower income countries that would be hardest hit. Ironically, by reducing their economic growth it may even reduce their ability and willingness to pay for environmental improvements.

What if the «domestic» issues are being internationalized instead by foreign groups or governments asserting their jurisdiction over the country's environmental priorities? Here the answer regarding the role of trade policies is different because the underlying issue is different. The primary question is not one of efficiency, but of enforcement. Is a trade measure the best instrument for getting an «uncooperative» country to change its environmental practices and policies?

Again the risk is that such a use of trade measures would lead to similar actions based on international differences in priorities in a wide range of other areas of economic and social life. And, since the trade measures would be necessarily discriminatory, their unilateral use would raise serious questions regarding their consistency with GATT obligations. Alternatively, if there is a shared consensus on a particular problem which leads to a multilateral agreement, the issue of using trade policy to ensure compliance by non-parties to the agreement may have to be addressed. This question is precisely the one that arises when environmental issues involving transborder physical spillovers are at issue.

4. Physical spillovers and multilateral cooperation

What if the pollution does not remain within the country's borders? Pollutants can contaminate a lake, river or sea that is shared by other countries, or cause acid rain in countries located far down wind. The discharge of carbon dioxide (CO_2) and CFCs into the atmosphere may cause global warming or ozone depletion. Once transborder or global physical spillovers become a serious concern to people in other countries, governments will seek to control or eliminate them.

Since what one nation does or does not do can be seen to impact directly on another's health, safety and domestic environment – even if the scientific evidence can be a matter of dispute – inter-governmental cooperation is likely to be essential to finding a solution. In addition to resolving disputes about the direction and magnitude of these impacts, both efficiency and equity considerations must be addressed as part of the solution.

Efficiency issues arise because if different countries have different costs of abatement, then global efficiency would require that those differences be taken into account in minimizing the cost of reducing the environmental damage. The contribution to be made by each country to the solution of the environmental problem would then vary, the incidence falling more where the costs of abatement are less. Equity issues arise, in turn, because each country's contribution to the globally efficient clean-up effort may not match either its share of the pollution being emitted or its ability to pay. In such instances, securing multilateral cooperation will not be easy, even if awareness of the environmental effects is acute and the necessity for a multilateral solution is agreed.

These issues, and the question of the appropriate role of trade policy in multilateral solutions, are illustrated by the debate over deforestation and global warming. Indeed, this is an area where there is evidence both of contemplated unilateral actions (such as proposals to use import restrictions to persuade countries to reduce the cutting of their tropical forests) and of efforts at multilateral cooperation.

Debates on global warming have stressed a connection between deforestation and the increase in carbon dioxide in the atmosphere. While it is generally accepted that reducing

[54] See OECD (1991) for a discussion of environmental labelling in the OECD countries.

CO_2 levels is likely to involve both reduced CO_2 emissions and action to slow or reverse deforestation, opinions differ as to which approach to emphasize. Countries which consume large amounts of fossil fuels (the principal source of CO_2 emissions) stress the need to preserve the forests. Other countries, concerned about foreign pressure to curtail the commercial exploitation of their forests, argue instead for a primary focus on reducing CO_2 emissions in high energy consumption countries.

One way of viewing this situation is that forests provide carbon absorption services to a world that is dumping increasing amounts of carbon into the atmosphere. Countries with a high ratio of forests to domestic carbon emissions effectively export carbon absorption services to the rest of the world. But because they are not paid for the exported services, they have little incentive to take such services into account when deciding how to use their forests. The result is most likely a faster rate of deforestation than would otherwise occur, which in turn creates concern among other countries.

Given that the countries which are home to large tropical forests are currently exporting carbon absorption services (and biodiversity services) to the rest of the world free of charge, there is a certain logic to the view that they should be offered compensation for reducing the rate of exploitation, rather than be threatened with restrictions on their exports. Yet in many importing countries the discussions have tended to focus on proposals to ban or tax imports of tropical timber in order to protect forests abroad.[55] Furthermore, as Box 6 suggests, even a complete ban on trade in tropical logs would have at best only a very minor effect on the pace of global deforestation. Compensation, in contrast, represents a general inducement for exporting countries to reform the full range of policies and activities which are currently depleting their forests.[56]

Imposing unilateral trade restrictions in pursuit of environmental goals is likely to be inefficient – as in the case just cited – and it raises problems of legal consistency and bad precedent for the trading system.

Trade measures in multilateral agreements

There can be little doubt that cooperative action among countries is superior to unilateral action in the case of a transborder spillover. This has implications for trade and trade policies because it is evident from existing and proposed agreements, as well as from recent bilateral developments, that governments and environmental interest groups see a role for trade policy in the promotion and enforcement of international cooperation on environmental issues.

Augmenting the incentives to participate can be important, especially when there is an urgent need for an agreement. There are at least four reasons why a country might decline, at least initially, to join other countries in trying to solve an environmental problem: first, the country may find the scientific evidence unconvincing, and therefore either not accept that there is a problem, or believe that the risks are exaggerated, or that the proposed remedies will be ineffective; second, it may accept that a particular environmental problem exists, but attach a low priority to solving it; third, it may disagree with the proposed allocation of responsibility, among the countries involved, for dealing with the problem; and fourth, the country simply may be trying to free ride on the efforts of other countries to solve the problem.[57]

Fortunately, the difficulty of recruiting participants generally is not an unsurmountable obstacle since environmental agreements typically do not require that all countries actively participate in order for the agreement to deal effectively with the problem in question. Many countries' activities make only a marginal contribution to a particular problem, which usually means they can make only a marginal contribution to solving it. On the other hand, lack of participation can raise political problems related to reciprocity and fairness.[58]

[55] It is sometimes argued that a general export ban on raw timber would enable the producing countries to achieve a target level of foreign exchange earnings at a lower resource cost because it would stimulate the domestic processing industry, thereby increasing the amount of domestic value added associated with a given level of wood exports. As far as economic growth and rising per capita incomes are concerned, this is an unpromising proposal since it could lead a country to expand industries in which it does not have a natural comparative advantage. Moreover, a ban on the export of unprocessed timber may not even increase foreign exchange earnings for any given level of timber harvesting (or, what is the same thing, maintain a constant level of foreign exchange earnings for a reduced harvest). It is true that an export ban may achieve a sufficient reduction in the domestic price of raw timber to make a previously uneconomic timber processing industry privately profitable. But that industry requires capital and labour in addition to logs. Insofar as these resources are drawn from other sectors producing tradable goods, the foreign exchange earned or saved by those other sectors will diminish. This may well more than offset any increase in foreign exchange earnings from the processing of timber. In other words, maintaining a target level of net foreign exchange earnings will generally require more, not less, harvesting of raw timber if a ban is imposed on log exports.

[56] On policies which encourage deforestation, see for example Repetto and Gillis (1988), Mahar (1989), Binswanger (1991), Grut, Gray and Egli (1991), Southgate, Sierra and Brown (1991), Pearce (1991, Chapter 8), and Cairncross (1991).

[57] See Blackhurst and Subramanian (1992) for additional details. See also Cooper (1989) for an examination of how a lack of agreement on scientific issues blocked international cooperation in controlling the spread of contagious diseases for nearly seventy years. Regarding the income distribution effects of alternative environmental policies on the distribution of income, see Lloyd (1992), Snape (1992), Winters (1992) and Hoekman and Leidy (1992). The free rider situation is considered in Piggott, Whalley and Wigle (1992) and Enders and Porges (1992).

[58] *See, for example, MacNeill, et al.* (1991 p. 106), and Hahn and Richards (1989).

Promoting cooperation on environmental issues

Promoting cooperation involves creating incentives which can be negative or positive. Negative incentives can take various forms, including discriminatory trade measures that penalize exports of products which are unrelated to the environmental problem at hand. In any individual situation, it may be tempting to rely on such measures. But it is very unlikely that such an approach would be a sustainable way of dealing over time with the variety of environmental issues facing the world community.[59] Among other things, by generating resentment and commercial frictions in the case at hand, it reduces the prospects for inter-governmental cooperation on future problems. This and other drawbacks no doubt explain why none of the existing multilateral environmental agreements contain provisions for discriminatory trade measures to be taken against unrelated products in the case of non-participation or defection. It may also be that governments recognise that their own economies are likely to be damaged by new trade barriers.

When cooperation is not voluntarily forthcoming, positive incentives are the best way to achieve sustained inter-governmental cooperation. Positive incentives can include offers of financial assistance and transfers of environmentally friendly technology directly related to the problem at hand, as well as more broadly based offers, for example, to increase foreign aid, to lessen debt problems and to make non-discriminatory reductions in trade barriers.[60]

It is useful to distinguish between (a) negative and positive trade measures applied to products which are unrelated to the environmental problem at hand, and (b) trade provisions applicable to related products. The distinction is useful because the scope for the latter type of trade measures is relatively limited, whereas there is essentially no limit to the use of trade measures on unrelated goods and services.[61]

Probably the best-known example of trade provisions in an environmental agreement are those in the Montreal Protocol on CFCs, though many earlier agreements covering fauna and flora contain similar trade provisions. The primary purpose of trade provisions in such agreements is to prevent trade between non-participants and participants from undermining the effectiveness of the agreement. Trade provisions often also have the incidental effect of treating non-participants less favourably than participants. Again, what distinguishes this from the use of negative incentives is that the products affected by the trade provisions are directly related to the environmental problem in question.

Trade provisions which are not essential to prevent the undermining of an agreement would be, of course, de facto negative incentives. Recalling the discussion of GATT rules in Part 2 above, it is also important to keep in mind that as long as participation in an environmental agreement is not universal, trade provisions will be, like negative trade incentives, discriminatory.

5. Protection and the environment

There are many examples, from many countries, of current government policies in such areas as agriculture, forestry, transportation and energy that have led to environmentally damaging behaviour.[62] It hardly needs to be added that the policy makers did not set out deliberately to create policies that would harm the environment. Nonetheless, that was the result. In such situations, policy reform would increase income and improve the environment at the same time. A case in point – and one which is particularly relevant to the interaction between trade and the environment – is agricultural policies in many of the developed countries.

Agriculture and the environment

There is little doubt that modern agricultural production often degrades the natural environment. Water, air and soil are subject to pollution by chemical fertilizers and pesticides, as well as by concentrations of manure from intensively farmed livestock. Chemical and pesticide residues in food are also a growing concern to consumers. When sloped land is ploughed, the result can be soil erosion and silting of downstream dams, and irrigation can create salinity problems. Would then the effect of trade liberalization be to accentuate these adverse effects or to diminish them?[63]

[59] Authors either fail to mention negative incentives when they discuss ways of encouraging participation in agreements or explicitly caution against the use of such measures. See Sand (1991), MacNeill, *et al.*, (1991), Chayes and Chayes (1991), Mohr (1990) and Stern (forthcoming).

[60] See, for example, MacNeill, *et al.* (1991, pp. 85-86).

[61] In practice, it may not always be easy to draw a line between unrelated and related products. For example, the Montreal Protocol on CFCs contains provisions covering not only trade in CFCs; but also imports of semiconductors that have been washed with CFCs and exports of CFC-related technology.

[62] In MacNeill *et al.* (1991, p. 33, footnotes omitted), the authors note that

> Energy subsidies can, and usually do, favour large supply projects and undermine funding for biomass and renewables. Tax concessions for logging, settlement, and ranching can accelerate deforestation, species loss, and soil and water degradation. Pesticide subsidies can promote excessive use and thereby threaten human health, pollute water, and increase the number of pesticide-resistant species. Subsidies for water-resource development and water use can lead to overuse for irrigation and industrial and municipal purposes.

They go on to cite specific examples from Germany, Japan, the United States, Canada, Brazil, Indonesia, China and India.

[63] See Eckholm (1976) and OECD (1989) for details on these and other environmental problems associated with agricultural production. A recently released joint study by two Dutch research institutes (RIVM and RIZA, 1991) concludes that much of the groundwater under farms in the European Communities is seriously polluted with pesticides and nitrates. According to the study, which fed samples from around the EC into a statistical model, farming is by far the most important source of the water pollution.

The answer to this question clearly depends in part on the impact of liberalization on the distribution of agricultural production around the world. Broadly speaking, current policy distortions in food production have led to high prices and other forms of support for farmers in most high income countries and low relative prices for farmers in many low income countries.[64] Reductions in farm support and increases in market access in highly-protected countries would cause a partial shift of agricultural production from farms in those countries to more competitive producers, including ones in the low income countries.[65] Clearly, this relocation of production would bring income gains to both groups of countries, with the gains being even larger if there were also policy reforms in the countries whose policies tax their farmers.[66]

The environmental effects of agricultural trade liberalization are more difficult to predict because it requires information on, for example, likely shifts in input use. However, several empirical studies offer insights into what might be expected to occur. One aspect concerns the use of chemical fertilizers and pesticides, which is highly correlated with prices received by producers. For example, countries with relatively low producer prices (such as Argentina, Australia and Thailand) use less than one-tenth the amount of chemical fertilizer per hectare used by high price countries in Europe.

Further, a study of rice production in several Asian countries in the late 1970s revealed that both fertilizer and pesticide use were highly correlated with the domestic producer price of rice. In the United States, land set-aside programs have caused farmers to devote more effort to increasing yields on remaining land, which almost certainly has involved increased per-acre use of chemicals. High support prices in land-scarce countries, backed-up by protection at the border, have a similar impact on chemical use. Moreover, support prices and deficiency payments in both North America and Europe have discouraged crop rotation and diversification which are natural alternatives to the intensive use of fertilizers.[67]

It is not unreasonable to conclude from such evidence that the positive environmental effects of the decline in the use of chemical inputs in the high income countries are likely to be substantially greater than the adverse environmental effects of the increased use of such inputs in the low income countries following a liberalization of world food trade. In other words, these several findings point to the conclusion that existing agricultural protection not only fails to help the environment, but almost certainly is an important source of environmental degradation.

There are fears that a partial shift of farm production from high income to low income countries would lead to large-scale deforestation. Such fears appear to be exaggerated. Evidence from Argentina and forest-abundant Brazil, for example, indicates that while the use of labour and capital equipment is reasonably responsive (and fertilizer use, starting from a low level, very responsive) to increases in prices received by farmers, the amount of land in cultivation is not. Recent studies of the agricultural sectors in China and Thailand point to the same conclusion.[68] In other words, in many countries most of the additional output would come from a more efficient use of existing farm land. It is also necessary to keep in mind that clearing land for farming in response to higher prices is only one of several causes of deforestation (see Box 6).

[64] In its *World Development Report 1986* the World Bank observes: Developing countries clearly tend to tax agricultural commodities and thus encourage imports and discourage exports ... Industrial countries, in contrast, tend to support domestic production and thereby inhibit imports and encourage exports ... Agricultural prices and costs are the key to the profitability of investment in agriculture. In industrial countries, resources are diverted from other sectors to agriculture. In developing countries, ... resources are diverted from agriculture to industry ... This makes developing countries export less and import more, even though they could become – if they are not already – efficient producers by making investments to acquire the necessary technology. (pages 11, 125)

As Krueger *et al.* (1988) demonstrate, most of the «taxation» of agriculture in the eighteen developing countries in their study occurred indirectly as a result of (i) an overvalued exchange rate, and (ii) industrial protection which depressed the prices of agricultural commodities relative to those of nonagricultural tradable goods.

[65] The following discussion of liberalizing trade in food products draws heavily on Anderson (1992a, b), where interested readers can find a more detailed development of the analysis as well as the supporting empirical data.

[66] Many food-importing low income countries would be among the gainers, either because they switch to the status of food exporters at the higher relative price of food or because their gains from higher domestic food prices (which attract labour and capital into agriculture and away from less efficient but protected manufacturing industries) more than offset the decline in their terms of trade. Those current net-food importers which would not become food exporters would, nonetheless, experience an increase in food self-sufficiency (see Anderson and Tyers, 1991).

[67] See Anderson (1992a,b), Avery (1991, p. 216) and Barbier and Burgess (1991).

[68] The study by Fan (1991) found that in China during the 1965-85 period – when real prices received by farmers increased very substantially – none of the growth in farm output was attributable to land expansion and only 8 per cent to increased labour use. A quarter of the output growth was attributed to increased fertilizer, a quarter to the introduction of the household responsibility system from the late 1970s, one fifth to greater machinery use and one sixth to technological change (Fan, 1991). Phantumvanit and Panayotou (1990) estimated that for the period 1962 to 1989, the elasticity of demand for cultivated land with respect to the lagged price of agricultural crops was only 0.08. That is, a 10 per cent aggregate output price increase would result in less than a 1 per cent increase in cultivated area.

Box 6 – Restricting trade in tropical timber

One especially unconvincing case for trade restraints on environmental grounds involves tropical timber. A number of groups have called for export or import restraints on tropical timber because of various concerns, including the effect of commercial logging in alienating the land of aboriginal peoples living in tropical forests, in contributing to the loss of genetic diversity of timber species and to the potential extinction of plants and animals, and in reducing the absorption of $CO2$ from the atmosphere.

Attention to date has focused on tropical log trade. To what extent would a general ban on trade in tropical logs reduce deforestation? The answer is: hardly at all, for the following reasons:

– only 0.5 per cent of log production in developing countries is exported in log form;[1]

– a ban on log exports would simply encourage logs to be sawn and perhaps processed into panels before being exported from developing countries (but with more wasting of timber and other resources because of relatively poor sawmill technology and management);[2]

– even if a ban on trade were extended to include sawn wood and wood panels made from tropical logs, it would have only a minuscule effect on felling, because even the sum of log plus processed timber exports amounts to less than 1 per cent of the trees felled in developing countries;

– through lowering the price of tropical timber, such a ban would reduce the incentive to protect existing forests and to establish new ones in developing countries;

– four-fifths of trees felled in developing countries are used as fuel directly or in the form of charcoal. This is largely because people are too poor to be able to purchase other fuels such as kerosene and need, in any case, to clear land (often slash-and-burn style) to be able to produce food for their growing population in the absence of enough paid employment opportunities; and

– little more than half the world's timber comes from tropical countries, so attention also needs to focus on forest management in industrial countries.

Should a developing country nonetheless take account of the concerns of other (including industrial) countries when determining its policy on forests? A country with a low ratio of carbon emissions per hectare of forest is effectively exporting, free of charge, «carbon absorption services» to the rest of the world. However, since it is not paid for those services (and for maintaining wilderness areas and a diversity of species), it has little or no incentive to take such services into account in deciding on the optimal management of its forest resource. The argument that it should maintain its forests because «they belong to the world at large» is unpersuasive to many people. After all, the argument goes, almost 80 per cent of the greenhouse gas emissions resulting from human activities are generated in industrial countries, so it is those countries which should look to solutions to global warming rather than ask lower-income countries to provide the solution.

Reducing emissions of greenhouse gases is obviously the most direct way to reduce the threat of global warming. But if deforestation is considered undesirable for other reasons, then some form of international agreement and possibly compensation to lower-income countries which are home to large forests needs to be considered. Perhaps the most effective way to slow the deforestation of tropical countries, however, is to promote employment and income growth for rural people in those countries, for example through economic policy reform at home and access to markets abroad.

[1] These and other trade data are taken from the Food and Agriculture Organisation's *Forest Products 1978-1989*, Rome, 1991.

[2] In 1978 more than 95 per cent of Indonesia's wood exports were in the form of logs, whereas now more than 90 per cent are in the form of sawn wood and wood panels. In its 10 August 1991 edition, *The Economist* noted that Swedish sawmills use 98 per cent of a tree whereas Malaysian mills use only 40 per cent.

Liberalizing protectionist agricultural policies in the high income countries is therefore likely to (i) cause the world's food to be produced with fewer chemicals, which in turn would reduce chemical residues in food and in the natural environment; and (ii) have at most a very modest impact on the rate of deforestation. It would also increase the availability of land for recreational and aesthetic uses – including the replanting of forests – in several high income countries as marginal farm land was taken out of production. Thus, in all likelihood there would be a substantial increase in global environmental quality following agricultural trade liberalization, even if no new environmental policies were introduced. Policy reforms in lower income countries which reduce the taxation of agriculture and improve forest management would add to these world-wide environmental gains.[69]

Interaction among environmental and trade policies

The situation in agriculture illustrates the general point that current restrictions on international trade can be bad for the environment. As regards future policies, there is concern

[69] Assuming high consumer prices for coal are maintained in high income countries, a similar environment-improving outcome is highly likely if global coal trade were to be liberalized (Anderson 1992a). An example from the manufactures area is discussed in Feenstra (1988). He shows how the voluntary export restraint agreement between the United States and Japan on automobiles led to an increase in the relative importance of heavier, less fuel efficient automobiles in the United States. See Birdsall and Wheeler (1991) for an analysis which concludes that openness to trade and foreign investment has been associated with less pollution intensity in Latin American countries.

that the growing interest in the linkages between trade and the environment brings with it a potentially serious source of new protectionism. More specifically, the past success of particular producer groups in manipulating domestic environmental policies to benefit themselves at the expense of both the rest of the economy and ultimately even the environment, and the successes of inefficient producers in obtaining protection against imports, suggests that the risks of inefficient policies being implemented in the area where environment and trade intersect are especially great.[70]

As was noted in Part 3, adoption of an environmental policy can cause direct pressure for additional protection, as the domestic industry may now claim that there is no longer a «level playing field». Alternatively, pressure may be exerted to amend existing unfair trade legislation to take into account asymmetric environmental regulatory regimes. In addition, firms may find that the impact of new environmental regulations on their profitability increases the likelihood that they can obtain protection under unfair trade laws or rules for emergency protection.[71] In the case of environmental, health and safety problems associated with consumption (rather than production), standards may be «strategically» manipulated by producer groups whose main aim is to put foreign rivals at a competitive disadvantage.[72]

The issue of political support for inappropriate policies becomes even more acute when protectionists attempt to draw environmental groups into implicit or explicit alliances. For example, a particular industry which is resigned to the inevitability of stricter environmental controls may try to avoid or resolve conflicts with environmental groups by indicating a willingness to clean-up, provided they are allowed to design the «fair» policy for doing so (there are elements of this in the proposals for countering so called «ecological dumping»). A similar process can be at work when the proposal is for tougher product standards. When this happens, it can substantially reduce the prospects of the appropriate environmental policy being adopted, since the policy which ranks first on efficiency grounds often ranks near the bottom of the industry's list of «fair» policy options.[73]

The dilemma for those concerned with the environment is that the political support of the affected industry for an economically costly environmental policy may increase the probability that at least some policy will be adopted. If this is the case, it may appear reasonable, in the short-term, for environmental groups to support the less appropriate environmental policy, despite the risk that their support of a higher cost policy will work against the environment in the medium and long term.

As has already been noted, non-discriminatory domestic policies offer the most efficient approach to dealing with nearly all environmental problems. Interference with trade is seldom, if ever, the first-best way of achieving a particular domestic environmental objective. If the efficient policy is believed not to be politically feasible, and the less efficient (protectionist oriented) policy is blocked by the GATT rules, the GATT rules can easily appear to be «environmentally unfriendly». But revising GATT rules to «legalize» inferior policies has serious drawbacks. Along with setting a bad precedent – the slippery slope argument – it would also remove an important incentive for countries to adopt appropriate domestic environmental policies.

[70] See, for example, Krueger (1974), Bhagwati (1982), Hillman (1989) and Magee, Brock and Young (1989) and the references cited there in. For an analysis of how the emergence of environmental lobbying groups can affect trade policy outcomes, see Hillman and Ursprung (1992). See also Van Grasstek (1991).

[71] See Hoekman and Leidy (1992). See also Finger and Murray (1990), Kaplan (1991) and Bovard (1991) on the point that the injury criteria established under existing legislation offer substantial discretion in evaluating the health of an industry.

[72] For a general discussion see Salop and Scheffman (1983).

[73] The history of the United States Clean Air Act provides a concrete example of the interaction between producers and environmental groups in the case of domestic environmental policies. See Ackerman and Hassler (1981), Maloney and McCormick (1982), Yandle (1989), Tietenberg (1988), Daly and Mayor (1986) and S. Fred Singer, «The Answer on Acid Rain Falls on Deaf Ears», *Wall Street Journal,* 6.3.90. Commenting on another example, involving the decision to build a major desalting plant in Arizona, Kneese (1988, pp. 7 and 13) notes that the option selected was most likely «about 15 to about 150 times» as costly as an available alternative, leading him to observe later in the paper that «there simply was no effective advocate for efficiency in the loop, and the result is a wildly uneconomic approach to the problem of reducing salinity in the Mexicali Valley.»

Part V
Settling Disputes

[20]

DISPUTE SETTLEMENT AND CONFLICTING TRADE AND ENVIRONMENT REGIMES

*James Cameron**

I. INTRODUCTION

Dispute settlement has become the ground upon which the trade and environment conflict is being fought. The failure of the Committee on Trade and Environment (CTE) to produce policy solutions at the First Ministerial Conference in Singapore has left the Dispute Settlement Body (DSB) with no new principles or rules to decide the real issues States seek to settle through law.

This short paper seeks to do three things: (1) describe the continuing conflict between the regimes; (2) analyse that conflict from a substantive and procedural law perspective; and (3) propose potential policy solutions. The paper has been strongly influenced by the current dispute known as the *Shrimp/Turtle Case* which, in many ways, is emblematic of the conflict. An analysis of the arguments presented in an *amicus brief* by WWF[1] forms the centrepiece of the paper.

As I hope to make clear, the dispute between Thailand, Malaysia, India and Pakistan against the US on shrimp and turtles can be characterised as a conservation dispute; even a conservation and development dispute. It has been characterised as a trade dispute — the WTO is now seized of the case, a Panel formed, briefs submitted, oral arguments made and an interim decision delivered. On the basis of the interim report, which remains confidential and is not widely available for comment, the US has failed to succeed with their environmental justification for the measure, which was held to be so unacceptable to the trade regime that it did not even warrant consideration under the Article XX (b) and (g) jurisprudence.

The decision, when made final, will almost certainly be appealed and although it is unlikely that the Appellate Body (AB) will find in favour of the US they may choose to apply different reasoning so that the US can take something away from the dispute which could go some way to appeasing a very unhappy domestic conservation community.[2] I am afraid this decision is going to be interpreted as another assault on democratically produced conservation law by the unelected decision-makers of the

WTO. It could not come at a worse time given the impending fast-track negotiations in the US.[3] The arguments which follow reveal my own sense of frustration that this case has become another "bad news" story for the trade and environment debate. It could have been otherwise. Perhaps it still could, with a very bold AB decision.

II. JURISDICTION

When conflicts arise between legal systems in private international law, there is a rational, if complex, system for determining which tribunal should hear the dispute. International law does not have such a system. It depends, or has traditionally depended on the consent of States to choose whether to use a tribunal at all and if so which one. Where there are conflicts between obligations freely undertaken by States in differing regimes — such as trade and environment — the tribunals operating under international law make use of the Vienna Convention on the Law of Treaties. The WTO has done this regularly in order to come to a decision on matters such as interpretation of the GATT and Covered Agreements. There are frequent references to Article 31 in particular. It is perfectly possible that the practice of using the Vienna Convention for interpretation be extended to assist in determinations of compatibility between trade and environment regimes; Article 31(3)(c) comes to mind.

However these rules were not designed to allocate jurisdiction. They cannot adequately deal with the circumstances such as the *Shrimp/Turtle Case* where obligations arise through both treaty and custom and where there are competing jurisdictions available to hear the case were it to be characterised as a conservation law case or even a mix of competing public international law obligations. Private international law has rules governing the characterisation of the dispute — is it contract or tort? What is the proper law of the contract or tort? What proportion of the dispute is governed by the foreign law and what by the domestic law? These rules complement the jurisdictional disciplines which enable a judge in one jurisdiction to decline to hear the case, to determine that there is some other clearly more appropriate forum or to receive the case and hear arguments in the foreign law as proved by witnesses.

Public international law, so dominated by the doctrine of consent, has not developed as such a system. If you believe all that matters is that States be free to choose whether and where they settle disputes simply because they are sovereign, then any irrationality in the allocation of judicial resources or legal competencies is accepted, because the sovereign creates the law and is not subject to it. I think we can do better than that.

States, representing the generalised will of their citizens, acting on their behalf, create layers of obligation in international law. Sometimes there are clear legal hierarchies, such as between a treaty and UN General Assembly Resolutions but often the layers overlap like cloth producing a different colour and texture. A tribunal seized of a dispute might be given a choice by the international legal system either to consider the richness and density of the overlapping layers or rationally separate them out, what it should not be entitled to do is ignore the existence or relevance of one of the layers — in this case environmental obligations.

The problem for the environmental regimes is compounded because they lack the power of the WTO, specifically, the WTO's Dispute Settlement Understanding (DSU) which compels Members to settle (trade) disputes. The DSU has been astoundingly popular with States, in part, because it offer rewards for use. You can win in the WTO and get economic and political benefits which you can cash in. The system is fast and effective. Rules are generally respected, decisions whether by Panel or the AB are adhered to. There is no comparable mechanism in multilateral environmental agreements (MEAs). The Montreal Protocol has a compliance mechanism which works but it does not adjudicate in the same way the AB does. Nor do its decisions have such far-reaching social and economic ramifications as the body of decisions which would emerge from the WTO in a year.

There are good reasons to explain why various MEAs have the dispute mechanisms they have, but none that I have seen or heard to explain why we do not have an international agreement to avoid the kind of forum shopping which private international law has taken such strides to limit or prevent.

III. DISPUTE SETTLEMENT REGIMES

MEAs have their own compliance and dispute settlement regimes designed for their own purposes. They match the nature of the obligations and the range of interests of the Parties. It should be remembered that the major MEAs have significantly more parties than the WTO. Many of the obligations are not subject to judicial application — they are simply too general, leaving too much discretion to Parties on how they choose to implement. There is no point having a judicial or quasi-judicial dispute settlement mechanism if your rules are not justiciable. The MEAs, focused as they are on grand objectives, like stabilising concentrations of greenhouse gases in the atmosphere, are more likely to offer carrots than sticks if countries fail to meet their obligations, at least for now. This will change over time as the obligations get tougher and clearer. The Kyoto Protocol to the Climate Change Convention is an important step in that direction. If the specialised regimes have their own specialised dispute settlement systems, the norm in MEAs is to have some way out to the International Court of Justice (ICJ). It has never been used but it is available. The Law of the Sea Convention (LOSC) has its own Tribunal in Hamburg, now finally receiving cases, where States have options including arbitration, use of the Tribunal or the ICJ. Since the LOSC has a significant conservation and marine pollution jurisdiction it could conceivably attract quite a range of disputes from other potential environmental fora.

Depending on how the dispute was characterised, the parties to the *Shrimp/Turtle* dispute could have made use of the dispute settlement regimes in APEC, the Convention on Biological Diversity (CBD) (provided the US, as a participating non-party, had submitted to its jurisdiction), the LOSC Tribunal (provided the US submitted), the WTO, the Court of Arbitration or even the ICJ. They could have constructed their own form of mediation or used arbitration. They could have chosen to arbitrate under the auspices of the WTO or the CBD. The complainants chose the WTO, no doubt because the forum would accept the characterisation of the dispute as a trade dispute but also because of the compulsory jurisdiction[4] between Members, the efficiency of the process and the availability of sanctions. The environmental regime cannot compete with this list of attributes.

The Kyoto Protocol on Climate Change's dispute settlement regime does not bear any resemblance to the WTO. At the moment it is woefully inadequate to deal with existing commitments, let alone those that will follow agreement on the trading mechanisms for those implementing[5] commitments to reduce greenhouse gas emissions by 5.2 per cent from a 1990 baseline. As the rules get clearer and closer to carrying real economic cost, pressure will mount for sanctions to be used to punish those that cheat. Unless the climate change regime creates a plausible system for settling conflicts of that nature, or allocates the responsibility to some other respected tribunal, there will be a contest between jurisdictions. If the law cannot offer a sure and a certain place to settle the dispute, the risk will rise of more brutal and less ordered solutions being used. Law is, after all, designed to transform natural power into legal power. If it dodges the responsibility of creating the right forum for settling conflicts of this kind it will have abdicated its essential function to keep the peace. What the environmental community must pay attention to in this instance is that the WTO will remain open and available to settle trade related climate change disputes, if countries choose to make claims in the language of WTO law.

IV. INTEGRATION

Given the powerful lure of the WTO for dispute settlement, what prospect is there of environmental issues, of fact and law, being considered and applied by the tribunal? There is some experience in the new, post 1994, system. In the *Reformulated Gasoline Case*, the AB stated (1) that the GATT "should not be read in clinical isolation from public international law"; (2) that "Article XX contains provisions designed to permit important State interests — including the protection of human health as well as the conservation of exhaustible natural resources — to find expression"; (3) that clean air was an exhaustible natural resource; (4) the balance between affirmative commitments under Articles I, III, and XI and the policies and interests embodied in the exceptions listed in Article XX needed to be interpreted and judged on a case by case basis; and (5) that the modern test of "relating to" in Article XX is that the measure must be more than inadvertently aimed at conservation of exhaustible natural resources.

Article 31(3)(c) of the Vienna Convention says:

> *There shall be taken into account, together with the context* [emphasis added]
> (c) any relevant rule of international law applicable in the relations between the parties

Surely this includes environmental obligations in a trade context — why wouldn't it? Why wouldn't established principles of international environmental law or obligations drawn from MEAs be relevant? The AB has shown itself capable of applying the Vienna Convention for very detailed questions of interpretation in order to decide disputes between States, and it is therefore perfectly capable of applying the same skills to the enterprise anticipated by the drafters of Article 31(3)(c).

In the *Beef Hormone Case*[6] the AB made extensive use of general principles of international law, and in particular, the principle of *in dubio mitius*[7], to aid their interpretation of the scope of the EU's discretion to apply its own health and environment standards even though they were higher than international standards. It is in effect a deference test and one which is wise for the WTO to adopt. Additionally, the AB embarked on a review of the precautionary principle, which whilst not resulting in any authoritative ruling on its status in international law did end with a determination that the principle was incorporated in Article 5 of the Sanitary and Phytosanitary (SPS) Agreement and had general application in the trade regime.

I take these rulings to represent the first steps towards integration of environmental policy and law through the practice of the WTO DSU. The Preamble of the WTO Agreement and the definite trend of contemporary international law expects such a step. The CTE should be tracking these events and asking itself why it finds it so hard to make policy recommendations when they do not have to deal with the exigency of disputed facts. It could be so much clearer for the DSU if the Committee on Trade and Environment (CTE) could craft a rule which would update Article XX and deal expressly, and at the very least, with the implementation of MEAs. In a sense the diplomatic failure of those who have argued for reform of the WTO rules leaves the DSB both free and exposed when making judgments on contentious trade and environment matters.

V. THE *SHRIMP/TURTLE CASE*: FACTS AND LAW

The *Shrimp/Turtle* dispute is a recent iteration of the well known *Tuna/Dolphin* cases. In this case, India, Pakistan, Malaysia and Thailand have complained to the WTO that Section 609 of the US Endangered Species Act violates various provisions of the GATT 1994 (Articles I, XI and XIII). This section effectively places an import ban on shrimp and shrimp products not harvested by trawlers using methods which protect marine turtles from incidental drowning. The legislation requires the use of Turtle Excluder Devices (TEDs) in shrimp fisheries where shrimp are exported to the US market.

It is difficult to discuss a case which has not yet been resolved. The story is not over and cannot be told now without a tone of advocacy entering into the text. There is no doubt that it is contentious, and a dangerous case for the WTO as an institution. A great deal of scientific analysis, political capital and legal argument has gone into establishing a rule to protect a much honoured animal which people care passionately about. The debate about safeguarding the various species of turtle at the centre of this dispute cannot be bounded by nationality or sovereignty. Interests cannot be neatly bundled up into the political and legal units we call States. The WTO has been presented with a communications challenge of some magnitude to deal with the sustained criticism which will be launched at the organisation, and the trade negotiators, from its Members, if the complainants win and legislation designed to protect turtles from extinction is held to be incompatible with the WTO rules.

Having said that, these are the essential facts, from my point of view, in the dispute:

(i) Sea turtles are highly migratory animals that do not respect national boundaries. Turtles travel between the complainant States.

(ii) Sea turtles are a global resource and/or part of the common heritage of humankind, and/or subject to the stewardship of all international societies depending on one's particular perspective, but they are not wholly and exclusively the resource of any single State.

(iii) Sea turtle mortality rates increase rapidly during the shrimping season.

(iv) There is a complex interaction between the gestation period for turtles, the maturation period, the loss of adult turtles and the rate of decline of turtle populations.

(v) Conservation programmes which provide protected coastal habitats and fishing restrictions as well as breeding programmes are of value but not sufficient to prevent the further decline of turtle populations.

(vi) The turtle excluder device is inexpensive and effective. It has a proven ability to save turtle life and does not affect the shrimp catch, which remains economically viable.

(vii) In order to further assuage concerns about any economic impact of TEDs, these devices have been provided by the US Government through their aid programme and US corporations trading in shrimp have offered to provide such devices free of charge to their suppliers including those within the complainants' jurisdictions.

In my view the US legislation is clearly related to the conservation of exhaustible natural resources. The measures chosen by the US have been made effective in conjunction with restrictions on domestic production or consumption. The US shrimp fishery has been under an obligation to use TEDs for approximately six years and has done much to develop the technology to the point at which it has become cheaper and more effective.

The facts established above make it clear beyond doubt that the measure is necessary to protect turtles from shrimp fisheries. There is no more effective alternative than the application of the TED, a measure which is designed to protect a global resource and to remove any incentives provided by access to a large market for States to ignore their obligations under international law by failing to protect such a resource. The international community has determined the necessity of taking steps, including trade measures, to protect sea turtles and whilst it has not authorised the US measure through some specific decisions agreed multilaterally, the US has acted in a manner consistent with its obligations and has taken reasonable measures to reflect the will of the international community.

There is nothing in the reasoning of the AB in the *Reformulated Gasoline Case* which would inhibit the US from proclaiming the necessity of the measure designed to protect turtle health, even outside US jurisdiction, or its desire to legislate for the conservation of a living resource threatened with extinction. The AB will however look closely at the headnote to Article XX and judge whether the US has acted in a manner which is transparent, justifiable and not in any way arbitrary. When it does consider the headnote or *chapeau* it will do so in order to judge whether the measure which fits within subparagraphs (b) or (g) is arbitrary or unjustifiable, not whether to consider the environmental arguments advanced at all.

Given the facts stated above it is clear beyond doubt that there is an urgent situation requiring significant intervention by the international community, including the actions of individual states, to prevent a valued species from disappearing in consequence of, in large part, shrimp fisheries. The evidence put forward by the complainants as to the spiritual and/or cultural worth of the turtle adds a layer of value to that identified by the US legislature in promulgating the legislation which is subject to complaint.

International law, including conventional law (MEAs such as CITES, CBD and the Bonn Convention on Migratory Species) and customary law has made sea turtles an object of protection. International law recognises that sea turtles are an endangered species and requires States to supervise and control activities within their jurisdiction which might undermine the conservation status of sea turtles. The harvesting of shrimp itself comes with obligations to conserve incidentally affected species.

It cannot reasonably be argued that fulfilling an obligation arising under customary international law, requiring consistent and uniform usage over a period of time, through a responsible and effective measure, could be arbitrary or unjustifiable. The arbitariness argument would have to rest on the manner of implementing the law.

The US has invited co-operation to protect these species through the use of TEDs. Three of the complainant States (Malaysia, India and Pakistan) have refused to participate in any multilateral process to promote the use of TEDs to protect sea turtles.

Here are the difficulties for policy makers, Panellists, or Members of the AB who would like to accept this line of argument — the US is not a party to the CBD or the LOSC so it is not a straight conflict between MEAs and the WTO. The irony is that the complainant countries are all parties to both. The US went too far in requiring certification to be carried out by their own inspectors — this kind of action offends. The US has an unfortunate history of extending the reach of its national law to other jurisdictions (the EU has done the same in many trade-related instances) and developing countries are right to be concerned about the strong forcing requirements on relatively weaker States which has the effect of closing markets for their goods.

VI. POLICY RECOMMENDATIONS

Given the desire of the US importers of shrimp to comply with Section 609 and their readiness to make TEDs available from their own resources, it would have been productive to have considered whether mediation would have been a more appropriate way to settle this dispute. It does seem possible that gathering all of the interested parties around a table, especially given the earnest commitments to turtle conservation manifest in the complainants briefs before this tribunal, and the desire, indeed established practice, of the US to make available aid and expertise to transfer the technology which was the subject of the US law, it is possible that a mediator could have succeeded in finding a just and rational settlement of this dispute.

Equally, given the discussion within APEC, as to the desire of many of the Asian members of that economic grouping to settle disputes by mediation rather than through adversarial dispute settlement procedures it is surprising that none of the complainants suggested making use of that form of settlement given that the defendant was also a member of APEC.

There are risks for all parties in going to the quasi-judicial AB to ultimately settle this dispute. The ruling is capable of laying down principles which would not be in the interest of either "side" of this case. The ruling could extend the reasoning of the *Reformulated Gasoline Case* to include general principles of law and principles of international environmental law. The ruling could narrow the scope for exception departing from the *Reformulated Gasoline Case* in a way that would make it less likely that States would be able to legislate to protect the environment and natural resources by use of measures which are either directly or indirectly trade related. It would have seemed sensible to concentrate resources on securing a settlement which enabled shrimp to be exported to the US of America and turtles to increase their chances of survival.

The WWF *amicus brief* itself demonstrates a willingness by non-governmental organisations to participate in dispute settlement processes. It does, I hope, demonstrate that there is some value in hearing the arguments both on scientific and legal grounds which NGOs are capable of representing. It is striking to note that following the WWF brief the WTO Panel organised the presentation of evidence to the Panel on the conservation facts from the experts that WWF had used.

WWF has previously called for a right of access to the DSU, a matter which ought to be the subject of discussion and thereafter negotiation in the context of the review of the DSU which takes place next year.

VII. CONCLUSION

Although the discussion in the CTE would not have produced a rule which could have been straightforwardly applied to resolve the particular facts of this case, nonetheless, an amendment of Article XX to include specific reference to "measures taken pursuant to" MEAs would have provided a better legal backcloth for the institutions of the DSU to work with.

There is a need for a rational system for distributing jurisdiction amongst competing regimes in international law. We need to learn from the private international law system and find ways of characterising disputes so as to choose the most appropriate forum. We need to do this not least to protect the WTO from taking on cases which it should not hear. The WTO/DSB ought to have ways of refusing jurisdiction or requiring mediation or arbitration instead of traditional trade dispute settlement.

Additionally, the further integration of environmental law and policy into the decision making process of the WTO would help build trust in the decision taken by trade tribunals within the environmental community.

NOTES

* LLB (Lon); LLM (Cantab); FRSA; FRGS; Barrister; Director FIELD (Foundation for International Environmental Law and Development); Of Counsel to Baker & McKenzie, Chicago; Professor, College of Europe, Bruges; Lecturer in law at SOAS, University of London; Director Global Environment and Trade Study (GETS); Member, Green Globe Task Force, advising Robin Cook MP, Foreign Secretary, UK, on global environmental policy; Member IUCN Commission on Environmental Law; Chairman, Cameron May Publishers.

[1] This is available from WWF International, Gland, Switzerland.

---

[2] The Panel Report was issued on 15 May 1998. Relevant sections of the Report can be found in Annex 3. The decision is currently in appeal.

[3] See S. Charnovitz, "US Fast Track and the Environment", Annex I in this publication.

[4] Is it rational that States should choose compulsory jurisdiction for trade disputes and not for environmental disputes?

[5] Annex I Parties — essentially, OECD plus Russia, Ukraine and the rest of the former Soviet controlled countries of Central Europe, such as the Czech Republic and Hungary, who are described as countries that are undergoing a process of transition to a market economy.

[6] *EC Measures Concerning Meat and Meat Products (Hormones)*, AB-1997-4, see *ITLR* Vol II, Iss.4.

[7] Similar to the margin of appreciation doctrine in human rights law.

Part VI
WTO and Multilateral Environment Agreements

[21]

Multilateral Environmental Agreements

An overview

Duncan Brack

Introduction

The aim of this paper is to explore the interrelationship between multilateral environmental agreements (MEAs) and the multilateral trading system (MTS), the complex of trade agreements centred around the General Agreement on Tariffs and Trade (GATT) and overseen by the World Trade Organization (WTO). The paper provides an outline proposal for a way forward in the context of the forthcoming High Level Meeting of trade and environment ministers and the subsequent Millennium Round of trade negotiations.

The paper starts from the assumption that the removal of barriers to international trade, and the protection of the global environment, are *both* desirable objectives. It is further assumed that in certain cases these two objectives do, or are likely to, come into conflict, and that it is desirable to derive a way to reach the optimal balance of trade liberalization and environmental protection in these instances.

Nearly 200 MEAs currently exist, with memberships varying from a relatively small group to about 170 countries – which means, effectively, the whole world. Over 20 of these incorporate trade measures, i.e. restraints on the trade in particular substances or products, either between parties to the treaty and/or between parties and non-parties. Although this is a relatively small number, it includes some of the most important, such as the 1973 Convention on International Trade in Endangered Species (CITES), the 1987 Montreal Protocol on Substances that Deplete the Ozone Layer and the 1989 Basel Convention on the Control of Transboundary Movements of Hazardous Waste. A series of MEAs recently signed or currently under negotiation, including the 1997 Kyoto Protocol on Climate Change, the Rotterdam Convention on the Application of the Prior Informed Consent Procedure for Certain Hazardous Chemicals and Pesticides in International Trade, the Convention on the Control of Persistent Organic Pollutants and the Biosafety Protocol to the Convention on Biological Diversity, may in due course come to contain trade measures.

Trade provisions in MEAs have been designed to realize four major objectives:

1. to restrict markets for environmentally hazardous products or goods produced unsustainably;
2. to increase the coverage of the Agreement's provisions by encouraging governments to join and/or comply with the MEA;
3. to prevent free-riding (where non-participants enjoy the advantages of the MEA without incurring its costs) by encouraging governments to join and/or comply with the MEA;
4. to ensure the MEA's effectiveness by preventing 'leakage' – the situation where non-participants increase their emissions, or other unsustainable behaviour, as a result of the control measures taken by signatories.

The experience of three of the major MEAs concerned – CITES, the Montreal Protocol and the Basel Convention – shows the value of trade measures. CITES and the Basel Convention are treaties aimed explicitly at controlling trade, which is identified as the source of the environmental harm in question; trade measures are thus the entire point of the treaties. In the case of CITES, no species listed in the appendices to the treaty have become extinct since their listing, and a few – notably, the African elephant – have moved further away from extinction. Since the Basel Convention entered into force, the worst forms of hazardous waste dumping on developing countries have largely ended. In the case of the Montreal Protocol, trade measures were adopted as an enforcement mechanism, providing an incentive for non-parties to join the MEA and ensuring that the production of ozone-depleting substances did not migrate to non-parties to evade the controls adopted by parties. In either case, uncontrolled production would undermine the implementation of the Protocol. There is direct evidence from some countries that the trade provisions were indeed an important factor in persuading them to accede to the treaty; and in general the Montreal Protocol has proved to be a highly effective MEA, with its aim – the recovery of the stratospheric ozone layer to its pre-industrial state – likely to be achieved in the next century.

There are a limited number of routes by which countries can affect the actions of other countries: political/diplomatic pressure; provision of financial and technological assistance; trade sanctions; and military force. While the first two of these are clearly preferable, they have obvious limits. One can assume that use of the military option is unlikely to be helpful. Trade measures are therefore likely to continue to play a role as one component of effective environmental agreements, particularly where trade itself is identified as the source of the environmental harm, and/or where effective enforcement mechanisms are essential to their success, for example by preventing industrial migration or encouraging universal participation. The growing scope and importance of MEAs such as the Kyoto Protocol means that effective methods of implementation have to be found – which in turn means that the inclusion of trade measures at the very least has to be contemplated.

Can the use of trade measures in this way be regarded as an infringement of national sovereignty? The classical doctrines of sovereignty, originating in the seventeenth century, have little of use to say about relations between states, or of the 'rights' of states to expect other states to engage in international trade with them. It is clear, however, that the unrestrained output of pollution that is transboundary or global in scope *does* constitute an infringement of sovereignty, in that it inflicts direct physical harm on the populations and/or territories of other states. The unrestrained depletion of the global commons, for example, or of non-territorial species can, though more arguably, be regarded similarly. The responsibility of individual nations for the protection of the global environment and for the promotion of development that is environmentally sustainable have of course been accepted in many international agreements, most notably Agenda 21. Once again, the use of trade measures in MEAs must be contemplated if the global environment is to be protected effectively.

Interrelationship with the multilateral trading system

Disregarding these more general considerations, and accepting the value of trade measures, the next question is whether the use of MEA trade measures against WTO members can be regarded as an infringement of their rights under the MTS. It seems fairly clear that there is a potential for conflict.

In the first place, GATT Articles I ('Most Favoured Nation' Treatment) and III (National Treatment) outlaw discrimination in trade: WTO Members are not permitted to discriminate between traded 'like products' produced by other WTO members, or between domestic and international 'like products'. Yet all the three major MEAs referred to above discriminate between countries on the basis of their environmental performance, requiring parties to restrict trade to a greater extent with non-parties than they do with parties; indeed, such discrimination is one of the points of these MEAs, since they are aimed to promote sustainable activities while punishing unsustainable behaviour.

Second, GATT Article XI (Elimination of Quantitative Restrictions) forbids any restrictions other than duties, taxes or other charges on imports from and exports to other WTO members; yet each of the three MEAs requires precisely such quantitative restrictions.

Third, Article III requires imported and domestic 'like products' to be treated identically. The meaning of the term 'like product' has become one of the most difficult issues in the trade–environment arena. Originally incorporated into the GATT in order to prevent discrimination on the grounds of national origin, GATT and WTO dispute panels have interpreted the term more broadly to prevent discrimination in cases where process methods, rather than product characteristics, have been the distinguishing characteristic of the product and the justification for trade measures – for example the US embargo on imports of shrimp caught by methods that kill sea turtles. Yet the Montreal Protocol envisages restrictions on trade in products made with but not containing ozone-depleting substances (originating from non-parties), while domestic products produced in this way are not subject to such regulation – although so far this provision has not been put into practice.

It is possible, however, that an MEA trade measure could be 'saved' by the General Exceptions clause of the GATT, Article XX, which states that:

> Subject to the requirement that such measures are not applied in a manner which would constitute a means of arbitrary or unjustifiable discrimination between countries where the same conditions prevail, or a disguised restriction on international trade, nothing in this Agreement shall be construed to prevent the adoption or enforcement by any contracting party of measures:
> ... (b) necessary to protect human, animal or plant life or health ...
> ... (g) relating to the conservation of exhaustible natural resources if such measures are made effective in conjunction with restrictions on domestic production or consumption.

Unlike many MEAs, where terms tend to be defined in the treaty or in subsequent decisions of conferences of the parties, interpretation of the MTS usually proceeds through a case-law-type approach, relying on the findings of dispute panels in particular cases. Since there has never been a dispute case brought before a GATT or WTO panel involving an MEA trade measure, it is impossible to say for certain whether it would be found to be incompatible with the MTS.

It is possible, however, to extrapolate from the arguments and findings in a series of trade–environment disputes that were brought before panels – involving, in this case, unilaterally imposed trade measures. In each of these cases, the panel found the environmental measures in question not to be justifiable, because either:

- the measures were not 'necessary' (Article XX(b)) to the achievement of the environmental goal, because the panel believed that there were less trade-restrictive or GATT-inconsistent measures also available; or
- the measures did not 'relate to the conservation of exhaustible natural resources' (Article XX(g)), because the policies in question were extra-jurisdictional: they attempted to modify the behaviour of other WTO members and could not therefore be considered to be primarily aimed at conserving the natural resources of the country applying the trade measures; or
- the measures represented 'arbitrary or unjustifiable discrimination' (Article XX headnote), in that there were less discriminatory methods available that could have been employed.

It is of course dangerous to extrapolate from arguments used in cases of trade measures imposed *unilaterally* to those involving the application of trade measures mandated by or in pursuance of the requirements of *multilateral* agreements. In any case, it is difficult, even from an environmental viewpoint, to defend most of the measures taken in the relevant disputes. The way in which the United States applied its embargo on shrimp imports from a number of South Asian and Southeast Asian countries, for instance, does appear to be 'arbitrary and unjustifiable discrimination' when compared with the much more gradual and participatory way in which it applied measures to protect sea turtles in the Caribbean region.

Furthermore, WTO dispute panels, and the WTO Appellate Body, have become steadily more sophisticated in their arguments, and more conscious of the environmental debate. The recent Appellate Body decision in the *Shrimp/Turtle* dispute, for example, used the reference in the Preamble to the Marrakesh Agreement establishing the WTO – 'allowing for the optimal use of the world's resources in accordance with the objective of sustainable development, seeking both to protect and preserve the environment and to enhance the means for doing so …' – to dispose of the argument that species protection was not a legitimate objective for trade measures.[1] It also stressed, as have several panels before it, the desirability of multilateral agreements as opposed to unilateral measures.[2]

Unsurprisingly, however, neither panels nor the Appellate Body have ever speculated as to the acceptability of trade measures taken under such agreements under the MTS. It is therefore still not clear as to how panels would rule. Even some of the arguments used in the *Shrimp/Turtle* Appellate Body finding suggest that they might rule against an MEA trade measure:

> Perhaps the most conspicuous flaw in this measure's application relates to its intended and actual coercive effect on the specific policy decisions made by foreign governments …[3]

[1] *United States – Import Prohibition of Certain Shrimp and Shrimp Products*, paras. 131–4 WT/DS58/AB/R, 12 October 1998.

[2] Ibid., paras. 166–72.

[3] Ibid., para. 161.

> However, it is not acceptable, in international trade relations, for one WTO Member to use an economic embargo to require other Members to adopt essentially the same comprehensive regulatory program, to achieve a certain policy goal, as that in force within that Member's territory.[4]

Trade measures employed under the three main MEAs cited above are now unlikely to be challenged in the WTO because of the wide international acceptability they enjoy – though this is perhaps less true of the Basel Convention, where the amendment banning trade in waste between OECD and non-OECD countries (not yet in force) has aroused hostility among some of the industries involved. The possible MTS incompatibility of the amendment has been raised explicitly by those opposed to the principle as an argument against adopting or ratifying it.

This 'political chill' argument is also relevant to other MEAs. Attempts to include trade provisions in the International Convention for the Conservation of Atlantic Tuna, and in agreements to control driftnet fishing, were shelved because of a fear that they would be inconsistent with GATT rules. The same issue was raised in last year's negotiations over the Kyoto Protocol and in discussions this year over the Rotterdam Convention on Prior Informed Consent.

The continuation of this potential conflict between the MTS and MEAs is undesirable for a number of reasons including the following:

- the fact that is not known for certain how a dispute panel would rule on an MEA trade measure creates an unstable and uncertain situation. On the face of it, it does appear absurd that the operation of an important element of international law should be subject to a panel of three individuals deciding what they think ten lines of printed text (the relevant sections of GATT Article XX) written fifty years ago could mean in a vastly changed international environment;
- it creates the spectre of a potential challenge to an existing MEA, bringing the two international regimes of trade liberalization and environmental protection directly into conflict;

[4] Ibid., para. 165.

- it increases the likelihood of conflict over the negotiation of future MEAs with trade measures, potentially weakening their effectiveness – the 'political chill' argument;
- finally, the perception that the WTO threatens environmental sustainability, already widespread in some quarters, assists neither the growth of the MTS nor the further spread of trade liberalization, even where this would have environmental benefit.

Resolution of the problem is therefore required.

Resolving the conflict

When two systems of law come into conflict, actually or potentially, there are three potential methods of dealing with the situation:

1. create some superior balancing mechanism;
2. determine that one legal system is superior to another, either wholly or in part;
3. modify either or both legal systems to bring them into harmony.

The first option, the creation of a balancing mechanism, would be the most desirable solution in a perfect world. This is effectively the system that operates inside the European Union, where trade liberalization and environmental protection are both objectives of the Treaty of Rome. Any conflict between the two objectives can be resolved by the European Court of Justice, which has the power to rule on the appropriate balance between trade and environmental measures in any particular case. In the well-known Danish bottles dispute of 1986, for example, the Court upheld the core of the Danish law requiring a collection system for returnable drinks containers while striking down some of the details of the regulations as unnecessarily trade-restrictive, given the environmental objective in question.

The creation of an equivalent system at a global level would require substantial reform of the entire system of international institutions, however, and is not a realistic prospect in the short term. Having said that, there have been calls for such a reform, perhaps using the International

Court of Justice as the superior body. Proposals for a new World Environmental Organization (for instance by Chancellor Kohl at the UN General Assembly Special Session, 'Earth Summit 2', in June 1997) have had at least partly in mind the objective of creating a balancing institution to the WTO, though the interrelationship between such a WEO and the WTO was not, and has not been, explored in any detail. It is interesting to note that the 1948 Charter for the International Trade Organization (ITO) (the intended third leg of the Bretton Woods tripod, never in fact adopted because of US opposition) did provide that a member prejudiced by an ITO decision could seek an advisory opinion from the ICJ, whose opinion would then bind the ITO. If Thomas Cottier's analysis of the WTO as increasingly assuming 'constitutional functions in a globalising economy' (WTO Symposium, 17–18 March 1998) is accurate, then this argument may need to be addressed sooner rather than later.

The second option, determining that one legal system is superior to the other, is *de facto,* even if not *de jure*, the position as it stands at present. As noted above, the validity of trade measures in MEAs could be challenged under the WTO, and a WTO dispute panel would then rule on their compatibility with the MTS. Although panels have become steadily more aware of and more open to environmental arguments (the decision of the Appellate Body in the *Shrimp/Turtle* case to accept 'non-requested information from non-governmental sources'[5] is a useful step forward), they are nevertheless composed of international trade experts who reach decisions in accordance with a body of international trade law – indeed, they cannot do otherwise, since this is the function of the WTO. The MTS has been constructed by trade negotiators with relatively little awareness of environmental requirements and policies, and, despite a number of references to environmental objectives in some of the WTO agreements, it is not well attuned to environmental imperatives even though it cannot avoid interacting with policies for environmental protection.

Equally, of course, it could be argued that MEAs are constructed by environmental negotiators with little awareness of trade law and the

[5] Ibid, paras. 104–10.

desirability of liberalized trade. But that would be unfair. Many delegations to MEA negotiations routinely include trade department representatives, and in a number of instances (including the Montreal Protocol and Basel Convention) negotiators have sought advice from the GATT/WTO Secretariat in designing particular features of their treaties. Some MEAs, including the UN Framework Convention on Climate Change, contain text drawn more or less straight from the GATT.

More generally, trade departments tend to wield greater political clout within national governments than do environmental departments and agencies; environmental policy objectives are not well integrated into policy across the board; and at the international level the MTS and the WTO (and in particular its dispute settlement system) are considerably more powerful and influential than are MEAs and the various environmental institutions such as the UN Environment Programme and the UN Commission on Sustainable Development. The trade implications of particular MEA requirements can in theory be subject to scrutiny by the institutions of the MTS, but there is no provision anywhere for the environmental implications of the MTS – or, for example, of the agreements likely to be reached in the forthcoming Millennium Round of trade negotiations – to be subjected to scrutiny by environmental institutions.

The existing hierarchy of international law therefore favours, in practice even if not in theory, the MTS over MEAs. For the reasons described above, this is an undesirable situation if one accepts that the two objectives of trade liberalization and environmental protection are of equal validity. The conclusion reached, therefore, is that the third option – modification of one of both of the existing systems of international law, for which priority should be given to the modification of the MTS – is required.

Resolution through the Millennium Round

The approach of the Millennium Round, due to begin at the end of 1999, and the proposed High Level Meeting between trade and environment ministers, provisionally scheduled for spring or early summer 1999, lends urgency to this analysis. And out of the very wide range of issues that could be considered under the 'trade–environment' heading, resolution of the MEAs–MTS conflict has always been regarded as one of the most pressing – as evidenced by the attention given to it by the WTO Committee on Trade and Environment (CTE) during the preparation of its first report, to the Singapore WTO Ministerial Meeting in December 1996.

It is important, however, to avoid a repeat of that sterile and long drawn-out debate. Although it was kicked off mainly by the EU's proposal for an amendment to GATT Article XX, proposals put forward by other WTO members became successively more and more restrictive. Increasingly, they aimed to limit the scope for trade measures in existing and future MEAs, by adding extra requirements to the trade measures under scrutiny. Any or all of 'necessity', 'effectiveness', 'least trade-restrictiveness', 'proportionality' or 'sound scientific basis' were suggested as criteria that trade measures would have to fulfil, and which WTO panels would judge whether they satisfied. In practice, this would have reinforced the existing international hierarchy, rendering MEAs even more subject to WTO scrutiny, and tilting the balance even further towards the MTS and away from MEAs.

Any solution to the conflict needs to satisfy the following criteria:

- There must be certainty about the MTS-compatibility of trade measures under existing MEAs, both those specifically mandated by the MEA in question ('specific measures') and those not specifically required by the MEA but taken in pursuance of its aims ('non-specific measures'). (The Montreal Protocol, for example, leads to both: the bans on trade with non-parties are specific measures mandated by the treaty, whereas parties have introduced a range of controls on trade with other parties in order to meet the requirements of the control measures ('non-specific measures').)
- There must be certainty over the MTS-compatibility of trade measures that might be incorporated in future MEAs or those currently under negotiation.
- There must be flexibility for MEA negotiators to incorporate trade measures in future MEAs where they consider them necessary to the fulfilment of their objectives.

- If trade measures are required by MEA negotiators, they must be applied in as non-discriminatory a way as possible; i.e., they should employ only such discrimination as is required to fulfil the aims of the MEA, and should not provide an opportunity for trade protectionism which is unrelated to environmental objectives.
- If disputes arise, it must be clear in which forum they can be resolved.

There are four main possible routes to resolving the issue:

1. a waiver from the obligations of the existing MTS;
2. modification of the MTS to create an 'agreement-specific' exemption from MTS provisions;
3. & 4. modification of the MTS to create a 'criteria-specific' exemption from MTS provisions; this could be achieved either via amendment of the GATT itself and/or through a new WTO Agreement on MEAs.

The use of waivers has been referred to as the *ex post* approach. Article XXV of the GATT provides for the granting of a waiver from other GATT obligations 'in exceptional circumstances'; Article IX of the WTO Agreement extends this to the MTS as a whole. Such waivers, however, are usually time-limited, can be considered only on a case-by-case basis, and require a three-quarters majority of WTO members to vote for them. Once again, they reinforce the existing hierarchy, firmly placing the WTO in judgment over MEAs; they cannot contribute to certainty about the relationship between MEAs and the MTS; and they do not fulfil any of the criteria set out above.

In contrast, the so-called *ex ante* approach implies modification of the MTS in some way. One possible method is a 'listing' of those particular MEAs whose provisions are deemed to be compatible with the MTS. This is similar to the approach taken by the North American Free Trade Agreement (NAFTA), which provides that, in the event of conflict between itself and CITES, the Montreal Protocol or the Basel Convention (or other MEAs where all NAFTA parties agree), the provisions of the MEA should take precedence over the MTS – though it also adds that parties must use the means least inconsistent with the NAFTA in implementing the MEAs. While more attractive than the waiver approach, this nevertheless involves the WTO in reaching a decision over which MEAs it considers acceptable and which it does not; it still does not create any certainty over the relationship with MEAs in general.

A broader solution is preferred, dealing with MEAs as a category rather than one by one. This implies a 'criteria-specific' modification of the MTS. The clearest political message would be to achieve this via amendment of the GATT. The EU proposal in the CTE, for example, was for a new sub-paragraph of Article XX, covering measures 'taken pursuant to specific provisions of an MEA complying with the "Understanding on the relationship between measures taken pursuant to MEAs and the WTO rules"'.[6] The proposed Understanding included a simple definition of an MEA and stated that measures taken pursuant to the specific provisions of the MEA should be presumed to be 'necessary' for the achievement of its environmental objectives, though they still remained subject to the requirements of the *chapeau* to Article XX.

This particular approach now looks a little dated; since the EU proposal was put together, a number of WTO panels have found trade measures in unilateral trade–environment cases to be justified under either paragraphs (b) or (g) of Article XX, but then failed them under the *chapeau*. (Earlier panels had failed them under (b) and (g), and never reached the *chapeau*.) If it is accepted that MEA trade measures would be likely to be treated similarly, then there is little point in adding a new paragraph: what would be required is amendment of the headnote itself. Since this would have implications for every category of exceptions to the GATT, and for unilateral as well as multilateral trade measures, it would be exceptionally difficult – to put it mildly – to negotiate. Finally, the procedures for amendment of the GATT are themselves quite stringent and time-consuming.

[6] WTO CTE, Non-paper by the European Community, 19 February 1996.

A new WTO Agreement on MEAs

The alternative route for 'criteria-specific' modification of the MTS is through a new WTO Agreement, similar in status to other WTO Agreements such as those on Subsidies and Countervailing Measures, on Technical Barriers to Trade or on Agriculture. The advantages of this approach are that it avoids attempting to amend existing rules, with probable implications for a wide range of topics; it creates a very clear set of rules which apply only to MEAs (i.e. which would not encourage further unilateral actions); and it is probably easier to negotiate.

What would the new Agreement need to cover? An outline of topics is provided here; further work would of course be necessary to develop detailed proposals.

- *The definition of an 'MEA'*, including criteria for its subject matter (possibilities include the promotion of sustainable development, the conservation of natural resources, the avoidance of transboundary pollution and/or the protection of human, animal plant life or health) and for its openness to participation by all parties affected and concerned.
- *The definition of trade measures*, and treatment of different categories of measures. It would seem logical that specific measures – for example the bans on trade with non-parties mandated by the Montreal Protocol, or the import and export licences required by CITES – should fall within the scope of the Agreement and thereby be exempted completely from the other requirements of the MTS.
- *Non-specific measures*, on the other hand, such as the controls on trade with parties implemented by Montreal Protocol parties (including measures such as taxation, labelling requirements, and total or partial import bans), could be covered by the *chapeau* to Article XX, as there seems little reason to think that they would need to be discriminatory to achieve their objectives. If discriminatory measures are required, it seems reasonable to insist that they should be specific, i.e. included in the text of the MEA. What is decided here therefore would have implications for the design of future MEAs.
- *Linkage of burdens and offsets*. Developing countries have tended, as a whole, to be most vociferously opposed to any modification of

the MTS for environmental purposes, including in the context of the MEAs debate. Given the record of Western protectionism against developing country exports, still enshrined in parts of the MTS (such as the Agreement on Textiles and Clothing), one can hardly blame them. It is important that trade measures are not used to force countries into implementing an agreement that unfairly retards their development – bearing in mind, of course, that in many cases the environmental harm at which the MEA is aimed may well retard their development anyway if it proceeds unchecked. The presence of trade measures *as one component* of a range of implementing measures in a particular MEA (including, for example, provisions for finance and technology transfer) is therefore an important feature of MEA design. To what extent this should be specified in a WTO Agreement is questionable, however; one would wish to avoid a situation in which a WTO panel found against the use of trade measures because the MEA's financial provisions were not working well.

- *Dispute settlement.* Finally, the Agreement would need to be clear about where disputes over the application of MEA trade measures should be resolved. In line with earlier CTE discussions, it seems logical for disputes between MEA parties to be resolved by the MEA, and for disputes between an MEA party and a non-party that is a WTO member to be resolved by the WTO. (This in turn has implications for WTO dispute settlement procedures and their ability to consider adequately environmental issues.) There also needs to be some agreed procedure for cases where it is not completely clear whether a trade measure is MEA-related or not; the US actions in the *Shrimp/Turtle* case, for example, could arguably be considered to be justified by a range of MEAs, including CITES, the Biodiversity Convention and the Bonn Convention on the Conservation of Migratory Species of Wild Animals.

Conclusion

The Millennium Round offers an excellent opportunity for the resolution of the potential conflict between the MTS and MEAs with trade provisions. It creates the wider political and negotiating environment, notably lacking within the CTE discussions, within which trade-offs can be reached, and all participants in the debate end up with perceived gains to offset perceived losses. It is the conclusion of this paper that the opportunity should be taken to open negotiations on a new WTO Agreement on MEAs with Trade Provisions. The High Level Meeting of trade and environment ministers provides an initial forum in which this idea can be tested and refined.

The biggest danger in this debate is that no political impetus will be given to it and nothing will in the end be resolved. It is entirely possible to argue, for example, that most MEAs do not contain trade provisions, that there has never been a WTO dispute involving an MEA, and that recent panel and Appellate Body findings have shown that the WTO is sensitive to the environmental imperative; therefore, no action is required. This would be a profound mistake. MEAs are growing in number, in scope and in importance, matching the growing evidence of global environmental degradation. In some cases they will need to impact international trade if they are to be implemented effectively. There have already been instances of MTS incompatibility arguments being used as weapons in MEA negotiations.

Trade liberalization and environmental protection are both desirable objectives. But the legal regimes that govern them are developing largely in isolation. A failure to resolve the *potential* conflict between them can only lead to actual conflict, undermining both. The time to act is now.

[22]

Effective Multilateral Environment Agreements and Why the WTO Needs Them

Gary P. Sampson

1. INTRODUCTION

SINCE its establishment, one of the most actively discussed topics in the World Trade Organisation (WTO) has been the relationship between its provisions and the use of trade measures in multilateral environmental agreements (MEAs). The debate has centred on the possibility of a conflict arising over trade-related measures contained in MEAs: namely, their potential inconsistency with WTO rules, and how conflict in these rules could be avoided or dealt with.

In a broad perspective, it could be argued that no real problem exists. Only a small proportion of MEAs contain trade provisions, and no trade dispute has arisen in the WTO over their use. It is also argued that the WTO rules already provide for non-consistent WTO trade measures to be taken to protect the environment, and the existing architecture of the WTO is adequate to deal with any potential problems. The counter-argument runs along the lines that uncertainty over the relationship between the two sets of rules is increasingly affecting MEA negotiations; uncertainty unnecessarily exacerbates tensions between MEAs and WTO. Additional concerns are that the objectives of some MEAs are frustrated by WTO rules. For example, the definition of patents in the Trade-related Intellectual Property Rights (TRIPS) Agreement of the WTO is seen by some to be at variance with the objectives of the Convention on Biological Diversity; protection of the rights of indigenous people; transfer of

GARY P. SAMPSON is Professor of International Economic Relations at the Institute of Advanced Studies at the United Nations University in Tokyo. He is also Visiting Academic at the London School of Economics and Visiting Professor at the Melbourne Business School. This article is part of a project supported by the Ford Foundation Project inquiring into the Role of the WTO in Global Governance.

environmentally sound technology; and, to the extent that patents apply to life forms, a loss of biodiversity.[1]

While there is no agreement about how to settle the debate on these matters, there is no disagreement among governments that belong to the WTO that MEAs are the best way to co-ordinate policy action to tackle global and trans-boundary environmental problems.[2] WTO member governments do not want the WTO to become an environment policy-making organisation or environmental standards enforcement agency. Indeed, WTO rules provide for governments to adopt whatever trade measures they wish to protect their domestic environment. When it comes to environmental problems beyond their borders, the expectation is that governments will agree to – and enforce – environmental regulations through regional or international environment agreements and not unilateral coercion through WTO inconsistent measures.

As the WTO and MEAs represent two different bodies of international law, the relationship between them should be coherent and fully understood by all concerned. This is not – it is argued – the case at the moment. In this article I express the view that MEAs do – and should – have the possibility to invoke WTO inconsistent measures to achieve their goals. Given the importance of the global trade and environment regimes, any clash over the application of rules agreed to among nations would have unfortunate ramifications for both regimes. To remove this possibility, and to avoid the WTO being the arbiter of environmental disputes, any WTO inconsistent measures should be clearly spelled out and agreed to by the parties to a broad-based multilateral environment agreement. Disagreement as to the legality of MEA measures in any MEA should then be dealt with by the compliance mechanism in the MEA itself and should not be left to interpretation by a WTO dispute panel or appellate body report as has been the case recently. This course of action requires effective MEAs, characterised by clearly specified trade measures that may be taken for environmental purposes, broad-based support in terms of country membership and a robust dispute settlement system. The theme of this article is, therefore, that effective MEAs are critical to avoid environmental disputes gravitating towards the WTO and inhibiting the smooth functioning of the WTO itself.

The outline of this article is as follows. In the first section, I very briefly describe the institutional response to the trade and environment debate in the

[1] All these points have been made in discussions in the WTO Committee on Trade and Environment (CTE). See also Dutfield (2000). The CTE and its terms of reference are discussed in the body of the text. For records of the discussions of the CTE, secretariat background documentation for meetings and national submissions, see WWW.WTO.Org.

[2] The recent discussion in the CTE stands as testimony to the spectrum of views among WTO Members regarding the need for clarification of the relationship between the WTO and MEAs and what to do about it. See, for example, the recent discussion in Committee on Trade and Environment, in WTO (12 December, 2000).

WTO; namely, the Committee on Trade and Environment (CTE). This is followed by a description of some of the characteristics of trade and environment regulations, policies and approaches to negotiations that go at least some way to explaining why it has been difficult on occasion to formulate coherent trade and environment policies. I then discuss why it is important to have clarity in MEAs when trade-related measures are provided for, and the consequences of any lack of clarity. There is also a discussion of the options already available for trade-related environmental measures to be considered as exceptions to WTO rules. Recent experience in the WTO dispute settlement process is also drawn on to illustrate how in the course of settling disputes it has become clear the extent to which effective MEAs can be beneficial to the WTO. I then advance a number of policy proposals with a view to avoiding, and eventually dealing with, future disputes. The article closes with a conclusion.

2. INSTITUTIONAL RESPONSE: CTE

The Committee on Trade and the Environment (CTE) was established in January 1995.[3] The Committee reports to the WTO General Council. It is mandated to address a variety of areas of work and to recommend whether any modifications to the rules of the multilateral trading system are required to permit a positive interaction between trade and environment measures. The CTE includes all WTO members and a number of observers from intergovernmental organisations.[4] There are no observers from non-governmental organisations (NGOs) despite a number of requests to be present at CTE meetings. The CTE has a standing agenda, and meets formally at least two times a year and in an informal mode whenever considered necessary. It addresses – *inter alia* – the relationship between the provisions of the multilateral trading system and trade measures for environmental purposes; in particular, the relationship between WTO rules and compliance procedures, and those of the multilateral environmental agreements.[5]

[3] Concern over the conflict of trade and environment policies arose after the launching of the Uruguay Round negotiations and did not find a place on that agenda. Nevertheless, discussions toward the end of the Round led to a Ministerial Decision on Trade and Environment (adopted in Marrakech in April 1994) calling for the creation of a Committee on Trade and Environment (CTE).

[4] There are presently over 140 governments that constitute the membership of the WTO. In what follows, these will be referred to as the WTO members. While the 15 countries of the European Union are individual members, they are represented at WTO meetings (with the exception of the WTO Budget Committee) by the European Commission, which speaks on behalf of the 15 member states.

[5] A number of MEAs have trade-related provisions that raise questions with respect to their WTO conformity. A detailed description of the WTO relevant measures in eleven environment conventions containing trade measures can be found in WTO (19 September, 2000).

In other words, its mandate embraces the need to determine if the WTO should change its rules to accommodate those in MEAs.

While the work of the CTE has been criticised for failing to recommend modifications to WTO rules, much of its work has been useful in increasing the understanding of the complexity of the issues at hand, particularly relating to MEA and WTO rules.[6] It could be argued, for example, that one of the reasons that there has never been a dispute relating to an MEA brought to the WTO is because of the increased understanding created through information sessions in the CTE where the secretariats of environmental agreements have been invited to present relevant information with respect to the rules of their agreements.[7] These sessions have clearly facilitated a mutual understanding of the linkages between the multilateral environment and trade agendas, and built awareness of the use of trade-related measures in MEAs.

At the time of its inception, there was active discussion in the CTE on the relationship between the WTO and MEAs. This debate has recently been enlivened with a number of far-reaching formal proposals on how to deal with potential problems by governments.[8] This is perhaps a reaction to the commercial, political and social importance of some recent MEAs that could well impact on trade, and the claim that the lack of clarity between WTO and MEA rules has led to confusion in the negotiation of the MEA. It has been argued that the negotiations surrounding the Bio-safety Protocol, for example, proved to be difficult, 'precisely because of the lack of clarity with regard to the relationship of the Protocol to the WTO'.[9] The renewed interest could also be due to high profile trade and environment disputes that have come to the WTO in recent times, and recognition of the fact that they probably never would have arisen had an effective MEA been in place. An additional consideration is that the debate in the WTO has been enriched with a large amount of useful work being undertaken by reputable non-governmental organisations, intergovernmental institutions and academics.[10]

[6] For a critique of the work of the committee at the time of the Singapore Ministerial meeting see Charnovitz (1997).

[7] The most recent of these information sessions was held on 24 October, 2000. The following Secretariats responded to questions from CTE Members: the Convention on the International Trade in Endangered Species of Wild Fauna and Flora; the Basel Convention on the Control of Trans-boundary Movements of Hazardous Wastes and their Disposal; UNEP Chemicals on the Rotterdam Prior Informed Consent Convention and the draft Persistent Organic Pollutants Convention; the Intergovernmental Forum on Forests; and the UN Framework Convention on Climate Change. The International Tropical Timber Organisation also contributed a paper and the Executive Secretary of the Convention on Biological Diversity attended this session. For a report on the meeting see WTO (12 December, 2000).

[8] These include, in particular, WTO (19 October, 2000a), WTO (19 October, 2000b); and WTO (10 October, 2000).

[9] See, WTO (19 October, 2000a). This view is also expressed in WTO (19 October, 2000b).

[10] See, for example, Brack (2000).

3. SOME FUNDAMENTALS

Approaches to the formulation of trade and environment policies are at times very different. Many policies designed to protect the environment are based on government intervention through the regulation of production activities: taxes, quantitative restrictions, and subsidies. GATT and the WTO, in contrast, have a long tradition of negotiating away such government measures when they adversely affect trade (e.g. subsidies affecting exports, export bans, restrictions on imports). In addition, the rules governing international trade are based on non-discrimination, whereas much of the regulation relating to environmental protection is justified on the grounds that discrimination between products and how they are produced is important.

More particularly, WTO rules do not, in general, inhibit governments from protecting (as they wish) against damage to the environment resulting from the manufacture and consumption of goods produced and used within national boundaries. This flexibility, however, only extends to the regulation of domestic products and processes, and not to the processes used to produce imported products. The underlying thesis is that should any country wish to influence the manner in which goods are produced in other countries – regardless of how appropriate it may seem to interest groups in the importing country – this should not translate into discriminatory trade measures.

In general, WTO rules treat products that have the same physical form as 'like' products even if they have been produced in very different ways.[11] From the perspective of the environment, environmentally unfriendly goods and services – and the processes that produce them – are categorically different from environmentally friendly ones. Thus, while the rationale for environmental regulation is to make discrimination between goods and services mandatory (based, for example, on life-cycle analysis), the rationale for WTO rules is to avoid it, at least for those goods that enter into international trade.

Another characteristic of multilateral trade rules is their contractual nature backed up with a powerful dispute settlement system. Unlike many environmental agreements, the dispute settlement process with the threat of retaliation and compensation is the Damocles' sword hanging over those that have to live with the interpretation of new rules. There is nothing of a 'best endeavours' nature about WTO rights and obligations. Not surprisingly, WTO members are far from eager to change rules that could bring uncertain outcomes unless it is absolutely necessary; thus, there have been only two instances of changes to GATT 1994 rules over the past fifty-five years.[12] It seems unlikely that future

[11] Exceptions to the rules include certain instances where 'like' goods are produced with subsidies or without meeting specified standards with respect to the protection of intellectual property rights.
[12] See Jackson (1998). There were, however, Understandings negotiated in the Uruguay Round that elaborated the interpretation of some of the principal GATT articles.

rule change (and the requisite agreement among WTO members that it is necessary to achieve it) will be forthcoming to accommodate hypothetical problems such as those relating to potential conflicts of WTO provisions with MEA rules. This reticence to change rules is sometimes interpreted by critics of the CTE as inertia or lack of concern, when it may be a reflection of the realisation on the part of trade officials of the complexity of the issues at hand and the binding nature – and therefore the potential consequences – of changes in rules.

On the other hand, GATT and WTO rules have proven to be very flexible instruments where 'changes' have been possible through techniques that have included simple non-enforcement, acceptance of 'constructive ambiguity' in the text of various agreements to permit negotiations to continue (or conclude) while keeping options open relating to future interpretation, and a variety of relatively informal actions agreeing to allow some deviations from rules.[13] It has been argued that the inexact status of the final actions taken by WTO members represents a practical answer to policy issues on which it is not possible to reach total agreement. The reasoning is that trade ministries have a certain degree of mutual trust allowing them to leave long-term answers open while short-term pragmatic solutions are found. They are confident that there is enough common interest among members to make it likely that something will be worked out in the long run.[14]

This WTO affinity for ambiguous solutions to legal issues does not, however, seem to provide a solution to the trade and environment debate. In reality, the alternatives to addressing the problems environmentalists have with WTO rules have been couched in terms of two rather rigid alternatives: the need for formal decisions involving amendments or waivers, or changes and interpretation to the rules through the dispute settlement procedures. The conclusion has been drawn that environmentalists resist the common WTO pragmatic solutions to the interpretation of rules, perhaps believing that trade ministries do not share the same ultimate values as they do. They are therefore not prepared to trust the WTO to achieve a solution for them in the long run.[15]

4. UNCLEAR AND INCONSISTENT MEASURES

At the most fundamental level, the potential problems surrounding the inconsistency of measures found in trade and environment agreements fall into

[13] Article XXIV of GATT 1994, which provides for an exception from the fundamental most favoured nation principle for preferential regional trading agreements, is an excellent example of WTO members' non-enforcement of rules.

[14] This thinking is developed in an excellent article on this and related topics by Hudec (1996).

[15] The reasoning in this paragraph draws on Hudec (1996).

just two groups. The first is when a trade-related measure is taken by a party to an MEA against another party. The problem arises when the measure is not specifically provided for in the MEA itself, but is 'justified' by the party taking the measure as necessary to achieve the objectives of the environment agreement. The necessity of this measure may be challenged by the party against which the measure is taken. In this case, both parties could be members of the WTO and the measure could violate WTO rights and obligations. This could lead to a dispute as to the legitimacy of the measure in terms of either the MEA or the WTO.

It seems reasonable that such a dispute should be pursued under the dispute settlement procedures of the MEA. In this respect, it would be helpful if MEA parties stipulated from the outset that they intended trade disputes arising out of implementation of the obligations of the MEA to be settled under the MEA's provisions. It could be argued that this approach could help ensure the convergence of the objectives of MEAs and the WTO, while safeguarding their respective spheres of competence, thus overcoming problems arising from overlapping jurisdictions.

This, however, requires an effective compliance mechanism to be available to MEA parties. As with the Dispute Settlement Understanding of the WTO, MEAs emphasise the avoidance of disputes. They include provisions to increase transparency through the collection and exchange of information, co-ordination of technical and scientific research, and collective monitoring of implementing measures, as well as consultation provisions. Most of the MEAs with trade-related provisions also contain mechanisms for resolving disputes, but these lack the power of the WTO dispute settlement process. In the words of one informed observer commenting on the dispute settlement system of the WTO:

> The speed, power, and efficiency of the system are both frightening and fascinating to environmental groups. It is the very power and authority of the system that has led to calls for reforms.[16]

In the absence of an effective dispute settlement system in the MEA, the dispute could gravitate to the WTO. It has been suggested on numerous occasions in the CTE that there would be value in strengthening MEA dispute settlement mechanisms. This, of course, is outside the terms of reference of the CTE.

In short, if an MEA does not specifically provide for the trade measures under dispute, and if it does not have a sufficiently effective dispute settlement mechanism to deal with the dispute, then the litigation could gravitate towards the WTO. If the measure is challenged in the WTO, trade officials have the task of determining if the measure is necessary to achieve the objectives of the environment agreement; a task that neither trade officials, nor environmentalists, think should fall to the WTO.

[16] The remarks are by the President of World Wide Fund for Nature International. See Martin (2001).

The second group of problems relates to potentially WTO inconsistent measures, which are *specifically* provided for in an MEA and taken by a party to the MEA against a non-party. A problem may then present itself if the measure is against a WTO member, which challenges the legitimacy of the measure in the WTO dispute settlement process.

Dealing with this group of problems involves a decision about the importance to ascribe to the existence of the MEA in determining if the measure in question is really necessary. In fact, even the ostensibly simple first step of determining what is an MEA has led to only very general definitions in the WTO that have proved to be of little help in determining which MEAs should be assigned a special importance in the WTO. One such definition is:

> a legally binding instrument, the aims of which include environmental protection, open to all countries concerned, and relevant to the aims set out in the head-note of GATT Article XX and sub-paragraphs (b) and (g).[17]

However, definition apart, the likelihood of a positive decision on the necessity of the measure is presumably enhanced if the goals of the environment agreement are accepted globally in a broad based MEA to which all, or most, WTO members belong. In fact, most proposals relating to the relationship between WTO and MEA rules are based on the notion that subject to specific conditions being met, certain trade measures taken pursuant to MEAs should benefit from special treatment under WTO provisions. This approach has been described as creating 'an environmental window' in the WTO. However, determining what is an acceptable MEA from the perspective of receiving greater WTO acceptability, has proved to be far from a simple task.

In both the cases described above, however, the WTO finds itself in the role of an arbiter in environment matters; a role WTO member governments have specifically stated that they do not wish to assume. In both instances, effective MEAs with precise language, broad based membership and a robust dispute settlement process would avoid environmental matters of this nature finding their way onto the WTO agenda.

5. CLARITY OF MEASURES

To appreciate the potential importance for the WTO of the lack of specificity in the provision of trade measures in an MEA, it is perhaps instructive to look at a particular case. The United Nations Framework Convention on Climate Change (FCCC), which entered into force on 21 March, 1994, is illustrative in this respect.[18]

17 See WTO (19 October, 2000b).

18 Possible conflicts between the rights and obligations of the WTO the Climate Change Convention are addressed in Goldberg (1995). See also Stewart, Wiener and Sands (1996).

All the more so, as the parties to the FCCC formally recognise that measures taken to address climate change problems have the potential to be used for trade protectionist purposes. In fact, in wording borrowed from the GATT 1994, the treaty specifically states that measures taken to combat climate change, including unilateral ones, should not:

> constitute a means of arbitrary or unjustifiable discrimination or a disguised restriction on international trade.[19]

The convention does not provide for any specific trade-related measures to deal with the environment.

However, in achieving the objectives of the Convention, a wide variety of measures will be taken that may well affect the costs of production of traded goods and therefore the competitive position of producers in the world market. Examples include energy, carbon, and other taxes; mandatory and voluntary standards; subsidies for environmentally friendly production processes; labelling and certification schemes; and the sale and transfer of emission permits within or between groups of countries. Offsetting measures will be called for by those whose competitive position is adversely affected by cheaper imports not subject to the same measures in the country of origin. All of these measures have potential implications for the WTO: they may violate WTO rules, or at least, some of the most contentious aspects of WTO concepts and rules may be thrown onto centre stage.[20]

The Convention is – as its name indicates – a framework only, and specific provisions on the nature of commitments by members and legal instruments (such as compliance procedures) are being elaborated in subsequent protocols. The Conference of the Parties (COP) – the decision-making body of the convention – held its third session in December 1997, during which 160 industrial and developing countries adopted the Kyoto Protocol by consensus. Its centre-piece is the commitment for industrial countries to reduce their collective emissions of greenhouse gases by at least five per cent below 1990 levels by 2008–12. The protocol will enter into force following the ratification from 55 countries that accounted for at least 55 per cent of carbon emissions in 1990. In November 1998, at its fourth session, the COP agreed on the Buenos Aires Plan of Action for finalising the Protocol's outstanding details by the end of 2000. This fifth COP session was held in The Hague in November 2000 and ended in disarray. The future of the climate change agreements look uncertain, to say the least. Nevertheless, the FCCC and Kyoto Protocol are instructive for present purposes.

[19] See Article 3.5 of the Climate Change Convention.

[20] In fact, enforcement mechanisms have already been proposed that would provide for measures that would clearly violate the WTO rules; for example, trade sanctions being used to enforce emission targets in other countries. See WWF International (June 1998).

The Kyoto Protocol provides for mechanisms through which parties can implement their emissions commitments. The signatories may take measures to promote the:

> progressive reduction or phasing out of market imperfections, fiscal incentives, tax and duty exemptions and subsidies in all greenhouse gas emitting sectors that run contrary to the objective of the Convention and application of market instruments.

This is certainly very much in line with the WTO objective of the progressive removal of trade restrictions and distortions, and more particularly, with the discussion in the CTE of the need to remove restrictions and distortions that can adversely affect both trade and the environment. The protocol provides further formal assurance that the intention is to avoid use of trade-distorting measures. As with the FCCC itself, the Kyoto Protocol does not provide for any trade measures; in fact, parties shall strive to implement policies and measures 'in such a way as to minimise adverse effects ... on international trade.'[21]

Notwithstanding these general assurances, the Kyoto Protocol also states that each party:

> in achieving its quantified emission limitation and reduction commitments (and) ... in order to promote sustainable development, shall implement and/or further elaborate policies and measures in accordance with its national circumstances.

These include vague objectives (in terms of acceptable measures) such as enhancement of energy efficiency in relevant sectors, protection and enhancement of sinks, and promotion of sustainable forms of agriculture.

Thus, parties will develop their national response strategies to reduce emissions, and impose, for example, environmental taxes that apply directly to production processes. Environmental charges and taxes are increasingly used for the pursuit of national environment policy objectives and for 'internalising' domestic environmental costs. WTO rules discipline the way in which governments impose internal taxes and charges on traded goods, either when imposed on imported products or when rebated on exports. This is of considerable importance to trade and environment policymakers in the context of proposals to increase taxes on environmentally sensitive inputs to production, such as energy and transportation. When the international competitiveness of products is affected by such taxes, it would be surprising if there was not domestic pressure for them to be rebated. The rebating of such taxes is one of the most sensitive areas of unresolved legal interpretation of WTO rules; namely, in the WTO debate on how to deal with border tax adjustments.

As far as WTO rules are concerned, governments are in principle free to operate their fiscal regime according to national preferences and constraints. They are, however, subject to rules governing the application of domestic taxes and charges on goods traded internationally. Through border tax adjustment,

[21] Both quotations in this paragraph come from the Kyoto Protocol, Article 2.

countries may impose domestic taxes and charges on imports, and exempt or reimburse them on exports. The objective is to preserve the competitive equality between domestic and imported products. Which taxes can be imposed or rebated is, however, an area of considerable controversy in the WTO.[22]

While it is clear that border tax adjustment is possible for taxes levied on *products*, the extent to which taxes on inputs, incorporated or exhausted in the *production process* can be adjusted at the border, whether on exports or on imports, remains to be clarified (see Roessler, 1996). This has important implications for measures to reduce greenhouse gas emissions when applied to traded goods. Taxes levied directly on products because of their physical characteristics are eligible for tax adjustment under WTO rules. In the case of imports, this could be the imposition of equivalent domestic taxes on imported 'like' products; domestic taxes, for example, on the same imported coal and petroleum. As far as exports are concerned, taxes could be rebated if they were levied on the product at the domestic level; rebates of domestic taxes on exported coal and petroleum. This same understanding does not, however, extend to taxes paid in the process of producing the good (i.e. according to its life cycle); for example, rebating domestic taxes applied to processes, such as indirect taxes levied because of the energy consumed or the carbon emitted in the production process.[23] Thus, a domestic tax can be applied legitimately to imported fuel, but a tax cannot be applied on the energy consumed in producing a ton of steel.[24] In short, under existing GATT rules and jurisprudence, 'product' taxes and charges can be adjusted at the border, but 'process' taxes and charges probably cannot. Since environmental taxes and charges are at least as much process-oriented as product-oriented, WTO rules have caused concern about the competitiveness implications for domestic producers.[25]

---

[22] In 1968, a Working Party on Border Tax Adjustments was established in GATT to examine the provisions of the General Agreement relevant to border tax adjustments, the practices of contracting parties in relation to such adjustments, as well as their possible effects on international trade. The Working Party's report was adopted on 2 December, 1970. For a comprehensive discussion see WTO (2 May, 1997).

[23] Other such taxes include consumption taxes on capital equipment, auxiliary materials, and services used in the transportation and production of other taxable goods (e.g., taxes on advertising, energy, machinery, and transport).

[24] The view that taxes levied on non-product-related production methods are not eligible for adjustment has been challenged in the CTE on the grounds that GATT jurisprudence remains unclear on this point, and that certain important environmental taxes and charges might fall into the category of taxes *occults* on which the 1970 Working Party did not reach a firm conclusion. See WTO (12 November, 1996).

[25] The 1970 Working Party Report noted that 'there was a divergence of views with regard to the eligibility for adjustment of certain categories of tax', such as those which encompass consumption taxes on capital equipment auxiliary materials and services used in the transportation and production of other taxable goods, as well as taxes on advertising, energy, machinery and transport. The Working Party did not investigate the matter for it felt that 'while this area of taxation was unclear, its importance – as indicated by the scarcity of complaints reported in this connection – was not such as to justify further examination'.

This distinction also has implications for WTO obligations relating to subsidies.[26] The rebate of taxes in one country, which is not permitted in another, can have the same effect from a commercial perspective as a subsidy. Different views have been expressed on the likely treatment under the Agreement on Subsidies of a rebate for exported products of indirect environmental taxes on a process (and which are not incorporated into the characteristics of the product) in excess of the tax rebated on like products when sold for domestic consumption.[27]

Another important consideration is that the Technical Barriers to Trade (TBT) Agreement provides flexibility by recognising that priorities with respect to the environment differ between countries and that this can be fully reflected in domestic regulations. Therefore, it permits the adoption of different standards and regulations by WTO members. This could relate to the amount of energy used in the production of a good, or the level of carbon emissions within national borders. If a country chose not to adopt a certain standard that had an important effect on emissions reduction, this may give it a certain cost advantage over competitors in the world market. This raises a number of issues. First, the importing country cannot apply standards requirements to the processes outside its own borders. Standards can apply to domestic processes, but not those in other countries. Further, labelling imports with respect to production methods is certainly controversial in the WTO (see Abdel Motaal, 2000). As noted, there is also a subsidy issue involved. If a country were not to invoke exacting standards with respect to an energy intensive production process, for example, would this not constitute a subsidy to the country with the lower process standards?

Where MEAs have clearly mandated the Parties to take specific action against each other in agreed circumstances, the normal rules of international law and treaty interpretation would provide little room for a party to such Agreements to contest the legality of the measures on WTO grounds. If the agreed solution involves a loss of rights under the WTO (e.g. being discriminated against on the grounds of production methods), then providing all WTO members agree to forgo those rights, it is difficult to see where there could be a problem. If measures taken to meet the objectives of the MEA are not clearly provided for in the MEA itself – that is, both what is and what is not permitted in terms of measures to meet the objectives of the MEA – the issues to be settled may well gravitate to the WTO and could include some of the most sensitive WTO legal ambiguities.

---

[26] These discussions relate primarily to the WTO Agreement on Subsidies and Countervailing Measures, in particular its provisions on 'Prohibited Subsidies' (Article 3 and Annex I) and its 'Guidelines on Consumption of Inputs in the Production Process' (Annex II). The WTO Secretariat document referred to above also addresses the legitimacy of process related subsidies.

[27] One view is that energy taxes appear to be covered by Footnote 61 of the SCM Agreement. Another is that the principle of physical incorporation remains the basis upon which border tax adjustment is applied.

6. INCONSISTENT MEASURES

In general terms, measures to protect the environment can be taken by WTO members even if this means a violation of WTO rights and obligations. However, a waiver or an exception has to be sought for such measures with the approval of WTO members (for a waiver) or rather strict conditions being fulfilled (for an exception).

a. Waivers

In special circumstances a waiver can be granted to a WTO obligation, subject to approval by at least three-quarters of WTO members. This could provide a measured, case-by-case response to non-conforming measures taken for environmental purposes. It could also apply to a waiver, which is more general, such as special treatment for all measures specifically provided for in certain MEAs. While this process may appear attractive, it has not received general support from either trade or environment officials. There are a number of reasons for this. A waived obligation is time-limited and must be renewed periodically; and a trade measure applied pursuant to a waiver could still be challenged in WTO dispute settlement on the grounds of non-violation, nullification, and impairment of WTO rights.

It has been proposed in the CTE that the waiver approach could be modified to make it more attractive for environmental purposes.[28] Provision could be made for a special 'multi-year' waiver for trade measures applied pursuant to MEAs. All such measures taken under MEAs would be eligible for a waiver, provided they meet specified criteria. A 'negative vetting' approach could be adopted whereby the waiver would be automatically renewed if no new developments affect the exceptional circumstances that justified it in the first place. Specific trade measures contained in existing and future MEAs, whether among parties or against non-parties, could also be granted a waiver on a case-by-case basis subject to non-binding guidelines. The waiver would be extended annually until its termination, as long as the WTO requirements are met, and the 'exceptional circumstances' referred to in that provision would cover the specific trade measures included in certain MEAs.

As WTO members vote on waivers, presumably there would be little resistance to a waiver being accepted if there were broad-based support for the MEA, and as long as there was effective co-ordination between different parts of national administrations. Nevertheless, given the legal certainty sought by environmentalists (and discussed above), resort to any test of voting on a waiver in the WTO would probably fail to provide MEA negotiators with the required degree

[28] These and other proposals can be found in WTO (12 November, 1996).

of security, or predictability, in their negotiations. Even worse, it might be seen to entail the WTO passing judgement over other international legal instruments.

b. Exceptions

Exceptions to WTO rules for environmental purposes are provided for in the GATT 1994 Exceptions Article (i.e. Article XX). In this article, non-conforming measures can be taken for environmental purposes if they are necessary to protect human, animal, or plant life or health (Article XX(b)), or if they relate to the conservation of exhaustible natural resources and are made effective in conjunction with restrictions on domestic production or consumption (Article XX(g)). If at least one of these conditions is fulfilled, then the remaining requirement is specified in the head-note to Article XX: that the measures not be applied in an arbitrary or unjustifiable manner in order to discriminate between countries where the same conditions prevail or constitute a disguised restriction on international trade.

7. GUIDANCE FROM DISPUTES

Some insight can be obtained in addressing the interface between MEAs and WTO provisions by looking at recent Panel and Appellate Body rulings. Paradoxically, the most informative case is one where an MEA was not in existence: the so-called Shrimp-Turtle case.[29] This dispute was first dealt with by a WTO panel and then appealed through the Appellate Body.

The brief facts of the case are as follows. In 1997, India, Malaysia, Pakistan and Thailand brought a joint complaint against a ban imposed by the US on the importation of certain shrimp and shrimp products. Under US legislation, wild-caught shrimp products cannot be imported in the US if they do not meet US standards regarding the protection of sea turtles. More specifically, the US requires that shrimp trawlers install a 'turtle excluder device' in their nets when fishing in areas where there is a significant likelihood of encountering sea turtles: countries wishing to export their shrimp products to the US must impose the same requirement on their fishermen. The complaining countries challenged the ban as violating WTO rules through the unjustified imposition of an import embargo. The bigger issue at play was whether the extraterritorial application of domestic standards on the production processes in the exporting country (as a requirement for importing the product) was acceptable in terms of seeking an exception. In this sense, the case was as much about labour standards as it was about the environment.

[29] The reference for the Appellate Body Report is WTO (12 October, 1998). The relevant aspects of the panel report can be found in the Appellate Body Report.

The Panel concluded that the scope of Article XX, when read in the light of the object and purpose of the WTO Agreement, did not encompass measures whereby a member conditioned access to its market for a given product on the adoption of certain conservation policies by the exporting member(s). This, they said, could have far-reaching implications for the maintenance of the multilateral trading system. The Panel noted that the issue at stake in this dispute was not the urgency of protecting sea turtles, as all the parties agreed that sea turtles needed to be protected. The parties had indeed implemented conservation programmes for that purpose. Moreover, it was not the Panel's role to review either the desirability or necessity of WTO governments' environmental objectives on sea turtle conservation. The Panel concluded that the GATT exception only allows members to derogate from GATT provisions so long as, in doing so, they do not undermine the WTO multilateral trading system. What was important for the panel was that the measure in question was unilateral in nature, and there was no existing MEA to deal with the situation.[30] The panel noted that:

> by its very nature, the WTO Agreement favours a multilateral approach to trade issues

and that such unilateral action could undermine the multilateral trading system. On these grounds it could not be considered a legitimate exception from WTO obligations.

The Appellate Body ruled against the panel in this respect, and noted that while maintaining the multilateral trading system is necessarily a fundamental and pervasive premise underlying the WTO Agreements, it is neither a right nor an obligation, nor is it an interpretative rule which can be employed in the appraisal of a measure to protect the environment under Article XX. In the view of the Appellate Body, the panel did not look into the object and purpose of the head-note of Article XX. Rather, it looked into the object and purpose of the whole of the GATT 1994 and the WTO Agreement, the object and purpose of which it described in an overly broad manner. Thus the Panel arrived at the very broad formulation that measures that 'undermine the WTO multilateral trading system' must be regarded as 'not within the scope of measures permitted under the chapeau of Article XX.' In over-ruling the Panel decision in this respect, the Appellate Body clearly accepted the legitimacy of seeking exceptions for environmental purposes without first considering whether they 'undermined the multilateral trading system', or were applied in an arbitrary or discriminatory manner.

Some specific aspects of this case provide useful insights into the positive benefits that accrue to the WTO through the existence of effective MEAs; or the negative implications of governments having failed to negotiate an effective

[30] As there was no trade in turtles in this case, the Convention on Trade in Endangered Species could not be resorted to.

regional or multilateral environment agreement. This section discusses some of these.

It is of relevance that the Appellate Body spelled out the *sequence of steps* they thought appropriate in seeking an exception under the GATT 1994. It held that this is a two-tiered process: first, it must be assessed whether a measure qualifies for provisional justification as an exception. Second, it must be appraised whether such a measure meets the requirement that it is not applied in an arbitrary or unjustifiable manner or as a disguised restriction on international trade.[31]

With respect to the first tier, the Appellate Body had to determine if the measure related to the conservation of an *exhaustible natural resource* and therefore qualified for provisional justification under the exceptions article. At issue was whether a living creature should be considered to be an exhaustible natural resource. This interpretation is of importance in determining how future environment related disputes – particularly dealing with endangered species should they arise – will be dealt with at the WTO.

The Appellate Body ruled that in the light of contemporary international law, living species, which are in principle renewable:

> are in certain circumstances indeed susceptible of depletion, exhaustion and extinction, frequently because of human activities.

In taking this decision, the existence of an MEA was critical. As:

> all of the seven recognised species of sea turtles are listed in Appendix 1 of the Convention on International Trade in Endangered Species of Wild Fauna and Flora (CITES),

the Appellate Body concluded that the five species of sea turtles involved in the dispute constitute 'exhaustible natural resources' within the meaning of Article XX(g) of the GATT 1994.[32]

The Preamble to the Agreement Establishing the WTO was also considered to be relevant in this respect, and the Appellate Body was further influenced by existing agreements dealing with the environment.[33] The WTO preamble is, according to the Appellate Body, to give:

> colour, texture and shading to the rights and obligations of Members under the WTO Agreement.

[31] That is first with respect to Article XX(a) to (j) of GATT 1994 and then the head note of Article XX of GATT 1994.

[32] See paragraph 128 of WTO (12 October, 1998).

[33] Unlike the preamble to the GATT, the Preamble to the Agreement Establishing the World Trade Organisation conditions WTO Members actions on allowing 'for the optimal use of the world's resources in accordance with the objective of sustainable development, seeking both to protect and preserve the environment and to enhance the means for doing so in a manner consistent with their respective needs and concerns at different levels of economic development.'

In this 'colouring-in' exercise, the Appellate Body noted that:

> [g]iven the recent acknowledgement by the international community of the importance of concerted bilateral or multilateral action to protect living natural resources, and recalling the explicit recognition by WTO Members of the objective of sustainable development in the preamble of the WTO Agreement, we believe it is too late in the day to suppose that Article XX(g) of the GATT 1994 may be read as referring only to the conservation of exhaustible mineral or other non-living natural resources.[34]

Thus, the preservation of turtles was, on the basis of the facts of this case, an acceptable measure for which to seek an exception.

However, a further step to be taken was determining whether WTO members can take otherwise non-conforming measures to protect the environment (in this case the turtles) not only in their own countries, but also in the commons of their trading partners. Can WTO obligations be breached to ensure that certain standards deemed appropriate by the importing country are applied in the exporting country as a precondition for doing business?

Whether such *extraterritorial action* is permissible is not formally established by the text of the GATT exceptions provision itself. It is a matter for interpretation by panels and the Appellate Body. Much to the chagrin of many environmentalists, the traditional interpretation has been that trade measures relating to environmental standards should be taken only with respect to the fauna and flora and natural resources within the boundaries of the country taking the action.[35] The implications are clear. Countries are free to adopt whatever regulations they wish to reflect standards within their own borders, but they cannot restrict trade on the grounds that other countries do not apply these standards domestically.

In the Shrimp-Turtle case, the Appellate Body did not rule directly on the question of extraterritoriality and there is considerable confusion as to where matters now stand. One view is that some of the statements found in the report might be interpreted as implying that it would be possible to adopt measures including non-process and product-related production requirements, unilaterally decided by the importing country which are applied to imported comply with WTO requirements.[36] For others, the view is that by ruling on the case without addressing this issue, the Appellate Body had not accepted the complainants' argument that some sort of jurisdictional limitations would prevent the use of Article XX(g) with respect to the measures in question. For others, if this was the

[34] The Preamble to the Agreement Establishing the World Trade Organisation, paragraphs 127–34.
[35] While there has been flexibility in the WTO with respect to extraterritoriality, this has been circumscribed by the requirement that the objective of the measure is not to change the policy toward the environment in the exporting country. This, however, is the very purpose of most environmental measures of this nature.
[36] The following views are all expressed by national delegations in WTO (14 December, 1998).
[37] See paragraph 161, WTO (12 October, 1998).

case, this was a fundamental and impermissible alteration of the present balance of the rights and obligations of Members under the WTO Agreement, as this could open the door to unilateral measures aimed at discrimination based on non-product related process and production methods. The complaining countries had all agreed that turtles were an endangered species, that they should be protected, and therefore had their national conservation strategies in place.

However, the Appellate Body noted that the most conspicuous flaw in the application of the trade sanction related to its intended and actual coercive effect on the specific policy decisions made by foreign governments. It considered that:

> it is not acceptable, in international trade relations, for one WTO Member to use an economic embargo to require other Members to adopt essentially the same comprehensive regulatory program, to achieve a certain policy goal, as that in force within that Member's territory, without taking into consideration different conditions which may occur in the territories of those other Members.[37]

Thus, the question of extraterritorial application of domestic process standards appears to be left open.

In the final analysis, the Appellate Body ruled against the measure taken by the United States to restrict imported shrimp on the grounds that it was applied in a manner, which amounts to a means not just of unjustifiable discrimination, but also of 'arbitrary' discrimination between countries where the same conditions prevail. This, it was concluded, was contrary to the requirements of the head-note of the GATT exceptions article. Thus, the absence of an MEA to deal with turtle protection through trade measures proved critical. While the Appellate Body recognised the importance of protecting and preserving an exhaustible natural resource, it also made clear that WTO Members must also fulfil their obligations and respect the rights of other Members under the WTO. On the facts of the case, it found that, among other things, the failure to have established an environmental agreement as an instrument of environmental protection policy had resulted in unilateralism which was discriminatory and unjustifiable, and that a rigid and inflexible application of the measure in question resulted in arbitrary discrimination. From the perspective of the Appellate Body, it is critical when negotiating an MEA, that parties ensure that trade measures are not included in the MEA if they are unnecessary, or applied in an arbitrary, protectionist or unjustifiably discriminatory manner.[38]

[38] The Appellate Body found the United States to be in error with respect to its failure to enter into multilateral or bilateral talks with the complaining countries in order to conclude an agreement protecting sea turtles. The United States did not enter into negotiations before imposing the import ban. The government did negotiate and conclude one regional agreement, the Inter-American Convention, which proved that alternative courses of action to the imposition of an embargo were available.

[39] See WTO (19 October, 2000a). This view is also expressed by the European Community in

8. INNOVATIVE APPROACHES

The view commonly expressed in the CTE is that amending the Exceptions Article XX would open a debate and entail the risk that the whole Article – which was the balanced result of long negotiations – would have to be reconsidered. However, a number of innovative ideas have emerged that capture some of the concerns discussed above, but which fall short of a textual change to the Exceptions Article.[39]

In order to make sure that specifically mandated trade measures taken pursuant to MEAs are recognised as being necessary and justified under WTO rules, a proposal has been made to 'reverse the burden of proof' when seeking an exception from WTO rules to protect the environment.[40] The proponents of this approach draw a parallel with the WTO Sanitary and Phyto-sanitary Agreement and the Technical Barriers to Trade Agreement, where the country challenging the measure would have to prove the measures imposed by the other party do not meet the conditions of the exceptions article. Therefore, the trade measure, itself provided for by an MEA, should benefit from a presumption of WTO conformity; that is, to be 'necessary' to protect the environment; not to be arbitrarily or unjustifiably discriminating, and not to be a disguised restriction on international trade. The conditions such MEAs must fulfil to be able to avail themselves of such presumptions would have to be agreed to and, *inter alia*, these criteria should ensure that the MEAs are supported by all interested parties and that their provisions concerning trade-related measures are drafted precisely. In this respect, there are a number of important practical issues. For example, if a country chose not to accept a certain standard, who would judge the appropriateness of that decision? The country may not adopt the more rigorous standard as it may find the scientific evidence unconvincing, have a high absorptive capacity for the environmental damage concerned or have other social and economic priorities.

The 'savings clause' has been recognised in the Vienna Convention as a way for parties to an agreement to clarify their intentions *vis-à-vis* other agreements. If all parties to a negotiation were clear that no conflict was intended, they could agree to reflect this in a savings clause. The formal insertion of such a clause could be an effective way of preventing governments from changing their intentions and prevent disputes from arising at the WTO. However, agreeing on a savings clause is not always a simple matter as the negotiation of the Bio-safety Protocol made clear.

The agreed text on the Bio-safety Protocol which emerged from Montreal last year addresses the concerns raised by the trans-boundary movement, transit,

---

WTO (19 October, 2000b).

[40] See WTO (19 October, 2000).

[41] See the Appellate Body Report, paragraphs 127–34 (WTO, 1998a).

handling and use of all living modified organisms with adverse effects on the conservation and sustainable use of biological diversity, and on human health. Much has been asked about the relationship between WTO rules and the Bio-safety Protocol, and in particular their compatibility or incompatibility with the Protocol. The case has been made that conflicts over potential inconsistencies during the negotiation of the Bio-safety Protocol clearly highlighted the need for a savings clause to clarify the basic parameters of the agreements.

However, the text, which emerged from the Montreal negotiations, does not appear to clarify matters at all. It states that:

> this Protocol shall not be interpreted as implying a change in the rights and obligations of a party under any existing international agreement.

This in itself would appear clear enough – WTO rights and obligations stay intact. The following paragraph, however, states that:

> the above recital is not intended to subordinate this Protocol to other international agreements.

This reads that they do not.

9. THE WAY FORWARD

a. Avoiding Disputes

It should not be beyond the competence of governments, given the existing knowledge about the trade provisions of MEAs, their objectives, and WTO rules to ensure that no formal dispute should arise between the provisions of the MEAs and WTO rules. A number of steps could be taken, however, to increase this likelihood of avoiding an environmental dispute finding its way to the WTO.

It should be possible to enhance transparency, dialogue, and co-operation between MEAs, relevant international organisations, and the WTO from the initial stage of negotiation of an MEA to its implementation. This co-operation could contribute to dispute avoidance if it involved an exchange of information, mutual participation in meetings, access to documents and databases, and briefing sessions, as necessary. It has been proposed in the CTE that a guide containing WTO principles could be compiled by the WTO Secretariat that could be used by MEA negotiators in their consideration of proposed trade measures. It has also been suggested that there could be co-operation agreements between the WTO and MEA institutions providing for the WTO secretariat to respond to requests for technical information about relevant WTO provisions. There has also been a proposal for the establishment of an informal mechanism for dialogue to discuss and exchange information on trade and environment issues.[41] This could involve,

[42] See Martin (2001).

inter alia, the United Nations Environment Program (UNEP), the WTO and MEA Secretariats, the members of the WTO and parties to the environmental agreements, as well as NGOs and industry. Such a mechanism would allow interested parties to develop a better understanding of trade and environment-related issues, in a forum which is not mandated to negotiate rules, but is rather aimed at preventing conflict and improving co-operation and co-ordination amongst policy makers.

It would seem important in MEA negotiations that representatives of both the environmental and trade ministries are present to ensure that MEAs utilise only those trade measures which are necessary for the protection of the environment, and which do not constitute a means of arbitrary or unjustifiable discrimination or a disguised restriction on international trade. In fact, newer MEAs, such as the Prior Informed Consent (PIC) Convention, or the Cartagena Protocol on Biosafety, explicitly refer to the principle of mutual supportiveness, and have involved both trade and environment officials.

In this manner, environmental standards for agreed production and process methods and products could be established within the context of the MEA; if there are grounds for discrimination in trade because of the characteristics of what is being traded (endangered species) or how a product is produced (carbon-emitting production processes), the appropriate standards should be established through agreement by the appropriate experts. There should be no objection to this approach. In fact, as this procedure would relieve the WTO of many concerns relating to difficult concepts such as like products and non-product-related product and production methods, it is not surprising that WTO members, as well as panel and Appellate Body reports, have strongly promoted the use of multilateral or other agreements to deal with these matters.

If the agreed solution involves a loss of rights under the WTO (that is, being discriminated against), then providing all WTO members agree to forgo those rights, it is difficult to see where there could be a problem. The text of the MEA should make clear that if the membership of the MEA coincides with that of the WTO, then disputes over a trade measure used for environmental purposes, in accordance with the MEA, should be dealt with through the MEA compliance mechanism.

b. An Alternative Approach to Settling Disputes

The President for World Wide Fund for Nature International recently observed that the Shrimp-Turtle dispute illustrates that, because of its adversarial nature, formal WTO dispute settlement may not be the best means to resolve disputes of this kind. He suggested that WTO members should explore the establishment of multi-stakeholder consultative processes in which relevant facts could be put on the table by all interested parties from governments, non-governmental organisations, industry, academia and local communities.[42] In fact, the Dispute Settlement Understanding formally creates the option of parties to the potential dispute to request the good offices of the Director-General to engage in consultations to settle the dispute. Such a consultative process could assist in providing the countries involved with an opportunity to consider a range of policy instruments suitable to resolve any trade related environmental issue which may have arisen.

Should agreement not be reached, a possible approach – that would require no textual changes to WTO Agreements – would be for the Director General of the WTO, in collaboration with his counterpart in the relevant MEA in terms of the subject matter being contested, to jointly hold consultations with the governments concerned.[43] To meet the criticisms of lack of transparency confronting the WTO in these maters, there could also be public hearings involving all interested parties: governments, non-governmental organisations, industry, academia and local communities. In this respect, it is worthy to note that in the shrimp-turtle case, the good offices of the Director-General were not sought.

This course of action would not be an obligation imposed on disputing parties, but it would constitute an alternative available to them. If it was resisted on the grounds that a public hearing would delay the settling of a dispute that could be urgent from an environmental perspective, it could be counter-argued that the absence of a formal procedure would expedite the process of bringing the parties together informally; and if there were no definitive outcome, presumably the consultations under the good offices of the Director-General would not be required.

Even if there were not a positive outcome in terms of a clear decision, this process would be totally transparent – something sought by many non-governmental organisations. The possibility of providing inputs from technical experts is another advantage. And the more WTO formal dispute settlement process would be avoided if the mediation were successful; the normal WTO channel of dispute settlement would, however, still remain open. While no country's rights and obligations would be affected in this process, it could be argued that the technical information provided could eventually influence the conclusion of the panel or the Appellate Body, if the process went that far. Yet it is hard to argue that additional factual information is a handicap if a well-informed decision is the ultimate objective.

The question could also be posed: What is so special about environmental disputes that merits an approach such as this? The answer is: Nothing. The process is equally applicable to all potential disputes if the defending and complaining countries agree. Indeed, such a process could be carried out by an

[43] This proposal is further elaborated in Sampson (2000).
[44] See Sampson (1998).

MEA outside the WTO or in collaboration with the WTO, for example if the idea was not adopted by the WTO.

c. Future Trade Negotiations

At the time of writing, the Director General of the WTO and a number of governments remain optimistic that a new round of multilateral negotiations will be launched in Qatar. With respect to the issues addressed in this article, and past experience in the Uruguay Round, it would seem appropriate to consider the creation of at least two specific groups in any new round of negotiations to deal with problems relating to trade and the environment.

First, in future negotiations, it would seem appropriate to establish a Group to review the Articles of the GATT (the Articles Group), as was the case in the Uruguay Round. The outcome of this process was a series of Understandings relating to individual articles to clarify their application in the light of four decades of experience. In this process, no Understanding with respect to the interpretation of the exceptions provision of GATT (Article XX) was thought necessary. Given the discussion in recent years, and the controversy over the interpretation of the exceptions provisions, it could be argued that it is appropriate to consider if an understanding or an interpretation is now required, and if not, then to settle the issue definitively. As many of the matters involved in the Article XX disputes have been of considerable importance from a policy perspective, the GATT/WTO tradition of deciding policy through debate and consensus is far preferable to what seems to have emerged in recent years involving evolutionary policy formulation through litigation in the dispute settlement process.

Second, a Group could be established to bring coherence between multilateral trade and multilateral environment policies. Here too, a precedent exists. In the Uruguay Round, a negotiating group was created to examine ways to bring greater coherence to global economic policy-making. The 'so-called' FOGS (Functioning of the GATT System) Group produced a Ministerial Declaration on the Contribution of the World Trade Organisation to Achieving Greater Coherence in Global Economic Policy-making. Ministers recognised that:

> difficulties, the origins of which lie outside the trade field can not be redressed through measures taken in the trade field alone.

They acknowledged that the:

> inter-linkages between the different aspects of economic policy require that the international institutions with responsibilities in each of these areas follow consistent and mutually supportive policies.[44]

[45] I have argued elsewhere that it is time to look seriously and objectively as to what is the

As the declaration called for the WTO to develop co-operation with other international organisations, it served as the basis for the comprehensive and formal agreements that were struck between the WTO, the World Bank and the International Monetary Fund. While the FOGS group concentrated on bringing greater coherence to economic policymaking, it would seem reasonable that a similar group give guidance as to how to establish a mutually supportive relationship between the WTO and various environmental agreements. This could well be the objective of a FOWTOG (Functioning of the World Trade Organisation Group).

d. WTO and Global Governance

The time has come to consider a way to deal with a number of non-traditional trade related problems that seem to be gravitating to the WTO. This could be done outside the negotiating context and by those with the capacity to adopt a broader vision of the role of the world trading system in global governance.[45]

A fundamental question that the group could address is the conditions according to which trade measures can be used to discriminate between like products made with different production processes. The answer to this question is relevant in ethical matters such as defining the role of precaution in the absence of scientific evidence and the use of unilateral trade measures to enforce nationally preferred environmental standards. It also underpins the concerns of developing countries with respect to the eventual inclusion of matters relating to labour standards, and a new 'justification' for protection on moral grounds.

Unlike other institutions, the WTO has had extremely limited recourse to High Level or Eminent Persons Groups to deal with matters beyond the normal business of negotiations. One exception has been the Leutwiler Group which addressed a number of systemic issues prior to the launching of the Uruguay Round and issued an influential report entitled 'Trade Policies for a Better Future; Proposals for Action'.[46] Few would deny the important contribution of this group to the Uruguay Round negotiations in terms of new policy orientations.[47]

appropriate role of the WTO in global governance. See Sampson (2001).

[46] See GATT (1985).

[47] The group recommended, for example, that 'trade policy and the functioning of the trading system should be made more open. Countries should be subject to the regular oversight or surveillance of their policies and actions, about which the GATT secretariat should collect and publish information.'

10. CONCLUSION

While the range of potential conflicts between MEAs and the WTO Agreements is somewhat circumscribed, questions will continue to arise when provisions of an MEA are unclear as to the action they mandate, even among the Parties to it, or in situations where the Parties to an MEA are applying trade measures against a non-party. Change in WTO rules and processes to accommodate the concerns of environmentalists will not come easily and certainly not outside of the context of a new round of broad-based multilateral negotiations. The WTO is a consensus-based organisation and many WTO members see no need for change in this respect. Notwithstanding that, eventual conflict between the rules of MEAs and the WTO remains a real possibility and a collision between regimes as important as those protecting the environment and the trading system should certainly be avoided.

What I have argued in this article is that in order to operate in a credible and efficient manner, the WTO needs effective, broad-based and consensus-driven MEAs including all interested WTO members. If WTO inconsistent measures are provided for in the MEA they should be clearly defined and enforced by a robust dispute settlement system within the MEA itself. If the political will of the international community falls short of what is necessary to agree on MEAs with these characteristics, a heavy price will be paid. Trade-related environmental disputes will gravitate to the WTO, as no alternative mechanism will be available to deal with them. In the absence of a world government to settle global environment problems and the division of responsibilities between different international organisations, we are confronted with a problem of global governance. It should not be beyond the capabilities of the world's leaders to decide on what is to be the role of the WTO in global governance.

REFERENCES

Abdel Motaal, D. (2000), 'The Agreement on Technical Barriers to Trade, the Committee on Trade and the Environment and Eco-labeling', in G. P. Sampson and B. Chambers (eds.), *Trade Environment and the Millennium* (Tokyo: United Nations University Press).

Brack, D. (2000), 'Environmental Treaties and Trade: Multilateral Environment Agreements and the Multilateral Trading System', in G. P. Sampson and B. Chambers (eds.), *Trade Environment and the Millennium* (Tokyo: United Nations University Press).

Charnovitz, S. (1997), 'A Critical Guide to the WTO's Report on Trade and the Environment', *Arizona Journal of International and Comparative Law*, **14**, 2.

Dutfield, G. (2000), *Intellectual Property Rights, Trade and Bio-diversity* (United Kingdom: Earthscan Publications Ltd.).

GATT (1985), 'Trade Policies for a Better Future; Proposals for Action', in *Leutwiler Report* (Geneva: GATT Secretariat).

Goldberg, D. M. (1995), 'The Framework Convention on Climate Change', in R. Housman et al. (eds.), *The Use of Trade Measures in Select Multilateral Environment Agreements* (UNEP and CIEL).

Hudec, R. E. (1996), 'The Gatt/WTO Dispute Settlement Process: Can it Reconcile Trade Rules and Environment Needs?', in R. Wolfrum (ed.), *Enforcing Environmental Standards: Economic Mechanisms as Viable Means* (Berlin: Springer-Verlag).
Jackson, J. (1998), *The World Trade Organization: Constitution and Jurisprudence* (London: The Royal Institute of International Affairs).
Martin, C. (2001), 'The Relationship Between Trade and Environment Regimes: What Needs to Change', Chapter 7 in G. P. Sampson (ed.), *The Role of the WTO in Global Governance* (Tokyo: United Nations University Press).
Roessler, F. (1996), 'Diverging Domestic Policies and Multilateral Trade Integration', in J. Bhagwati and R. Hudec (eds.), *Fair Trade and Harmonization Prerequisites for Free Trade?* (Cambridge, Massachusetts: The MIT Press).
Sampson, G. P. (1998), 'Greater Coherence in Global Economic Policy Making', in A. O. Krueger (ed.), *The WTO as an International Organization* (Chicago and London: The University of Chicago Press).
Sampson, G. P. (2000), *Trade Environment and the WTO: The Post-Seattle Agenda* (Washington: Overseas Development Council and Johns Hopkins University Press).
Sampson, G. P. (ed.) (2001), *The Role of the WTO in Global Governance* (Tokyo: United Nations University Press).
Stewart, R. B., J. B. Wiener and P. Sands (1996), *Legal Issues Presented by a Pilot International Greenhouse Gas Trading System* (Geneva: UNCTAD).
WTO (12 November, 1996), *Report of CTE to Singapore Ministerial Conference*, WT/CTE/1.
WTO (2 May, 1997), *Taxes and Charges for Environmental Purposes: Border Tax Adjustment*, WT/CTE/W/47.
WTO (12 October, 1998) *United States – Import Prohibition of Certain Shrimp and Shrimp Products*, Appellate Body Report, WT/DS58/AB/R.
WTO (14 December, 1998), *Minutes of Meeting of the Dispute Settlement Body*, WT/DSB/M/50.
WTO (19 September, 2000), *Matrix on Trade Measures Pursuant to Selected MEAs*, Note by The WTO Secretariat, WT/CTEW/160.
WTO (10 October, 2000), *The Relationship Between the Provisions of the Multilateral Trading System and Trade Measures for Environment Purposes including those Pursuant to Multilateral Environment Agreements*, Communication from New Zealand, WT/CTE/W/162.
WTO (19 October, 2000), *Clarification of the Relationship Between the WTO and Multilateral Environmental Agreements*, Submission by Switzerland, WT/CTE/W/168.
WTO (19 October, 2000), *Resolving the Relationship Between WTO Rules and Multilateral Environmental Agreements*, Submission by the European Community, WT/CTE/W/170.
WTO (12 December, 2000), *Minutes of the Meeting on 24–25 October 2000*, WT/CTE/M/25.
WWF International (June, 1998), *Climate Change and Compliance*, WWF Discussion Paper (Gland, Switzerland).

[23]

Sharing the Benefits of Biodiversity

Is there a Role for the Patent System?

Graham DUTFIELD*

"Patents shield the collective interests of all participants."

Jeff Kushan[1]

"... there is no 'bioprospecting' only 'biopiracy'."

Pat Mooney[2]

I. INTRODUCTION

The Convention on Biological Diversity (CBD), which entered into force in 1993, has, as its three objectives:

> "... the conservation of biological diversity, the sustainable use of its components and the fair and equitable sharing of the benefits arising out of the utilization of genetic resources."

Intellectual property rights (IPRs), and particularly patents, are considered to be most relevant to the third of these objectives, that of fair and equitable benefit-sharing. This article seeks to answer three questions. First, do patents promote the sharing of benefits between the commercial users of genetic resources and associated traditional knowledge and the provider States and indigenous communities? Second, if they do not, why not? Third, how might the patent system be made more compatible with the CBD, bearing in mind the obligations that countries have accepted through their membership of the World Trade Organization (WTO) and adherence to the Agreement on Trade-Related Aspects of Intellectual Property Rights (TRIPS)?

The article begins by explaining how benefit-sharing emerged as a political issue and the way it was incorporated into the CBD. This opening Section also covers the

* Herchel Smith Senior Research Fellow, Queen Mary Intellectual Property Research Institute, University of London; Senior Research Associate, Oxford Centre for Intellectual Property Research, St Peter's College, University of Oxford; Academic Director, International Centre for Trade and Sustainable Development—UN Conference on Trade and Development (ICTSD–UNCTAD) Capacity Building Project on TRIPS and Development (2001-2003).

I am grateful to Maiko Ozawa for helping me to better understand the Japanese patent system, to Richard Tarasofsky for his helpful comments on an earlier version of this article, and to Geertrui van Oyerwalle for kindly sending me two articles relevant to the discussion on disclosure of origin.

The author may be contacted at: «g.dutfield@qmul.ac.uk».

1 Former U.S. Negotiator on trade, intellectual property rights and the Convention on Biological Diversity (CBD). This statement is taken from the notes of a presentation made by Jeff Kushan on *Patents and Biopiracy: Getting to the Bottom of the Debate*, at the WIPO Conference on the International Patent System, Geneva, March 2002.

2 Executive Director of Action Group on Erosion, Technology and Concentration (ETC Group). Quoted from, P.R. Mooney, *Why we call it Biopiracy*, in H. Svarstad and S.S. Dhillion (eds.), *Responding to Bioprospecting: From Biodiversity in the South to Medicines in the North*, Spartacus Forlag, Oslo, at 38.

CBD's treatment of IPRs. The next Section identifies and describes three ways that the patent system seems to hinder the implementation of the CBD's benefit-sharing objective. The article goes on to describe the current state of international negotiations on the access and benefit-sharing (ABS)/patent relationship and the proposals put forward to harmonise the two. The final Section evaluates the main proposals that have been put forward by governments at the relevant forums to make the patent system more supportive of the CBD's ABS provisions.

II. Access and Benefit-Sharing in the CBD: How it Got There and What it Means

Since the CBD came into force, ABS has been one of the main topics for discussion during the meetings of the Conference of the Parties (COP), which usually take place every two years. This is hardly surprising considering the negotiating history of the Convention. It is worth describing the history because it explains a great deal about why ABS is treated as such an important issue, especially for developing country parties. It also explains why the text of the CBD is unbalanced, in the sense that so much of it deals with matters that are not directly related to conservation of biological diversity.

When the CBD was first conceived there was little expectation that negotiations would become as politicized as they did. The United States had initially proposed to the Governing Council of the United Nations Environment Programme (UNEP) that there be a convention on biological diversity in 1987. By this time, the International Union for the Conservation of Nature (IUCN), a major international environmental non-governmental organization (NGO) had already begun drafting a convention on the *in situ* conservation of biological diversity. The Council adopted a Resolution supporting the IUCN's efforts, and requesting that UNEP's Executive Director:

> "... establish an *ad hoc* working group ... to establish the desirability and possible form of an umbrella convention to rationalise current activities in this field."[3]

Two years later, the Governing Council followed up by authorizing the Executive Director to establish:

> "... an *ad hoc* working group of legal and technical experts with a mandate to negotiate an international legal instrument for the conservation of the biological diversity of the planet."[4]

Neither the U.S. government nor the IUCN envisaged that their efforts would spawn an agreement dealing not only with conservation but also with biotechnology, technology transfer and IPRs. In fact, the United States would hardly have proposed it if it could have foreseen the outcome!

Agreeing a text acceptable to governments of the biodiversity-poor industrialized

[3] In W.E. Burhenne, *Foreword*, in V. Sánchez and C. Juma (eds.), *Biodiplomacy: Genetic Resources and International Relations*, ACTS Press, Nairobi, 1994, at x.

[4] Ibid., at xi.

world and of the biodiversity-rich developing countries turned into an unexpectedly long, difficult and contentious process. Some developing countries, initially Malaysia and India, complained that it was unfair for influential conservation organizations (like the IUCN) and developed country governments to expect them to protect their forests and forgo the economic benefits from selling timber or converting them to other uses. These countries argued vociferously that a *quid pro quo* for biodiversity preservation was fair and necessary. Realising the potential economic value of their biodiversity wealth and needing to improve their scientific, technological and financial capacities to exploit it, their position was that they had the right to set conditions on those seeking access to *their* resources, including the fair and equitable sharing of benefits such as the transfer of technology and financial resources. Needless to say, perhaps, developed countries and transnational corporations wanted as few restrictions and conditions as possible on access to biological resources.

While the position of these developing countries seems very reasonable, it introduced some major difficulties. First, although not directly stated, the CBD's language is based on an inherent assumption that the main users of genetic resources are pharmaceutical and biotechnology firms. It is important to underline here that the rights and responsibilities in relation to ABS arise in connection with "genetic resources"[5] rather than the broader term "biological resources".[6] Second, the emphasis on national sovereignty and the authority of governments to regulate access suggests that bilateral negotiations are to be the normal means by which biodiversity-rich but technologically-poor countries can benefit fairly from the commercial use of resources acquired from them.

What is wrong here? First, the pharmaceutical corporations are primarily interested in pharmacologically active biochemical substances that do not contain DNA and are therefore not genetic resources. Biotechnology firms, it is true are interested in genes, and not just therapeutic proteins. But these latter businesses are generally small, short of cash and have no products to sell or license (except patents). There is nothing to stop governments from extending their ABS regimes to cover biochemical resources, and some of them do, but the choice of terminology seems to reflect a lack of realism, which becomes more apparent when discussing the second point. This is that when it comes to plant genetic resources for food and agriculture, no country is completely self-sufficient, not even countries like Brazil and India. In fact, these resources have generally been exchanged quite openly, and it is in the interests of all countries, as well as farmers and plant breeders, that this situation should continue. This is why countries generally exercise their national sovereignty rights in a way that places few access restrictions on this category of biological resource, and why the new Food and Agriculture Organization (FAO) International Treaty on Plant Genetic Resources for

[5] Defined in the CBD as "genetic material of actual or potential value" (Article 2).

[6] Defined in the CBD as including "genetic resources, organisms or parts thereof, populations, or any other biotic component of ecosystems with actual or potential use or value for humanity" (Article 2).

Food and Agriculture establishes a multilateral system of facilitated access to plant genetic resources for food and agriculture and benefit-sharing.

In other words, the CBD promotes bilateral agreements between providers and users of resources for which a multilateral approach is more mutually beneficial *and* encourages countries to withhold access to resources that should probably be circulated freely for the benefit of all countries.[7] And even if governments extend their ABS regulations to cover biological resources, their bargaining position is not all that strong. The same resources may exist in two or more countries. Also, natural product research is one of several competing approaches to drug discovery. In this context it is worth bearing in mind that chemists have created ten million new molecules since the nineteenth century, and also that nowadays they can make twenty-five thousand variants of the same molecule.[8] As long as companies have plenty of lead compounds to investigate, bioprospecting may not be as important as many people think.

Third, there is surprisingly little information on the economic potential of *in situ* genetic resources. Yet, designing an appropriate ABS regulatory regime without having any idea of how much the resources are likely to be worth means founding it on guesswork and assumptions that may be completely false.

The relationship between IPRs and the CBD tends to be treated as most relevant to the regulation of access to genetic resources and the development of measures to ensure fair and equitable benefit-sharing with States and the holders of traditional knowledge. The most important parts of the Convention here are Articles 15 and 8(j). Article 15 recognizes the sovereign rights of States over their natural resources and their authority to determine access to generic resources, and that access, where granted, shall be on mutually agreed terms and subject to prior informed consent of the provider party. Article 8(j) requires parties to:

> "... respect, preserve and maintain knowledge, innovations and practices of indigenous and local communities embodying traditional lifestyles relevant for the conservation and sustainable use of biological diversity and promote their wider application with the approval and involvement of the holders of such knowledge, innovations and practices and encourage the equitable sharing of the benefits arising from the utilization of such knowledge, innovations and practices."

In spite of this, intellectual property is only explicitly referred to in the context of technology transfer, which is supposed to be one of the main kinds of benefit for provider countries to receive.[9] Article 16, on access to and transfer of technology, requires parties to the Convention to undertake to provide and/or facilitate access and transfer of technologies to other parties under fair and most favourable terms. The only technology referred to is biotechnology, but Article 16 is concerned with any

[7] See D. Charles, *Seeds of Discontent*, Science 294, 2001, 773–775.

[8] B. Bensaude-Vincent and I. Stengers, *A History of Chemistry*, Harvard University Press, Cambridge and London, 1996, at 255.

[9] Along with appropriate access to genetic resources and appropriate funding (Article 1).

technologies "that are relevant to the conservation and sustainable use of biological diversity or make use of genetic resources and do not cause significant damage to the environment." Recognizing that technologies are sometimes subject to patents and other IPRs, access to such technologies must be "on terms which recognize and are consistent with the adequate and effective protection of intellectual property rights ...".[10] Clearly this is nothing for the life-science industries to feel too concerned about. Indeed, the clause beginning "adequate and effective protection" was specifically to establish a link with the draft TRIPS Agreement, which also used this language as did the final version.

Paragraph 16.5 is a little more controversial, requiring the parties to co-operate to ensure that patents and other IPRs "are supportive of and do not run counter to" the CBD's objectives. This reflects the profound disagreement during the negotiations between those who believed that IPRs conflict with the CBD's objectives, and others that saw no contradiction. While the language is not particularly threatening, life-science firms in the United States were nonetheless unhappy with the CBD's coverage of IPRs and with the Convention more generally, and persuaded President George Bush that it was not in America's best interests to sign it. Although the United States did so a few years later in the latter part of the 1990s, it remains one of the few countries in the world not to have ratified it.[11]

III. The Problems with Patents

For the sake of a proper discussion on the problems with patents it is helpful to clarify what the current international patent standards are in relation to biochemical compounds, genetic resources and life-forms. Article 27.1 of the TRIPS Agreement requires WTO Members to allow patents to:

> "... be available for any inventions, whether products or processes, in all fields of technology, provided that they are new, involve an inventive step and are capable of industrial application ...".

But Article 27.3(b) allows Members to exclude from patentability the following:

> "(b) plants and animals other than micro-organisms, and essentially biological processes for the production of plants or animals other than non-biological and microbiological processes. However, Members shall provide for the protection of plant varieties either by patents or by an effective *sui generis* system or by any combination thereof ...".

In terms of products, then, micro-organisms must be patentable and plant variety rights must come under some kind of IPR system (see *Table 1*, which summarizes what Article 27.3(b) requires Members to do and allows them not to do).

But what about genetic and biochemical resources? Must these also be patentable? Since they are not expressly excluded patents must, in principle, be made available for

[10] Article 16.2.

[11] Thailand is another notable non-party.

TABLE 1: SUMMARY OF TRIPS ARTICLE 27.3(B) PROVISIONS

WTO members must provide protection for:	WTO members may exclude from patent protection:
Micro-organisms	Plants
Non-biological processes	Animals
Microbiological processes	Essentially biological processes for the production of plants or animals.
Plant varieties (by an intellectual property right system which may be patents, a *sui generis* alternative, or a combination).	Plant varieties

these. But this should be subject to the conditions that they be new, involve an inventive step and be capable of industrial application. Do these requirements mean that resources existing in nature cannot be patented? As will be explained below, they do not in the United States and Europe,[12] though arguably they should.

Before going further, the reader should be reminded of the opening quote of this article, which implies that patents may be necessary to ensure that commercial benefits can be shared fairly and equitably between all parties. What are the grounds for believing this to be the case? The main argument is that patents, as with other kinds of property, provide exclusive rights that allow markets for certain things—in this case, valuable information in the form of inventions—to operate where they otherwise could not do so. As Paul Geroski puts it:

> "... patents are designed to create a market for knowledge by assigning propriety rights to innovators which enable them to overcome the problem of non-excludability while, at the same time, encouraging the maximum diffusion of knowledge by making it public."[13]

The "public goods" justification for patents posits that such rights are likely to have various beneficial effects. Several economists and others have countered convincingly that knowledge is not exactly like other public goods and that such justifications need to be qualified.[14] Persuasive as these counter-arguments may be, let us, for the sake of argument, accept that knowledge is a public good.

Accordingly, two such beneficial effects should be mentioned here. The first is that they encourage investment in invention and the research and development needed to turn inventions into marketable innovations. The second—and this takes us back to Kushan's point—is that the partners can exploit the market value of an invention in ways they could not do without a patent.

---

[12] In the United States inventions must be new, useful and non-obvious to be patentable. Novelty, however defined, is a universal requirement but not the other two. In Europe, for example, the two other requirements (apart from novelty) are industrial application and inventive step.

[13] P. Geroski, *Markets for Technology: Knowledge, Innovation and Appropriability*, in P. Stoneman (ed.), *Handbook of the Economics of Innovation and Technological Change*, Blackwell, Oxford and Malden, 1995, at 97; see also K.J. Arrow, *Economic Welfare and the Allocation of Resources in Invention*, in NBER, *The Rate and Direction of Innovative Activity*, Princeton University Press, Princeton, 1962, at 619.

[14] See P. David, *Intellectual Property Institutions and the Panda's Thumb: Patents, Copyrights, and Trade Secrets in Economic Theory and History*, in M.B. Wallerstein, R.A. Schoen and M.E. Mogee (eds.), *Global Dimensions of Intellectual Property Rights in Science and Technology*, National Academy Press, Washington, D.C., 1993, at 27–28.

How would this work? Ownership of the patent could be shared, or it could be held by one party on behalf of the others by an arrangement that all would benefit from successful appropriation of the patent's market value, either by developing a product or selling or licensing the patent to someone else interested in doing so. Since many innovations and patents are dependent upon earlier patents, it is conceivable also that the patent could be used to engage profitably in transactions with follow-on innovators.

So much for the theory. What about the practice? In reality, while patents could indeed shield the collective interests of all parties and no doubt often do, when it comes to bioprospecting this very rarely happens.[15] Why is this? One reason—and this would be consistent with Geroski's perspective—is that indigenous communities tend not to enjoy legal property rights over their valuable (or potentially valuable) knowledge. It would certainly help if they did, though the fact they do not is really a matter of social injustice rather than one of economic inefficiency. Another possible reason for the failure to distribute benefits fairly is that companies using genetic material and associated traditional knowledge (TK) prefer to deal with governments and indigenous communities at arm's length, if at all. However, certain features and trends in patent law itself are also responsible, and it is to this matter—which is the main focus of this article—that the discussion now turns.

One can identify three closely related issues that potentially, and almost certainly in reality, make the patent system unhelpful in promoting fair and equitable benefit-sharing. These are the extension of patents to substances discovered in nature, and the problem of patents being granted that would not be if the novelty and inventive-step criteria were properly applied; the latter is a particularly serious problem in the United States. The third issue is the opportunity that the system provides for businesses and researchers to acquire sole patent rights for inventions that could not have been achieved without their having first accessed traditional knowledge. Let us now consider these issues in some detail.

A. *Patenting Natural Products: Discovery or Invention?*

In Europe and North America, which have the most experience in the patenting of such apparently natural substances, there has never been any kind of blanket exclusion of inventions on the basis that because they were not one-hundred percent human-made they cannot be inventions. For example, adrenaline was first patented in 1903,[16]

[15] It is worth noting in passing that rarely—if ever—are indigenous communities invited to jointly own a patent, or are traditional healers named as inventors.

[16] H.K. Mulford and Co. actually held two patents: for a glandular extractive product in the form of a purified form of adrenaline; and for this compound in a solution with salt and a preservative. In a 1911 court case, Parke Davis and Co., which was accused by H.K. Mulford of infringing its patents, defended itself on a number of grounds, one of which was that the inventions were mere products of nature and that this made the patents invalid. The Judge, ruling in favour of Mulford, held that "Takamine [i.e. the inventor] was the first to make it available for any use by removing it from the other gland-tissue in which it was found, and, while it is of course possible logically to call this a purification of the principle, it became for every practical purpose a new thing commercially and therapeutically.": see *Parke Davis and Co. v. H.K. Mulford and Co.*, 189 Fed. 95 (S.D.N.Y. 1911), affirmed, 196 Fed. 496 (2nd Circuit 1912).

and insulin in 1923.[17] Shortly after the Second World War, Merck was granted patents on two products extracted from a micro-organism called streptomyces griseus: the antibiotic streptomycin, and vitamin B_{12}.[18] While there was a general assumption that living things could not be patented, patents were occasionally granted in some countries on plants and micro-organisms; the United States even had a plant patent system from as early as 1930. But for most of the twentieth century the legal situation in Europe and North America was uncertain. From the 1970s, though, things became clearer as the scope of patent protection was extended not just to micro-organism products but to micro-organisms themselves, followed later on by plants and animals. As for DNA sequences, they started appearing in patent applications in about 1980.

How can such products, some of which are obviously discoveries, be protected by patents as if they are inventions? The technical explanation is that patent law treats them as if they are chemical substances, and these have been patentable for at least one-hundred and fifty years. It is well established in the patent laws of Europe and North America that while you cannot claim as an invention something as it occurs in nature, it is possible to do so if you extract it from nature and thereby make it available for industrial utilization for the first time. This argument may not always convince a patent examiner or a court, though; but it almost certainly will if you change the substance or life-form in some way such as by adding something to it (e.g. a gene), subtracting something from it (i.e. purifying it), mixing it with something else to create a new or synergistic effect, or structurally modifying it so that it differs in an identifiable manner from what it was before.[19] It also appears to be possible in some jurisdictions to get a patent on a natural substance by simply being the first to describe it in the language of biochemistry. Thus the South African Council for Scientific and Industrial Research (CSIR) has, in several countries, patented certain compounds found in a plant called hoodia, which has traditionally been used by certain groups of Bushmen people known as Xhomani as an appetite suppressant. The CSIR has high hopes that it will form the basis of a successful anti-obesity treatment and will become Africa's first blockbuster drug. The patent specification may well provide the first biochemical description of how the plant produces its commercially promising effect.[20] But the intended use of the plant would hardly be considered as novel by the

[17] U.S. Patent No. 1,469,994 (issued 9 October 1923): extract obtainable from the mammalian pancreas or from the related glands in fishes, useful in the treatment of diabetes mellitus, and a method of separating it.

[18] U.S. Patent No. 2,446,102 (issued 27 July 1948): complex salts of streptomycin and process for preparing same; U.S. Patent No. 2,563,794 (issued 7 August 1951): Vitamin B_{12}.

[19] G. Dutfield, *Intellectual Property Rights and the Life Science Industries: A Twentieth Century History*, Ashgate, Aldershot, forthcoming; see also K. Bozicevic, *Distinguishing "Products of Nature" from Products derived from Nature*, Journal of the Patent and Trademark Office Society 69(8), 1987, 415–426, at 422–423.

[20] See WIPO/PCT International Publication No. WO 98/46243, *Pharmaceutical Compositions having Appetite Suppressant Activity*.

Bushmen groups who are not mentioned at all in the patent.[21] According to the European Patent Convention's standards, however, the CSIR has a legitimate claim. The European Patent Office Guidelines for Examination state that:

> "... if a substance found in nature has first to be isolated from its surrounding and a process for obtaining it is developed, that process is patentable. Moreover, if the substance can be properly characterized either by its structure, by the process by which it is obtained or by other parameters ... and it is 'new' in the absolute sense of having no previously recognized existence, then the substance *per se* may be patentable."[22]

It may not be obvious to everybody that allowing patent claims to cover natural substances that have been isolated, purified or merely just described in chemical terms is necessarily a bad thing, at least as far as benefit-sharing is concerned. In the above case, the CSIR has agreed to share benefits with the Bushmen (although it only agreed to do so after being heavily criticized for initially failing to make such a commitment). The patents certainly place the institution in a better position to do this.

But let us consider the following scenario, which seems quite common. A substance is taken from a country and a foreign patent is granted claiming the substance or a close derivative. The substance is not acquired in accordance with the provider country's ABS regulations, and the patent owner has made no legal commitment to share the benefits from commercialization.[23] In addition, the country granting the patent imposes no requirement that the owner should share benefits with the provider country either at the point of patent grant or commercialization. How have the Convention's terms been violated?

Arguably, in three ways. First, the patent ownership itself can be said to conflict with the sovereign rights of States over their natural resources. Second, the owner inventor, company, university or research agency has broken the law in the provider country by failing to agree to share benefits in accordance with its regulations. Third, the country granting the patent may be failing in its obligation under Article 15.7 of the CBD which requires all State parties to:

> "... take legislative, administrative or policy measures ... with the aim of sharing in a fair and equitable way the results of research and development and the benefits arising from the

[21] Ironically, the head of Phytopharm, which is developing hoodia as an anti-obesity drug, was reported as saying that "the evidence seems to show that they [i.e. the Xhomani] used the plant as a food supplement and didn't even think about obesity." See F. Kapner, *Finding an Answer to the West's Big Problem*, Financial Times, 4 January 2002, 18; also see A. Barnett, *Bushmen Victory over Drug Firms*, The Observer, 31 March 2002, 19. The latter article notes that "although the details of the agreement have to be hammered out, the San are likely to be involved in farming and cultivating hoodia and to be offered scholarships to study so that their ancient botanical knowledge may lead to other commercial products." If the drug turns out to fulfil its commercial promise, the Xhomani would certainly deserve much more than this.

[22] European Patent Office, *Guidelines for Examination in the European Patent Office*, EPO, Munich (n.d.), at Part C-IV, 2.3. It is worth comparing this with the rather different Article 15(b) of the Andean Community's Common Intellectual Property Regime (Decision 486), which entered into effect in December 2000. The following (among others) are not considered to be inventions: "Any living thing, either complete or partial, as found in nature, natural biological processes, and biological material, as existing in nature, or able to be separated, including the genome or germplasm of any living thing."

[23] Note here that commercialization does not refer only to when products developed from the patented invention are placed on the market. Patents themselves are products for many companies, since they can be sold and licensed.

commercial and other utilization of genetic resources with the Contracting Party providing such resources ...".

Of course, the scenario raises concerns beyond the inadequacies of the patent system. But to the extent it describes conventional business practice, it shows that patents do legitimize the monopolization of benefits in the hands of single institutions or firms in cases where ABS regulations are lacking or not complied with, and are not supported by complementary measures in the countries where genetic resources are used for commercial ends.

B. *Patent Quality Problems*

As the volume of patent applications rapidly increases each year and the ability of national and regional patent offices to process them properly becomes an ever more acute concern, the granting of patents for "inventions" that privatize parts of the public domain has become a huge controversy that has brought the whole patent system into serious disrepute. So the problem caused by patent rules allowing discovered natural substances to be protected is compounded by the increasing numbers of patents being granted for "inventions" that lack novelty and inventive step and are essentially reformulations of existing knowledge with claims covering products that differ minimally, if at all, from those that already exist. The U.S. Patent and Trademark Office, in particular, has been severely condemned for its granting of patents that should have been rejected and for turning the patent system into what to the outsider appears almost to be a quasi-registration system. In addition, the law is that undocumented knowledge held only in foreign countries does not form the state of the relevant art.[24] Although an applicant is not allowed to receive a patent if "he did not himself invent the subject-matter sought to be patented",[25] there are concerns that this loophole sometimes allows people to copy such undocumented foreign knowledge and claim that they have come up with a new invention.[26]

---

[24] See 35 U.S.C. §102: "A person shall be entitled to a patent unless:
(a) the invention was known or used by others in this country, or patented or described in a printed publication in this or a foreign country, before the invention thereof by the applicant for patent, or
(b) the invention was patented or described in a printed publication in this or a foreign country or in public use or on sale in this country, more than one year prior to the date of the application for patent in the United States ...".

[25] See 35 U.S.C. §102(f).

[26] How foreign prior art may be used in determining the novelty of an invention varies from one legal jurisdiction to another. In some countries inventions cannot be patented if prior knowledge, use or publication exists anywhere in the world. Elsewhere, only unpublished foreign use or knowledge cannot be taken into account in prior art searches. But in a few countries, only domestically-held knowledge, use or knowledge manufacture is accepted. Philip Grubb, a corporate patent lawyer, helpfully refers to these different conceptions of novelty as, respectively, absolute novelty, mixed novelty and local novelty: see P.W. Grubb, *Patents for Chemicals, Pharmaceuticals and Biotechnology*, Clarendon Press, Oxford, 1999, at 54. According to Maiko Ozawa of the Institute of Intellectual Property in Tokyo, mixed novelty operates in Australia, China, India, the Republic of Korea, and, of course, the United States. Local novelty operates in Egypt, Fiji, New Zealand and Panama: see M.Ozawa, *Study on Protection of Traditional Knowledge and Intellectual Property: From an Era of Preservation to the Utilization of Genetic Resources and Traditional Knowledge*, Institute of Intellectual Property, Tokyo, 2002, at 46, Appendix A, available at: «http://www19.u-page.so-net.ne.jp/qc5/michelle/emaikoozawa.pdf»; «http://www19.u-page.so-net.ne.jp/qc5/michelle/appendixa.pdf»; and «http://www19.u-page.so-net.ne.jp/qc5/michelle/appendixb.pdf».

The notorious patent on the use of turmeric powder for wound healing[27] granted to the University of Mississippi Medical Center may be an example of this.[28] The patent provoked considerable anger in India because such use of turmeric was common knowledge there. Yet the Indian government agency that challenged the patent had to do more than persuade the U.S. Patent and Trademark Office that this was true. It had to provide published documentation. Because it was able to do so the patent was revoked,[29] yet the patent should never have been granted in the first place.

Many such patents do not really do any harm except to waste the time of patent examiners.[30] But some are potentially harmful and others are actually harmful. Two potentially harmful patents concern a plant related to mustard called maca (lepidium meyenii). Maca, sometimes dubbed "natural viagra", is a traditional crop that Andean populations have cultivated for centuries for use as a food and as the basis for several medicinal formulations. One of the U.S. patents—owned by Pure World Botanicals Inc.—is for an isolated maca extract which, it is claimed, can be used to treat cancer and sexual dysfunction, as well as for the process of preparing it.[31] The latter use is already well known; indeed, the company has, for several years, been importing maca into the United States and selling it for this very purpose.[32] The other patent—which Biotics Research Corporation owns[33]—covers a mixture of powdered maca and antler and the process of increasing testosterone levels in men by administering this mixture in various forms. The consumption of both maca and antler is already known to be associated with increased testosterone levels. This casts doubt on whether the company has a genuinely patentable invention.

While suggestions that Peruvian maca farmers depending on exports could be harmed by these patents are purely speculative, consider the case of a patent granted in 1999 on a field bean cultivar dubbed "enola" by its "inventor" Larry Proctor.[34] Proctor's company Pod-Ners has been using the patent to block the sale of imported beans with the same colour as the one described in the patent, whose description would cover several not very novel traditional bean varieties. The patent claims not only a certain yellow-coloured phaseolus vulgaris bean seed, plants produced by growing the

---

[27] U.S. Patent No. 5,401,504 (issued 28 March 1995): use of turmeric in wound healing.

[28] It is worth emphasizing the words "may be". Many patents are granted that should not be and the problem seems largely due to the failure of the system to more efficiently enable examiners to identify novelty-destroying prior art published even in the United States.

[29] P. Ganguli, *Intellectual Property Rights: Unleashing the Knowledge Economy*, Tata McGraw Hill, New Delhi, 2001, at 156.

[30] Examples are legion, but IBM deserves an honourable mention for U.S. Patent No. 6,329,919 (issued 11 December 2001): system and method for providing reservations for restroom use, as does Wen Ya-Yeh for U.S. Patent No. 6,257,248 (issued 10 July 2001): both-hand hair-cutting method, and Dale Miller's U.S. Patent No. 5,616,089 (issued 1 April 1997): method of putting.

[31] U.S. Patent No. 6,267,995 (issued 31 July 2001): extract of lepidium meyenii roots for pharmaceutical applications.

[32] ETC Group, *Peruvian Farmers and Indigenous People denounce Maca Patents*, ETC Group, 3 July 2002, available at: «http://www.etcgroup.org/documents/macafinall.pdf».

[33] U.S. Patent No. 6,093,421 (issued 25 June 2000): maca and antler for augmenting testosterone levels.

[34] U.S. Patent No. 5,894,079 (issued 13 April 1999): field bean cultivar named enola.

seed as well as all other plants with the same physiological and morphological characteristics, but also the breeding methods employed.

Two things are extraordinary about this patent. The first is that many bean cultivars exist and the specification provides no evidence that none of these cultivars possess the same characteristics falling within the patent's rather broad claims.[35] The second is that Mr Proctor employed conventional crossing and selecting breeding methods that are in no way novel. This prevents others from using the bean, as well as other beans with similar characteristics, in their own breeding programmes. None of this would necessarily matter if the owner had not decided to assert the patent aggressively.

Soon after receiving the patent, Proctor sued a company called Tutuli that had been importing Mexican yellow bean cultivars called mayocoba and peruano from that country since 1994, and with customs inspectors disrupting supplies Tutuli began to suffer financially, as did Mexican farmers that had been selling their beans to this firm. His company has since then filed lawsuits against various other small bean companies and farmers.[36] The patent is being challenged by the International Center for Tropical Agriculture (CIAT), which holds the largest collection of bean varieties, and claims that six of its two-hundred and sixty yellow-bean accessions very closely resemble enola and may well fall within its claims. CIAT's Director, Dr Joachim Voss, reportedly called the patent "both legally and morally wrong" and claimed to have "solid scientific evidence that Andean peasant farmers developed this bean first, together with Mexico."[37] The Mexican government has also condemned the patent. But according to one report, the patent owner will get his revenge on Mexico if he loses: "Proctor warns that if his patent is reversed he'll flood the Mexican market with beans, depressing an already-weak bean price."[38]

In short, it is easier than it should be to receive a patent. This is because in many countries—and the United States is a very good example of this—the examination process is not as thorough as it should be. This is largely because too few examiners are handling too many applications with the result that a lot of bad quality patents are being issued. It would be wrong to make scapegoats out of the patent examiners for this unacceptable state of affairs. Like World Cup referees that can hardly meet the impossibly high competence standards expected of them in the face of rampant gamesmanship and cheating by players, we should rather blame the system and its many unscrupulous users whose behaviour makes their work so difficult, if not impossible. Given the controversies in other fields like software and business methods, the cases

---

35 In fact, Proctor indicated in his application for a Plant Variety Protection Certificate on enola (that was subsequently granted) that "the yellow bean, enola variety, is most likely a landrace from the [Mexican] azufrado-type varieties.": ETC Group, *Proctor's Gamble*, News Release, 17 December 2001.

36 Id.

37 In T. Pratt, *Small Yellow Bean sets off International Patent Dispute*, New York Times, 20 March 2001.

38 In L. Carlsen, *Little, Yellow ... Different?* 2001, available at: «http://www.latintrade.com/newsite/content/archives.cfm?topicid=3&storyid=1385».

described are clearly not isolated ones. We are not dealing with the odd bad patent. The problem is systemic.

C. *Patents and Misappropriation of Traditional Knowledge*

As is well known, patents are supposed to protect only those inventions that are new. Yet, novelty is to some extent a relative rather than absolute term, especially when viewed from a cross-cultural perspective. This was nicely explained by Lord Hoffman of the British House of Lords in a 1995 patent appeal case:

> "There is an infinite variety of descriptions under which the same thing maybe known. Things may be described according to what they look like, how they are made, what they do and in many other ways. Under what description must it be known in order to justify the statement that one knows that it exists?"[39]

He went on to use the example of quinine:

> "The Amazonian Indians have known for centuries that cinchona bark can be used to treat malarial and other fevers. They used it in the form of powdered bark. In 1820, French scientists discovered that the active ingredient, an alkaloid called quinine, could be extracted and used more effectively in the form of sulphate of quinine. In 1944, the structure of the alkaloid molecule ($C^{20}H^{24}N^{2}O^{2}$) was discovered ... Does the Indian known about quinine? My Lords, under the description of a quality of the bark which makes it useful for treating fevers, he obviously does. I do not think it matters that he chooses to label it in animistic rather than chemical terms. He knows that the bark has a quality which makes it good for fever and that is one description of quinine. On the other hand, in a different context, the Amazonian Indian would not know about quinine. If shown pills of quinine sulphate, he would not associate them with the cinchona bark. He does not know quinine under the description of a substance in the form of pills. And he certainly would not know about the artificially synthesised alkaloid."[40]

The hoodia patent case exemplifies this point, as do the patents relating to maca, and another one based upon phyllanthus niruri, a medicinal plant used in India for treating various ailments including jaundice, which was discovered in tests to show effectiveness against viral hepatitis-B and E. The Fox Chase Cancer Center, which had carried out these tests, was awarded a U.S. patent[41] for a pharmaceutical preparation comprising an extract of the plant. While the invention was sufficiently new, useful and non-obvious to be patentable, Indian Ayurvedic healers are unlikely to be as impressed as the Patent and Trademark Office examiner who granted the patent.

It seems that while a plant or animal extract or mixture of extracts known by an indigenous group to have a useful characteristic cannot be patented due to its lack of novelty, the achievement of being first to explain the extract's effectiveness by way of

---

[39] *Merrell Dow v. H.N. Norton*, Intellectual Property Reports, 33: 1–14, 1996, at 10.

[40] Id.

[41] U.S. Patent No. 4,673,575 (issued 16 June 1987): a pharmaceutical preparation comprising the methanol extractable components of phyllanthus niruri L, administered to patients suffering from hepatitis B virus infection to inhibit the growth of the virus.

some tests, by describing its mode of action in the language of chemistry, or even by just modifying the mixture in some modest way, seems to be sufficient in some jurisdictions to merit the award of a patent. Often such patents make no reference to the relevant TK (e.g. the hoodia patent) or merely mention it in a cursory manner as if it is of little importance (e.g. the turmeric patent). Under these circumstances, it is not really surprising that indigenous groups believe the patent system to be exploitative and predatory. This is hardly an ideal state of affairs for industry either. Such patents make it so much harder for trusting relationships to be developed between indigenous groups and researchers and businesses that could benefit all parties.

Disappointingly, the business sector generally fails to take this problem seriously except for issuing the occasional public statement.[42] The fact that some companies get attacked even when they sincerely try to do the right thing does not excuse the passive stance of these corporations, many of which continue to abuse the patent system by seeking—all too often successfully—to patent the unpatentable, and by stretching out their patent monopolies on money-spinning drugs for periods that are sometimes far longer than is reasonable.[43] By their inaction, they give support to the rather extreme cynicism of those such as Pat Mooney who believe that equitable bioprospecting partnerships are impossible.[44]

IV. PATENTS, ABS AND TRADITIONAL KNOWLEDGE AT THE CBD CONFERENCE OF THE PARTIES, THE WORLD INTELLECTUAL PROPERTY ORGANIZATION, AND THE WTO

In the past few years, high-level discussions have been taking place at the Conference of the Parties to the CBD and the World Intellectual Property Organization (WIPO) that aim, among other things, to explore ways to make the IPR system and the

[42] Among those business associations that have issued constructive public statements are the European Chemical Industry Council (CEFIC) and the International Chamber of Commerce (ICC). See CEFIC, *The Chemical Industry Comments on the Legal Protection of Traditional Knowledge and Access to Genetic Resources—Patenting (Adopted in November 2000 and updated in July 2002)*, 2002, available at: «http://www.cefic.org/templates/shwpublications.asp?nid=2&t=3&s=6»; ICC, *Discussion Paper: Protecting Traditional Knowledge—Prepared by the Commission on Intellectual Property*, 2001, available at: «http://www.iccwbo.org/home/statements_rules/statements/2001/protecting_traditional_knowledge.asp». Also, the Biotechnology Industry Organization is developing a set of principles on respecting local cultures and ensuring fair compensation for indigenous peoples. In addition, the World Business Council for Sustainable Development has engaged in some fruitful and worthwhile dialogues with stakeholders to discuss the issue of traditional knowledge. Otherwise, industry tends to be overly defensive and makes few, if any, constructive proposals of its own. In sum, industry's contribution to the debate has mainly been limited to restating its support for the CBD, pointing out what it considers to be the unfeasibility of proposals that others have made, and warning against over-regulation in national and regional access regimes.

[43] As Correa explains: "Only a few (several dozen) 'new chemical entities' ... are developed and patented each year. Nonetheless, thousands of patents are granted annually in this sector. This paradox can be explained by the enormous capacity that the sector's major firms have built up not only for developing authentic inventions, but also for taking out patents on secondary, occasionally trivial developments, in order to extend their monopoly over a product or process, beyond that allowed by the original patent.": C.M. Correa, *Trends in Drug Patenting: Case Studies*, Corregidor, Buenos Aires, 2001, at 11.

[44] See the following publication for evidence that equitable partnerships are possible and do take place, and that some indigenous groups at least are actively involved, suggesting an unexpected degree of "eco-paternalism" on Mooney's part: S.A. Laird, *Biodiversity and Traditional Knowledge: Equitable Partnerships in Practice*, Earthscan, London, 2002.

CBD's provisions on ABS and traditional knowledge more mutually supportive. The WTO has also provided a forum for negotiations on the same subject. The discussions, proposals and outcomes—which are actually rather similar to each other—are briefly described below.

A. *The CBD Conference of the Parties and the Bonn Guidelines*

To review implementation of the CBD, the COP (composed of all Contracting Parties) meets periodically (usually biannually). As suggested earlier, IPRs are most frequently discussed in deliberations on such topics as access to genetic resources, benefit-sharing, and the knowledge innovations and practices of indigenous and local communities, and not so much transfer of technology. The COP has become a forum in which IPRs and the TRIPS Agreement are debated, critiqued (and defended) in a fairly open way. There are two reasons for this. First, the national delegations consist largely of civil servants from environment ministries. They tend to be concerned mostly about conservation, sustainable development and food security, and often have little contact with their trade ministry counterparts. Second, there are close links between many of the national delegations and well-organized networks of highly articulate and politically astute activists representing international civil society organizations that attend virtually all inter-governmental meetings relating to the CBD. The openness of the CBD forums, not just the COP but the other bodies set up to assist the COP in its works,[45] has made the buildings of such links easier. Sometimes activists are even invited onto the official delegations. "Biopiracy", a word coined by Mooney, is frequently invoked by developing country delegations to condemn transnational corporations, evidencing the extent to which the term has served to inspire critical perspectives and political activism relating to the role of IPRs in determining the skewed distribution of benefits from the commercial use of biological and genetic resources.

At the Sixth Meeting of the Conference of the Parties (COP 6), which took place in The Hague in May 2002, the Bonn Guidelines on Access to Genetic Resources and Fair and Equitable Sharing of the Benefits Arising out of their Utilization were officially adopted.[46] The Guidelines, which are intended to be used when developing and drafting legislative, administrative or policy measures on ABS and contracts, have a number of provisions relating to IPRs. They suggest that parties with genetic resource users under their jurisdiction consider adopting:

> "... measures to encourage the disclosure of the country of origin of the genetic resources and of the origin of traditional knowledge, innovations and practices of indigenous and local communities in applications for intellectual property rights."[47]

[45] These include the *Ad Hoc* Open-Ended Working Group on Access and Benefit-Sharing and the *Ad Hoc* Open-Ended Inter-Sessional Working Group on Article 8(j) and Related Provisions.

[46] Secretariat of the Convention on Biological Diversity, *Report of the Sixth Meeting of the Conference of the Parties to the Convention on Biological Diversity*, UNEP/CBD/COP/6/20, 2002.

[47] Bonn Guidelines, paragraph 16(d)(ii).

As means to implement the CBD provision that benefit-sharing be upon mutually agreed terms, two elements to be considered as guiding parameters in contracts and as basic requirements for mutually agreed terms are that "provision for the use on intellectual property rights include joint research, obligation to implement rights on inventions obtained and to provide licences by common consent", and "the possibility of joint ownership of intellectual property rights according to the degree of contribution".[48] COP Decision VI/24, to which the Bonn Guidelines were annexed, also called for further information gathering and analysis regarding several matters including:

- the impact of intellectual property regimes on access to and use of genetic resources and scientific research;
- the role of customary laws and practices in relation to the protection of genetic resources and TK, innovations and practices, and their relationship with intellectual property rights;
- the efficacy of country of origin and prior informed consent disclosures in assisting the examination of IPR application and the re-examination of IPRs granted;
- the feasibility of an internationally recognized certification of origin system as evidence of prior informed consent and mutually agreed terms;
- the role of oral evidence of prior art in the examination, granting and maintenance of IPRs.

B. *WIPO's Intergovernmental Committee on Intellectual Property and Genetic Resources, Traditional Knowledge and Folklore*

In September 1999, WIPO's Standing Committee on the Law of Patents (SCP) held its third session, which was to be devoted mainly to discussing a draft Patent Law Treaty (PLT). The PLT was intended to harmonise certain patent procedures while steering clear of matters relating to substantive patent law. The Colombian delegation at the session submitted a brief document entitled *Protection of Biological and Genetic Resources*[49] that turned out to be quite controversial. The delegation proposed that the PLT include an Article based on the two proposals that the document comprised. The first was that:

> "All industrial property protection shall guarantee the protection of the country's biological and genetic heritage. Consequently, the grant of patents or registrations that relate to elements of that heritage shall be subject to their having been acquired legally."

The second was that:

[48] Ibid., paragraph 43(c) and (d).

[49] World Intellectual Property Organization, Standing Committee on the Law of Patents, *Protection of Biological and Genetic Resources: Proposal by the Delegation of Colombia*, SCP/3/10, WIPO, Geneva, 1999.

> "Every document shall specify the registration number of the contract affording access to genetic resources and a copy thereof where the goods or services for which protection is sought have been manufactured or developed from genetic resources, or products thereof, of which one of the member countries is the country of origin."

This idea of linking patent filing with ABS regulations gained the support of Bolivia, Paraguay, China, Namibia, Cameroon, Mexico, South Africa, Chile, Cuba, India, Kenya, Costa Rica and Barbados. Predictably, it did not go down well with some of the other delegations, including the United States, the European Community, Japan and Korea, all of which argued that the proposed Article related to substantive patent law and therefore had no place in the PLT. As things turned out, Columbia's proposal did not fail completely in that the concerns behind it were given other opportunities for expression within WIPO.

As a compromise, the SCP invited WIPO's International Bureau to do two things. The first was to include the issue of protection of biological and genetic resources on the Agenda of that November's meeting of the Working Group on Biotechnological Inventions. The second was to arrange another meeting specifically on that issue. This Meeting on Intellectual Property and Genetic Resources took place in April 2000 and reached a consensus that:

> "WIPO should facilitate the continuation of consultations among Member States in co-ordination with the other concerned international organizations, through the conduct of appropriate legal and technical studies, and through the setting up of an appropriate forum within WIPO for future work."[50]

Two months later, the Diplomatic Conference for the Adoption of the Patent Law Treaty took place. While the main purpose was, of course, to agree upon and formally adopt the PLT, there were also consultations on genetic resources. Based upon these consultations, WIPO's Director-General, Kamil Idris, read out an agreed statement announcing that:

> "Member State discussions concerning genetic resources will continue at WIPO. The format of such discussions will be left to the Director-General's discretion, in consultation with WIPO Member States."[51]

After the Conference, Idris continued to consult with Member States on how such discussions could continue.

For the 25th Session of WIPO's General Assembly, the Secretariat prepared a document which invited Member States to consider the establishment of an Intergovernmental Committee on Intellectual Property and Genetic Resources, Traditional Knowledge and Folklore (IGC). The WIPO Secretariat suggested that the IGC

---

[50] In World Intellectual Property Organization, *Matters concerning Intellectual Property and Genetic Resources, Traditional Knowledge and Folklore: Document prepared by the Secretariat*, WO/GA/26/6, WIPO, Geneva, 2000.

[51] Id.

constitute a forum for Members to discuss three themes that it had identified during the consultations. These were:

> "Intellectual property issues that arise in the context of:
> (i) access to genetic resources and benefit-sharing;
> (ii) protection of traditional knowledge, whether or not associated with those resources; and
> (iii) the protection of expressions of folklore."[52]

This suggestion was enthusiastically supported by a large number of developing countries and was approved without formal opposition.

The first three sessions of the IGC convened in April and December 2001, and in June of the following year. At the third IGC, substantive discussion relating to how patent law might more effectively promote benefit-sharing and prevent the misappropriation of TK focused mainly on two possible approaches. The first was to require patent applicants to disclose the origin of genetic resources and/or associated TK in related patent applications. Some delegations believe such applicants should also provide documentary evidence of prior informed consent and compliance with the ABS regulations of provider countries. The U.S. delegation stated that such requirements would conflict with TRIPS by creating another substantive condition on patentability beyond those already provided by the latter. Countries such as India and Brazil have repeatedly stated that such a measure is necessary to make patents supportive of the CBD. They claim that mandatory disclosure of origin would do this by preventing private monopoly rights from extending to illegally acquired genetic resources.[53]

The second approach was to improve the availability of public-domain TK to patent examiners to prevent cases where patents whose claims extend to traditional knowledge are improperly awarded. Two possible ways to do this are to provide an inventory of publications that regularly document TK, and to compile databases of public-domain TK. India is a very keen proponent of such databases and is already setting up its own Traditional Knowledge Digital Library. The specifics of these proposals and their feasibility are considered in the next Section of this article.

C. *ABS and Traditional Knowledge at the WTO*

TRIPS is silent on ABS and TK, and makes no reference to the CBD. But this has not prevented developing countries from referring to the TRIPS/CBD relationship and portraying it in a negative light. In October 1999, twelve developing countries from

---

[52] Id.

[53] See World Intellectual Property Organization, *Intergovernmental Committee on Intellectual Property and Genetic Resources, Traditional Knowledge and Folklore, Third Session, Geneva, 13 to 21 June 2002; Draft Report prepared by the Secretariat*, WIPO/GRTKF/IC/3/17 Prov., WIPO, Geneva, 2002.

Asia, Africa and Latin America submitted two joint papers to the WTO General Council detailing the implementation issues they were seeking solutions to.[54]

The two papers put forward several TRIPS-related proposals. One of these argued that TRIPS is incompatible with the CBD and sought a clear understanding that patents inconsistent with Article 15 of the CBD, which vests the authority to determine access to genetic resources in national governments, should not be granted. Several other proposals were directed to TRIPS Article 27.3(b) and the review of its substantive provisions. One proposal was that the paragraph should be amended in light of the provisions of the CBD taking fully into account the conservation and sustainable use of biological diversity, and the protection of the rights and knowledge of indigenous and local communities.

Traditional knowledge has become an especially important concern for many developing countries. On 6 August 1999, the African Group of countries[55] proposed to the WTO General Council that in the sentence on plant variety protection in Article 27.3(b):

> "... a footnote should be inserted stating that any *sui generis* law for plant variety protection can provide for [*inter alia*]: (i) the protection of the innovations of indigenous farming communities in developing countries, consistent with the Convention on Biological Diversity and the International Undertaking on Plant Genetic Resources."

This Communication also warned that:

> "... by mandating or enabling the patenting of seeds, plants and genetic and biological materials, Article 27.3(b) is likely to lead to appropriation of the knowledge and resources of indigenous and local communities."

At the fourth meeting of the WTO Ministerial Conference which took place in Doha in November 2001, a Ministerial Declaration was adopted according to which the WTO Member States instructed:

> "... the Council for TRIPS, in pursuing its work programme including under the review of Article 27.3(b), the review of the implementation of the TRIPS Agreement under Article 71.1 and the work foreseen pursuant to paragraph 12 of this Declaration, to examine, *inter alia*, the relationship between the TRIPS Agreement and the Convention on Biological Diversity, the protection of traditional knowledge and folklore ...".[56]

---

[54] See World Trade Organization, General Council, *Preparations for the 1999 Ministerial Conference: Implementation issues to be addressed before/at Seattle. Communication from Cuba, the Dominican Republic, Egypt, El Salvador, Honduras, India, Indonesia, Malaysia, Nigeria, Pakistan, Sri Lanka and Uganda*, WT/GC/W/354, WTO, Geneva, 1999; World Trade Organization, General Council, *Preparations for the 1999 Ministerial Conference: Implementation issues to be addressed in the first Year of Negotiations. Communication from Cuba, the Dominician Republic, Egypt, El Salvador, Honduras, India, Indonesia, Malaysia, Nigeria, Pakistan, Sri Lanka and Uganda*, WT/GC/W/355, WTO, Geneva, 1999.

[55] World Trade Organization, General Council, *Preparations for the 1999 Ministerial Conference: The TRIPS Agreement. Communication from Kenya on behalf of the African Group*, WT/GC/W/302, WTO, Geneva, 1999.

[56] World Trade Organization, Ministerial Conference, Fourth Session, Doha, 9–14 November 2001, Ministerial Declaration, WT/MIN(01)/DEC/W/1, WTO, Geneva, 2002, Paragraph 19. Also noteworthy is Paragraph 31 which states, in part, that: "With a view to enhancing the mutual supportiveness of trade and environment, we agree to negotiations, without prejudicing their outcome, on: (i) the relationship between existing WTO rules and specific trade obligations set out in multilateral environmental agreements (MEAs) ..."

As a contribution to this examination, Brazil, China, Cuba, the Dominican Republic, Ecuador, India, Pakistan, Thailand, Venezuela, Zambia and Zimbabwe jointly submitted a paper to the Council for TRIPS in June 2002.[57] The paper, noting the relevant provisions of the Bonn Guidelines, proposed that TRIPS be amended to provide that WTO Member States must require:

> "... that an applicant for a patent relating to biological materials or to traditional knowledge shall provide, as a condition to acquiring patent rights:
> (i) disclosure of the source and country of origin of the biological resource and of the traditional knowledge used in the invention;
> (ii) evidence of prior informed consent through approval of authorities under the relevant national regimes; and
> (iii) evidence of fair and equitable benefit-sharing under the national regime of the country of origin."

V. ARE SOLUTIONS POSSIBLE WITHIN THE PATENT SYSTEM?

The patent system is coming under intense scrutiny and heavy criticism. The same may be said for industry which, to be fair, has much less to be ashamed of when it comes to destruction of biodiversity and exploitation of indigenous peoples than many governments, but which benefits considerably from being able to access the biological (including genetic) resources of developing countries. Adopting confidence-building measures would help to build a climate of trust between users and providers of biological resources. At present this trust is seriously lacking, and this situation benefits nobody.

This final Section of the article discusses the feasibility of some of the proposed measures described earlier.

A. *Disclosure Requirements and Certification of Origin*

The compulsory disclosure of genetic resources and associated TK in patent applications was originally mooted by civil society organizations, but has now been adopted by a number of countries. The proposal is intended to help realise fair and equitable benefit-sharing as required by the CBD. It is supposed to do this by ensuring that the resources and TK were acquired in accordance with biodiversity ABS regulations in the source countries.[58]

Proposals relating to disclosure have weak, medium and strong forms. The weak form is that such disclosure would be encouraged or even expected but not required, and

[57] World Trade Organization, TRIPS Council, *The Relationship between the TRIPS Agreement and the Convention on Biological Diversity and the Protection of Traditional Knowledge. Communication from Brazil on behalf of the Delegations of Brazil, China, Cuba, the Dominican Republic, Ecuador, India, Pakistan, Thailand, Venezuela, Zambia and Zimbabwe*, IP/C/W/356, WTO, Geneva, 2002.

[58] This idea appears first to have been suggested in print by Frédéric Hendrickx, Veit Koester and Christian Prip in *Access to Genetic Resources: A Legal Analysis*, Environmental Policy and Law 23(6), 1993, 250–258. See also M. Gadgil and P. Devasia, *Intellectual Property Rights and Biological Resources: Specifying Geographical Origins and Prior Knowledge of Uses*, Current Science 69(8), 1995, 637–639. The Danish government, with the support of some activist groups, sought unsuccessfully to have the EU Biotechnology Inventions Directive incorporate the mandatory disclosure idea.

its omission would not disqualify the patent from being granted. The medium form is that disclosure of origin would be mandatory. The International Chamber of Commerce supports the weak version,[59] which was adopted in the 1998 European Union Directive on the Legal Protection of Biotechnological Inventions. Its Recital 27 states that:

> "Whereas if an invention is based on biological material of plant or animal origin or if it uses such material, the patent application should, where appropriate, include information on the geographical origin of such material, if known; whereas this is without prejudice to the processing of patent applications or the validity of rights arising from granted patents."[60]

It is interesting to note that Belgium is seeking to implement Recital 27 by linking compliance with the CBD to requirements that exploitation of an invention not be contrary to *ordre public* and morality. In 2000, a draft proposal to modify the 1984 Belgian Patent Act was prepared which:

> "... stipulates that the exploitation of an invention is contrary to *ordre public* and morality when the invention is developed on the basis of biological material that was collected or exported in breach of Articles 3, 8(j), 15 and 16 of the CBD."[61]

In addition:

> "... a patent application should contain, not only a formal request, a description, one or more claims, drawings and an abstract, but also *the geographical origin of the plant or animal material on the basis of which the invention was developed*." (emphasis added).[62]

India has actually introduced the medium form into the Patents (Amendment) Act, 2002, which adds two new grounds for revocation, which are that patents may be revoked on the ground:

> "... that the complete specification does not disclose or wrongly mention the source or geographical origin of biological material used for the invention.",

and

---

[59] See ICC, 2002, Policy Statement, *Should Patent Applicants disclose the Origin of Biological Materials on which they File Patents? Should they demonstrate Prior Informed Consent (PIC) for their Use?* Prepared by the Commission on Intellectual Property, available at: «http://www.iccwbo.org/home/statements_rules/statements/2002/should_patent_applicants.asp».

[60] Legal opinion differs as to whether the Recitals of EU Directives are legally binding or not. Whichever is the case, the word "should" does not suggest an absolute legal requirement. It is worth noting that Recital 27 resulted from a compromise between Denmark, which had originally proposed that such information disclosure be the subject of an Article of the Directive, and other EU Members that considered that making it mandatory would add another substantive condition on patentability and would therefore violate the TRIPS Agreement. See G. Van Overwalle, *Belgium goes its Own Way on Biodiversity and Patents*, European Intellectual Property Review 5, 2002, 233–236, at 233.

[61] Article 3, which was not mentioned earlier, states that: "States have, in accordance with the Charter of the United Nations and the principles of international law, the sovereign right to exploit their own resources pursuant to their own environmental policies, and the responsibility to ensure that activities within their jurisdiction or control do not cause damage to the environment of other States or of areas beyond the limits of national jurisdiction." The citation is from Van Overwalle, *supra*, footnote 60, at 234. This approach has been criticized on the basis of both legality and practicality. With respect to the former, Van Overwalle (ibid., at 234–235) notes that the legal basis for such an application of the *ordre public* and morality concepts is very weak. She argues that there is no precedent in Belgium, or in civil-law countries more generally, for construing *ordre public* and morality concepts so broadly or for applying them to acts such as these which, wrong as they may seem to many people, would not be considered as extreme examples of intolerable or publicly unacceptable behaviour.

[62] Id.

"... that the invention so far as claimed in any claim of the complete specification was anticipated having regard to the knowledge, oral or otherwise, available within any local or indigenous community in India or elsewhere."

In addition, a significant new item is added to the list of things that are not inventions within the meaning of the Act:

"... an invention which, in effect, is traditional knowledge or which is an aggregation or duplication of known properties of traditionally known component or components."

Similarly, Article 31 of Brazil's Provisional Measure No. 2.186-16 stipulates that:

"The grant of industrial property rights by the competent bodies for a process or product obtained using samples of components of the genetic heritage is contingent on the observance of this Provisional Measure, the applicant being obliged to specify the origin of the genetic material and the associated traditional knowledge, as the case may be."

The strong form goes beyond disclosure in the patent specification to require—like the first of the new provisions being considered in Belgium—that patent applicants comply with the CBD's ABS provisions. One way to implement this is to require applicants to submit official documentation from provider countries proving that genetic resources and—where appropriate—associated TK were acquired in accordance with the ABS regulations, including conformity with such obligations as prior informed consent and benefit-sharing. Applicants unaccompanied by such documentation would automatically be returned to the applicants for re-submission with the relevant documentation. The Bonn Guidelines refer to "a legally recognized certification of origin system as evidence of prior informed consent and mutually agreed terms." The idea here is that if provider countries were to agree on some common requirements and procedures, standardized certificates of origin could be used which all national and regional patent offices would recognize.[63]

Three questions arise here. First, is compulsory disclosure of origin incompatible with TRIPS? Second, if it is, is an amendment of TRIPS to incorporate it feasible and desirable? Third, could disclosure of origin work in practice? In other words, is it actually a good idea anyway?

The answer to the first question depends upon whether we are talking about the medium or strong versions. Clearly there is no problem whatsoever with the weak version since there is no compulsion to disclose. As for the medium version, some developed countries, including the United States, hold that compulsory disclosure is TRIPS-incompatible because it establishes another substantive condition. Is this correct? To deal with this question, it is necessary for a moment to separate discussion on the

[63] The certification-of-origin idea was devised by Brendan Tobin, then of the Peruvian Society for Environmental Law: see B. Tobin, *Certificates of Origin: A Role for IPR Regimes in Securing Prior Informed Consent*, in J. Mugabe, C.V. Barber, G. Henne, L. Glowka and A. La Viña (eds.), *Access to Genetic Resources: Strategies for Sharing Benefits*, ACTS Press, Nairobi, 1997.

requirement to disclose the origin of the genetic material from the requirement to disclose the associated TK.

Let us deal with the latter first. Patent applicants are normally required to cite or describe the relevant prior art in the specification. So, there is absolutely nothing wrong with requiring a description of the relevant TK. In fact, it should be compulsory, whether or not the patent legislation or the patent office examiners' guidelines explicitly refer to TK. The point here is that the patent examiner needs to know what the relevant state of the art is so that he or she can compare it with the claimed invention and determine whether an inventive step exists or not. It is not important to know where the relevant TK comes from but it is vital to know what the knowledge covers. So it is TRIPS-compatible to require a description of the relevant TK as part of the novelty determination and the examination for inventive step. But it may not be TRIPS-compatible to require the disclosure of its source. As we will see below, this is where the strong version can save the situation.

As for the disclosure of the source of genetic material, it seems reasonable to suggest that a proper description of an invention should include a detailed disclosure of how it was achieved including a statement of how the genetic material was required. Nonetheless, there is a compelling counter-argument which states that if failure to conform would result in a rejection of the application, then the requirement would be TRIPS-incompatible. To one legal expert, the main issue is what the consequences of non-compliance with a disclosure requirement would be for the patent holder. If the consequence would be a rejection of the application or a post-grant revocation, there would be a conflict. Consequently, the way to avoid a conflict with TRIPS is not to make the disclosure requirement a condition for granting the patent but a condition for its enforceability after it has been granted.[64] The expert suggests that framing the disclosure requirement as a condition for enforcement could be adopted multilaterally in the framework of WIPO and then, perhaps, incorporated into TRIPS.

However, a careful application of the strong version may provide a more satisfactory resolution. There is no compelling reason at all why the compulsory submission of a document, such as a certificate of origin, would impose another substantive condition as long as it is not linked to determining the patentability of the invention. After all, examination and renewal fees normally have to be paid by patent applicants and owners, and TRIPS does not prevent them merely because they are not mentioned in the Agreement. Similarly, the submission of documentation attesting to the fact that the applicant had complied with the relevant ABS regulations, such as a certificate of origin, would be just another administrative requirement.

[64] N.P. de Carvalho, *Requiring Disclosure of the Origin of Genetic Resources and Prior Informed Consent in Patent Applications without Infringing the TRIPS Agreement: The Problem and the Solution*, Washington University Journal of Law and Policy 2, 2000, 371–401.

In short, the following interpretation seems plausible: it would not be a violation of TRIPS for countries to require patent applicants (i) to describe the relevant genetic material and TK in the specification and (ii) to submit documentary evidence that the ABS regulations were complied with. But it probably would be to require patent applicants also to disclose the geographical origin of the relevant genetic material and associated TK in the specification. Consequently, imposing such a requirement will entail a revision of TRIPS. Alternatively, these requirements could be introduced outside of the search and examination processes as administrative measures.

The problem is that a patent applicant may be tempted to omit disclosure of the relevant TK. There is no particular reason for an examiner to suppose that a given invention is based on TK unless the applicant discloses the fact. So, in most cases, his or her suspicions are unlikely to be aroused and the patent will then be granted—assuming it is deemed to fulfil the normal requirements.

It is noteworthy that some countries have decided not to wait for the WTO to determine the legality of these kinds of measures. For example, the Andean Community's Common Intellectual Property Regime (Decision 486), which took effect in December 2000, requires that patent applications must contain:

> "... a copy of the contract for access, if the products or processes for which a patent application is being filed were obtained or developed from genetic resources or by-products originating in one of the Member Countries; [and]
> if applicable, a copy of the document that certifies the license or authorization to use the traditional knowledge of indigenous, African American, or local communities in the Member countries where the products or processes whose protection is being requested was obtained or developed on the basis of the knowledge originating in any one of the Member countries."[65]

On the feasibility and desirability of revising TRIPS, one possibility is to amend Article 29 of TRIPS, which deals with conditions on patent applications, and which the Indian government has proposed in the past.[66] Brazil favours amending Article 27.3(b).[67] Given the subject-matter of Article 29, the Indian proposal seems more logical, but the Brazilian one may be better strategically. This is because a review of Article 27.3(b) is currently on-going, and also because the Doha Ministerial Declaration refers to the CBD-TRIPS relationship in the context of this review. But it is difficult to be certain that either proposal is realistic or advantageous. Ideally, the demandeurs need to examine the practical complexities as presented here as well as their implications[68] and then to reflect on the economic advantages that could be gained from a successful outcome, and to

[65] Article 26(h) and (i).

[66] World Trade Organization, General Council, *Preparations for the 1999 Ministerial Conference: Proposals on IPR Issues. Communication from India*, WT/GC/W/147, WTO, Geneva, 1999.

[67] World Trade Organization, TRIPS Council, *Review of Article 27.3(b). Communication from Brazil*, IP/C/W/228, WTO, Geneva, 2000.

[68] Given the possibility that small- and medium-sized businesses (SMEs) could conceivably find these measures burdensome, it may be a good idea for demandeur governments to consult with their domestic SMEs if they have not already done so.

balance such advantages with the disadvantages from the concessions that would need to be made in exchange. No doubt this is much easier said than done. But it is important to try to gain a reasonably clear idea of how much is at stake economically as well as politically just in case the demand succeeds and something has to be given up in return.

Turning to the third question, mandatory disclosure could probably work quite well for resources with health applications, especially pharmaceuticals. The pharmaceutical industry generally bases its new drugs on single compounds, and tracing and declaring the sources of these should not normally be a particularly onerous task. The measure would still need to determine the extent to which the obligation would extend to synthetic compounds derived from or inspired by lead compounds discovered in nature.

But in the case of plant varieties—which can be patented in some countries—genetic material may come from numerous sources, some of which may no longer be identifiable because of the lack of documentation and the length of time between its acquisition and its use in breeding programmes. Since new varieties may be based on genetic material from many different sources, the value of individual resources is relatively low. In addition, the seed industry is much smaller than the pharmaceutical industry and will never generate as many benefits to share anyway. Besides, it is by no means certain whether provider countries are the actual countries of origin or whether they had themselves acquired the resources in conformity with the CBD. One might add also that many of these countries are likely not to be developing countries. So for plant varieties developed through conventional breeding methods, the system may be unworkable, and may not necessarily benefit developing countries if it were. The patent applicants may simply be unable to comply and the examiners would be unable to verify whether the identities of the countries and indigenous communities of origin have been fully disclosed and are the true ones. It is possible also that the requirement could reinforce the tendency for plant breeders to rely on material in existing collections rather than to search for hitherto undiscovered resources from the countries of origin. This would have the effect of increasing the genetic uniformity of new plant varieties. The FAO International Treaty on Plant Genetic Resources for Food and Agriculture may offer a solution. This is because facilitated access to plant genetic resources for food and agriculture of those crop species covered under the multilateral system is to be subject to a standard material transfer agreement (MTA). The MTA will require benefits to be shared from the use, including commercial use, of the resources acquired. Article 13(d) of the International Treaty requires that:

> "… a recipient who commercializes a product that is a plant genetic resource for food and agriculture and that incorporates material accessed from the Multilateral System, shall pay to [a financial mechanism to be established] an equitable share of the benefits arising from the commercialization of that product, except whenever such a product is available without restriction to others for further research and breeding, in which case the recipient who commercializes shall be encouraged to make such payment."

In effect, this means that a recipient that sells a food or agricultural product incorporating material from the multilateral system is obliged to pay monetary or other benefits from commercialization under the following circumstance: that he/she owns a patent on the product and—as is normally the case—there is no exemption in the patent law of the relevant jurisdiction that would freely allow others to use it for further research and breeding. If the product is a plant variety protected under an International Union for the Protection of New Varieties of Plants (UPOV) Convention-type system with such a research exemption, the recipient selling the product would be encouraged to pay benefits.

As for the certification-of-origin system, one of the practical complications, as the International Chamber of Commerce has correctly noted, is that many countries still do not have ABS regulations.[69] In fact, one country has even decided not to have any such regulations, though it must be said that the country in question (Denmark) is not exactly noted for its biodiversity-richness.[70] If the patent must be accompanied by official documentation from the source country, no authority may exist to provide it. In this case, presumably the requirement for a certification would have to be waived. But if so, what is to stop a company from claiming that a resource was obtained from such a country when it was actually collected illegally from another country with ABS regulations?

In short, mandatory disclosure and certification of origin are promising ideas that can help enhance compatibility between the CBD and the patent system; but the practicalities still need to be thought out carefully.[71]

B. *TK Databases*

India has been a particularly strong demandeur on TK databases and has already begun to develop a Traditional Knowledge Digital Library (TKDL), which is a searchable database of already documented information related to traditional health knowledge of the Ayurvedic system and to medicinal plants used by practitioners. The government wants to make the TKDL available to patent examiners in India and elsewhere. Clearly, the question of TRIPS incompatibility does not arise. Such databases would simply be used to improve the efficiency of prior art searches. Moreover, no country involved in the WIPO IGC has opposed the idea in principle, although there have been some

[69] ICC, *supra*, footnote 59.

[70] Id. This is not to suggest that bioprospecting would necessarily be a waste of time in a country like Denmark. Several valuable antibiotic-producing micro-organisms were discovered in temperate-zone countries, including penicillin, cephalosporin, neomycin, nystatin, novobiocin and lincomycin: see J. Le Fanu, *The Rise and Fall of Modern Medicine*, Little, Brown and Co., London, 1999, at 13.

[71] It is noteworthy that CBD-COP Decision VI/24 invited WIPO to prepare a technical study and to report its findings to COP 7 "on methods consistent with obligations in treaties administered by the World Intellectual Property Organization for requiring the disclosure within patent applications of, *inter alia*:

- genetic resources utilized in the development of the claimed inventions;
- the country of origin of genetic resources utilized in the claimed inventions;
- associated traditional knowledge, innovations and practices utilized in the development of the claimed inventions;
- the source of associated traditional knowledge, innovations and practices; and
- evidence of prior informed consent."

differences of opinion on whether TK databases should be made publicly available only or provided for the exclusive use of patent offices (see below).[72]

But would TK databases actually be useful? They could certainly stop patents like the turmeric one from being granted, but it is by no means certain that they would have prevented the other controversial patents described above. They may have narrowed their scope but even this is by no means certain. Take the hoodia patent. The problem here is that the relevant TK was known about but was apparently unrecorded in any published document. Therefore it would not be in the database anyway. But let us suppose for a moment that it was. How would it have had to be described in order to constitute novelty-destroying prior art? If the published description came, say, from an anthropologist untrained in chemistry, it is possible that the examiner would have treated the TK relating to the hoodia so described as being quite distinct from the CSIR's patent specification.

In this context, it is important to note that national and regional patent laws vary with respect as to how information or material in the public domain should be presented or described in order that they constitute novelty-defeating prior art.[73] In Japan, for example, industrially applicable inventions are patentable except for:

"(i) inventions which were publicly known in Japan or elsewhere prior to the filing of the patent application;
(ii) inventions which were publicly worked in Japan or elsewhere prior to the filing of the patent application; [and]
(iii) inventions which were described in a distributed publication or made available to the public through electric telecommunication lines in Japan or elsewhere prior to the filing of the patent application."[74]

According to the examiners' guidelines:

"... 'an invention described in a publication' means an invention which a person skilled in the art can identify on the basis of matters both described and essentially described, though not literally, in a publication."[75]

---

[72] See World Intellectual Property Organization, *supra*, footnote 53.

[73] This matter was the subject of a questionnaire carried out by WIPO's Standing Committee on the Law of Patents that was sent to governments and regional patent offices: World Intellectual Property Organization, Standing Committee on the Law of Patents, *Information provided by Members of the Standing Committee on the Law of Patents (SCP) concerning the Definition of Prior Art—Brief Summary*, Prepared by the International Bureau, SCP/6/INF/2 WIPO, Geneva, 2001. One of the questions was as follows: "A ship is displayed at a quay for sale. Does a screw propeller of the ship, which is under water, constitute prior art?" This is somewhat analogous to the question whether a patented chemical substance with a therapeutic effect is anticipated by public use of a plant-based treatment whose effectiveness derives from the chemical's existence. WIPO summarized the responses thus: "Some of the countries that responded positively indicated that the screw propeller formed part of the prior art provided the visitors were able to see the screw propeller, or they could be given any explanation about the screw propeller. Three countries that responded negatively expressly mentioned that it was not considered prior art because of the concealed feature of the object. Three countries considered that the fact that the ship was for sale would satisfy the requirement of 'accessibility to the public'. Further, two countries replied that if the quay was accessible to the public, for example in a public harbour, the screw propeller would constitute prior art. One country explained that, even if the screw propeller were hidden from view, as long as its use was without limitation, restriction or obligation of secrecy, it would be considered public use."

[74] Article 29 of the Japanese Patent Law of 1959 as amended by Law No. 220 of 22 December 1999.

[75] Japan Patent Office, *Examination Guidelines for Patent and Utility Model in Japan, Part II—Requirements for Patentability*, JPO Examination Standard Office, Tokyo, 2001, at 10.

In practice, this means that:

> "... novelty-defeating disclosure ... has to be enabling, i.e. it teaches those skilled in the art how to make and use the claimed invention. If novelty-defeating disclosure fails to provide such information, the disclosure will not be a novelty-defeating bar ...".[76]

This "enabling disclosure" requirement also operates in the United Kingdom and Germany, among other countries.[77] It appears to imply that if published TK is not disclosed in a way that would teach someone to come up with an invention similar to or exactly as described in the specification of the actual patent, the latter's validity would not be threatened.

As for Europe, the European Patent Convention considers an invention "to be new if it does not form part of the state of the art", which is "held to comprise everything made available to the public by means of a written or oral description, by use, or in any other way, before the date of filing of the European patent application."[78] This indicates that articles which are publicly available may form the state of the art whether or not they have been described in writing or even orally.

Consistent with this principle, in the House of Lords appeal case referred to earlier, Lord Hoffman spoke of the Amazonian Indians' knowledge of the cinchona bark and their use of it to treat fevers. The point of doing so was to argue that the 1977 U.K. Patents Act "does not confine the state of the art about products to knowledge of their chemical composition".[79] In other words, it is not necessary for a chemical to have been described or even known about for it to be part of the state of the art, i.e. to have been made available to the public. Since his speech was accepted by the other Law Lords as sufficient to dismiss the case, his interpretation is authoritative. This suggests that despite its enabling disclosure requirement, the United Kingdom may perhaps be a promising place for those opposing the misappropriation of TK, even that which has not been documented. And perhaps the rest of Europe, too. The European Patent Office Technical Board of Appeal has ruled that:

> "... the concept of novelty must not be given such a narrow interpretation that only what has already been described in the same terms is prejudicial to it ... There are many ways of describing a substance."[80]

It is noteworthy also that in Europe:

> "... the information disclosed by a product is not limited to the information that is immediately apparent from looking at the product. Importantly, the information available

---

[76] M.A. Morneault and B.F. Rademaker, *A Maze of Laws and Exceptions: Examples of Novelty Around the World*, 4 J.W.I.P. 1, January 2001, 27–32, at 28.
[77] L. Bently and B. Sherman, *Intellectual Property Law*, Oxford University Press, Oxford, 2001, at 422.
[78] Article 54.
[79] *Merrell Dow v. H.N. Norton*, *supra*, footnote 39, at 11.
[80] In Bently and Sherman, *supra*, footnote 77, at 421.

to the public also includes information that a skilled person would be able to derive from the product if they analysed or examined it."[81]

The House of Lords judgment and the above text suggest that the CSIR's U.K. and European patents on the hoodia compounds[82] may be vulnerable to a challenge on the basis of lack of novelty. However, one should also be cautious about this because:

> "... any information that is obtained as a result of an analysis undertaken by a person skilled in the art must be obtained without undue burden or without the need to exercise any additional inventive effort."[83]

This analysis of how Japan and Europe define and assess novelty-defeating prior art suggests that many so-called biopiracy cases could not be legally challenged in those parts of the world (despite the promising European legal interpretations cited above), and that TK databases will make little difference. But what about patents covering traditional plant varieties like the Pod-Ners one, as is allowed in certain countries such as the United States? Preventing these patents would require the database to provide descriptions of all existing landraces. This may not be feasible, which reinforces some scepticism that while TK databases would prevent some of the really bad patents, many would not be affected. This is not to deny their usefulness, but to caution that without other reforms to the patent system they would only deal with the most egregious cases of TK misappropriation, and not even all of these.

The discussion so far should make it evident that, among other things, a definite cultural bias is inherent to patent law. And as long as patent systems privilege certain sources of knowledge and forms of expression over others,[84] databases will go only so far in preventing behaviour that indigenous groups find exploitative. In fact, they may even be counter-productive since they could also provide opportunities for further biopiracy.

This latter concern is certainly a valid one if the TK databases are to be made available not only to patent offices but to the general public. Then they would become a valuable resource for industry, which would otherwise have to conduct far more time-consuming literature searches to acquire the same quantity of information. It is even more valid if the decision were also made to document hitherto unrecorded TK and place it in the databases. Indeed, in the last few decades, many thousands of patents have been granted in China for formulations based on medicinal plants which have been used for centuries in Chinese traditional medicine.

---

81 Ibid., at 419–420.

82 U.K. Patent No. 2,338,235 and EP No. 1,222,927.

83 Bently and Sherman, *supra*, footnote 77, at 420.

84 There are, of course, very sound reasons for privileging certain forms of expression over others. In fact, we all do it and we can hardly expect patent examiners to be any different. Yet favouring the discourse of synthetic chemists over traditional healers is bound to seem grossly unfair to the latter. There is also a cultural bias in treating TK as part of the public domain from which businesses may derive legal and economic monopolies without having to compensate the TK holders. Somehow we need to recognize this and do something about it.

As yet, there is no consensus among delegates at the WIPO IGC that only published TK should be entered and that the databases should be available only to patent examiners. This is unfortunate, not because access to all TK databases should be restricted to patent examiners—ideally, such decisions should be left to the TK holders themselves—but if *the* purpose of the database is to present published information to examiners so they do not grant patents in error, then restricted access is necessary to prevent further abuses.

The lack of agreement on this point reflects a fundamentally different view among the delegates about whose interests they are advancing. In countries like India, the predominant view is that the nation itself is the "victim" of biopiracy. For Africa, the perception seems to be that the continent as a whole is prey to the biopiracies. But in the Americas, Australia and New Zealand, the victims are seen generally as indigenous peoples who usually—though not always—represent minority populations. It is important to be aware of these differing perceptions and the reasons for them. Some countries feel quite nationalistic about this issue and consider biopiracy as a manifestation of neo-colonialism. For them, TK is national (or perhaps continental) knowledge, and while some of it may rightfully belong to minority groups, most of it does not. For the New World countries established by European settlers, TK belongs to certain discrete communities and falls outside the dominant culture. For them, dealing with this issue in forums like WIPO is, one hopes, a matter of doing the right thing by their indigenous groups, who they admit have been subjected to oppression in the past and continue to be marginalized.

These matters will no doubt be debated further and one can only hope that the right decisions are made. But even if they are, the economic benefits of TK databases may not be all that great. Proponents should try to weigh the advantages of investing in such databases against the costs of allowing the problem of patents being granted that they find offensive to continue.

C. *Banning Patents on Life*

Beginning as a campaign by activists and NGOs, opposition to the patenting of life-forms including plants, animals, micro-organisms, cells, proteins and genes has been adopted as a negotiating position by some developing countries including—as shown earlier—the African Group which, in its 1999 WTO Submission proposed that:

> "The review process [of Article 27.3(b)] should clarify that plants and animals as well as micro-organisms and all other living organisms and their parts cannot be patented, and that natural processes that produce plants, animals and other living organisms should also not be patentable."

This would constitute a very broad exception indeed, and while there may be some strategic advantage in adopting such a position, it has no chance whatsoever of being adopted—at least for the time being. The economic power and political influence of businesses that gain from patenting in these areas is irresistable. In any case, for Europe and the United States, a century of patent-law evolution and jurisprudence underpinning the extension of patent law to these kinds of substance would have to be reversed. It is not realistic to suppose that the U.S. and European governments would all agree to such a reversal through a revision of TRIPS. A more debatable question is whether a more modest widening of the Article 27.3(b) exceptions, either in an optional or mandatory form, would have more chance of success. In the mandatory form, again, the chance of success seems virtually non-existent. But for those countries that feel strongly about this, they could consider drawing the line between the patentable and the unpatentable in the biotechnology field as they see fit—whether or not this is TRIPS-compliant—and sticking to their guns as a matter of principle. A dispute settlement panel may well find against them, but the developed countries are becoming keener not to be seen as bullies on TRIPS and may choose not to make a challenge that could provoke widespread condemnation.[85] But even in this case, the kinds of patents that the developing countries object to would still be granted in the United States, Europe or Japan.

The "no-patents-on-life" position of course assumes that patents cannot or will not shield the collective interests of bioprospecting partners, including indigenous peoples, and that in consequence the best that can be done is to keep patents out of bioprospecting transactions and natural product-based research, development and commercialization more generally. This position may be too negative. But whether or not patents can only be a problem and never a solution in the ABS context, decisions on where to draw the patentability line need to take many other factors into account, including science and technology capacity-building, foreign direct investment and technology transfer. The interests of individual developing countries in this respect are likely to vary, but further discussion about this would fall outside the scope of this article and will therefore not be pursued.

---

[85] It is worth noting here that the United States and the European Union are to some extent side-stepping the WTO and directly pressing developing countries to raise their IPR standards beyond those required by TRIPS, using sticks such as threats to remove trade concessions, and carrots like bilateral IPRs and free trade agreements. These agreements require developing country partners to undertake such commitments as: to introduce TRIPS standards before the expiry of the transitional periods; to provide higher standards of protection than TRIPS requires; and to extend the subject-matter of IP protection in ways that TRIPS may not necessarily require. One such bilateral agreement, whose IPR provisions are considered a model for others to follow by IPR lobbyists and by Joseph Papovich, Assistant U.S. Trade Representative for intellectual property, is the 2000 "Agreement between the United States of America and the Hashemite Kingdom of Jordan on the Establishment of a Free Trade Area". The Agreement requires patents to be available for any invention in all fields of technology *without including the exceptions contained in Article 27.3(b) of TRIPS*. Jordan must also join UPOV. The number of these kinds of agreements is rapidly increasing, and many have provisions relating to biotechnology and plant breeding. See Bureau of National Affairs, *Co-operation, Enforcement, TRIPS Case will help Protect IP Rights, Leader Says*, BNA Daily Report for Executives, 1 October 2001, A-20; Genetic Resources Action International, *"TRIPS-Plus" through the Back Door: How Bilateral Treaties impose much Stronger Rules for IPRs on Life than the WTO*, GRAIN, Barcelona, 2001.

D. *Improving Patent Quality*

The first two proposed solutions do not address all of the three problems with patents described earlier, but only the third—and by no means comprehensively at that. The third would solve all three, but is politically not feasible, and might not necessarily be in the wider development interests of at least some developing countries. So what else can be done that is politically feasible?

Let us first be clear that these three problems are linked to the fact that the rules determining patentability have been bent to accommodate the wishes of certain industrial sectors (especially biotechnology) to the extent that the discovery-invention distinction has become so blurred that the two words are almost treated as synonymous; and also that these rules are not being rigorously applied even in their weakened form, especially in jurisdictions like the United States. This is disturbing. The world's most economically powerful nation seems no longer to have the will to ensure that the patents it grants are for geniune inventions and is more interested in exporting its flawed model than in doing something about it. Some might argue that the additional time and resources necessary to maintain high standards can be hard to justify on economic efficiency grounds, and that final validity decisions should be made in litigation.[86] Yet the economic costs of allowing the present situation to persist must surely be very high too. And for those who consider themselves to be victims of biopiracy, such a defence invites derision.

Policy-makers and politicians ought to be asking whether the behaviour of companies that patent discoversies or free-ride on TK and then assert their patents aggressively is something their patent system should be encouraging, and what kinds of innovation ought better to be promoted. For a start, the novelty and inventive step/non-obviousness requirements should be applied strictly, and tightened up in jurisdictions where they have been loosened too much. It is difficult and expensive to challenge patents, even very bad ones, and it would be much better if more (and preferably all) patent applications for bogus inventions were simply returned to sender. And for another, the invention-discovery distinction should be clarified or re-established where it has been completely eroded. So given that the most controversial patents are granted mainly in the United States, and in Europe and Japan to a lesser extent, action should be addressed at improving patent quality in those parts of the world.

The question is, would compaigning for better patent quality have any effect? As with the other possible solutions discussed above, the feasibility of achieving change is again questionable? Yet, sooner or later, the problem of poor patent quality is certainly going to stifle innovation if it is not doing so already, and the interests of some businesses

[86] See M.A. Lemley, *Rational Ignorance at the Patent Office*, Northwestern University Law Review 95(4), 2001, 1495–1532. As the title suggests, Lemley is one who takes such a view.

will be affected negatively. The life-science corporations are already complaining about the patenting practices of small biotechnology firms which amass sizeable patent portfolios covering basic research tools. Even though many of these patents would struggle to survive a legal challenge, they are asserted aggressively because they are the only assets many of these companies have. The history of patent-law evolution and the life-science industries over the last one-hundred and fifty years strongly suggests that whenever regulatory reforms were made, it was because commercial interests were at stake and powerful businesses supported them.[87] Therefore, any successful lobby coalition is likely to have to include business representatives. Unfortunately it is still unclear who these representatives might be. At present the life-science corporations have also been accused of engaging in some of the practices they criticize biotechnology firms for. But until something is done, biodiversity-rich developing countries and indigenous peoples will continue, justifiably, to feel victimised by the patent systems of the United States and Europe, and by those who use them to claim what is not theirs to claim, and hoarding benefits which should be shared.

[87] See Dutfield, *supra*, footnote 19.

Part VII
Developing Country Concerns

[24]

Environmental Labelling Schemes Revisited: WTO Law and Developing Country Implications

Arthur E. Appleton

1. Introduction

Traditionally product labelling schemes have been employed to alert consumers to health and safety considerations. Increasingly labels are also being employed to provide information reflecting social policy concerns, for example environmental or labour attributes associated with a particular product. This chapter, revised and updated since the first edition of this book, explores the developing country implications of environmental labelling schemes. Labour-related labelling issues are also touched upon when relevant. Recent Appellate Body decisions are examined.

Environmental labelling schemes alert consumers to particular environmental issues and serve to popularize environmental issues among producers, consumers, and government officials. Examples include eco-labelling schemes (labels reflecting environmental characteristics associated with various stages in a product's life cycle) and single-issue labels (labels that relate to one aspect in a product's life cycle), e.g. that a can of tuna is "dolphin safe" or a product recyclable.

The proliferation of environmental labelling schemes has raised economic concerns among developing countries. There is fear that meeting the norms furthered by foreign labelling schemes will be technically difficult. There is also concern that it will be financially costly to meet developed country norms – particularly if labelling standards differ among importers. Finally, there is a preoccupation that the labelling of certain products will result in consumer discrimination against unlabelled products, many of which will be from countries in the developing world that have not met environmental or labour standards applied in the developed world. Many developing country WTO members fear that this will have adverse economic implications for them. Indeed, the purpose of many labelling schemes is to make it easier for consumers to discriminate against products that do not meet selected environmental or labour norms. Because such norms, or higher norms, are often more likely to be found in the developed world, manufacturers of products in the developing world, as well as their government officials, are inclined to view such measures as potentially protectionist. Opinions are therefore split, frequently along North–South lines, concerning the acceptability of labelling schemes for social policy purposes, in particular the furtherance of environmental or labour goals.

For some time there has been a growing likelihood of a trade dispute wherein the legality under the Marrakesh Agreement Establishing the World Trade Organization ("WTO Agreement")[1] of an eco-labelling scheme will be tested. It is only a matter of time before a WTO member challenges an eco-labelling programme that it views as discriminatory. Such a dispute would pose risks to the WTO as an institution, pitting developing country growth, consumer rights, environmental and social norms, free speech considerations, and trade rules against one another. Regardless of the outcome, respect for the WTO will diminish, either among developing countries or in the environmental and labour communities of the developed world. The alternative is that the members negotiate a solution to labelling questions before the Appellate Body is asked to find one.

In this chapter, relevant terms are defined, policy issues examined, applicable WTO rules discussed, and suggestions offered on how labelling questions might be addressed in future multilateral trade negotiations. In order to prevent the discussion from becoming too technical, legal issues are simplified. Nevertheless, certain important trade law concepts are addressed.

2. Terminology

Labelling terminology

There is no agreed terminology applicable to environmental labelling schemes. Recent experience with environmental labelling schemes and studies of such schemes by various organizations have however begun to yield some accord on the use of terms.[2] Environmental labelling schemes, whether voluntary or mandatory, are often divided into three groups: single-issue labels, negative labels, and eco-labels. These terms are explained below.

1. *Single-issue labels:* alert consumers about a particular issue, for example whether a product is recyclable, biodegradable, or "dolphin safe." They can also inform consumers about a particular performance-related characteristic; for example, automobile gas mileage, emissions, or electricity consumption.
2. *Negative labels:* alert consumers about dangerous or other negative characteristics; for example, "cigarettes are dangerous to your health," "drinking during pregnancy can cause foetal damage," "poison," or "do not inhale fumes."
3. *Eco-labels:* are granted by a public or private body to particular products based on a life-cycle analysis.[3] Eco-labels are awarded to what a granting authority deems to be environmentally superior products in a particular category (usually not more than 10–15 per cent of the products in a category). In theory, eco-labels rely on market forces (consumers) to promote products determined to be environmentally friendlier. Participation in eco-labelling schemes is assumed to be voluntary. The first eco-labelling scheme, the "Blue Angel," was created in Germany in 1977. Eco-labelling programmes, in various forms, are now prevalent throughout the developed world and increasingly in

the developing world.[4] They remain controversial, in part because domestic schemes have the potential to influence foreign production practices.

The above terminology, although frequently repeated in the literature, is not entirely satisfactory. First, there is potential for overlap between single-issue and negative labels. Should a label reading "Made from genetically modified organisms" or "Cattle fed natural hormones" be classified as a single-issue or a negative label? The answer to this question may depend on scientific analyses that are not yet conclusive, or even more likely on consumer perception. Secondly, there is a growing realization that the term "environment" is now being applied very broadly. Growth in scientific understanding has led to an expansion of what is considered to be environmental in nature. The result is an increase in what is scientifically perceived to relate to the environment and what might be reflected on a label. Thirdly, there is no guarantee that the life-cycle analysis used in a given eco-labelling scheme will take into consideration only factors that are strictly environmental in nature; for example, certain labour issues (perhaps with distant environmental implications) might be assessed. It is conceivable that a labelling authority could examine production-related working conditions (e.g. employee exposure to hazardous chemicals or child labour issues) when deciding whether to award an eco-label. One reason certain developing countries oppose eco-labelling schemes is fear that the continued growth in the popularity of eco-labelling schemes will open the door wider for other forms of labelling, in particular labels that reflect labour-related issues. This fear is reinforced by the realization that certain child labour practices are already the subject of labelling campaigns. This point will be returned to when policy issues are discussed.

PPM terminology

Among the most controversial trade issues is whether a WTO member should be permitted to apply its trade policy to influence the selection of manufacturing processes in other countries – so-called foreign "process and production methods" (PPMs). Certain environmental labelling schemes provide a means of discriminating between products based on how they are made by informing consumers when production methods do not meet particular environmental, labour, or other criteria. Changes in demand for a product may influence the selection of production methods.

From the trade law perspective, this issue is intertwined with the "like product" distinction made, among other places, in Articles I:1 and III:4 of the 1947 General Agreement on Tariffs and Trade (GATT 1947).[5] The concept of "like products" is critical for an understanding of the PPM question because the GATT Agreement restricts the right to discriminate between and among foreign and domestic like products, and past GATT/WTO practice has generally relied upon an examination of a product itself (as opposed to how it is made) in determining whether two products are "like products".[6] The result has been that "process and production methods" that cannot be detected in the final product are generally not examined in a like product determination.

If a PPM causes a change detectable in the product itself, trade experts classify the PPM as "product related" or "incorporated." If a PPM cannot be identified in the product itself, it is said to be "non product related" (NPR-PPM) or "unincorporated." PPM questions must be seen against the background that, with a few notable exceptions (e.g. intellectual property matters and products made by prison labour), goods have not generally been distinguished for purposes of the WTO Agreement based on PPMs unless the PPMs are detectable in the final product ("product related"). In other words, a widget is a widget regardless of how it is made, unless the manufacture of the widget changes some important characteristic detectable in the widget itself. More specifically, for WTO purposes trade lawyers might distinguish automobiles based on fuel efficiency or exhaust emissions, but not based on the sulphur dioxide emissions used to make the steel in a given vehicle.

Whereas from an environmental or labour perspective the disregard for non-product-related PPMs in the like product determination may be subject to criticism, from the trade perspective it is justified on the grounds that differentiating between goods based on NPR-PPMs would increase trade barriers and result in increased trade discrimination. Treating a car differently based on how it is made, as opposed to how efficiently it operates, would provide a new basis for trade discrimination. Developing countries have been particularly adamant in opposing trade restrictions based on NPR-PPMs out of fear that they would lose economically. In part this is because the technical capacity and capital to meet the stringent production standards that exist in certain developed countries may be lacking. This opposition is also based on the realization that, if standards for NPR-PPMs differed greatly among countries, economies of scale would diminish. If Countries A and B establish different production-related environmental standards for widgets, a widget producer in Country C might need to build two separate production lines in order to export to both Country A and Country B.

WTO members have little problem with the idea that a particular member can regulate production processes within its own jurisdiction, or that a member can establish reasonable performance-related environmental standards applicable to products within its own jurisdiction. Controversies arise when a member seeks to apply its laws to influence production processes and methods outside its jurisdiction. These problems tend to be more serious when the member seeking to apply its standards abroad is a major market for the product in question.

Eco-labelling schemes (schemes based on a life-cycle analysis) have aroused particular concern among developing country members because they provide a means of permitting consumers to discriminate against goods based, in part, on NPR-PPMs. This issue will be returned to in the discussion of policy issues that follows.

3. Policy issues

Several important policy issues have already been introduced. Most readers will readily see that, at least in theory, eco-labelling schemes rely on market forces (changes in consumption patterns) to influence production practices. Products are labelled to affect consumer purchasing habits, i.e. demand. By affecting demand, changes may occur relative to supply – producers and suppliers may choose to become more environmentally "responsible" when consumers become environmentally more discerning. Thus viewed, one goal of eco-labelling schemes is to foster demand-side discrimination against certain products in order to alter the supply side of the economic equation.

Most evidence on the effectiveness of eco-labelling schemes is anecdotal in nature. Nevertheless, developing countries fear the potential discriminatory implications of these schemes. Providing consumers with the ability to discriminate against products perceived to be less environmentally sound is a source of worry for developing countries for the technical and financial reasons alluded to above. Producers in developing countries may also lack the resources and political expertise to influence the development of foreign labelling criteria, and may find it difficult from a linguistic and cultural perspective to inform themselves about the requirements of foreign labelling schemes and to participate in these schemes.[7] In other words, information asymmetries may influence participation in particular schemes. Local manufacturers are more likely to be aware of the criteria being applied in a particular scheme, and are often better positioned politically to influence the selection of applicable criteria.

Developing countries are also concerned because of the perceived tendency of developed countries to formulate eco-labelling criteria based on conditions in the developed world, or only in the labelling state.[8] Flexibility is necessary to assure that labelling criteria also reflect the conditions prevailing in developing countries, particularly with respect to PPMs. This flexibility may be lacking in certain developed country programmes, particularly when protectionist interests influence the drafting of labelling criteria.

Complicating the problem are questions of comparative advantage. Wage considerations, regulatory requirements, and the lax enforcement of regulations are often viewed as sources of comparative advantage. Labelling schemes that alert consumers to serious discrepancies in the above may disadvantage developing countries that benefit from low wages or a less rigorous regulatory environment.

Another potential criticism is that eco-labelling schemes are likely to be of greater interest to the residents of developed countries – from the perspective of both demand and supply. From the demand perspective, increased discretionary income brings the luxury of selecting products based on factors other than price, including social and moral considerations. Assuming that many labelled products are more expensive to produce, and that they may command a premium price, it is probable that labelled products will be more expensive than competing unlabelled products, and as a result less likely to attract consumer interest in developing countries that have labelling schemes. On the supply side, to the extent that the market for a product labelled by a developed country is of interest to a developing country (often not the case because primary goods and agricultural products are frequently not labelled), for reasons mentioned above it may be difficult for developing countries to participate in foreign labelling schemes.

From the developing country perspective, eco-labelling schemes give rise to serious economic concerns. This is because, by definition, eco-labelling programmes evaluate environmental aspects of production processes – an area of potential weakness for some developing countries. Although the overall goal of such labelling schemes (using market forces to improve the environment) is laudable, producers face risks which can result from very subjective factors. For example:

- What should receive a greater weighting in a life-cycle analysis – factors associated with a product's production, use, or disposal?
- Should one evaluate transport-related criteria, given that this would seem to discriminate against many imports?
- How do you evaluate products produced using dirty or dangerous sources of energy?

- How do you evaluate foreign production processes that may be more suitable given a particular country's geographical, climatic, and other circumstances?
- More specifically, how do you evaluate products coming from countries at different levels of development and with different levels of technology?

Concern about the economic implications of single-issue labelling schemes is also present in certain special interest communities in the developed world, particularly those in industrial sectors, such as agribusiness, which fear labelling schemes will be used to discriminate against products in which they have invested heavily. For example, the labelling of foodstuffs produced with the aid of hormones or genetic engineering has those in the agribusiness, chemical, and biotechnology sectors worried. Products with health risks, in particular tobacco and alcohol, have long been subject to various single-issue labelling schemes. This has raised economic concerns in those industries.

The policy considerations presented above are serious, but at this point there is little evidence to suggest that eco-labelling schemes have significantly altered consumer buying habits or manufacturing practices. Instead, fears concerning labelling schemes currently appear exaggerated. From the developing country perspective, the strong opposition in many quarters to labelling schemes may be a strategic decision. By keeping the attention of the trade community focused on eco-labelling, other more important issues, such as the internalization of environmental externalities and labour-related labelling, have been kept off the agenda.

Government officials and business people in the developing world and certain constituencies in the developed world may be preoccupied with the trade effects of environmental labelling schemes, but this is not to suggest that labelling schemes have received universal opposition, or that there are not important arguments in support of these schemes. Many in the environmental, labour, and consumer advocacy communities strongly support labelling schemes. The potential environmental advantages seem clear. To the extent that labelling informs consumers, influences consumption habits, and changes production processes in favour of environmentally superior products, labelling can play a beneficial role. The success of such schemes will, however, depend on many variables, including consumer acceptance, the willingness of manufacturers to change production processes, the availability of reasonably priced products of sufficient quality, adequate publicity, and effective developing country participation.

The potential benefits of eco-labelling programmes have led environmentalists to question uncertainties that arise pursuant to the WTO Agreement concerning the legal treatment of these schemes, in particular with respect to the treatment of NPR-PPMs. Environmentalists, as well as labour activists, would like WTO members to have the freedom to use trade as a means of influencing foreign environmental and labour practices. They do not see why a consumer should be forced to buy a product manufactured in a manner that he or she would find objectionable if the PPMs were revealed through labelling.

Environmentalists have a second concern that is also rooted in a criticism of the WTO Agreement. They recognize that many environmental problems are trans-boundary or global in nature. This is because resources such as air and water are migratory, and production processes in one state may affect resources in another state. For example, forest resources, animal resources, and coastal and marine resources can be affected by environmental decisions taken in other countries. Environmentalists tend not to accept what they view as a jurisdictional limitation present in interpretations of the GATT/WTO Agreement (even if from the WTO perspective the limitation is framed otherwise) restricting a state's use of trade measures to protect the environment.

Consumer sentiment also favours environmental labelling programmes. From the consumer perspective, labelling furthers consumer awareness, empowers consumers to make better-informed choices, satisfies certain moral, political, and social convictions, and provides economic and social pressure, which may compel manufacturers to change production processes. Furthermore, some consumers view labelling as a form of advertising supported by freedom of speech considerations.

To what extent should those in one state be able to influence production methods in another state? From the perspectives of state sovereignty and trade policy, one might be inclined to take a restrictive view. Trade policy remains an essentially state-centric system. From an environmental or consumer perspective, however, the scope for action is arguably broader. Environmental issues, like human rights issues, challenge fundamental notions of state sovereignty and jurisdiction, owing in large part to their cross-border implications. The intersection between trade and environmental issues is, from a strictly legal perspective, an instance of two cultures colliding. Environmental labelling, or more correctly the questions of international trade and environmental law that lie beneath labelling questions, is not necessarily clear or logical when viewed from the perspective of the other system or culture. The WTO perspective, including the uncertainties that have arisen in the application of international trade law to labelling, is examined below.

4. Legal issues – the WTO Agreement

No eco-labelling scheme has ever been challenged before the GATT or the WTO, although a single-issue labelling scheme was challenged in the first *Tuna-Dolphin* dispute,[9] and labelling did arise as an issue in the *Malt Beverages* panel.[10] In light of the limited GATT/WTO practice concerning labelling, the comments that follow are somewhat speculative in nature but should offer insight into various potential challenges and possible results. They are meant to provide an overview of the applicable law and the points left to be resolved, either through dispute settlement proceedings or, preferably, through future negotiations.

One starting point in an analysis of the legality of eco-labelling schemes is the Report of the WTO Committee on Trade and Environment (CTE) produced for the 1996 Singapore Ministerial Meeting. Paragraph 183 of this report (containing Conclusions and Recommendations applicable to labelling programmes) reads in part: "Well-designed eco-labelling schemes/programmes can be effective instruments of environmental policy to encourage the development of an environmentally-conscious consumer public."[11] This statement is both non-binding and carefully drafted. Not only does it say nothing about the WTO-legality of eco-labelling schemes, but paragraph 185 of the same report reveals the discord in the CTE with respect to the treatment of the NPR-PPM component of eco-labelling schemes.

Three other points of departure offer better starting points for an analysis of the legality of eco-labelling schemes: the Preamble to the WTO Agreement,[12] the relevant provisions of GATT 1947, which is now a part of GATT 1994,[13] and the Agreement on Technical Barriers to Trade (TBT Agreement).[14] The Preamble will be discussed first. Then the legality of labelling schemes will be addressed first from the perspective of GATT (where many of the principles found in the TBT Agreement originate), and then from the perspective of the TBT Agreement. This mirrors the approach of recent WTO dispute settlement reports, which have avoided examining TBT issues despite the fact that the TBT Agreement enjoys a higher legal precedence than GATT 1994 in the event of a conflict between the two.

Preamble

The Preamble of the WTO Agreement acknowledges the need to allow "for the optimal use of the world's resources in accordance with the objective of sustainable development, seeking both to protect and preserve the environment."[15] In an earlier work, I concluded that the inclusion of environmental language in the Preamble was probably not intended to alter the fundamental balance of rights and obligations that existed pursuant to GATT 1947, in particular with respect to developing country members.[16] This conclusion must now be re-examined in light of the Appellate Body's decision in the *Shrimp-Turtle* dispute.[17] In *Shrimp-Turtle*, the Appellate Body found that the Preamble's environmental language "reflects the intentions of negotiators of the WTO Agreement" and "must add colour, texture and shading to our interpretation of the agreements annexed to the WTO Agreement, in this case, the GATT 1994."[18] It then took account of the Preamble's language as part of the context of GATT Article XX's chapeau.[19]

It is difficult to second guess to what extent the Appellate Body will be influenced by the Preamble's language when confronted with a challenge to an environmental labelling scheme. Suffice it to say that the Appellate Body is now on record as having recognized the importance of the Preamble when interpreting the rights and obligations of members under the WTO Agreement (which includes the TBT Agreement) and under GATT 1994 (which includes GATT 1947). This would suggest that, in borderline situations, environmental labelling schemes may receive the benefit of the doubt.

GATT Article I ("General Most-Favoured-Nation Treatment")

GATT Article I, which provides for most-favoured-nation (MFN) treatment, ensures that a trade privilege extended to one member is extended to all members. Article I:1 prohibits a member from using financial and regulatory measures as a means of discriminating against "like products" from one member in favour of like products from another member. With respect to mandatory labelling requirements, the effect of Article I:1 is to assure that labelling requirements applicable to the imports of one member are applicable to like products imported from all members. Likewise, a voluntary labelling programme open to one member must generally be open to like products from all members on similar terms.[20]

A voluntary environmental labelling scheme reflecting an NPR-PPM (whether or not tuna was "dolphin safe") withstood a challenge based on Article I:1 in the 1991 *Tuna-Dolphin* report.[21] The panel found that the voluntary federally promulgated US scheme at issue did not prevent tuna products from being sold freely with or without the "dolphin-safe" label; nor did the scheme establish requirements that had to be met to obtain an advantage from the US government. Any advantage that occurred resulted from consumer choice.[22]

The 1991 *Tuna-Dolphin* report was never adopted by the GATT contracting parties. Unadopted GATT panel reports have been found by the Appellate Body to have "no legal status in the GATT or WTO system," but the Appellate Body has found that a panel "could nevertheless find useful guidance in the reasoning of an unadopted panel report that it considered to be relevant."[23]

GATT Article III ("National Treatment on Internal Taxation and Regulation")

GATT Article III contains the "national treatment" obligation. This provision is intended to ensure that imported like products are treated no less favourably than like domestic products with respect to the application of internal taxes, charges, "laws, regulations and requirements affecting the internal sale, offering for sale, purchase, transportation, distribution or use of products." The goal is to prevent internal measures from being applied so as to afford protection to domestic production.[24] The Appellate Body noted in the *Alcoholic Beverages* report that:

> The broad and fundamental purpose of Article III is to avoid protectionism in the application of internal tax and regulatory measures. More specifically, the purpose of Article III "is to ensure that internal measures 'not be applied to imported or domestic products so as to afford protection to domestic production.'" Toward this end, Article III obliges Members of the WTO to provide equality of competitive conditions for imported products in relation to domestic products. "[T]he intention of the drafters of the Agreement was clearly to treat the imported products in the same way as the like domestic products once they had been cleared through customs. Otherwise indirect protection could be given." . . . Article III protects expectations not of any particular trade volume but rather of the

equal competitive relationship between imported and domestic products. Members of the WTO are free to pursue their own domestic goals through internal taxation or regulation so long as they do not do so in a way that violates Article III or any of the other commitments they have made in the WTO Agreement.[25]

Article III:4 has particular relevance for mandatory labelling schemes. This provision assures that laws, regulations, and requirements affecting the internal sale, offering for sale, purchase, transportation, distribution, or use are not applied so as to accord less favourable treatment to imported over domestic like products. The concepts of "like products" and "treatment no less favourable" are essential elements of Article III:4, and are also found in the TBT Agreement, although this does not mean that these concepts are interpreted the same throughout the WTO Agreement.

Like products

The like products decision in the *Asbestos*[26] case is the most significant Article III:4 decision interpreting "likeness." This controversial decision takes into account past GATT/WTO practice interpreting likeness, but nevertheless constitutes a step towards a more economic interpretation of Article III:4 likeness.

In *Asbestos*, the Appellate Body side-stepped certain textual implications of Article III. Based on its interpretation of a "general principle" said to be articulated in Article III:1 and which it elaborated in *Alcoholic Beverages*, the Appellate Body opted for a broader interpretation of Article III:4 likeness, which, if not "co-extensive" with its interpretation of Article III:2, appears to approach the breadth of Article III:2.[27] In *Asbestos* the Appellate Body again recognizes that likeness must be interpreted on a case-by-case basis, and that no one approach is appropriate for all cases.[28] With reference to the Working Party on Border Tax Adjustments[29] and the findings of the Appellate Body in *Alcoholic Beverages* (Art. III:2) and *Reformulated Gasoline*[30] (Art. III:4), the Appellate Body recognizes the same four criteria that together provide a framework ("simple tools") for analysing likeness. They are (1) the properties, nature, and quality of the products, (2) the end-uses of the products, (3) consumers' tastes and habits ("consumers' perceptions and behaviour"), and (4) tariff classifications. To these four criteria the Appellate Body adds (5) an examination of all pertinent evidence, and (6) an examination of the competitive relationship of the products in the market place.[31] These last two criteria are, at least in the *Asbestos* decision, interwoven with the first four criteria. This interpretation permits the Appellate Body to examine the *competitive relationship* of products as a consideration intertwined with the four-part test applied in *Alcoholic Beverages*.

The Appellate Body found in *Asbestos* that the panel should have examined all of the evidence relating to each of the four criteria separately, and weighed all relevant evidence when making an overall determination on likeness.[32] The Appellate Body also found that the panel, in its analysis of the physical properties of asbestos, should have examined the carcinogenity of asbestos fibres. It termed this carcinogenity a "defining element" of the physical properties of asbestos.[33]

The *Asbestos* decision represents a move towards an interpretation of likeness that is on the one hand more sensitive to economic considerations (conditions of competition), but on the other hand more pragmatic to the extent that it examines a broader group of product-related characteristics, including health considerations.

Article III:4 is applicable to product-related labelling requirements. Many in the environmental community would also like to see NPR-PPMs included in an Article III:4 assessment of "likeness." Past and recent GATT/WTO practice suggests that this is not a realistic expectation. This conclusion is supported by the findings of the unadopted 1991 and 1994 *Tuna-Dolphin* panels,[34] whose reasoning is at best a source of "useful guidance." Nevertheless, the reasoning of these panels appears to have won some acceptance from the United States, as evidenced by its decision not to argue at the panel stage that Article III:4 was applicable in the *Shrimp-Turtle* dispute.[35]

Excluding NPR-PPMs from the Article III:4 determination of likeness prevents members from arguing that a labelling scheme reflecting NPR-PPMs applied equally to domestic and foreign products ("like products") would be in conformity with the national treatment obligation (and would not instead be subject to the requirements of GATT Article XI). From the perspective of international trade, this is a prudent outcome. If all products could be differentiated for likeness purposes based on NPR-PPMs, the WTO would become an international arbitrator of a broad range of "trade-related" social and political differences, be they environmental, labour, religious, or political in nature. This could rapidly undermine the effectiveness of the international trading system.

Treatment no less favourable

Assume we are dealing with a product-related labelling requirement applicable to two like products, one domestic and one imported; for example, the mandatory labelling of domestic and imported automobiles based on fuel consumed or emissions produced. Pursuant to Article III:4, there is an obligation to assure that the imported product is accorded "treatment no less favourable" than the like domestic product. This requires an examination of the conditions of competition – whether imported products are afforded "effective equality of opportunity" (treatment at least equal to that accorded like domestic products).[36]

Do labelling requirements affect the conditions of competition and have implications for the maintenance of effective equality of opportunity? This problem can be viewed from two perspectives: in terms of the general labelling requirements, and in terms of the specific information yielded by these requirements. Strictly speaking, mandatory product-related labelling requirements designed to reveal information, if applied in a fair, open, non-discriminatory, and transparent manner, do not *directly* affect the conditions of competition, nor do they have *direct* implications for the maintenance of effective equality of opportunity. This is because they do not prevent the sale of the good in question provided that it is labelled. They also do not have a *direct* effect on price, as would a tax. Furthermore, they do not impose less favourable regulatory treatment on imported products. All products, whether domestic or imported, would be subject to the same regulatory regime – they would each be required to bear a label revealing the same product-related characteristics.

Questions arise only when the analysis is taken one step further and the contents of the label are examined. Mandatory product-related labelling requirements are likely to reveal information that could result in consumer discrimination against a particular product (domestic or imported) based on performance-related characteristics. Viewed in this light, labelling schemes can have an *indirect* effect on price and competitiveness, and might *indirectly* affect the conditions of competition. Developing countries might find it particularly difficult to compete in such an environment if they lack the necessary financial and technical resources to manufacture products that meet the environmental expectations of consumers in the developed world.

Such a labelling requirement would not prevent products from being sold freely, nor would it establish requirements needed to procure a government-accorded advantage. It would only further the ability of consumers to make an informed decision based on product-related characteristics, and to discriminate against products based on this information. Successfully challenging such a scheme could be difficult. One approach might be to prove that a particular labelling requirement was purposefully designed by a government to reveal environmental deficiencies in foreign like products, with the expectation that consumers would accord these products less favourable treatment. This could require a showing of intentional abuse.

This is not necessarily a surprising result. WTO members have historically recognized the need to retain a certain degree of domestic policy autonomy. For example, there is acceptance among members that states must be able to apply domestic regulations to preserve natural resources and to protect the health and safety of their citizens.[37] In the *Malt Beverages* and *Automobiles* reports, this autonomy was assured by ruling that certain goods, distinguished on the basis of product-related characteristics for reasons other than protectionism, were not like products (therefore Article III did not apply). As a result of the Appellate Body decision in the *Alcoholic Beverages* dispute, this line of argument (aim and effect) now appears to be closed,[38] but the need to retain a degree of domestic policy autonomy still exists, and it is possible that such autonomy may be preserved in the interpretation and application of the "treatment no less favourable" test.[39]

The GATT Article III legality of voluntary product-related labelling schemes, including the product-related portion of eco-labelling schemes, has been treated to some extent above, but requires a few additional comments. Some trade specialists argue that, like mandatory labelling requirements, voluntary labelling can discriminate against members with fewer technical and financial capabilities and thus affect the conditions of competition.[40] Although certain developing countries will find this argument attractive, it would probably be difficult to sustain before a panel or the Appellate Body.

First, it would need to be proven that voluntary labelling schemes constitute regulations or requirements for the purposes of Article III:4. This has not been established. Secondly, for the reasons noted above, it seems unlikely that a panel or the Appellate Body would find that likeness can be dependent on an NPR-PPM. This would suggest that NPR-PPMs in eco-labelling schemes would not be considered for Article III purposes in the event that the regulations or requirements establishing a voluntary eco-labelling scheme were deemed to fall within Article III. Thirdly, if certain mandatory labelling schemes are GATT consistent, it is probable that voluntary schemes are more likely to be GATT consistent. Voluntary labelling programmes do not prevent products from being sold freely, nor do they establish requirements needed to procure a government-accorded advantage. They are designed to further the ability of consumers to make informed decisions. They are therefore less likely to affect the conditions of competition than mandatory schemes.

In conclusion, without a showing of purposeful abuse of a voluntary labelling scheme, in particular purposeful government abuse, a finding by a dispute settlement body against a voluntary scheme based on Article III:4 is unlikely. Given the large number of eco-labelling schemes already in existence, and the reputation of the WTO concerning environmental issues, ruling against an eco-labelling scheme could pose political risks for the WTO system. In light of the above, a member that chooses to oppose a voluntary labelling scheme should instead be prepared to give greater emphasis to arguments arising under the TBT Agreement, particularly technical arguments concerning necessity, harmonization, notice, and transparency (discussed below), as opposed to broad policy arguments that are likely to raise controversial political issues.

GATT Article XI ("General Elimination of Quantitative Restrictions")

GATT Article XI sets forth a general prohibition on import and export restrictions other than duties, tariffs, and other charges. The intent of Article XI is to limit import restrictions to tariff-based measures, and to prohibit "most non-tariff measures from being applied against imports at the point of importation."[41] GATT Article III and Article XI are usually viewed as mutually exclusive. Article III governs internal measures, including internal measures applied against imports at the point of importation,[42] whereas Article XI governs the importation of products. Article XI is generally deemed to be comprehensive, and is even applicable to non-mandatory measures where sufficient government incentives exist to encourage implementation.[43]

As noted in the discussion of Article III, it is probable that it is GATT Article XI and not GATT Article III that is applicable to non-product-related environmental labelling requirements. If this is the case, import restrictions, such as a requirement that NPR-PPMs be labelled as a prerequisite to import, would violate Article XI. Prohibiting the import of products that do not bear an eco-label would also violate Article XI to the extent that NPR-PPMs are part of the labelling criteria.

Voluntary labelling schemes, including the NPR-PPM component of eco-labelling schemes, are unlikely to violate Article XI. The only conceivable exception would be when there are sufficient government incentives to discourage the import of goods that do not bear the label in question – perhaps in the form of a government programme that stigmatizes the import of unlabelled goods.

GATT Article XX ("General Exceptions")

Much has already been written about Article XX, so it will be only briefly mentioned here. Assuming that a labelling scheme has been alleged to violate one of the Articles discussed above, the scheme would probably be defended on the basis of GATT Article XX (b) or (g), two of the general exceptions to the GATT Agreement.

Until recently, GATT Article XX(b)[44] has never been successfully invoked, casting doubts on its viability. Previous interpretations of the term "necessary" were so strict that the standard seemed virtually impossible to satisfy.[45] The Appellate Body's recent decision in the *Asbestos* case is noteworthy because it constitutes the first time that the Appellate Body has made a finding that a given trade measure satisfies the conditions of Article XX(b), and more specifically the "necessary" test. This decision is all the more surprising because, having found that Article III:4 had not been violated, the Appellate Body could have avoided the Article XX(b) question based on the doctrine of judicial economy. This suggests that its Article XX(b) analysis was politically motivated.

The *Asbestos* report emphasizes that a measure is "necessary" if no alternative GATT-consistent measure or less GATT-inconsistent measure is *reasonably* available.[46] Relying in part on its report in *Korea–Beef*,[47] the Appellate Body found in *Asbestos* that whether a measure is "reasonably" available requires a weighing and balancing process that must take into consideration whether an alternative measure would contribute to the realization of the end pursued. The more vital the common interest or value pursued, the easier it will be for the Appellate Body to accept that a particular measure is necessary.[48]

Absent a factual background, the applicability of the *Asbestos* reasoning to an eco-labelling scheme alleged to violate a substantive GATT provision is difficult to assess. Assuming that a particular eco-labelling scheme does violate a substantive GATT provision, it is arguable that it will be viewed as being reasonable and among the least GATT-inconsistent trade measures available. Article XX(b) could conceivably save certain eco-labelling schemes.

Prior to the *Asbestos* report, Article XX(g)[49] was the focus of much attention. Two Appellate Body reports, *Shrimp-Turtle* and *Reformulated Gasoline*, demonstrate the viability of Article XX(g),[50] but in each case the environmental measure at issue was found not to satisfy the conditions present in Article XX's chapeau. The fact that the *Shrimp-Turtle* case concerned NPR-PPMs was not an express barrier to the application of Article XX(g) or the chapeau. Were an Article XX(g) labelling case to arise, it is likely that the decision would rest on the application of the chapeau. This makes the Appellate Body's decisions in *Shrimp-Turtle* and *Reformulated Gasoline*, each of which interprets the chapeau, potentially important for the "application" of labelling schemes that take NPR-PPMs into consideration. Both reports stress the need for a cooperative resolution to international environmental problems, suggesting that labelling schemes that conform with international standards would be more acceptable. Both reports also examine the administration of the law or regulation in question, suggesting the need for a fair, equal, and transparent administration of labelling schemes.

The Agreement on Technical Barriers to Trade

The TBT Agreement is the most important instrument applicable to environmental labelling in the WTO Agreement. The TBT Agreement was drafted with labelling regulations and standards in mind.

As evidenced by the *Asbestos* decision, there has been a general reluctance on the part of both panels and the Appellate Body to rule based on the TBT Agreement when confronted with the possibility of basing a decision on the GATT Agreement. Given the unanswered questions arising from the GATT Agreement with respect to labelling schemes, a developing country seeking to challenge a labelling scheme would be better served by basing its challenge on both the GATT and the TBT Agreements, or on the TBT Agreement alone. This being said, there is also a degree of uncertainty concerning the application of the TBT Agreement to labelling schemes.

The principal uncertainty concerns the treatment of labels reflecting NPR-PPMs.[51] This point is of particular importance for voluntary eco-labelling schemes and for other voluntary schemes that reflect environmental and labour-related considerations. This confusion arises from the definitions of "technical regulation" and "standard" provided in Annex 1 of the Agreement. The generally accepted rule is that only product-related PPMs are covered by the TBT Agreement, but this point remains open to debate. Some developing countries have taken the view that the TBT Agreement prohibits the labelling of NPR-PPMs, and therefore eco-labels, whereas other members have taken the view that eco-labels fall within the TBT Agreement.[52] A middle position – that only the product-related portion of an eco-label falls within the TBT Agreement – is tenable, but from a practical viewpoint unworkable.

The TBT Agreement is important and complex, and because of its potential "rigidity" a politically sensitive instrument. Much of the foundation required for an understanding of this agreement has been set forth in the above discussion of GATT Articles I, III, and XI. It is not possible to undertake a thorough analysis of the TBT Agreement in a short chapter of this nature, but the provisions of greatest interest for developing countries are outlined below.

The TBT Agreement differentiates between technical regulations (mandatory provisions) and standards (voluntary provisions) and establishes provisions applicable to both. Environmental labelling programmes can fall into either category depending upon whether or not a label is mandatory or voluntary. The distinction between mandatory and voluntary labelling requirements is important for ascertaining which provisions of the TBT Agreement apply.

Article 2 of the TBT Agreement is applicable to mandatory labelling requirements. Many important GATT principles that have already been discussed are incorporated into this provision. Article 2.1 provides for MFN and national treatment (treatment no less favourable for like products). Article 2.2 requires that technical regulations do not create "unnecessary" obstacles to international trade, and that such regulations are not more trade restrictive than necessary to fulfil legitimate objectives, taking account of the risks that non-fulfilment would create. Certain legitimate objectives are identified, including the protection of human, animal, and plant life or health and the environment. Article 2.4 requires the use of relevant international standards as a basis for technical regulations, unless they would be ineffective or inappropriate for the fulfilment of a legitimate objective. Article 2.5 provides that technical regulations that are in conformity with the international standards mentioned in Article 2.4 are "rebuttably presumed not to create unnecessary obstacles to international trade." Other portions of Article 2 set forth important notice and transparency requirements. In Article 3, rules for the application of these provisions by local governments and non-governmental bodies are set forth.

Article 2 recognizes the protection of human, animal, and plant life and health as legitimate objectives that might justify technical regulations, but trade measures to protect such legitimate objectives may not constitute "unnecessary" obstacles to international trade. This parallels the necessary test applied in conjunction with GATT Article XX(b), as evidenced by the fact that Article 2.2 incorporates a "least trade-restrictive measures" provision.[53] This provision is designed to minimize the burden to technical regulations and to prevent the abuse of technical regulations for protectionist purposes. The earlier characterization of the TBT Agreement as "rigid" is due to the incorporation of this "necessary" test. Past GATT/WTO experience with this standard suggests that certain non-protectionist measures may not easily satisfy this test owing to the frequent availability of reasonable less trade-restrictive alternatives.

This raises the question of whether or not mandatory labelling requirements are necessarily trade restrictive. By their very nature, labelling requirements that simply provide product-related information, even if mandatory, are not a particularly trade-restrictive measure. Instead, product-related labelling tends to play an informative role. Despite the fact that labelling may result in consumers choosing not to purchase certain products based on the information provided, as noted above, such product discrimination is indirect and, for many people (particularly those in the developed world), well within what they would view as necessary for informed decision-making and consumer choice.

There is one instance when a mandatory labelling requirement could be deemed trade restrictive. An import ban directed at goods that do not bear a mandatory label could, depending on the circumstances, operate to restrict trade and, based on the Appellate Body decision in *Asbestos*,[54] could be susceptible to review under the TBT Agreement as a technical regulation.

From the developing country perspective, one point should be noted. Article 2 places considerable emphasis on the promulgation of technical regulations in accordance with international standards. Although this provision is intended to encourage international harmonization, developing country interests will be served only if they participate actively in the harmonization process. If they do not, it is conceivable that harmonized standards may be promulgated that are significantly more difficult for developing countries to meet. This means the capacity of developing countries to participate in the international harmonization process must be enhanced, and developing country resources must be directed toward participation in such activities. This will mean participation in certain international harmonization activities that may have no immediate benefit for certain developing countries.

With respect to voluntary labelling schemes, including eco-labelling schemes, the situation is somewhat less straightforward.

These schemes fall under Article 4 of the TBT Agreement, which incorporates the "Code of Good Practice for the Preparation, Adoption and Application of Standards" (Annex 3 of the TBT Agreement). The Code of Good Practice contains the principal TBT obligations applicable to voluntary labelling schemes. Pursuant to Article 4.1, *only* central government standardizing bodies are bound by the provisions contained in the Code. Other standardizing bodies have the option to accept and apply the Code. However, members are obligated to take "reasonable measures" to assure that local and non-governmental standardizing bodies do indeed accept and comply with the Code. This leaves a risk that labelling standards that do not comply with the Code will be promulgated by various subnational governmental authorities (or non-governmental bodies), particularly in countries with decentralized political systems. If the intent of the members is to widen the application of the Code, a goal that is probably in the interest of developing countries, attention should be given to defining what constitutes the "reasonable measures" required by a member to assure that subnational governmental and non-governmental bodies accept and comply with the Code.

With respect to voluntary labelling schemes, the obligations set forth in the Code generally parallel those of Article 2 of the TBT Agreement: MFN and national treatment provisions exist, standards are not permitted to create unnecessary obstacles to international trade, deference is given to international standards,[55] harmonization is encouraged, and notice and transparency obligations receive considerable attention.

As already noted, the treatment of NPR-PPMs for the purposes of the Code is a point of contention that the members have not been able to resolve. The area of greatest preoccupation for developing countries has, not surprisingly, been the labelling of non-product-related environmental criteria, particularly the criteria found in eco-labelling schemes. Although the problem is not serious yet, if eco-labelling schemes become a well-accepted marketing tool, and if eco-labelling schemes attribute particular importance to NPR-PPMs, labelling could eventually undermine what some perceive to be a comparative advantage in certain countries. This means that the concern of developing countries with respect to the NPR-PPM question is legitimate, but that present fears are overstated given the paucity of data demonstrating the effectiveness of eco-labelling schemes in increasing a product's market share.

Other concerns revolve around the fact that few products from developing countries are currently labelled, and that the industries that tend to be found in the least developed countries are frequently not those that will benefit, at least for now, from labelling schemes. This again suggests that much of the fear that developing countries have about eco-labelling schemes is not warranted. Yet, the vigorous opposition to eco-labelling programmes on the part of some developing country members is not without purpose. Opposition to voluntary eco-labelling schemes has slowed down progress in the WTO's Committee on Trade and Environment (CTE), preventing more controversial issues (such as internalization) from receiving serious consideration. It has also made members realize that environmental issues are a stalking horse for labour-related issues, in particular "core labour standards." By blocking the resolution of the environmental questions now on the CTE's agenda, some countries are hoping that they are also blocking the advancement of labour issues up the WTO's agenda.

5. Concluding comments: Seattle and beyond

Environmental issues transcend national borders and are not solely a developed country concern. Developing countries are beginning to experience serious environmental difficulties, and these problems will grow. The continued deterioration of environmental conditions world-wide means that eco-labelling and other product-related labelling programmes are not going to disappear from the international trade agenda. Yet the polarized manner in which environmental issues are being addressed in the CTE has left little hope for progress in this forum. Although this may be in accord with certain developing country interests, it is inevitable that pressure will increase on developing countries during the next round of trade talks to reach a compromise, particularly with respect to less controversial environmental issues, such as eco-labelling.

The dramatic failure to launch a new round of trade talks in Seattle offers little encouragement that the members are ready to reach a consensus on the treatment of environmental issues, including environmental labelling questions. There is still not enough on the negotiating table to give the developing world an incentive to consider concessions in the politically charged and economically problematic environmental area.

The commitment of the United States to achieving a compromise on trade-related environmental questions is also now in doubt. The new administration in Washington has shown little support for, or interest in, either international or domestic environmental protection. If this continues to be the case, it is doubtful that the United States will support what "civil society" would view as environmental improvements (in the form of amendments) to the WTO Agreement. This means that, at least in the short term, it is probable that confrontation between the WTO and "civil society" will continue to characterize the trade-related environmental debate.

For many developing countries, environmental issues remain a luxury, and green protectionism is a legitimate concern. They realize that environmental agreements are possible only if all sides are willing to make concessions, and they are waiting for movement from the members in the developed world. If, as is likely, certain environmental issues are going to be on the agenda of the next round of trade talks, it may be time for the developing countries to take advantage of this fact, and to begin to line up concessions from the developed country members, perhaps in areas such as agriculture and textiles, in exchange for movement on environmental issues such as eco-labelling.[56] Despite opposition among many developing countries to eco-labelling programmes, negotiating a solution where trade concessions are won for developing countries may be preferable to "rolling the dice" and letting the Appellate Body resolve the unanswered GATT Article III and TBT questions.

Uncertainty concerning the treatment of NPR-PPMs in the TBT Agreement will remain the focus of attention for the developing world. This is not because eco-labelling poses an economic threat, but instead because of the "slippery slope" argument. Authorizing an evaluation of foreign NPR-PPMs for labelling purposes could open the door to other more effective means of influencing foreign NPR-PPMs. Going further down the "slippery slope," it could even open the WTO's doors to labour-related issues, human rights issues, and other sensitive social and political concerns. This is something most members want to avoid. Neither the use of trade as an economic lever to compel social change nor the use of the WTO's dispute settlement mechanism as a means of resisting social change is perceived as being in the best interests of the WTO, or of most of its members.[57]

With the exception of some uncertainty regarding the treatment of NPR-PPMs, the TBT Agreement seems adequate to prevent most cases of "green protectionism" arising from voluntary eco-labelling programmes. There are nevertheless improvements, already discussed at length in the CTE, that could lead to broader support for eco-labelling schemes. For example, assuming that they are permissible, voluntary eco-labelling schemes that reflect NPR-PPMs should take local geographic, environmental, economic, and developmental conditions into consideration. Furthermore, the need for developing country input in the drafting of criteria for labelling schemes is important. Lastly, maximum transparency in all stages of the labelling process must be assured. Progress on labelling issues is possible only if all sides recognize that legitimate aspirations and concerns are at stake and are prepared to work together towards a compromise that reflects these mutual interests.

Notes

1. Marrakesh Agreement Establishing the World Trade Organization, 15 April 1994 (hereinafter WTO Agreement); reprinted in GATT, *The Results of the Uruguay Round of Multilateral Trade Negotiations: The Legal Texts*, 5, 1994.
2. The International Standards Organization (ISO) has a system of classification that utilizes a different nomenclature. "Type I" labels are voluntary life-cycle labels based on pre-set criteria established by third parties. "Type II" labels are based on manufacturers' claims concerning individual environmental characteristics. "Type III" labels do not imply a product preference. They are

based on an independent scientific assessment of environmental information. Arthur E. Appleton, *Environmental Labelling Programmes: International Trade Law Implications*, London: Kluwer Law International, 1997, p. 4.

3. A life-cycle analysis ("LCA" or "cradle-to-grave analysis") is an assessment of environmental factors present in the production, use, and disposal of a product. By definition it includes the production processes used to make a product, use of the product (emissions, noise, etc.), and disposal (recyclability, biodegradability, etc.). From an environmental perspective the concept of life-cycle analysis is of considerable importance, given that every stage in a product's life can have environmental consequences.

4. Schemes exist or have existed in Austria, Canada, Croatia, the Czech Republic, the European Union, Finland, France, Germany, Iceland, India, Israel, Japan, the Netherlands, New Zealand, Norway, Republic of Korea, Singapore, Spain, Sweden, and the United States. Schemes were under consideration (and may have now been implemented) in Brazil, Chile, Colombia, Indonesia, Poland, and Thailand. An attempt to implement a scheme failed in Australia. Appleton, *Environmental Labelling Programmes*, op. cit., p. 6. The most famous schemes are probably the Nordic White Swan and the German Blue Angel.

5. The General Agreement on Tariffs and Trade, opened for signature 30 October 1947, 55 *UNTS* 187, entered into force 12 January 1948; reprinted in GATT, *Basic Instruments and Selected Documents* [*BISD*] 4/1, 1969.

6. GATT Article I provides for most-favoured-nation (MFN) treatment. GATT Article III provides for national treatment. Together these provisions make up GATT's "non-discrimination" obligation.

7. This being said, certain developing country products may qualify for a label based on their naturalness, lack of chemical processing, etc. Stores such as the Body Shop and Magasins du Monde and certain "fair trade" organizations are capitalizing on the marketing potential of developing country products.

8. Depending on geological or climatic considerations, certain production or disposal techniques may be adequate in one state but not in another. For example, the suitable use of hydrological power and the safe disposal of hazardous chemical substances may require geological or climatic considerations that can vary region by region.

9. *United States–Restrictions on Imports of Tuna*, Report of the Panel, GATT Document DS21/R, 3 September 1991 (unadopted), *BISD* 40S/155 (hereinafter *Tuna* Panel Report); reprinted in 30 *ILM* 1594 (1991), paras. 5.41–5.44.

10. *United States–Measures Affecting Alcoholic and Malt Beverages*, Report of the Panel, GATT Document DS23/R, adopted 19 June 1992, *BISD* 39S/206 (hereinafter *Malt Beverages* Panel Report), paras. 5.70–5.76.

11. WTO Document Press/TE 014, 14 November 1996.

12. WTO Agreement, op. cit., p. 6.

13. Ibid., p. 485.

14. Ibid., p. 138.

15. Ibid., p. 6.

16. Appleton, *Environmental Labelling Programmes*, op. cit., p. 91.

17. *United States–Import Prohibition of Certain Shrimp and Shrimp Products*, AB-1998-4, WT/DS58/AB/R, 12 October 1998 (hereinafter *Shrimp-Turtle* Appellate Body Report).

18. Ibid., para. 153.
19. Ibid., para. 155.
20. Appleton, *Environmental Labelling Programmes*, op. cit., pp. 141–142.
21. *Tuna* Panel Report, op. cit., paras. 5.41–5.44. See also Appleton, *Environmental Labelling Programmes*, op. cit., pp. 142–145.
22. *Tuna* Panel Report, op. cit., para. 5.42.
23. *Japan–Taxes on Alcoholic Beverages*, AB-1996-2, WT/DS8, 10 & 11/AB/R, 4 October 1996 (hereinafter *Alcoholic Beverages* Appellate Body Report), §E.
24. Appleton, *Environmental Labelling Programmes*, op. cit., p. 147. GATT Articles III and XI ("General Elimination of Quantitative Restrictions") are mutually exclusive. Article III applies even if the internal measures at issue are applied at the point of importation against like imported products. See GATT Annex I, "Notes and Supplementary Provisions," ad Article III.
25. *Alcoholic Beverages* Appellate Body Report, op. cit., §F (footnotes omitted).
26. *European Communities–Measures Affecting Asbestos and Asbestos-Containing Products*, AB-2000-11, WT/DS135/AB/R, 12 March 2001 (hereinafter *Asbestos* Appellate Body Report).
27. Ibid., para. 99.
28. Ibid., para. 101.
29. *Border Tax Adjustments*, *Report of the Working Party*, GATT Doc. L/3464, adopted 2 December 1970, *BISD* 18S/97, para. 18.
30. *United States–Standards for Conventional and Reformulated Gasoline*, AB-1996-1, WT/DS2/AB/R, 29 April 1996 (hereinafter *Reformulated Gasoline* Appellate Body Report).
31. *Asbestos* Appellate Body Report, op. cit., paras. 101–103.
32. Ibid., paras. 109, 111.
33. Ibid., para. 114.
34. *Tuna* Panel Report, op. cit., para. 5.14; and *United States–Restrictions on Imports of Tuna*, Report of the Panel, GATT Doc. DS29/R, 16 June 1994 (unadopted), reprinted in 33 *ILM* 842, 1994, paras. 5.8–5.9. Both reports found that Article XI would be applicable because Article III (Note ad Article III) does not permit an assessment (in the determination of like products) at the point of importation of policies and practices that do not have an effect on a product's physical characteristics (NPR-PPMs).
35. *United States–Import Prohibition of Certain Shrimp and Shrimp Products*, Report of the Panel, WT/DS58/R, 15 May 1998, para. 3.143.
36. Appleton, *Environmental Labelling Programmes*, op. cit., pp. 105 and 149.
37. See e.g. Agreement on Technical Barriers to Trade (hereinafter TBT Agreement), in Agreement Establishing the World Trade Organization, Marrakesh, 15 April 1994, Annex 1a, Article 2.
38. Mr. Lacarte signed both the *Malt Beverages* and *Alcoholic Beverages* reports. This change in practice is therefore somewhat surprising.
39. The Appellate Body recognized the right of members to pursue certain domestic goals in a WTO-consistent manner in the *Alcoholic Beverages* report (*Alcoholic Beverages* Appellate Body Report, op. cit., §F). In making such an evaluation, it is possible that considerations of domestic policy autonomy, in such areas as health, safety, and the environment, will enter into the analysis.
40. See e.g. C. Tietje, "Voluntary Eco-labelling Programmes and Questions of

State Responsibility in the WTO/GATT Legal System," *Journal of World Trade* 29(123), October 1995, 139–141.
41. Appleton, *Environmental Labelling Programmes*, op. cit., p. 159.
42. See GATT, Annex I, "Notes and Supplementary Provisions," ad Article III.
43. Appleton, *Environmental Labelling Programmes*, op. cit., pp. 159–160.
44. Article XX(b) provides an exception for measures "necessary to protect human, animal or plant life or health."
45. A measure is not "necessary" for GATT purposes if a GATT-consistent measure can be applied or if a trade measure that is less trade restrictive can be implemented.
46. *Asbestos* Appellate Body Report, op. cit., paras. 170–171.
47. *Korea–Measures Affecting Imports of Fresh, Chilled and Frozen Beef*, AB-2000-8, WT/DS161/AB/R, WT/DS169/AB/R, 10 January 2001.
48. *Asbestos* Appellate Body Report, op. cit., para. 172.
49. Article XX(g) provides an exception for measures "relating to the conservation of exhaustible natural resources if such measures are made effective in conjunction with restrictions on domestic production or consumption."
50. See *Shrimp-Turtle* Appellate Body Report, op. cit., and *Reformulated Gasoline* Appellate Body Report, op. cit.
51. See, generally, Doaa Abdel Motaal, "Eco-labelling and the World Trade Organisation," paper prepared for the International Conference Green Goods V: Eco-labelling for a Sustainable Future, Berlin, Germany, 26–28 October 1998 (on file with the author).
52. Ibid., p. 5.
53. TBT Agreement, Article 2.2, reads in part "technical regulations shall not be more trade-restrictive than necessary to fulfil a legitimate objective."
54. *Asbestos* Appellate Body Report, op. cit., paras. 59–77.
55. Unlike TBT Agreement, Article 2.5, no rebuttable presumption of validity is created in the Code for national and subnational standards based on international standards, nor are legitimate objectives for standardization set forth as in Article 2.2.
56. To this list can be added the treatment of multilateral environmental agreements that incorporate trade measures.
57. A preferable solution would be to strengthen international and regional agreements governing areas such as environment, labour, and human rights, and to create effective enforcement mechanisms. There is, however, no consensus on such a step.

[25]

Trade and Environment: How Real Is the Debate?

Magda Shahin

Globalization and liberalization are the twin processes marking the beginning of the twenty-first century. Today, we are confronted with maxims such as "Making Globalization Social and Green"[1] or "Globalization with a Human Face." A myriad of new standards is in the making to handle the devastating effects of globalization on developed and developing countries alike. Yet, without a doubt, developed countries are the front-runners. Green consumers, healthy consumers, and safe consumers are now in the driving seat. Today, trade wars are erupting even between the United States and the European countries on genetically altered crops and modified food, threatening trade and investment flows accounting for more than US$2,000 billion annually and providing 14 million jobs on both sides of the Atlantic.[2] What are the underlying motives? Are they truly anxiety and concern for food safety, the environment, morality, and human kind? Or are these kinds of trade wars driven by world hegemony and by commercial interests with billions of dollars at stake? Is linking trade to environment a justified concern with genuine environmental goals? Or are additional protection measures at play? Where do the developing countries fit into all this, with their resource constraints, poor information flows, and lack of scientific knowledge?

1. Background

The relationship between trade and environment is complex and critical. It is over-burdened with suspicion and strained by misunderstandings that need to be addressed and clarified. To that end, it is appropriate to go back as far as the issuing of the Brundtland report in the mid-1980s. Brundtland, the Prime Minister of Norway at that time, chaired a group of eminent personalities. In her famous report, she drew the attention of the international community to the interface between environment and development in the newly introduced phrase "sustainable development." When introduced at the 39th General Assembly in 1985, it was met with a great deal of scepticism on the part of developing countries in general. The notion of sacrificing today's development to preserve the environment for the development of future generations was viewed with resentment and misgivings. It took the international community several years and a huge effort to work out a smooth relationship between development and environment and to establish close linkages between them. This culminated in an Agreement at the UN Conference on Environment and Development (UNCED) held in Rio de Janeiro in 1992. The Agreement has established fundamental principles to be observed and specific measures to be undertaken for the attainment of environmental goals, all framed in a detailed programme of action: Agenda 21. Some of the key principles of the Rio Declaration are particularly pertinent to our discussion:

> The right to development must be fulfilled so as to equitably meet developmental and environmental needs of present and future generations. (Principle 3)
>
> Eradicating poverty is an indispensable requirement for sustainable development. (Principle 5)
>
> States have common but differentiated responsibilities in regard to promoting sustainable development. (Principle 7)
>
> There should be a diffusion and transfer of technologies. (Principle 9)

States should co-operate to promote a supportive and open international economic system that would lead to economic growth and sustainable development in all countries. (Principle 12)[3]

Agenda 21 set out specific measures on trade; in particular, the promotion of "an open, non-discriminatory and equitable multilateral trading system that will enable all countries – in particular, the developing countries – to improve their economic structures and improve the standard of living of their populations through sustained economic development."[4] In addition, a range of measures was agreed for the transfer of technology and the provision of new and additional financial resources to the developing countries for the implementation of the programme. Hence Agenda 21 set the basic principles as well as the overall framework within which the international community shoulders its burden of responsibility and has to work in order to protect, preserve, and enhance the environment together with the development process, particularly in developing countries.

Nevertheless, in parallel to that event and far away in Geneva, while trade representatives were busy negotiating the Uruguay Round Agreements of the soon to be World Trade Organization, environmentalists were determined to integrate environment in the trade debate. Their intentions and motives were questioned at a time when the Rio Conference had just been successfully concluded. Were developed countries thinking of backtracking on the commitments and obligations they had agreed to within the framework of the UN Conference? Were developing countries justified in their apprehensions about the trade debate? Were these apprehensions legitimate? It did not take long for such doubts to be proved well founded. In addition to the persisting divisions in the ongoing debate in the World Trade Organization, the lack of progress in the mid-term review of the Rio Programme of Action in New York in 1997 was yet further proof of the doubts and suspicions aired by developing countries. There has been obvious, and regrettable, backtracking on the obligations undertaken by the developed countries, especially in regard to improving market access for developing country exports, the transfer of technology, and the provision of new and additional resources. (In regard to financial resources, it was estimated that the developing countries would require US$125 billion, in the form of grants and concessions, from the international community to implement the activities specified in Agenda 21. This requirement remains unmet.) Moreover, in the view of many developing countries, developed countries are in effect retreating from the holistic approach to sustainable development agreed at Rio. Their focus is now on unilateral measures and on environmental conditionalities attached to trade and investment. This trend is inimical to the attainment of both developmental and environmental goals.[5]

2. The trade and environment debate in the WTO

Though initially developing countries resisted debating the trade/environment relationship in the World Trade Organization (WTO), they reluctantly came to an agreement towards the end of the Uruguay Round. A decision was issued at the Marrakesh Ministerial Conference (1994) to that effect. A Committee on Trade and Environment was established to cool the heat created by the non-governmental organizations (NGOs) and to allow for a smooth signing and ratification of the Uruguay Round Agreements and the creation of the WTO. Dealing with the relationship between trade and environment in the WTO has gone through various phases, at some points being a leading priority in the framework of the WTO work, at other times being less attractive and thus occupying a lower profile. At no time were developing countries the *demandeurs*; on the contrary, they succumbed to pressure on many occasions.

In all this, the central question remained how to bring the trade and the environmental systems closer together without undermining either system, knowing that they are not necessarily always compatible. In fact, the two regimes are often even in conflict. The environmental regime allows for measures that go beyond a country's borders, for the sake of protecting the environment, whereas such a measure would amount to a flagrant violation of WTO rules and regulations, which do not allow for extra-territorial measures. The problem goes even further. Today we see growing concern by environmental groups at the national level forcing the issue of *national sovereignty* against the country's obligations to abide by WTO judgements. A case in point is the well-known dispute regarding "Import Prohibition of Certain Shrimp and Shrimp Products" between the United States on the one hand and Thailand, India, Pakistan, and Malaysia on the other hand. Unhappy with rulings on the matter by the WTO dispute settlement panel and the Appellate Body, a coalition of US environmental groups raising the issue of national sovereignty succeeded in winning a ruling from the US Court of International Trade that went against the WTO panel. There is no doubt that this ruling from the Court of International Trade will handicap US efforts to comply with the WTO panel and Appellate rulings.[6] The environmentalists believe that the United States is compromising its national sovereignty for the sake of its international obligations.

Today, after five years of intensive discussion and learning about the relationship between trade and environment, many continue to have mixed feelings about how to go about this relationship. Traders and environmentalists have many a time stood helpless and perplexed in front of this conundrum, which turns on how to accommodate environmental concerns in trade policy without tampering with the trade rules. Striking a balance between the need for governments to protect and preserve the environment, on one hand, and avoiding the usage of environmental measures as a new trade protection measure, on the other hand, remains a sensitive and highly controversial issue.

It was only after long and informed reasoning that many realized beyond a doubt that the two systems could not remain under the same roof, because their objectives vary as well as their methods of implementation. That does not mean, however, that trade and environment are not mutually supportive. In many instances they are. Nevertheless, all the efforts to incorporate environment within the WTO system were to no avail. Based on this, Renato Ruggiero, the outgoing WTO Director-General, was brave enough to come up with a solution, which is – to my mind – straightforward and simple. He explained that all we need is a multilateral rules-based system (similar to that of the WTO) for environment – a World Environment Organization to be the institutional and legal counterpart to the WTO. Such a proposal has been put forward on a number of occasions, the last being the High Level Symposium on Trade and Environment in the WTO on 15 March 1999.[7] There has been agreement with this viewpoint. "Indeed, nothing would advance 'trade and environment' harmony more than the creation of a Global Environmental Organization to work alongside the WTO," wrote Daniel C. Esty of Yale University in his presentation to the High Level Symposium.[8]

Realizing the immense difficulties involved in resolving the trade and environment relationship and easing the tension that had developed in the WTO in this regard, the European Commission proposed a high-level "political" conference to bring trade and environment ministers together in the WTO. Because the debate in the WTO seemed burdened with suspicion and scepticism, developing country representatives in Geneva felt that the timing was not propitious, especially in light of the fact that many issues remained unsolved in this relationship. In their mind, this needed further technical work before it could be brought to a political forum. Together with developed country delegations, they agreed after long deliberations to turn the high-level "political" conference into a non-official, non-conclusive symposium involving a wider spectrum of the public, notably NGOs and academia, in a brainstorming session with a view to airing all positions, including those of civil societies.

It is astonishing that, in spite of the general view that further work needs to be undertaken on all items of the agenda of the CTE, pre-determined positions are still taken. Such positions continue to press for amending the WTO rules to accommodate environment or call for the legitimization of the process and production methods approach in the GATT system, irrespective of the wide-ranging and serious implications for developing countries and their methods of production. In addition, little tribute is paid to the concerns of developing countries in general. Market access and the new environmental conditions are key in this respect. The pretext that competition among nations is creating downward pressure on environmental standards is causing new protectionist measures to be arbitrarily imposed. The debate has revolved around these and other issues for the past few years. Developing countries have defended their interests and stood firm for positions that today might warrant more explanation and definition. The next phase of negotiations will be not less but certainly more controversial, and developing countries will again have to aggressively defend their positions.

3. The basis of the WTO trade/environment debate

It is worth noting that the trade and environment debate in the WTO is set within a consensual framework and based on three essential premises. These I would call the three Cs: Consistency with the level of development, the Competence of the world trading system, and allaying fears of additional Conditionality. Let me elaborate further.

First, no one denies the importance assigned to the protection and preservation of the environment in the Preamble of the Marrakesh Agreement Establishing the World Trade Organization.[9] But, it is equally true that the Preamble emphasized that this be done in a manner consistent with the needs and concerns of countries at different levels of economic development. What is of significance here is that the importance accorded to environment was not absolute, but linked to countries' levels of development. I could even argue that priority was given to development, because the protection and preservation of the environment can be achieved only to the extent that this is consistent with the level of development.

It is not difficult to draw a comparison between the WTO Preamble and Rio Principle 7, cited earlier, concerning the common but differentiated responsibilities of states in regard to promoting sustainable development. This principle was the anchor for the

UNCED. It accepted that the Northern countries had a greater responsibility for meeting the costs of adjustment because of their larger role in environmental degradation as well as their economic capacity to absorb more costs. The developing countries still needed to grow and develop (sustainably, of course) to meet their people's needs. The North also made a commitment to provide adequate financial resources and technology transfer to facilitate the South's transition to sustainable development.[10]

Secondly, the Marrakesh Ministerial Decision on Trade and Environment[11] was clear in setting the terms of reference for WTO work on trade and environment. The fourth paragraph of the Preamble stipulates that the coordination of policies in the field of trade and environment should be done without exceeding the competence of the multilateral trading system. Again of utmost significance here is that the negotiators were adamant that the "competence of the multilateral trading system" is limited to trade policies and those aspects of environmental policies that may result in significant trade effects for its members.

Thirdly, in order to allay any possible fears of a new "green conditionality" attached to market access opportunities, thus nullifying the benefits accruing from trade liberalization within the context of the Uruguay Round, the 1996 Singapore Ministerial Report on Trade and Environment[12] stressed the following:

1. the WTO is not an environmental protection agency and it is assumed that the WTO itself does not provide an answer to environmental problems;
2. environmental problems require environmental solutions, not trade solutions;
3. no blank cheque for the use of trade measures for environmental purposes;
4. trade liberalization is not the primary cause of environmental degradation, nor are trade instruments the first-best policy for addressing environmental problems;

5. GATT/WTO agreements already provide significant scope for members to adopt national environmental protection policies, provided that they are non-discriminatory;
6. secure market access opportunities are essential to help developing countries work towards sustainable development;
7. increased national coordination as well as multilateral cooperation are necessary to address trade-related environmental concerns adequately.

It is worth stressing that the first WTO Ministerial Conference was keen to elucidate the reality of the relationship and its rightful stance in the multilateral system. It was clear from the ongoing debate at the time that there was no quarrel with depicting the WTO as an environment-friendly organization. In fact, the GATT allows for any action to be taken at the national level to protect the environment, provided it is in compliance with its basic rules and regulations. Article XX ("General Exceptions"),[13] the Agreement on Technical Barriers to Trade (TBT),[14] and the Agreement on the Application of Sanitary and Phytosanitary Measures (SPS)[15] are all cases in point: they give each country the right to set the level of protection that it deems appropriate on environment, provided it does not act against the basic principles of the WTO as stipulated by Article I ("Most-Favoured-Nation Treatment") and Article III ("National Treatment"). In addition, it should not constitute an unnecessary barrier to trade. I should emphasize that the Trade and Environment Report adopted at the first Ministerial Conference remains as valid as ever and constitutes the backbone of the ongoing debate on trade and environment. However, one thing developing countries were keen to elucidate was that the report does not represent a legal instrument, hence does not alter or touch upon the rights and obligations of WTO members.

I shall now turn to a few of the specific issues that were subject to intensive debate at the CTE. I start with the interrelationship between multilateral environmental agreements and the WTO, followed by the complex relationship between the Agreement on Trade-related Intellectual Property Rights (TRIPS) and environment. I then deal with eco-labelling as a life-cycle analysis and the problem of process and production methods. Finally, I address market access and competitiveness as prime issues of interest to developing countries in the trade and environment debate.

4. Some specific issues in the debate

The relationship between multilateral environmental agreements and the WTO

The relationship between the provisions of the multilateral trading system and trade measures for environmental purposes, including those pursuant to multilateral environmental agreements (MEAs), was a topic that was extensively debated and subject to the most controversy. In spite of the long and tedious discussions throughout the previous five years or so, little rapprochement, if any, was achieved. Views on a number of issues were and remain wide apart; the definition of MEAs, Article XX, the issue of process and production methods, the effectiveness of trade restrictions and whether they were the most appropriate instruments to advance environmental policies are but a few of these issues.

The relationship between the multilateral trading system and the multilateral environmental agreements raised numerous difficulties and controversies. These ranged from issues of hierarchy and compatibility between the two entities to the comprehensive framework of the MEAs, which combine a mixture of incentives and trade measures to deal with environmental externalities. In the framework of MEAs, positive measures – such as improved market access, capacity-building, additional finance, and access to and transfer of technology – were considered to be effective instruments to assist developing countries to meet multilaterally agreed environmental targets. This was in sharp contrast to the much-disputed effectiveness of trade measures applied as sanctions under the purview of the WTO. The scope for trade measures pursuant to MEAs under WTO provisions and their unilateral application to address environmental problems that lie outside a country's national jurisdiction led to wide disagreement and were strongly contested.

In this debate, developing countries had to defend themselves on a number of fronts. First, developing countries continued to argue against developed countries' intentions of arming the WTO with additional power to protect the environment, because this would have the effect only of elevating trade measures, i.e. sanctions to be considered as priority tools for the environment. This would undermine the international consensus reached on a whole range of positive measures negotiated at length within the framework of the multilateral environmental agreements. Isolating the trade measures would not serve the purpose and could prove to be detrimental to the environment because they deprive developing countries of an assured source of resources. Such resources could be directed, among other things, towards the protection of the environment. Furthermore, in order to determine the necessity and effectiveness of the trade measures, these would have to be assessed together with other measures in a holistic framework, such as the one provided for by the multilateral environmental agreements. Countries cannot press for the use of trade measures just because they are less expensive and hence more appealing to politicians, without weighing the pros and cons of such usage in an objective and comprehensive manner. On the contrary, MEAs should provide developing countries with the "carrot" to entice them to comply with their obligations under such agreements, if – as proclaimed – the ultimate goal is to preserve and protect the environment.

Secondly, regarding the issue of hierarchy, at the Singapore Ministerial Conference of the WTO in December 1996,[16] developing countries succeeded in undermining the attempts by developed countries to give the MEAs superiority over the WTO's settlement of disputes. The underlying reasons were clear: developing countries refused the dominance of environmental considerations, as advocated in the MEAs, over the WTO Dispute Settlement Understanding (DSU) as guided by the key principles of the trading system, notably most-favoured-nation and national treatment, as well as the rejection of unilateral measures. Developing countries felt that on no account should they give up or weaken their inalienable rights to have recourse to the WTO DSU by giving primacy to settling disputes through the MEA. That did not mean, however, that MEAs were disregarded. They remain a viable option for disputants to settle their disputes, if they so wish.

The repeated attempts by the European Commission to reinterpret or even add an amendment to the WTO rules that would prioritize environment or make it an exception through what they would like to perceive as an "environmental window" were doomed to failure. Developing countries have stood firm against any amendments to the WTO rules in order to legitimize inconsistent trade measures in the WTO. They insisted that any effort to reopen the WTO rules would mean imposing environmental conditionality on trade and would give sufficient ground for unilateral measures that would amount to protectionism and restriction of market access under the disguise of protecting the environment. It was also recognized that, in principle, trade measures taken pursuant to MEAs were not to be challenged by the WTO membership, because the majority are also members of the MEAs. Furthermore, trade measures within the MEAs – as multilaterally agreed upon – were tolerated, and many of them were even pushed by developing countries themselves. This was the case with the Basel Convention and the Prior Informed Consent Convention on Hazardous Chemicals.

It is surprising that voices are still raised in favour of effecting substantive changes in the GATT. The first of these would involve amending Article XX on the pretext that, as it is currently applied, it gives prominence to trade goals over environmental ones. In my view this is the wrong way to look at things. The WTO's main concern is implementing trade goals. It is entitled to rectify any wrong-doings in the area of trade, but it is not within the competence of the organization or its trade representatives to deal with issues going beyond trade and trade-related issues, be they environment, human rights, child labour, or other social issues. In addition, it has been stated that Article XX is flexible enough to accommodate legitimate environmental concerns. It was precisely with this in mind that negotiators stressed the competence of the multilateral trading system in the fourth paragraph of the Preamble of the Marrakesh Ministerial Decision on Trade and Environment.

Another substantive amendment to the current GATT structure that would facilitate peace between the trade and environment camps would involve the recognition by GATT that, in an ecologically interdependent world, *how* things are produced is often as important as *what* is produced. In particular, environmental standards that relate to process and production methods (PPMs) cannot always be rejected and judged indiscriminately to be violations of GATT.[17] On the other hand, accepting the introduction of PPMs in GATT/WTO would amount to the imposition of a country's domestic environmental values or policies on other countries. As environmental standards and PPMs are based on values that differ from one society to another, it would be difficult to internationalize PPMs and require all countries to follow the same production methods. On the other hand, we have to distinguish between environmental standards that are product related, such as disposal and handling, with which I have no quarrel, and non-product-related standards, which do not affect the final product.

The risks of setting and accepting ecological standards for PPMs in GATT today are twofold. First, these standards would most likely be the ones used in developed countries, thus allowing environmental standards to be easily manipulated for protection purposes. Second, setting ecological standards for PPMs could be used as an opening for over-stretching the concept in the future and taking it as a precedent to incorporate other non-trade-related goals, such as labour standards, human rights, good governance, and all sorts of other domestic pressures that have hardly any relationship with the WTO.

The Shrimp-Turtle *dispute*

It is worth referring briefly to the *Shrimp-Turtle* dispute. In this case, the two rulings (by the dispute settlement panel as well as by the Appellate Body) are precedent setting. The dispute was the first concerning a trade embargo based solely on domestic environmental legislation forced by the United States as the only country that interprets Article XX so broadly as to allow for extra-territorial measures to protect the environment beyond its territories. It was obvious from the very beginning that the issue at stake was not a trade measure mandated by an MEA (in this case the Convention on International Trade in Endangered Species of Wild Fauna and Flora [CITES]), but a measure to address a global environmental concern applied unilaterally by one country.

For the United States, the case involved the right of WTO members to take measures under Article XX (b) and (g)[18] of GATT 1994 to conserve and protect natural resources, as reaffirmed and reinforced by the Preamble to the WTO Agreement. For the complainant, it was a case about the imposition of unilateral trade measures designed to coerce other members to adopt environmental policies that mirrored those in the United States. The United States based its entire defence on Article XX, which allows countries to take measures contrary to GATT obligations when such measures (a) are necessary to protect human, animal, or plant life or health; (b) relate to the conservation of exhaustible natural resources.

In this case, the United States argued that a trade measure was necessary because sea turtles were threatened with extinction and the use of turtle excluder devices on shrimp nets was the only way effectively to protect them from drowning in shrimp nets. The panel, however, stressed the WTO's preference for multilaterally negotiated solutions.[19] Furthermore, the panel focused its analysis on the headnote or "chapeau" of Article XX, which requires legitimate trade restrictions to be applied "in a manner, which would not constitute a means of arbitrary or unjustifiable discrimination between countries where the same conditions prevail or a disguised restriction on international trade." The panel found that interpreting the chapeau in a way that would allow importing countries to restrict market access according to exporters' adoption of "certain policies, including conservation policies" would mean that "GATT 1994 and the WTO Agreement could no longer serve as a multilateral framework for trade among Members." Such an interpretation, the panel felt, could lead to "conflicting policy requirements" because exporting countries would need to conform with different domestic policies in importing countries, thus threatening the "security and predictability of trade relations" under WTO agreements. It therefore drew the conclusion that "certain unilateral measures, insofar as they could jeopardize the multilateral trading system, could not be covered by Article XX."[20]

The panel reaffirmed the logic of developing countries that the WTO cannot be made responsible for safeguarding all kinds of different interests. This would give leeway to members to pursue their own trade policy solutions unilaterally, thus reinstating power politics. This would certainly amount to an abuse of Article XX exceptions, as the panel put it, and thus threaten the preservation of the multilateral trade system based on consensus and multilateral cooperation. It is worth recalling at this juncture that to do away with a power-based system and replace it with a rule-based one was an essential objective of the seven-year Uruguay Round of negotiations, which hardly anyone would want to give up today.

Without much ado, the Appellate Body also concluded that the US measure was "unjustifiably discriminatory."[21] In its ruling, the Appellate Body was more cautious and less blunt than the panel. Trying to find some "political" justification for the US measure, it characterized the ban "as an appropriate means to an end," although its application was at fault. It attributed the unjustifiable nature of the discrimination to the failure of the United States to pursue negotiations for consensual means of protecting and conserving sea turtles, resulting in the "unilateral" application of its trade measure. The Appellate Body further agreed that the United States had applied the measure in an "arbitrary and discriminatory" manner between countries where the same conditions prevail, contrary to the requirements of the chapeau of Article XX. The application was discriminatory in giving a longer grace period to Caribbean countries than to Asian nations, in not transferring technology to them on similar terms, in its lack of transparency, etc.

The Appellate Body then stressed that it had not decided that the sovereign nations that are members of the WTO cannot adopt effective measures to protect endangered species, such as sea turtles; "Clearly, they can and should."[22] It stressed that protection and preservation of the environment are of significance to WTO members, provided that "they [sovereign states] act together bilaterally, plurilaterally or multilaterally, either within the WTO or in other international forums." Finally the Appellate Body decided that, "although the measure of the US in dispute in this appeal serves an environmental objective that is recognized as legitimate under paragraph (g) of Article XX of GATT 1994, this measure has been applied by the US in a manner which constitutes arbitrary and unjustifiable discrimination between Members of the WTO, contrary to the requirements of the chapeau of Article XX."[23]

Although the US ambassador to the WTO hailed the Appellate Body's ruling as a success for the US position, a similar sense of victory was neither felt nor expressed by US environmental NGOs, which, as mentioned earlier, had brought the case to the US Court. The Appellate Body ruling, in my view, does not amount to a reversal of the panel ruling, as some would like to have it, but rather falls under what the Singapore Ministerial Meeting attempted to elucidate. GATT/WTO agreements do provide significant scope for national environmental protection policies, provided they are not discriminatory in nature. Moreover, countries should seek joint and not unilateral action. This is how, I believe, the Appellate Body findings and conclusions should be regarded. This decision is an attempt not to overturn the consensus reached in the WTO CTE, but rather to strengthen it. In fact, the Appellate Body pronounced itself clearly against WTO-inconsistent trade measures applied unilaterally to address extra-jurisdictional environmental problems. It thus underlined what WTO members had succeeded in injecting into the factual part of the Singapore report. It was explicitly mentioned that "all delegations except one"[24] stated that they consider that the provisions of GATT Article XX do not permit a member to impose unilateral trade restrictions that are otherwise inconsistent with WTO obligations for the purpose of protecting environmental resources that lie outside its jurisdiction. In any event, arguments in favour of reinterpreting Article XX to address environmental concerns (as put forcefully by those who want to see Article XX amended or reinterpreted), for fear of the trend by the Appellate Body to expand – on its own – the meaning of Article XX, remain void. There is no doubt that neither the Appellate Body nor the panels are entitled to attempt to interpret the WTO rules. *Interpretation of the rules is the sole right of the membership.*

The environment and trade-related intellectual property rights

The relationship between environment and trade-related intellectual property rights (TRIPS) is yet another example of the underlying conflict in the WTO between the urge to protect the environment on the one hand and the tools made available for such an objective in the framework of the TRIPS Agreement, on the other hand. Here the case is quite the reverse. The TRIPS Agreement as negotiated and pushed for by the developed countries has proven to be unfriendly to the environment. In fact, reading carefully through the TRIPS Agreement, one cannot fail to realize that environmental concerns did not really occupy a priority at the negotiating table then. It has become clear only over the past few years that a number of provisions in the TRIPS Agreement go against the objectives of Agenda 21 and the various multilateral environmental agreements in regard to access to and transfer of technology to help maintain and protect the environment. The outcry came first from non-governmental organizations engaged in development and environment in developed and developing countries alike.

India was one of the few countries that, at an early stage in the work of the CTE, recognized the real problem in reconciling intellectual property protection, as laid down in the TRIPS Agreement, with the objectives and provisions on transfer of technology incorporated in some of the MEAs.[25] It failed, however, to summon the necessary backing on the part of the developing countries on this topical issue. The primary reason was the complexity of the issue itself. Hardly any developing countries were grabbed by this difficult and composite relationship, because they were still struggling with other outstanding commitments emanating from the Uruguay Round. Coping with the various provisions of the TRIPS Agreement was not a priority, because they felt they had ample time until the transitional period expired.

As we get closer to the implementation of the TRIPS Agreement and with environment looming as a topic in the Millennium Round, developing countries ought to look more seriously at this issue. Let me hasten to say that at no point in my argument should it be taken that developing countries are trying to back-pedal on their commitments. It none the less remains a fact that the TRIPS Agreement as negotiated was put in a very narrow context and with limited objectives, i.e. to lay down minimum standards for the protection of the owner, the titleholder, and the patentee, conferring on them exclusive rights. This goes against a whole myriad of legitimate and valid concerns; topping the list are socio-economic and developmental issues, the environment, technology transfer, and fair and open competition. It is no secret that, for these as well as other reasons, developing countries remained inimical to such an agreement until the eleventh hour. It was only under pressure of the "Single Undertaking" commitment that they were obliged to accede to it.

Addressing the relationship between the TRIPS Agreement and environment, the CTE focused in its deliberations on two main issues:

1. the generation of, access to, and transfer of environmentally sound technologies, and
2. the contradiction between the TRIPS Agreement and the Convention on Biological Diversity.

In regard to the first issue, the question concerns what happens if TRIPS put such technologies beyond the reach of developing countries. This would undoubtedly have a negative impact on the environment and on the stringent efforts developing countries are making to cope with the environmental requirements. It is true that Article 7 of the TRIPS Agreement stipulates that patenting should encourage the promotion of technological innovation and the transfer and dissemination of technology, to the mutual advantage of producers and users and in a manner conducive to social and economic welfare. This, however, has not yet materialized owing to the fact that developing countries are still benefiting from the transitional period of the implementation of the Agreement. Nor has any empirical evidence sustained this argument so far. Hence, the question remains how TRIPS link up with the objective of facilitating access to and transfer of technology "on fair and most favourable terms"[26] to assist in the conservation of the environment and promote sustainable development.

As for the relationship between the TRIPS Agreement and the Convention on Biological Diversity (CBD), this heads the list of concerns of developmental and environmental NGOs in the North as well as in the South. The contradiction between TRIPS and the CBD is not implicit. There are doubts about the compatibility of the various provisions of the TRIPS Agreement with the clear objectives of the Convention as it relates to the conservation and sustainable use of genetic resources. The underlying disparity between the timely transfer of relevant biotechnology as agreed in the CBD and Article 33 of TRIPS, which provides for a term of protection of at least 20 years, remains a point of contention and a source of serious concern. This is even more so for developing countries when they start implementing the TRIPS Agreement by the year 2000.

It was only after the conclusion of the TRIPS Agreement and after its adoption within the framework of the Uruguay Round that questions regarding the compatibility between TRIPS and the CBD started to surface. Equitable sharing of the benefits arising out of the utilization of the knowledge systems of indigenous communities and fair trade-offs between access to genetic resources and the transfer of technology remain the essence of the CBD, as agreed notably in Articles 15 and 16 of the Convention.[27] However, concerns were expressed about the negative impact of TRIPS in the fields of agriculture, nutrition, and health care, because they would inevitably lead to an extension of the monopoly control of transnationals over production and distribution in these vital areas for developing countries. Moreover, the TRIPS Agreement does not try to curb the commercial exploitation of genetic resources or deal with the sharing on a fair and equitable basis of the benefits arising out of the patenting of genetic resources. Much has been said with respect to the usage and applicability of Article 31(k) of the TRIPS Agreement regarding compulsory licensing for the public domain, as permitting the necessary flexibility. With all the strings attached to this article, however, the question arises whether it truly serves the purpose of facilitating access to and transfer of technology, including biotechnology, on fair and most favourable terms, as stipulated by Article 16.2 of the Biodiversity Convention. This issue undoubtedly requires more in-depth study.

Because of these fundamental controversies and whether or not environment becomes an issue in the next multilateral trading round or is mainstreamed in the various agreements, environment will have to be an integral part of any review process of the TRIPS Agreement. The different available alternatives should be weighed and carefully studied. Three main options, which set the framework for the overall trade and environment debate, come to mind:

1. to agree on the relevance of Article XX as a general exception in the context of the TRIPS Agreement when specifically addressing biodiversity and the sustainable use of genetic resources;
2. to decide whether the TRIPS Agreement or the Convention would prevail in the event of a dispute and how it would work out between parties and non-parties to either; and
3. to keep the issue open, to be addressed and settled on an ad hoc basis by panels in the event of a dispute.

It is worth stressing at this juncture that developmental and environmental NGOs from the North as well as from the South latched on to the issue that developing countries should have been tackling in depth much earlier. Their views should not be neglected, otherwise developing countries might at some point find themselves on the defensive and be confronted with the same kind of arguments raised against the TRIPS Agreement, namely that it was negotiated entirely out of the public view; it might then perhaps be too late. The recent failure of the lengthy negotiations on the Multilateral Agreement on Investment in the Organisation for Economic Co-operation and Development (OECD) is a case in point. It clearly denotes the strength and skills of environmental NGOs and, if they feel sidelined, TRIPS could be next in turn.

Eco-labelling

Eco-labelling is another highly controversial issue. Compared with other voluntary standards, such as packaging, labelling, or even recycling requirements, it has attracted much attention in the trade and environment debate in the WTO. In spite of the fact that it was discussed extensively prior to the Singapore Ministerial Conference as well as in the framework of the review process of the Agreement on Technical Barriers to Trade, hardly any decision has materialized to date. The issue has raised a number of practical, conceptual, and systemic problems. It might sound strange and be difficult to comprehend, but the more the debate is focused on the core of the issue at hand, the more the gap between the various views widens.

The complexity of the issue arises from the fact that eco-labelling schemes are based on life-cycle analysis, which involves process and production methods (PPMs). In other words, eco-labelling is interested in the product during its entire life cycle: the sourcing of raw materials, production, consumption, and disposal.[28] This approach requires, in and of itself, large amounts of information when products or materials are imported, which may cause enormous practical problems, especially for developing countries.[29] In addition, specific PPM-related criteria based on domestic conditions and priorities in the importing country may be less appropriate in other countries. Whereas there is no question that each country has the right to institute domestic regulations on eco-labelling, the concern is that it should not be used for protectionist purposes – applied by some countries selectively to products that are imported or that compete with their own products.

The principal fear of developing countries in dealing with the issue of eco-labelling in the WTO is that an attempt will be made to extend the coverage of such labelling – even though voluntarily – to non-related PPMs. They fear not only the whole range of implications for their exports that such an extension would produce but more the systemic problem it raises in the WTO. It would amount to writing new rules for a system that has so far served the international community and the world trading system well. The problem of subjecting eco-labelling to WTO rules and disciplines lies in the conflict that would arise with the product-based rules of the GATT/WTO trading system. Discriminating between "like products" and making market access conditional on complying with PPMs, thus legitimizing unincorporated PPMs, which are not product related, would upset the entire multilateral trading system and would have devastating effects, in particular on developing country exports.

Developing countries have recognized that what is being put into question – through using eco-labelling as a litmus test – is the basic criteria and characteristics that have so far governed the multilateral trading system. Through eco-labelling, the WTO would become more and more deeply involved in the realm of domestic policy and intervention from the outside would be allowed to set national priorities. On this basis, most developing countries have insisted that eco-labelling is inconsistent and should not be accommodated within the WTO system. This was strongly supported by the fact that the negotiating history of the TBT Agreement upheld their view that unincorporated PPMs were not covered by the Agreement.[30] While admitting the role that equivalence and mutual recognition could play in helping them meet the requirements of foreign schemes, they insisted that accommodating unincorporated PPMs would amount to creating scope for the extraterritorial imposition of national standards. This, they felt, would have significant consequences for the trading system as a whole.[31]

Furthermore, as stated earlier and as emphasized by the Preamble of the WTO Agreement, environmental objectives should be *consis-*

tent with the level of development. The prevention of product differentiation on the basis of unincorporated PPMs allows countries to set standards, whether environmental or otherwise, that are appropriate for their level of development. In other words, it allows countries to trade their developmental needs against their needs for environmental protection in a manner that is consistent with how they themselves value these needs (and not on the basis of how others value them for them).[32]

What I would like to add here is that the debate in the CTE on eco-labelling schemes has triggered a similar heated debate between environmentalists and business groups. The former have criticized what they consider to be the narrow perspective of international trade rules, noting that PPMs are fundamental to minimizing the environmental impact of a product during its life cycle. Business groups see trade rules that distinguish between products solely on the characteristics of end products as relevant and appropriate. Like many developing countries, they view the introduction of PPMs into the trade debate as the beginning of a slippery slope, where loosely related production factors would become the basis for trade barriers.

Lastly, it is essential to recall Principle 11 of the Rio Declaration in this context, which stipulates that environmental standards, management objectives, and priorities should reflect the environmental and developmental context to which they apply. The standards applied by some countries may be inappropriate and of unwarranted economic and social cost to other countries, in particular developing countries.[33] Accordingly, the disciplining of eco-labelling schemes should be on the basis of equivalencies and mutual recognition, where each country sets its standards according to its own values, as stipulated by Agenda 21. The aim of harmonizing or internationalizing PPMs on the basis of any set of multilateral guidelines is in contradiction to what the international community agreed upon unanimously in Agenda 21. What is even more risky is that such an attempt would be detrimental to the trading system, at a time when all countries are embracing and respecting its rules.

Market access and competitiveness aspects of the trade/ environment debate

One cannot address the interface between trade and environment without looking at the market access and competitiveness aspects of this relationship. These aspects tended to be underplayed and even overlooked at the beginning of the debate, for the obvious reasons stated earlier. It is needless to reiterate that the whole debate was triggered by developed countries targeting specific issues of concern to themselves. As developing countries gradually became aware of the underlying reasons and objectives of this debate, they rightly pushed issues of their own to the fore. It should be stressed, however, that this move by developing countries was on no account aimed at eventually achieving trade-offs. On the one hand, their refusal to amend or reinterpret Article XX or to introduce non-related PPMs was based on systemic principles, which cannot be subjected to bargaining, because this would alter the very essence of the system. On the other hand, the purpose of bringing in market access and competitive concerns was to add balance to the lopsided debate, and put it in its proper perspective.

From the very beginning the debate on this issue was set in a North–South context. This has harmed rather than helped the debate advance. False allegations continue to be made by firms in countries with high environmental standards and high costs of compliance that they are often undercut by competition from companies based in countries with less strict regulation and lower costs. In theory, this could lead to entire industries departing for countries with lower standards, the so-called "pollution havens." So far, however, there is no evidence of this happening. The reverse – that high environmental standards were a factor in location decisions or have led to the relocation of industry – has also not occurred on a large scale.

The debate on market access from the perspective of developing countries tends to be twofold. They want to ensure first that existing market access conditions are not eroded by emerging environmental requirements and second that additional market access – through what can be perceived as win–win situations – will help promote environmental protection and sustainable development. In this context developing countries have tried to concentrate on identifying sectors of export interest to them. These could be textiles and clothing, leather, footwear, furniture and other consumer goods, and other labour-intensive sectors, where environmental measures could affect existing market access opportunities and thus possibly nullify or impair the Uruguay Round results. In fact, empirical studies, mostly done by the UN Conference on Trade and Development (UNCTAD), show that the sectors of interest to developing countries are those most affected by environmental standards often set unilaterally by the importing governments. Such standards negatively influence developing countries' market access, even though the environmental effects of, say, textile production might mainly be local and do not affect the final characteristics of the product. In addition, there are few – if any – trans-boundary externalities.

Furthermore, UNCTAD's studies have also demonstrated that small and medium enterprises (SMEs) in developing countries have encountered difficulties in complying with environmental policies emerging in the above-mentioned sectors. Such policies have had significant effects on the competitiveness of SMEs in developing countries and have in many instances acted as barriers to trade. A number of reasons have been cited, among them the following:

- The possibility of compensating for the loss of competitiveness in some sectors by gains in others is higher in economies that are diversified and dynamic, which are not necessarily the main characteristics of developing countries' economies.
- Developing country exporters are normally price-takers, because they compete on price rather than on non-price factors such as technology and ideas. Consequently, any environmental requirement resulting in cost increases reduces export competitiveness. This nevertheless may vary from one industry to another as well as among developing countries at different stages of development and with varying capability to integrate innovative approaches.
- The problems of adjustment are higher for SMEs in developing

countries, especially as they are important players in the export promotion strategy for sectors such as textiles, clothing, and footwear. Thus the need to examine the possible conflict between the export promotion strategies of developing countries and the need to comply with environmental requirements and their effects on competitiveness becomes all the more relevant.

- The variable cost component of complying with environmental standards is higher in some sectors than in others. Again, evidence has shown that it is higher in sectors of interest to developing countries, especially leather and footwear, as well as textiles and garment sectors. For example, in leather tanning, the cost of the chemicals required to meet international standards is approximately three times the cost of conventional chemicals.[34]

Two additional topics are germane to the market access and competitiveness debate: the internalization of environmental costs, and charges and taxes for environmental purposes. Though these topics are not new and have in fact been debated at length, they remain contentious and difficult, especially if the idea is to add them to the trading agenda.

The concept of internalization remains difficult to adopt in GATT on the grounds that it interferes with the efficiency of the comparative advantage principle, which is central to the free trading system. The tendency to consider the lack of internalization as a kind of "implicit subsidy" that would be actionable under GATT/WTO is a non-starter. Furthermore, environmental externalities are in principle not distinguishable from other factors, such as education, infrastructure, and social policy, that contribute to the comparative advantages and thus competitiveness edge of an economy. Are we to conclude that the costs of all these factors are to be integrated in production processes under the auspices of the multilateral trading system? The internalization of environmental costs by domestic producers in no way conflicts with GATT principles. However, it becomes problematic under GATT if countries start implementing trade policies on the basis of whether or not foreign producers have internalized their environmental costs. GATT would be more concerned with the trade-distorting or discriminatory effect of such a policy, and with its necessity and effectiveness, rather than with its environmental objectives.

As for charges and taxes for environmental purposes, no one can deny the validity and effectiveness of imposing taxes as such. But what is occurring here is the imposition of taxes on a phenomenon that is not quantitative. Forcing producers to incorporate environmental externalities by imposing taxes on products made with polluting processes is based on the assumption that the costs to the polluting firm and the damage caused by the pollution are known. Moreover, if this is true at the national level, it can only be more complex and difficult if an importing country aims at adjusting such costs at its borders by imposing border tax adjustments on its "like" imports. In addition, the question of what would be an appropriate tax for pollution that would be accepted internationally is still open.

Border tax adjustments (BTAs) should pass the necessity and effectiveness test to find out how pertinent they are to the environment, before even debating how to impose them at the border. The effectiveness of border tax adjustment is doubted and even contradicts the view, widely acknowledged by developing and developed countries alike, that environmental problems should be addressed at source. So how can a tax imposed on final products, as a border tax adjustment, be effective for problems that should be dealt with as far upstream in the production process as possible?[35] As rightly pointed out by UNCTAD, it is generally better if the tax is levied on the production and extraction process causing the environmental problems rather than on the resulting product. In other words, a tax levied internally by the producing country would be more effective at dealing with environmental problems at their source. GATT neither prohibits nor prevents a country from pursuing a policy of taxation or regulation with regard to environmental protection as long as these policies apply only to its domestic consumers and producers. In fact, one can even go one step further. For BTA on imports to pass the compatibility test in GATT, it has to meet the following conditions:

(a) the tax is product related;
(b) the imported product has not been taxed in the country of origin, to avoid double taxation;
(c) the imported product has caused trans-boundary pollution and the polluting input was not consumed domestically.

Similarly to their stance on process and production methods in eco-labelling, developing countries insist that there should be an explicit reference to addressing charges and taxes that relate only to products or product characteristics that are covered by WTO provisions. In any event, the environmental effectiveness and potential trade effects of levying environmental taxes and charges, particularly on market access and competitiveness, remain questions open for debate.

Before concluding, let me state that no one can deny the fact that the relationship between trade and environment has been debated extensively in the WTO. This has undoubtedly helped clarify the status of this relationship in the framework of the organization and shape positions in response to the underlying motives and objectives. Today, even before settling this complex relationship, other more difficult and cumbersome issues are emerging, such as linking trade to labour standards. Though from the very beginning such an inclusion has met with strong objections, it will continue to be pushed in the WTO mainly by the United States – for obvious reasons, which neither time nor space permit to be addressed here. One thing is clear, however. Developing countries have to stand firm on their positions on trade and environment as regards changing the rules. Such a move would only serve as a prelude to the integration of the "social clause" in the WTO, which has wider implications for developing countries and should be of more serious concern.

5. Conclusion

The Seattle Ministerial Conference in December 1999 and the proposed Millennium Round will be a turning point for the trade and environment debate. It will decide on the future course of the debate. One thing remains clear. A great deal of work and education continue to be needed before drawing conclusions or reaching the stage of negotiating rules and disciplines, not to mention changing the rules, as some would like to happen. The trade and environment relationship continues to be an area prone to difficulties, complexities, and most of all sensitivities. Throughout this chapter I have tried to show that so far the CTE has worked within a consensual framework. To try to tamper with this framework in order to incorporate additional objectives will necessitate a new consensual framework. The attempts by the international community to forward some alternatives remain in the very early stages and will need further in-depth study. The following are a few of the options:

1. To carry the debate forwards in the CTE in parallel with the Millennium Round, with a view to bringing the two ends closer. This option is hardly likely to achieve results because, in the view of many people, the CTE has exhausted the debate.
2. The so-called "Ruggiero" option presented earlier: a World Environment Organization to be the counterpart to the WTO. This is a pragmatic and likely workable option in view of the difficulties encountered so far, though it is still resisted by mainly developed countries and their NGOs. Some developed countries, notably the EU countries, Norway, Switzerland, and Canada, continue to believe that the WTO, with its strong and enforceable dispute settlement mechanism, is an appealing instrument for policy makers, particularly in the field of environment. Many NGOs continue to be convinced that the trading systems should provide the necessary flexibility for the sake of the environment, which is undoubtedly their priority.
3. Mainstreaming environment in the various agreements, such as Agriculture, TRIPS, Textiles and Clothing, and others. The degree of complexity and controversy inherent in this option, which is still to be tested, is difficult to anticipate. However, care should be taken because this option carries with it the inherent risk of doing away with the sensitive balance carefully

negotiated in the CTE between issues of interest to developing and developed countries alike, thus thwarting the possibility of trade-offs, if any. With this option, issues of market access would be spread thinly over different agreements, leaving the two topics of concern to developed countries, i.e. the relationship between trade and environment and PPMs, to be negotiated separately.

In spite of tremendous efforts not to label the trade and environment debate as a North–South issue, these have hardly borne fruit. No one can deny that there is evidence of a conflict between developed and developing countries, which will continue and deepen unless the existing doubts about linking environmental interests with protectionism dissipate. *The challenge is to separate protectionism from environment.* The environment cannot be safeguarded and enhanced through trade sanctions. Benefiting the environment must be through access to technology, increased awareness, financial resources, and access to markets, without which developing countries will find it extremely difficult to generate the resources necessary to protect their domestic environments and the global commons.

Let me conclude by stating how Rubens Ricupero, the Secretary-General of UNCTAD, perceives the trade/environment relationship:

> Trade and Environment are two poles in a dialectical thesis, where the resulting synthesis should conciliate the two ends. Unlike many would like to believe, linking trade to environment does not come as something natural. To reconcile these two ends necessitates tremendous efforts – and not without sacrifices – where environment should not be treated as a late consideration or an afterthought.[36]

The way to deal with environmental problems is to go to their roots and integrate environment in the decision-making process from the very beginning. This requires the provision of the necessary technology and making available the necessary financing, knowledge, and expertise for the preservation and protection of the environment.

Postscript

Today, after the Seattle débâcle of December 1999 and when preparations for the fourth WTO Ministerial Conference to be held in November 2001 in Doha are in top gear, the trade and environment debate is again surfacing as an issue for the next round of multilateral trade negotiations. At the risk of disheartening the environmentalists, this debate figures only as a side dish to the main plate of constraints on initiating a new round. To many it seems that environment has been relegated to a second-class category of issues in the framework of the ongoing preparations in Geneva. Many feel that the trade and environment debate could be dispensed with, so that it does not lead the already protracted and cumbersome preparations to a dead end.

The constraints are twofold. First, there are constraints pertaining directly to the trade and environment debate and the unpreparedness of many to start negotiating rules and disciplines, not to mention the new issues, such as genetically modified organisms (GMOs), with all their complexities. Second, there are constraints of a more general and comprehensive nature relating to the Round itself and the new pressures emerging around it, amidst which the trade and environment debate looks even more complex.

Although many of the constraints in the trade and environment debate date back to Seattle and before, others are more recent and in turn need to be studied before they are ready to be negotiated. I will not enumerate the pre-Seattle ones, as they have been addressed in detail in my chapter, and continue to be as germane and pertinent to our discussion as ever. Looking more closely at the post-Seattle problems, however, environment is introduced on a number of counts.

First, there are trade-related environmental problems in the area of agriculture. Whether they are real or fictitious, this is a highly sensitive issue, because negotiators on both sides of the fence are going to summon environment to their support. On the one hand, agricultural exporters will continue to blame the subsidizing producers for the misuse and abuse of the environment and for the highly damaging effect of subsidized food and agriculture on it. On the other hand, the European Union is already preparing a counter-strategy and looking for ways to continue subsidizing agriculture in its member states. This is no longer under the superannuated pretext of maximizing output and aiding its farmers but rather under a seemingly more "noble" excuse of promoting quality and taking account of the environment.

Secondly, the issue of environment and trade-related intellectual property rights, which I touched upon in my chapter, will appear anew and much more forcefully than in the pre-Seattle phase. The issue is gaining in profile and importance owing to the determined move by many of the developing countries, headed by Brazil, South Africa, and India, to find satisfactory solutions to the drugs patenting and pricing problem – a move that could very well result in the reopening of the TRIPs Agreement, where technology transfer and the environment would figure high.

Last but not least is the highly explosive issue of genetically modified organisms. What we have here is an undisguised clash in the relationship between environment, trade, agriculture, and health. Power politics at the national and international levels will find a way to decide on this very sensitive issue. Is this yet another environmental problem that will be brought to the WTO in the not so distant future? How can we start negotiating so-called synergies when these and other problems are still wide open in the framework of the trade and environment debate? Should we not be more resolute in preserving the multilateral trading system we have all worked hard to establish, rather than burden the next round with highly controversial environmental issues? Have we not agreed that the Committee on Trade and Environment should first exhaust the debate before it is put on the negotiating table?

As for the more general set of constraints, topping them are the clear signals from the new US administration, which has started questioning the overarching priority of environmental protection and is attempting to separate the objectives of economic progress from environment preservation. It is beyond any doubt that the US administration is having second thoughts about the extent and desire of integrating environment in the multilateral trading system. It is said that President Bush is a passionate free trader who will resist efforts to restrain globalization with environmental and worker safeguards. Developing countries could rejoice in their new ally. This is, however, yet another problem – not to be taken lightly – which is overshadowing the next round of multilateral trade negotiations and widening the already existing and growing gap between the United States and the European Union. Needless to say, the expansion of the North American Free Trade Agreement is a priority for the Bush administration, and the awaited fast-track authority is nowhere in sight. Needless to say also, and pre-eminently, the European Union is professionally manoeuvring to cover its reluctance to liberalize trade in its agriculture by dumping all sorts of issues on the next round for the sake of horse-trading and exchanging concessions to balance its liberalization in agriculture. Finally, the developing countries are increasingly aware of the implications of a new round for their economies. They will not be ready to budge from their positions unless they see some satisfactory responses by developed countries to the so-called implementation issues.

In view of all these constraints, which seem insurmountable (at least for the foreseeable future), I believe that many negotiators are increasingly unenthusiastic about environment appearing as yet another hard nut to crack for the next round. Environmentalists need to find adequate solutions for their imminent and very serious problems not in the multilateral trading system but in a multilateral environmental system of their own.

Acknowledgements

Although I am indebted to René Vossenaar, UNCTAD, and Doaa Abdel Motaal, WTO, for their valuable comments and suggestions, which have sharpened the exposition, I wish to exonerate them from any responsibility for the final product. This chapter is my own responsibility and is not meant to reflect Egypt's position.

Notes

1. *Herald Tribune*, 15 March 1999.
2. Stuart E. Eizenstat, US Undersecretary of State for Economic Affairs, "Why We Should Welcome Biotechnology," *Financial Times*, 16 April 1999.
3. Rio Declaration on Environment and Development, United Nations Conference on Environment and Development, Rio de Janeiro, June 1992.
4. "Report of the United Nations Conference on Environment and Development," Rio de Janeiro, 3–14 June 1992, Chapter 1, Objectives 2.9 (a), p. 3.
5. "Trade and Environment: A Developing Countries' Perspective," a paper presented by the Dominican Republic, Egypt, Honduras, and Pakistan to the WTO High Level Symposium on Trade and Environment, 15–16 March 1999.
6. "Legal Wrangle Engulfs US Shrimp Dispute," *Financial Times*, 14 April 1999.
7. Opening remarks by Renato Ruggiero to the WTO High Level Symposium on Trade and Environment, 15 March 1999.
8. Daniel C. Esty, "Economic Integration and Environmental Protection: Synergies, Opportunities, and Challenges," Yale University, 5 March 1999 (draft presented to the WTO High Level Symposium).
9. GATT, *The Results of the Uruguay Round of Multilateral Trade Negotiations, The Legal Texts*, 1994, p. 6.
10. Martin Khor, "Trade, Environment and Sustainable Development: A Developing Country View of the Issues Including in the WTO Context," paper presented to the WTO High Level Symposium on Trade and Environment, 15 March 1999.
11. Final Act Embodying the Results of the Uruguay Round of Multilateral Trade Negotiations, signed Marrakesh, 15 April 1994.
12. WTO CTE, *Report (1996) of the Committee on Trade and Environment*, WT/CTE/1, 12 November 1996.
13. Article XX ("General Exceptions") gives ample opportunity to use measures to protect (a) public morals, (b) human, animal, or plant life or health, etc. The chapeau of the Article stipulates that these measures should not be applied in a manner that would *constitute a means of arbitrary or unjustifiable discrimination between countries where the same conditions prevail, or a disguised restriction on international trade.*
14. The Agreement on Technical Barriers to Trade deals basically with technical regulations and international standards, including packaging, marking, and labelling requirements, and procedures for assessment of conformity. It further makes sure that these regulations and standards should not constitute a means of arbitrary or unjustifiable discrimination between countries where the same conditions prevail or a disguised restriction on international trade.

15. The Agreement on the Application of Sanitary and Phytosanitary Measures forms an integral part of the Agreement on Agriculture. It reaffirms in its Preamble that no member should be prevented from adopting or enforcing measures necessary to protect human, animal, or plant life or health. These measures are subject to the requirement that they are not applied in a manner that would constitute a means of arbitrary or unjustifiable discrimination between members where the same conditions prevail or a disguised restriction on international trade.
16. The 1996 Singapore Ministerial Conference was the first ministerial meeting of the WTO.
17. Esty, "Economic Integration," op. cit.
18. Article XX (b) (g) stipulates that any country subject to the requirement that such measures are not applied in a manner that would constitute a means of arbitrary or unjustifiable discrimination could take measures: (b) necessary to protect human, animal, or plant life or health; (g) relating to the conservation of exhaustible natural resources if such measures are made effective in conjunction with restrictions on domestic production or consumption.
19. *United States–Import Prohibition of Certain Shrimp and Shrimp Products*, Report of the Panel, WT/DS58/R, 15 May 1998, paras. 278–300.
20. Ibid.
21. *United States–Import Prohibition of Certain Shrimp and Shrimp Products*, Appellate Body Report, WT/DS58/AB/R, adopted 6 November 1998.
22. Ibid., para. 185.
23. Ibid.
24. It is no secret that the "one" delegation was the United States.
25. Non-paper by India for the Committee on Trade and Environment, "The Relationship of the TRIPS Agreement to the Development, Access and Transfer of Environmentally-sound Technologies and Products," 20 June 1996.
26. This is a term used in some MEAs and is of particular interest to developing countries because it is interpreted by many of them as meaning "on preferential and non-commercial terms." Indian Non-paper, op. cit.
27. Article 15 emphasizes the sovereign rights of states over their natural resources. It further stresses that access to genetic resources is to take place on terms that are environmentally sound and on a mutually agreed basis, and to be subject to prior informed consent of the party providing the resources, unless otherwise determined by that party. Article 16 implies a central role for access to and transfer of technology in the conservation and sustainable use of biodiversity resources. It further stipulates that such transfer of technology shall be provided on favourable terms, including concessional and preferential treatment as mutually agreed.
28. See Chapter 9 in this volume, and *Report (1996) of the Committee on Trade and Environment*, op. cit.
29. R. Vossenaar and R. Mollerus, "Eco-labelling and International Trade: Possible Effects on Developing Countries," UNCTAD, ITC/233/1B/96-II-TP, 1996.
30. *Negotiating History of the Coverage of the Agreement on Technical Barriers to Trade with Regard to Labelling Requirements, Voluntary Standards, and Processes and*

Production Methods Unrelated to Product Characteristics, WT/CTE/W/10 and G/TBT/W/11, 29 August 1995.
31. Chapter 9 in this volume, pp. 278–9.
32. Ibid., p. 275.
33. This should also apply to ISO schemes, especially ISO-1400, because their unbiased formation is highly doubted by many developing countries. Such schemes cannot be forced into the WTO as internationally agreed ones, as long as developing countries in practice remain outside the effective frame of decision-making in such standard-setting bodies and organizations.
34. UNCTAD, "Environmental Policies, Trade and Competitiveness: Conceptual and Empirical Issues," TD/B/WG.6/6, 29 March 1995.
35. Ibid.
36. Rubens Ricupero, UNCTAD Workshop, Viet Nam, July 1997.

Part VIII
Systemic

[26]

NON-GOVERNMENTAL ORGANIZATIONS AT THE WORLD TRADE ORGANIZATION: COOPERATION, COMPETITION, OR EXCLUSION

*by Daniel C. Esty**

INTRODUCTION

Recent efforts by non-governmental organizations (NGOs), especially environmental groups, to participate in international trade policy-making activities have been met with hostility from the trade community. This article argues that this negative reaction is a mistake. Non-governmental organizations offer the World Trade Organization (WTO) a mechanism by which to 'connect' to citizens around the world in whose interest trade liberalization initiatives are advanced. Improved responsiveness and representativeness on the part of the WTO and better understanding of the international trading system on the part of the public would enhance the WTO's legitimacy and strengthen its position as a central element of the emerging structure of international economic governance. Non-governmental organizations offer, moreover, a source of analytic 'competition' to governments that promises to fortify the WTO's capacity to regulate in a manner that avoids market failures and to improve the organization's decision-making more generally, further augmenting the WTO's credibility and authoritativeness. The arguments for excluding NGOs from the WTO, particularly the fear that NGO participation in decision-making will result in special interest manipulation of outcomes, are largely misplaced.

* Yale Law School and Yale School of Forestry and Environmental Studies; formerly Deputy Chief of Staff and Deputy Assistant Administrator for Policy, Planning, and Evaluation at the US Environmental Protection Agency. Thanks to Judson Jaffe, Hari Osofsky, Raj Patel, Sonja Petersen, and Shalini Ramanathan for research assistance and to the Global Environment and Trade Study and its funders (Ford Foundation, MacArthur Foundation, Pew Charitable Trusts, Rockefeller Brothers Fund and Turner Foundation) and the Avina Foundation for support. Thanks as well to Bruce Ackerman, Frederick Abbott, Steve Charnovitz, André Dua, Jeffrey Dunoff, Phil Levy, William Nordhaus, Gus Ranis, William Rapp, William Rhoads, Susan Rose-Ackerman, Bruce Russett, Peter Spiro, Joel Trachtman, Thomas Weiss, and the participants in the Avina Foundation Workshop on Changing Roles of NGOs, the University of Michigan Conference on the Representation of Constituent Interests in US Trade Policymaking, and Yale International Political Economy Seminar for comments on earlier drafts.

The magic of markets is now widely understood and appreciated.[1] But markets sometimes fail, and when they do, governmental intervention is required to avoid allocative inefficiency and welfare losses.[2] Markets fail for a number of reasons. Most notably, when externalities, such as unregulated pollution, exist, the 'invisible hand' cannot be counted upon to maximize social welfare. In addition, the well-known problems of 'free riding' and the 'tragedy of the commons' mean that market forces cannot be relied upon to generate optimal results with regard to the delivery of public goods or the management of open-access resources.[3] In these cases, economic theory teaches that some sort of governmental intervention is required at a scale commensurate with the failure to be addressed, the public good to be provided, or the resource to be managed.[4] In some circumstances, the scope of the problem will span several countries or even the entire world, making an international response at least optimal and sometimes essential.

From the greenhouse gas emissions that blanket the planet, to the need to protect biodiversity, to the unsustainable consumption of fish and other resources from the global commons, transboundary environmental problems frequently go unattended by national governments since no individual jurisdiction has an incentive to act. When national governments do attempt to regulate international market failures, however, disputes often erupt. American trade restrictions imposed on Mexican tuna caught using nets that killed large numbers of dolphins in the Eastern Tropical Pacific Ocean provide one such example.[5] National government regulation to address domestic concerns also may have trade or other economic spillovers that become contentious. The European Union's restrictions on hormones in beef,

[1] See Paul A. Samuelson and William D. Nordhaus, Economics 22, 43, 136 (15th edn, 1995); Robin Berman Schwartzman, Programs of the United States Government and Multinational Organizations Supporting Trade and Investment in Eastern Europe and the Former Soviet Union, 789 PLI/CORP. 497, 499 (1992); Kim Reisman, 'Note, The World Bank and the IMF: At the Forefront of World Transformation', 60 Fordham L Rev S349 at S349–51 (1992).

[2] See William J. Baumol and Wallace E. Oates, The Theory of Environmental Policy (2nd edn, 1988) [hereinafter Baumol and Oates, Theory].

[3] See Mancur Olson, The Logic of Collective Action: Public Goods and The Theory of Groups 28 (1965) [hereinafter Olson, Logic]; Garrett Hardin, 'The Tragedy of the Commons', 162 Science 1243, 1244–5 (1968); Carol Rose, 'The Comedy of the Commons: Custom, Commerce and Inherently Public Property', 53 U Chi L Rev 711 (1986); Gordon Tullock, 'Federalism: Problems of Scale', 6 Pub Choice 19 at 25–8 (1969).

[4] See Baumol and Oates, Theory, above n. 2; Olson, Logic, above n. 3 at 48, 53–7; Daniel C. Esty, 'Stepping Up to the Global Environmental Challenge', 8 Fordham Env L Rev 103 at 105 (1996) (discussing the persistence of environmental threats 'because there is no international authority with the requisite breadth of authority to impose effective and equitable responses on the violators'); Richard B. Stewart, 'Pyramids of Sacrifice?: Problems of Federalism in Mandating State Implementation of National Environmental Policy', 86 Yale LJ 1196 at 1210–20 (1977) [hereinafter Stewart, Pyramids].

[5] See Steve Charnovitz, 'Dolphins and Tuna: An Analysis of the Second GATT Panel Report', 24 Env L Rep 10 at 567 (1994).

recently deemed inconsistent with international trade rules by a WTO dispute settlement panel, fit within this category.[6]

Into this regulatory breach has stepped the WTO. As the key global-scale institution with a mandate to manage the terms of international economic exchange and to set the behavioural boundaries for trade, the WTO cannot escape responsibility for helping to address market failures in its domain. In fact, the need for and value of a global regulatory structure is widely understood.[7] But the WTO faces numerous tensions and difficulties in fulfilling its role as part of the international economic management structure and as the response mechanism to global-scale market failures.

Against the backdrop of these challenges, this article argues that the WTO will be able to carry out its economic management role better if it embraces NGOs[8] and establishes formal procedures for NGO participation in the international trading system.[9] Specifically, NGOs offer the promise of serving as 'connective tissue' that will help to bridge the gap between WTO

[6] See 'Europe's Ban on Beef from US Held Illegal', New York Times, 2 July 1997, at D2.

[7] See Jagdish Bhagwati and T.N. Srinivasan, 'Trade and Environment: Does Environmental Diversity Detract from the Case for Free Trade?' in Jagdish Bhagwati and Robert Hudec (eds), Fair Trade and Harmonization: Prerequisites For Free Trade? (1996) [hereinafter Bhagwati and Srinivasan, Trade and Environment]; Daniel C. Esty, 'The Case for a Global Environmental Organization' in Peter B. Kenen (ed.), Managing The World Economy: Fifty Years After Bretton Woods (1994) 287 [Hereinafter Esty, Geo]; Daniel C. Esty, 'Revitalizing Environmental Federalism', 95 Mich L Rev 57 at 613–53 (1996) [hereinafter Esty, Revitalizing]; John H. Jackson, 'Reflections on Constitutional Changes to the Global Trading System', 72 Chi-Kent L Rev 511 at 512–15 (1996) [hereinafter Jackson, Reflections]; William D. Nordhaus, Locational Competition and the Environment, Discussion Paper No. 1079, at 5–8 Cowles Foundation for Research and Economics, Yale University (1994).

[8] There is considerable debate over what groups should be considered 'non-governmental organizations'. Some observers would include only 'non-profit' entities such as environmental groups. Others would include all non-governmental entities including corporations. See Martin A. Olz, 'Non-Governmental Organizations in Regional Human Rights Systems', 28 Colum Hum Rts L Rev 307 at 313–21 (1997) (discussing the struggle to define NGOs). A further question arises as to whether to exclude non-profit business organizations such as the International Chamber of Commerce. See Steve Charnovitz, 'Two Centuries of Participation: NGOs and International Governance', 18 Mich J Int'l L 183 at 186–7 (1997) (defining the term NGO) [hereinafter Charnovitz, Two Centuries.] For the purposes of this article, I shall focus on all private (non-governmental) organizations that seek to shape decision-making at the national or international level with special reference to public interest groups such as environmental organizations.

[9] The WTO has taken some steps to become more transparent and open to NGOs. In 1995, the WTO launched a worldwide web site (http://www.wto.org). In July 1996, the WTO released a set of 'Guidelines for Arrangements on Relationships with Non-Government Organizations' and made a renewed commitment to 'transparency', in part, in support of easier communications with NGOs. See *General Council Decision on Ttransparency* (18 July 1996). The WTO Committee on Trade and the Environment has held seminars to which environmental NGOs were invited. But all WTO General Council, Committee meetings and dispute settlement panel sessions remain closed to the public. Minutes of these meetings are not released. Non-governmental organizations have no right to make presentations or even submit written comments on issues under debate. Dispute panel decisions are not made public until the General Council adopts the decision. See Steve Charnovitz, 'Participation of Nongovernmental Organizations in the World Trade Organization', 17 U Pa J Int'l Econ L 331 at 332–4 (1996) [hereinafter Charnovitz, Participation].

decision-makers[10] and the distant constituents which they are meant to serve, thereby ensuring that the WTO's actions are perceived as responsive and fair. Non-governmental organizations also can act as 'competition' to governments in international trade debates. In doing so, they could broaden the base of information and thinking upon which decisions are made, and thus improve the quality, authoritativeness, and perceived fairness of the policy choices and judgments emanating from the WTO.

1. CHALLENGES FACING THE WORLD TRADE ORGANIZATION

The issues facing the WTO as it seeks to fulfill its role at the centre of the international economic system have been reviewed and discussed at length elsewhere.[11] Fundamentally, the WTO must facilitate collective action among nations to support liberalized trade and investment and simultaneously overcome market failures which would otherwise disrupt the efficient workings and welfare-enhancing potential of the international marketplace.[12] The WTO efforts in this respect involve negotiations to reduce tariffs and non-tariff barriers to liberalized trade, the setting of trade rules to keep markets open, and the adjudication of disputes when differences arise.

In carrying out these functions, the WTO faces a number of critical challenges. First, in its adjudicatory role, the WTO needs to be recognized for its authoritativeness.[13] The vitality of international organizations in general, and of the WTO in particular, depends on a capacity to produce 'correct' answers to the issues with which they must deal.[14] In its core work involving trade liberalization and the settlement of traditional trade disputes, the WTO has an outstanding track record.[15] Over the past 50 years, the international trading system has developed a clear underlying theory,

[10] These decision-makers are fundamentally the national representatives at the WTO, but also should be understood to include the WTO staff who often shape the context of decisions.

[11] See, e.g., Pitou van Dijck and Gerrit F. Faber, Challenges To The New World Trade Organization (1996) 1 at 24; Jeffrey J. Schott (ed.), The World Trading System: The Challenges Ahead (1996); Jackson, Reflections, above n. 7 at 519–20.

[12] See Robert Gilpin, The Political Economy of International Relations 171 (1987); John H. Jackson, World Trade and The Law of GATT (1994) (discussing the operation of the international trading system) [hereinafter Jackson, Law of GATT]; John H. Jackson, The World Trading System: Law and Policy of International Economic Relations (1992) [hereinafter Jackson, World Trading]; Jackson, Reflections, above n. 7 at 512–15.

[13] For a discussion of the importance of authoritativeness, see W. Michael Reisman, 'Myres S. McDougal: Architect of a Jurisprudence for a Free Society', 66 Miss LJ 15 at 20–1 (1996).

[14] See Jeffrey L. Dunoff, ' "Trade And": Recent Developments in Trade Policy and Scholarship–And Their Surprising Political Implications', 17 NW J Int'l L Bus 759 at 767 (1996–97) (arguing that poor WTO 'trade and environment' decisions could prompt a backlash against the WTO more broadly) [hereinafter Dunoff, Trade And]; see also Philip M. Nichols, 'Trade Without Values', 90 NW L Rev 658, 659–719 (1996).

[15] See Robert Hudec, Enforcing International Trade Law (1995); E.U. Petersmann (ed.), International Trade Law and The GATT/WTO Dispute Settlement System (1997); Pierre Pescatore *et al.*, Handbook of GATT Dispute Settlement (1996) (providing an overview of GATT dispute settlement).

well-established rules, and a body of case experience to follow.[16] The WTO has in-house staff and access to outside experts who are well-versed in all of these dimensions of support for the trading system and international economic law.

Yet increasingly, trade disputes involve issues at the intersection of trade and other policy arenas, such as the environment.[17] In these cases, the WTO often lacks ready access to the necessary expertise for making well-regarded and broadly accepted decisions. Beyond the limited depth of the WTO's knowledge base, the organization's dispute settlement mechanisms lack credibility and legitimacy outside the realm of trade issues. In brief, the WTO faces serious questions about its capacity to deliver substantively correct decisions with respect to trade and environment disputes and to other conflicts arising on the periphery of trade law.[18]

In addition to substantive correctness, the WTO faces a further challenge of being, and of being perceived as, fair. Fairness has procedural and substantive requirements which must be met if WTO decisions, both in dispute settlement cases and in the negotiation of trade rules, are to have legitimacy.[19] Procedurally, those who believe that they have an interest in the outcomes of decisions must have an opportunity to be part of the process, with opportunities to submit views and to observe how a particular outcome is reached. Substantively, the established rules and precedents must be applied even-handedly over time and across issues, and in ways that do not appear to advantage systematically any particular group or nation.

16 See Jackson, Law of GATT, above n. 12; see also Philip M. Nichols, 'GATT Doctrine', 36 Va J Int'l Law 379 (1996). But note that by GATT tradition, past decisions are not meant to have precedential value. See *WTO Report of the Appellate Body in Japan-Taxes on Alcoholic Beverages*, W1.1EL.-1-B-81, WT/DS 8FAB1R, WT/DS10/AB/R, WR/DS11/R (25 September 1996); Barry Eichengreen and Peter B. Kenen, 'Managing the World Economy Under the Bretton Woods System: An Overview', in Peter B. Kenen (ed.), Managing The World Economy: Fifty Years After Bretton Woods (1994) 3 (examining changes in the international system after World War II); Chi Carmody, 'Of Substantial Interest: Third Parties Under GATT', 18 Mich J Int'l L 615, 652–3 (1997).

17 See, e.g., Jeffrey L. Dunoff, 'Institutional Misfits: The GATT, the ICJ and Trade-Environment Disputes', 15 Mich J Int'l L 1043 (1994) (reviewing how ill-equipped the WTO is to handle such disputes) [hereinafter Dunoff, Misfits]; Dunoff, Trade And, above n. 14 at 762–4 (discussing the WTO's 'expansion into new substantive areas'); GATT Report by Amb. H. Ukawa, Chairman, Group on Environmental Measures and International Trade, 49th Session of the Contracting Parties 3 (25 January 1994) (acknowledging that 'GATT is not equipped to become involved in the tasks of reviewing national environmental priorities, setting environmental standards, or developing global policies on the environment').

18 Note that with no more in-house expertise than the WTO (and arguably less), the US Supreme Court renders 'trade and environment' opinions without stirring deep controversy of the sort that has sparked demonstrations against 'GATTzilla' in Washington. See Daniel C. Esty, Greening the GATT: Trade, Environment, and The Future (1994) 115 (questioning 'GATT's legitimacy, technical capacity, and neutrality in cases that involve environmental issues') [hereinafter Esty, Greening the GATT]; Dunoff, Misfits, above n. 17 at 1063–5 (arguing that the WTO is inescapably a 'trade' body and cannot therefore ever be seen as a fair broker); Dunoff, Trade And, above n. 14 at 763.

19 See Peter J. Spiro, 'New Global Communities: Nongovernmental Organizations in International Decisionmaking Institutions', 18 Wash Q 4 at 52–4 (1994) [hereinafter Spiro, Global Communities] (making the case for 'process legitimacy').

A third concern – the responsiveness and representativeness of those making the decisions – shapes impressions about the authoritativeness and fairness of the decision-making process.[20] Whenever political choices derive from higher (more centralized) levels of government, which are inescapably more distant from the localized citizenry, issues of representation and fears of a 'democratic deficit' emerge.[21] The trading system historically has been quite vulnerable on this point, facing regular attacks because of the perception that a secretive cabal of 'faceless international bureaucrats' in Geneva makes decisions without fully appreciating their impacts at the local level in countries around the world.[22]

Finally, the WTO faces a challenge of effectiveness. Because the organization has a small staff, it cannot hope to implement by itself the policy directions set in Geneva. The international trading system thus depends on others, particularly national governments, to carry out the decisions that it makes. In addition, the WTO has limited resources for oversight and auditing of its own performance or for forcing the compliance of national governments with internationally agreed goals. These limitations further constrict the WTO's capacity to shape trade policy and to implement it effectively.[23]

2. NON-GOVERNMENTAL ORGANIZATIONS AT THE WORLD TRADE ORGANIZATION

Non-governmental organizations can help the WTO to be more authoritative, fair, responsive, representative, and effective. Historically, NGOs have contributed to the efficacy and legitimacy of international organizations in a range of ways which should be instructive for the international trading system.[24] Non-governmetnal organizations are currently part of the fabric of international decision-making in many realms outside of trade – again, with

[20] See Jackson, Reflections, above n. 7 at 517–18.

[21] See Naomi Roht-Arriaza, 'The Committee on Regions and the Role of Regional Governments in the European Union', 20 Hastings Int'l Comp L Rev 413 at 413–15 (1997) (discussing the 'simultaneous integration and decentralization' in the European Union context); Sol Picciotto, 'Networks in International Economic Integration: Fragmented States and the Dilemmas of Neo-Liberalism', 17 NW J Int'l L Bus 1014 at 1038 (1996–97) [hereinafter Picciotto, Networks] (describing democratic deficit problems in international institutions).

[22] See Esty, Greening the GATT, above n. 18 at 35–6 (reviewing these attacks); Ralph Nader, 'Free Trade and the Decline of Democracy' in Ralph Nader (ed.), The Case Against Free Trade: GATT, NAFTA, and The Globilization of World Power (1993); Walter Russell Mead, 'Bushism Found', Harper's 285 (September 1992).

[23] See Jackson, Reflections, above n. 7 at 517–18 (discussing WTO struggles with transparency and participation).

[24] See Hilary French, 'The Role of Non-State Actors' in Jacob Werksman (ed.) Greening International Institutions (1996) 251; Charnovitz, Two Centuries, above n. 8; Kal Raustiala, 'States, NGOs, and International Environmental Regimes', 41 Int'l Studies Q (1997); A. Dan Tarlock, 'The Role of Non-Governmental Organizations in the Development of International Environmental Law', 68 Chi-Kent L Rev 61 (1993) [hereinafter Tarlock, Role].

lessons applicable to the WTO.[25] As I explain below, the participation of NGOs represents a crucial opportunity for the WTO in the organization's quest for strength and legitimacy. Yet, the recent entry of new types of NGOs, especially environmental groups, onto the trade stage has produced discomfort and even hostility within the trade community.[26] The following sections examine the reasons for this response and review the various roles that NGOs might play at the WTO. Specifically, the case for NGOs as co-operators and competitors with governments at the WTO is advanced, and arguments for excluding NGOs from more active participation in international trade policy-making are reviewed.

Non-governmental organization co-operation

The potential for NGOs to play a co-operative role in assisting international decision processes is supported by a growing body of literature. Non-governmental organizations can serve as service providers (either acting independently or as government subcontractors); mobilizers of public opinion; defenders of view points that governments do not represent or under-represent; watchdogs or private enforcement agents; policy analysts and expert advisors to governments; and bridges between state and non-state actors connecting local and global politics.[27]

25 See Thomas G. Weiss and Leon Gordenker (eds), NGOS, The UN, and Global Governance (1996) [hereinafter Global Governance]; Charnovitz, Two Centuries, above n. 8; Daniel C. Esty, 'Why the World Trade Organization Needs Environmental NGOs', 1 Public Participation in The International Trading System 11–15 (1996) [hereinafter Esty, Why NGOs]. But see Philip M. Nichols, 'Realism, Liberalism, Values, and the World Trade Organization', 17 U Pa J Int'l Econ L 851 at 856–60 (1996) (rejecting 'undisciplined comparison of international organizations') [hereinafter Nichols, Realism].

26 The 1994 agreement establishing the WTO allows for 'consultation and co-operation with non-governmental organizations'. Final Act Embodying the Results of the Uruguay Round of Trade Negotiations, art. 5, § 2, (15 April 1994), reprinted in 33 ILM 1125 at 1146 (1994). But little has been done to give form or content to this provision. See Charnovitz, Participation, above n. 9 at 332–4; Daniel C. Esty, 'Greening World Trade' in Jeffrey J. Schott (ed.), The World Trading System: Challenges Ahead (1996) 78–9 [hereinafter Esty, Greening Trade]; Esty, Why NGOs, above n. 25 at 3–4.

27 See Thomas Prince and Matthias Finger, Environmental NGOs in World Politics: Linking the Global and the Local (1994); A. Bebbington and J. Farrington, 'Governments, NGOs and Agricultural Development: Perspectives on Changing Inter-Organizational Relationships', 29 J Dev Stud 199 (1993); Charnovitz, Participation, above n. 9; P.O. Eikland, 'US Environmental NGOs: New Strategies for New Environmental Problems?', 19 J Soc Pol Econ Stud 259 (1994); Leon Gordenker and Thomas G. Weiss, 'Pluralizing Global Governance: Analytical Approaches and Dimensions' in Global Governance, above n. 25 [hereinafter Gordenker and Weiss, Pluralizing]; Philippe Sands, 'The Role of Environmental NGOs in International Environmental Law', 2 Dev J Soc Int'l Dev 28–32 (1996); Philippe Sands and Albert P. Bedecarre, 'Convention on International Trade in Endangered Species: The Role of Public Interest Non-Governmental Organizations in Ensuring the Effective Enforcement of the Ivory Ban', 17 BC Env Aff L Rev 799 (1990); Paul Wapner, 'Politics Beyond the State: Environmental Activism and Civil World Politics', 47 World Politics 311 (1995); S. Zadek and M. Gatword, 'Transforming the Transnational NGOs: Social Auditing or Bust?' in Michael Edwards and David Hulme (eds), Beyond the Magic Bullet: NGO

In the WTO context, several of these roles are especially prominent. Notably, the WTO's reputation for responsiveness and representativeness as well as fairness will be shaped, in part, by its relationship with non-governmental bodies. As discussed above, one of the central tensions facing the WTO arises from concerns, as a matter of political theory, about decision-making in general that occurs at a great distance from the affected public and about the representativeness of WTO decision-making mechanisms in particular. Much stress is placed in the USA on *federalism*, with an emphasis on keeping political choices as close to the people as possible.[28] Similarly, in the European Union, *subsidiarity* is a byword and a rallying cry for those who seek decentralized decision-making.[29]

Despite the preference for decentralized decision-making, in some circumstances, economic efficiency and the demands of effective governance require that policy-making occur at higher levels of authority.[30] In particular, international regulation is necessary when salient externalities arise on a worldwide scale.[31] That governmental intervention is both necessary and advisable in these circumstances, however, does not mean that it will happen.[32]

Unless governments are convinced to surrender a bit of sovereignty to make international collaboration possible, collective action will not occur, no

---

Performance and Accountability in the Post Cold War World (1996); Spiro, Global Communities, above n. 19; James Cameron and Ross Ramsay, Participation by Non-Governmental Organizations in the World Trade Organization, Global Environment and Trade, Study Working Paper No. 1 (New Haven) [hereinafter Cameron and Ramsay, Participation].

28 See Esty, Revitalizing, above n. 7 at 605–13 (reviewing the arguments for decentralized decision-making).

29 See George A. Bermann, 'Taking Subsidiarity Seriously: Federalism in the European Community and the United States', 94 Colum L Rev 331 (1994); Denis J. Edwards, 'Fearing Federalism's Failure: Subsidiarity in the European Union', 44 Am J Comp L 537 (1996); Paul D. Marquardt, 'Subsidiarity and Sovereignty in the European Union', 18 Fordham Int'l LJ 616 (1994); Joel P. Trachtman, 'Etat C'est Nous: Sovereignty, Economic Integration and Subsidiarity', 33 Harv Int'l LJ 459 (1992); W. Gary Vause, 'The Subsidiarity Principle in European Union Law – American Federalism Compared', 27 Case W Res J Int'l L 61 (1995).

30 See Esty, Revitalizing, above n. 7 at 613–52 (explaining when centralized decision-making, including international regulation, will sometimes be necessary); see also Stewart, Pyramids, above n. 4.

31 See Andre Dua and Daniel C. Esty, Sustaining the Asia Pacific Miracle: Environmental Protection and Economic Intergration (1997) (arguing that economic integration inevitably requires non-economic integration to some degree – and thus some structure of international regulation); Robert Lawrence *et al.*, A Vision For the World Economy: Openness, Diversity, and Cohesion (1996); Dani Rodrick, Has Globalization Gone Too Far (1997); Bhagwati and Srinivasan,Trade and Environment, above n. 7; Nordhaus, Locational Competition, above n. 7.

32 Of course, political interventions may fail too, requiring comparative institutional analysis and a search for solutions that promise least failure. See Neil K. Komesar, Imperfect Alternatives: Choosing Institutions in Law, Economics, and Public Policy (1994) (explaining the need for comparative institutional analysis); Joel Trachtman, 'The Theory of the Firm and the Theory of the International Economic Organization: Toward Comparative Institutional Analysis', 17 NW J Int'l Bus 470 (1996–97) (reviewing this theory in the context of international organizations); Dua and Esty, above n. 31 (discussing the range of market and regulatory failures).

matter that the result is suboptimal regulation or even persistent market failure. Whether governments can be persuaded to co-operate through international organizations such as the WTO depends on these bodies being able to demonstrate a capacity to deliver collective action gains[33] and a responsiveness and representativeness that protects the national governments from criticism by their domestic constituents about the ceding of decision-making to distant and unresponsive officials.[34]

The WTO's need for *connectedness* to people around the world creates a special opportunity for NGOs. In fact, while national representatives in Geneva officially represent their governments – and thus their publics–at the WTO, individuals for a variety of reasons may not feel adequately represented by their governments. First, states are imperfect representatives of public opinion. Governments systematically disregard minority viewpoints. As the public choice literature amply demonstrates, a position that is in the minority across many jurisdictions may, in fact, enjoy a plurality of support at a higher level of aggregation in voting.[35] Permitting NGOs to participate in WTO discussions thus might allow the organization to hear important voices which would otherwise be unrepresented or under-represented in Geneva.[36]

Second, many people today do not have their identities determined by the geographic political jurisdiction in which they happen to live.[37] Non-governmental organizations cut across political boundaries and define 'communities of interest', uniting individuals who are committed to human rights, animal welfare, peace, or any number of other causes or view points. In doing so, they offer an alternative form of 'representation' that may, in some

[33] Many analysts believe that governmental efforts to address market failures are likely to lead to worse rather than better results. See, e.g., Peter S. Menell, 'Institutional Fantasylands: From Scientific Management to Free Market Environmentalism', 15 Harv JL Pub Poly 489 (1992); Maxwell L. Stearns, 'The Misguided Renaissance of Social Choice', 103 Yale LJ 1219 at 1229 (1994).

[34] Indeed, whatever sovereignty is ceded will be reclaimed to the extent that emerging international institutions such as the WTO are perceived to serve alien interests. See Peter J. Spiro, 'New Global Potentates: Nongovernmental Organizations and the "Unregulated" Marketplace', 18 Cardozo L Rev 957 at 958 (1996) [hereinafter Spiro, Potentates]; see also Henry N. Butler and Jonathan R. Macey, 'Externalities and the Matching Principle: The Case for Reallocating Environmental Regulatory Authority', 14 Yale J Reg 23 at 25–9 (1996) (arguing for a more decentralized environmental governance structure).

[35] See Herbert Hovenkamp, 'Legislation, Well-Being and Public Choice', 57 U Chi L Rev 63 at 75 (1990) (providing an example of this problem) [hereinafter Hovenkamp, Legislation.]

[36] A number of today's global NGOs, from Amnesty International to the Worldwide Fund for Nature, clearly represent transnational interest groups that unite people across the globe who share common interests. See Paul Wapner, Environmental Activism and World Civic Politics (1995); see also, Wendy Schoener, 'Note, Nongovernmental Organizations and Global Activism: Legal and Informal Approaches', 4 Ind J Global Legal Stud 537 at 564 (1997) (describing Amnesty International as transnational).

[37] In at least some circumstances, the author might be better understood as an 'environmental law professor' than as a 'resident of Connecticut'.

instances, allow for a more refined and closely tailored reflection of an individual's views in relevant decision-making bodies than will be obtained through his or her government. Participation in NGOs also allows individuals to express an intensity of preference that simple voting mechanisms do not permit.[38] A citizen who cares very deeply about ending whaling, for instance, almost certainly will find his or her views better represented in international fora by the Worldwide Fund for Nature than by his or her own government, which has many goals it must simultaneously pursue. At the very least, listening to NGOs offers a cut across the grain of territorial representation which may awaken WTO decision-makers to the complexity and nuances of the issues they face or otherwise provide an additional perspective on what is at stake.

Our growing appreciation of the richness and diversity of 'civil society' reinforces the suggestion that it would be a mistake to think that all interactions among people can be mediated through the narrow channel of national governments. Indeed, one of the cornerstones of the liberal critique of traditional realist international relations theory centres on the assumption that states are the prime (or even the only) actors on the international stage.[39] A wide variety of transnational forces now operate internationally, NGOs among them.[40] It would be an error for the WTO not to take cognizance of this transformation or to continue to act as though international affairs were solely a contest among the wills of governments.[41]

The participation of NGOs in WTO debates also can help to compensate for deficient representativeness at the national level. In many countries, weak democratic institutions and other public choice flaws mean that national government policies do not fairly and accurately represent the citizenry's views. In some cases, authoritarian regimes seek to maintain their hold on power with little regard for public opinion. In other countries, leaders are corrupt. And in every country, public choice distortions – special interest manipulation,

[38] See Hovenkamp, Legislation, above n. 35 at 75 (providing an example of this problem).

[39] Marvin S. Soros, Beyond Sovereignty: The Challenge of Global Policy (1986) 75–119 (describing international actors and including both states as traditional actors and IGOs); Thomas J. Biersteker and Cynthia Wever (eds), State Sovereignty as Social Construct (1996) 444 (describing recent scholarly discussion of state sovereignty); Harold Hongju Koh, 'Why Do Nations Obey International Law', 106 Yale LJ 2599 at 2604–41 (1997) (describing evolving conceptions (of international law) and actors within it).

[40] See Barbara J. Bramble and Gareth Porter, 'Non-Governmental Organizations and the Making of US International Environmental Policy' in Andrew Hurrell and Benedict Kingsbury (eds), The International Politics of the Environment (1992) 31 at 313 (describing the role of NGOs in international environmental politics).

[41] See, e.g., G. Richard Shell, 'The Trade Stakeholders Model and Participation by Nonstate Parties in the World Trade Organization', 17 U Pa J Int'l Econ L 359 at 371 (1996) (critiquing 'realist' views of international law that leave trade matters under the control of diplomats and states) [hereinafter Shell, Stakeholders]; Weiss and Gordenker, Global Governance, above n. 25 (reviewing the role of NGOs in a broadened concept of international law).

campaign contributions, asymmetries of resources and political activity among interest groups, etc. – cause policies to deviate to some degree from the true will of the people. It may seem ironic to suggest that the WTO, often criticized for its 'democratic deficit', could improve the representativeness of decision-making.[42] But, in many cases, the WTO offers a potentially more open, transparent, and pluralistic decision-making forum than would be available at the national level. In brief, upgrading the quality of the WTO's political debates – through greater transparency and an organized role for NGOs – may substitute for the lack of liberal democracy in a considerable number of countries around the world.

An inclusive approach to NGOs at the WTO also offers important advances from the perspective of the political economy of trade liberalization. Notably, if environmental groups (especially those in North America) and others who have felt excluded from trade policy-making perceive themselves as included in the process and are given a fair opportunity to shape decisions, they are much less likely to obstruct trade liberalization efforts.[43] The benefits of a strategy of inclusiveness were demonstrated during the course of the North Atlantic Free Trade Agreement (NAFTA) debate in the USA. Both the Bush and Clinton Administrations worked hard to ensure that environmental groups were briefed regularly, included in the US Trade Representative's advisory groups, and given access to the negotiation process. In the end, a number of environmental groups supported the treaty.[44]

A regularized channel of information that flows *up* from NGOs to the WTO also would be beneficial, especially insofar as it might strengthen the WTO's decision-making capacity. When decisions require an understanding of policy in areas outside of the WTO's existing zones of expertise, such as in 'trade and environment' cases, the opportunity to tap data, information,

[42] See E.U. Petersmann, Constitutional Functions and Constitutional Problems of International Economic Law (1991) 166–7 (describing democratic deficit in EU GATT participation); Picciotto, Networks, above n. 21 at 1037–8 (discussing democratic deficit in international institutions); E.U. Petersmann, 'National Constitutions, Foreign Trade Policy, and European Community Law', 46 Aussenwirtschaft 197 (1991); Frieder Roessler, 'The Constitutional Function of the Multilateral Trade Order' in M. Hilf and E. U. Petersmann (eds), National Constitution and International Economic Law (1992); Guy de Jonquie'res and Michael Smith, 'EU Farm Chief Rebuked Over Swipe at WTO', Financial Times 4, 5 September 1997 (reporting on EU farm commissioner Franz Fischler's 'suggestion that the WTO lacked democratic accountability').

[43] For a review of the political economy of trade liberalization in the United States, see Daniel C. Esty, 'Environmentalists and Trade Policymaking', in Alan V. Deardorff and Robert M. Stern (eds), Representation of Constituent Interests in the Design and Implementation of US Trade Policies (1997). The difficulty President Clinton faced in getting approval for 'fast track' negotiating authority in 1997 – and especially the opposition of environmentally oriented congressmen – demonstrates the saliency of this political economy argument.

[44] See Frederick M. Abbott, 'Foundation-Building for Western Hemispheric Integration', 17 NW J Int'l L Bus 900 at 924–6 (1997); John Audley, Green Politics and Global Trade (1997) (reviewing the NGO role in NAFTA); Esty, Greening the GATT, above n. 18 at 27–8 (describing environmental NGOs' approach to NAFTA negotiations).

studies, option assessments, and views from the NGO community broadens the base of analysis on which decisions rest.[45] In some realms, such as environmental policy, the high degree of scientific flux and other uncertainties makes the capacity to triangulate on the truth especially valuable. As noted earlier, the more clearly that WTO decisions are recognized to be substantively on the mark – appropriately regulating to avoid market failures in the international economic domain and faithfully advancing goals such as environmental protection – the greater the authoritativeness and legitimacy of the organization.

Non-governmental organizations provide the WTO not only with a mechanism to hear views beyond governmental ones, but also with a means for sharing information about what is happening within the international trading system. Many NGOs are ideally situated to play this dissemination role insofar as they have connections to millions of individuals with whom government officials have no direct method of contact. Explaining what is happening within the trade regime and developing a public appreciation of the work that goes on at the WTO are essential prerequisites for broader public support for trade liberalization in general and for the decisions of the WTO in particular.

Regular communication *down* to people at the grassroots level through the medium of NGOs promises to go a considerable distance toward dispelling the trading system's image as mysterious, distant, and unresponsive. That which people understand they are less likely to react negatively toward. Regular contact with groups around the world also might help governments to mobilize public opinion in favour of freer trade when it comes time to hold congressional or parliamentary votes on free trade agreements or other trade and investment liberalization efforts.[46]

Non-governmental organizations also provide an additional oversight and audit mechanism. Well-informed citizen groups can act as watchdogs of national governments and report on whether they are fulfilling their obligations under international economic law. With better access to documents and meetings, NGOs also would be in a position to review and critique WTO performance. While this may not seem intuitively attractive to those in

[45] The same logic would argue for expanded co-operation between the WTO and other international bodies with substantive expertise, such as the UN Environment Program (UNEP). An argument could also be made that a better answer would be to have the WTO incorporate by reference environmental analyses undertaken elsewhere, such as within UNEP, as GATT Article XV contemplates guidance from the International Monetary Fund on certain issues. This author has, in fact, argued for creation of a Global Environmental Organization that could play this role. See Esty, Geo, above n. 7 at 287. But the strengthening of the international environmental regime necessary to make this approach work does not seem imminent.

[46] See A.M. Clark, 'Non Governmental Organizations and Their Influence on International Society', 48 J Int'l Affairs 504 at 518–21 (1995) (discussing NGO information sharing role); P. Ghils, 'International Civil Society: International Non-Governmental Organizations in the International System', 44 Int'l Sci J 417 (1992).

Geneva, the value of peer review is now widely appreciated.[47] It would therefore be in the public interest to have WTO decisions carefully scrutinized and analysed to ensure that, at every turn, preferred policy directions are being selected.

Broader public participation in the WTO with communication both up from NGOs and down through these organizations would yield a stronger, more democratic, and more durable international trading system. A richer 'WTO politics' offers the promise of a more responsive, representative, authoritative, and effective WTO.

Non-governmental competition

As noted above, the WTO makes many complex and technically difficult decisions. The WTO's in-house expertise becomes severely strained when the Secretariat must untangle trade and environment questions, trade and labour issues, or any number of other matters that overlap from the trade domain into other policy areas. In many of these decisions, the capacity of the WTO to produce good policy outcomes – that contribute to its reputation for authoritativeness and responsiveness – depends on having its deliberations enriched through 'outside' information and multiple policy perspectives. In short, there is great value in considering *competing* policy options.[48]

The benefits of competition are well established in general economic theory.[49] Increasingly, the gains from bringing competitive forces to bear in the regulatory domain are being understood.[50] In the context of the WTO decision-making, this theory could translate into national governments advancing competing visions of international trade policy. But the limits of horizontally arrayed governments as the *competitors* in the regulatory arena also are being recognized.[51]

47 The OECD, for example, has benefited considerably from having NGOs participate in many (if not all) of its meetings and workshops. See generally Robert F. Housman, 'Democratizing International Trade Decision-Making', 27 Cornell Int'l LJ 699 at 717–18 (1994) (discussing various ways in which NGOs have been allowed participation in the OECD).

48 The benefits of multiple perspectives which permit triangulation on the truth are especially significant in the environmental realm because the field is marked by particularly dramatic uncertainties and technical complexity. See Esty, Revitalizing, above n. 7 at 578–80.

49 See, e.g., Samuelson and Nordhaus, Economics, above n. 1 at 136–43 (discussing the equity and efficiency of competitive markets).

50 See William A. Fischel, 'Fiscal and Environmental Considerations in the Location of Firms in Suburban Communities' in Edwin S. Mills and Wallace E. Oates (eds), Fiscal Zoning and Land Use Controls (1975) 119; Richard L. Revesz, 'Rehabilitating Interstate Competition: Rethinking the "Race to the Bottom" Rationale for Federal Environmental Regulation', 67 NYUL Rev 1210 (1992); W. E. Oates and Robert M. Schwab, 'Economic Competition Among Jurisdictions: Efficiency Enhancing or Distortion Inducing', 35 J Pub Econ 333 (1988); Charles M. Tiebout, 'A Pure Theory of Local Expenditures', 64 J Pol Econ 416 (1956).

51 See Kirsten A. Engel, 'State Environmental Standard-Setting: Is There a "Race" and is it "To the Bottom"?', 48 Hastings LJ 271 at 297–347 (1997); Joshua D. Sarnoff, 'Overcoming Uncooperative Federalism', 39 Ariz L Rev 205 at 215 (1997); Esty, Revitalizing, above n. 7 at 627–38 (discussing arguments over whether regulatory races to the bottom occur).

In many realms, governments do not generate serious intellectual competition. This weakness is especially acute when the ability to generate policy alternatives turns on technical capacity. Environmental policy-making, for example, often requires careful problem identification, fate and transport analyses, epidemiological and ecological studies, risk assessment, policy design and options development, and cost–benefit analyses. Not many governments in the world are positioned to carry out this type of analytically intensive activity. Hence, few serve as serious idea generators and thus policy competitors at the WTO.

There are other reasons to be sceptical about achieving better international policies through intergovernmental regulatory competition. Notably, international bodies often have narrow mandates and therefore narrowly focused secretariats and national representatives. The WTO's mission, for example, is trade liberalization. When trade policies overlap into other domains, the tendency is for all those at the WTO – both staff and those representing capitals – to see the problem through a trade lens. Thus, debates over issues such as 'trade and the environment' go forward within a limited band of viewpoints. Too often both the international civil servants and government officials are happy to ignore issues that fall beyond their bailiwick. It is thus helpful, if not essential, that NGOs, drawing on a wider array of perspectives and expertise, be available to prod governments into paying attention to 'peripheral' – but not unimportant – issues such as protection of the environment.[52]

In many cases, NGOs are better positioned to serve as intellectual competitors than governments. These organizations often have the requisite analytic and technical skills to delve into the matters at hand. Their success and rewards derive from being recognized as contributors to improved policy outcomes.[53] In addition, NGOs frequently are more nimble than governments in spotting new issues and shifting their resources quickly in response. In an ideal world, governments might be expected to re-evaluate their policies regularly and then be positioned to bring fresh thinking to the fore, making a prominent NGO role unnecessary. But in the real world, governmental

[52] See Elizabeth Dowdeswell and Steve Charnovitz, 'Globalization, Trade, and Interdependence' in Marian Chertow and Daniel Esty (eds), Thinking Ecologically: The Next Generation of Environmental Policy (1997) 91 at 99; see also Dunoff, Trade And, above n. 14 at 763–4 (discussing the limitations of the WTO in addressing 'trade and' issues).

[53] In this sense, market forces discipline NGOs. Groups perceived to be doing a poor job (and not undergirding their environmental campaigning with rigorous analysis) suffered reduced contributions and forced cut-backs in staffing, while those who were perceived as valuable contributors to current debates found their membership and support surging. The contrast between Greenpeace, which recently was forced to close ten of its US regional offices as a result of a budget shortfall, see Greenpeace Protest Group Slashing US Budget, Staff, Wash Post, 10 August 1997 at A4, and the Environmental Defense Fund, which has seen its membership rise six-fold over the past ten years, is instructive. See Environmental Defense Fund, Memo on Membership Growth 1967–1996 (on file with author).

inertia is overwhelming. Thus, regulatory competition from outside the governmental domain becomes essential to a sound policy-making process.

The logic of *horizontal* competition – between governments and NGOs at the WTO – builds on the basic economic understanding that welfare gains can be achieved by having competing options available. Political theory suggests, similarly, that *vertical* competition among levels of government – local, state, national, and global – will produce benefits. Specifically, the dispersion of power across various levels of authority provides useful 'checks and balances' on mistakes and abuses of power.[54] An NGO-enriched WTO decision process would offer better competition for national governments in the search for optimal policies. To the extent that national trade debates disregard issues or useful perspectives, a more robust WTO political process would ensure a full airing of the issues and options.

If national debates prove to be systematically limited,[55] WTO discussions, fueled by the intellectual competition of NGO participation, might well take on increased significance over time. The end result would be an international trading system that has greater legitimacy and effectiveness as well as broader political and public support.

Fears about the role of non-governmental organizations at the World Trade Organization

Despite these benefits, many in the trade community continue to resist NGO involvement at the WTO. The desire to exclude NGOs from a formal role in the international trade regime can be traced to a number of concerns. In brief, those who would exclude NGOs from international trade policy-making believe that an increased presence for environmental groups and other non-governmental entities within the halls of the WTO headquarters on Lake Geneva would distort rather than improve the decision-making process.[56] While the concerns about NGOs at the WTO are real, they are not unanswerable. Indeed, in recent years, many of the fears expressed above have

[54] See 5 Writings of James Madison 27 [G. Hunt (ed.) 1901]; Akhil R. Amar, 'A Neo-Federalist View of Article III: Separating the Two Tiers of Federal Jurisdiction', 65 BUL Rev 205 at 247 (1985) (arguing a strong federal government represents a bulwark 'against overweening state governments'); Akhil R. Amar, 'Of Sovereignty and Federalism', 96 Yale LJ 1425 at 1444–65 (1987) (outlining the Framers' theories of competition in government).

[55] See the 'public choice' discussion in Section A, above n. 35 and accompanying text, for a review of why national trade policy-making might be systematically sub-optimal.

[56] Curiously, there is little academic literature arguing against a broader role for NGOs at the WTO. Government officials seem to be the leading critics of expanded NGO participation. For the best arguments against participation, see Bhagawati and Srinivasan, Trade and Environment at 195; Nichols, Realism, above n. 25 (explaining potential problems of NGO participation at the WTO); William Diebold, 'Reflections on the International Trade Organization', 14 N Ill UL Rev 335 (1994) (discussing major business groups refusing to follow ITO charter agreements); William M. Reichert, 'Note, Resolving the Trade and Environment Conflict: The WTO and NGO Consultative Relations', 2 Minn J Global Trade 219 at 230 (1996) (cataloguing problems with NGO participation) [hereinafter Reichert, Resolving].

been narrowed or even put to rest.[57] Steve Charnovitz demonstrates, moreover, that NGOs have a long history of involvement in international economic relations.[58] Thus, the current limited role at the WTO represents an historical anomaly and a low point in an evolutionary cycle.[59]

1. Special interest manipulation

Whenever lobbying of a decision-making body is permitted, there exists a risk that certain interests will exert disproportionate influence.[60] Some analysts suggest that interest group participation slows decision-making processes and leads to inefficient results.[61] Thus, critics of a broader role for NGOs at the WTO worry that the presence of environmental groups or of other organizations lobbying WTO officials or governmental representatives at the WTO will result in distorted policy outcomes.[62] One commentator, Peter Spiro, warns that NGO leaders, armed with fattened bank accounts and with the leverage of large but docile memberships, have emerged as a new class of modern day potentates.[63]

A more refined version of the special-interest-domination fear stems from governments' need to trade off competing domestic interests to strike agreements that liberalize trade. In many cases, trade officials must give up the particularized interests of certain industries or groups – especially inefficient industries hiding behind tariff barriers or other protectionist walls – to obtain benefits for the general public they represent.[64] It is often easier to go behind closed doors to cut these deals. Indeed, severe 'public choice' problems,

[57] See, e.g., Charnovitz, Participation, above n. 9 (rebutting the arguments against NGO participation); Shell, Stakeholders, above n. 41 (offering a model for NGO participation at the WTO and refuting various concerns about such a role); Esty, Why NGOs, above n. 25 at 4–7.

[58] See Charnovitz, Two Centuries, above n. 8. As Charnovitz points out, NGOs played a major role in leading the world toward the abolition of slavery in the 19th century. They have also been strong advocates for peace and for worker rights for more than a hundred years. NGOs have had a long-standing involvement in international trade policy-making, including promoting free-trade and the end of the British corn tariffs in the mid-nineteenth century. See ibid. at 189–95.

[59] The post-Second World War international leaders who crafted the GATT, the forerunner of today's World Trade Organization, clearly anticipated a significant role for NGOs. In fact, Sir Eric Wyndham White, the first head of the GATT, advanced a quite specific NGO agenda. Specifically, he proposed that the International Trade Organization (ITO): (1) draw up a list of NGOs to be given consultative status; (2) invite NGO observers to ITO conferences and allow them to propose agenda items and to speak; (3) consult with NGOs with competence in particular fields of activity related to ITO efforts; and (4) appoint an advisory committee of NGO representatives. See Steve Charnovitz and John Wickham, 'Non-Governmental Organizations and the Original International Trade Regime', J World Trade 111 at 117–18 (1995); Charnovitz, Participation, above n. 9 at 338–9.

[60] See e.g., Anthony Downs, An Economic Theory of Democracy (1957); Olson, Logic, above n. 3; James M. Buchanan and Gordon Tullock, The Calculus of Consent (1971); Elmer E. Schattschneider, Politics, Pressures and the Tariff (1935).

[61] See Mancur Olson, The Rise and Decline of Nations (1982) 41–5; Nichols, Realism, above n. 22 at 861–6.

[62] Nichols, Realism, above n. 25 at 860–66.

[63] See Spiro, Potentates, above n. 34 at 963.

[64] See Esty, Why NGOs, above n. 25 at 4–5; Jackson, Reflections, above n. 7 at 511.

arising from the visibility of the gains to narrow groups from closed markets and from the relative invisibility of the diffuse benefits of open markets, are endemic in the trade domain.[65] Many trade experts fear that an expanded role for NGOs at the WTO therefore would exacerbate the tendency to hear protectionist voices, making the pursuit of trade liberalization more difficult.

Free traders' concerns are heightened by a perception that many NGOs are unsympathetic to trade liberalization efforts and perhaps even protectionist.[66] These fears have some basis in fact; a number of environmental groups and many labour unions are fundamentally opposed to free trade.[67] Almost by definition, the groups that historically have not had entree to the WTO and now want access are not trade-oriented. Thus, they bring to trade debates no special commitment to open markets and, in most cases, their core interests centre on some other agenda such as environmental protection.

The fear of NGOs acting as special interests, and manipulating WTO outcomes is, however, overblown. Special interests, representing (often protectionist!) business entities, already inhabit the WTO. Adding additional NGO perspectives, likely would counteract and blunt the influence of existing interests and therefore reduce, not increase, the risk of special-interest-driven policy outcomes. Indeed, the presence of a more diverse set of interests within the WTO decision process largely would be self-policing as the various groups could monitor each other, exert countervailing pressures, and generally diminish the prospect of the 'capture' of the WTO by narrow interest groups.[68]

[65] Groups representing special interests that have a great deal at stake in trade policy often will invest considerable resources to protect their positions. On the other hand, the general public, which benefits broadly but not deeply from freer trade, is much harder to activate politically. Thus, there exists a significant asymmetry between those who benefit from open markets (a diffuse and not well organized public) and those who seek protectionism (concentrated groups which are often easier to mobilize). See Philip M. Nichols, 'Extension of Standing in the World Trade Organization Disputes to Non Governmental Entities', 17 U Pa J Int'l Econ L 295 at 319–20 (1996) [hereinafter Nichols, Extension]; Nichols, Realism, above n. 25 at 860; E.U. Petersmann, 'Settlement of International and National Trade Disputes Through the GATT: The Case of Antidumping Law' in E. U. Petersmann and G. Jaenicke (eds), Adjudication of International Trade Disputes in International and National Economic Law (1992); see also Alan V. Deardorff and Robert M. Stern, 'An Overview of the Modeling of Choices and Consequences of US Trade Policies' in Alan V. Deardorff and Robert M. Stern (eds), Representation of Constituent Interests in the Design and Implementation of US Trade Policies (1997).

[66] See Esty, Why NGOs, above n. 25 at 5; Reichert, Resolving, above n. 56 at 220–1.

[67] See Daniel C. Esty, Greening the GATT, above n. 18 at 27–29; Reichert, Resolving, above n. 56 at 221.

[68] See Arvind Subramanian, 'Trade Measures for Environment: A Nearly Empty Box', 15 World Economy 135 (1992) (reviewing the risk of capture of the trading system); Spiro, Potentates, above n. 34 at 962, 962–8 (concluding that institutionalizing the role of NGOs could work to improve international institutional decision-making while avoiding the risk of 'interest group capture of the global marketplace'); Kevin Stair and Peter Taylor, 'Nongovernmental Organizations and the Legal Protection of the Ocean: A Case Study' in Andrew Hurrel and Benedict Kingsbury (eds), The International Politics of the Environment (1992) 110 at 134 (discussing general benefits to international law of NGO participation).

The suggestion, furthermore, that more open processes would make achieving trade liberalization harder because governments could not cut deals rests on two faulty assumptions. First, it is by no means clear that the current non-transparent negotiating style promotes freer trade. To the contrary, many protectionist results have emerged from the WTO and from the General Agreement on Tariffs and Trade (GATT) before it.[69] Second, public choice distortions generally become more severe not less so, when decisions are made out of public view.[70] Transparent decision processes, in which positions are openly disclosed and debated, represent a powerful force in support of outcomes that track the public interest.[71]

The observation that many of the groups that seek access to the WTO are closet, if not overt, protectionists may be true, but it offers no real argument for closed door meetings. World Trade Organization secrecy only serves to heighten anxiety about trade liberalization. Many environmental groups, in particular, are highly sensitive to process issues – and their opposition to freer trade might well be more muted if they better understood how trade policy decisions are made.

2. The World Trade Organization is an intergovernmental body

A second major argument against an expanded NGO role in the international trading regime derives from the belief that the WTO should be an *intergovernmental* body. According to this view, the trade policy process works best when governments can speak clearly to each other without a cacophony of other voices. As Philip Nichols suggests, it can be confusing to have domestic constituencies opposing the positions of the governments that are supposed to represent those constituencies.[72] Another strand of this argument recoils at the prospect of NGOs getting two bites at the apple. Why, critics ask, should NGOs be able to lobby both at the national level in the debate over their government's WTO approach and again at the WTO itself?

Other observers argue that the essence of international affairs is relations among sovereign states. To the extent that international bodies must deal with other actors as well, their decision processes become murky and the foundation for their legitimacy uncertain.[73] While this state-centric view of

[69] The Multi-Fiber Agreement and dispute settlements that codify Voluntary Restraint Agreements are the examples of this tendency. See, e.g., James Bovard, The Fair Trade Fraud (1991).

[70] To ensure further transparency, the WTO should develop procedures to require the disclosure of all lobbying activities and to prohibit its staff from accepting gratuities from those with interests in the outcome of their work. See Esty, Why NGOs, above n. 25 at 6.

[71] See, e.g., J. Oloka-Onyango, 'Beyond the Rhetoric: Reinvigorating the Struggle for Economic and Social Rights in Africa', 26 Cal W Int'l LJ 1, 71 (1995) ('In order to have honest agencies that serve the public interest, transparency is crucial . . . ').

[72] See Nichols, Extension, above n. 65 at 308–9; see also Esty, Why NGOs, above n. 25 at 5.

[73] See Esty, Why NGOs, above n. 25 at 5; Nichols, Extension, above n. 65 at 308; Nichols, Realism, above n. 25 at 874–8 (arguing for 'institutionalism' as a more refined version of realist international relations theory). But see Shell, Stakeholder, above n. 41 at 371–9 (criticizing Nichols' narrow institutionalist view of international relations).

the world might be critiqued as passé,[74] it is a mistake to gainsay the important role states play in international relations[75] or to deny that the presence of NGOs complicates state-to-state relations.

The argument that the WTO is meant to be an intergovernmental body is both superficially true and beside the point. Giving NGOs a voice at the WTO, and more importantly, the opportunity to observe WTO debate and dispute settlement proceedings, does not preclude governments from discussing some issues behind closed doors. The WTO need not be a purely state-to-state institution.[76] To suggest, moreover, that all NGO influence should occur at the national level misunderstands the complexity of the modern world. As noted earlier, some NGOs are international in scope. Telling these groups that they must exert influence only at the national level is to deprive them of their transnational essence.[77] In addition, some political debates are conducted better at the international level because the underlying issues involve questions of global governance.[78] Institutions, such as the WTO, that play a role in setting and enforcing the rules of international behaviour, will be strengthened to the extent that they encourage a full and rich debate over the directions to be taken.[79]

3. Unrepresentativeness of non-governmental organizations

A third set of concerns about the role of NGOs in the WTO relates to their representativeness and accountability.[80] In fact, it may well be difficult to ascertain how many and which people a particular group represents.

[74] See Cameron and Ramsay, Participation, above n. 27 at 11; Reichert, Resolving, above n. 56 at 221–3; see also Gordenker and Weiss, Pluralizing, above n. 27 at 34; David Scott Rubinton, 'Toward a Recognition of the Rights of Non-States in International Environmental Law', 9 Pace Env L Rev 475 at 487–91 (describing the movement from a state-centric approach in the environmental realm).

[75] See Ian Brownlie, Principles of Public International Law (1990) 287–8 (discussing traditional sovereignty and equality of states in the international system); Gordenker and Weiss, Pluralizing, above n. 27 at 34; Anne-Marie Slaughter, 'The Real New World Order', 76 Foreign Affairs 183 (1997); Nichols, Realism, above n. 25 at 877.

[76] Even institutionalist critics of an expanded role for NGOs at the WTO acknowledge that hybrid institutions – in which governments share the stage with non-governmental entities – are not only conceivable but sometimes even useful. See Nichols, Realism, above n. 25 at 877–8.

[77] Amnesty International is not a British organization but a worldwide one. The World Wildlife Fund – as its very name suggests – is an international organization made up of representatives from more than a 100 countries. See generally Gordenker and Weiss, Pluralizing, above n. 727 at 27–8; Michael H. Posner and Candy Whittome, 'The Status of Human Rights NGOs', 25 Colum Hum R L Rev 269 at 270–2 (1994) (examining human rights NGOs).

[78] See Steve Charnovitz, 'A Critical Guide to the WTO's Report on Trade and Environment', 14 Ariz J Int'l Comp L 341 at 367 (1997); Tarlock, Role, above n. 24 (describing the complicated nature of transboundary environmental problems and the benefit of international debate over responses).

[79] As Part II above explains in detail, there are a number of reasons to believe that governments systematically do not bring forward all of the perspectives and arguments which should be considered in setting the course for international bodies such as the WTO.

[80] See Spiro, Potentates, above n. 34 at 963; Tarlock, Role, above n. 24 at 75.

Non-governmental organizations with ostensibly similar constituencies might present conflicting view points. This raises a number of questions. To whom should officials in international bodies listen? How do we know if the things NGOs say are true? What disciplines do NGOs face which ensure their responsible behaviour? Would increased NGO participation in debates at the WTO not give more weight to views from the developed north as opposed to those of the developing south?[81]

It is no doubt true that certain perspectives (especially those backed by money) will be represented more fully if the WTO were opened up to NGOs. Concerns about the representativeness of NGOs should not, however, be taken too seriously. World Trade Organization decision-makers more often are swayed by the quality of arguments made than by the quantity of noise they hear from a particular quarter. Just as national officials learn over time which groups represent important perspectives and will provide useful information, so too would officials of the WTO. In the international domain, as in national political discourse, the credibility and weight given to NGO positions would vary with the political mobilization potential of the group and the quality of its past contributions to public dialogues. Moreover, fears of a North–South imbalance in the participation of NGOs in Geneva already have begun to subside as the developing world gains new groups and advances in information technology make it possible to participate in WTO decision-making from a great distance at ever lower costs.[82] Indeed, the internet and e-mail have dramatically lowered the cost of staying on top of WTO activities.

4. Practicalities of non-governmental organization participation

Other worries centre on the practical difficulties of credentialling NGOs and controlling their activities within the international trading system. Who would determine which groups actually constitute NGOs? How would the right to speak be allocated? Would not the already limited time available to governments in open meetings be further diluted? Other observers worry that the presence of NGOs in the room at WTO meetings would chill candour. Governments, they fear, would resist exposing their underlying policies to greater scrutiny and perhaps criticism at home, which are inevitable byproducts of more transparent decision processes that include NGOs.[83]

[81] See Nichols, Extension, above n. 65 at 318–19; Charnovitz, Participation, above n. 9 at 343; see also Reichart, Resolving, above n 56 at 244–6 (discussing worries about NGOs being biased toward Northern interests).

[82] See Gordenker and Weiss, Pluralizing, above n. 27 at 25; see also Richard H. Steinberg, 'Trade-Environment Negotiations in the EU, NAFTA, and WTO: Regional Trajectories of Rule Development', 91 Am J Int'l Law 231 (1997) (arguing that the power of developed country 'green' interests will be relatively low at the WTO because their influence must be spread widely).

[83] See Nichols, Extension, above n. 65 at 319; see also Jackson, Reflections, above n. 7 at 517 (noting the tendency of international organizations to prefer secrecy). But see Charnovitz, Participation, above n. 9 at 343–5 (arguing that the WTO should not seek to maintain anonymity).

These practical concerns can be addressed. Models for managing the participation of NGOs in international meetings abound.[84] In fact, as the WTO matures and evolves as a governance mechanism, it needs a more fully developed administrative law structure that spells out rules and procedures for its decision processes.

Not only is the current exclusion of NGOs from substantive participation in the WTO historically anomalous from the perspective of the trade domain, it is entirely inconsistent with the relationship between NGOs and intergovernmental organizations in other realms.[85] Even within the international economic domain, the WTO lags behind other bodies. The World Bank, for example, has developed a series of procedures to permit NGOs access to its meetings and decision processes.[86] Likewise, the Organization for Economic Co-operation and Development has broadened its outreach considerably to NGOs in recent years.

In sum, there are practical issues to overcome if NGOs are to participate effectively, efficiently, and appropriately in WTO activities. But fears of a cacophony of voices need not take on a magnified importance, nor should worries about the dilution of governmental influence be exaggerated.[87]

3. A PRACTICAL PROPOSAL FOR CO-OPERATION AND COMPETITION

By arguing for an expanded role for NGOs at the WTO – to promote connections from the organization to distant publics and to expand the data and

[84] See Esty, Why NGOs, above n. 25; Charnovitz, Two Centuries, above n. 8.

[85] Non-governmental organizations played a major role in the UN Conference on Environment and Development, including the many preparatory meetings that led up to the June 1992 Earth Summit in Rio de Janeiro. More recent UN conferences – the 1994 Cairo Population Conference, the 1995 Beijing Woman's Conference, and the 1996 Copenhagen Conference on Human Habitats – similarly have involved thousands of NGOs. See, e.g., Charnovitz, Two Centuries, above n. 8 at 266; Charnovitz, Participation, above n. 9 at 335–6, 336 n. 25; Wendy Shoerer, 'Note, Non-Governmental Organizations and Global Activism: Legal and Informal Approaches', 4 Ind J Global Leg Stud 537, 569 n. 76 (1997). But see Nichols, Realism, above n. 25 at 856–7 (arguing against opening the WTO to NGOs and noting that just because every other international body 'jumps off a roof' the WTO should not follow). Note, however, that Nichols, while dismissing Charnovitz's comparisons, makes no effort to explain what makes the WTO unique or especially unsuited to NGO participation.

[86] See Paul Nelson, The World Bank and Non-Governmental Organizations (1995); Barbara J. Bramble and Gareth Porter, 'Non-Governmental Organizations and the Making of US International Environmental Policy', C990 Ali-Aba 407, 415–21 (1995); David Reed, 'The Global Environmental Facility and Non-Governmental Organizations', 9 Am U J Int'l L Policy 191 at 202–4 (1993); Tarlock, Role, above n. 24 at 71–2.

[87] Of course, designing working mechanisms for NGO participation at the WTO will require some accommodation on the part of NGOs. If NGOs are to be effective in their roles as co-operators and competitors with governments, they must also change how they carry out their business. In particular, NGOs will need to sharpen their educational activities to ensure that they are capable of playing the information flow role. And if these groups are to succeed as competitors to government, they must become more analytically rigorous. For a discussion of the variance in strength and quality of NGOs, see Esty, Why NGOs, above n. 25 at 6; Reichert, Resolving, above n. 56 at 239–41.

analysis which underlie WTO decisions, especially when trade policy decisions spill over into other realms such as the environmental domain – I do not mean to suggest that all NGO activity at the WTO would be welcome or helpful. It is important that access permitted in the name of transparency or public participation not devolve into manipulation of the international trade policy-making process by special interests.

Creating the right sort of NGO role is not a trivial matter. In establishing the parameters for non-governmental participation in the international trading system, it is important to distinguish, at the outset, between: (1) WTO adjudicatory processes, (2) WTO legislative activities, and (3) trade negotiations *per se*. The logic for non-governmental participation, the exposure to the risk of special interest distortions, and the difficulty of managing the practicalities of NGO involvement varies considerably across these different activities.

World Trade Organization dispute resolution

The arguments for allowing NGO observation of and limited participation in the WTO dispute settlement process are overwhelming.[88] Permitting NGOs to watch the proceedings when parties give evidence to dispute panels and to have access to written submissions would go a considerable distance toward dispelling fears about the unexplained 'black box' that hides WTO decisions emanating from the shores of Lake Geneva.

The Uruguay Round Dispute Settlement Understanding[89] moves the WTO dispute resolution process solidly in the direction of more formal adjudication. Opening the proceedings to non-governmental observers would be a useful additional step – at no risk to the integrity of the process. Indeed, it is hard to imagine how the presence of NGOs would distort the outcome of the panel process, except to the extent that governments could not say one thing to the panelists and something else publicly.[90]

[88] The opening up of the dispute settlement process to non-governmental entities has already begun. Many governments, for example, employ private attorneys to help them prepare their briefs and arguments. See WTO Report of the Appellate Body European Communities–*Regime for the Importation, Sale and Distribution of Bananas*, AB-1997-3, WT/DS27/AB/R (9 September 1997) at 11 (noting the extensive role played by 'private counsel'). Jeffrey Dunoff argues that many trade disputes (e.g., the recent Kodak–Fuji film dispute and the US–Venezuela reformulated gasoline case) are better understood as disputes between private parties. This reality further weakens the argument for excluding non-governmental actors. See Jeffrey L. Dunoff, The Death of the Trade Regime (1998) at 64–8.

[89] See General Agreement on Tariffs and Trade – Multilateral Trade Negotiations (The Uruguay Round): Understanding on Rules and Procedures Governing the Settlement of Disputes (15 December 1993) reprinted in 33 ILM 112 (1994) (setting up new procedures including an appellate process).

[90] To the extent that governments want to 'negotiate' solutions to disputes, they would, of course, continue to be free to do so. That the dispute process would not be available as a forum for such discussions is of little consequence. All of the governments at the WTO know how to set up intergovernmental meetings.

The practicalities of assigning seats in the audience for panel hearings represents an inconsequential administrative burden. Limited space might be allocated by lottery or given in turn to credentialed NGOs.[91] Any group that creates a disruption can be, and should be, barred from future WTO access.

Allowing NGOs to make submissions to the panels also would be constructive. In many cases, WTO dispute panels would benefit from having outside views available. In cases where the scope of a case goes beyond the boundaries of trade law, e.g., environmental questions or other scientific and technical issues are at play, non-governmental view points might be especially illuminating. Not only would NGO submissions thus be available to provide competing data, science, risk or cost–benefit analyses, and policy conclusions which would broaden the information base on which the panelist must rely, but the NGO participation in the decision process also would help to legitimize the panel's decision and broaden public acceptance of the outcome.

If rules prohibiting *ex parte* contacts with panel members are in place and all submissions must be in writing and open to scrutiny and rebuttal, the risk of manipulation by special interests is virtually non-existent. World Trade Organization decisions would rely on NGO submissions only to the extent that the arguments and information presented assists the members of the dispute panel with their analyses. The administrative burden would be easy to manage through page limits, form requirements, and the provision of legal assistants to the panelists in any case in which the outside submissions were large in number.[92]

World Trade Organization legislative functions

Defining the bounds of NGO participation in WTO policy development, review, and rule-making activities would require a somewhat more complicated structure. With respect to formal meetings such as the General Council or to the sessions of subgroups like the Committee on Trade and Environment (CTE), allowing NGO observers might broaden public understanding of the work of the WTO. If NGOs were permitted to watch the proceedings, they could, with their networks of contacts, help to disseminate information on policy issues under discussion. If they were given (carefully circumscribed) opportunities to present material, they also could add to the knowledge base of the WTO Secretariat and of the government officials participating in the work of the WTO.

[91] I would envision a credentialing process that gives WTO access to any non-governmental group that agrees to abide by the WTO's rules and procedures.

[92] Many models exist for such submissions, including the *amicus curiae* (friend of the court) procedures under US law. See Sup Ct R 37.

The risk of outcome manipulation by special interests is not especially serious in the course of formal meetings. The fact that information must be presented publicly, records are kept on what is said, and any material offered is open to scrutiny and debate minimizes the risk of inappropriate influence being exerted.

The real danger of special interest distortion comes from informal contacts and private meetings. Of course, lobbying by special interests of the WTO staff or national representatives occurs today. Establishing formal roles for NGO participation in WTO activities would not add to, and might even diminish, the risk of inappropriate pressure being brought to bear. In particular, if formal procedures for the airing of NGO views were in place, WTO officials could steer those seeking to meet with them privately toward these public sessions where attempts to win special favours would be harder to execute.

The opening of formal WTO meetings to NGOs also might present an opportunity to introduce lobbying disclosure requirements that mandate public reporting of all informal contacts between NGOs (including business as well as public interest groups) and WTO officials. At the same time, rules on gifts to officials also might be put in place. As the WTO matures into a more important element of our global governance structure, it is reasonable to expect that it will have to adopt operating procedures which improve the transparency and perceived fairness of its decision processes.

In any case, the salient fact is that excluding NGOs from the WTO does not shelter the organization from special interest manipulation. Likewise, establishing a formal role for NGOs within the WTO creates no *additional* risk of protectionist results emerging from the organization's decision processes. Thus, the argument that excluding NGOs creates a useful 'buffer' between decision-makers and special interest groups has no foundation whatsoever.[93]

Trade negotiations

Actual trade negotiations remain fundamentally a government-to-government bargaining process and thus present the strongest case for a measure of secrecy. Given the complexity of making trade deals and the added degree of difficulty 'open' negotiations would entail, WTO mandates on NGO involvement in negotiating sessions would be misguided. Whether national authorities want to share their negotiating positions and strategies with non-governmental entities must be left to each country individually. While many countries have found it useful to consult with interested parties in the course

[93] See Nichols, Realism, above n. 25 at 860.

of negotiations,[94] whether and how such discussions take place should remain a matter of national policy.

CONCLUSION

The WTO is emerging as an institution of considerable importance in the international economic realm. Managing the flow of trade, setting the boundaries for appropriate behaviour in international commercial transactions, and guarding the global economic system against market failures represents a significant responsibility.

If the WTO is to discharge its obligations in a way that builds legitimacy and respect and that minimizes market failures, it must take more seriously the opportunity represented by an active role for NGOs. Indeed, if the organization is to produce consistently 'correct' answers to the policy problems that it is asked to address, it must have input from NGOs. For the decisions that emerge from this body to be viewed as representative, authoritative, and fair, the WTO must provide mechanisms for expanded public participation in its decision-making processes.

In a co-operative role, NGOs can facilitate a flow of information to and from decentralized citizens and thereby diffuse concerns about the WTO's democratic deficit. In addition, by competing with governments in the WTO analytic realm, NGOs can help to ensure that the WTO makes well-informed and carefully considered decisions. While the risk of special interest manipulation of WTO decision-making is real and should be taken seriously, excluding NGOs from a formal role at the WTO does nothing to address the danger. Disclosure requirements and rules that spell out when and where lobbying is appropriate are the answer to this problem. In sum, a WTO that includes NGOs will be stronger, more durable, and better able to perform its essential functions.

[94] For example, the US Trade Act of 1974 provides mechanisms for consultation in trade negotiations. See Oscar C. Sattinger, 21 Am Jur 2d Customs Duties and Import Regulations § 20 (1981); see also Jonathan I. Miller, 'Comment, Prospects for Satisfactory Dispute Resolution of Private Commercial Disputes Under the North American Free Trade Agreement', 21 Pepp L Rev 1313 at 1313 n. 23 (1994) (discussing the extensive consultations with the private sector during NAFTA negotiations).

[27]

NAFTA and the Environment: Lessons for the Future

Howard Mann*

I. INTRODUCTION

In 1990, Mexico, the United States, and Canada (the Parties) began negotiating an agreement for a continent-wide free trade zone. The completion of negotiations for the North American Free Trade Agreement (NAFTA) in 1992 provoked what was probably the first major public debate on the relationship of trade to environmental issues.[1] Ultimately, after becoming a serious issue in the U.S. presidential campaign of 1992, the NAFTA process was re-engaged to develop two so-called side agreements, the North American Agreement on Environmental Cooperation (NAAEC), and another on

---

* Lawyer and consultant in Ottawa, Canada, specializing in international law for sustainable development; Associate with the Trade and Environment program of the International Institute for Sustainable Development; 1992-1993, Counsel to Environment Canada, acting as a negotiator and legal advisor with the Canadian delegation negotiating the North American Agreement on Environmental Cooperation. The views expressed here are solely those of the author, and do not necessarily reflect the views of Environment Canada or the Government of Canada.

1. *See* North American Free Trade Agreement, Dec. 17, 1992, Can.-Mex.-U.S., 32 I.L.M. 289 (pts. 1-3) and 32 I.L.M. 605 (pts. 4-8, annexes) [hereinafter NAFTA] (entered into force Jan. 1, 1994).

labor.[2] The environmental negotiation was the first multilateral negotiation between developed and developing countries specifically mandated to establish institutional and substantive linkages between the development and implementation of trade law, and the development and implementation of national or international environmental law.

This Article considers the results of the NAFTA environmental negotiations that concluded in the signing of the NAAEC. Part II of this Article begins with a look at the conceptual approach to international law, trade, and the environment that underlies this Article, focusing on these relationships in the context of the ongoing formulation of international law for sustainable development. Part III then discusses the events that led to the side agreements. Next, Part IV focuses on some precise examples of the linkages made between trade and the environment through the special environmental side agreement, with an eye to an initial evaluation of their success. These examples lead to some specific conclusions on the successes and failures of the NAFTA/NAAEC model as an integrative approach to trade and environmental issues. The Article concludes with some suggestions for integrating the trade and environmental issues in future negotiations.

The major conclusions of this Article can be summarized as follows. First, the NAFTA model has not yet led to a significant increase in the sensitivity of trade officials to the impacts of their work on environmental law and management. In some cases, the creation of a separate environmental organization appears to have actually slowed the process of achieving the necessary interaction on trade and environmental issues by allowing trade officials to argue that the environment is being addressed under another agreement. This has tended to solidify, rather than help break down, the "two solitudes" approach to trade and the environment often apparent at the global level.

A review of the success of the NAFTA model is extremely timely. Environmental and sustainable development issues have assumed a high public and political profile in recent events. Such issues were in the spotlight during the collapse of the Organization for Economic Cooperation and Development (OECD) negotiations for a Multilateral Agreement on Investment in October 1998, and in the

2. *See* North American Agreement on Environmental Cooperation, Sept. 14, 1993, Can.-Mex.-U.S., 32 I.L.M. 1480 [hereinafter NAAEC] (entered into force Jan. 1, 1994); *see also* North American Agreement on Labor Cooperation, Sept. 14, 1993, Can.-Mex.-U.S., 32 I.L.M. 1499.

aborted World Trade Organization (WTO) attempt to initiate a new round of multilateral trade negotiations in Seattle in December 1999.[3] Concurrent with these events, several environmentally related arbitration cases were initiated by private investors under Chapter 11 of the NAFTA.[4] These cases, and the failure of NAFTA institutions to address the issues they raised regarding environmental protection, have contributed significantly to supporting the legitimacy of the concerns of civil society groups that focus on environmental issues in the trade law arena. These events highlight the ability of environmental issues to become significant factors in the liberalization of trade and investment, potentially stopping such liberalization from proceeding further. Unresolved environmental implications also risk eroding the legitimacy of the existing agreements, as well as the public support for them.

II. THE CONTEXT: DEVELOPING INTERNATIONAL TRADE LAW FOR SUSTAINABLE DEVELOPMENT

Building linkages between trade law and environmental law and management is not an easy process. One reason is the lack of a broadly accepted underpinning for this task. This Article examines the NAFTA/NAAEC experience from the perspective of developing international law for sustainable development. But what does this mean? The brevity of this Article does not allow an extensive exploration of views on this question. It is relevant to refer to the general understanding of sustainable development recently espoused by the WTO Appellate Body (the Appellate Body) in the "Shrimp-Turtle" case, as it is popularly known: "This concept has been generally accepted as integrating economic and social development and environmental protection."[5] The Appellate Body at the same time declared that this concept informs all the WTO-covered agreements

3. *See* Marc Selinger, *Nations Drop Efforts on Global Investment Deal*, WASH. TIMES, Dec. 5, 1998, at CI, *available in* 1998 WL 3465468; Richard Gwyn, *Giving Voice to Our Fears About Seattle Trade Talks*, TORONTO STAR, Nov. 28, 1999, *available in* 1999 WL 24005870; *Seattle Trade Talks Suspended*, CINCINNATI POST, Dec. 6, 1999, at 3A, *available in* 1999 WL 21785789.

4. *See infra* notes 71-80 and accompanying text.

5. WTO Appellate Body Report, United States—Import Prohibition of Certain Shrimp and Shrimp Products, AB-1998-4, WT/DS58/AB/R, ¶ 129, n.107, 38 I.L.M. 118, 155 (Oct. 12, 1998) [hereinafter Shrimp-Turtle Appellate Body Report], *available at* (visited May 11, 2000) <http://www.wto.org/dispute/distab.htm>.

and applied it as a principle of interpretation to the terminology found therein.[6]

It is interesting to note that the Appellate Body did not articulate a static, definitional approach of the type that was used by the Brundtland Commission.[7] Rather, it adopted a more process-oriented, dynamic understanding, reflecting the role of "sustainable development as the over-riding policy objective" to be achieved over time.[8] Adopting a dynamic approach rather than a static one imposes specific responsibilities for the development of the different branches of international law being called upon to support this process, including trade law.

How can this dynamic approach be applied to the formation and implementation of trade law? The answer may have both negative and positive components. On the negative side, it should be clear that no trade body, whether the NAFTA, the WTO, or any other, should be developing either international or national environmental laws. These organizations do not have the expertise or the mandate to do so, and few would suggest such an expansion to environmental protection work.

On the positive side, while trade bodies should not make environmental laws, it is readily apparent that they have a large and growing influence on others whose function it is to protect the environment. Trade law itself has expanded enormously over the past twenty to thirty years, moving from its original focus primarily on tariffs to a much broader interplay with all forms of laws that do, or may, have an impact on trade in goods or services.[9] These areas of interplay include environmental and natural resource management, intellectual property rights, investment, government procurement,

---

6. *See id.* ¶¶ 129-31, 153-55; Howard Mann, *Of Revolution and Results: Trade and Environment Law in the Afterglow of the* Shrimp-Turtle *Case*, 9 Y.B. INT'L ENVTL. L. 28 (1998).

7. From 1983 to 1987, the World Commission on Environment and Development, headed by Gro Brundtland, the Prime Minister of Norway, conducted public hearings throughout the world to review the concept of sustainability. The "Brundtland Commission," as it is commonly known, defined sustainable development as "development that meets the needs of the present without compromising the ability of future generations to meet their own needs." THE WORLD COMMISSION ON ENVIRONMENT AND DEVELOPMENT, OUR COMMON FUTURE 43 (1987).

8. Günther Handl, *Sustainable Development: General Rules versus Specific Obligations*, *in* SUSTAINABLE DEVELOPMENT AND INTERNATIONAL LAW 37, 41 (Winfried Lang ed., 1995). This is the only article referenced by the Appellate Body in this context. *See* Shrimp-Turtle Appellate Body Report, *supra* note 5, ¶ 129, n.107.

9. Many recent developments are the results of the Uruguay Round of Multilateral Trade Negotiations. *See* Final Act Embodying the Results of the Uruguay Round of Multilateral Trade Negotiations, Apr. 15, 1994, LEGAL INSTRUMENTS—RESULTS OF THE URUGUAY ROUND, 33 I.L.M. 1125 (1994).

workplace health and safety, and more.[10] Given this expansion, trade negotiators and trade bodies must consider the consequences of their activities and rules on the environment, on environmental management processes and decision-making, and, more broadly, on sustainability issues.

This consideration needs to extend beyond the conventional use of trade laws and principles to prevent protectionist abuses of environmental laws. It must extend to a positive reflection, in the texts of the agreements, of the need to ensure that trade laws are, in practice, supportive of environmental laws and lawmaking. Preventing protectionist abuses through environmental laws may well remain a legitimate trade law goal, especially when protectionist practices are deployed "against" developing countries. Yet, preventing abuses should not be the only aspect of the relationship considered and, arguably, should not even be the predominant aspect trade bodies or negotiators consider in terms of their participation in developing the international and national infrastructure for sustainable development.

The very success of trade law underlies its importance in expanding the capacity of trade officials to consider trade law, not as an end in itself, but as a part of a broader, multifaceted international law geared toward achieving sustainable development. In particular, one has to appreciate international trade law's unique level of success in establishing a binding dispute resolution process with economic sanctions. The increased scope of trade law and its impacts on all areas of lawmaking, combined with its binding dispute resolution process, have given the trade law system what can be referred to as a quasi-constitutional (if not fully constitutional) legal status: Under threat of financial penalties, trade law requires governments to act in certain ways and to withdraw or modify certain measures when rulings go against them.[11] This quasi-constitutional status now applies

10. This interplay comes form different sources. One such source is the inclusion of new agreements under the WTO umbrella. *See, e.g.*, Agreement on Trade-Related Aspects of Intellectual Property Rights, Apr. 15, 1994, Marrakesh Agreement Establishing the World Trade Organization [hereinafter WTO Agreement], Annex 1C, LEGAL INSTRUMENTS—RESULTS OF THE URUGUAY ROUND, 33 I.L.M. 1197 (1994). A different source is the expanded coverage of more traditional trade law disciplines through such agreements as the Agreement on the Application of Sanitary and Phytosanitary Measures, Apr. 15, 1994, WTO Agreement, *supra*, Annex 1A, LEGAL INSTRUMENTS—RESULTS OF THE URUGUAY ROUND (1994); and the Agreement on Technical Barriers to Trade, Apr. 15, 1994, WTO Agreement, *supra*, Annex 1A, LEGAL INSTRUMENTS—RESULTS OF THE URUGUAY ROUND (1994).

11. For example, the WTO has wide-reaching supervisory power through its dispute resolution process, as evidenced in the Understanding on Rules and Procedures Governing the

even in countries where international law is not otherwise automatically of a constitutional nature, such as Canada.[12] The problem today is that, given this very significant quasi-constitutional role, trade law does not have the breadth of inputs necessary to adequately balance the trade values and approaches upon which it is based, with its impacts on other aspects of governance. Addressing this problem, it is submitted, is fundamental to trade law having the capacity to fully develop its role as part of the corpus of international law for sustainable development.

III. The Origins of the NAFTA/Environment Model

Environmental issues were considered in the initial discussions for structuring the NAFTA negotiations.[13] A major question was whether to have negotiations leading to one agreement that would encompass all trade and environmental issues, or to have two parallel but contemporaneous negotiations leading to two agreements.[14] The negotiators and members chose to take the "parallel tracks" approach; more precisely, the original design of the process was analogous to two parallel rails of the same train track, both beginning and ending their journey at the same time and place. However, when the negotiations finished in 1992, only one agreement was completed, the NAFTA, and while it did include some specific environmental provisions, the broader notion of parallel negotiations and agreements was never realized.[15]

The environmental train had been sidetracked, but it did not derail. To pursue the analogy further, it is useful to think of the children's book character, "The Little Engine That Could." Refusing to give up the battle no matter how steep the hill, the environmental train kept creeping forward. Fueled mainly by the 1992 presidential campaign in the United States, and to a lesser extent by Canadian elections anticipated throughout the spring of 1993, the negotiations

---

Settlement of Disputes, Apr. 15, 1994, WTO Agreement, *supra* note 10, Annex 2, LEGAL INSTRUMENTS—RESULTS OF THE URUGUAY ROUND, 33 I.L.M. 1226 (1994).

12. *See* David Schneiderman, *NAFTA's Takings Rule: American Constitutionalism Comes to Canada*, 46 U. TORONTO L.J. 499 (1996).

13. For a detailed review of the history of the environmental dimensions of the NAFTA, and of the trade law provisions with an environmental dimension in the NAFTA, see PIERRE MARC JOHNSON & ANDRÉ BEAULIEU, THE ENVIRONMENT AND NAFTA: UNDERSTANDING AND IMPLEMENTING THE NEW CONTINENTAL LAW (1996).

14. *See id.* at 24-34.

15. The NAFTA negotiations themselves were concluded in 1992, with no ancillary environmental accords. The negotiation of these separate agreements, as events unfolded, was to begin several months later. *See id.*

on the "environmental side agreement" began to catch up to the bigger, faster NAFTA train. For, while the NAFTA train had run most of its course, it was stalled short of its final destination: ratification by the United States Congress.

The inability of the NAFTA to receive approval in Congress without the environmental and labor components essentially overrode the orientations of the trade ministers and their negotiators not to include them in the original package concluded in 1992.[16] However, public and political pressure on the trade officials and negotiators finally helped "The Little Engine That Could" catch up, and the NAAEC was concluded in September 1993, with both trains reaching the ratification station and coming into force on January 1, 1994. Nevertheless, they were two very separate agreements, on separate tracks, not the close parallel rails first described and envisioned. From both the institutional and substantive perspectives, this put a high premium on their points of intersection or overlap.

IV. Some Specific Results of the NAFTA/NAAEC Model

A. *Making the Environment Count*

In retrospect, perhaps the most significant result of the NAFTA process was the nature of the public reaction to the trade deal in the United States and Canada, and to a lesser extent in Mexico. Instead of focusing on the minutiae of the agreement or the narrow interests of individual stakeholders as winners and losers, public reaction encompassed the broader issues of the relationship of trade agreements to, in particular, the protection of the environment and labor rights.[17] The need to address these areas as part of the NAFTA package reflected a wide, and early, public appreciation of the potential scope of impact of trade liberalization. What at the time seemed to this author like almost daily media coverage of the environmental and social problems in the Maquiladora special trading region along the Mexico-United States border solidified the largely negative public perception of the links between trade liberalization, the environment, and labor standards.

---

16. *See id.*

17. It is important to separate out two time periods here. The first is the period between the signing of NAFTA without the side agreements, for which this statement is particularly relevant. The second is the final stages of public debate after the side agreements were concluded in September, 1993, for which the statement may be somewhat less accurate. *See id.*; Daniel Magraw, *NAFTA'S Repercussions: Is Green Trade Possible?*, 36 ENV'T 14 (1994).

These concerns about the impact of trade on the environment led directly to the creation of the Commission for Environmental Cooperation (CEC) under the NAAEC.[18] The CEC is charged with addressing environmental issues per se from a continental perspective.[19] The CEC surely would not have been established so soon, if at all, without the impetus of the public reaction to the NAFTA. Although the organization is still young, the CEC does have the potential to achieve significant environmental results over the long run. An independent review of the operation of the CEC in 1998 noted its distinct roles as an environmental organization and as an organization with the mandate to link trade and environment issues.[20] The review stressed the need for both parts to succeed.[21]

The NAFTA negotiations also led to the creation of two Mexico-United States border institutions, the North American Development Bank (NADBank) and the Border Environmental Cooperation Commission (BECC).[22] Unlike the NAAEC and its institutions, these two bodies were given much more limited and functional mandates relating to the repair and improvement of the infrastructure in the border region.[23] While critical to environmental improvement in the region, and ultimately to achieving passage of the NAFTA, the mandates of these two bodies did not extend to the more general relationships of trade law and environmental management. Given that this latter area is the primary subject of this Article, these two institutions will not be part of the discussion below.[24]

---

18. *See* NAAEC, *supra* note 2, pt. III.

19. The broad environmental cooperation mandate of the CEC is set out mainly in Article 10 of the NAAEC. *See* NAAEC, *supra* note 2, Art. 10. The CEC functions as a traditional intergovernmental organization in this regard, acting by consensus; it has no independent, binding "lawmaking" capacity. *See id.* art. 9(6). Provisions relating to the enforcement of environmental laws, a key aspect of the environmental negotiations, are found in Articles 5, 6, 14-15, and Part V of the NAAEC.

20. *See* COMMISSION FOR ENVTL. COOPERATION, FOUR YEAR REVIEW OF THE NORTH AMERICAN AGREEMENT ON ENVIRONMENTAL COOPERATION: REPORT OF THE INDEPENDENT REVIEW COMMITTEE (June 1998), *available at* (visited May 11, 2000) <http://www.cec.org/pubs_info_resources/law_treat_agree/cfp3.cfm?varlan=english>.

21. *See id.*

22. Agreement Concerning the Establishment of a Border Environment Cooperation Commission and a North American Development Bank, Nov. 16, 18, 1993, Mex.-U.S., 32 I.L.M 1545 (1993).

23. *See id.* ch. I, art. I, § 2 (prescribing functions of the BECC); *id.* ch. II, art. I, § 2 (prescribing functions of the NADBank).

24. At the same time, it is recognized by the author that these two bodies do indeed play a large, and generally constructive role today, and can be seen as positive consequences of the public linkages drawn between the trade and environmental areas during the NAFTA debate. Indeed, in many ways, these two bodies, and the costs of the infrastructure projects they have promoted and/or financed, can be seen as having arisen as a consequence of the absence of trade

In essence, the political debate at the end of the NAFTA negotiations was a forerunner of the debate over the WTO that took place in Seattle and around the world, over the Internet and through other media, in November and December of 1999.[25] In the NAFTA process, environmental and other public interest groups were able to muster the political support to complete what they saw as lacking, or at least sufficient parts of what they saw as lacking, in the environmental and labor aspects of the agreement. The WTO trade talks in Seattle brought to a head increased antipathy towards trade negotiators either unwilling or unable to address these issues. Coming at what was intended to be the beginning of a new round of global trade talks, the outcry effectively delayed them, certainly now past the upcoming 2000 U.S. presidential election. In effect, the focus on the environmental and social dimensions attached to the regional NAFTA experience was expanded and applied very early in the effort to initiate an expanded global trade agenda.

B. *The Absence of Immediate Substantive Legal Linkages*

The NAFTA text expressly includes some substantive environmental provisions. Whether these constituted an improvement on previous trade law disciplines and made the NAFTA the "greenest" trade agreement need not be discussed here. Rather, given our present focus on the interaction between trade and environment regimes, it may be more useful to note the two types of environmentally related provisions that the NAFTA can be understood to contain.

1. Type 1

The first type of provision contains the traditional trade disciplines and their impact on environmental law and management practices. Examples of this type of provision include: (1) provisions identifying environmental protection as a legitimate purpose for which trade-impacting measures may be taken in relation to services, technical barriers to trade and sanitary and phystosanitary measures, and the conditions under which the measures might be taken;[26] and (2) a special provision that sets out a specific regime for

---

and environmental linkages being drawn in the design and implementation of free trade area along the border in the first place.

25. *See supra* note 3 and accompanying text.

26. *See, e.g.*, NAFTA, *supra* note 1, arts. 1201-05, 904-07, 712, 713, 715.

environmental measures taken pursuant to international environmental agreements.[27]

In its final form, the environment agreement contained no provisions designed to have an immediate legal impact on trade law disciplines or their application to environmental measures. It did, however, possess the potential to develop such linkages through the work program it created.[28] In the menu of broad cooperative functions given to the Council of the CEC (the Council) to work on,[29] two items are particularly noteworthy. Article 10 of the NAAEC lists among the Council's functions the ability to consider and develop recommendations addressing "the environmental implications of goods throughout their life cycles."[30] This was a euphemistic way to bring the vexing trade and environmental issue of nonproduct-related process and production methods within the scope of the CEC mandate. Article 10 also brings ecological labeling (eco-labeling) into the potential range of CEC functions and Council recommendations.[31] Both of these issues were the subject of much debate over trade law at the time of the conclusion of the NAAEC.[32] The wording of Article 10(2) provides the Council with the ability, but not the mandate, to place these issues on their agenda: "The Council *may* consider, and develop recommendations regarding" the environmental implications of goods and eco-labeling.[33] For those areas where recommendations are adopted, they are not legally binding on the parties as a matter of international law unless further adopted in the form of an international agreement.

To date, the most aggressive action of the CEC regarding product-life cycle issues and eco-labeling has been in the context of specific issues. This is best seen in the promotion of "green products," such as shade-grown coffee, bringing the environmental

27. *See* NAFTA, *supra* note 1, art. 104.

28. *See* NAAEC, *supra* note 2, art. 10.

29. *See id.* arts. 9-10 (defining the structure, procedures, and functions of the Council).

30. *Id.* art. 10(2)(m).

31. *See id.* art. 10(2)(r).

32. The discussions on NAFTA and the environment began shortly after the first General Agreement on Tariffs and Trade (GATT) "Tuna-Dolphin" case, which addressed U.S. measures to protect dolphins being killed as a consequence of certain tuna fishing methods and ruled that the measures were inconsistent with trade law. This case focused on both trade and environmental issues. *See* GATT Dispute Panel Report on U.S. Restrictions on Imports of Tuna, 30 I.L.M. 1594 (1991). The Tuna-Dolphin case was to become a *cause celebre* for environmentalists, developing countries, and many developed countries for much of the 1990s. *See Beyond the Agreements: The Tuna-Dolphin Dispute* (visited May 11, 2000) <http://www.wto.org/about/beyond5.htm>.

33. NAAEC, *supra* note 2, art. 10(2) (emphasis added).

dimensions of the production process together with the labeling of such products.[34] Activities such as this are largely touted under the rubric of "win-win" trade and environment issues, where trade promotion can be used to help promote environmentally sounder products.[35]

The CEC has not yet attempted to address the trade law disciplines relating to process and production methods and eco-labeling. The potential ability of the CEC to consider the substantive relationship of trade law disciplines to these issues is controlled through the decision-making approach established by the NAAEC: The Council can only enter into a review of specific issues if it has agreed by consensus to do so.[36] This requires a political consensus in the capitals of the three Parties as well as among the three Parties.[37] Government trade ministries can and do have significant input into what subjects the CEC actually addresses under its general mandate.

2. Type 2

The second type of substantive environmental provision found in the NAFTA is essentially limited to a nonbinding provision stating that the Parties should not waive or derogate from existing environmental protection standards, or their enforcement, in order to maintain or attract investment.[38] This provision was designed to address the concern that trade and investment liberalization would lead to a "race to the bottom" in environmental standards, with each party either deregulating or not enforcing standards in order to attract or maintain investments.[39] The nonbinding nature of the provision, however, left it open only to political consultations, rather than the

---

34. *See generally* Commission for Envtl. Cooperation, Supporting Green Markets: Environmental Labeling, Certification and Procurement Schemes in Canada, Mexico and the United States (1999), *available at* (visited May 11, 2000) <http://www.cec.org/pubs_info_resources/publications/enviro_trade_econ/labels.cfm?varlan=english>.

35. *See, e.g.*, Commission for Envtl. Cooperation, Report of the Informal Workshop of Experts and Government Officials on Environment and Trade 3-4 (1999) [hereinafter Informal Workshop Report] (on file with the *Tulane Environmental Law Journal*).

36. *See* NAAEC, *supra* note 2, art. 9(6).

37. *See id.*; *see also id.* art. 9(1) (providing that "cabinet-level or equivalent representatives of the Parties, or their designees," shall comprise the Council).

38. *See* NAFTA, *supra* note 1, art. 1114(2).

39. In an interesting analysis, Gareth Porter has recently considered the concept of "stuck at the bottom," as opposed to a "race to the bottom," as a more appropriate description of the environment-versus-trade/investment issue. *See* Gareth Porter, *Trade Competition and Pollution Standards: "Race to the Bottom" or "Stuck at the Bottom"?* 8 J. ENV'T & DEV. 133 (1999). While Porter's analysis is aimed mainly at developing countries, it may also be applicable in some areas in North America.

formal dispute resolution process otherwise applicable throughout the NAFTA.

The NAAEC, on the other hand, did create a direct overlap between the two regimes by making the effective enforcement of environmental laws mandatory.[40] The Article 5 obligation to "effectively enforce" environmental laws does not include a requirement to maintain any existing laws or regulations, nor does the agreement establish a specific substantive standard.[41] This policy followed from the presumption that underpinned most of the NAAEC negotiations: that the laws of the three Parties were roughly consistent, but that under-enforcement or nonenforcement was a major concern, at least in Mexico.[42]

In addition to making the enforcement of environmental laws mandatory, the NAAEC established two separate processes to monitor implementation of this obligation. One such process is the Citizen Submission process, which allows individual citizens or nongovernmental organizations in the three Parties to file a submission with the Secretariat of the CEC to review government actions aimed at enforcing a specific environmental law or group of laws.[43] The second mechanism is a more traditional state-to-state dispute resolution process that can lead to trade sanctions or pecuniary penalties against a party that persistently fails to effectively enforce its environmental laws.[44] This process has not been used to date, and the Parties are continuing to develop rules of procedure in the event it is used.[45]

40. *See* NAAEC, *supra* note 2, art. 5(1).

41. *Id.* The legal meaning of "effectively enforce" has not been clearly defined in the NAAEC or by the parties.

42. *See* JOHNSON & BEAULIEU, *supra* note 13; Magraw, *supra* note 17.

43. *See* NAAEC, *supra* note 2, arts. 14-15. The process does not lead to a determination of compliance or noncompliance with the enforcement obligation, but, if the process is followed to completion, the Secretariat may determine the facts surrounding government action or inaction in relation to the subject of the submission. Since 1995, 27 submissions have been received, one factual record has been completed, another is being developed, and the Secretariat has informed the Council that several other submissions warrant developing a factual record. Of this latter group of submissions, the Council of the CEC on May 16, 2000, voted to reject one recommendation for a factual record, suspend consideration of another recommendation, and accept a third, leaving several environmental groups to question the value of the process. *See* COMMISSION FOR ENVTL. COOPERATION, CITIZEN SUBMISSIONS ON ENFORCEMENT MATTERS—STATUS (visited May 11, 2000) <http://www.cec.org/citizen/status/index.cfm?varlan=english>; *see also* Barrie McKenna, *Environmental Probes Derailed by NAFTA Nations*, GLOBE & MAIL, May 18, 2000, at A-11.

44. *See* NAAEC, *supra* note 2, pt. V.

45. *See id.* art. 28(1) (providing that "[t]he Council shall establish Model Rules of Procedure" for dispute resolution). The preamble to CEC Council Resolution 99-06, adopted June 28, 1999, indicated that the process of developing the rules of procedure for Part V was

C. Other Process and Procedural Links

The enforcement of environmental laws provides a significant example of the substantive and procedural overlap that is possible between the environment and trade agreements, with the NAAEC turning at least part of the NAFTA's political obligation into an international legal obligation. The text of the NAAEC addresses other process and procedural issues, particularly in Article 10(6).[46] Article 10(6) is a critical point of intersection for the establishment and future development of the relationship between the NAFTA and the NAAEC, and between trade law and environmental law. It expressly calls for cooperative interaction on trade and environmental issues, particularly with regard to public access to the process and to dispute avoidance and resolution.[47] The CEC is called upon, inter alia, to: (1) act "as a point of inquiry and receipt for comments" on trade and environment issues;[48] (2) provide assistance in any consultations under NAFTA Article 1114(2) on issues concerning the possible waiver of or derogation from environmental standards in order to attract or maintain an investment;[49] (3) contribute "to the prevention or resolution of environment-related trade disputes by seeking to avoid disputes between the Parties, making recommendations to the Free Trade Commission [(FTC)] with respect to the avoidance of such disputes, and identifying experts able to provide information or technical advice to NAFTA committees" and

continuing. *See* COMMISSION FOR ENVTL. COOPERATION, COUNCIL RESOLUTION: 99-06, ADOPTION OF THE REVISED GUIDELINES FOR SUBMISSIONS ON ENFORCEMENT MATTERS UNDER ARTICLES 14 AND 15 OF THE NORTH AMERICAN AGREEMENT ON ENVIRONMENTAL COOPERATION (1999), *available at* (visited May 11, 2000) <http://www.cec.org/citizen/guide_submit/index.cfm?varlan=english>.

46. *See* NAAEC, *supra* note 2, art. 10(6).

47. *See id.* The language of Article 10(6) of the NAAEC is somewhat elliptical here, referring to cooperation of the Council and "the NAFTA Free Trade Commission to achieve the environmental goals and objectives of the NAFTA." *Id.* As there is no specific section in the NAFTA spelling out its environmental goals and objectives, and none are set out in the "Objectives" section of the NAFTA, *see* NAFTA, *supra* note 1, art. 102, one is left to consider the environmental dimensions established in the Preamble and other articles with an environmental aspect to establish the environmental goals and objectives of the NAFTA. This can be a somewhat difficult and tortured process, one that is beyond the scope of this Article. The concepts used in the present discussion take a fairly liberal view of these goals, drawing on the Preamble and the breadth of NAAEC Article 10(6) as a basis for doing so. *See* NAFTA, *supra* note 1, pmbl., art. 102; NAAEC, *supra* note 2, art. 10(6).

48. NAAEC, *supra* note 2, art. 10(6)(a).

49. *See id.* art. 10(6)(b). No such consultations have been sought since the NAFTA came into force in 1994.

other bodies;[50] and (4) otherwise assist the FTC on environmentally related matters.[51]

To date, neither the CEC nor the FTC has developed or utilized these cooperative opportunities, nor have they established systems for doing so. The implementation of Article 10 provides the clearest systemic example of the "two solitudes" approach suggested in Part I of this Article. As partners in a cooperative process, both the FTC and the CEC must make the necessary efforts. However, to date, trade officials, for the most part, appear to have taken quite the opposite approach: The trade agreement is the trade agreement and the environment agreement is the environment agreement, and there is little if any need for the environmental regime to address matters within the trade regime. In effect, the approach has been largely one of "keep your environmental hands off our trade agreement."[52]

As is the case with implementing the general policy mandate of the CEC, the development of relations between the FTC and the CEC, and of legal bridges between the two agreements, is not just a commission-to-commission issue. In reality, it is primarily a policy issue within government capitals. The consensus has not existed either within or amongst the three NAFTA capitals to enable environment Ministers or officials to address these issues in the CEC. This domestic political situation, however, also reflects the failure of the NAFTA/NAAEC model to promote a more constructive intersection of the trade and the environment arenas.

---

50. *Id.* art.10(6)(c). As part of its implementation program, the NAFTA established a series of committees, working groups, and other bodies to oversee the implementation of the existing obligations and/or to assist in the development of further obligations. *See, e.g.*, NAFTA, *supra* note 1, art. 913 (Committee on Standards-Related Measures), annex 913.5.a-1 (Land Transportation Standards Subcommittee), .a-3 (Automotive Standards Council). The CEC has identified a number of such committees or entities with environmental dimensions, including the automotive sector, and committees linked to more general chapters of the NAFTA, such as the Committee on Standards-Related Measures, all of which could potentially be cooperatively linked with the environmental expertise available through the CEC under Article 10(6) of the NAAEC. *See* NAAEC, *supra* note 2, art. 10(6)(c)(iii); COMMISSION FOR ENVTL. COOPERATION, ENVIRONMENT AND TRADE SERIES NO. 5, NAFTA'S INSTITUTIONS: THE ENVIRONMENTAL POTENTIAL AND PERFORMANCE OF THE NAFTA FREE TRADE COMMISSION AND RELATED BODIES 13-14 (1997), *available at* (visited May 11, 2000) <http://www.cec.org/pubs_info_resources/publications/enviro_trade_econ/insindex.cfm?varlan=english>. To date, however, the CEC has identified no experts, and the agencies and committees of the FTC have not sought environmental input.

51. *See* NAAEC, *supra* note 2, art. 10(6)(e). This final paragraph of Article 10(6) also supports a broad reading of the potential for interaction set out in the NAAEC.

52. This is subject, however, to some more recent efforts through a Secretariat initiative on trade and environmental issues, and the operation of a less than well-known CEC Article 10(6) Environment and Trade Officials Group composed of representatives of the three Parties. *See infra* Part VII.

Article 10(6) of the NAAEC also includes the CEC's own mandate to consider, on an ongoing basis, the environmental effects of the NAFTA.[53] Since the NAAEC and the NAFTA came into effect, this program mandate has resulted in the publication of six studies that provide a framework for analyzing the ongoing effects of the NAFTA.[54] However, attempts to measure these effects have achieved limited success, due in part to real difficulties in attempting to distinguish the effects of the NAFTA from those of other economic, political, or international trade law forces that have evolved over the same period.[55]

While success in quantifying the NAFTA's effects may be limited, such attempts are significantly more advanced than in the other areas of potential interaction between the two regimes. A critical factor is the difference between the two types of mandates involved. By the very nature of what is meant by cooperation, the first set of cooperative mandates requires the FTC to take a participatory role.[56] The FTC or, more specifically, the trade ministries have not been prepared to do this in any kind of systematic way. While a strict interpretation of the NAAEC would allow the Council of the CEC to initiate cooperative processes and recommendations without the support of the FTC, this is not politically feasible. By contrast, measuring the environmental effects

---

53. *See id.* art. 10(6)(d). It is important to recognize, as noted *infra* in the text accompanying note 57, that this is an independent mandate of the CEC, not one linked to cooperation with the FTC as an institutional requirement.

54. *See* COMMISSION FOR ENVTL. COOPERATION, ENVIRONMENT AND TRADE SERIES NO. 1, NAFTA EFFECTS—POTENTIAL NAFTA ENVIRONMENTAL EFFECTS: CLAIMS AND ARGUMENTS, 1991-1994 (1996); COMMISSION FOR ENVTL. COOPERATION, ENVIRONMENT AND TRADE SERIES NO. 2, NAFTA EFFECTS—A SURVEY OF RECENT ATTEMPTS TO MODEL THE ENVIRONMENTAL EFFECTS OF TRADE: AN OVERVIEW AND SELECTED SOURCES (1996); COMMISSION FOR ENVTL. COOPERATION, ENVIRONMENT AND TRADE SERIES NO. 3, DISPUTE AVOIDANCE: WEIGHING THE VALUES OF TRADE AND THE ENVIRONMENT UNDER THE NAFTA AND THE NAAEC (1996); COMMISSION FOR ENVTL. COOPERATION, ENVIRONMENT AND TRADE SERIES NO. 4, BUILDING A FRAMEWORK FOR ASSESSING NAFTA ENVIRONMENTAL EFFECTS: REPORT OF A WORKSHOP HELD IN LA JOLLA, CALIFORNIA ON APR. 29 AND 30, 1996 (1996); COMMISSION FOR ENVTL. COOPERATION, ENVIRONMENT AND TRADE SERIES NO. 5, NAFTA'S INSTITUTIONS: THE ENVIRONMENTAL POTENTIAL AND PERFORMANCE OF THE NAFTA FREE TRADE COMMISSION AND RELATED BODIES (1997); COMMISSION FOR ENVTL. COOPERATION, ENVIRONMENT AND TRADE SERIES NO. 6, ASSESSING ENVIRONMENTAL EFFECTS OF THE NORTH AMERICAN FREE TRADE AGREEMENT (NAFTA): AN ANALYTIC FRAMEWORK (PHASE II) AND ISSUE STUDIES (1999). All six studies are available at (visited May 11, 2000) <http://www.cec.org/pubs_info_resources/publications/all_pubs/index.cfm?varlan=english>. In addition to these six major studies, a number of working papers have also been published by the CEC in this area. *See generally Publications and Information Resources—CEC Publications* (visited May 11, 2000) <http://www.cec.org/pubs_info_resources/publications/all_pubs/index.cfm?varlan=english>.

55. *See generally* sources cited *supra* note 54.

56. *See* NAAEC, *supra* note 2, art. 10(6).

of the NAFTA was specifically mandated as a requirement for the CEC to undertake.[57]

The lack of progress in implementing Article 10(6) reflects the bifurcated nature of the trade and environmental regimes. Rather than promoting their constructive interaction, the separation of the FTC and the CEC has largely reinforced the division between the two. Trade officials perceive the environmental issues raised by the trade disciplines and other implementing provisions of the NAFTA as "our responsibility," and not as a matter of concern for the CEC or the Council. The view that predominates is that the CEC deals with environmental issues per se, while the FTC deals with trade issues, including environmental issues associated with the content of the trade agreement.

V. THE CONCRETE PROBLEM OF CHAPTER 11

It is useful to illustrate the general conclusions described above with the specific situation created by Chapter 11 of the NAFTA.[58] Chapter 11 concerns international investment and was emulated in the aborted attempt by the Organization for Economic Cooperation and Development (OECD) to develop the Multilateral Agreement on Investment (MAI).

The theory behind Chapter 11 is that when investors have security they are more inclined to invest in a wider range of countries, and therefore development is more likely to occur in more places. To Mexico, attracting investment was an important goal of the NAFTA.[59] And, indeed, the inclusion of Chapter 11 in the NAFTA is widely viewed as a critical factor in the rapid expansion of foreign direct investment in Mexico.[60] For Canada and the United States, Chapter 11 was attractive because it would provide protection to investors in Mexico, where the judicial process was generally considered corrupt or at least compliant with the will of the state.[61] Hence, Chapter 11

---

57. *See id.* art. 10(6)(d).

58. *See* NAFTA, *supra* note 1, ch. 11. *See generally* HOWARD MANN & KONRAD VON MOLTKE, INTERNATIONAL INST. FOR SUSTAINABLE DEV., NAFTA'S CHAPTER 11 AND THE ENVIRONMENT: ADDRESSING THE IMPACTS OF THE INVESTOR-STATE PROCESS ON THE ENVIRONMENT (1999), *available at* <http://iisd1.iisd.ca/trade/chapter11.htm >.

59. *See* Gloria Sandrino, *The NAFTA Investment Chapter and Foreign Direct Investment in Mexico: A Third World Perspective*, 27 VAND. J. TRANSNAT'L L. 259 (1994); MANN & VON MOLTKE, *supra* note 58, § 2.

60. *See* GOVERNMENT OF MEXICO, *Private Sector Shows Confidence in Mexico's Economy*, 4 NAFTA WORKS No. 3 (1999).

61. *See* MANN & VON MOLTKE, *supra* note 58, § 2, at 12.

was also seen as a good thing for businesses in Canada and the United States.

To deliver these benefits, Chapter 11 created the most expansive combination of rights and remedies ever given to the private sector in an international agreement. The rights are defined in a series of nine articles covering such matters as the right to national treatment,[62] the right not to have performance requirements imposed upon private investors,[63] the right to be treated in accordance with minimum international standards,[64] and protection against expropriation or measures tantamount to expropriation imposed against an investor without a proper public purpose and payment of full compensation.[65]

In order to support these rights, Chapter 11 provides a special remedy for foreign investors in the form of mandatory and binding arbitration.[66] The initiation of arbitration is subject to a preliminary ninety-day consultation period requirement and certain other fairly limited procedural requirements.[67] The process can be initiated at the sole discretion of the foreign investor.[68]

The problem that has appeared in relation to Chapter 11 arises from the combination of very broad but often vague rights along with mandatory remedies. The result has been described by one former U.S. trade negotiator as "unprecedented," "remarkable," and "an as yet untapped source of extensive private investor rights."[69] Other trade lawyers similarly referred it to as "revolutionary".[70]

62. *See* NAFTA, *supra* note 1, art. 1102; *see also id.* art. 1103 (providing for "most-favored-nation treatment"). The NAFTA-provided right to national treatment is similar to the traditional trade discipline of national treatment and prohibits discrimination against foreign investors by host states. *See id.* art. 1102.

63. *See id.* art. 1106. Performance requirements are obligations imposed on an investor, which require the investor to undertake all or some of its operations, purchasing, or sales in a specific manner as prerequisite to acceptance of the investment by the host country. *See id.* Additional requirements may also relate to foreign currency or corporate governance structures. *See id.*

64. *See id.* art. 1105.

65. *See id.* art. 1110. The full scope of this article is the subject of some debate, given that it actually includes three protections: protection from direct expropriation, indirect expropriation, and from measures tantamount to expropriation. *See* MANN & VON MOLTKE, *supra* note 58, § 3.7, at 38. The scope of these three terms is not defined.

66. *See id.* art. 1115.

67. *See id.* art. 1119.

68. *See id.* arts. 1116-17.

69. *See* Gary N. Horlick & Alicia L. Marti, *NAFTA Chapter 11B—A Private Right of Action to Enforce Market Access through Investments*, 14 J. INT'L ARB. 43, 53-54 (1997).

70. *See* Hope H. Camp, Jr. & Andrius R. Kontrimas, *Direct Investment Issues (Including Competition and U.S./Mexico Taxation Treaty)*, *in* NAFTA AND BEYOND: A NEW FRAMEWORK FOR DOING BUSINESS IN THE AMERICAS 87, 104 (Joseph J. Norton & Thomas A. Bloodworth eds., 1995).

As of December 31, 1999, some thirteen cases have been initiated under Chapter 11. Of these, eight relate to lawmaking or administrative decision-making in the environmental field by governments bound by Chapter 11.[71] In other words, environmental issues have been the subject of over half the actions brought to enforce Chapter 11 rights and remedies.

Four of these eight cases have arisen in Canada. As of the time of writing, Canada had withdrawn one piece of environmental legislation that effectively banned the import, and hence the use of, a specific gasoline additive, MMT,[72] following a Chapter 11 challenge by its sole manufacturer, the Ethyl Corporation of the United States.[73] In addition, Canada paid thirteen million dollars in compensation to Ethyl.[74] A second piece of Canadian legislation banning the transboundary movements of PCB wastes on a temporary basis is the subject of a pending Chapter 11 case.[75] Two other cases relating to the management of forest resources and fresh water are also pending.[76]

---

71. *See infra* notes 72-80 and accompanying text. Due to a lack of transparency requirements under Chapter 11, it is possible that more cases were initiated but remain unknown.

72. *See* Manganese-based Fuel Additives Act (MMT Act), S.C. 1997, ch. 11 (effective June 24, 1997), *available at* <http://canada.justice.gc.ca/cgi-bin/folioisa.dll/estats.NFO/query=*/doc/{@62651}?>. MMT is an acronym for "methylcyclopentadienyl maganese tricarbonyl."

73. *See* Ethyl Corp. v. Canada, Jurisdiction, NAFTA ch. 11 Arb. Trib., ¶ 6 (June 24, 1998) [hereinafter Jurisdictional Decision], *reprinted in* 38 I.L.M. 708 (1999); *see also* Alan C. Swan, Note, *Ethyl Corporation v. Canada, Award on Jurisdiction (Under NAFTA/UNCITRAL)*, 94 AM. J. INT'L L. 159, 159 (2000). The primary documents in the case include: Ethyl Corp., Notice of Intent to Submit a Claim to Arbitration Under Section B of Chapter 11 of the North American Free Trade Agreement (Sept. 10, 1996); Ethyl Corp., Notice of Arbitration Under the Arbitration Rules of the United Nations Commission on International Trade Law and the North American Free Trade Agreement (Apr. 14, 1997); Ethyl Corp., Statement of Claim (Oct. 2, 1997); Gov't of Canada, Statement of Defence (Nov. 27, 1997); Ethyl Corp. v. Canada, Place of Arbitration, NAFTA Ch. 11 Arb. Trib. (Nov. 28, 1997), *reprinted in* 38 I.L.M. 700 (1999). For a description of the settlement conditions, see *News Release: Government to act on Agreement on Internal Trade (AIT) Panel Report on MMT* (visited May 15, 2000) <http://www.ec.gc.ca/press/mmt98_n_e.htm>. MMT remains banned in over half of the states in the United States.

74. *See* Jurisdictional Decision, *supra* note 73, ¶ 18.

75. *See* S.D. Myers Inc., Notice of Intent to Submit a Claim to Arbitration Under Section B of Chapter 11 of the North American Free Trade Agreement (July 21, 1998); S.D. Myers Inc., Notice of Arbitration Under the Arbitration Rules of the United Nations Commission on International Trade Law and the North American Free Trade Agreement (Oct. 30, 1998); S.D. Myers Inc, Statement of Claim Under the Arbitration Rules of the United Nations Commission on International Trade Law and the North American Free Trade Agreement (Oct. 30, 1998).

76. The forestry resource-related claim is the *Pope & Talbot* case. *See* Pope and Talbot, Inc., Notice of Intent to Submit a Claim to Arbitration Under Section B of Chapter 11 of the North American Free Trade Agreement, (Dec. 24, 1998); Pope and Talbot, Inc. v. Canada, Executive Summary, NAFTA Investor-State Dispute Claim by Pope and Talbot, Inc. (forthcoming). The *Sunbelt Water* case concerns water exports. *See* Sunbelt Water Inc., Notice of Intent to Submit a Claim to Arbitration Under Section B of Chapter 11 of the North American

In Mexico, at least three cases relating to decisions made by environmental authorities have been challenged under Chapter 11. The first of these cases was recently decided in Mexico's favor.[77] The other decisions are pending.[78]

The United States, in June of 1999, received a notice of intent to submit a Chapter 11 claim from Canadian-based Methanex Corporation after the State of California adopted a law banning MTBE, a gasoline additive Methanex helps to produce, from being sold in California after the year 2002.[79] The claim in this case is for 970 million dollars.[80]

The issues relating to these cases are discussed in detail in a working paper of the International Institute for Sustainable Development (IISD), completed in June of 1999.[81] Beyond the individual cases, however, it is critical to understand the impact that Chapter 11 has begun to have on environmental authorities in the NAFTA countries. It is increasingly apparent that the private rights of foreign investors are being used not as a defensive protection against government abuse because an investor is a foreign-owned company, but as a strategic offensive threat to be wielded against government decision-makers rendering or considering decisions adverse to the interests of the company involved. The cases demonstrate the lobbying capacity attached to Chapter 11, a capacity never envisaged when the NAFTA negotiations took place.[82]

The IISD working paper concluded that, as a result of these aggressive uses of Chapter 11, environmental regulators must contend with vague rights supported by multimillion dollar claims against the

---

Free Trade Agreement (Nov. 27, 1998). A formal Notice of Arbitration had not, to this author's knowledge, been issued at the time of writing.

77. *See* Robert Azinian et al. v. United Mexican States, 14 ICSID (W. Bank) Rev.-FILJ 538, Case No. ARB (AF)/97/2 (Arb. Trib. 1999), *available at* (visited May 12, 2000) <http://www.worldbank.org/icsid/cases/mexico-e.pdf>.

78. As of the time of writing, the next anticipated ruling is in the case of *Metalclad Corp. v. United Mexican States*, ICSID (W. Bank) Case No. ARB(AF)/97/1. The final Mexican case is *Waste Management Inc. v. United Mexican States*, ICSID (W. Bank) Case No. ARB(AF)/98/2. For a list of cases pending before the International Centre for Settlement of Investment Disputes (ICSID), see (visited May 12, 2000) <http://www.worldbank.org/icsid/cases/pending.htm>.

79. *See* Methanex Corp. v. United States of America, Notice of Intent to Arbitrate, June 15, 1999; *see also* Samrat Ganguly, Note, *The Investor-State Dispute Mechanism (ISDM) and a Sovereign's Power to Protect Public Health*, 38 COLUM. J. TRANSNAT'L L. 113, 150-51 (1999) (discussing *Methanex Corp.*). A formal notice of arbitration was anticipated as this article was finalized.

80. *See* Methanex Corp. v. United States of America, Notice of Intent to Arbitrate, June 15, 1999; Ganguly, *supra* note 79, at 150.

81. *See* MANN & VON MOLTKE, *supra* note 58.

82. *See* ALAN RUGMAN ET AL., ENVIRONMENTAL REGULATIONS AND CORPORATE STRATEGY: A NAFTA PERSPECTIVE (1999) (documenting these strategic opportunities and uses).

actual or proposed decisions that regulators may make.[83] The result is the creation of a strong "regulatory chill" that is preventing regulators from taking steps they believe need to be taken to protect the environment. In essence, the uncertainty of the law combined with the potential amounts of the claims involved has created an atmosphere that is frustrating environmental management activities.[84]

The government of Canada raised the issue with the FTC in an effort to develop a special interpretive statement to address uncertainties in the text.[85] The NAFTA specifically authorizes such a statement.[86] The United States offered ambiguous support, while Mexico opposed the effort and continues to block any further discussions on the issue.[87] The situation remains unchanged despite the clear statement of the three environmental Ministers acting as the Council of the CEC. At its June 1999 meeting, the Council recognized the need to address this issue and that the avenues to do so, which are built into Chapter 11, do not require amending the NAFTA.[88] For the first time, the Ministers' annual communiqué as the Council of the CEC specifically addressed a NAFTA text-based issue, not suggesting a solution, but offering to assist in finding one.[89]

To summarize, the Chapter 11 story finds: (1) NAFTA obligations having significant impacts on environmental laws and lawmaking; (2) that such impacts were not intended, but are widely understood to have been accidental; (3) that, at minimum, the government of Canada and the United States Environmental Protection Agency have expressly supported taking action that is specifically permitted under Chapter 11 to address this situation; and (4) the Council of the CEC expressly sought to employ the broad cooperative framework of Article 10(6) in order to achieve such action.

83. *See* MANN & VON MOLTKE, *supra* note 58, § 6, at 62.

84. *See id.* § 2, at 12-18.

85. *See* Government of Canada, NAFTA Chapter 11 Issues Paper on Expropriation, *reprinted in* Nihal Sherif, *Canadian Memo Identifies Options for Changing NAFTA Investment Rules*, INSIDE U.S. TRADE, Feb. 12, 1999, at 1, 20-21; Government of Canada, NAFTA Chapter 11 Issues Paper on Transparency, *reprinted in* Nihal Sherif, *Canadian Memo Identifies Options for Changing NAFTA Investment Rules*, INSIDE U.S. TRADE, Feb. 12, 1999, at 1, 21-23.

86. *See* NAFTA, *supra* note 1, art. 1132(2).

87. *See* MANN & VON MOLTKE, *supra* note 58, § 1.4, at 10-11; Government of Canada, NAFTA Chapter 11 Issues Paper on Expropriation, *supra* note 85, at 1, 20-21; Government of Canada, NAFTA Chapter 11 Issues Paper on Transparency, *supra* note 85, at 1, 21-23.

88. *See* COMMISSION FOR ENVTL. COOPERATION, FINAL COMMUNIQUÉ, 6TH ANNUAL MEETING OF THE COUNCIL OF THE COMMISSION FOR ENVIRONMENTAL COOPERATION (1999) (on file with author).

89. *See id.*

The response to this situation has been the most specific rejection of a constructive interaction between the two regimes to date. Trade officials have simply closed the door to further discussion with the CEC on the matter. To some extent, this is due to the view on the part of Mexico that the existing cases will resolve the concerns. Perhaps a stronger Mexican goal is showing its commitment to investment liberalization by refusing to use any tools (other than the arbitration process) that might be seen as limiting the new rights of investors, given the success Mexico has experienced under Chapter 11. The Methanex claim against the United States has been initiated since the discussions ended, and there is an ongoing concern that regulatory action to protect the environment will continue to be hampered as a result of claims under Chapter 11.[90] Returning to a previous thought, the approach of the FTC and trade ministries has clearly been to maintain a distance between the CEC and the FTC on this issue: They continue to take a "keep your environmental hands off of our trade agreement" approach.

VI. Some Specific Lessons for Future Trade Negotiations

The conclusions reached in this Article are not based on an antitrade agenda and do not lead to a rejection of trade agreements. In this author's view, trade agreements will continue to play a very important role in broadening opportunities for achieving sustainable development. But increased trade is not the end in itself; rather, it is part of the means to an end of globally equitable and environmentally sound and sustainable development. A failure to address the full range of impacts of trade law on other issues that are equally critical to achieving sustainability, it may be argued, does not fully reflect this critical distinction between means and ends.

The failures of the NAFTA/NAAEC model should not tarnish its successes. The specific suggestions presented below are intended to address those failures. However, the most critical failure is also the area in which success is most necessary: the ability of the trade regime to understand and address its impacts on environmental management and protection. Five specific suggestions below address this concern.

First, an independent environmental impact assessment should be conducted for trade agreements as they are being developed.

---

90. *See supra* note 80; *How International Trade and Investment Rules Affect the Environment: A Look at the Gasoline Additive MTBE* (visited May 15, 2000) <http://www.nwf.org/nwf/trade/mtbe.html>.

Proposals and options to address all issues being negotiated should be considered for their various impacts, if any, on the environment and environmental management. This process should be independent of government because the dynamics within governments prevent one agency from publicly questioning the work of another. One suggestion is for a panel of independent, nonstakeholder experts to come together to act as "friends of the Chair" and advise negotiators of the environmental implications of various proposals. By integrating an assessment process into the ongoing negotiating process, a review will be timely, add value to the process, and help prevent unintended consequences, such as those resulting under Chapter 11. Assessment should not be left to individual governments or stakeholders to conduct after negotiations end. At that point there is virtually no hope for changes to be made because the size and complexity of agreements prevent reopening sections without the risk of the whole process collapsing as a result. If sustainable development is the overarching goal, this suggestion should be seen as a process that supports and complements the role of trade law in contributing to that goal.

This type of assessment should not be understood as opposed to development. Indeed, development opportunities will undoubtedly underlie most of the suggestions for further trade liberalization, which this Article does not argue against. It remains this author's view, however, that understanding and forestalling significant negative environmental consequences of trade agreements will contribute to sustainable development in a more, rather than less, equitable manner.

Second, the expansion of private sector trade rights and remedies should be approached with caution. Investment and market access security can have significant benefits, but remedies given uniquely to the private sector under international law that bypass domestic legal systems present significant risks. Trade officials have recognized that business stakeholders have self-interests that they need not balance against other interests, as governments must.[91] In such circumstances, providing rights and remedies, particularly in the absence of corresponding obligations, can lead to significant consequences. Again, a proper assessment of any proposals in this regard may help clarify desired goals and the means to achieve them without unanticipated consequences.[92]

91. *See, e.g.*, Jonathan Fried, *Globalization and International Law—Some Thoughts for Citizens and States*, 23 QUEEN'S L.J. 259, 274 (1997).

92. For some advanced thinking on this, see Konrad von Moltke & Howard Mann, *Misappropriation of Institutions: Some Lessons from the Environmental Dimension of the*

Third, the implementation process for trade agreements should mandate the use of independent environmental expertise in all committees or other agencies with an environmental dimension. The NAFTA/NAAEC model of an offer to identify appropriate expertise has failed to produce results. It is critical that decision-makers be informed of the environmental dimensions, including relationships to environmental management processes, of trade agreements at the time of the initial negotiation of those agreements, as well as at the implementation stage. It is here that the trade, development, and environment dimensions can most effectively be balanced.

Fourth, all actors must recognize that no technical fixes can address the political failure to integrate environmental issues into the mainstream of trade work. The events in Seattle demonstrated the costs of reluctance to do so. However, these costs are felt not only at specific negotiating junctures, but also when day-to-day decisions on implementing agreements are made in a manner that is not fully informed. The impact of trade agreements on sustainable development requires that the environment be treated as an issue that is "over here," inside the agreement, not "over there" in another agreement.

Finally, trade law must reconcile its scope of impact with what has been referred to earlier in this Article as its quasi-constitutional impacts. The European Union (EU) has addressed this constitutionalization problem by establishing a constitutional equality between trade and other values in the context of the expanding structures of the EU.[93] Under this process, the European Court, when considering any given trade issue, must also consider relevant environmental issues on equal footing. Trade principles and rules do not have automatic priority as they do when a tribunal deals only with issues raised by trade rules and considered from the perspective of those rules. Under the European model the trade origins of the union have expanded to reflect not just human rights, the first major social issue addressed on a pan-European basis, but nearly all areas of social and environmental governance.

European governance structures may not be appropriate for North America or for broader global arrangements. However, ensuring equivalent constitutional applicability for different values is

NAFTA Investor-State Dispute Settlement Process, *in* 1 INTERNATIONAL ENVIRONMENT AGREEMENTS (forthcoming 2000).

93. *See generally* Marina Wheeler, *Greening the EEC Treaty*, *in* GREENING INTERNATIONAL LAW 85 (Philippe Sands ed., 1994).

a critical issue that must be considered further if the development of an extended trade and investment regime is to be realized.

VII. CONCLUSION

As this Article was being finalized, the CEC held the first informal Workshop on Environment and Trade, bringing together trade, environmental, business, academic, and other professionals working in the field. The session covered four specific topics: the precautionary approach, building "win-win" economy-environment links, investment liberalization and the environment, and environmental assessments of trade.[94] It concluded with a discussion of the future agenda and role for the CEC in this area.[95]

This workshop was followed the next day by a private session of government officials from both trade and environmental departments. This closed session identified two areas for specific follow-up work: the precautionary approach and eco-labeling.[96] The FTC was to be formally involved in some aspects of this work, although the precise details and scope of this work had not been finalized at the time of writing.[97]

The workshop constituted the first major move toward a cooperative work product between the two halves of the NAFTA/NAAEC regime. As such, its importance should not be underestimated. The precautionary principle, in particular, is a highly controversial issue at the heart of the intersection of trade law disciplines and environmental management. The full scope of the work and its results remain, of course, to be seen. As a result, a review of the general conclusion that the NAFTA/NAAEC model has not succeeded to date in fostering a constructive interaction between trade law and environmental law and management must be awaited.

94. *See* INFORMAL WORKSHOP REPORT, *supra* note 35, at 1-6.

95. *See id.* at 6-7. The Secretariat prepared a background paper for the session that included independent presentations by nongovernmental participants. *See* COMMISSION FOR ENVTL. COOPERATION, BACKGROUND NOTE: INFORMAL WORKSHOP ON ENVIRONMENT AND TRADE (Dec. 13, 1999) (on file with author).

96. *See* Letter from Scott Vaughan, Head of Division, Environment, Economy and Trade, CEC, to Howard Mann, Consultant, IISD (Jan. 28, 2000) (on file with the *Tulane Environmental Law Journal*).

97. *See id.* (noting plans for a joint meeting of the CEC and relevant working groups and committees of the FTC to support work on eco-labeling and certification).

[28]

Journal of World Trade **35(4)**: 399–426, 2001.

A Global Environment Organization (GEO) and the World Trading System

C. Ford RUNGE*

I. INTRODUCTION

This article argues that a Global Environmental Organization (GEO) is an idea whose time will surely come. A GEO should be considered as one in a set of efforts to better coordinate international environmental policy, whilst protecting and insulating the World Trade Organization (WTO) from responsibilities for which it is both disinclined and unprepared. At the failed trade ministerial meeting in Seattle at the end of 1999, and at several subsequent international meetings, strident criticisms have been levelled at the WTO, IMF and World Bank, described as faceless international bureaucracies with programmes harmful to the environment.[1] Although hostile to multilateral institutions, these criticisms raise the obvious question: if not *these* institutions, then what others?[2] While many criticisms of the global economy and global institutions may have merit, it is hard to think of a future in which trade and global institutions, or issues of the natural environment, will play little or no part. Accordingly, the task is to *redefine* objectives in a global economy, and to *restructure* institutions to meet these objectives.

A GEO is an important part of this global institutional restructuring, and could play a major role in defusing criticisms of global institutions. Such global restructuring is necessary today at an international level, much as in the 1780s, the weaknesses of the Articles of Confederation in the United States were increasingly apparent at the national level. Madison, Hamilton and Jay (writing as "Publius" in *The Federalist*) recognized the need to persuade others that the nation would not endure without substantial institutional innovations. A central element in this school of thought was that free and unfettered commerce should be encouraged between states, coordinated by bodies

---

* C. Ford Runge, Distinguished McKnight University Professor of Applied Economics and Law, Center for International Food and Agricultural Policy, Department of Applied Economics, University of Minnesota. This article is based in part on a revised Policy Paper for the Center for Strategic and International Studies (CSIS), Washington, DC for the Twenty-first Century Commission on US Foreign Policy in a Globalized Economy. Reprinted with permission. "A Global Environmental Organization and the World Trading System," a CSIS Policy Paper by Ford Runge. © 2001 by the Center for Strategic and International Studies, Washington D.C. Thanks to Scott Barrett, Steve Charnovitz, Todd Sandler, Gregory Shaffer and Justin Ward for comments and suggestions. Responsibility remains with the author.

[1] For a critique of the Seattle debacle in the context of food security, see C. Ford Runge and Benjamin Senauer, "A Removable Feast", *Foreign Affairs* (May–June 2000) 39–51. For an environmental critic's view of Seattle see Henry Holmes, "The World Trade Take-Over", *Earth Island Journal* 14: 4 (Winter 1999–2000) 38.

[2] See John Mickelthwait and Adrian Wooldridge, *A Future Perfect: The Challenge and Hidden Promise of Globalization*, London: Heinemann, 2000.

which derived their authority from the consent of the same states. The concept of a GEO defended here has exactly such features, although the states are nations.

This article traces the evolution of the debate over a GEO, and analyses the problems and opportunities it poses for the world trading system. It considers the genesis of proposals for a GEO, and provides a short historical account (Section II). Next, it offers one view of what a GEO might entail (Section III). The following two Sections (IV and V) offer a brief summary of some of the main arguments for and against such a body. Section VI discusses issues of implementation, and the relationship between a GEO and existing institutions with environmental or trade responsibilities, such as UNEP and the WTO. It also considers whether a GEO should be built up incrementally, or whether a "grand stroke" would be more effective in establishing it. Section VII takes up three related issues: the role of developing countries, issues of sovereignty and the effective use of sanctions or conditionality. The eighth and final section is a summary and conclusion.

II. Genesis of Proposals for a GEO

In the early 1990s, transnational environmental policy challenges led to calls for a Global Environmental Organization (GEO).[3] By 2000, support extended from French Prime Minister Jospin and President Jacques Chirac to former WTO Director General Renato Ruggiero, the *Economist* magazine, and others.[4] Even so, many remain unconvinced of the need for yet another international organization.[5]

The argument for a GEO arose in the 1990s primarily from trade policy participants who felt that the GATT/WTO system was ill-equipped to respond when trade questions intersected with environmental issues. While sympathetic to stronger national environmental safeguards, they recognized that governments required coordinated multilateral responses to transnational environmental issues, not only when trade conflicts were apparent, but also where trade was largely unaffected. Even if the GATT/WTO system could be "greened," they felt that international environmental challenges required their own multilateral responses. Just as the GATT/WTO system had evolved out of growing *commercial* interdependence following World War II, and had helped to foster a set of rules by which the trade game should be played, so growing *ecological* interconnections now created the need for a set of global environmental rules.[6] The

[3] The idea of a GEO, broadly defined, is much older. Those who created the U.N. Environmental Programme (UNEP) envisioned it as a kind of GEO, and many UNEP advocates continue to see a new organization as unnecessary.

[4] Daniel C. Esty, "The Value of Creating a Global Environmental Organization," *Environment Matters*, Annual Review, Washington, DC. The World Bank, 2000.

[5] See, for examples, Calestous, Juma, "The Perils of Centralizing Global Environmental Governance", *Environmental Matters*, Annual Review, Washington, DC. The World Bank, 2000.

[6] See G. Maggi, "The Role of Multilateral Institutions in International Trade Cooperation", *American Economic Review* (March, 1999), 190–214. K. Bagwell and R.W. Staiger, "An Economic Theory of GATT", *American Economic Review* (March, 1999), 215–248. For a longer history of trade-environment interactions, see Charles S. Pearson, *Economics and the Global Environment*. Cambridge, UK, Cambridge University Press, 2000, pp. 258–306.

parallelism of trading rules and environmental rules arose from the fact that interdependent states could not cope with commercial *or* environmental challenges through unilateral or *ad hoc* solutions. A more stable and predictable system must be rule-based, although the coexistence of a set of multilateral trade and environmental rules would give rise to questions of priority and consistency.[7]

These calls for a GEO also emerged from criticisms of the impacts of trade liberalization on the natural environment in the debate over the North American Free Trade Agreement (NAFTA) during 1992 and 1993. The early phases of this debate found traders and environmentalists in hostile camps (where many remain). Environmentalists, influenced by a number of critiques of expanded economic growth on the natural environment, tended to equate trade, and thus growth, with pressures on natural ecosystems.[8] Traders, in contrast, focused on the potential role of environmental safeguards as non-tariff barriers to trade, the inevitable differences across nations in environmental regimes, and the necessity of income growth if environmental protection was to be afforded.[9] In addition, a growing number of multilateral environmental agreements (MEAs) stimulated discussion of the need for enforcement mechanisms, some of which involved explicit trade sanctions. This raised questions of how, and whether, such MEAs should be granted exceptions to the principles of the GATT articles.[10]

The politics of NAFTA brought these interests into sharp conflict, especially over the environmental degradation evident in factories along Mexico's pre-NAFTA free trade zone with the US NAFTA also brought into relief the north/south divide over environmental policy, with richer northern countries such as the US and Canada calling for higher levels of transborder environmental protection. LDCs such as Mexico perceived other motives in these calls, including old-fashioned protectionism disguised as "environmental conditionality". Many LDCs remain convinced that northern environmental restrictions will serve as non-tariff barriers to market access, or will condition such access on developing countries' adherence to costly environmental measures.

In the volatile political atmosphere of the 1992 US Presidential election, many Democrats were critical of NAFTA, while most Republican supporters attempted to protect the agreement from environmental criticisms or the opposition of labour. Given this political dilemma, a small number of scholars and a few environmental organizations saw an opportunity for linkage between trade and environment, proposing that an

---

[7] John Jackson, *World Trade and the Law of GATT*, New York: Bobbs-Merrill Co., 1969. John Jackson, "World Trade Rules and Environmental Policies: Congruence or Conflict?" *Washington and Lee Law Review* 49: 4 (Fall, 1992) 1227–1278.

[8] Herman E. Daly, "The Perils of Free Trade", *Scientific American* 269: 5 (November, 1993) 50–57.

[9] J. Bhagwati and T.N. Srinivasan, "Trade and Environment: Does Environmental Diversity Detract from the Case for Free Trade?" in J. Bhagwati and Robert E. Hudec (eds), *Fair Trade and Harmonization: Prerequisites for Free Trade? Vol. 1. Economic Analysis*. Cambridge: MIT Press, 1997.

[10] See discussion in C. Ford Runge (with Francois Orlalo-Magne and Philip Van de Kamp), *Freer Trade, Protected Environment: Balancing Trade Liberalization and Environmental Interests*, New York: Council on Foreign Relations Press, 1994; and Gary Sampson, *Trade, Environment and the WTO: The Post-Seattle Agenda*, Overseas Development Council, Policy Essay no. 27, ch. 6. Washington, DC, 2000.

"environmental protocol" be attached to the NAFTA treaty to safeguard and support environmental initiatives, especially in the US/Mexico border region.[11] Such a protocol could reassure NAFTA's environmental critics while preserving the gains from trade in the agreement itself. This proposal rapidly evolved into an environmental "side-agreement" (one of three ultimate side-agreements to NAFTA). Candidate Clinton, seeking a way to square pro-NAFTA and pro-environment positions, gave his support. While the government of Mexico regarded the side-agreement with considerable anxiety, their larger interest in expanded trade with a US economy 25 times the size of Mexico's caused them, after intense negotiations, to agree to its basic provisions. Despite fears of "protectionism in green disguise" and threats to its sovereignty, the promise of substantially expanded access by Mexico to the markets of the US and Canada ultimately proved too great a prize to reject the side-agreement.

The provisions of the side-agreement evolved from the environmental guarantees given by President George Bush in May 1991 in order to gain renewed trade negotiating authority for NAFTA and the GATT Round. On 16 September 1992, the environment ministers of Canada, Mexico and the US initiated a new round of negotiations directed at creating a trilateral North American environmental council. From April of 1993 until 13 August 1993, negotiations continued, leading to a signed side-agreement to the NAFTA text, the North American Agreement on Environmental Cooperation (NAAEC) on 13 September 1993.[12]

With the successful negotiation of the environmental side-agreement, a number of key environmental organizations threw their support to NAFTA, although a number continued to oppose it, some vociferously.[13] In the end, pro-NAFTA environmental groups helped garner sufficient support from Democratic members of Congress to ensure NAFTA's eventual passage. On 17 November 1993, NAFTA was ratified by the US Congress, together with provisions that would create the North American Commission for Environmental Cooperation (CEC), and it was signed by President Clinton on 8 December 1993.

The specific linkages from the side-agreement's NAAEC to the main NAFTA text (from which it remained separate), are worth noting in relation to the larger issues surrounding a GEO and world trade rules. The centrepiece of NAAEC was the creation

[11] C. Ford Runge and Peter Emerson circulated a memo proposing an environmental protocol in 1991. Emerson was the Environmental Defense Fund's point man on NAFTA, and headed EDF's Austin office. A similar proposal was circulated by Justin Ward, of the Natural Resources Defense Council (NRDC) in Washington, DC. Other groups, such as the Center for International Environmental Law (CIEL), the National Wildlife Federation, and Sierra Club were actively involved in debating whether a side-agreement could justify support for NAFTA. On the strategic structure of trade/environment linkages, see Grant Hauer and C. Ford Runge, "Trade–Environment Linkages and the Resolution of Transboundary Externalities", *The World Economy* 22: 1 (January 1999) 25–39.

[12] For a comprehensive history and assessment see Pierre Marc Johnson and André Beaulieu, *The Environment and NAFTA: Understanding and Implementing the New Continental Law*, Island Press, 1996. See also Steve Charnovitz, "NAFTA: An Analysis of its Environmental Provisions", *Environmental Law Reporter* 23: 2 (1993) 10067–10073.

[13] Among the dedicated opponents were Ralph Nader's Public Citizen, the Sierra Club, the Fair Trade Campaign, and Greenpeace. Environmental supporters included the Environmental Defense Fund (now Environmental Defense), the Natural Resources Defense Council, Conservation International, the National Wildlife Federation, National Audubon Society and World Wildlife Fund.

of the North American Commission on Environmental Cooperation (CEC), overseen by a small Secretariat headquartered in Montreal, with a budget of US$ 9 million—smaller than many academic departments. Despite its small size, its mandate extended beyond the trade effects of NAFTA on the environment, to include an array of transborder ecological issues. It also provided for a dispute settlement mechanism for environmental questions. From a legal perspective, NAAEC and the CEC derived from an executive agreement, which "steers clear of the normative realm and concerns itself with things institutional, primarily because it is the product of an intergovernmental process between entities that each want to set their own standards".[14] It was thus largely detached from the NAFTA trade agreement, seeking to achieve its goals primarily through new institutions to foster environmental cooperation and new environmental obligations.[15]

The dynamics leading to the NAFTA environmental side-agreement illustrated the double-edged nature of trade–environment linkages. On the one hand, the creation of the NAAEC and CEC showed that an implicit bargain is reachable between rich northern states and LDCs such as Mexico, in which environmental commitments are made by LDCs in return for expanded market access to the north. This process has been described as a win–win outcome for both trade and the environment.[16] But it also underscored the point that LDCs are generally unwilling and unable to make such commitments in the absence of the kind of growth in income which trade can bring.[17] Unfortunately, the same logic can be interpreted as a form of environmental conditionality, in which the engine of trade is hooked to environmental requirements which LDCs might well prefer to avoid. In the so-called "Tuna–Dolphin" dispute between the US, Mexico and other LDCs, for example, an embargo on dolphin-unsafe tuna was seen as a bald attempt by US interests (including the US fishing fleet) to close off market access until Mexico and other countries stopped the use of dolphin-unsafe (and lower-cost) fishing gear.[18] How trade–

[14] Johnson and Beaulieu, 1996, p. 128. The NAAEC was recognized under US Executive Order 12915 of 13 May, 1994.

[15] Ibid., p. 130.

[16] See David Vogel, *Trading Up: Consumer and Environmental Regulations in a Global Economy*, Cambridge: Harvard University Press, 1995.

[17] See Runge, 1994.

[18] *United States—Restrictions on Imports of Tuna*, GATT Doc. No. DS21/R, 3 September 1991. This US action was challenged by Mexico and several other GATT contracting parties as an unwarranted reach into the commerce of the embargoed nations, or "extrajurisdictionality". In the first case (*Tuna–Dolphin I*), neither the United States nor Mexico asked the GATT Council to adopt the decision, which found the United States in violation of the GATT Articles, in part because delicate NAFTA negotiations were under way. Subsequently, the European Economic Community requested a second dispute resolution panel (*Tuna–Dolphin II*) to review again the US restrictions on tuna imports from countries failing to meet provisions of the US Marine Mammal Protection Act (MMPA). On 20 May 1994, the panel found that the US embargo violated GATT prohibitions on quantitative restrictions and did not fall under any of the exceptions to the GATT's general obligations. However, as some environmental commentators noted, there are "significant differences between the analytical paths taken in the two decisions" (CIEL, 1994). Similar issues of "extrajurisdictionality" arose prominently in the *Shrimp–Turtle* case, in which the United States banned the importation of shrimp and shrimp products from countries found to be in violation of Section 609 of US Public Law 101-162, which authorizes such bans if sea turtles are caught and adversely affected incidental to shrimp fishing. In a report of a panel formed under challenge to the US action, the ban was found in violation of Art. XI:I of the GATT, and was not justified as an exception under Art. XX. The WTO Appellate Body reversed the finding concerning the application of Art. XX, and found that Art. XX(g), "relating to the conservation of exhaustible natural resources", did in fact apply, but that the US measure nonetheless failed to meet the requirements of the chapeau to Art. XX.

environment linkages are designed will thus affect their reception as either win–win outcomes or as economic leverage to wrest environmental or trade concessions.[19]

III. The Proposal: One View

One of the proponents of the NAFTA environmental side-agreement was Daniel Esty, who served under President George H. W. Bush's Administrator to EPA, William Rielly. After leaving the government, Esty wrote *Greening the GATT: Trade, Environment and the Future* (1994), which developed the argument for a GEO. At the same time, *Freer Trade, Protected Environment: Balancing Trade Liberalization and Environmental Interests* (1994) was published by the Council on Foreign Relations in New York, based on the work of the Council's Study Group on Trade and the Environment. In it, the present writer developed a case similar to Esty's, arguing that the CEC and NAFTA side-agreement could be generalized from a trilateral to a multilateral environmental secretariat. Such a body would function separately from, but in tandem with, the World Trade Organization (WTO).[20]

The basic design of a GEO advanced by Runge (1994) was composed of a Secretariat and a Multilateral Commission on Environment (MACE). The Secretariat would be the formal, ministerial-level body of government representatives, meeting periodically to affirm certain policies. The Commission would be a policy-oriented group of environmental experts drawn from NGOs, academia, business and government (see Figure 1). While the representatives to the GEO Secretariat would, like WTO representatives, be government officials, expert environmental and business involvement was also proposed, similar to the International Labour Organization (ILO), via the Commission. The Commission would thus be composed of a standing group of environmental experts, government and business representatives from all member countries. Its meetings would be open to the public, and would allow worldwide access to the data and analysis underlying its work. The primary focus of this work would be to propose ways to "harmonize up" national environmental standards, while carefully considering the technical issues and problems of this process for developing countries. The GEO Commission would issue regular reports and related documents proposing improved policies, identifying environmental "hot spots," and recommend special projects for national governments. This process would allow for public comments from

[19] See C. Ford Runge. "A Conceptual Framework for Agricultural Trade and the Environment – Beyond the 'Green Box'", *Journal of World Trade* 33: 6 (Dec. 1999) 47–68.

[20] Other early advocates of a GEO were Steve Charnovitz and Jeffrey Dunoff, who suggested modelling it on the International Labour Organization (ILO), as well as Geoffrey Palmer. See Steve Charnovitz, "The Environment versus Trade Rules: Defogging the Debate", *Environmental Law* 23 (1993) 511–517; Jeffrey Dunoff, "International Misfits: The GATT, the ICJ, and Trade-Environment Disputes", *Michigan Journal of International Law* 15 (1994) 1043–1127; Geoffrey Palmer, "New Ways to Make International Environmental Law", *American Journal of International Law* 86 (April, 1992) 259–283. See also Daniel C. Esty, "GATTing the Greens", *Foreign Affairs,* vol. 72, no. 5 (Nov/Dec, 1993) 132–136. More recently see John Whalley and Ben Zissimos, "A World Environmental Organization?" mimeo, University of Western Ontario, University of Warwick and National Bureau of Economic Research, October, 2000; and Frank Biermann, "The Case for a World Environmental Organization", *Environment* 42: 9 (November, 2000) 23–31.

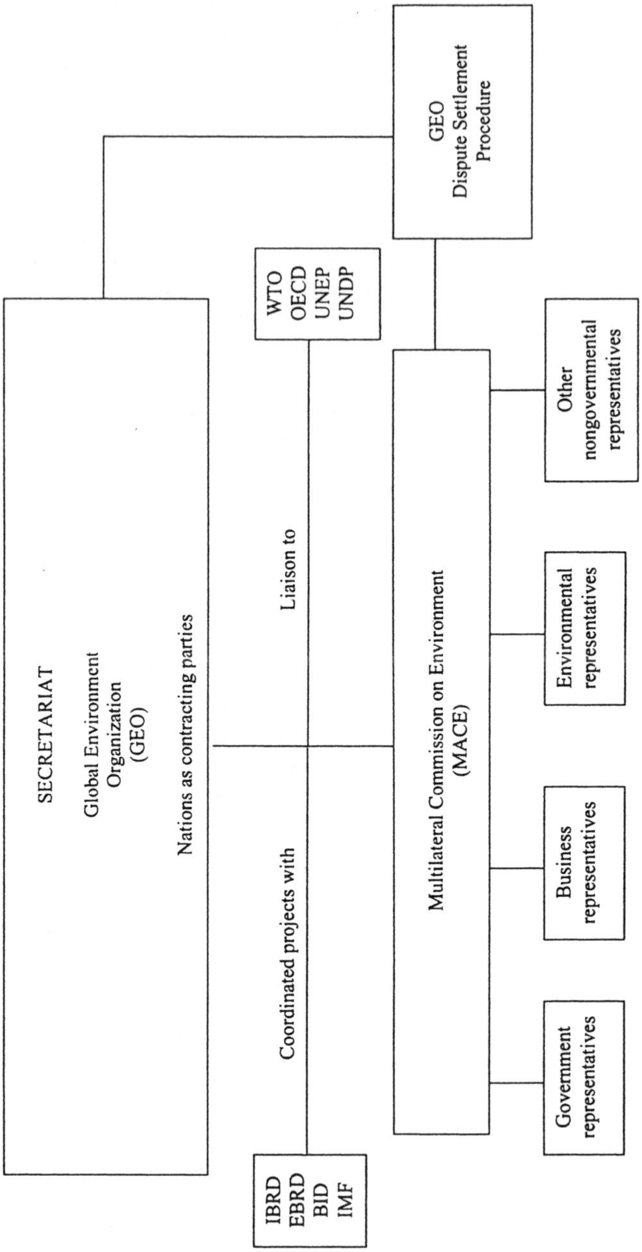

FIGURE 1: STRUCTURE OF A GLOBAL ENVIRONMENTAL ORGANIZATION (GEO) (ADAPTED FROM RUNGE, 1994)

any group, governmental or non-governmental. The effect would be to open the GEO Commission to full public participation and review.

The GEO and its Commission would work closely with the World Bank (IBRD) and other multilateral lending agencies, such as the European Bank for Reconstruction and Development (EBRD) and the Inter-American Bank (BID), as well as the International Monetary Fund (IMF), to develop funding for environmental projects to upgrade national infrastructure, especially for waste water treatment, sanitation, and hazardous waste disposal. National governments would be encouraged to establish an initial tranche of $10 billion for these purposes to operate on a revolving basis through the Global Environmental Facility.[21] This funding would focus primarily on projects in developing countries in Latin America, Asia, Africa, and in Eastern Europe and the former Soviet Union, where national resources for environmental improvements are most scarce.

The GEO would also work jointly with the WTO and the Organization for Economic Cooperation and Development (OECD) to identify trade measures that threaten environmental quality, and to develop environmental policies that are least burdensome to trade expansion. It could also serve as a general "chapeau" for the growing number of multilateral environmental agreements, such as the Montreal Protocol, just as the ILO serves as an umbrella over a large number of special labour agreements and arrangements. The overall effect would be to relieve the WTO of major institutional demands to accommodate a "green agenda." Since the WTO is not an environmental organization, and should not become one, a well-engineered GEO would reduce pressure to "reform GATT", which would be diverted constructively into the development of instruments directly aimed at environmental targets. In cases in which trade burdens due to environmental policies come before WTO dispute settlement panels, the GEO Commission would utilize its expertise to offer evidence, analysis, and proposed alternatives to the policies in dispute. In addition the GEO could have its own dispute resolution procedures, to be discussed in greater detail below.

While a highly elaborated plan will require a great deal of analysis and consultation, it is well to ask whether such an organization is really needed, in light of the UNEP and related work by development agencies such as the United Nations Development Programme and the Commission on Sustainable Development created as a result of the 1992 Rio Conference. While supplementing and drawing on the work of these groups, knowledgeable observers and participants still support a

[21] The Global Environmental Facility was launched in 1991 as a three-year pilot programme to allow for actions where no international agreement had yet been negotiated. It is jointly managed by the World Bank, the United Nations Environment Programme, and the United Nations Development Programme. Its role was further elaborated at the 1992 Rio Conference, and it has complex links to the Biodiveristy and Climate Conventions, as well as to the Montreal Protocol. Its further role, however, is still the subject of debate among all of the organizations involved. See Kenneth Piddington, "The Role of the World Bank", in Andrew Hurrell and Benedict Kingsbury (eds), *The Institutional Politics of the Environment: Actors, Interests and Institutions.* Oxford: Clarendon Press, 1992, pp. 212–227.

GEO.[22] The late Elliot Richardson argued forcefully in the context of climate change for a permanent environmental multilateral body, whether a "beefed-up UNEP" or an entity patterned on the WTO, noting that "it may not make a crucial difference whether an old agency is given new duties or a new one is brought into existence".[23] As Richardson argued, a GEO

> "would create substantial incentives for member states to improve their environmental performance. Nongovernmental organizations would be watching, exhorting and pushing. Domestic awareness of the national effort would be heightened by the international attention it attracted. Media coverage would be correspondingly intensified. The attention thereby focused on the government's response would generate pressure to raise its level. It is arguable, indeed, that the self-reinforcing process thus set in motion could become a formidable substitute for official action—more effective than regulation and far less expensive than its enforcement. If this happens, what has generally been called 'soft law' will become progressively harder".[24]

The linking of the environmental activities of a GEO to market access and trade reform in the WTO, the OECD, and the multilateral lending agencies would also create additional incentives for LDCs to support it. Susskind and Ozawa have noted that "environmental negotiations, up to now, have been conducted largely in isolation from negotiations on other international issues such as debt, trade, or security". Linking these issues properly can enhance the potential for mutual gains, since "the goal of a well-structured negotiation is not to encourage compromise but to find ways of ensuring that all parties will be better off if they cooperate".[25] How such linkage occurs is important, and will be considered in the sections to follow.

IV. The Arguments in Favour

The argument for a GEO was thus built around a number of common themes. The first was that the GATT/WTO institutions were unable and largely unwilling to shoulder major environmental responsibilities in conflicts between trade and the environment. This argument has been supported by developments inside the WTO throughout the 1990s. The WTO, concerned over the use of environmental measures as trade barriers, had been stung by criticisms from environmentalists of various WTO

[22] For a discussion of the role of the UN agencies in global environmental affairs, see Peter S. Thacher, "The Role of the United Nations", in Hurrell and Kingsbury, *International Politics*, pp. 183–211. A cautionary note on the need for new institutions in the context of NAFTA is given in Stephen P. Mumme, "New Directions in United States–Mexican Transboundary Environmental Management: A Critique of Current Proposals", *Natural Resources Journal*, vol. 31 (summer 1992) 539–562. The range of supporters for a GEO has nonetheless continued to expand.

[23] Richardson's analysis and call for a Multilateral Environmental Agency was developed in the context of climate change, although the arguments he advanced are general ones. See Elliot L. Richardson, "Climate Change: Problems of Law-Making", in Hurrell and Kingsbury, *International Politics*, pp. 166–182.

[24] Richardson, "Climate Change", ibid. pp. 176–177.

[25] Lawrence Susskind and Connie Ozawa, "Negotiating More Effective International Environmental Agreements", in Hurrell and Kingsbury, *International Politics*, pp. 110–141. See also Scott Barrett, "International Agreements for the Protection of Environmental and Agricultural Resources: An Economics Perspective", London: London Business School, 1992.

rulings, notably the *Tuna–Dolphin* and *Shrimp–Turtle* cases.[26] Concerned that it show some response to environmental critics, the WTO General Council created a Committee on Trade and the Environment (CTE) in 1995. The CTE was set up to follow the recommendations of the Ministerial Decision on Trade and Environment adopted in 1994 in Marakesh.[27] While defenders of the CTE claimed that it demonstrated the "greening" of the WTO, it faced a barrage of criticism after release of its heavily negotiated report to Ministers in Singapore in December 1996.[28] It had, critics argued, failed to recommend modifications in multilateral trade rules "to enhance a positive interaction between trade and environmental measures ... ".[29] It was precisely the unwillingness of trade ministers to redefine trade rules for environmental ends that revealed their essentially (and understandably) conservative posture. Sampson argues that the Singapore report of CTE shows how wary trade officials are of entering into environmental policy. Instead, those who have the appropriate environmental expertise—both nationally and internationally—should play a larger role. However, this introduces the question of how they should play such a role.

In general, the CTE's limited terms of reference clearly indicated an unwillingness by the WTO to venture too far into the environmental domain. As Sampson notes: "WTO members do not want a role in environmental policymaking and enforcement, nor do they take lightly changing rules that could give them this role."[30] In short, the members of the WTO and its secretariat in Geneva have not been enthusiastic about assuming added responsibilities for the environment. Only in those cases in which trade is explicitly affected by environmental measures is the WTO likely to become engaged.[31] Moreover, many environmentalists mistrust the capacity and willingness of WTO panels or trade ministries to give sufficient weight to environmental concerns. This leaves a substantial institutional gap both in terms of trade-related environmental measures and transnational environmental issues posing global challenges of policy coordination which can only be filled by a separate body such as a GEO.[32]

[26] See note 20 above.

[27] See Gary P. Sampson, *Trade, Environment and the WTO: The Post-Seattle Agenda*, Overseas Development Council, Policy Essay No. 27 pp. 26–29. Washington, DC, 2000. Shaffer (2001) emphasizes that the motivation behind the CTE was not simply pressure from groups concerned over the environmental impact of trade but primarily fears by WTO members, especially LDCs, over the growing number of environmental regulations with potential trade effects. From the point of view of trade ministers the latter dominated the former. See Gregory C. Shaffer, "The World Trade Organization Under Challenge: Democracy and the Law and Politics of the WTO's Treatment of Trade and Environment Matters", *Harvard Environmental Law Journal* 25: 1 (2001). All citations of pages are to the manuscript version.

[28] Steve Charnovitz, "A Critical Guide to the WTO's Report on Trade and the Environment", *Arizona Journal of International and Comparative Law* 14: 2 (1997) 341–378.

[29] Sampson, note 27, p. 27.

[30] Sampson, note 27, pp. 27–28.

[31] Even in such cases, the WTO is wary of an explicit environmental role. In the famous *Shrimp–Turtle* dispute, the appellate body of the WTO ruled that the US should have sought an international environmental agreement to deal with fishing practices, rather than bringing the matter before the trade body as a result of a trade embargo. See Sampson (2000), p. 83 and note 7 on p. 98.

[32] Esty (1994, p. 80) refers to this gap in terms of a "lack of parallelism" between trade and environmental institutions at the international level and as an asymmetry in the rules of trade versus those for environment, under the general heading of "institutional imbalance".

A second argument in favour of a GEO concerns these transnational challenges, which are often described as "global public goods", and which may or may not have direct linkages to trade.[33] Issues such as atmospheric ozone pollution, degradation and loss of plant genetic resources, transboundary shipments of hazardous wastes, and threats to endangered animal and plant species are all examples of such problems. Because they respect no national boundaries, their solution requires joint participation and commitments by sovereign states. Absent a "global Leviathan," agreements must be reached which call upon each affected country in the "global commons" to adopt policies that contribute to a general solution.[34] Thus far, the mode adopted most often is a multilateral environmental agreement (MEA), such as the Montreal Protocol (1989) respecting atmospheric ozone, the Cartagena Protocol (2000) respecting biosafety and plant genetic modification, the CITES agreement (1972) respecting endangered species and the Basel Convention (1992) respecting hazardous wastes.

Each of these MEAs has important provisions which raise questions over their compatibility with international trade rules. The Montreal Protocol, with 161 signatories, requires bans or phase-outs on any production of ozone-depleting substances, including chlorofluorocarbons. Signatories are prohibited from trading in these products with any non-signatory that cannot prove that it otherwise meets the requirements of the protocol. The Cartagena Protocol respecting biosafety created an informed agreement procedure for importing or exporting living organisms that have been genetically modified, allowing countries to restrict market access to these products. The Convention on International Trade in Endangered Species (CITES), with 132 signatories, bans trade in either live endangered species or the parts of dead ones. The Basel Convention, with 113 signatories, imposes bans on trade in hazardous wastes for final disposal between OECD countries and non-OECD countries.[35] The UNEP's *Register* lists more than 200 multilateral agreements (including protocols and amendments) on environmental issues.[36] The four cited above are perhaps most salient in respect to trade restrictions, but many others have the potential to run afoul of WTO rules. While it is arguable that such MEAs are an adequate response to these environmental problems, two fundamental questions arise. First, should the MEAs themselves somehow fall outside the trade disciplines of the GATT/WTO system, or

[33] See Inge Kaul, Isabelle Grunberg and Marc A. Stern, *Global Public Goods: International Cooperation for the 21st Century*, New York: Oxford University Press, 1999; Todd Sandler, *Global Challenges: An Approach to Environmental, Political and Economic Problems*, New York: Cambridge University Press, 1997.

[34] See Oran Young, *The Effectiveness of International Environmental Regimes: Causal Connections and Behavioral Mechanisms*. Cambridge: MIT Press, 1999.

[35] Sampson, 2000, note 5 on p. 98, citing Donald M. Goldbery *et al.*, *Effectiveness of Trade and Positive Measures in Multilateral Environmental Agreements: Lessons from the Montreal Protocol*, Washington: CIEL, 1998; Dale Andrews, *Experiences in the Use of Trade Measures in CITES*, Joint Session of Trade and Environmental Experts, OECD/GD (97) 106, Paris: OECD, 1997; Jonathan Kreuger, *The Basel Convention and Transboundary Movements of Hazardous Wastes*, Briefing Paper No. 45, Royal Institute of International Affairs, London, May 1998.

[36] See United Nations Environment Programme, *Register of Treaties and Other Agreements in the Field of the Environment*, Nairobi, 1991; and UNEP, *Environment and Trade: A Handbook*, International Institute for Sustainable Development, Winnipeg, Canada, 2000. See also Andrew Hurrell and Benedict Kingsbury (eds), *The International Politics of the Environment: Actors, Interests, and Institutions*, Oxford: Clarendon Press, 1992, note 20 on p. 10.

(especially when they involve explicit trade measures or sanctions) are they in fact in violation of the principles of free trade? Second, can the hundreds of existing MEAs, and the scores which can be anticipated in the coming decades, be adequately managed without creating an institutional umbrella to help oversee the linkages among them, and their potential conflicts with WTO rules?

The first question relates primarily to the scope and application of the "exceptions clause", or GATT Article XX.[37] A subsection (Article XX(g)) allows for agreements concerned with the "conservation of exhaustible natural resources" to be treated as an exception to the general GATT/WTO principles of non-discrimination and reciprocity "if such measures are made in conjunction with restrictions on domestic production or consumption". If this or other subsections of Article XX, such as those related to "human, animal or plant life or health" in Article XX(b), are interpreted broadly to apply to most MEAs, then actions undertaken to protect the environment may distort trade and still be allowed so long as they are "necessary" (i.e. alternative measures are not available or practicable). But this broad interpretation of Article XX, supported by many environmentalists as one form of "environmental window", is viewed with extreme apprehension in trade circles. Such a wide window invites the use of MEAs as non-tariff barriers to trade, leading to environmental protectionism rather than environmental protection. These concerns have been advanced, for example, in relation to the 2000 Cartagena Protocol on biosafety and genetically modified (GM) plants, which seems to allow for trade restrictions on the basis of wide application of the somewhat ill-defined "precautionary principle".[38]

A more conservative approach, creating a case-by-case environmental window, would be to provide for waivers to WTO rules for some MEAs, renewable over regular time intervals.[39] Such waivers would require a supporting vote by three-quarters of the WTO Contracting Parties. However, the presumption that trade ministers should vet each MEA would seem to place them in regular and recurring judgment of environmental policy measures, a position which they have said they prefer to avoid.

In practice, the WTO has been very gingerly in granting exceptions to environmental measures under Article XX, since many of the cases brought involve questionable efforts to disguise protectionism as conservation.[40] In general, the right to

---

[37] For an early treatment, see Steve Charnovitz, "Exploring the Environmental Exceptions in GATT Article XX", *Journal of World Trade* 25 (October, 1991) 37–55.

[38] See C. Ford Runge and Lee Ann Jackson, "Labeling, Trade and Genetically Modified Organisms: A Proposed Solution", *Journal of World Trade* 33 (6) (2000) 111–122.

[39] See Sampson, 2000, pp. 95–97.

[40] See, for example, the US/Canada dispute over salmon and herring catch and count limits. In this case, Canada demanded that US salmon and herring boats land and have their catch fully counted in Canada before proceeding to canneries and further processing. The United States argued that this policy was not necessary to conserve exhaustible natural resources under Article XX(g), as claimed by Canada, and was an unjustified burden on the commercial conduct of the US fisheries industry. After a series of disputes, settlement panels heard the case (under both the US–Canada Free Trade Agreement and the GATT/WTO process), and the US position was upheld. This case illustrated a clear line of reasoning from a finding of trade burden to a lack of justification for the burden in terms of environmental protection. For a discussion, see Runge, 1994, pp. 80–87.

invoke an exception has been granted only if it applies within the country taking the action, and not if it involves measures that reach into other countries, such as embargoes or border restrictions. This, of course, fails to answer the important question: what if MEAs *must* have such extrajurisdictional reach in order to respond to transboundary environmental challenges?[41]

The second question, related to the first, concerns the arguable need for an umbrella organization overarching the proliferating number of MEAs. As noted in the previous section, a GEO secretariat, comparable to the WTO secretariat in Geneva, would offer such a "chapeau". It could help to coordinate disparate environmental efforts and MEAs, and function as a go-between and buffer relating MEAs or other environmental policies to the GATT/WTO system. One function, for example, could be to help design MEAs (and national environmental programmes) with minimal trade-distorting effects, and to help advance market-based environmental initiatives such as trading schemes. When obvious conflicts with GATT/WTO rules arose, a GEO could help to prepare sound arguments in favour either of an Article XX exception, based on the necessity of trade measures in an MEA, a waiver if deemed appropriate, or some other GATT-legal "window" allowing an exception for the environmental measure. An even more significant function might be the consolidation of claims made under myriad environmental agreements into a unified dispute settlement process, in which NGOs and other interested parties could participate.

A third argument in favour of a GEO arises from the need for exactly this kind of independent authority in international environmental policy making. In many circles, this has been termed the "targets and instruments" issue.[42] A principle of economic

[41] Other possible "environmental windows" have been explored in various WTO cases. For example, another justification for environmental measures appears in the chapeau, or headnote, to Article XX, relating to "unjustifiable discrimination" or a "disguised restriction" on international trade. These justifications have been developed in the light of recent cases before the Appellate Body of the WTO, notably the *Reformulated Gasoline* cases, in which a US claim that a discriminatory regulation had been enacted for a *bona fide* regulatory purpose was rejected because the United States had alternative measures available that could have accomplished the regulatory objective without employing discrimination. When the discriminatory element of a regulation is found to be unnecessary to the policy objective it is meant to serve, that measure can be classified as "unjustified discrimination" or a "disguised restriction" to international trade (Hudec, 1998, p. 638). The issue also arose in the *Shrimp–Turtle* case (see note 20 above). Yet another basis for justifying environmental measures derives from Article 2.2 of the 1994 Standards Code, which discusses "unnecessary obstacles" to trade. Although the WTO dispute settlement system has not rendered any decisions applying the Article, it appears to be especially useful in relation to measures that are neutral on their face (or "origin neutral") but in which *de facto* discrimination is alleged; in contrast to *de jure* discrimination, which could be handled more readily under Article XX (Hudec, 1998, p. 644). A final basis for justifying environmental measures related to food quality and health risks in the food system, of especial relevance to new issues of biotechnology and genetically modified organisms, is the Sanitary and Phytosanitary (SPS) Agreement made in the Uruguay Round. Controversy currently surrounds the application of the SPS Agreement to the risks that may be posed by genetically modified (GM) foods, and whether measures designed to ban imports of GM products can be justified by demonstrating that they might promote plant or insect pests, antibiotic resistance, or other threats to human, animal or plant life or health. See Michael Trebilcock and Julie Soloway, "International Trade Policy and Domestic Food Safety Regulations: The Case for Substantial Deference by the WTO Dispute Settlement Body Under the SPS Agreement", paper presented at the Conference, "The Political Economy of International Trade", University of Minnesota, 15–16 September 2000.

[42] See C. Ford Runge, "A Conceptual Framework for Agricultural Trade and the Environment: Beyond the 'Green Box'", *Journal of World Trade* 33: 6 (December, 1999) 58–63.

planning developed by economist Jan Tinbergen (1950) is that in general each target of policy merits a separate instrument. This principle can be interpreted to mean that environmental targets are generally best met first by environmental policies, and trade targets by trade policies. If an appropriately balanced combination of environmental and trade policy measures is found, the result can be gains both from the trade reforms *and* from improvements in the level of environmental quality. In general, therefore, some *combination* of trade and environmental policies will be most efficient. Conversely, the advantages of trade policy reform can be lost if appropriate environmental actions are not undertaken jointly.[43]

Precisely because an independent entity such as a GEO is lacking, a greater temptation exists to use trade measures to enforce environmental obligations, violating the targets and instruments principle and threatening the world trading system. Trade interests may condemn the use of such measures for environmental goals (such as dolphin-safe tuna), but in the absence of effective multilateral environmental rules and an overarching entity such as the GEO, environmentalists will claim that they have no recourse. Here it is useful to remember that by structuring a separate institutional entity in the form of the NAAEC and the CEC, Canada, Mexico and the US were honouring the principle of separate instruments and attempting to disentangle environmental from trade politics.

It is naive to imagine that these two realms of policy can be entirely disjoint, but the creation of a GEO would assist in separating many issues that do not need to be in conflict. However, the weaker the perceived ability of environmental groups to influence international policies, the greater their incentive to use "linkage" destructively: to threaten the trading system in order to gain environmental concessions.[44] By drawing environmental expertise and energy into the functioning of a GEO, the GATT/WTO system would be largely left to pursue its own trade agenda, mindful of environmental concerns, and in cooperation with a GEO secretariat, but not as a functioning "green" trading body.

Together, the three arguments described above constitute the core rationale for a GEO. They are: (1) the unwillingness and inappropriateness of the GATT/ WTO system as a centre for transnational environmental expertise and activity; (2) the widespread number of environmental issues which are inherently multilateral because of their scale and multiple jurisdictions, making them "global public goods" which cannot be adequately managed through existing agencies or ever-proliferating and uncoordinated MEAs; and (3) the logical necessity of separate institutional authority for what are substantively separate environmental problems,

---

[43] Kym Anderson, "The Standard Welfare Economics of Policies Affecting Trade and the Environment", in K. Anderson and Richar Blackhurst (eds), *The Greening of World Trade Issues*, New York: Harvester-Wheatsheaf, 1992; Kerry Krutilla, "Environmental Regulation in an Open Economy", *Journal of Environmental Economics and Management* 20 (1991) 127–142.

[44] Grant Hauer and C. Ford Runge, "Trade-Environment Linkages in the Resolution of Transboundary Externalities", *The World Economy* 22: 1 (January, 1999) 25–39.

which pose a set of targets for policy that require their own instruments at an international level.[45]

V. The Arguments Against

The arguments against a GEO may be grouped around three main claims. The first is that it is unnecessary—that existing institutions, suitably augmented, are adequate to respond to transnational environmental challenges. The second is that it is unwieldy—another international bureaucracy which may prove just as unresponsive as existing ones to the concerns and interests of member states and may actually challenge their sovereignty over national environmental issues. The third, and most potent, is that its creation would reflect the same "rich man's club" priorities which, in the view of many LDCs, have dominated the GATT/WTO system, tilting its functioning toward priorities of the north rather than the south.

The first is that the panoply of existing UN agencies, NGOs and MEAs together constitute a sufficient response to transboundary environmental issues. These include the UN Environment Programme (UNEP), the UN Commission on Sustainable Development (CSD) and the hundreds of MEAs noted above. Others include the UN Development Programme (UNDP), the World Bank, the World Meteorological Organization (WMO) and the Global Environmental Facility (GEF). In addition, a growing number of NGOs, such as the World Resources Institute (WRI) in Washington, DC, the World Wildlife Fund (WWF), and the Center for International Environmental Law (CIEL) have become active participants in the trade/environment agenda.[46] Juma (2000) notes that because of the diversity of environmental problems, specialized institutional responses are often required, reflected in the MEAs and other agreements that deal with these questions issue by issue. While coordination may be desirable, "centralization" is not.

The second claim levelled at a GEO is that it is likely to be an unwieldy and unresponsive international bureaucracy which simply adds another layer to the many and diverse responses to global environmental problems noted above. Below the surface of this argument are GEO opponents who are relatively comfortable with their

[45] In a brief opposed to a GEO, Calestous Juma, 2000, asserts that Esty's arguments in favour revolve around "administrative efficiency" claims. A careful reading of Esty's 1994 volume, and the arguments developed here suggest that administrative efficiency, even if improved by a GEO, is not a central argument in its favour, especially in light of the struggles it would face from existing UN agencies.

[46] For a broad analysis of an emerging global culture, see John Boli and G.M. Thomas (eds), *Constructing World Culture: International Nongovernmental Organizations Since 1875* (1999). Cited in Schaffer, 2000, note 13. See also Barbara J. Bramble and Gareth Porter, "Non-Governmental Organizations and the Making of US International Environmental Policy", in Hurrell and Kingsbury, *International Politics*, pp. 313–353. See also Nancy Lindboug, "Non-Governmental Organizations: Their Past, Present and Future Role in International Environmental Negotiations", in Lawrence E. Susskind, Eric Jay Dolin, and J. William Breslin (eds), *International Environmental Treaty Making*, Cambridge, Mass.: Harvard University Program on Negotiation Books, 1992; Daniel C. Esty, "Non Governmental Organizations at the World Trade Organization: Cooperation, Competition or Exclusion", *Journal of International Economic Law* 12: 3 (1998) 135–137. For a more critical evaluation of the role of NGOs, see Peter Spiro, "New Global Potentates: Nongovernmental Organizations and the 'Unregulated' Marketplace", *Cardozo Law Review* 18: 3 (1996) 957–969.

influence over existing institutions, and who fear that they would lose this influence in a new body. These groups include not just bureaucrats at bodies such as UNEP, but state agencies and NGOs as well. It is arguable that member states of any multilateral body, as well as stakeholders such as environmental NGOs, seek to capture it for their own purposes. Such investments in capture, once made, are defended against new and uncertain prospects.[47] A GEO that is less subject to capture, and therefore "unresponsive", is also less subject to special interests. By increasing the scope for coordinated approaches to global environmental issues, a GEO may reduce opportunities for exercising such influence, and thus arouse concerted opposition from defenders of the *status quo*.

A related issue concerns the many national agencies and ministries to which existing MEAs and agreements are tied back. At an administrative level, the authority for various aspects of international environmental policymaking emanates from these different parts of national governments. In the United States, while the Executive Office of the President is ultimately responsible, duties for international environmental policy are parcelled out across a large number of executive agencies, from the Environmental Protection Agency (EPA), to the National Oceanic and Atmospheric Administration (part of the Department of Commerce), the State Department, Department of Energy, Office of the US Trade Representative, and Department of Agriculture among others. Each agency will defend its role in *status quo* agreements against any "coordination" that diminishes it.[48]

The third and most potent forces arrayed against a GEO are developing countries convinced that it may force northern priorities on southern interests. These include not only environmental goals regarded as lower priorities in LDCs, but trade protection in "green" disguise. As Juma (2000, p. 15) notes, "many developing countries are concerned that a new environmental agency would only become another source of conditions and sanctions". These concerns were amply revealed in the WTO's Committee on Trade and Environment (CTE). In opposing even the formation of the CTE, spokesmen for ASEAN such as Thailand, and other LDC representatives from Morocco, Tanzania and Egypt all questioned the need for it. Shaffer (2001) notes that none of them wanted "to be pressured into signing an environmental side-agreement analogous to NAFTA's".[49] When the CTE agenda was finally settled, it reflected a variety of issues of direct concern to LDCs, notably a cluster of issues that linked LDC environmental initiatives to the achievement of expanded access to northern markets.[50]

---

[47] See Shaffer, 2001, note 27. A more recent analysis of the links from domestic political interest to trade and environment issues at the international level is Gregor Shaffer, "WTO Blue-Green Blues: The Impact of US Domestic Politics on Trade-Labour, Trade-Environment Linkages for the WTO's Future", *Fordham International Law Review*, forthcoming 2001.

[48] See, for example, "Administration Unclear on Policy for WTO Environment Committee", *Inside US Trade* 26 Jan. 1996 for a discussion of internal dissension over goals and responsibilities in the CTE.

[49] Shaffer, 2001, p. 10.

[50] Ibid., p. 14.

However, even these concessions did little to assuage nervousness of LDCs concerning the possible growth of environmental conditionality. Of particular concern was the widespread sense that environmental demands would join similar demands by labour interests in the north to justify shutting off LDCs' market access, a view reinforced by the political alliances struck between greens and labour on display during the trade protests in Seattle in late 1999 and at subsequent world economic fora. Discussing the idea of opening the Article XX exceptions to broaden allowances for environmental measures, for example, Brazil's Deputy Permanent Representative to the WTO stated in 1998 that "We [developing countries] cannot be in favour of a change in Article XX. We think that this would create an imbalance in terms of a whole set of disciplines and commitments and would set a precedent for other issues." As Shaffer notes, the other issues he had in mind were trade restrictions based on "unfair" labour standards.[51] It is particularly noteworthy that Mexico, after acceding to the NAFTA environmental side-agreement with the US and Canada, led the opposition to many US proposals in the CTE. When the US delegation questioned whether Mexico's representatives to the CTE were speaking for the Mexican government, Mexico City quickly confirmed that these opposing views were indeed official positions.[52]

In summary, three major claims raise questions over the possibility of successfully launching a GEO. They are (1) that existing bodies and agreements respecting international environmental issues are adequate, and do not require a centralized overarching entity; (2) that a GEO would, in any case, be unwieldy, simply adding another layer of bureaucracy to existing agencies and groups, most of whom will oppose any attempts at coordination that diminishes their influence; and (3) that most LDCs will oppose any new body which may pressure them to conform to higher environmental norms or standards or risk reduced access to northern markets. Together, these three claims pose serious challenges to a GEO, requiring that any successful argument in its favour demonstrate (1) that existing arrangements are *not* in fact adequate and that coordination may not imply centralization; (2) that a GEO can be implemented in a way which accommodates existing institutional arrangements; (3) that LDCs' suspicions and reservations can be overcome.

A final reservation, somewhat external to the question of a GEO *per se*, concerns the prospects for a new MTN round. In the two years since the breakdown of talks in Seattle in December 1999, forward progress has been slow, although various working groups and WTO committees continue to meet. In part, this is the result of various election cycles, especially in the US. It is clear that the new US administration will support renewed efforts at liberalization, and will have different priorities and approaches than its predecessor. Rewriting and recasting a script for a new trade round

[51] Shaffer, 2001, p. 21.

[52] Interview with Ricardo Barba, Deputy Permanent Representative to the WTO from Mexico, quoted in Shaffer, 2001, p. 26.

will take time, and Congress must be prepared to extend trade negotiating authority. Meanwhile, other trading blocs and nations are showing increasing irritation with the way the US and EU have handled the liberalization process. Countries in Asia, for example, are moving to rebuild their economies through numerous bilateral and multilateral trade pacts, and Latin economies are not far behind. In 1990, there were 50 regional trade groupings compared with 200 today, and 70 are under discussion.[53]

It is far from clear how a GEO, and "green trade" issues generally, might fit into a new round, and whether enthusiasm for them will be found in the new US administration or among developing countries. Unless LDC interests and concerns can be confronted realistically and fully, and real commitments made to them for greater market access, whatever progress might occur towards a GEO may result from bilateral or regional commitments rather than a multilateral deal. Even here, the prospects seem dim. Although President Bush signalled a desire to move rapidly towards a hemispheric US free trade agreement after the April 2001 summit in Quebec City, the Latin countries have been among the most vocal opponents of environmental or labour conditions attached to such accords.[54] The probability that bilateral or regional agreements will lead to a GEO thus seems remote.

An alternative model, suggested by a recent bilateral deal, is the US free trade agreement with Jordan, which incorporates labour and environmental provisions in the main text, but essentially calls on both parties to observe and enforce their own national environmental norms and standards.[55] The "Jordan model" was proposed for prospective US agreements with Singapore and Chile late in the Clinton Administration. However, these proposals prompted a harshly worded letter from the Republican leadership to the White House in December 2000, warning that internalizing labour and environmental provisions in bilateral trade deals "will severely undermine the ability of the next president to craft a bipartisan trade program".[56]

In one respect, however, opposition to the "Jordan model" may actually improve the prospects for a separate entity such as a GEO. Charnovitz has compared a GEO to an expanded and strengthened International Labour Organization (ILO). As suggested in previous sections, like the ILO, a GEO might be organized to reflect business, environmental and governmental representation.[57] Echoing this idea, some Republicans have recently argued that business might favour moving environmental issues into a separate body in a manner similar to ILO's treatment of labour disputes. The essential question is whether such an approach, in which environmental issues are

53 Elizabeth Olson, "Regional Trade Pacts Thrive as the Big Players Fail to Act", *New York Times*, 28 Dec. 2000. p. W1.

54 Edward Alden, "Bush Faces Huge Trade Divide", *Financial Times* 3 January 2001, p. 5.

55 Sherman Katz. Center for Strategic and International Studies, Washington, DC, personal communication, 10 December 2000.

56 Quoted in Edward Alden, note 54 above.

57 Steve Charnovitz, "Environmental Harmonization and Trade Policy", in Durwent Zaelke (ed.), *Trade and the Environment: Law, Policy and Economics*, Washington, DC: Island Press, 1993. A more fully developed comparison of a GEO and the ILO is contained in Frank Biermann, "The Case for a World Environment Organization", *Environment* 42: 9 (November 2000) 23–31.

linked but separate, necessarily implies the creation of a body such as the GEO, at the same level as the ILO.

VI. Issues of Implementation

It is clear that the creation of a GEO would pose difficult issues of implementation, among them: (1) What duties of existing bodies would be assumed by a GEO, and what would these bodies then do? (2) What new responsibilities would be assigned to a GEO by its members, and by whom would these duties be performed? (3) What would be the relationship between a GEO and the WTO? While no definitive answers can be given to these complex legal and administrative questions in an article of this length, some general comments are in order.

First, it is probable that a GEO would assume some of the responsibilities of UNEP and the Commission on Sustainable Development (CSD). This is in part, Esty (2000) argues, because UNEP as a programme agency "tries to do too much".[58] The CSD is similarly overstretched. In addition, there are responsibilities of the UNDP and the World Bank related to environment and development in which the GEO might assist, assuming development projects remained the province of these groups. The GEO could, for example, assist in the planning of expanded irrigation schemes involving interbasin and/or international transfers of water so as to minimize environmental disruptions. A major function of the GEO would be to provide a transparent source of information on global environmental issues, assisting what is now often the task of NGOs. As currently arranged, Esty (1999, p. 1564) notes that someone attempting to track environmental decisions at the WTO "would find out a great deal more by reading newsletters from the World Wildlife Fund than communiqués from the Office of the US Trade Representative".[59] Although groups such as UNEP and even some NGOs might feel threatened by a GEO, it is probable that enough work will remain to keep every group fully engaged in international environmental affairs. However, to the extent that budgetary resources are drawn off existing agencies and programmes to support a GEO, internecine competition will be intense.

The new responsibilities assigned to a GEO are of special importance in developing a rationale for its creation. As noted above, one of these would be to offer a "chapeau" for the growing number of MEAs, especially in the context of dispute settlement. While it can be argued that each MEA responds to different needs and

---

[58] UNEP has recently been reorganized under its executive director, Klaus Töpfer, former German environment minister. Even so, its weaknesses have led other international bodies such as the UN Food and Agriculture Organization (FAO) and the UN Educational, Scientific and Cultural Organization (UNESCO) to initiate their own environmental programmes. As Biermann (2000, p. 25) observes, "it remains to be seen whether this incrementalism in strengthening UNEP will deliver the necessary results in the future or whether more fundamental reforms are needed."

[59] Daniel C. Esty, "Toward Optimal Environmental Governance", *New York University Law Review* 74: 6 (Dec. 1999) 1495–1574. Indeed, the total budget resources devoted to these efforts by NGOs considerably exceed those of sub-agencies in UNEP responsible for environmental information. Shaffer (2001, p. 32 note 97) notes that Greenpeace's annual income in 1998 was $125 million, and that of the World Wildlife Fund was $53 million.

constituencies, there is a strong argument for coordinating many of these efforts. This does not imply any necessary changes in the MEAs, or in the lines of authority stretching back to national governments. One analogy is the role played (since 1967) by the World Intellectual Property Organization (WIPO), headquartered in Geneva. The WIPO was established in part to help unsnarl the "treaty congestion" that surrounded intellectual property and patent rights, and to help rationalize and coordinate these efforts.[60]

It is also arguable that a GEO would help to offset the perception in LDCs that MEAs and exceptions granted to WTO contracting parties under GATT Article XX or other headings are heavily tilted in the direction of the northern states. The Indian NGO Centre for Science and the Environment, for example, has "characterized the use of trade measures in MEAs as an inequitable lever available only to stronger countries".[61] As noted above, so long as this perception continues, southern countries will remain sceptical of global environmental initiatives. Yet a GEO may be precisely the mechanism needed to give added weight to these southern concerns.

One of the most pressing needs, at present unmet, to which a GEO could contribute is preparation and technical support available to developing countries in the formulation of trade, development and environmental initiatives. If a GEO is to succeed, it must treat these needs as of paramount importance. In particular, a GEO should take as its responsibility the implementation of the primary principles emerging from the 1992 Rio Declaration on Environment and Development (ostensibly the current responsibility of the Commission on Sustainable Development):

- that developing and developed countries have differing responsibilities to enact domestic measures to protect the environment;
- that international transfers are necessary to assist developing countries to upgrade their environmental protection measures;
- that unilateral measures are to be avoided.[62]

In the context of a GEO, these three principles have the following implications:

(1) A form of "special and differential treatment" in environmental policies is to be expected as part of an international body of multilateral environmental rules, in which the differing capacities of the north and south to mount programmes of environmental protection are realistically acknowledged.

(2) The resources to undertake environmental programmes are substantial. The estimated 2000 budget authority of the US EPA ($7.6 billion), Interior ($8.3 billion), USDA-Forest Service ($1.2 billion), USDA-Fish and Wildlife ($715 million), USDA-Natural Resources Conservation ($661 million) and NOAA ($1.8 billion) together total $20.6 billion.[63] This may be compared with 1998

[60] See Esty, 1994, p. 96.

[61] Quoted in Shaffer, 2001, p. 36. Biermann (2000, pp. 25–26) argues that improving technology transfers to developing countries for environmental improvements could be a major GEO function.

[62] Quoted in Shaffer, 2001, p. 47 note 132.

[63] Budget of the US Govt., fiscal year 2001: http://w3.access.gpo.gov/usbudget/fy2001/pdf/budget.pdf

total GNP for Uruguay of $20 billion, Vietnam of $26.5 billion, and Bangladesh of $44.2 billion.

This clearly implies the need for expanded technical assistance through US agencies such as AID. But more important may be a recognized payoff to LDCs willing to promote environmental protection in the form of expanded market access to developed country markets. This issue will be taken up in greater detail below.

(3) Just as unilateralism in trade policy is ultimately self-defeating, so is it in environmental policy, at least where transborder issues are concerned. Naturally, a GEO would not require all national environmental measures to be subjected to oversight, but where these measures affect the "global commons", multilateralism should provide a foundation principle.

Finally, the GEO/WTO interface will be all-important. Perhaps, paradoxically, if it is to take environmental pressures off the WTO, a GEO should be located in Geneva. There, it could assist the WTO (analogous again to WIPO), and would be situated to work in cooperation with the World Health Organization (WHO) and the growing number of environmental NGOs who have found it useful to use Geneva as a base.

A last set of implementation issues concerns timing and phasing. It is very unlikely, given the problems and potential opposition facing a GEO, that it could be implemented in a single "grand stroke". Such an achievement would only be likely to emerge from a more general agreement to reform and revitalize all of the major multilateral institutions: the World Bank, IMF, WTO and UN system, in a single exercise analogous to the momentous post-war conferences of the late 1940s. There seems little current enthusiasm for such an effort.

A less ambitious, but still daunting, possibility would be to launch a GEO as part of some final agreement in a new MTN round. Such an outcome assumes that a new round can be successfully launched and negotiated, with side-negotiations over a GEO contributing part of the final package. This will require general acceptance of the arguments in favour of a GEO, and overcoming the arguments and factors weighing against it, notably those related to LDC interests.

A third approach, consistent with a new round of MTN talks, but not reliant upon them, would be to open negotiations over a GEO as a multilateral environmental effort, *linked to but separate from* MTN negotiations. This would follow, in general form, the NAFTA side-agreement model and would place GEO talks on a separate path. A difference might be that while the NAAEC environmental side-agreement would surely not have succeeded had NAFTA failed, GEO talks might proceed and even succeed without a successful MTN. However, for a variety of reasons, related especially to market access requirements of LDCs, this outcome also seems unlikely.

A fourth, scaled-down proposal would establish not a GEO, but a "Standing Conference on Trade and Environment". This approach, advocated by UNCTAD's Rubens Ricupero, would be an expansion of the informal *ad hoc* sessions so far organized by the WTO Secretariat for delegates, various international organizations and NGOs. The result would be to create a body of interested parties which might, over time, evolve into a more formal negotiating group.[64]

Sampson (2000, pp. 140–141) in somewhat the same spirit, has advocated the use of an "eminent persons group", for trade and environment issues on the model of the Leutwiler Group in the run-up to the Uruguay Round. In addition, he has suggested that a new MTN negotiation might include sub-negotiating groups similar to the GATT Articles subgroup and the Functioning of the GATT System (FOGS) subgroup during the Uruguay Round. The GATT Articles type of subgroups would reconsider the exceptions under Article XX, while the FOGS subgroup would contemplate linkages from the WTO to various environmental agreements. It is notable that nowhere in his recent treatment of trade/environment linkages does Sampson mention a GEO.[65]

VII. Three Issues: LCDs, Sovereignty and Conditionality

Considerable attention has already been given to the role and interests of LDCs in successfully negotiating a GEO. Yet it is critical to understand that as a group, the developing countries feel left out of the many rewards promised in return for their support of a Uruguay Round Agreement. Since the completion of the round in 1994, global trade has risen significantly faster than GDP, but the share of LDC exports has fallen relative to those of the US and EU.[66] While this is partly a function of relative growth rates, protectionist subsidies and price supports have grown along with GDP, leaving many developing countries feeling short-changed. As the *Economist* recently noted, the failure of the Seattle trade talks was due not to the presence of disgruntled demonstrators so much as to "a failure of the self-appointed vanguard of America and Europe to respond to the concerns of developing countries".[67]

---

[64] Shaffer (2001, notes 110 and 111) discusses the five NGO Symposia held by the WTO, and Ricupero's proposal (note 136). See Rubens Ricupero, "UN Reform: Balancing the WTO with a Proposed World Environment Organization", in *Policing the Global Economy*, 2000.

[65] Biermann offers three "models" for a GEO: a cooperation model, a centralization model and a hierarchization model. The cooperation model would essentially retain all existing bodies in their current state, but would elevate UNEP to a leading and coordinating role, becoming in effect a GEO. The centralization model would grant greater authority to a central institutional actor (again probably UNEP) to oversee and direct the environmental activities of other UN bodies. This model would make the GEO similar to the WTO, and would bring MEAs into a reporting relationship with the GEO. This GEO would have a double-weighted voting procedure in which decisions would require a two-thirds majority of both developed and developing countries. The hierarchization model would grant the GEO enforcement authority like the Security Council, and would constitute the most *dirigiste* of the alternatives—approaching a global government. Of the three alternatives, a hybrid of the first two, "cooperation" and "centralization", is closest in spirit to that discussed here. One might call this hybrid the "coordination model". See Frank Biermann. "The Case for a World Environment Organization", *Environment* 42: 9 (November, 2000) 23–31.

[66] The IMF reports that in 1993, the US share of world exports was 15.7 percent, the EU 34.7 percent, and the rest of the world 49.6 percent. In 1999, the US share was 17.7 percent, the EU 38 percent and the rest of the world 44.3 percent.

[67] *The Economist*. "A Different, New World Order", 357: 8196 (12 November 2000) 83–84, 89.

These concerns go beyond environmental measures, but tend to reinforce LDCs' suspicions that such measures are yet another excuse to restrict market access. It is expanded market access, above all else, which constitutes their main preoccupation. Brazil has made a market access agreement in agriculture a precondition to its involvement in a new round. India has agreed that commitments it made on intellectual property rights have not been matched by the expanded market access in agriculture and textiles which it expected to ensue. This was, after all, to have been the "Development Round" of MTN talks.[68]

Given this state of affairs, a GEO can only succeed if it is linked to a larger set of real expansions in market access opportunities for LDCs. Like NAFTA and its side-agreements, this is in part because such linkage offers the only prize sufficient to induce LDCs to take a GEO seriously. Second, such linkage will tend to undercut the suspicion that a GEO is a protectionist Trojan horse. Third, it will underscore the obvious need for economic growth and expansion if LDCs are to make the many investments required to protect their environments.

Notwithstanding such a need for *linkage*, there is no reason that negotiations over a GEO could not be *separated* from the formal MTN talks, in the same manner as the NAFTA side-agreements. This would allow the MTN talks to proceed without the threat posed by the length and complexity of GEO discussions. In general, such a view argues against the "Jordan model", in which environmental commitments are internalized in larger trade agreements.

In one respect, however, the "Jordan model" is of special relevance to LDCs' interest in a GEO. By treating the separate environmental goals of Jordan and the US as mutually acceptable, the bilateral accord was endorsing the proposition that environmental policy should be conducted by sovereign states at an appropriate level of competency and jurisdiction. In the context of LDC interests, such policy should also recognize the differential capacity of lower-income countries to undertake expensive environmental programmes. This is closely tied to special and differential treatment of LDCs in the conduct and performance of environmental programmes. By emphasizing these special and differential circumstances in relation to environmental policy, a GEO would help to build support for added technical assistance for environmental improvements. Unfortunately, a key area in which the Jordan model fails is in cases of obvious transboundary or public goods problems. Such transboundary issues affecting the US and Jordan are very small in number, but this would not be true of a multilateral undertaking such as a GEO.

A last, and especially thorny, issue concerns the potential role of a GEO as an imposer of sanctions and conditionality on countries unwilling or unable to comply

[68] See J. Michael Finger and Philip Schaler, "Implementation of Uruguay Round Commitment: The Development Challenge", *The World Economy* 23: 4 (April, 2000) 511–525; Rubens Ricupero, "A Development Round: Converting Rhetoric into Substance", Background note to the Conference on Efficiency, Equity and Legitimacy: The Multilateral Trading System at the Millennium, John F. Kennedy School of Government, Harvard University, 1–2 June 2000.

with norms or standards. This is, of course, an old and contentious issue in trade policy.[69] Most multilateral agreements, including a GEO and its rules, are likely to carry penalties for noncompliance. However, there is no reason in the case of a GEO why such penalties need to take the form of *trade* sanctions, as opposed to fines, denial of voting rights, or other measures "decoupled" from trade itself. This argument can be employed in order to *separate* environment from trade measures, reducing the potential use (and abuse) of trade sanctions to enforce multilateral environmental compliance.

The experience of sanctions in trade policy suggests that they are far less important to the maintenance of world trade rules than the dispute settlement mechanisms of the WTO, which are in turn modelled on those established in 1919 by the ILO.[70] If a GEO were to come into being, the opportunity to create a separate environmental dispute resolution process might be of special help in separating multilateral environmental issues from those of trade. Such a process could function as a conduit for disputes under the many MEAs or bilateral environmental agreements (including regional agreements such as NAAEC) so that *ad hoc* dispute resolution mechanisms for each such agreement could be consolidated. In addition, such a process would allow NGOs to enter disputes as "friends of the court". While not a formal sanction, the capacity of NGOs to focus international attention on countries found to have violated environmental norms might have important impacts on compliance.

VIII. Conclusions

Despite the necessary limits of this analysis, a number of conclusions emerge. The first is that a GEO holds opportunities for both the trading system and the global environment. To the trading system, it offers the opportunity to disentangle trade from environmental matters, allowing the WTO to focus where it should: on expansion of market access and reductions in trade protectionism, saving attention for environmental measures only in cases of obvious trade distortion. A GEO could be of considerable assistance to the WTO in clarifying where environmental exceptions to the GATT articles were justified (under Article XX or other headings) and providing guidelines for minimally trade-distorting MEAs. At the same time, a GEO could help fill the institutional gap in dispute resolution and coordination surrounding the many MEAs

[69] See Robert Hudec, *Enforcing International Trade Law: The Evolution of the Modern GATT Legal System*, Salem, NH: Butterworth Legal Publishers, 1993. In the case of environmental obligations and sanctions, see Scott Barrett, *Environmental and Statecraft*, forthcoming. In a 1997 theoretical article, Barrett argues that the existence of trade sanctions in environmental agreements may nudge countries towards compliance, so long as a sufficient number of countries are committed to their enforcement. See Scott Barrett, "The Strategy of Trade Sanctions in International Environmental Agreements", *Resource and Energy Economics* 19 (1997) 345–361.

[70] Steve Charnovitz, personal communication, 10 January 2001. See Steve Charnovitz, "Rethinking WTO Trade Sanctions", a paper at the Conference, "The Political Economy of International Trade", University of Minnesota, 15–16 September 2000. For a review of different types of carrots and sticks, see the appendix in Daniel C. Esty, *Greening the GATT: Trade, Environment and the Future* (1994), and Howard Chang, "Carrots, Sticks and International Externalities", *International Review of Law and Economics* 17:3 (September 1997) 309–324. For a broader assessment of compliance issues see A. Chayes and A. Chayes, *The New Sovereignty: Compliance with International Regulation Agreements*, Cambridge: Harvard University Press, 1995.

and institutions now responsible for global environmental issues, especially UNDP, the CSD and certain activities of the World Bank, WHO, WMO, FAO, among others. This coordination need not imply centralization, nor the usurpation of authority from these bodies or national governments.

Second, a GEO could channel needed attention to a wide range of global public goods and global commons issues—from ozone depletion to biodiversity to air and water pollution to overfishing. These issues are in need of greater focus and attention independent of the trading system, suggesting a need for separate multilateral instruments such as a GEO.

Third, overcoming opposition to a GEO will require a twofold undertaking involving the politics and posture of both developed and developing countries. In the north, opposition to multilateral institutions generally—arising from both right and left—must change. Conservatives will need to overcome their distrust of global environmental initiatives. The environmental left, meanwhile, must overcome its strident opposition to all things multinational. In developing countries, environmental improvements are an urgent need, which can now be deflected by claims that environmental issues are rich men's concerns. Unless a GEO clearly offers specific commitments to special and differential treatment of LDC problems, expanded technical assistance, and ample LDC representation, it will be easily discredited as a form of environmental conditionality and a disguised mechanism of northern protectionism.

Fourth, it is unlikely that LDCs will find a GEO attractive unless it is linked to commitments for expanded market access, especially in key areas such as agriculture and textiles. This suggests a model in which a GEO is *linked* to but *separate* from a new round of MNT negotiations. The virtue of linkage is that LDCs will see that market access will enable them seriously to contemplate environmental improvements in the context of economic growth. The virtue of separation is that a successful MTN negotiation will not have to internalize questions of multilateral environmental policy.

The overall conclusion is that despite serious hurdles, a GEO can be envisioned which is both pro-trade and pro-environment, strengthening the global trading system and its rules, while carving out new areas of international environmental competency. Achieving this vision will be difficult, but it is this author's view that we are condemned to succeed.

References

Alden, Edward, "Bush Faces Huge Trade Divide", *Financial Times* 3 January 2001, p. 5.

Anderson, Kym, "The Standard Welfare Economics of Policies Affecting Trade and the Environment", in K. Anderson and Richar Blackhurst (eds), *The Greening of World Trade Issues*, New York: Harvester-Wheatsheaf, 1992.

Andrews, Dale, *Experiences in the Use of Trade Measures in CITES*, Joint Session of Trade and Environmental Experts, OECD/GD (97) 106, Paris: OECD, 1997.

Bagwell, K. and R.W. Staiger, "An Economic Theory of GATT", *American Economic Review* (March 1999) 215–248.

Barrett, Scott, "International Agreements for the Protection of Environmental and Agricultural Resources: An Economic Perspective", London: London Business School, 1992.

Barrett, Scott, "The Strategy of Trade Sanctions in International Environmental Agreements", *Resource and Energy Economics* 19 (1997) 345–361.

Barrett, Scott, *Environment and Statecraft*, forthcoming.

Bhagwati, J. and T.N. Srinivasan, "Trade and Environment: Does Environmental Diversity Detract from the Case for Free Trade?" in J. Bhagwati and Robert E. Hudec (eds), *Fair Trade and Harmonization: Prerequisites for Free Trade? Vol 1, Economic Analysis*, Cambridge: MIT Press, 1997.

Biermann, Frank, "The Case for a World Environmental Organization", *Environment* 42: 9 (November 2000) 23–31.

Boli, John and G.M. Thomas (eds), *Constructing World Culture: International Nongovernmental Organizations Since 1875*, Stanford, CA: Stanford University Press, 1999.

Bramble, Barbara J and Gareth Porter, "Non-Governmental Organizations and the Making of U.S. International Environmental Policy", in Hurrell and Kingsbury (eds), *International Politics*, pp. 313–353.

Center for International Environmental Law (CIEL), "GATT Tuna–Dolphin II: Environmental Protection Continues to Clash with Free Trade", CIEL Brief No. 2, Washington, DC, June 1994.

Chang, Howard, "Carrots, Sticks and International Externalities", *International Review of Law and Economics* 17:3 (September 1997) 309–324.

Charnovitz, Steve, "Exploring the Environmental Exceptions in GATT Article XX", *Journal of World Trade* 25 (October 1991) 37–55.

Charnovitz, Steve, "Environmental Harmonization and Trade Policy", in Durwent Zaelke (ed.) *Trade and the Environment: Law, Policy and Economics*, Washington, DC: Island Press, 1993.

Charnovitz, Steve, "NAFTA: An Analysis of its Environmental Provisions", *Environmental Law Reporter* 23: 2 (1993) 10067–10073.

Charnovitz, Steve, "The Environment versus Trade Rules: Defogging the Debate", *Environmental Law* 23 (1993) 511–517.

Charnovitz, Steve, "A Critical Guide to the WTO's Report on Trade and the Environment", *Arizona Journal of International and Comparative Law* 14: 2 (1997) 341–378.

Charnovitz, Steve, "Rethinking WTO Trade Sanctions", a paper at the Conference, "The Political Economy of International Trade", University of Minnesota, 15–16 September 2000.

Chayes, A. and A. Chayes, *The New Sovereignty Compliance with International Regulation Agreements*, Cambridge: Harvard University Press, 1995.

Daly, Herman E., "The Perils of Free Trade", *Scientific American* 269: 5 (November 1993) 50–57.

Dunoff, Jeffrey, "International Misfits: The GATT, the ICJ, and Trade–Environment Disputes", *Michigan Journal of International Law* 15 (1994) 1043–1127.

Economist, "A Different, New World Order", 357: 8196 (12 November 2000) 83–84; 89.

Esty, Daniel C., "GATTing the Greens," *Foreign Affairs*, vol. 72, no. 5 (Nov./Dec. 1993) 132–136.

Esty, Daniel C., *Greening the GATT: Trade, Environment and the Future*, Washington, DC: Institute for International Economics, 1994.

Esty, Daniel C., "Non Governmental Organizations at the World Trade Organization: Cooperation, Competition or Exclusion", *Journal of International Economic Law* 12: 3 (1998) 135–137.

Esty, Daniel C., "Toward Optimal Environmental Governance", *New York University Law Review* 74: 6 (Dec. 1999) 1495–1574.

Esty, Daniel C., "The Value of Creating a Global Environmental Organization", *Environment Matters*, Annual Review, Washington, DC: The World Bank, 2000.

Finger, J. Michael and Philip Schaler, "Implementation of Uruguay Round Commitment: The Development Challenge", *The World Economy* 23: 4 (April 2000) 511–525.

Goldbery, Donald M. et al., *Effectiveness of Trade Measures in Multilateral Environmental Agreements: Cessous from the Montreal Protocol*, Washington, CIEL, 1998.

Hauer, Grant and C. Ford Runge, "Trade–Environment Linkages in the Resolution of Transboundary Externalities", *The World Economy* 22: 1 (January 1999) 25–39.

Holmes, Henry, "The World Trade Take-Over", *Earth Island Journal* 14: 4 (Winter 1999–2000) 38.

Hudec, Robert, *Enforcing International Trade Law: The Evolution of the Modern GATT Legal System*, Salem, NH: Butterworth Legal Publishers, 1993.

Hudec, Robert, "GATT/WTO Constraints on National Regulation: Requiem for an 'Aims and Effects' Test", *The International Lawyer* 32 (1998) 619–649.

Hurrell, Andrew and Benedict Kingsbury (eds), *The International Politics of the Environment: Actors, Interests, and Institutions*, Oxford: Clarendon Press, 1992.

Jackson, John, *World Trade and the Law of GATT*, New York: Bobbs-Merrill Co., 1969.

Jackson, John, "World Trade Rules and Environmental Policies: Congruence or Conflict?" *Washington and Lee Law Review* 49: 4 (Fall 1992) 1227–1278.

Johnson, Pierre Marc and André Beaulieu, *The Environment and NAFTA: Understanding and Implementing the New Continental Law*, Island Press, 1996.

Juma, Calestous, "The Perils of Centralizing Global Environmental Governance", *Environment Matters*, Annual Review, Washington, DC: The World Bank, 2000.

Katz, Sherman, Center for Strategic and International Studies, Washington, DC, personal communication, 10 December 2000.

Kaul, Inge, Isabelle Grunberg and Marc A. Stern, *Global Public Goods: International Cooperation for the 21st Century*, New York: Oxford University Press, 1999.

Kreuger, Jonathan, *The Basel Convention and Transboundary Movements of Hazardous Wastes*, Briefing Paper no. 45, Royal Institute of International Affairs, London, May 1998.

Krutilla, Kerry, "Environmental Regulation in an Open Economy", *Journal of Environmental Economics and Management* 20 (1991) 127–142.

Nancy Lindboug, "Non-Governmental Organizations: Their Past, Present and Future Role in International Environmental Negotiations", in Lawrence E. Susskind, Eric Jay Dolin and J. William Breslin (eds), *International Environmental Treaty Making*, Cambridge, MA: Harvard University Program on Negotiation Books, 1992.

Maggi, G., "The Role of Multilateral Institutions in International Trade Cooperation", *American Economic Review* (March 1999) 190–214.

Mickelthwait, John and Adrian Wooldridge, *A Future Perfect: The Challenge and Hidden Promise of Globalization*, London: Heinemann, 2000.

Mumme, Stephen P., "New Directions in United States–Mexican Transboundary Environmental Management: A Critique of Current Proposals", *Natural Resources Journal*, vol. 31 (Summer 1992) 539–562.

Olson, Elizabeth, "Regional Trade Pacts Thrive as the Big Players Fail to Act", *New York Times* 28 Dec. 2000, p. W1.

Palmer, Geoffrey, "New Ways to Make International Environmental Law", *American Journal of International Law* 86 (April 1992) 259–283.

Pearson, Charles S., *Economics and the Global Environment*, Cambridge, UK: Cambridge University Press, 2000.

Piddington, Kenneth, "The Role of the World Bank" in Hurrell and Kingsbury (eds), *The Institutional Politics of the Environment: Actors, Interests and Institutions*, Oxford: Clarendon Press, 1992, pp. 212–227.

Richardson, Elliot L., "Climate Change: Problems of Law-Making", in Hurrell and Kingsbury (eds), *The International Politics of the Environment: Actors, Interests and Institutions*, Oxford: Clarendon Press, 1992.

Ricupero, Rubens, "A Development Round: Converting Rhetoric into Substance", background note to the Conference on Efficiency, Equity and Legitimacy: The Multilateral Trading System at the Millennium, John F. Kennedy School of Government, Harvard University, 1–2 June 2000.

Ricupero, Rubens, "UN Reform: Balancing the WTO with a Proposed World Environment Organization" in *Policing the Global Economy*, Stanford, CA: Stanford University Press, 2000.

Runge, C. Ford (with Francois Orlalo-Magne and Philip Van de Kamp), *Freer Trade, Protected Environment: Balancing Trade Liberalization and Environmental Interests*, New York: Council on Foreign Relations Press, 1994.

Runge, C. Ford, "A Conceptual Framework for Agricultural Trade and the Environment—Beyond the 'Green Box'", *Journal of World Trade* 33: 6 (Dec. 1999) 47–68.

Runge, C. Ford and Lee Ann Jackson, "Labeling, Trade and Genetically Modified Organisms: A Proposed Solution", *Journal of World Trade* 33: 6 (2000) 111–122.

Runge, C. Ford and Benjamin Senauer, "A Removable Feast", *Foreign Affairs* (May–June 2000) 39–51.

Sampson, Gary P., *Trade, Environment and the WTO: The Post-Seattle Agenda*, Overseas Development Council, Policy Essay no. 27, Washington, DC, 2000.

Sandler, Todd, *Global Challenges: An Approach to Environmental Political and Economic Problems*, New York: Cambridge University Press, 1997.

Shaffer, Gregory C., "The World Trade Organization Under Challenge: Democracy and the Law and Politics of the WTO's Treatment of Trade and Environment Matters", *Harvard Environment Law Journal*, 25:1 (2001).

Spiro, Peter J., "New Global Potentates: Nongovernmental Organizations and the 'Unregulated' Marketplace", *Cardozo Law Review* 18: 3 (1996) 957–969.

Susskind, Lawrence and Connie Ozawa, "Negotiating More Effective International Environmental Agreements," in Hurrell and Kingsbury (eds), *The International Politics of the Environment: Actors, Interests and Institutions*, Oxford: Clarendon Press.

Thacher, Peter S., "The Role of the United Nations", in Hurrell and Kingsbury (eds), *International Politics*, pp. 183–211.

Tinbergen, Jan, *On the Theory of Economic Policy*, Amsterdam: Elsevier, North Holland, 1950.

Trebilcock, Michael and Julie Soloway, "International Trade Policy and Domestic Food Safety Regulations: The Case for Substantial Deference by the WTO Dispute Settlement Body Under the SPS Agreement", paper presented at the Conference, "The Political Economy of International Trade", University of Minnesota, 15–16 September 2000.

United Nations Environment Programme, *Register of Treaties and Other Agreements in the Field of the Environment*, Nairobi, 1991.

United Nations Environment Programme, *Environment and Trade: A Handbook*, International Institute for Sustainable Development, Winnipeg, Canada, 2000.

Vogel, David, *Trading Up: Consumer and Environmental Regulations in a Global Economy*, Cambridge: Harvard University Press, 1995.

Whalley, John and Ben Zissimos, "A World Environmental Organization?" mimeo, University of Western Ontario, University of Warwick and National Bureau of Economic Research, October 2000.

Young, Oran, *The Effectiveness of International Environmental Regimes: Causal Connections and Behavioral Mechanisms*, Cambridge: MIT Press, 1999.

Name Index